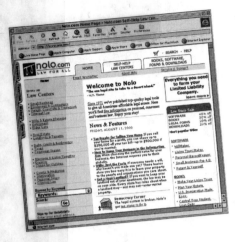

An Important Message to Our Readers

This product provides information and general advice about the law. But laws and procedures change frequently, and they can be interpreted differently by different people. For specific advice geared to your specific situation, consult an expert. No book, software or other published material is a substitute for personalized advice from a knowledgeable lawyer licensed to practice law in your state.

1st edition

Federal Employment Laws:

A Desk Reference

by Amy DelPo & Lisa Guerin

Keeping Up-to-Date

To keep its books up-to-date, Nolo issues new printings and new editions periodically. New printings reflect minor legal changes and technical corrections. New editions contain major legal changes, major text additions or major reorganizations. To find out if a later printing or edition of any Nolo book is available, call Nolo at 510-549-1976 or check our website at www.nolo.com.

To stay current, follow the "Update" service at our website at www.nolo.com/lawstore/update/list.cfm. In another effort to help you use Nolo's latest materials, we offer a 35% discount off the purchase of the new edition of your Nolo book when you turn in the cover of an earlier edition.

FIRST EDITION	JULY 2002
Illustrations	MARI STEIN
Cover Design	TONI IHARA
Book Design	TERRI HEARSH
Proofreading	ROBERT WELLS
Index	THÉRÈSE SHERE
Printing	BERTELSMANN SERVICES INC.

DelPo, Amy, 1967-
    Federal employment laws : a desk reference / by Amy DelPo and Lisa Guerin.
        p.   cm.
    Includes index.
    ISBN 0-87337-798-2
    1. Labor laws and legislation--United States--Popular works. I. Guerin, Lisa, 1964- II. Title.

KF3455.Z9 D45 2002
344.7301--dc21   2002018883

For information on bulk purchases or corporate premium sales, please contact the Special Sales Department. For academic sales or textbook adoptions, ask for Academic Sales. Call 800-955-4775 or write to Nolo, 950 Parker Street, Berkeley, CA 94710.

Acknowledgments

The authors would like to thank:

Jake Warner, who came up with the idea that turned into this book. His encouragement and advice were invaluable.

Janet Portman, for helping us trim the fat, explain the technicalities and bring this material down to earth.

Albin Renauer, for his amazing database, his help in organizing the book and his assistance in pulling together so much of the information contained herein.

Ella Hirst, for her unsurpassed research skills and for creating most of the 50-state charts that appear in this book.

Stan Jacobsen, for his research assistance and general good cheer.

Terri Hearsh, for making the book look good.

Thanks also go to attorney Dan Feinberg of Sigmund, Lewis and Feinberg in Oakland, California, for his keen eye in reviewing the ERISA material in this book.

Table of Contents

Part I: Overview

1 Getting the Information You Need

Part 2: Federal Laws

2 Americans With Disabilities Act of 1990 (ADA)

3 Age Discrimination in Employment Act (ADEA)

4 Consolidated Omnibus Budget Reconciliation Act (COBRA)

5 Equal Pay Act (EPA)

6 Employee Polygraph Protection Act (EPPA)

7 Employee Retirement Income Security Act (ERISA)

8 Fair Credit Reporting Act (FCRA)

9 Fair Labor Standards Act (FLSA)

16 Personal Responsibility and Work Opportunity Reconciliation Act (PRWORA)

17 Civil Rights Act of 1866 (Section 1981)

18 Title VII of the Civil Rights Act of 1964 (Title VII)

19 Uniformed Services Employment and Reemployment Rights Act (USERRA)

20 Worker Adjustment and Retraining Notification Act (WARN)

Appendix

State Resources

Index

Part 1:
Overview

Chapter 1

Getting the Information You Need

*C*hances are good that you've opened this book because you have a question about something that's come up at your workplace. If you're an employer, manager or human resources professional, you might be wondering how to handle an employee's request for medical leave, a complaint of sexual harassment or a question about continuing health insurance benefits for a former employee. If you're an employee, you might be concerned about unsafe working conditions, how to get your job back when you return from leave for military service or what your rights are if you get laid off.

No matter where you fall in your work hierarchy—from the boss right on down to the lowest-paid worker—you can use this book to find the answers to your questions. This book explains all of the major federal employment laws: whom they protect, who has to follow them, what they require and what they prohibit. We let you know what obligations you have under each law, what your rights are and where to go for more help.

Each of the following chapters explains the ins and outs of a single federal employment law. But before diving into those details, read this chapter to learn the basic information you will need to get the most out of this book. Here, we will cover:

- the basic framework of employment law, including how to determine which employment laws you need to follow and how to discover what the law means (Section A)

- how to use this book to get information on federal employment laws (Section B), and
- how to find additional information beyond this book (Section C).

What This Book Doesn't Cover

Some employment situations aren't covered in this book. If you fall into one of these categories, you won't find the information you need here.

- **Government employers and employees.** Although we explain which (if any) federal, state and local government workers are protected by each law, we don't detail the special rules that may apply to public employees. For example, although federal government workers are protected from certain types of discrimination by Title VII (see Chapter 18), they have to follow a special complaint process that doesn't apply to private employees. We don't cover that process here.

- **Federal contractors.** Private employers who contract to do work for the federal government are subject to additional employment laws. We don't cover those laws here.

A. Understanding Employment Law

Employment law comes from many sources and can be found in many different places—including the major federal employment laws, or statutes, which this book explains. But many employment questions can't be fully answered by looking at federal employment statutes alone. Even if you understood every detail of a federal employment statute, you might not have all the information you need to answer the question that brought you to this book in the first place.

In this book, we explain each of 19 major federal employment laws, in detail. This information synthesizes not only the text of each law, but also any regulations issued by the agency that enforces the law and the major court cases that interpret the law (see Section 1, below).

So why would you need even more information? For two reasons: first, there may be state and even local laws that cover the topic of your question. If so, you will have to follow those laws if you are an employer—and you may have additional rights under those laws, if you are an employee—as well as any federal laws that apply to you (see Section 1, below, for information on state and local laws). Second, the meaning of a federal law can change, as courts issue new decisions and agencies write new regulations interpreting what the law requires (see Section 2, below, for information on the role of courts and agencies in interpreting laws).

In this section, we explain how all of these components—federal laws, state and local laws, court decisions and agency regulations—combine to create "the law" that governs employment questions.

1. Finding the Law That Answers Your Question: Federal, State and Local Laws

The laws that we explain in this book are federal statutes. They started out as bills passed by the U.S. Congress and were signed into law by the president. They are written down in a series of books called the United States Code. (You can learn more about the U.S. Code in Section C.) For every law that we explain in this book, you'll need to know whether the law *applies* to you and then whether you must *follow* it. We'll explain these two threshold questions below.

a. Does the federal statute apply to you?

Because employment laws explained here are federal statutes, they apply throughout the country, regardless of what state the employer or the employee is in. This means that every federal law in this book has the potential of applying to you if you operate your business in the United States or if you work in the United States. We say "potential" because no law described here applies to *every* employer and employee. Instead, most laws specify which employers need to follow them and which employees are covered by them.

The Special World of Unions

If your workplace is unionized, the first place to look for answers to your employment questions isn't the law, believe it or not. Instead, direct your attention to the collective bargaining agreement (CBA) between the union and the employer. If the CBA gives workers more rights in certain areas (most commonly, wage and hour issues, leave, discipline and termination procedures), the CBA trumps the law.

For example, let's say you are an employer who wants to know how much leave you have to give to an employee who is about to have a baby. You look up the Family and Medical Leave Act in this book and see that it requires you to give the employee up to 12 weeks of unpaid leave. When you look at your CBA, however, you find that you must give the employee 16 weeks of paid leave. No matter how much you may want to save money, you must give the paid leave required by the CBA.

Generally, unions are not allowed to bargain away their members' federal rights in a collective bargaining agreement—that is, the CBA usually can't provide workers less than the federal law requires. However, there are some exceptions to this rule. For example, most courts have upheld a common CBA provision that requires workers to make certain workplace claims only through the union grievance procedure, rather than bringing them to court (which they would otherwise have the right to do). And some laws allow unions and management to bend the rules in a CBA—for example, although some state laws require employers to give workers specified meal and rest breaks, many of them don't apply to workplaces governed by a CBA.

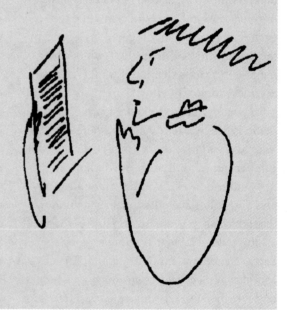

Usually, laws will apply to employers who have a minimum number of employees (for example, 15) or to employees who have certain characteristics (for example, a disability). We explain this issue in more detail in Section B.

b. Which law must you follow?

Unfortunately, determining whether a federal law applies to you is only the first step in discovering "the law" that you must follow. This is because state and local governments have their own laws that often overlap with federal laws—and when these laws apply to you, you must follow them as well. It's not as confusing as it may seem, because it boils down to this rule of thumb: When two or more laws apply in any given situation, the employer must follow the law that is most beneficial to employees

For example, if a federal and a state law both apply to your question and the state law is more beneficial to the employee, the state law controls. Or, when a federal and a local law both apply but the local law is less beneficial, the federal law applies. And if a federal law does not apply to your question (perhaps the employer is too small) but state and local law do, the law that is more beneficial to the employee (state or local) must be followed.

c. Identifying the law you must follow

Understanding that there may be multiple laws that pertain to any employment question can seem a bit daunting. But it needn't be if you methodically approach the problem. If you are an employer, you must check all of the following laws to determine your legal obligations to your employees:

- the federal laws that apply to you
- the laws of the state in which you operate your business that apply to you, and
- the laws of the locality (city and county, for example) in which you operate your business that apply to you.

Similarly, if you are an employee, you must check all of the following laws to determine what your workplace rights are:

- the federal laws that apply to you and your employer
- the laws of the state in which you work that apply to you and your employer, and
- the laws of the locality (city and county, for example) in which you work that apply to you and your employer.

Let's look at an example to see how this works in the real world. Assume that you are a private employer with 11 employees and that you operate your business in California. You want to know what your obligations are to employees in your workplace who have a disability. There is a federal law called the Americans with Disabilities Act that governs this issue. (You can learn more about the ADA in Chapter 2.) Because the ADA is a federal law, all employers in the United States are potentially covered by this law. To find out if you are in fact covered by it, you have to look at the law itself (or, in the case of this book, at the part of the chapter that describes which employers are regulated by the law at issue). If you look at Chapter 2, Section A2, you will see that the ADA applies to private employers with 15 or more employees. Thus, you don't need to worry about following the ADA because you have only 11 employees.

But you're not done yet. As we explained above, your state law might apply to you even though the federal law doesn't. Since you are a California employer, you follow California's disability law if it applies to you. In this book, we often list state laws at the end of each chapter. If you look at Chapter 2, Section F, you'll see a note referring you to the list of fair employment laws at the end of Chapter 18. When you look at that list, you see that California's disability law applies to employers with five or more employees. Thus, you must follow California's law.

Of course, you still aren't done. Your final step is to find out what your local governments have to say on the subject. In California, local governments are divided into cities and counties. You should contact both sets of government offices to see if there are any ordinances that you must follow when it comes to employees who have disabilities. If there are, you will have to follow the stricter of the state or local law—that is, the law that provides the most protection to your disabled workers.

Thus, you have a three-step process to follow every time you want to determine what your legal obligations or rights are:

1. Check federal law.
2. Check state law.
3. Check local ordinances.

This book can help you mainly with the first step—checking federal law. Although each chapter gives some guidance on state law, not all of them do. Thus, you must undertake the second and third steps on your own. Although this may sound daunting, it usually isn't in reality. The federal government and most state governments have agencies designed to help you through this process. You can find out more about those agencies—and other useful resources—in Section C of this chapter.

Often, understanding how to follow similar federal, state and local laws can be rather straightforward. For example, if your state requires employers to pay a minimum wage that is higher than the $5.15 per hour currently required by federal law, you have to pay the higher state minimum wage—easy enough. Sometimes, however, it can get complicated. If you are covered by two laws that say different things, you may need some help figuring out what to do. We recommend contacting one of the resources listed in Section C. If that fails, you may have to consult with an attorney.

2. Understanding What the Law Means

Once you determine which laws apply to you, your next task will be to figure out exactly what that law means. You can usually accomplish this through the fairly simple process of picking up a book—this book for federal laws, or a similar source for state laws—

and reading what it has to say. Or you might contact a state agency or other organization for information. As we explain in Section C, these resources—called "secondary sources" by lawyers—can be invaluable to you in understanding the law. We especially recommend the government agencies as secondary sources of first resort. For the vast majority of questions, you won't need to look at anything but secondary sources to understand the law well enough to follow it or use it.

Sometimes, however, you may need—or want—to discern the meaning of a law on your own, without relying on books or agencies or other secondary sources. To do that, you will have to turn to what are called "primary resources," which are:

- the text of the law itself
- court decisions interpreting the law, and
- agency regulations interpreting the law.

Before you decide to tackle primary sources on your own, think again: This book has already done this work for you when it comes to the major federal employment laws. The authors have looked at the primary resources and distilled the information so that you have everything you need in this handy reference. The vast majority of readers will never need to delve into primary resources in order to obey the law, if they are employers, or to assert their rights under the law, if they are employees.

Nonetheless, understanding how to use primary resources can be valuable to understanding the information you learn in books and from agencies. And you might just be adventurous enough to want to tackle legal interpretation yourself. For brave souls like you, this subsection examines how you can discern the meaning of a law on your own.

a. Reading the text of a law

It may seem almost too obvious to mention, but if you really want to know what a law has to say, the first place to look is at the law itself. In this book, we provide the text of most of the federal laws. (In Section C, below, we also give you instructions on finding the text of the law on the Internet or in a law library.) As you will see, laws can be rather dense and difficult reading. If you work through them slowly, however, making sure to refer to the definitions and the cross references, you can usually get a pretty good sense of what is going on.

Employment laws or "codes"—called "statutes" when they come from the federal or state government and known as "ordinances" when they come from a local government—are typically structured the same way:

- The law usually has a name (for example, the Americans With Disabilities Act).
- Near the beginning of the law is a list of definitions. These definitions are very important and often have meanings that are different from what Webster's would say. For this reason, don't assume you know the meaning of a word just because you use it every day. When interpreting a law, the word means what the law says it means—regardless of what everyone else thinks. Even a word as simple as "employer" will have its own meaning depending on which

law you are looking at. Always read the definitions first so you know what you are dealing with.

- The law's main provisions usually come after the definitions and describe what actions are required or prohibited by those who are covered by the law.
- There are usually provisions setting the penalties for violating the law. There might also be a provision empowering an agency to define the penalties.
- Finally, there may be language authorizing a specific government agency to enforce the statute and to write regulations—detailed explanations of how, in practice, employers and employees must carry out the broad purposes of the statute. These regulations, unfortunately, aren't right there next to the law—as we'll explain below, you have to look elsewhere for these materials.

If you still feel lost after reading the text of the law, don't worry. Sometimes it's not possible to understand a law completely just by reading what it says. That's why we have courts and agencies to interpret laws. We look at their roles in the next two subsections.

b. Reading court decisions

Courts have many tasks, but for your purposes in understanding the law, only one—interpreting statutes, and recording that interpretation in a written opinion—is important. Sometimes, a judge might clarify the meaning of a term in a law (for example, what does "reasonable" really mean?). Other times, a court might clarify which of two or more laws

applies in a given situation. The written form of that decision (a court opinion) can be very enlightening to people with similar questions.

As a nice bonus, courts will often summarize a law while they are interpreting it. These court decisions are usually a lot easier to read and understand than the laws themselves.

If you need help understanding a federal law like the employment statutes covered in this book, you must look at federal court decisions. There are three sources of court decisions, corresponding to the path a case might take as it wends its way through the court system:

- **The trial court.** A case starts in the federal district court, which is a trial court, and sometimes ends with an opinion from the trial judge. Some, but not all, of these opinions are published for the public. These cases are "the law" only for the parties to the case itself, though

judges in the same geographic area will often follow their colleague's interpretation of the law.

- **The first appeal.** The losing side can usually appeal the case to a federal circuit court (also called an "appellate court"), which normally writes an opinion explaining its decision. These decisions are always published. The appellate court's opinion must be followed by the parties and by trial courts and appellate courts within the court's geographic area. "Federal Appellate Courts: Which One Applies to You," below, lists the circuit courts and the states that they preside over.
- **The last word.** Finally, the party that loses in the circuit court can ask the Supreme Court to hear the appeal, but the Court doesn't have to take the case unless it wants to. When the Supreme Court takes a case, it always writes an opinion. Everyone in the country must abide by the Supreme Court's decision.

The best court decisions to consult are those from the U.S. Supreme Court, because they apply everywhere. If those cases aren't helpful (or if the Supreme Court hasn't decided a case involving your question), you can also look at circuit court decisions. For the most part, any circuit court decision, regardless of where the court is located, can help you understand a law. If you are dealing with a controversial question about which courts disagree, however, you should follow what the courts in your geographical area (your "circuit") have to say on the subject.

Federal Appellate Courts: Which One Applies to You?	
Federal Appellate Court	**States**
First Circuit	Maine, Massachusetts, New Hampshire, Puerto Rico and Rhode Island
Second Circuit	Connecticut, New York and Vermont
Third Circuit	Delaware, New Jersey, Pennsylvania
Fourth Circuit	Maryland, North Carolina, South Carolina, Virginia and West Virginia
Fifth Circuit	Louisiana, Mississippi and Texas
Sixth Circuit	Kentucky, Michigan, Ohio and Tennessee
Seventh Circuit	Illinois, Indiana and Wisconsin
Eighth Circuit	Arkansas, Iowa, Minnesota, Missouri, Nebraska, North Dakota and South Dakota
Ninth Circuit	Alaska, Arizona, California, Hawaii, Idaho, Montana, Nevada, Oregon and Washington state
Tenth Circuit	Colorado, Kansas, New Mexico, Oklahoma, Utah and Wyoming
Eleventh Circuit	Alabama, Florida and Georgia
D.C. Circuit	District of Columbia

You can find court decisions from all of the above three sources (trial, appellate and Supreme courts) by looking in the United States Code Annotated—Section C gives you more information on how to find them.

If you need help understanding a state law, you need to read cases from courts in your state. To find those, you can look in your state's equivalent of the United States Code Annotated (see Section C, below, for more on this).

c.   Reading agency regulations

When Congress passed each federal law in this book, it also designated a federal agency whose job it is to interpret and enforce that law. One way agencies do this is by issuing regulations that summarize what they think the law says.

When laws use broad, vague terms such as "significant" or "reasonable," Congress will often direct the appropriate agency to supply the definitions. Sometimes the lawmakers just don't want to be bothered with these details; other times, they are relying on the expertise of the agency members to put the lawmakers' intentions into clear, practical language.

Although regulations are supposed to make it easier to understand and apply the law, they are often voluminous and excruciatingly detailed—indeed, much longer than the statutes they interpret. Depending on which agency issued the regulations, they may be very easy or very difficult to understand. Most readers won't need to consult the regulations, because we studied them for you in order to explain the statutes in this book. If you'd like to do your own research, however, regulations are a good place to look when trying to understand what a law means. We explain how to find regulations in Section C, below.

One word of caution: Sometimes, courts and agencies will disagree over what a law means. This leaves the rest of us in a bit of a bind, because we need to choose which interpretation to follow. Often, the rules for deciding who trumps whom can be quite complicated. If you find yourself in this situation, your safest course of action is to simply take the most conservative approach, acting in a way that is safe and legal under both interpretations. For example, if the regulations interpreting a law places obligations on employers beyond what the law requires, an employer's best course of action is to follow the regulations—even if the employer thinks they go beyond the scope of the law.

B. How to Use This Book

This book is designed to be used as a desk reference. You can use it to quickly look up the answer to a particular question about a law or an employment situation. Of course, you can also read the book from cover to cover, if you like.

1. What Each Chapter Includes

To make it easy for you to find what you need, each chapter has the same basic structure that provides the following information about each law:

- **The name of the law.** Generally, the name of the law is either the official title given to it by Congress or a popular name based on the law's location in the United States Code (the collection of all the federal laws).

- **The law's citation.** The law's citation is somewhat like its address in the U.S. Code. It tells you how to find the law by giving you the particular volume and section of the Code where it resides. We also provide you with one or more URLs where you can find the law on the Internet.

- **Citations to any regulations interpreting the law.** As explained above in Section A2, federal agencies that enforce and administer these laws sometimes draft regulations explaining the law's provisions. We give you the official citation to the volume and section of the Code of Federal Regulations (C.F.R.) where you can find these regulations, as well as a URL to locate these regulations on the Internet.

- **Definitions of important terms that are used in the law.** As we explained in Section A, above, words mean what the law says they mean; and the same term (like "independent contractor") can have different meanings under different laws. In each chapter, the terms that are specially defined for that law are italicized —this is your cue to look the term up

in the list of definitions at the beginning of the chapter, if you haven't done so already.

- **Whom the law covers.** For each law, we let you know which employers must follow the law and which employees are protected by it.

- **What the law requires and prohibits.** For each law, we explain to you what obligations the law imposes on employers and employees—and what the law forbids.

- **Exceptions.** Most laws have exceptions to their provisions. For each law, we give you information on any exceptions or exclusions from the law's requirements.

- **Enforcement.** When Congress passed each of the laws in this book, it also created mechanisms for enforcing the law. In each chapter, we provide you with information on how the law is enforced, including contact information for the federal agency that administers the law and the rules (if any) for bringing lawsuits under the law.

- **Information for employers.** We tailored this section just for employers, giving them practical advice on what they need to know to comply with the law, including any recordkeeping requirements, posting requirements and the penalties for failing to obey the law.

- **Information for employees.** We tailored this section just for employees, giving them practical advice on how to enforce their rights under the law, including where to start and what forms to use.

- **Agency resources.** Each chapter includes a list of resources (such as fact sheets, forms, posters and special guidance on how to apply the law) available from the federal agency that enforces the law—and the URL where you can find these resources on the Internet.

- **State law information.** Some chapters include 50-state charts that detail each state's law on the same topic; others include information on where to find your state's laws.

- **The actual text of the law.** Most of the time, you won't need to read this material. But if you want to see the language of the law for yourself, we've included it here.

2. Finding the Laws You Need

This book is organized law by law—which will work just fine if you know that you need information about the Americans With Disabilities Act or the Occupational Safety and Health Act, for example. But what if you just have an employment-related question—and no idea which law, if any, might apply?

The table below, "Laws That Apply to Common Employment Issues," should help you get started. Across the top, we've listed common employment issues. Once you find the issue that best describes your situation, follow that column down to find out which federal laws might apply.

3. Figuring Out Whether a Law Applies to You

Once you find the federal law or laws that apply to your situation, you're well on your way to getting the information you need. But even if a particular law covers the subject matter of your question, it may not cover *you*. That's because many laws exclude certain employers and employees—and some contain exceptions for specific situations.

To figure out whether a particular law applies, ask yourself each of the following questions. If the answer to each question is "yes," then you know that the law applies to your situation (for your convenience, these questions are summarized in a checklist at the end of this section).

a. Is the employer big enough?

Many employment laws apply only to employers that have more than a certain number of employees. Under the heading "Regulated Employers" in every chapter, you'll find information about minimum employer size. For example, an employer with only ten employees is not covered by the Age Discrimination in Employment Act—only employers with 20 or more employees have to comply with that law. (See Chapter 3 for more about the ADEA.)

b. Does the employer meet any other requirements imposed by the law?

Not every employment law applies to every employer, even if the employer meets the size requirement discussed above. Some employment laws don't apply to government

Laws That Apply to Common Employment Issues

Law	Acronym	Wages & Hours	Leave	Health & Safety	Privacy	Firing & Layoffs	Benefits	Discrimination	Unions & Organizing
Age Discrimination in Employment Act	ADEA							✓	
Americans With Disabilities Act	ADA			✓			✓	✓	
Civil Rights Act of 1866 (Section 1981)	§ 1981							✓	
Consolidated Omnibus Budget Reconciliation Act	COBRA					✓	✓		
Employee Polygraph Protection Act	EPPA				✓				
Employee Retirement Income Security Act	ERISA					✓	✓		
Equal Pay Act	EPA	✓							
Fair Credit Reporting Act	FCRA				✓			✓	
Fair Labor Standards Act	FLSA	✓							
Family and Medical Leave Act	FMLA		✓						
Immigration Reform and Control Act	IRCA							✓	
National Labor Relations Act	NLRA	✓			✓	✓		✓	✓
Occupational Safety and Health Act	OSH Act			✓					
Older Workers Benefit Protection Act	OWBPA						✓	✓	
Personal Responsibility & Work Opportunity Act of 1996	PRWOA								
Pregnancy Discrimination Act	PDA		✓		✓		✓	✓	
Title VII	Title VII							✓	
Uniformed Services Employment and Reemployment Rights Act	USERRA		✓				✓	✓	
Worker Adjustment and Retraining Notification Act	WARN					✓			

employers or religious schools, for example. You can also find this information under "Regulated Employers." For example, the Employee Polygraph Protection Act applies only to private employers—not to state, local or federal governments—so those employers do not need to concern themselves with following this particular law. (See Chapter 6 for more about the EPPA.)

c.   Is the employee covered?

Some employment laws apply only to employees who have worked for the employer for a certain period of time. Or, the law might apply only to employees in certain occupations. Each chapter has a heading called "Covered Workers," which gives you this information. For example, the Family and Medical Leave Act protects only those employees who have worked for the employer for at least a year and have worked at least 1,250 hours during that year. (See Chapter 10 for more about the FMLA.)

d.   Do all of the law's provisions apply?

Some laws have provisions that apply only to some workers. For example, the provisions of the Fair Labor Standards Act that require employers to pay overtime and the minimum wage don't apply to certain types of employees, including certain computer specialists, seamen and criminal investigators. Each chapter includes a section called "Covered Workers" that gives you this information on any additional coverage restrictions. (See Chapter 9 for more about the FLSA.)

e.   Is your situation covered by the law?

You've already figured out which laws deal with the general subject matter of your question. But that doesn't necessarily mean that the law applies to your situation. Each of these laws covers a limited spectrum of employment issues—and may not extend to the problem or question you're facing. You can find this information under the headings "What's Prohibited: Employers," "What's Required: Employers" and "What's Required: Employees." For example, if you have a question about discrimination, our chart shows you that both the Civil Rights Act of 1886 and the Equal Pay Act prohibit discrimination in employment. However, the Civil Rights Act of 1886 prohibits only race discrimination, and the Equal Pay Act prohibits only sex-based wage discrimination.

In addition, some laws carve out certain situations that are not covered. You can find this information under the heading "Exceptions." For example, although the Worker Adjustment and Retraining Notification Act generally requires certain employers to give employees advance notice of a layoff, employers don't have to give notice if the layoff results from a strike or the closing of a temporary facility. (See Chapter 20 for more about the WARN Act.)

Having read through th ese five questions, you should have a good idea as to whether your question will be answered by one of the laws we summarize in this book.

Does This Law Apply to Me?		
Question	Yes	No
1. Is the employer big enough?		
2. Does the employer meet any other requirements imposed by the law?		
3. Is the employee covered?		
4. Do all of the law's provisions apply?		
5. Is your situation covered by the law?		

C. Where to Find More Information

You may need more information than we provide here—for example, you may want to look up your state's law, either because no federal law covers your situation or because our chapter on the law that applies to you indicates that your state has a law covering the same topic. Or, you may want to find out how courts in your area have interpreted a particular law; or you may want to read the regulations that apply to a law. If so, you'll be pleased to learn that it isn't very difficult to do your own legal research—in fact, you can get lots of legal information without ever leaving your home or office by using the Internet.

Here, we give you a few tips on finding employment law materials. For more information on doing your own research, see *Legal Research: How to Find & Understand the Law*, by Steve Elias and Susan Levinkind (Nolo).

1. Check With a Government Agency First

Your first stop on the information highway should be the federal or state agency that administers and enforces the law you're interested in. At the end of our discussion of each law, we give you a list of resources available from the federal agency that interprets and enforces the law. But these lists aren't exhaustive—some of these agencies have dozens of fact sheets, guidance memoranda and special bulletins for employers, small businesses and workers that can help you figure out the law's requirements. And they also have staff members available to help answer your questions or point you toward the information you need.

If your question has to do with state law, you can start your research by contacting the state agency that enforces the law—generally the state fair employment practices agency for discrimination questions and the state labor department for all other inquiries.

2. Finding a Statute

If you want to look up a state or federal statute, the first thing you need to know is how to decipher legal citations. Most citations to federal statutes look like this: 29 U.S.C. §§ 2101-2108. The "U.S.C." stands for the United States Code, the set of books in which all current federal laws eventually appear. The number before U.S.C.—"29," in this example—indicates which "title" of the Code that law appears in. Each title of the Code deals with a particular subject, such as civil rights or labor. There may be several volumes of books that all cover one title. The numbers after U.S.C. are the section numbers in which the law appears.

Now that you know how to read a federal statute citation, where do you find the federal statutes? The easiest place to find them is on Nolo's website, at http://www.nolo.com. At the top of our home page, click on the tab marked "Plain English Law Centers." Then click on "Statutes and Cases" to enter our legal research area. Choose "Federal Laws" from the menu on the legal research page, then click on "U.S. Code" and follow the instructions for searching.

If you're more of an ink-on-paper type, you can find federal statutes at your local law library. First, ask the law librarian to direct you to the United States Code. Then find the set of volumes that covers the title you're searching for. Finally, find the volume that includes the sections you want. You'll notice that most volumes include a "pocket part"—a soft-cover pamphlet tucked into the back of the bound volume. This contains any recent changes that have been made to the law since the bound volume was printed. Always look at the pocket part to make sure you're reading the most current version of the law.

You can decipher state law citations in much the same way. States use a variety of formats to cite their laws. But all of them include the name, title or volume of the state's laws in which the statute appears; and the section or chapter number of the statute itself. You can find links to state statutes on our website, at http://www.nolo.com. Follow the instructions, above, to get to the legal research area. Then click on "State Laws," select your state and follow the instructions for searching. Or, you can go to your local law library.

3. Finding a Regulation

For many (but not all) of the laws in this book, we have included a citation to the federal regulations interpreting the law. These regulations are issued by the federal government agency that administers the law—and they can be enormously helpful if you are trying to understand how the law applies to real-life situations.

Citations to regulations look like this: 29 C.F.R. § 1625. The "C.F.R." stands for the Code of Federal Regulations, a very sizable collection of softbound volumes of all the current regulations issued by every federal agency. The number before the C.F.R. (in this example, "29") again refers to the title where the regulation appears. And the number after the C.F.R. refers to the section number of the regulation. You can find regulations online at our website at http://www.nolo.com. Follow the instructions, above, for finding a federal statute, but click on "Code of Federal Regulations" instead of "U.S. Code." Then follow the instructions for searching. You can also find regulations at your local law library.

4. Finding a Case

If you want to see how courts in your area have interpreted a certain law, you will have to look at some actual cases—the written decisions issued by courts. But how do you figure out which cases to look at? One good way to find cases that interpret federal employment statutes is to use the United States Code Annotated.

If you're thinking that the name sounds familiar, you're right—the United States Code Annotated ("U.S.C.A.") includes the entire United States Code. But it also includes citations to cases that interpret particular sections of the code. For example, if you're interested in whether and how courts have interpreted the leave requirement of the Family and Medical Leave Act, you can look up 29 U.S.C.A. § 2612 (the section of the law dealing with that topic). If any cases have been decided on that issue, they will be listed after the text of the statute itself, along with a short blurb describing what the case says.

Unfortunately, there is currently no easy way to access the U.S.C.A. for free on the Internet. This means you'll probably have to take a trip to your local law library. Ask the librarian where the U.S.C.A. is—the books are organized just like the United States Code. Once you find the section that interests you, be sure to check the pocket part to find the most recent cases.

Once you find a case that looks interesting, you can read the case itself. You can find many cases online at www.findlaw.com or www.lawsource.com/also. To use either of these sites, you must know the case's citation, which should be listed directly after the case's name in the Annotated Code. You can also find cases from the United States Supreme Court at our website, at http://www.nolo.com. Once you get to the Legal Research page, click on "Supreme Court Cases" and follow the search instructions.

If you're in the law library, you can look up a case using its citation. Although cases are collected in many different sets of books (usually called "reporters"), most case citations follow the same general format. For example, if you are looking for a case with the citation 33 F.3d 333, the first number, "33," is the volume number where the case appears. The middle of the citation, "F.3d," refers to the name of the reporter in which the case appears—here, the Federal Reporter, Third Series. And the last number, "333," tells you the page on which the case starts.

If you decide to do your research in the law library, don't be afraid to ask for help. Most law librarians are more than happy to help you find the material you need—and can probably give you some good pointers on finding additional helpful information.

Part 2:

Federal Laws

Chapter 2

Americans With Disabilities Act of 1990 (ADA)

Statute: 42 U.S.C. § 12101 and following
http://www.eeoc.gov/laws/ada.html

Regulations: 29 C.F.R. § 1630 and following
http://lula.law.cornell.edu/cfr/cfr.php?title=29&type=part&value=1630

Definitions

Direct threat

A significant risk to the health or safety of the disabled person or others that is the result of the person's *disability* and that cannot be resolved by a *reasonable accommodation*. For more, see Section A6.

Disability

A physical or mental impairment that *substantially limits* a *major life activity*. For more, see "With a Disability" in Section A3.

Essential functions

The fundamental, not marginal, duties of a job. For more, see "Qualified for the Position" in Section A3.

Illegal drug use

The use of illegal drugs and the improper use or abuse of prescription and over-the-counter drugs.

Major life activities

Activities that are of essential importance to daily life. For more, see "With a Disability" in Section A3.

Qualified individual with a disability

An individual who has a *disability* and who, with or without a *reasonable accommodation*, can perform the *essential functions* of a job that the individual holds or would like to have. The ADA covers only qualified individuals with a disability. To find out more, see Section A3.

Reasonable accommodation

Providing assistance or making changes in the job or workplace that will enable a worker to do her job despite the worker's *disability*. To find out more, see Section A5.

Retaliation

Any adverse action taken by an employer (or someone who works for the employer) against an employee for complaining about harassment or discrimination. For more about this, see "Retaliation" in Section A4.

Substantially limits

A person is substantially limited by an impairment when he or she is either unable or less able to perform a *major life activity* that an average person can perform. For more about this, see "With a Disability" in Section A3.

A. Overview of the ADA

1. Summary

The Americans With Disabilities Act of 1990 (ADA) is a sweeping civil rights law that protects people with *disabilities* in many contexts, including employment, government services, public accommodations and tele-communications. This discussion is limited to the ADA's employment provisions, which can be found in Title I of the Act.

The ADA's main employment provisions prohibit covered employers from discriminating against *qualified individuals with a disability*. This prohibition applies to all terms, conditions and privileges of employment, and it protects both applicants and current employees.

In addition, the ADA requires employers to evaluate whether they can accommodate a qualified individual's *disability* so that the individual can perform the job.

2. Regulated Employers

The following employers must comply with the ADA's employment provisions:

- private employers with 15 or more employees
- employment agencies
- labor organizations
- joint labor/management committees
- local governments, their agencies and subdivisions.

When Congress passed the ADA in 1990, it intended the law to cover state employers as well. In 2001, however, the U.S. Supreme Court ruled that this was an unconstitutional use of federal power over the states. The Court ruled that the states do not have to make special accommodations for individuals with *disabilities* so long as the state's treatment of those individuals has a rational basis. The Court also ruled that state employees cannot sue their government employers for money damages in the event that the state violates the law.

Although the ADA does not cover the federal government, a similar law—the Rehabilitation Act of 1973 (29 U.S.C. § 701 and following)—does. To find out more about the Rehabilitation Act, contact the U.S. Equal Employment Opportunity Commission (see Section E, below, for contact details).

The ADA has special provisions for covered employers that operate in foreign countries. Those provisions are beyond the scope of this discussion.

3. Covered Workers

The ADA covers all *qualified individuals with a disability* who are either current or prospective employees of a covered employer.

Thus, the individual must meet a three-part test to get the benefits of the ADA's employment provisions:

- the individual must be a current or prospective employee of a covered employer
- the individual must be qualified for the position, and
- the individual must have a *disability* within the meaning of the ADA.

The sections below explain these requirements.

Current or Prospective Employee

Only people who are current employees of a covered employer or who have applied to be employees of a covered employer can fall within the ADA's employment provisions. (See Section A2, above, for a list of covered employers.) Independent contractors, vendors and customers cannot (though they may be covered by some of the ADA's other provisions, such as those mandating access to public accommodations).

Qualified for the Position

An individual is qualified for a position if both of the following are true:

- the individual satisfies the prerequisites for the position (for example, has the right level of education, employment experience, skills, licenses), and
- the individual is able to perform the *essential functions* of the position, with or without a *reasonable accommodation* from the employer.

The term *essential functions* refers to the fundamental, as opposed to marginal, duties of a job. A job duty is an *essential function* if:

- the reason the job exists is to perform that function (for example, an *essential function* of a pilot is to fly the plane)
- only a few employees can perform the function, or
- the function is so highly specialized that the employer hires people into the

position specifically because of their expertise in performing that function.

The following types of information are relevant to determining whether a job duty is an *essential function*:

- written job descriptions prepared before advertising or interviewing for a position
- the employer's opinion
- the amount of time that people who hold that job have to spend performing that duty
- the consequences of someone holding the job who could not perform that duty
- the terms of a collective bargaining agreement
- the work experience of people who have held the job in the past
- the work experience of people who are currently holding the job.

Although the analysis may sound complicated, it's rooted in common sense. A good question to ask when trying to determine whether a job duty is an *essential function* is whether removing that job duty would fundamentally alter the job.

With a Disability

Not all physical or mental impairments are *disabilities* under the law. A worker is legally disabled only if he or she falls into one of these three categories:

- The worker has a physical or mental impairment that *substantially limits* a *major life activity*. (For more information about these terms, see immediately below.) Courts tend not to categorically characterize certain conditions as disabilities. Instead, they consider the effect of the particular condition on the particular employee.

- The worker has a record or history of such an impairment.
- The employer erroneously regards the worker as having a *disability*.

For an impairment to be a legal *disability*, it must be long term. Temporary impairments, such as pregnancy or broken bones, are not covered by the ADA (but they may be covered by other laws).

The EEOC's regulations say specifically that the following are not *disabilities*: transvestism, transsexualism, pedophilia, gender identity disorders (other than those that result from a physical impairment), other sexual behavior disorders, compulsive gambling, kleptomania, pyromania, psychoactive substance use disorders resulting from current *illegal drug use*, homosexuality and bisexuality.

Physical or Mental Impairment

A physical or mental impairment means a physiological disorder, condition, cosmetic disfigurement or anatomical loss that affects one or more of the following systems in the human body:

- neurological
- musculoskeletal
- sensory
- respiratory (including speech organs)
- cardiovascular
- reproductive
- digestive
- genitourinary
- hemic or lymphatic
- skin
- endocrine.

Physical or mental impairment also includes any mental or psychological disorder—for example, mental retardation, organic brain syndrome, emotional or mental illness and learning disabilities.

An impairment is different from a condition or trait. This is an important distinction to understand, because only impairments can be *disabilities;* conditions and traits cannot. For example, eye color and hair color are traits, not impairments. Height and weight, when they are in the normal range, are traits, not impairments. Personality traits such as poor judgment or a quick temper are also not impairments (unless they are a symptom of a mental or psychological disorder).

Substantially Limits

A person is *substantially limited* by an impairment when he or she is either:

- unable to perform a *major life activity* that an average person can perform, or
- less able to perform a *major life activity* than an average person.

The following factors are important to determining whether a person is *substantially limited* by an impairment:

- the impairment's nature and severity
- the impairment's duration or expected duration
- the impairment's long-term or permanent impact.

Major Life Activity

Major life activities are activities that are of essential importance to daily life. They include such things as caring for oneself, performing manual tasks, walking, seeing, hearing, speaking, breathing, learning and working.

Illegal Drug Use

If an individual is currently engaged in *illegal drug use*, that person is not a *qualified individual with a disability* and is therefore not entitled to the ADA's protections.

This exception only applies to individuals who are *currently* using drugs illegally. The ADA still protects the following individuals:

- those who have successfully completed a drug rehabilitation program and who are no longer engaging in *illegal drug use*
- those who are currently participating in a drug rehabilitation program and who are no longer engaging in *illegal drug use*, or
- those whom people erroneously believe use drugs illegally but who, in reality, do not.

4. What's Prohibited: Employers

Discrimination

Covered employers may not discriminate against *qualified individuals with a disability* in any aspect of employment, including:

- recruitment
- job application procedures
- hiring
- promotion and training

- leave
- job assignments
- benefits
- wages
- layoff and termination.

Covered employers also may not discriminate against a person for associating with a person with a *disability*. For example, a covered employer cannot refuse to hire someone just because that individual is married to someone who suffers from AIDS.

Segregation

Employers may not segregate individuals with disabilities. For example, if co-workers feel uncomfortable working with an individual who has a *disability*, the employer cannot ask that individual to work at home. The employer should instead educate and desensitize the co-workers.

Medical Examinations

Covered employers may not conduct medical examinations of job applicants. However, employers may conduct a medical examination after making a conditional offer of employment to an applicant if both of the following are true:

- all entering employees must take the examination regardless of *disability*, and
- the employer keeps the information gathered in the examination in a separate and confidential medical file.

A test for *illegal drug use* is not a medical examination and is therefore not governed by the ADA.

Inquiries About Disabilities

Covered employers may not ask job applicants questions about whether they have a *disability* or about the nature or severity of a *disability*. However, employers can explain to applicants what the application process involves and ask if the applicant will need a *reasonable accommodation*.

They can also explain what the job entails and ask applicants whether they are capable of performing job-related functions.

Retaliation

Covered employers may not take any adverse action against individuals for asserting their rights under the ADA. Adverse action includes demotion, discipline, firing, salary reduction, negative evaluation, change in job assignment or change in shift assignment.

Retaliation can also include hostile behavior or attitudes toward an employee. In some circumstances, the employer will be liable for the hostile acts and attitudes of other employees and supervisors.

5. What's Required: Workers

If an applicant or employee needs a *reasonable accommodation*, it is that individual's responsibility to request it. The employer does not have to anticipate this need. Someone other than the individual (such as a spouse, friend or co-worker) can request the accommodation on the worker's behalf.

Workers do not have to make the request in writing (though it is a good idea to do so, if possible), nor do they have to use any magic legal words—for example, they don't have to mention the ADA or use the words "reasonable accommodation." They simply need to request that some change be made because of a medical condition or impairment.

Once the request is made, the employer does not have to automatically grant the request. Instead, the employer and the individual must talk and work together to see if a *reasonable accommodation* is possible.

If the *disability* or need for accommodation is not obvious and if the employee has not previously provided documentation, the employer may request that the employee document the *disability* and limitations.

6. Exceptions

Direct Threat

Covered employers may refuse to hire *qualified individuals with a disability* if hiring them for the job would pose a *direct threat* to their own health or safety or to the health or safety of other individuals in the workplace.

A *direct threat* means more than simply an increased risk. The threat must pose a significant risk—that is, a high probability of substantial harm. The threat must be immediate, and it must be based on real information, not stereotypes or assumptions.

Religious Institutions

Religious institutions may give preference to individuals of a particular religion. They may also require that the individual be able to conform to the tenets of the religion.

Infectious Diseases

If a job requires food handling, an employer can refuse to hire an individual who has an infectious or communicable disease that is transmitted through food handling, but only if a *reasonable accommodation* cannot eliminate the risk of transmitting the disease.

B. How the ADA Is Enforced

1. Individual Complaints

The ADA is enforced under the same procedures as Title VII. See Section B1 of the chapter on Title VII.

2. Agency Enforcement

The ADA is enforced under the same procedures as Title VII. See Section B2 of the chapter on Title VII.

C. For Employers: Complying With the ADA

1. Reporting Requirements

The reporting requirements for the ADA are the same as those for Title VII. See Section C1 of the chapter on Title VII.

2. Posting Requirements

Covered employers must post notices informing current and prospective employees about the ADA.

3. Recordkeeping Requirements

The recordkeeping requirements for the ADA are the same as those for Title VII. See Section C2 of the chapter on Title VII.

4. Practical Tips

For advice about complying with anti-discrimination laws in general, see Section C3 of the chapter on Title VII.

A good rule of thumb is to ask only about an individual's abilities, not disabilities. This way, you can find out if the individual is capable of doing the job without running afoul of the ADA's prohibition against asking questions that will elicit information about *disabilities*. During the hiring process, attach to the application form a list of the essential functions of the job. Then ask applicants how they would perform each function.

Although it is up to the employee to come to you with a request for a accommodation, it is your job to work with that employee to see if the two of you can find something suitable. Be open-minded and understanding. The vast majority of accommodations that employers make are easy and inexpensive (for example, raising the height of a desk, purchasing a special keyboard for a computer, putting special lighting in an employee's workspace).

The EEOC is eager to help employers comply with the ADA. The agency staff will respond to requests for information and assistance (and employers who ask for information and assistance will not be prosecuted because of their inquiries).

5. Penalties

The ADA incorporates the same penalties as Title VII. See Section C4 of the chapter on Title VII.

In addition to the Title VII penalties, a court might order an employer to *reasonably accommodate* an individual's *disability*.

6. What's Required: Employers

Covered employers must make *reasonable accommodations* for known physical or mental limitations of *qualified individuals with a*

disability unless the accommodation would impose an *undue hardship* on the employer.

Employers must provide a *reasonable accommodation* for an applicant who needs it to apply for a job, to perform a job or to access work facilities and benefits.

Reasonable Accommodation

Accommodating a worker means providing assistance or making changes in the job or workplace that will enable the worker to do a job despite the *disability*. For example, an employer might lower the height of a desktop to accommodate a worker in a wheelchair, provide TDD telephone equipment for a worker whose hearing is impaired or provide a quiet, distraction-free workspace for a worker with Attention Deficit Disorder.

Reasonable accommodations fall into three broad categories:

- changes in the job application process that enable a *qualified individual with a disability* to apply and be considered for the position
- changes in the work environment, the circumstances in which the job is performed or the manner in which the job is performed that enable a *qualified individual with a disability* to perform the job's *essential functions*
- changes that enable an employee with a *disability* to enjoy the same benefits and privileges that other employees enjoy.

Employers must provide *reasonable accommodations* to all employees with *disabilities*, regardless of whether the employee works part time or full time or is probationary.

It is the employee's responsibility to request the accommodation. (For more about this, see Section D1, below). Once an employee makes this request, employers must engage in an informal interactive discussion with the individual to find a *reasonable accommodation*.

Accommodations that employers do not have to make because they are not reasonable include the following:

- Employers do not have to eliminate an *essential function* of the job.
- Employers do not have to lower production or performance standards.
- Employers do not have to provide personal use items, such as a wheelchair, eyeglasses, hearing aid or prosthetic limb.

The employer does not have to grant the specific accommodation that the employee requests, as long as the employer works with the employee to find an effective accommodation.

Undue Hardship

An accommodation creates an *undue hardship* if it would involve significant difficulty or expense for the employer or if it would fundamentally alter the nature or operation of the business. Whether an accommodation creates an *undue hardship* depends on a number of factors, including:

- the accommodation's cost
- the size and financial resources of the business
- the business structure, and
- the effect the accommodation would have on the business.

An *undue hardship* can be financial, but it doesn't have to be. For example, suppose a library clerk with a hearing disability requested a loud bell and speaker be added to the telephone, which would enable that person to be a receptionist there. Although the accommodation is probably inexpensive, it would destroy the quiet atmosphere of the library and make it difficult for patrons to use it. This means that the accommodation probably creates an *undue hardship* for the library.

D. For Workers: Asserting Rights Under the ADA

1. Where to Start

If You Need an Accommodation

If you need an accommodation, you must ask your employer for it. Your employer has no obligation to anticipate your needs. Although the law does not require you to make the request in writing, you'd be wise to do so. If you ever get to the point where you have to prove your case to a judge or jury, that document will come in quite handy.

If your employer fails to provide you with a *reasonable accommodation*, your next step is to file a complaint (also called a charge) with your local fair employment office (see the chapter on Title VII, Section E for contact information) or with the EEOC. (For more about this agency, see Section E, below). You can file a charge by mail or in person at your nearest EEOC office. To find the office closest to you, call 800-669-4000 or refer to the agency's website at http://www.eeoc.gov/teledir.html.

If You Think You Are Being Discriminated Against

If you think that your employer is discriminating against you because of your disability, and if this discrimination is unrelated to *reasonable accommodation* issues, you must start with your employer. If your employer has written complaint procedures, follow them. If there are no written complaint procedures, complain to the human resources department and any manager or supervisor.

If your employer does not act to stop the discrimination or harassment, your next step is to file a charge.

Whatever you do, don't let too much time pass before filing your charge. Strict time limits apply, and if you miss the deadline, you will not be allowed to sue your employer. The deadlines depend on whether your state also has an anti-discrimination agency. In states without an anti-discrimination agency, you have 180 days from the date of the discriminatory act to complain. In states with an anti-discrimination agency, you have 300 days to complain. (See the chapter on Title VII, Section F for a list of states with anti-discrimination laws.) Even if the deadline has passed, you will sometimes be able to file suit depending on the reasons for your delay. However, if you can file a charge before the deadline, you should absolutely do so. Courts only allow more time in very limited and complicated circumstances.

The agency will investigate your complaint. It will try to resolve the situation or inform you that it didn't find any evidence of discrimination.

Regardless of what the agency does, you may also contact an attorney about negotiating a settlement or filing a lawsuit on your behalf.

2. Required Forms

Not applicable.

3. Practical Tips

For practical tips about dealing with discrimination in general, see the chapter on Title VII, Section C3.

If you need a *reasonable accommodation* from your employer, remember that your employer is not required to give you everything you ask for, nor is your employer required to spend a lot of money or endure a lot of inconvenience. Being aware of your employer's needs and limitations when you propose an accommodation increases the likelihood that the two of you will find something acceptable.

There are quite a number of resources available for people with disabilities. Before requesting a *reasonable accommodation*, do your homework. A good place to start is the Job Accommodation Network, a consulting service that provides free information and assistance. You can call them at 800-526-7234 (V/TTY) or visit their website at http://janweb.icdi.wvu.edu.

E. Agency Charged With Enforcement & Compliance

Equal Employment Opportunity Commission (EEOC)
1801 L Street, NW
Washington, DC 20507
202-663-4900
http://www.eeoc.gov
To find your local EEOC office, refer to http://www.eeoc.gov/teledir.html

Agency Resources for Employers and Employees
(These can be obtained either at the Web addresses listed below or at the address and phone number listed above.)
- Information for employers about their obligations under the ADA
  The ADA: Your Responsibilities As an Employer
  http://www.eeoc.gov/facts/ada17.html
- Brief and general information about the ADA
  Facts About the Americans With Disabilities Act
  http://www.eeoc.gov/facts/fs-ada.html
- A detailed yet easy-to-understand discussion of reasonable accommodation and undue hardship
  Enforcement Guidance: Reasonable Accommodation and Undue Hardship Under the Americans With Disabilities Act
  http://www.eeoc.gov/docs/accommodation.html
- Answers to some common questions about the ADA
  The ADA: Questions and Answers
  http://www.eeoc.gov/facts/adaqa1.html
- Information about different types of discrimination, including national origin discrimination and race discrimination
  Fact Sheets
  http://www.eeoc.gov/eeoinfo.html
- Information on complying with federal anti-discrimination laws
  Information for Small Employers
  http://www.eeoc.gov/small/index.html
- A description of the EEOC and how it works
  The U.S. Equal Employment Opportunity Commission: An Overview
  http://www.eeoc.gov/facts/overview.html

- Information about anti-discrimination laws
  Federal Laws Prohibiting Job Discrimination: Questions and Answers
  http://www.eeoc.gov/facts/qanda.html
- Instructions on how to file a charge of discrimination with the EEOC
  Filing a Charge
  http://www.eeoc.gov/facts/howtofil.html

F. State Laws Relating to Disability Discrimination

See the chapter on Title VII, (Title VII) Section F, for state laws relating to all forms of employment discrimination, including disability discrimination.

G. Text of the ADA

Selected portions that deal with private sector employment.

U.S. Code
Title 42: The Public Health and Welfare
Chapter 126: Equal Opportunity for Individuals With Disabilities

§ 12101. Findings and purpose.
§ 12102. Definitions.
...
Subchapter I—Employment
§ 12111. Definitions.
§ 12112. Discrimination.
§ 12113. Defenses.
§ 12114. Illegal use of drugs and alcohol.
§ 12115. Posting notices.
§ 12116. Regulations.
§ 12117. Enforcement.

...

§ 12101. [§ 2] Findings and Purposes

(a) Findings.—The Congress finds that—

(1) some 43,000,000 Americans have one or more physical or mental disabilities, and this number is increasing as the population as a whole is growing older;

(2) historically, society has tended to isolate and segregate individuals with disabilities, and, despite some improvements, such forms of discrimination against individuals with disabilities continue to be a serious and pervasive social problem;

(3) discrimination against individuals with disabilities persists in such critical areas as employment, housing, public accommodations, education, transportation, communication, recreation, institutionalization, health services, voting, and access to public services;

(4) unlike individuals who have experienced discrimination on the basis of race, color, sex, national origin, religion, or age, individuals who have experienced discrimination on the basis of disability have often had no legal recourse to redress such discrimination;

(5) individuals with disabilities continually encounter various forms of discrimination, including outright intentional exclusion, the discriminatory effects of architectural, transportation, and communication barriers, overprotective rules and policies, failure to make modifications to existing facilities and practices, exclusionary qualification standards and criteria, segregation, and relegation to lesser services, programs, activities, benefits, jobs, or other opportunities;

(6) census data, national polls, and other studies have documented that people with disabilities, as a group, occupy an inferior status in our society, and are severely disadvantaged socially, vocationally, economically, and educationally;

(7) individuals with disabilities are a discrete and insular minority who have been faced with restrictions

and limitations, subjected to a history of purposeful unequal treatment, and relegated to a position of political powerlessness in our society, based on characteristics that are beyond the control of such individuals and resulting from stereotypic assumptions not truly indicative of the individual ability of such individuals to participate in, and contribute to, society;

(8) the Nation's proper goals regarding individuals with disabilities are to assure equality of opportunity, full participation, independent living, and economic self-sufficiency for such individuals; and

(9) the continuing existence of unfair and unnecessary discrimination and prejudice denies people with disabilities the opportunity to compete on an equal basis and to pursue those opportunities for which our free society is justifiably famous, and costs the United States billions of dollars in unnecessary expenses resulting from dependency and nonproductivity.

(b) Purpose.—It is the purpose of this Act—

(1) to provide a clear and comprehensive national mandate for the elimination of discrimination against individuals with disabilities;

(2) to provide clear, strong, consistent, enforceable standards addressing discrimination against individuals with disabilities;

(3) to ensure that the Federal Government plays a central role in enforcing the standards established in this Act on behalf of individuals with disabilities; and

(4) to invoke the sweep of congressional authority, including the power to enforce the fourteenth amendment and to regulate commerce, in order to address the major areas of discrimination faced day-to-day by people with disabilities.

§ 12102. [§ 3] Definitions

As used in this chapter:

(1) Auxiliary aids and services.—The term "auxiliary aids and services" includes—

(A) qualified interpreters or other effective methods of making aurally delivered materials available to individuals with hearing impairments;

(B) qualified readers, taped texts, or other effective methods of making visually delivered materials available to individuals with visual impairments;

(C) acquisition or modification of equipment or devices; and

(D) other similar services and actions.

(2) Disability.—The term "disability" means, with respect to an individual—

(A) a physical or mental impairment that substantially limits one or more of the major life activities of such individual;

(B) a record of such an impairment; or

(C) being regarded as having such an impairment.

(3) State.—The term "State" means each of the several States, the District of Columbia, the Commonwealth of Puerto Rico, Guam, American Samoa, the Virgin Islands, the Trust Territory of the Pacific Islands, and the Commonwealth of the Northern Mariana Islands.

Subchapter I [Title I]—Employment

§ 12111. [§ 101] Definitions

As used in this subchapter:

(1) Commission.—The term "Commission" means the Equal Employment Opportunity Commission established by section 2000e-4 of this title [section 705 of the Civil Rights Act of 1964].

(2) Covered entity.—The term "covered entity" means an employer, employment agency, labor organization, or joint labor-management committee.

(3) Direct threat.—The term "direct threat" means a significant risk to the health or safety of others that cannot be eliminated by reasonable accommodation.

(4) Employee.—The term "employee" means an individual employed by an employer. With respect to employment in a foreign country, such term includes an individual who is a citizen of the United States.

(5) Employer.—

(A) In general.—The term "employer" means a person engaged in an industry affecting commerce who has 15 or more employees for each working day in each of 20 or more calendar weeks in the current or preceding calendar year, and any agent of such person, except that, for two years following the effective date of this subchapter, an employer means a person engaged in an industry affecting commerce who has 25 or more employees for each working day in each of 20 or more calendar weeks in the current or preceding year, and any agent of such person.

(B) Exceptions.—The term "employer" does not include—

(i) the United States, a corporation wholly owned by the government of the United States, or an Indian tribe; or

(ii) a bona fide private membership club (other than a labor organization) that is exempt from taxation under section 501(C) of Title 26 *[the Internal Revenue Code of 1986]*.

(6) Illegal use of drugs.—

(A) In general.—The term "illegal use of drugs" means the use of drugs, the possession or distribution of which is unlawful under the Controlled Substances Act *[21 U.S.C. 801 et seq.]*. Such term does not include the use of a drug taken under supervision by a licensed health care professional, or other uses authorized by the Controlled Substances Act or other provisions of Federal law.

(B) Drugs.—The term "drug" means a controlled substance, as defined in schedules I through V of section 202 of the Controlled Substances Act *[21 U.S.C. 812]*.

(7) Person, etc.—The terms "person", "labor organization", "employment agency", "commerce", and "industry affecting commerce", shall have the same meaning given such terms in section 2000e of this title *[section 701 of the Civil Rights Act of 1964]*.

(8) Qualified individual with a disability.—The term "qualified individual with a disability" means an individual with a disability who, with or without reasonable accommodation, can perform the essential functions of the employment position that such individual holds or desires. For the purposes of this subchapter, consideration shall be given to the employer's judgment as to what functions of a job are essential, and if an employer has prepared a written description before advertising or interviewing applicants for the job, this description shall be considered evidence of the essential functions of the job.

(9) Reasonable accommodation.—The term "reasonable accommodation" may include—

(A) making existing facilities used by employees readily accessible to and usable by individuals with disabilities; and

(B) job restructuring, part-time or modified work schedules, reassignment to a vacant position, acquisition or modification of equipment or devices, appropriate adjustment or modifications of examinations, training materials or policies, the provision of qualified readers or interpreters, and other similar accommodations for individuals with disabilities.

(10) Undue hardship.—

(A) In general.—The term "undue hardship" means an action requiring significant difficulty or expense, when considered in light of the factors set forth in subparagraph (B).

(B) Factors to be considered.—In determining whether an accommodation would impose an undue hardship on a covered entity, factors to be considered include—

(i) the nature and cost of the accommodation needed under this chapter;

(ii) the overall financial resources of the facility or facilities involved in the provision of the reasonable accommodation; the number of persons employed at such facility; the effect on expenses and resources, or the impact otherwise of such accommodation upon the operation of the facility;

(iii) the overall financial resources of the covered entity; the overall size of the business of a covered entity with respect to the number of its employees; the number, type, and location of its facilities; and

(iv) the type of operation or operations of the covered entity, including the composition, structure, and functions of the workforce of such entity; the geographic separateness, administrative, or fiscal relationship of the facility or facilities in question to the covered entity.

§ 12112. [§ 102] Discrimination

(a) General rule.—No covered entity shall discriminate against a qualified individual with a disability because of the disability of such individual in regard to job application procedures, the hiring, advancement, or discharge of employees, employee compensation, job training, and other terms, conditions, and privileges of employment.

(b) Construction.—As used in subsection (a) of this section, the term "discriminate" includes—

(1) limiting, segregating, or classifying a job applicant or employee in a way that adversely affects the opportunities or status of such applicant or employee because of the disability of such applicant or employee;

(2) participating in a contractual or other arrangement or relationship that has the effect of subjecting a covered entity's qualified applicant or employee with a disability to the discrimination prohibited by this subchapter (such relationship includes a relationship with an employment or referral agency, labor union, an organization providing fringe benefits to an

employee of the covered entity, or an organization providing training and apprenticeship programs);

(3) utilizing standards, criteria, or methods of administration—

(A) that have the effect of discrimination on the basis of disability; or

(B) that perpetuate the discrimination of others who are subject to common administrative control;

(4) excluding or otherwise denying equal jobs or benefits to a qualified individual because of the known disability of an individual with whom the qualified individual is known to have a relationship or association;

(5)

(A) not making reasonable accommodations to the known physical or mental limitations of an otherwise qualified individual with a disability who is an applicant or employee, unless such covered entity can demonstrate that the accommodation would impose an undue hardship on the operation of the business of such covered entity; or

(B) denying employment opportunities to a job applicant or employee who is an otherwise qualified individual with a disability, if such denial is based on the need of such covered entity to make reasonable accommodation to the physical or mental impairments of the employee or applicant;

(6) using qualification standards, employment tests or other selection criteria that screen out or tend to screen out an individual with a disability or a class of individuals with disabilities unless the standard, test or other selection criteria, as used by the covered entity, is shown to be job-related for the position in question and is consistent with business necessity; and

(7) failing to select and administer tests concerning employment in the most effective manner to ensure that, when such test is administered to a job applicant or employee who has a disability that impairs sensory, manual, or speaking skills, such test results accurately reflect the skills, aptitude, or whatever other factor of such applicant or employee that such test purports to measure, rather than reflecting the impaired sensory, manual, or speaking skills of such employee or applicant (except where such skills are the factors that the test purports to measure).

(c) Covered entities in foreign countries.—

(1) In general.—It shall not be unlawful under this section for a covered entity to take any action that constitutes discrimination under this section with respect to an employee in a workplace in a foreign country if compliance with this section would cause such covered entity to violate the law of the foreign country in which such workplace is located.

(2) Control of corporation

(A) Presumption.—If an employer controls a corporation whose place of incorporation is a foreign country, any practice that constitutes discrimination under this section and is engaged in by such corporation shall be presumed to be engaged in by such employer.

(B) Exception.—This section shall not apply with respect to the foreign operations of an employer that is a foreign person not controlled by an American employer.

(C) Determination.—For purposes of this paragraph, the determination of whether an employer controls a corporation shall be based on

(i) the interrelation of operations;

(ii) the common management;

(iii) the centralized control of labor relations; and

(iv) the common ownership or financial control, of the employer and the corporation.

(d) Medical examinations and inquiries.—

(1) In general.—The prohibition against discrimination as referred to in subsection (a) of this section shall include medical examinations and inquiries.

(2) Preemployment.—

(A) Prohibited examination or inquiry.—Except as provided in paragraph (3), a covered entity shall not conduct a medical examination or make inquiries of a job applicant as to whether such applicant is an individual with a disability or as to the nature or severity of such disability.

(B) Acceptable inquiry.—A covered entity may make preemployment inquiries into the ability of an applicant to perform job-related functions.

(3) Employment entrance examination.—A covered entity may require a medical examination after an offer of employment has been made to a job applicant and prior to the commencement of the employment duties of such applicant, and may condition an offer of employment on the results of such examination, if—

(A) all entering employees are subjected to such an examination regardless of disability;

(B) information obtained regarding the medical condition or history of the applicant is collected and maintained on separate forms and in separate medical files and is treated as a confidential medical record, except that—

(i) supervisors and managers may be informed regarding necessary restrictions on the work or duties of the employee and necessary accommodations;

(ii) first aid and safety personnel may be informed, when appropriate, if the disability might require emergency treatment; and

(iii) government officials investigating compliance with this chapter shall be provided relevant information on request; and

(C) the results of such examination are used only in accordance with this subchapter.

(4) Examination and inquiry.—

(A) Prohibited examinations and inquiries.—A covered entity shall not require a medical examination and shall not make inquiries of an employee as to whether such employee is an individual with a disability or as to the nature or severity of the disability, unless such examination or inquiry is shown to be job-related and consistent with business necessity.

(B) Acceptable examinations and inquiries.—A covered entity may conduct voluntary medical examinations, including voluntary medical histories, which are part of an employee health program available to employees at that work site. A covered entity may make inquiries into the ability of an employee to perform job-related functions.

(C) Requirement.—Information obtained under subparagraph (B) regarding the medical condition or history of any employee are subject to the requirements of subparagraphs (B) and (C) of paragraph (3).

§ 12113. [§ 103] Defenses

(a) In general.—It may be a defense to a charge of discrimination under this chapter that an alleged application of qualification standards, tests, or selection criteria that screen out or tend to screen out or otherwise deny a job or benefit to an individual with a disability has been shown to be job-related and consistent with business necessity, and such performance cannot be accomplished by reasonable accommodation, as required under this subchapter.

(b) Qualification standards.—The term "qualification standards" may include a requirement that an individual shall not pose a direct threat to the health or safety of other individuals in the workplace.

(c) Religious entities.—

(1) In general.—This subchapter shall not prohibit a religious corporation, association, educational institution, or society from giving preference in employment to individuals of a particular religion to perform work connected with the carrying on by such corporation, association, educational institution, or society of its activities.

(2) Religious tenets requirement.—Under this subchapter, a religious organization may require that all applicants and employees conform to the religious tenets of such organization.

(d) List of infectious and communicable diseases.—

(1) In general.—The Secretary of Health and Human Services, not later than 6 months after July 26, 1990 *[the date of enactment of this Act]*, shall—

(A) review all infectious and communicable diseases which may be transmitted through handling the food supply;

(B) publish a list of infectious and communicable diseases which are transmitted through handling the food supply;

(C) publish the methods by which such diseases are transmitted; and

(D) widely disseminate such information regarding the list of diseases and their modes of transmissibility to the general public. Such list shall be updated annually.

(2) Applications.—In any case in which an individual has an infectious or communicable disease that is transmitted to others through the handling of food, that is included on the list developed by the Secretary of Health and Human Services under paragraph (1), and which cannot be eliminated by reasonable accommodation, a covered entity may refuse to assign or continue to assign such individual to a job involving food handling.

(3) Construction.—Nothing in this chapter shall be construed to preempt, modify, or amend any State, county, or local law, ordinance, or regulation applicable to food handling which is designed to protect the public health from individuals who pose a significant risk to the health or safety of others, which cannot be eliminated by reasonable accommodation, pursuant to the list of infectious or communicable diseases and the modes of transmissibility published by the Secretary of Health and Human Services.

§ 12114. [§ 104] Illegal Use of Drugs and Alcohol

(a) Qualified individual with a disability.—For purposes of this subchapter, the term "qualified individual with a disability" shall not include any employee or applicant who is currently engaging in the illegal use of drugs, when the covered entity acts on the basis of such use.

(b) Rules of construction.—Nothing in subsection (a) of this section shall be construed to exclude as a qualified individual with a disability an individual who—

(1) has successfully completed a supervised drug rehabilitation program and is no longer engaging in the illegal use of drugs, or has otherwise been rehabilitated successfully and is no longer engaging in such use;

(2) is participating in a supervised rehabilitation program and is no longer engaging in such use; or

(3) is erroneously regarded as engaging in such use, but is not engaging in such use; except that it shall not be a violation of this chapter for a covered entity to adopt or administer reasonable policies or procedures, including but not limited to drug testing, designed to ensure that an individual described in paragraph (1) or (2) is no longer engaging in the illegal use of drugs.

(c) Authority of covered entity.—

A covered entity—

(1) may prohibit the illegal use of drugs and the use of alcohol at the workplace by all employees;

(2) may require that employees shall not be under the influence of alcohol or be engaging in the illegal use of drugs at the workplace;

(3) may require that employees behave in conformance with the requirements established under the Drug Free Workplace Act of 1988 (41 U.S.C. 701 et seq.);

(4) may hold an employee who engages in the illegal use of drugs or who is an alcoholic to the same qualification standards for employment or job performance and behavior that such entity holds other employees, even if any unsatisfactory performance or behavior is related to the drug use or alcoholism of such employee; and

(5) may, with respect to Federal regulations regarding alcohol and the illegal use of drugs, require that—

(A) employees comply with the standards established in such regulations of the Department of Defense, if the employees of the covered entity are employed in an industry subject to such regulations, including complying with regulations (if any) that apply to employment in sensitive positions in such an industry, in the case of employees of the covered entity who are employed in such positions (as defined in the regulations of the Department of Defense);

(B) employees comply with the standards established in such regulations of the Nuclear Regulatory Commission, if the employees of the covered entity are employed in an industry subject to such regulations, including complying with regulations (if any) that apply to employment in sensitive positions in such an industry, in the case of employees of the covered entity who are employed in such positions (as defined in the regulations of the Nuclear Regulatory Commission); and

(C) employees comply with the standards established in such regulations of the Department of Transportation, if the employees of the covered entity are employed in a transportation industry subject to such regulations, including complying with such regulations (if any) that apply to employment in sensitive positions in such an industry, in the case of employees of the covered entity who are employed in such positions (as defined in the regulations of the Department of Transportation).

(d) Drug testing.—

(1) In general.—For purposes of this subchapter, a test to determine the illegal use of drugs shall not be considered a medical examination.

(2) Construction.—Nothing in this subchapter shall be construed to encourage, prohibit, or authorize the conducting of drug testing for the illegal use of drugs by job applicants or employees or making employment decisions based on such test results.

(e) Transportation employees.—Nothing in this subchapter shall be construed to encourage, prohibit, restrict, or authorize the otherwise lawful exercise by entities subject to the jurisdiction of the Department of Transportation of authority to—

(1) test employees of such entities in, and applicants for, positions involving safety sensitive duties for the illegal use of drugs and for on-duty impairment by alcohol; and

(2) remove such persons who test positive for illegal use of drugs and on-duty impairment by alcohol pursuant to paragraph (1) from safety sensitive duties in implementing subsection (C) of this section.

§ 12115. [§ 105] Posting Notices

Every employer, employment agency, labor organization, or joint labor-management committee covered under this subchapter shall post notices in an accessible format to applicants, employees, and members describing the applicable provisions of this chapter, in the manner prescribed by section 2000e-10 of this title *[section 711 of the Civil Rights Act of 1964]*.

§ 12116. [§ 106] Regulations

Not later than 1 year after July 26, 1990 *[the date of enactment of this Act]*, the Commission shall issue regulations in an accessible format to carry out this subchapter in accordance with subchapter II of chapter 5 of title 5 *[United States Code]*.

§ 12117. [§ 107] Enforcement

(a) Powers, remedies, and procedures.—The powers, remedies, and procedures set forth in sections 2000e-4, 2000e-5, 2000e-6, 2000e-8, and 2000e-9 of this title *[sections 705, 706, 707, 709 and 710 of the Civil Rights Act of 1964]* shall be the powers, remedies, and procedures this subchapter provides to the Commission, to the Attorney General, or to any person alleging discrimination on the basis of disability in violation of any provision of this chapter, or regulations promulgated under section 12116 of this title *[section 106]*, concerning employment.

(b) Coordination.—The agencies with enforcement authority for actions which allege employment discrimination under this subchapter and under the Rehabilitation Act of 1973 *[29 U.S.C. 701 et seq.]* shall develop procedures to ensure that administrative complaints filed under this subchapter and under the Rehabilitation Act of 1973 are dealt with in a manner that avoids duplication of effort and prevents imposition of inconsistent or conflicting standards for the same requirements under this subchapter and the Rehabilitation Act of 1973. The Commission, the Attorney General, and the Office of Federal Contract Compliance Programs shall establish such coordinating mechanisms (similar to provisions contained in the joint regulations promulgated by the Commission and the Attorney General at part 42 of title 28 and part 1691 of title 29, Code of Federal Regulations, and the Memorandum of Understanding between the Commission and the Office of Federal Contract Compliance Programs dated January 16, 1981 (46 Fed. Reg. 7435, January 23, 1981)) in regulations implementing this subchapter and Rehabilitation Act of 1973 not later than 18 months after July 26, 1990 *[the date of enactment of this Act]*.

Chapter 3

Age Discrimination in Employment Act (ADEA)

Statute: 29 U.S.C. §§ 621-634
http://www.law.cornell.edu/uscode/29/ch14.html

Regulations: 29 C.F.R. §§ 1625-26
http://lula.law.cornell.edu/cfr/cfr.php?title=29&type=part&value=1625

Definitions

Bona fide employee benefit plan

A benefit plan that has been accurately described, in writing, to all employees and that actually provides the benefits promised.

Bona fide executive

A top level employee who exercises substantial executive authority over a significant number of employees and a large volume of business. Examples include the head of a substantial regional operation of a national employer or the head of a major corporate division.

Bona fide occupational qualification

An exception to ADEA that allows employers to discriminate on the basis of age if the nature of the job requires them to do so. For more on bona fide occupational qualifications (BFOQs), see Section A7, "Exceptions," below.

Bona fide seniority system

A seniority system that uses length of service with the employer as the primary criterion for deciding who will receive available employment opportunities and perquisites. For the system to qualify as "bona fide," its essential terms and conditions must be communicated to employees and applied uniformly to all workers, regardless of age. For more on bona fide seniority systems, see Section A7, "Exceptions," below.

Firefighter

An employee whose primary duties are to perform work directly connected with controlling and extinguishing fires or maintaining and using firefighting apparatus and equipment, including an employee engaged in any of these activities who is transferred to a supervisory or administrative position.

High policymaking position

A top level position that carries significant responsibility, held by someone who plays a substantial role in the development and effective implementation of corporate policy. This definition includes employees who do not supervise other workers, such as a company's chief research scientist or head economist.

Law enforcement officer

An employee whose primary duties are the investigation, apprehension or detention of individuals suspected or convicted of offenses against the criminal laws of a state, including an employee engaged in this activity who is transferred to a supervisory or administrative position. Prison guards and other employees assigned to guard incarcerated prisoners are law enforcement officers.

A. Overview of the ADEA

1. Summary

The Age Discrimination in Employment Act (ADEA) prohibits age discrimination against employees and applicants age 40 or older. Congress passed the ADEA in 1967 to address the difficulties older employees face in the workplace, including mandatory retirement cutoffs and discrimination in the hiring process. The ADEA outlaws age discrimination but does create a few limited exceptions, recognizing the fact that advanced age may, in some circumstances, affect a worker's ability to perform certain jobs effectively.

2. Regulated Employers

The ADEA covers the following employers:
- private employers with 20 or more employees (an employer has 20 or more employees if it has 20 or more employees on each working day in each of 20 or more calendar weeks in the current or preceding calendar year)
- state and local governments (but state employees may not sue their employer for ADEA violations—see Section A3, below)
- employment agencies, and
- labor organizations.

One section of the ADEA (29 U.S.C. § 633a) requires most federal agencies not to discriminate on the basis of age against employees or applicants who are at least 40 years of age.

3. Covered Workers

The ADEA covers those who work for regulated employers.

Although state government workers are protected by the ADEA, they do not have the right to sue their employers (the state for which they work) in court to enforce those rights—only the EEOC may sue a state to protect state employees from age discrimination.

The ADEA protects only workers who are at least 40 years old. Unlike other anti-discrimination laws, the ADEA does not prohibit "reverse discrimination"—workers under the age of 40 have no rights under the law.

4. What's Prohibited: Employers

The ADEA prohibits age discrimination against applicants and employees who are at least 40 years old. The ADEA applies to all aspects of employment, including:
- hiring
- firing
- compensation
- benefits
- job assignments and transfers
- employee classifications
- promotions
- layoffs and recalls
- training and apprenticeship programs
- retirement plans
- leave.

The ADEA also prohibits employers from retaliating against employees who complain of age discrimination or otherwise assert their rights under the law. For more on retaliation, see "Retaliation," below.

Discrimination

Among the practices that might constitute age discrimination under the ADEA are:

- requiring workers to retire once they reach a certain age
- treating older workers worse than younger workers by, for example, targeting them for layoffs or discipline
- giving younger workers higher pay, more favorable assignments or more responsibilities than older workers because of age
- making decisions based on stereotypes about older people (for example, refusing to include older workers in training programs because of a belief that they are set in their ways and unwilling or unable to learn new things).

The ADEA's prohibitions apply even if the "younger" workers who receive better treatment are over the age of 40. For instance, an employer who treats a 60-year-old worker more favorably than a 70-year-old worker because of age has violated the ADEA, even though both workers are protected from age discrimination under the law.

Disparate Impact Claims Are an Open Question

Most anti-discrimination laws, including Title VII (see the chapter on Title VII), prohibit not only intentional discrimination but also seemingly neutral practices that have a discriminatory effect on a particular group, even if the employer did not intend to discriminate. For example, a height requirement may disqualify disproportionate numbers of women and members of certain minority groups.

However, because the ADEA was written somewhat differently than Title VII and other anti-discrimination laws, courts disagree as to whether the ADEA prohibits employment practices that have a discriminatory effect (or "disparate impact"). Some courts allow employees to bring these claims; others don't.

This issue comes up frequently in the context of layoffs. For example, an employer who needs to cut costs might decide to lay off its most highly compensated employees. In most companies, these employees will be the workers who have the longest seniority at the company, and probably will be disproportionately older workers. If the employer's true purpose was not to discriminate but to cut costs, the laid-off workers' only available age discrimination challenge would be a disparate impact claim.

The U.S. Supreme Court heard arguments on this issue in 2002, but declined to decide the case—which means that the viability of age-based disparate impact claims is still and open question.

Harassment

Harassment occurs when an employee is forced to endure a hostile, offensive or intimidating work environment because of his or her age. Harassment might include:

- age-related slurs or offensive remarks
- offensive jokes about a worker's age

- cartoons or pictures that depict older people unfavorably
- threats, intimidation or hostility
- physical violence.

Although harassment has been recognized as a form of discrimination under Title VII (see the chapter on Title VII), there have been very few lawsuits by workers claiming age-based harassment. As a result, the U.S. Supreme Court and most of the federal Courts of Appeal have not explicitly said that harassment claims can be brought under the ADEA. Most legal scholars believe that age-based harassment is illegal under the ADEA. However, because the language of the ADEA is slightly different from the language of Title VII, some commentators still consider this an open question.

Advertising Prohibitions

The ADEA specifically prohibits employers from printing or publishing any job advertisement or notice that expresses a preference or limitation based on age. Terms such as "college student," "young" or "recent college graduate" all fall afoul of this rule. Job notices seeking applicants of a particular age are also illegal.

Retaliation

The ADEA prohibits employers from retaliating against employees who complain about age discrimination, file a charge of age discrimination with the Equal Employment Opportunity Commission, participate in an investigation of age discrimination, file or testify in a lawsuit alleging age discrimination or otherwise exercise their rights under the ADEA.

Retaliation means any negative job action an employer takes against an employee for exercising his or her legal rights. It might include firing, demotion, discipline, pay cuts or less favorable job assignments.

5. What's Required: Employers

See Section A4, "What's Prohibited: Employers," above.

6. What's Required: Workers

Not applicable.

7. Exceptions

Employers may use age as a basis for employment decisions in a few limited circumstances. If an employer who relies on one of these exceptions is sued for age discrimination, the employer will bear the burden of proving that its actions fell within the exception.

Bona Fide Seniority System

An employer may use a *bona fide seniority system* as a basis for employment decisions, even if that results in more favorable treatment of younger workers. For example, an employer can adopt a policy of laying off workers who have the least seniority with the company, even if older workers disproportionately lose their jobs as a result.

This exception is rarely used—because older workers tend to have greater seniority than younger workers, they are unlikely to be disadvantaged by an employer's decision to lay off workers who have little or no seniority. A "reverse" seniority system that benefits workers with less seniority or penalizes workers with more seniority does not qualify as a *bona fide seniority system* under the ADEA.

Bona Fide Occupational Qualification

An employer may discriminate on the basis of age in filling a particular job if age is a *bona fide occupational qualification* (BFOQ) for the position—that is, if the job, by its very nature, must be filled by an employee of a particular age. In age discrimination cases, the BFOQ defense comes up most often in the context of age limits, when an employer refuses to hire anyone over a certain age for certain positions.

An employer may use the BFOQ defense only if the age limit or other age-related policy is reasonably necessary to the essence of the employer's business, and

- all or substantially all persons over the age limit would be unable to perform the job, or
- some persons over the age limit would be unable to perform the job and testing each employee individually to determine whether he or she can perform the job would be impossible or highly impractical for the employer.

If the employer's goal in using the BFOQ is public safety, the employer must also show not only that the challenged age limit achieves that goal, but also that there is no acceptable alternative that is less discriminatory.

Bona Fide Employee Benefit Plan

- In some cases, an employer may reduce benefits paid to older workers if the employer acts in accordance with a *bona fide employee benefit plan*. This exception is discussed in detail in the chapter on the Older Workers' Benefits Protection Act (OWBPA).

Firefighters and Law Enforcement Officers

State and local governments may institute a mandatory retirement age of 55 or older for *firefighters* and *law enforcement officers*.

Bona Fide Executives and High Policymakers

Employers may require a high-ranking employee to retire or step down to a lesser position if all of the following conditions are met:

- the employee is 65 or older
- the employee has worked for at least the previous two years as a *bona fide executive* or in a *high policymaking position*, and
- the employee is entitled to an immediate, nonforfeitable annual retirement benefit of at least $44,000 from the employer. A benefit is immediate if payments start (or could have started, at the employee's election) within 60 days of the effective date of the employee's retirement. A benefit is nonforfeitable if no plan provisions could cause payments to cease. For example, if the plan requires payments to be suspended if the employee files a lawsuit, that benefit would be

forfeitable. In calculating whether a benefit pays at least $44,000 annually, employers may not count Social Security contributions, employee contributions, contributions of former employers or rollover contributions.

B. How the ADEA Is Enforced

1. Individual Complaints

Employees may file a charge (complaint) of age discrimination with the Equal Employment Opportunity Commission (EEOC). The deadlines for filing a charge depend on whether the state where the discrimination charge will be filed also has an anti-discrimination law. In states without anti-discrimination laws, an employee has 180 days from the date of the discriminatory act to complain. In states with an anti-discrimination law, this deadline is extended to 300 days. (See Section F of the chapter on Title VII for a list of states with anti-discrimination laws.)

An employee may also file a lawsuit for age discrimination. However, the employee must file a charge of discrimination with the EEOC and get a "right to sue" letter first (see Section B2, below). An employee must file the lawsuit within 90 days of receiving a right to sue letter from the EEOC.

2. Agency Enforcement

The federal agency responsible for investigating ADEA complaints is the EEOC. An employee usually initiates the process by filing a charge (complaint) of age discrimination with the EEOC, although the agency can also act on its own initiative. The EEOC has the power to investigate, negotiate with employers and bring lawsuits against employers to stop discriminatory practices.

Once an employee files a charge with the EEOC, the employee cannot file a lawsuit until the EEOC gives the employee a "right to sue" letter. The EEOC generally issues such a letter when it finishes processing the charge— and it must issue a right to sue letter if it has not filed its own lawsuit against the employer within 180 days after the charge is filed. However, an employee who wants to file a lawsuit before the EEOC has completed its investigation or before 180 days have passed can request a right to sue letter from the agency—the EEOC will generally comply with these requests.

C. For Employers: Complying With the ADEA

1. Reporting Requirements

The ADEA imposes no reporting requirements.

2. Posting Requirements

All regulated employers must post a notice regarding the ADEA. Employers must post this notice in a prominent location, where it can be easily seen and read by employees and job applicants. The Department of Labor has created a poster, "Equal Employment Opportunity Is the Law," which fulfills this requirement. You can access and print the poster at the Department of Labor's website, or you can order the poster in English, Spanish or Chinese from the Equal Employment Opportunity Commission (see "Agency Resources for Employers" in Section E, below).

3. Recordkeeping Requirements

Employers must make and keep records for three years that contain the following information for each employee:

- name
- address
- birth date
- occupation
- pay rate, and
- compensation earned each week.

Employers who make or use personnel records relating to the following topics must keep those records for one year after any personnel action to which the records relate:

- Job applications, resumes, responses to job advertisements, inquiries about jobs and any other records relating to the failure to hire any applicant.
- Promotion, demotion, transfer, selection for training, layoff, recall or termination.
- Job orders submitted by the employer to an employment agency or labor organization to recruit applicants for job openings.
- Test papers completed by applicants for any position.

- Results of any physical examination considered by the employer in connection with any personnel action.
- Job notices or advertisements relating to job openings, promotions, training programs or opportunities to work overtime.

Employers must also keep copies of any employment benefit plan and any written seniority system and merit system for one year beyond the date when the plan expires. If such a plan or system is not written, the employer must keep a memorandum fully outlining its terms and the manner in which it has been communicated to employees for the same time period.

4. Practical Tips

Here are some practical tips to consider:

- **Make employment-based decisions.** If you can show that you took a disputed work action (such as promoting one employee over another or laying off certain workers) for non-discriminatory reasons based on your legitimate business needs, an employee will have a tough time proving that you acted out of bias or prejudice.
- **Investigate complaints right away.** Adopt a written complaint policy, letting employees know how to raise concerns about discrimination. Once an employee complains, investigate immediately—and if your investigation shows that the employee was discriminated against, take quick action to remedy the situation.

- **Keep proper records.** It's important to have written records supporting your employment decisions. For example, if you decide to fire a worker for poor performance, you should have records documenting the reasons for your decision (like performance evaluations and disciplinary warnings). These records will come in handy if the employee later challenges your actions in court.

- **Don't rely on stereotypes.** It is discriminatory to make employment decisions based on stereotypes about a protected class rather than the merits of the individual employee. However, many managers still rely on age-based stereotypes—that older employees cannot learn new ways of working, will retire soon or are declining mentally, for example—when making workplace decisions.

5. Penalties

If a court finds that an employer has violated the ADEA, the employer may be ordered to do any or all of the following:

- Pay the employee all wages, benefits and other forms of compensation lost as a result of the discrimination.

- Take action to remedy the results of the discrimination by, for example, reinstating or promoting the worker. If the court finds that such action is warranted but impractical (for example, if the employee's position has been eliminated or the work relationship is irrevocably

poisoned), the court may require the employer to pay front pay—compensation for future earnings lost—instead.

- Pay a penalty (called "liquidated damages"), equal to all of the wages, benefits and other compensation owed the employee at the time of trial, if the employer knew that its conduct was illegal or showed reckless disregard as to whether its conduct violated the ADEA.

- Pay the employee's court costs and attorney fees.

D. For Workers: Asserting Rights Under the ADEA

1. Where to Start

If you believe your employer has violated the ADEA, your first course of action should be to make an internal complaint. Follow your company's complaint policy or, if there is no policy, complain to a human resources representative or a member of management. If you are a union member, talk to your shop steward or union representative.

If you no longer work for the employer whom you believe violated your rights, you may want to contact your former employer to see if you can resolve the problem informally. However, many former employees choose to go straight to the EEOC instead.

If internal and union complaints don't work, your next step is to file a charge of discrimination with the EEOC (see Section B1, above).

You can file a charge by mail or in person at your nearest EEOC office. To find the office closest to you, call 800-669-4000 or refer to the agency's website at http://www.eeoc.gov/teledir.html.

Once the EEOC has issued you a "right to sue" letter, you can also file a lawsuit in state or federal court against your employer.

2. Required Forms

If you decide to file a charge with the EEOC, you will have to use their charge form. This form is available at EEOC offices and through the EEOC's website (see Section 1, above).

3. Practical Tips

Here are some tips for protecting your rights:

- **Complain as soon as you believe that your rights have been violated.** If your company has a complaint policy, follow the procedures outlined there. If your company has no policy, complain to someone in human resources or a management official. The sooner you assert your rights, the sooner you will know whether the company will work with you to resolve the problem—or whether you will have to get some outside help.

- **Put everything in writing.** Handle important communications relating to your complaint in writing. Take notes of every action, statement or other incident that relates to your complaint. If you file a written complaint with your company, keep a copy. Keep copies of every document relating to your complaint (such as a termination letter or a denial of insurance benefits). If you later have to take your employer to court, these documents will help you prove your case.

- **Let the government work for you.** Some employees think that filing a charge of discrimination with the EEOC is a mere formality—the necessary prerequisite to bringing a lawsuit. But the EEOC can offer valuable help. Once you file a charge of discrimination with the EEOC, the agency will probably investigate your case and may try to resolve the matter with your employer. If the agency thinks you have an especially strong claim, it might even file a lawsuit on your behalf. But even if the EEOC can't settle the case and decides not to represent you in court, you can use what it discovers in its investigation in your own lawsuit.

E. Agency Charged With Enforcement & Compliance

Equal Employment Opportunity Commission
1801 L Street, NW
Washington, DC 20507
Phone: 202-663-4900
TTY: 202-663-4494
http://www.eeoc.gov

Agency Resources for Employers
(These can be obtained either at the Web addresses listed below or at the address and phone number listed above.)
- The official notice employers must post regarding the ADEA
  Equal Employment Opportunity Is the Law
  http://www.dol.gov/dol/esa/public/regs/compliance/posters/pdf/eeobw.pdf (download)
  http://www.eeoc.gov/publications.html (order online)
- Basic facts about the ADEA
  Facts About Age Discrimination
  http://www.eeoc.gov/facts/age.html
- Questions and answers about discrimination for small businesses
  Information for Small Employers
  http://www.eeoc.gov/small/index.html

Agency Resources for Workers
(These can be obtained either at the Web addresses listed below or at the address and phone number listed above.)
- Questions and answers about discrimination laws and EEOC charge processing procedures
  Federal Laws Prohibiting Job Discrimination: Questions and Answers
  http://www.eeoc.gov/facts/qanda.html
- How to file a discrimination charge at the EEOC
  Filing a Charge
  http://www.eeoc.gov/facts/howtofil.html
- Basic facts about the ADEA
  Facts About Age Discrimination
  http://www.eeoc.gov/facts/age.html

F. State Laws Relating to Age Discrimination

Most states have anti-discrimination laws—and many of these laws prohibit age discrimination. Some states follow the ADEA's lead by prohibiting discrimination only against older workers. Other states prohibit all age discrimination—including discrimination against younger workers. To find out whether your state has an age discrimination law, check Section F of the chapter on Title VII.

G. Text of the ADEA

US. Code
Title 29: Labor
Chapter 14: Age Discrimination in Employment

§ 621. [§ 2] Statement of Findings and Purpose

(a) The Congress hereby finds and declares that—

(1) in the face of rising productivity and affluence, older workers find themselves disadvantaged in their efforts to retain employment, and especially to regain employment when displaced from jobs;

(2) the setting of arbitrary age limits regardless of potential for job performance has become a common practice, and certain otherwise desirable practices may work to the disadvantage of older persons;

(3) the incidence of unemployment, especially long-term unemployment with resultant deterioration of skill, morale, and employer acceptability is, relative to the younger ages, high among older workers; their numbers are great and growing; and their employment problems grave;

(4) the existence in industries affecting commerce, of arbitrary discrimination in employment because of age, burdens commerce and the free flow of goods in commerce.

(b) It is therefore the purpose of this chapter to promote employment of older persons based on their ability rather than age; to prohibit arbitrary age discrimination in employment; to help employers and workers find ways of meeting problems arising from the impact of age on employment.

§ 622. [§ 3] Education and Research Program

(a) The Secretary of Labor *[EEOC]* shall undertake studies and provide information to labor unions, management, and the general public concerning the needs and abilities of older workers, and their potentials for continued employment and contribution to the economy. In order to achieve the purposes of this chapter, the Secretary of Labor *[EEOC]* shall carry on a continuing program of education and information, under which he may, among other measures—

(1) undertake research, and promote research, with a view to reducing barriers to the employment of older persons, and the promotion of measures for utilizing their skills;

(2) publish and otherwise make available to employers, professional societies, the various media of communication, and other interested persons the findings of studies and other materials for the promotion of employment;

(3) foster through the public employment service system and through cooperative effort the development of facilities of public and private agencies for expanding the opportunities and potentials of older persons;

(4) sponsor and assist State and community informational and educational programs.

(b) Not later than six months after the effective date of this chapter, the Secretary shall recommend to the Congress any measures he may deem desirable to change the lower or upper age limits set forth in section 631 of this title *[section 12]*.

§ 623. [§ 4] Prohibition of Age Discrimination

(a) It shall be unlawful for an employer—

(1) to fail or refuse to hire or to discharge any individual or otherwise discriminate against any individual with respect to his compensation, terms, conditions, or privileges of employment, because of such individual's age;

(2) to limit, segregate, or classify his employees in any way which would deprive or tend to deprive any individual of employment opportunities or otherwise adversely affect his status as an employee, because of such individual's age; or

(3) to reduce the wage rate of any employee in order to comply with this chapter.

(b) It shall be unlawful for an employment agency to fail or refuse to refer for employment, or otherwise to discriminate against, any individual because of such individual's age, or to classify or refer for employment any individual on the basis of such individual's age.

(c) It shall be unlawful for a labor organization—

(1) to exclude or to expel from its membership, or otherwise to discriminate against, any individual because of his age;

(2) to limit, segregate, or classify its membership, or to classify or fail or refuse to refer for employment any individual, in any way which would deprive or tend to deprive any individual of employment opportunities, or would limit such employment opportunities or otherwise adversely affect his status as an employee or as an applicant for employment, because of such individual's age;

(3) to cause or attempt to cause an employer to discriminate against an individual in violation of this section.

(d) It shall be unlawful for an employer to discriminate against any of his employees or applicants for employment, for an employment agency to discriminate against any individual, or for a labor organization to discriminate against any member thereof or applicant for membership, because such individual, member or applicant for membership has opposed any practice made unlawful by this section, or because such individual, member or applicant for membership has made a charge, testified, assisted, or participated in any manner in an investigation, proceeding, or litigation under this chapter.

(e) It shall be unlawful for an employer, labor organization, or employment agency to print or publish, or cause to be printed or published, any notice or advertisement relating to employment by such an employer or membership in or any classification or referral for employment by such a labor organization, or relating to any classification or referral for employment by such an employment agency, indicating any preference, limitation, specification, or discrimination, based on age.

(f) It shall not be unlawful for an employer, employment agency, or labor organization—

(1) to take any action otherwise prohibited under subsections (a), (b), (c), or (e) of this section where age is a bona fide occupational qualification reasonably necessary to the normal operation of the particular business, or where the differentiation is based on reasonable factors other than age, or where such practices involve an employee in a workplace in a foreign country, and compliance with such subsections would cause such employer, or a corporation controlled by such employer, to violate the laws of the country in which such workplace is located;

(2) to take any action otherwise prohibited under subsection (a), (b), (c), or (e) of this section—

(A) to observe the terms of a bona fide seniority system that is not intended to evade the purposes of this chapter, except that no such seniority system shall require or permit the involuntary retirement of any individual specified by section 631(a) of this title because of the age of such individual; or

(B) to observe the terms of a bona fide employee benefit plan—

(i) where, for each benefit or benefit package, the actual amount of payment made or cost incurred on behalf of an older worker is no less than that made or incurred on behalf of a younger worker, as permissible under section 1625.10, title 29, Code of Federal Regulations (as in effect on June 22, 1989); or

(ii) that is a voluntary early retirement incentive plan consistent with the relevant purpose or purposes of this chapter. Notwithstanding clause (i) or (ii) of subparagraph (B), no such employee benefit plan or voluntary early retirement incentive plan shall excuse the failure to hire any individual, and no such employee benefit plan shall require or permit the involuntary retirement of any individual specified by section 631(a) of this title, because of the age of such individual. An employer, employment agency, or labor organization acting under subparagraph (A), or under clause (i) or (ii) of subparagraph (B), shall have the burden of proving that such actions are lawful in any civil enforcement proceeding brought under this chapter; or

(3) to discharge or otherwise discipline an individual for good cause.

(g) *[Repealed]*

(h)

(1) If an employer controls a corporation whose place of incorporation is in a foreign country, any practice by such corporation prohibited under this section shall be presumed to be such practice by such employer.

(2) The prohibitions of this section shall not apply where the employer is a foreign person not controlled by an American employer.

(3) For the purpose of this subsection the determination of whether an employer controls a corporation shall be based upon the—

(A) interrelation of operations,

(B) common management,

(C) centralized control of labor relations, and

(D) common ownership or financial control, of the employer and the corporation.

(i) It shall not be unlawful for an employer which is a State, a political subdivision of a State, an agency or instrumentality of a State or a political subdivision of a State, or an interstate agency to fail or refuse to hire or to discharge any individual because of such individual's age if such action is taken—

(1) with respect to the employment of an individual as a firefighter or as a law enforcement officer and the individual has attained the age of hiring or retirement in effect under applicable State or local law on March 3, 1983, and

(2) pursuant to a bona fide hiring or retirement plan that is not a subterfuge to evade the purposes of this chapter.

(j)

(1) Except as otherwise provided in this subsection, it shall be unlawful for an employer, an employment agency, a labor organization, or any combination thereof to establish or maintain an employee pension benefit plan which requires or permits—

(A) in the case of a defined benefit plan, the cessation of an employee's benefit accrual, or the reduction of the rate of an employee's benefit accrual, because of age, or

(B) in the case of a defined contribution plan, the cessation of allocations to an employee's account, or the reduction of the rate at which amounts are allocated to an employee's account, because of age.

(2) Nothing in this section shall be construed to prohibit an employer, employment agency, or labor organization from observing any provision of an employee pension benefit plan to the extent that such provision imposes (without regard to age) a limitation on the amount of benefits that the plan provides or a limitation on the number of years of service or years of participation which are taken into account for purposes of determining benefit accrual under the plan.

(3) In the case of any employee who, as of the end of any plan year under a defined benefit plan, has attained normal retirement age under such plan—

(A) if distribution of benefits under such plan with respect to such employee has commenced as of the end of such plan year, then any requirement of this subsection for continued accrual of benefits under such plan with respect to such employee during such plan year shall be treated as satisfied to the extent of the actuarial equivalent of inservice distribution of benefits, and

(B) if distribution of benefits under such plan with respect to such employee has not commenced as of the end of such year in accordance with section 1056(a)(3) of this title *[section 206(a)(3) of the Employee Retirement Income Security Act of 1974]* and section 401(a)(14)(C) of title 26 *[the Internal Revenue Code of 1986]*, and the payment of benefits under such plan with respect to such employee is not suspended during such plan year pursuant to section 1053(a)(3)(B) of this title *[section 203(a)(3)(B) of the Employee Retirement Income Security Act of 1974]* or section 411(a)(3)(B) of title 26 *[the Internal Revenue Code of 1986]*, then any requirement of this subsection for continued accrual of benefits under such plan with respect to such employee during such plan year shall be treated as satisfied to the extent of any adjustment in the benefit payable under the plan during such plan year attributable to the delay in the distribution of benefits after the attainment of normal retirement age. The provisions of this paragraph shall apply in accordance with regulations of the Secretary of the Treasury. Such regulations shall provide for the application of the preceding provisions of this paragraph to all employee pension benefit plans subject to this subsection and may provide for the application of such provisions, in the case of any such employee, with respect to any period of time within a plan year.

(4) Compliance with the requirements of this subsection with respect to an employee pension benefit plan shall constitute compliance with the requirements of this section relating to benefit accrual under such plan.

(5) Paragraph (1) shall not apply with respect to any employee who is a highly compensated employee (within the meaning of section 414(q) of title 26 *[the Internal Revenue Code of 1986]*) to the extent provided in regulations prescribed by the Secretary of the Treasury for purposes of precluding discrimination in favor of highly compensated employees within the meaning of subchapter D of chapter 1 of title 26 *[the Internal Revenue Code of 1986]*.

(6) A plan shall not be treated as failing to meet the requirements of paragraph (1) solely because the subsidized portion of any early retirement benefit is disregarded in determining benefit accruals.

(7) Any regulations prescribed by the Secretary of the Treasury pursuant to clause (v) of section 411(b)(1)(H) of title 26 *[the Internal Revenue Code of 1986]* and subparagraphs (C) and (D) of section 411(b)(2) of title 26 *[the Internal Revenue Code of 1986]* shall apply with respect to the requirements of this subsection in the same manner and to the same extent as such regulations apply with respect to the requirements of such sections 411(b)(1)(H) and 411(b)(2).

(8) A plan shall not be treated as failing to meet the requirements of this section solely because such plan provides a normal retirement age described in section 1002(24)(B) of this title *[section 3(24)(B) of the Employee Retirement Income Security Act of 1974] and section 411(a)(8)(B) of title 26 [the Internal Revenue Code of 1986]*.

(9) For purposes of this subsection—

(A) The terms "employee pension benefit plan", "defined benefit plan", "defined contribution plan", and "normal retirement age" have the meanings provided such terms in section 1002 of this title *[section 3 of the Employee Retirement Income Security Act of 1974]*.

(B) The term "compensation" has the meaning provided by section 414(s) of title 26 *[the Internal Revenue Code of 1986]*.

(k) A seniority system or employee benefit plan shall comply with this chapter regardless of the date of adoption of such system or plan.

(l) Notwithstanding clause (i) or (ii) of subsection (f)(2)(B) of this section—

(1) It shall not be a violation of subsection (a), (b), (c), or (e) of this section solely because—

(A) an employee pension benefit plan (as defined in section 1002(2) of this title *[section 3(2) of the Employee Retirement Income Security Act of 1974]*) provides for the attainment of a minimum age as a condition of eligibility for normal or early retirement benefits; or

(B) a defined benefit plan (as defined in section 1002(35) of this title *[section 3(35) of such Act]*) provides for—

(i) payments that constitute the subsidized portion of an early retirement benefit; or

(ii) social security supplements for plan participants that commence before the age and terminate at the age (specified by the plan) when participants are eligible to receive reduced or unreduced old age insurance benefits under title II of the Social Security Act (42 U.S.C. 401 et seq.), and that do not exceed such old age insurance benefits.

(2)

(A) It shall not be a violation of subsection (a), (b), (c), or (e) of this section solely because following a contingent event unrelated to age

(i) the value of any retiree health benefits received by an individual eligible for an immediate pension;

(ii) the value of any additional pension benefits that are made available solely as a result of the contingent event unrelated to age and following which the individual is eligible for not less than an immediate and unreduced pension; or

(iii) the values described in both clauses (i) and (ii); are deducted from severance pay made available as a result of the contingent event unrelated to age.

(B) For an individual who receives immediate pension benefits that are actuarially reduced under subparagraph (A)(i), the amount of the deduction available pursuant to subparagraph (A)(i) shall be reduced by the same percentage as the reduction in the pension benefits.

(C) For purposes of this paragraph, severance pay shall include that portion of supplemental unemployment compensation benefits (as described in section 501(c)(17) of title 26 *[the Internal Revenue Code of 1986]*) that—

(i) constitutes additional benefits of up to 52 weeks;

(ii) has the primary purpose and effect of continuing benefits until an individual becomes eligible for an immediate and unreduced pension; and

(iii) is discontinued once the individual becomes eligible for an immediate and unreduced pension.

(D) For purposes of this paragraph and solely in order to make the deduction authorized under this paragraph, the term "retiree health benefits" means benefits provided pursuant to a group health plan covering retirees, for which (determined as of the contingent event unrelated to age)—

(i) the package of benefits provided by the employer for the retirees who are below age 65 is at least comparable to benefits provided under title XVIII of the Social Security Act (42 U.S.C. 1395 et seq.);

(ii) the package of benefits provided by the employer for the retirees who are age 65 and above is at least comparable to that offered under a plan that provides a benefit package with one fourth the value of benefits provided under title XVIII of such Act; or

(iii) the package of benefits provided by the employer is as described in clauses (i) and (ii).

(E)

(i) If the obligation of the employer to provide retiree health benefits is of limited duration, the value for each individual shall be calculated at a rate of $3,000 per year for benefit years before age 65, and $750 per year for benefit years beginning at age 65 and above.

(ii) If the obligation of the employer to provide retiree health benefits is of unlimited duration, the value for each individual shall be calculated at a rate of $48,000 for individuals below age 65, and $24,000 for individuals age 65 and above.

(iii) The values described in clauses (i) and (ii) shall be calculated based on the age of the individual as of the date of the contingent event unrelated to age. The values are effective on October 16, 1990, and shall be adjusted on an annual basis, with respect to a contingent event that occurs subsequent to the first year after October 16, 1990, based on the medical component of the Consumer Price Index for all urban consumers published by the Department of Labor.

(iv) If an individual is required to pay a premium for retiree health benefits, the value calculated pursuant to this subparagraph shall be reduced by whatever percentage of the overall premium the individual is required to pay.

(F) If an employer that has implemented a deduction pursuant to subparagraph (A) fails to fulfill the obligation described in subparagraph (E), any aggrieved individual may bring an action for specific performance of the obligation described in subparagraph (E). The relief shall be in addition to any other remedies provided under Federal or State law.

(3) It shall not be a violation of subsection (a), (b), (c), or (e) of this section solely because an employer provides a bona fide employee benefit plan or plans under which long-term disability benefits received by an individual are reduced by any pension benefits (other than those attributable to employee contributions)—

(A) paid to the individual that the individual voluntarily elects to receive; or

(B) for which an individual who has attained the later of age 62 or normal retirement age is eligible.

§ 624. [§ 5] Study by Secretary of Labor

(a)

(1) The Secretary of Labor *[EEOC]* is directed to undertake an appropriate study of institutional and other arrangements giving rise to involuntary retirement, and report his findings and any appropriate legislative recommendations to the President and to the Congress. Such study shall include—

(A) an examination of the effect of the amendment made by section 3(a) of the Age Discrimination in Employment Act Amendments of 1978 in raising the upper age limitation established by section 631(a) of this title *[section 12(a)]* to 70 years of age;

(B) a determination of the feasibility of eliminating such limitation;

(C) a determination of the feasibility of raising such limitation above 70 years of age; and

(D) an examination of the effect of the exemption contained in section 631(c) of this title *[section 12(c)]*, relating to certain executive employees, and the exemption contained in section 631(d) of this title *[section 12(d)]*, relating to tenured teaching personnel. (2) The Secretary *[EEOC]* may undertake the study required by paragraph (1) of this subsection directly or by contract or other arrangement.

(b) The report required by subsection (a) of this section shall be transmitted to the President and to the Congress as an interim report not later than January 1, 1981, and in final form not later than January 1, 1982.

Transfer of Functions

[All functions relating to age discrimination administration and enforcement vested by Section 6 in the Secretary of Labor or the Civil Service Commission were transferred to the Equal Employment Opportunity Commission effective January 1, 1979, under the President's Reorganization Plan No. 1.]

§ 625. [§ 6] Administration

The Secretary *[EEOC]* shall have the power—

(a) to make delegations, to appoint such agents and employees, and to pay for technical assistance on a fee for service basis, as he deems necessary to assist him in the performance of his functions under this chapter;

(b) to cooperate with regional, State, local, and other agencies, and to cooperate with and furnish technical assistance to employers, labor organizations, and employment agencies to aid in effectuating the purposes of this chapter.

§ 626. [§ 7] Recordkeeping, Investigation, and Enforcement

(a) The Equal Employment Opportunity Commission shall have the power to make investigations and require the keeping of records necessary or appropriate for the administration of this chapter in accordance with the powers and procedures provided in sections 209 and 211 of this title *[sections 9 and 11 of the Fair Labor Standards Act of 1938, as amended]*.

(b) The provisions of this chapter shall be enforced in accordance with the powers, remedies, and procedures provided in sections 211(b), 216 (except for subsection (a) thereof), and 217 of this title *[sections 11(b), 16 (except for subsection (a) thereof), and 17 of the Fair Labor Standards Act of 1938, as amended]*, and subsection (c) of this section. Any act prohibited under section 623 of this title *[section 4]* shall be deemed to be a prohibited act under section 215 of this title *[section 15 of the Fair Labor Standards Act of 1938, as amended]*. Amounts owing to a person as a result of a violation of this chapter shall be deemed to be unpaid minimum wages or unpaid overtime compensation for purposes of sections 216 and 217 of this title *[sections 16 and 17 of the Fair Labor Standards Act of 1938, as amended]*: Provided, That liquidated damages shall be payable only in cases of willful violations of this chapter. In any action brought to enforce this chapter the court shall have jurisdiction to grant such legal or equitable relief as may be appropriate to effectuate the purposes of this chapter, including without limitation judgments compelling employment, reinstatement or promotion, or enforcing the liability for amounts deemed to be unpaid minimum wages or unpaid overtime compensation under this section. Before instituting any action under this section, the Equal Employment Opportunity Commission shall attempt to eliminate the discriminatory practice or practices alleged, and to effect voluntary compliance with the requirements of this chapter through informal methods of conciliation, conference, and persuasion.

(c)

(1) Any person aggrieved may bring a civil action in any court of competent jurisdiction for such legal or equitable relief as will effectuate the purposes of this chapter: Provided, That the right of any person to bring such action shall terminate upon the commencement of an action by the Equal Employment Opportunity Commission to enforce the right of such employee under this chapter.

(2) In an action brought under paragraph (1), a person shall be entitled to a trial by jury of any issue of fact in any such action for recovery of amounts owing as a result of a violation of this chapter, regardless of whether equitable relief is sought by any party in such action.

(d) No civil action may be commenced by an individual under this section until 60 days after a charge alleging unlawful discrimination has been filed with the Equal Employment Opportunity Commission. Such a charge shall be filed—

(1) within 180 days after the alleged unlawful practice occurred; or

(2) in a case to which section 633(b) of this title applies, within 300 days after the alleged unlawful practice occurred, or within 30 days after receipt by the individual of notice of termination of proceedings under State law, whichever is earlier. Upon receiving such a charge, the Commission shall promptly notify all persons named in such charge as prospective defendants in the action and shall promptly seek to eliminate any alleged unlawful practice by informal methods of conciliation, conference, and persuasion.

(e) Section 259 of this title *[section 10 of the Portal-to-Portal Act of 1947]* shall apply to actions under this chapter. If a charge filed with the Commission under this chapter is dismissed or the proceedings of the Commission are otherwise terminated by the Commission, the Commission shall notify the person aggrieved. A civil action may be brought under this section by a person defined in section 630(a) of this title *[section 11(a)]* against the respondent named in the charge within 90 days after the date of the receipt of such notice.

(f)

(1) An individual may not waive any right or claim under this chapter unless the waiver is knowing and voluntary. Except as provided in paragraph (2), a waiver may not be considered knowing and voluntary unless at a minimum—

(A) the waiver is part of an agreement between the individual and the employer that is written in a manner calculated to be understood by such individual, or by the average individual eligible to participate;

(B) the waiver specifically refers to rights or claims arising under this chapter;

(C) the individual does not waive rights or claims that may arise after the date the waiver is executed;

(D) the individual waives rights or claims only in exchange for consideration in addition to anything of value to which the individual already is entitled;

(E) the individual is advised in writing to consult with an attorney prior to executing the agreement;

(F)

(i) the individual is given a period of at least 21 days within which to consider the agreement; or

(ii) if a waiver is requested in connection with an exit incentive or other employment termination program offered to a group or class of employees, the individual is given a period of at least 45 days within which to consider the agreement;

(G) the agreement provides that for a period of at least 7 days following the execution of such agreement, the individual may revoke the agreement, and the agreement shall not become effective or enforceable until the revocation period has expired;

(H) if a waiver is requested in connection with an exit incentive or other employment termination program offered to a group or class of employees, the employer (at the commencement of the period specified in subparagraph (F)) informs the individual in writing in a manner calculated to be understood by the average individual eligible to participate, as to—

(i) any class, unit, or group of individuals covered by such program, any eligibility factors for such program, and any time limits applicable to such program; and

(ii) the job titles and ages of all individuals eligible or selected for the program, and the ages of all individuals in the same job classification or organizational unit who are not eligible or selected for the program.

(2) A waiver in settlement of a charge filed with the Equal Employment Opportunity Commission, or an action filed in court by the individual or the individual's representative, alleging age discrimination of a kind prohibited under section 623 or 633a of this title *[section 4 or 15]* may not be considered knowing and voluntary unless at a minimum—

(A) subparagraphs (A) through (E) of paragraph (1) have been met; and

(B) the individual is given a reasonable period of time within which to consider the settlement agreement.

(3) In any dispute that may arise over whether any of the requirements, conditions, and circumstances set forth in subparagraph (A), (B), (C), (D), (E), (F), (G), or (H) of paragraph (1), or subparagraph (A) or (B) of paragraph (2), have been met, the party asserting the validity of a waiver shall have the burden of proving in a court of competent jurisdiction that a waiver was knowing and voluntary pursuant to paragraph (1) or (2).

(4) No waiver agreement may affect the Commission's rights and responsibilities to enforce this chapter. No waiver may be used to justify interfering with the protected right of an employee to file a charge or participate in an investigation or proceeding conducted by the Commission.

§ 627. [§ 8] Notice to be Posted

Every employer, employment agency, and labor organization shall post and keep posted in conspicuous places upon its premises a notice to be prepared or approved by the Equal Employment Opportunity Commission setting forth information as the Commission deems appropriate to effectuate the purposes of this chapter.

§ 628. [§ 9] Rules and Regulations

In accordance with the provisions of subchapter II of chapter 5 of title 5 *[United States Code]*, the Equal Employment Opportunity Commission may issue such rules and regulations as it may consider necessary or appropriate for carrying out this chapter, and may establish such reasonable exemptions to and from any or all provisions of this chapter as it may find necessary and proper in the public interest.

§ 629. [§ 10] Criminal Penalties

Whoever shall forcibly resist, oppose, impede, intimidate or interfere with a duly authorized representative of the Equal Employment Opportunity Commission while it is engaged in the performance of duties under this chapter shall be punished by a fine of not more than $500 or by imprisonment for not more than one year, or by both: Provided, however, That no person shall be imprisoned under this section except when there has been a prior conviction hereunder.

§ 630. [§ 11] Definitions

For the purposes of this chapter—

(a) The term "person" means one or more individuals, partnerships, associations, labor organizations, corporations, business trust, legal representatives, or any organized groups of persons.

(b) The term "employer" means a person engaged in an industry affecting commerce who has twenty or more employees for each working day in each of twenty or more calendar weeks in the current or preceding calendar year: Provided, That prior to June 30, 1968, employers having fewer than fifty employees shall not be considered employers. The term also means (1) any agent of such a person, and (2) a State or political subdivision of a State and any agency or instrumentality of a State or a political subdivision of a State, and any interstate agency, but such term does not include the United States, or a corporation wholly owned by the Government of the United States.

(c) The term "employment agency" means any person regularly undertaking with or without compensation to procure employees for an employer and includes an agent of such a person; but shall not include an agency of the United States.

(d) The term "labor organization" means a labor organization engaged in an industry affecting commerce, and any agent of such an organization, and includes any organization of any kind, any agency, or employee representation committee, group, association, or plan so engaged in which employees participate and which exists for the purpose, in whole or in part, of dealing with employers concerning grievances, labor disputes, wages, rates of pay, hours, or other terms or conditions of employment, and any conference, general committee, joint or system board, or joint council so engaged which is subordinate to a national or international labor organization.

(e) A labor organization shall be deemed to be engaged in an industry affecting commerce if (1) it maintains or operates a hiring hall or hiring office which procures employees for an employer or procures for employees opportunities to work for an employer, or (2) the number of its members (or, where it is a labor organization composed of other labor organizations or their representatives, posed of other labor organizations or their representatives,

if the aggregate number of the members of such other labor organization) is fifty or more prior to July 1, 1968, or twenty-five or more on or after July 1, 1968, and such labor organization—

(1) is the certified representative of employees under the provisions of the National Labor Relations Act, as amended [29 U.S.C. 151 et seq.], or the Railway Labor Act, as amended [45 U.S.C. 151 et seq.]; or

(2) although not certified, is a national or international labor organization or a local labor organization recognized or acting as the representative of employees of an employer or employers engaged in an industry affecting commerce; or

(3) has chartered a local labor organization or subsidiary body which is representing or actively seeking to represent employees of employers within the meaning of paragraph (1) or (2); or

(4) has been chartered by a labor organization representing or actively seeking to represent employees within the meaning of paragraph (1) or (2) as the local or subordinate body through which such employees may enjoy membership or become affiliated with such labor organization; or

(5) is a conference, general committee, joint or system board, or joint council subordinate to a national or international labor organization, which includes a labor organization engaged in an industry affecting commerce within the meaning of any of the preceding paragraphs of this subsection.

(f) The term "employee" means an individual employed by any employer except that the term "employee" shall not include any person elected to public office in any State or political subdivision of any State by the qualified voters thereof, or any person chosen by such officer to be on such officer's personal staff, or an appointee on the policymaking level or an immediate adviser with respect to the exercise of the constitutional or legal powers of the office. The exemption set forth in the preceding sentence shall not include employees subject to the civil service laws of a State government, governmental agency, or political subdivision. The term "employee" includes any individual who is a citizen of the United States employed by an employer in a workplace in a foreign country.

[The exclusion from the term "employee" of any person chosen by an elected official "to be on such official's personal staff, or an appointee on the policymaking level or an immediate advisor with respect to the exercise of the constitutional or legal powers of the office," remains in section 11(f). However, the Civil Rights Act of 1991 now provides special procedures for such persons who feel they

are victims of age and other types of discrimination prohibited by EEOC enforced statutes. See section 321 of the Civil Rights Act of 1991.]

(g) The term "commerce" means trade, traffic, commerce, transportation, transmission, or communication among the several States; or between a State and any place outside thereof; or within the District of Columbia, or a possession of the United States; or between points in the same State but through a point outside thereof.

(h) The term "industry affecting commerce" means any activity, business, or industry in commerce or in which a labor dispute would hinder or obstruct commerce or the free flow of commerce and includes any activity or industry "affecting commerce" within the meaning of the Labor Management Reporting and Disclosure Act of 1959 *[29 U.S.C. 401 et seq.].*

(i) The term "State" includes a State of the United States, the District of Columbia, Puerto Rico, the Virgin Islands, American Samoa, Guam, Wake Island, the Canal Zone, and Outer Continental Shelf lands defined in the Outer Continental Shelf Lands Act *[43 U.S.C. 1331 et seq.].*

(j) The term "firefighter" means an employee, the duties of whose position are primarily to perform work directly connected with the control and extinguishment of fires or the maintenance and use of firefighting apparatus and equipment, including an employee engaged in this activity who is transferred to a supervisory or administrative position.

(k) The term "law enforcement officer" means an employee, the duties of whose position are primarily the investigation, apprehension, or detention of individuals suspected or convicted of offenses against the criminal laws of a State, including an employee engaged in this activity who is transferred to a supervisory or administrative position. For the purpose of this subsection, "detention" includes the duties of employees assigned to guard individuals incarcerated in any penal institution.

(l) The term "compensation, terms, conditions, or privileges of employment" encompasses all employee benefits, including such benefits provided pursuant to a bona fide employee benefit plan.

§ 631. [§ 12] Age Limitation

(a) The prohibitions in this chapter *[except the provisions of section 4(g)]* shall be limited to individuals who are at least 40 years of age.

(b) In the case of any personnel action affecting employees or applicants for employment which is subject to the provisions of section 633a of this title *[section 15]*, the prohibitions established in section 633a of this title *[section*

15] shall be limited to individuals who are at least 40 years of age.

(c)

(1) Nothing in this chapter shall be construed to prohibit compulsory retirement of any employee who has attained 65 years of age and who, for the 2-year period immediately before retirement, is employed in a bona fide executive or a high policymaking position, if such employee is entitled to an immediate nonforfeitable annual retirement benefit from a pension, profit-sharing, savings, or deferred compensation plan, or any combination of such plans, of the employer of such employee, which equals, in the aggregate, at least $44,000.

(2) In applying the retirement benefit test of paragraph (1) of this subsection, if any such retirement benefit is in a form other than a straight life annuity (with no ancillary benefits), or if employees contribute to any such plan or make rollover contributions, such benefit shall be adjusted in accordance with regulations prescribed by the Equal Employment Opportunity Commission, after consultation with the Secretary of the Treasury, so that the benefit is the equivalent of a straight life annuity (with no ancillary benefits) under a plan to which employees do not contribute and under which no rollover contributions are made.

(d) Nothing in this chapter shall be construed to prohibit compulsory retirement of any employee who has attained 70 years of age, and who is serving under a contract of unlimited tenure (or similar arrangement providing for unlimited tenure) at an institution of higher education (as defined by section 1141(a) of title 20 *[section 1201(a) of the Higher Education Act of 1965]*).

§ 632. [§ 13] Annual Report

The Equal Employment Opportunity Commission shall submit annually in January a report to the Congress covering its activities for the preceding year and including such information, data and recommendations for further legislation in connection with the matters covered by this chapter as it may find advisable. Such report shall contain an evaluation and appraisal by the Commission of the effect of the minimum and maximum ages established by this chapter, together with its recommendations to the Congress. In making such evaluation and appraisal, the Commission shall take into consideration any changes which may have occurred in the general age level of the population, the effect of the chapter upon workers not covered by its provisions, and such other factors as it may deem pertinent.

§ 633. [§ 14] Federal-State Relationship

(a) Nothing in this chapter shall affect the jurisdiction of any agency of any State performing like functions with regard to discriminatory employment practices on account of age except that upon commencement of action under this chapter such action shall supersede any State action.

(b) In the case of an alleged unlawful practice occurring in a State which has a law prohibiting discrimination in employment because of age and establishing or authorizing a State authority to grant or seek relief from such discriminatory practice, no suit may be brought under section 626 of this title *[section 7]* before the expiration of sixty days after proceedings have been commenced under the State law, unless such proceedings have been earlier terminated: Provided, That such sixty-day period shall be extended to one hundred and twenty days during the first year after the effective date of such State law. If any requirement for the commencement of such proceedings is imposed by a State authority other than a requirement of the filing of a written and signed statement of the facts upon which the proceeding is based, the proceeding shall be deemed to have been commenced for the purposes of this subsection at the time such statement is sent by registered mail to the appropriate State authority.

§ 633a. [§ 15] Nondiscrimination on Account of Age in Federal Government Employment

(a) All personnel actions affecting employees or applicants for employment who are at least 40 years of age (except personnel actions with regard to aliens employed outside the limits of the United States) in military departments as defined in section 102 of title 5 *[United States Code]*, in executive agencies as defined in section 105 of title 5 *[United States Code]* (including employees and applicants for employment who are paid from nonappropriated funds), in the United States Postal Service and the Postal Rate Commission, in those units in the government of the District of Columbia having positions in the competitive service, and in those units of the legislative and judicial branches of the Federal Government having positions in the competitive service, and in the Library of Congress shall be made free from any discrimination based on age.

(b) Except as otherwise provided in this subsection, the Equal Employment Opportunity Commission is authorized to enforce the provisions of subsection (a) of this section through appropriate remedies, including reinstatement or hiring of employees with or without back pay, as will effectuate the policies of this section. The Equal Employment Opportunity Commission shall issue such rules, regulations, orders, and instructions as it deems necessary and appropriate to carry out its responsibilities under this section. The Equal Employment Opportunity Commission shall—

(1) be responsible for the review and evaluation of the operation of all agency programs designed to carry out the policy of this section, periodically obtaining and publishing (on at least a semiannual basis) progress reports from each department, agency, or unit referred to in subsection (a) of this section;

(2) consult with and solicit the recommendations of interested individuals, groups, and organizations relating to nondiscrimination in employment on account of age; and

(3) provide for the acceptance and processing of complaints of discrimination in Federal employment on account of age. The head of each such department, agency, or unit shall comply with such rules, regulations, orders, and instructions of the Equal Employment Opportunity Commission which shall include a provision that an employee or applicant for employment shall be notified of any final action taken on any complaint of discrimination filed by him thereunder. Reasonable exemptions to the provisions of this section may be established by the Commission but only when the Commission has established a maximum age requirement on the basis of a determination that age is a bona fide occupational qualification necessary to the performance of the duties of the position. With respect to employment in the Library of Congress, authorities granted in this subsection to the Equal Employment Opportunity Commission shall be exercised by the Librarian of Congress.

(c) Any person aggrieved may bring a civil action in any Federal district court of competent jurisdiction for such legal or equitable relief as will effectuate the purposes of this chapter.

(d) When the individual has not filed a complaint concerning age discrimination with the Commission, no civil action may be commenced by any individual under this section until the individual has given the Commission not less than thirty days' notice of an intent to file such action. Such notice shall be filed within one hundred and eighty days after the alleged unlawful practice occurred. Upon receiving a notice of intent to sue, the Commission shall promptly notify all persons named therein as prospective defendants in the action and take any appropriate action to assure the elimination of any unlawful practice.

(e) Nothing contained in this section shall relieve any Government agency or official of the responsibility to assure nondiscrimination on account of age in employment as required under any provision of Federal law.

(f) Any personnel action of any department, agency, or other entity referred to in subsection (a) of this section shall not be subject to, or affected by, any provision of this chapter, other than the provisions of section 631(b) of this title *[section 12(b)]* and the provisions of this section.

(g)

(1) The Equal Employment Opportunity Commission shall undertake a study relating to the effects of the amendments made to this section by the Age Discrimination in Employment Act Amendments of 1978, and the effects of section 631(b) of this title *[section 12(b)]*, as added by the Age Discrimination in Employment Act Amendments of 1978.

(2) The Equal Employment Opportunity Commission shall transmit a report to the President and to the Congress containing the findings of the Commission resulting from the study of the Commission under paragraph (1) of this subsection. Such report shall be transmitted no later than January 1, 1980.

Effective Date [§ 16]

[Section 16 of the ADEA (not reproduced in the U.S. Code)] This Act shall become effective one hundred and eighty days after enactment, except (a) that the Secretary of Labor may extend the delay in effective date of any provision of this Act up to an additional ninety days thereafter if he finds that such time is necessary in permitting adjustments to the provisions hereof, and (b) that on or after the date of enactment the Secretary of Labor *[EEOC]* is authorized to issue such rules and regulations as may be necessary to carry out its provisions.]

§ 634. [§ 17] Appropriations

There are hereby authorized to be appropriated such sums as may be necessary to carry out this chapter.

[Approved December 15, 1967.]

■

Chapter 4

Consolidated Omnibus Budget Reconciliation Act (COBRA)

Statute: 29 U.S.C. §§ 1161–1169

http://www4.law.cornell.edu/uscode/29/ch18schIstBp6.html

Regulations: 26 C.F.R. § 54.4980B-0 and following

http://frwebgate.access.gpo.gov/cgi-bin/get-cfr.cgi?TITLE=26&PART=54&SECTION=4980B-0&TYPE=TEXT

Definitions

Church plan

A *group health plan* that is established and maintained by a church or an association or convention of churches that is tax exempt under Internal Revenue Code Section 501(a).

Gross misconduct

Neither the statute nor the regulations define this term. The court decisions consistently hold that gross misconduct must be something more than mere negligence or incompetence. Rather, the conduct must be either willful, intentional, reckless or in deliberate indifference to the employer's interests.

Any of the following falls within gross misconduct:

- theft
- embezzlement
- violation of company policy
- lies
- driving a vehicle under the influence of alcohol
- off-site assault on a co-worker.

Group health plan

An employee benefit plan that provides medical care to participants (usually employees, their spouses and their dependents). Medical care typically includes inpatient and outpatient hospital care, physician care, surgery and other major medical benefits, prescription drugs, dental care and vision care. It does not include life insurance.

Amounts that an employer contributes to a medical savings account are not a *group health plan*. A medical savings account is a tax-exempt account in which employees can save money for medical expenses.

Initial notice

The notice that the plan administrator or the employer must give to employees when they become eligible to participate in an employer's *group health plan*. For more about *initial notice*, see Section A5.

Noncompliance period

The noncompliance period begins on the first day that the employer fails to continue coverage for a *qualified beneficiary*, and it ends on the earlier of: (1) the date the employer corrects the violation, or (2) six months after the last day of the *qualified beneficiary's* coverage period. For more, see "Excise Taxes" in Section C4.

Qualified beneficiary

An individual who is covered by an employer's *group health plan* on the day before a *qualifying event*. Individuals who are *qualified beneficiaries* are eligible to receive COBRA benefits. To learn more about *qualified beneficiaries*, see Section A3.

Qualifying event

An event—such as termination or layoff—that causes the employee to separate from the employer. To learn more about *qualifying events*, see Section A3.

Qualifying event notice

After a *qualifying event* has occurred, the plan administrator must send this notice to the *qualified beneficiaries* informing them of their rights under COBRA.

This notice typically consists of a cover letter explaining COBRA rights and obligations (including election, payment and notice deadlines), an election form and a premium schedule. For more about this notice, see Section A5.

A. Overview of COBRA

1. Summary

The Consolidated Omnibus Budget Reconciliation Act of 1985 (COBRA) enables employees and their families to continue healthcare coverage under the employer's *group health plan* even after they experience an event—such as a layoff or termination—that would have ended their coverage under ordinary circumstances. Usually, employees and their families must pay for the coverage, but they get to pay at the employer-negotiated group rate, which is usually less expensive than an individual rate.

The COBRA law amended both the Internal Revenue Code and the Employee Retirement Income Security Act of 1974 (ERISA). Thus, both statutes are important in understanding COBRA.

2. Regulated Employers

COBRA covers private employers with 20 or more employees. (See "Counting Workers," below, for information on how to count employees for coverage purposes.)

COBRA does not cover state and local governments. However, there is a parallel law—42 U.S.C. § 300bb-1—that imposes COBRA continuation requirements on *group health plans* sponsored by state and local governments. The U.S. Department of Health and Human Services administers and enforces that law.

COBRA does not cover the federal government. However, federal government employees and their families are covered by similar, but not parallel, provisions in the Federal Employees Health Benefits Amendments Act (5 U.S.C. § 8905a).

COBRA does not cover *church plans*.

Counting Workers

Knowing whether or not an employer has 20 or more employees for purposes of COBRA is not always as simple as counting heads in the office. The following are guidelines for counting employees to determine whether or not COBRA applies:

- Count both full- and part-time employees. Each part-time employee counts as a fraction of an employee, with the fraction being equal to the number of hours the part-time employee works divided by the number of hours a full-time employee works. For example, if a part-time employee works four hours a day, but full-time employees work eight hours a day, then the part-time employee would count as 4/8—or half—an employee.
- Even though they may be entitled to COBRA coverage (see Section A3), self-employed individuals, independent contractors and directors (in the case of a corporation) are not counted when determining whether COBRA applies.

3. Covered Workers

To be eligible to enjoy COBRA's benefits, a worker must:

- be a qualified beneficiary, and
- have a relationship with the employer that will be affected by a *qualifying event*. Individuals who have an employment-related connection to the employer consist of employees, former employees, the employer and others associated or formerly associated with the employer or in a business relationship (including members of a union who are not currently employees).

Qualified Beneficiary

A *qualified beneficiary* is an individual covered by the employer's *group health plan* on the day before a *qualifying event*. Employees who were not covered by their employer's *group health plan* prior to the *qualifying event* are not entitled to COBRA's coverage or notice rights.

Usually, the individual is an employee, an employee's spouse or an employee's dependent child.

Retired employees, their spouses and their dependent children can also be qualified beneficiaries if the employer files for certain types of bankruptcy. The intricacies of this rule are beyond the scope of this discussion.

If a child is born to a covered employee or placed for adoption with a covered employee while the employee is on COBRA, the child will be a *qualified beneficiary*.

Agents, independent contractors and directors who are not employees but who nonetheless participate in the *group health plan* can also be *qualified beneficiaries*.

Qualifying Event

There are many events that will affect an individual's relationship with an employer, but only a *qualifying event* makes the individual eligible for COBRA coverage.

Whether or not an event will be a *qualifying event* depends on what category an individual falls into: employee, spouse or dependent.

Employees

The following are the *qualifying events* for employees:

- voluntary termination of employment— for example, quitting.
- involuntary termination of employment for reasons other than *gross misconduct*— for example, termination because the employee wasn't skilled enough for the position, layoff.
- a reduction in the number of work hours to an amount that would otherwise make an employee ineligible for benefits. For example, let's say an employer only provides health insurance benefits to employees who work 40 hours a week. If a full-time employee chooses to switch to a 30-hour-a-week schedule, that employee becomes ineligible for health insurance benefits under the employer's rules. COBRA allows the employee to continue to participate in the health plan for a specified period of time. (See Section A5 to find out how long COBRA coverage lasts.)

Spouses

The following are *qualifying events* for spouses of employees:

- any of the reasons listed under "Employees," above
- the employee becomes entitled to Medicare
- the spouse and the employee separate or divorce
- the employee dies.

Dependent Children

The *qualifying events* for dependent children are the same as those listed above under "Spouses," with one addition: It is a *qualifying event* if the dependent child stops being a dependent under the plan. For example, if the plan states that children stop being dependents when they turn 18, a child's 18th birthday is a *qualifying event*.

4. What's Prohibited: Employers

Employers may not condition COBRA coverage of a *qualified beneficiary* on evidence of current insurability. If the *group health plan* covered the employee, spouse or dependent on the day before the *qualifying event*, then that individual is entitled to COBRA—regardless of whether the plan would choose to insure the individual in ordinary circumstances.

5. What's Required: Employers

Employer obligations under COBRA fall into two broad categories: notice requirements and coverage requirements.

Notice Requirements

An employer's notice obligations depend on whether the employer administers the plan itself or whether another entity administers the plan.

Combined Employer/Plan Administrator

In cases where the employer and the plan administrator are the same entity, the employer must provide two notices:

- The first is an *initial notice* to employees when they become eligible to participate in the plan—for example, when they are hired if their employer allows new hires to immediately be covered by health insurance. This notice informs employees of their rights and obligations under COBRA. This notice must be written. If the employee and any other *qualified beneficiaries* live at different addresses, the employer must send each of them a separate notice.
- The second is a *qualifying event notice* to *qualified beneficiaries* of their rights under COBRA after a *qualifying event* has occurred. These *qualifying events* trigger this notice: voluntary or involuntary termination of employment, reduction of hours, death of the covered employee or eligibility of the covered employee for Medicare. Although the law does not specify a time deadline for this notice when the employer and the plan administrator are the same, most commentators suggest within 45 days after the triggering event.

- In the case of other types of *qualifying events*—such as divorce—the employee has the burden of notifying the plan administrator that the *qualifying event* has occurred. (See Section A6.) The plan administrator/employer then has 14 days to give the *qualifying event notice* to the beneficiary.

Separate Employer/Plan Administrator

The notice rules work slightly differently when the employer and plan administrator are separate entities:

- The rules regarding the *initial notice* are unclear. Most commentators believe that the plan administrator—and not the employer—must send the *initial notice* described above.
- In the case of certain *qualifying events*, the employer has 30 days to notify the plan administrator of the occurrence of the *qualifying event*. These *qualifying events* trigger this notice: voluntary or involuntary termination of employment, reduction of hours, death of the covered employee, or eligibility of the covered employee for Medicare. The plan administrator then has 14 days to send a *qualifying event notice* to the *qualified beneficiaries* of the rights under COBRA.
- In the case of some *qualifying events*—such as divorce—the beneficiary has the responsibility of notifying the plan administrator of the *qualifying event*. (See Section A6.) Once the plan administrator receives that notice, it has 14 days to give the *qualifying event* notice to the beneficiary.

Coverage Requirements

If a *qualified beneficiary* chooses to take advantage of COBRA benefits, the *group health plan* must continue to cover the beneficiary for a period of time. How long a period of time depends on the type of beneficiary and the qualifying event as shown in the chart below.

Coverage Periods		
Qualifying Event	**Qualified Beneficiary**	**Coverage Period**
Voluntary termination Involuntary termination Reduction of hours	Employee Spouse Dependent child	18 months
Employee on Medicare Divorce Legal separation Employee's death	Spouse Dependent child	36 months
Loss of dependent child status	Dependent child	36 months

The law allows the employer to choose to extend COBRA benefits beyond the statutory coverage period.

The *qualified beneficiary*—and not the employer—is responsible for paying the premiums. The employer may charge a 2% administrative fee, making the total cost to the employee 102% of the coverage costs.

The employer must provide coverage to the COBRA beneficiary that is identical to the coverage the employer would have provided to the beneficiary if the *qualifying event* had not occurred.

See Section A7 for exceptions to the coverage periods.

6. What's Required: Workers

Qualified beneficiaries have three main obligations under COBRA: notice, election and payment.

Notice
Qualified beneficiaries must notify the plan administrator of the following *qualifying events:*

- divorce
- legal separation
- dependent child losing dependent status under the plan.

The deadline for this notice is 60 days from the *qualifying event*. (For other types of *qualifying events*, the employer has the responsibility for this notice. See Section A5 for more information.)

If a *qualified beneficiary* misses this deadline, the plan administrator has the right to deny COBRA coverage.

Once a *qualified beneficiary* provides this notice, the plan administrator has 14 days to give the beneficiary the *qualifying event notice*.

Election
To take advantage of COBRA rights, *qualified beneficiaries* must notify the plan administrator that they want to do so. This is called an election, and *qualified beneficiaries* must do it by the later of the following two dates:

- within 60 days after the date that plan coverage ends because of the *qualifying event*, or
- within 60 days after the *qualified beneficiary* received the *qualifying event notice*.

Each *qualified beneficiary* has individual election rights. This means that even within the same family, one *qualified beneficiary* could choose to elect coverage, while others could choose not to. For example, the employee could choose against coverage, but the spouse and child could decide that they want it.

Payment
Usually, the *qualified beneficiary*—and not the employer—pays for the continued health coverage. (Employers can choose to pay for the coverage, but the law does not require them to do so.)

The *qualified beneficiary* must make the initial premium payment within 45 days after electing coverage. If the beneficiary does not do so, the plan administrator can end the COBRA coverage.

Subsequent premium payments are due on the first of each month, subject to a 30-day grace period.

7. Exceptions

The coverage periods described in Section A5). above, may be lengthened if certain events occur. These events are:

- a disability
- a subsequent qualifying event
- when a covered employee becomes entitled to Medicare coverage
- the employer's bankruptcy.

Disability

Most of the time, if the *qualifying event* is voluntary or involuntary termination of employment or reduction in hours, the COBRA coverage lasts for 18 months. However, if a *qualified beneficiary* is disabled at the time of the *qualifying event* or becomes disabled during the first 60 days of COBRA coverage, that beneficiary can extend COBRA coverage to 29 months.

In order to qualify for this exception, the beneficiary must be disabled as defined by Titles II or XVI of the Social Security Act (42 U.S.C. § 401 and following or § 1381 and following, respectively).

The beneficiary must provide notice to the plan administrator of the disability.

The employer may increase the charge for the last 11 months of coverage from 102% of the premium to 150% of the premium.

Subsequent Qualifying Event

If a beneficiary is using the 18-month coverage period and another *qualifying event* happens during that coverage period (for example, a divorce that occurs several months after a termination), the beneficiary can extend the coverage period to 36 months from the date of the *first qualifying event*.

Medicare

If an employee is on an 18-month coverage period and the employee becomes eligible for Medicare benefits during that period, the employee will no longer be entitled to COBRA benefits for himself. However, Medicare will not cover the employee's family. Under COBRA, any *qualified beneficiaries* other than the employee (for example, the employee's spouse or the employee's child) can extend their own coverage to 36 months from the date the employee became eligible for Medicare.

B. How COBRA Is Enforced

1. Individual Complaints

Individuals may bring a civil action in court to enforce COBRA rights. These lawsuits fall under the civil enforcement provisions of the Employee Retirement Income Security Act of 1974 (ERISA). (See the chapter on ERISA for more information.)

2. Agency Enforcement

The Pension and Welfare Benefits Administration of the Department of Labor enforces COBRA's disclosure and notice provisions under the same rules that it enforces ERISA. (See the chapter on ERISA for more information.)

The Internal Revenue Service and the Department of Labor share jurisdiction for enforcement of COBRA's eligibility, coverage and premium provisions.

C. For Employers: Complying With COBRA

1. Reporting Requirements

COBRA has no specific reporting requirements. However, ERISA contains reporting requirements for health plans generally. (See Section C1 of the chapter on ERISA.)

2. Recordkeeping Requirements

COBRA has no specific recordkeeping requirements. However, ERISA contains recordkeeping requirements for health plans generally. (See Section D3 of the chapter on ERISA.)

3. Practical Tips

If a separate entity administers your *group health plan*, the law is unclear as to which one of you bears the ultimate responsibility

for issuing the *initial notice*. Make sure that your plan administrator issues this notice. If it doesn't, issue the notice yourself.

Given the lack of guidance from Congress, government agencies and the courts on what exactly *gross misconduct* means, you should consult with an attorney if you want to use this exception to deny COBRA benefits to an employee.

4. Penalties

Both COBRA and ERISA describe the penalties that employers will suffer if they fail to comply with COBRA.

A private sector employer that fails to comply with COBRA faces any or all of the following sanctions:

- excise taxes (see below for more information)
- fines for failing to satisfy COBRA's reporting and disclosure rules
- civil liability to individuals who suffered losses because they did not receive the health insurance coverage to which they were entitled
- attorneys fees.

See Section D5 of the chapter on ERISA for more about penalties under ERISA.

Excise Taxes

An employer must pay an excise tax (also called a penalty tax) for every day that it fails to meet the continuation rules during the *noncompliance period*.

This excise tax applies separately for each *qualified beneficiary* for whom the employer fails to provide the required coverage. However, if the affected *qualified beneficiaries* are in the same family, then the tax is capped at $200 per day for the family.

The noncompliance period begins on the first day of the violation and ends on the earlier of: (1) the date the employer corrects the violation, or (2) six months after the last day of the *qualified beneficiary's* coverage period.

The employer will not have to pay the excise tax in either of the following circumstances:

- when the failure is not intentional and the employer has a reasonable explanation, or
- when the employer corrects the violation within 30 days of finding out about the violation.

D. For Workers: Asserting Rights Under COBRA

1. Where to Start

Both the Department of Labor and the Internal Revenue Service have jurisdiction over COBRA. If you feel that your employer has not honored your COBRA rights, contact these agencies for assistance. (See Section E, below, for contact information.)

You may also bring a civil action in court to enforce COBRA rights. These lawsuits fall under the civil enforcement provisions of the Employee Retirement Income Security Act of 1974 (ERISA). (See the chapter on ERISA for more information.)

2. Required Forms

See Section D2 of the chapter on ERISA.

3. Practical Tips

Although COBRA gives you the important right to continue your healthcare coverage, that right comes at a cost: You must foot the bill for the premiums. For some families, this can take quite a chunk out of the budget. You will have to weigh your ability to pay these premiums against the dangers of going without health insurance (unless, of course, you can find cheaper coverage elsewhere).

If you are leaning toward foregoing your COBRA rights because you can't afford to pay the premiums or because you think that you will soon find a job with benefits, think hard and long before making this decision. If you have trouble finding a job, you may lose an important right under another law called the Health Insurance Portability and Accountability Act. That Act says that health insurance companies can't deny you insurance on the basis of a preexisting condition—so long as you haven't had more than a 63-day gap in coverage. This means that if you forego your COBRA coverage and don't obtain some other health insurance within 63 days, you risk being denied insurance in the future based on a preexisting condition (if you have one).

If you are thinking about switching to your spouse's plan because it is cheaper or free, compare the plans carefully. Your plan may offer more benefits and better access to doctors—and might be worth the premium you have to pay.

E. Agencies Charged With Enforcement & Compliance

Pension and Welfare Benefits Administration
U.S. Department of Labor
200 Constitution Ave., NW, Room N-5619
Washington, DC 20210
Phone: 202-219-8776
http://www.dol.gov/dol/pwba/welcome.html

Internal Revenue Service
U.S. Treasury Department
1500 Pennsylvania Avenue, NW
Washington, DC 20220
Phone: 202-622-2000
http://www.irs.gov

Agency Resources for Employers
None specific to COBRA. See Section E of the chapter on ERISA for resources about ERISA in general.

Agency Resources for Workers
(These can be obtained either at the Web addresses listed below or at the address and phone number listed above.)

- A detailed booklet describing worker rights and obligations under COBRA
  Health Benefits Under the Consolidated Omnibus Reconciliation Act
  http://www.dol.gov/dol/pwba/public/pubs/COBRA/cobra99.pdf
- A discussion of the implications of various life events on health benefits
  Life Changes Require Health Choices: Know Your Benefit Options
  http://www.dol.gov/dol/pwba/public/pubs/health/life-text.html
- Information about what happens to healthcare benefits when a worker loses a full-time job
  Pension and Health Care Coverage ... Questions and Answers for Dislocated Workers
  http://www.dol.gov/dol/pwba/public/pubs/disloc1.htm
- Information about asserting your rights to healthcare benefits after a job loss
  Protecting Pension and Health Care Benefits after Job Loss
  http://www.dol.gov/dol/pwba/public/pubs/disloc2.htm
- A discussion of the implications of various work events on healthcare coverage
  Work Changes Require Health Choices: Protect Your Rights
  http://www.dol.gov/dol/pwba/public/pubs/health/work-text.html

F. State Laws Relating to Health Coverage Continuation

Alabama	Ala. Code § 27-55-3
	No general continuation laws, but subjects of domestic abuse, who have lost coverage under abuser's plan and who do not qualify for COBRA, may have 18 months coverage (applies to all employers).
Arkansas	**Ark. Code Ann. § 23-86-114**
Employers affected	All employers who offer group health insurance.
Eligible employees	Employees continuously insured for previous 3 months.
Qualifying event	Termination of employment; death of employee; change in marital status.
Length of coverage for employee	120 days.
Length of coverage for dependents	120 days.
Time employee has to apply	10 days.
Special benefits	Excludes: dental care; prescription drugs; vision services.
California	**Cal. Health & Safety Code §§ 1373.6, 1373.621; Cal. Ins. Code § 10128.50**
Employers affected	Employers with 2 to 19 employees.
Eligible employees	Employees continuously insured for previous 3 months.
Qualifying event	Termination of employment; reduction in hours.
Length of coverage for employee	18 months. (29 months if disabled at termination or during first 60 days of continuation coverage.)
Length of coverage for dependents	18 months. (29 months if disabled at termination or during first 60 days of continuation coverage; 36 months upon death of employee, divorce or legal separation, loss of dependent status, employee's eligibility for Medicare.)
Time employer has to notify employee of continuation rights	15 days.
Time employee has to apply	31 days after group plan ends; 30 days after COBRA or Cal-COBRA ends.
Special benefits	Includes vision and dental benefits.
Special situations	Employee who is 60 or older and has worked for employer for previous 5 years may continue benefits for self and spouse beyond COBRA or Cal-COBRA limits.
Colorado	**Colo. Rev. Stat. § 10-16-108**
Employers affected	All employers who offer group health insurance.

Eligible employees	Employees continuously insured for previous 3 months. (If eligible due to reduction in hours, must have been continuously insured for previous 6 months.)
Qualifying event	Termination of employment; reduction in hours; death of employee; change in marital status.
Length of coverage for employee	18 months.
Length of coverage for dependents	18 months.
Time employer has to notify employee of continuation rights	Within 10 days of termination.
Time employee has to apply	31 days after termination.
Special benefits	Excludes: specific diseases; accidental injuries.
Connecticut	**Conn. Gen. Stat. Ann. § 38a-538; § 31-51o**
Employers affected	All employers who offer group health insurance.
Eligible employees	Employees continuously insured for previous 3 months.
Qualifying event	Layoff; reduction in hours; termination of employment; death of employee; change in marital status.
Length of coverage for employee	18 months.
Length of coverage for dependents	18 months. (36 months upon death of employee or divorce.)
Time employer has to notify employee of continuation rights	14 days.
Time employee has to apply	60 days.
Special benefits	Excludes: specific diseases; accidental injuries.
Special situations	Facility closes or relocates: employer must pay for insurance for employee and dependents for 120 days or until employee is eligible for other group coverage, whichever comes first. (Employee entitled to regular continuation coverage at the end of 120 days.)
District of Columbia	**D.C. Code Ann. § 32-731**
Employers affected	Employers with fewer than 20 employees.
Eligible employees	All insured employees are eligible.
Qualifying event	Any reason employee or dependent becomes ineligible for coverage.
Length of coverage for employee	3 months.
Length of coverage for dependents	3 months.
Time employer has to notify employee of continuation rights	Within 15 days of termination of coverage.
Time employee has to apply	45 days after termination of coverage.
Special benefits	Excludes: dental or vision only insurance.

Florida	Fla. Stat. Ann. § 627.6692
Employers affected	Employers with fewer than 20 employees.
Eligible employees	Full-time (25 hours/week) employees covered by employer's health insurance plan.
Qualifying event	Layoff; reduction in hours; termination of employment; death of employee; change in marital status.
Length of coverage for employee	18 months.
Length of coverage for dependents	18 months.
Time employer has to notify employee of continuation rights	Carrier notifies employee within 14 days of learning of qualifying event (employee is responsible for notifying carrier).
Time employee has to apply	30 days from receipt of carrier's notice.
Georgia	**Ga. Code Ann. §§ 33-24-21.1 to 33-24-21.2**
Employers affected	All employers who offer group health insurance.
Eligible employees	Employees continuously insured for previous 6 months.
Qualifying event	Termination of employment (except for cause).
Length of coverage for employee	3 months plus any part of the month remaining at termination.
Length of coverage for dependents	3 months plus any part of the month remaining at termination.
Special situations	Employee, spouse or former spouse, who is 60 or older and who has been covered for previous 6 months, may continue coverage until eligible for Medicare. (Applies to companies with more than 20 employees; does not apply when employee quits for reasons other than health.)
Illinois	**215 Ill. Comp. Stat. §§ 5/367e, 5/367.2**
Employers affected	All employers who offer group health insurance.
Eligible employees	Employees continuously insured for previous 3 months.
Qualifying event	Termination of employment.
Length of coverage for employee	9 months.
Length of coverage for dependents	9 months.
Time employee has to apply	10 days after termination or receiving notice from employer, whichever is later, but not more than 60 days from termination.
Special benefits	Excludes: dental care; prescription drugs; vision services; disability income; specified diseases.
Special situations	Upon death or divorce, 2 years coverage for spouse under 55; until eligible for Medicare or other group coverage for spouse over 55.

Indiana	**Ind. Code Ann. § 27-8-15-31.1**
Employers affected	Employers with 2 to 50 employees.
Eligible employees	Employed by same employer for at least one year and continuously insured for previous 90 days.
Qualifying event	Termination of employment; reduction in hours; dissolution of marriage; loss of dependent status.
Length of coverage for employee	12 months.
Length of coverage for dependents	12 months.
Time employer has to notify employee of continuation rights	10 days after employee becomes eligible for continuation coverage.
Time employee has to apply	30 days after becoming eligible for continuation coverage.
Iowa	**Iowa Code §§ 509B.3 to 509B.5**
Employers affected	All employers who offer group health insurance.
Eligible employees	Employees continuously insured for previous 3 months.
Qualifying event	Any reason employee or dependent becomes ineligible for coverage.
Length of coverage for employee	9 months.
Length of coverage for dependents	9 months.
Time employer has to notify employee of continuation rights	10 days after termination of coverage.
Time employee has to apply	10 days after termination of coverage or receiving notice from employer, whichever is later, but no more than 31 days from termination of coverage.
Special benefits	Excludes: dental care; prescription drugs; vision services.
Kansas	**Kan. Stat. Ann. § 40-2209(i)**
Employers affected	All employers who offer group health insurance.
Eligible employees	Employees continuously insured for previous 3 months.
Qualifying event	Any reason employee or dependent becomes ineligible for coverage.
Length of coverage for employee	6 months.
Length of coverage for dependents	6 months.
Time employee has to apply	31 days from termination.
Kentucky	**Ky. Rev. Stat. Ann. § 304.18-110**
Employers affected	All employers who offer group health insurance.
Eligible employees	Employees continuously insured for previous 3 months.
Qualifying event	Any reason employee or dependent becomes ineligible for coverage.

Length of coverage for employee	18 months.
Length of coverage for dependents	18 months.
Time employer has to notify employee of continuation rights	Employer must notify insurer as soon as employee's coverage ends; insurer then notifies employee.
Time employee has to apply	31 days from receipt of notice.
Special benefits	Excludes: specific diseases; accidental injury.

Louisiana	**La. Rev. Stat. Ann. §§ 22:215.7, 22:215.13**
Employers affected	All employers who offer group health insurance.
Eligible employees	Employees continuously insured for previous 3 months.
Qualifying event	Termination of employment.
Length of coverage for employee	12 months.
Length of coverage for dependents	12 months.
Time employee has to apply	Must apply and submit payment before group coverage ends.
Special benefits	Excludes: dental care; vision care; specific diseases; accidental injury.
Special situations	Surviving spouse who is 50 or older may have coverage until remarriage or eligibility for Medicare or other insurance.

Maine	**Me. Rev. Stat. Ann. tit. 24-A, § 2809-A**
Employers affected	All employers who offer group health insurance.
Eligible employees	Employees continuously insured for previous 3 months.
Qualifying event	Termination of employment.
Length of coverage for employee	One year (either group or individual coverage at discretion of insurer).
Length of coverage for dependents	One year upon death of insured, if original plan provided for coverage (either group or individual coverage at discretion of insurer).
Time employee has to apply	90 days from termination of group coverage.
Special situations	Temporary layoff or work-related injury or disease: Employee and dependents entitled to one year group or individual continuation coverage. (Must have been continuously insured for previous 6 months; must apply within 31 days.)

Maryland	**Md. Code Ann., [Ins.] §§ 15-402 to 15-409**
Employers affected	All employers who offer group health insurance.
Eligible employees	Employees continuously insured for previous 3 months.
Qualifying event	Involuntary termination of employment; death of employee; change in marital status.
Length of coverage for employee	18 months.

Length of coverage for dependents	18 months upon death of employee; upon change in marital status, 18 months or until spouse remarries or becomes eligible for other coverage.
Time employer has to notify employee of continuation rights	Must notify insurer within 14 days of receiving employee's request.
Time employee has to apply	45 days from termination of coverage. Employee begins application process by requesting an election of continuation notification form from employer.
Massachusetts	**Mass. Gen. Laws ch. 175, § 110G; ch. 176J, § 9**
Employers affected	All employers who offer group health insurance; special rules for employers with Small Group Health Insurance (2 to 19 employees).
Eligible employees	All insured employees are eligible.
Qualifying event	Involuntary layoff; death of insured employee. For Small Group Health Insurance employer add: reduction in hours; divorce or legal separation; loss of dependent status; employee's eligibility for Medicare; employer's bankruptcy.
Length of coverage for employee	39 weeks (but may not exceed time covered under original coverage). Small Group Health Insurance employer: 18 months. (29 months if disabled.)
Length of coverage for dependents	39 weeks. (Divorced or separated spouse entitled to benefits only if included in judgment decree.) Small Group Health Insurance employer: 18 months upon termination or reduction in hours; 29 months if disabled; 36 months on divorce, death of employee, employee's eligibility for Medicare, employer's bankruptcy.
Time employer has to notify employee of continuation rights	When employee becomes eligible for continuation benefits.
Time employee has to apply	30 days. Small Group Health Insurance employer, 60 days.
Special situations	Termination due to plant closing: 90 days coverage for employee and dependents, at the same payment terms as before closing.
Minnesota	**Minn. Stat. Ann. § 62A.17**
Employers affected	All employers who offer group health insurance.
Eligible employees	All insured employees are eligible.
Qualifying event	Termination of employment; reduction in hours.
Length of coverage for employee	18 months.

Length of coverage for dependents	18 months.
Time employer has to notify employee of continuation rights	Within 10 days of termination of coverage.
Time employee has to apply	60 days from termination of coverage or receipt of notice, whichever is later.
Mississippi	**Miss. Code Ann. § 83-9-51**
Employers affected	All employers who offer group health insurance.
Eligible employees	Employees continuously insured for previous 3 months.
Qualifying event	Termination of employment; divorce, employee's death; employee's eligibility for Medicare; loss of dependent status.
Length of coverage for employee	12 months.
Length of coverage for dependents	12 months.
Time employee has to apply	Must apply and submit payment before group coverage ends.
Special benefits	Excludes: dental and vision care; any benefits other than hospital, surgical or major medical.
Missouri	**Mo. Rev. Stat. § 376.428**
Employers affected	All employers who offer group health insurance.
Eligible employees	Employees continuously insured for previous 3 months.
Qualifying event	Termination of employment.
Length of coverage for employee	9 months.
Length of coverage for dependents	9 months.
Time employer has to notify employee of continuation rights	No later than date group coverage would end.
Time employee has to apply	31 days from date group coverage would end.
Special benefits	Excludes: dental and vision care; any benefits other than hospital, surgical or major medical. Must include: maternity benefits if they were provided under group policy.
Montana	**Mont. Code Ann. § 33-22-508**
Employers affected	All employers who offer group health insurance.
Eligible employees	Employees continuously insured for previous 3 months.
Qualifying event	Termination of employment; employer going out of business.
Length of coverage for employee	No time limit specified.
Length of coverage for dependents	No time limit specified.
Time employee has to apply	31 days from date group coverage would end.
Special situations	Reduction in hours: one year's coverage (if employer consents).

Nebraska	Neb. Rev. Stat. §§ 44-1640, 44-7406
Employers affected	Employers not subject to federal COBRA laws.
Eligible employees	All insured employees are eligible.
Qualifying event	Involuntary termination of employment (layoff due to labor dispute not considered involuntary).
Length of coverage for employee	6 months.
Length of coverage for dependents	One year upon death of insured employee.
Time employer has to notify employee of continuation rights	Within 10 days of termination of employment must send notice by certified mail.
Time employee has to apply	10 days from receipt of notice.
Special situations	Subjects of domestic abuse, who have lost coverage under abuser's plan and who do not qualify for COBRA, may have 18 months coverage (applies to all employers).

Nevada	Nev. Rev. Stat. Ann. §§ 689B.245 to 689B.246; 689B.0345
Employers affected	Employers with less than 20 employees.
Eligible employees	Employees continuously insured for previous 12 months.
Qualifying event	Involuntary termination of employment; involuntary reduction in hours; death of employee; divorce or legal separation; loss of dependent status; employee's eligibility for Medicare.
Length of coverage for employee	18 months.
Length of coverage for dependents	36 months.
Time employer has to notify employee of continuation rights	14 days after receiving notice of employee's eligibility.
Time employee has to apply	Must notify employer within 60 days of becoming eligible for continuation coverage; must apply within 60 days after receiving employer's notice.
Special situations	Leave without pay due to disability: 12 months for employee and dependents (applies to all employers).

New Hampshire	N.H. Rev. Stat. Ann. § 415:18(VII)
Employers affected	Employers with 2 to 19 employees.
Eligible employees	All insured employees are eligible.
Qualifying event	Any reason employee or dependent becomes ineligible for coverage.
Length of coverage for employee	18 months. (29 months if disabled at termination or during first 60 days of continuation coverage.)

Length of coverage for dependents	18 months. (29 months if disabled at termination or during first 60 days of continuation coverage; 36 months upon death of employee, divorce or legal separation, loss of dependent status, employee's eligibility for Medicare.)
Time employer has to notify employee of continuation rights	Within 15 days of termination of coverage.
Time employee has to apply	Within 31 days of termination of coverage.
Special benefits	Includes dental insurance.
Special situations	Layoff or termination due to strike: 6 months coverage with option to extend for an additional 12 months. Surviving, divorced or legally separated spouse who is 55 or older: may continue benefits until eligible for Medicare or other employer-based group insurance.

New Jersey	**N.J. Stat. Ann. §§ 17B:27-30, 17B:27-51.12, 17B:27A-27**
Employers affected	Employers with 2 to 50 employees.
Eligible employees	Employed full time (25 or more hours).
Qualifying event	Termination of employment; reduction in hours.
Length of coverage for employee	12 months.
Length of coverage for dependents	180 days upon death of employee (applies to all employers).
Time employer has to notify employee of continuation rights	At time of qualifying event employer or carrier notifies employee.
Time employee has to apply	Within 30 days of qualifying event.
Special benefits	Coverage must be identical to that offered to current employees.
Special situations	Total disability: Employee who has been insured for previous 3 months and dependents entitled to continuation coverage that includes all benefits offered by group policy (applies to all employers).

New Mexico	**N.M. Stat. Ann. § 59A-18-16**
Employers affected	All employers who offer group health insurance.
Eligible employees	All insured employees are eligible.
Qualifying event	Termination of employment.
Length of coverage for employee	6 months.
Length of coverage for dependents	May convert to individual policy upon death of employee, divorce or legal separation.
Time employer has to notify employee of continuation rights	Must give written notice at time of termination.
Time employee has to apply	30 days after receiving notice.

New York	**N.Y. Ins. Law §§ 3221(f), 3221(m)**
Employers affected	All employers who offer group health insurance.
Eligible employees	All insured employees are eligible.
Qualifying event	Termination of employment; death of employee; divorce or legal separation; loss of dependent status; employee's eligibility for Medicare.
Length of coverage for employee	18 months. (29 months if disabled at termination or during first 60 days of continuation coverage.)
Length of coverage for dependents	18 months. (29 months if disabled at termination or during first 60 days of continuation coverage; 36 months upon death of employee, divorce or legal separation, loss of dependent status, employee's eligibility for Medicare.)
Time employee has to apply	60 days after termination or receipt of notice, whichever is later.
Special situations	Employee who has been insured for previous 3 months and dependents may convert to an individual plan instead of group continuation (must apply within 45 days of termination). Employee who is 60 or older and has been continuously insured for at least 2 years is entitled to a converted policy with set maximum premium limits.
North Carolina	**N.C. Gen. Stat. § 58-53-25**
Employers affected	All employers who offer group health insurance.
Eligible employees	Employees continuously insured for previous 3 months.
Qualifying event	Termination of employment.
Length of coverage for employee	18 months.
Length of coverage for dependents	18 months.
Time employer has to notify employee of continuation rights	Employer has option of notifying employee as part of the exit process.
Time employee has to apply	60 days.
Special benefits	Excludes: dental care; prescription drugs; vision care; any benefits other than hospital, surgical or major medical.
North Dakota	**N.D. Cent. Code § 26.1-36-23**
Employers affected	All employers who offer group health insurance.
Eligible employees	Employees continuously insured for previous 3 months.
Qualifying event	Termination of employment.
Length of coverage for employee	39 weeks.
Length of coverage for dependents	39 weeks. 36 months if required by divorce or annulment decree.

Time employee has to apply	Within 10 days of termination or of receiving notice, whichever is later, but no more than 31 days from termination.
Special benefits	Excludes: dental care; prescription drugs; vision care; any benefits other than hospital, surgical or major medical.

Ohio	**Ohio Rev. Code Ann. §§3923.38; 1751.53**
Employers affected	All employers who offer group health insurance.
Eligible employees	Employees continuously insured for previous 3 months who are entitled to unemployment benefits.
Qualifying event	Involuntary termination of employment.
Length of coverage for employee	6 months.
Length of coverage for dependents	6 months.
Time employer has to notify employee of continuation rights	At termination of employment.
Time employee has to apply	Whichever is earlier: 31 days after termination; 10 days after termination if employer gave notice prior to termination; 10 days after employer gives notice.
Special benefits	Excludes: dental care; prescription drugs; vision care; any benefits other than hospital, surgical or major medical.

Oklahoma	**Okla. Stat. Ann. tit. 36, § 4509**
Employers affected	All employers who offer group health insurance.
Eligible employees	Insured for at least 6 months. (All other employees and their dependents entitled to 30 days continuation coverage.)
Qualifying event	Any reason coverage terminates.
Length of coverage for employee	3 months for basic coverage, 6 months for major medical.
Length of coverage for dependents	3 months for basic coverage, 6 months for major medical.
Special benefits	Includes maternity care.

Oregon	**Or. Rev. Stat. §§ 743.600 to 743.610**
Employers affected	Employers not subject to federal COBRA laws.
Eligible employees	Employees continuously insured for previous 3 months.
Qualifying event	Termination of employment.
Length of coverage for employee	6 months.
Length of coverage for dependents	6 months.
Time employee has to apply	10 days after termination or receiving notice, whichever is later, but not more than 31 days.
Special benefits	Excludes: dental care; prescription drugs; vision care; any benefits other than hospital, surgical or major medical.

Special situations	Surviving, divorced or legally separated spouse who is 55 or older and dependent children entitled to continuation benefits until spouse remarries or is eligible for other coverage. Must include dental, vision or prescription drug benefits if they were offered in original plan (applies to employers with 20 or more employees).
Pennsylvania	**40 Pa. Cons. Stat. Ann. § 756.2**
	No laws for continuation insurance. Employees who have been continuously insured for the previous 3 months may convert to an individual policy.
Rhode Island	**R.I. Gen. Laws § 27-19.1-1**
Employers affected	All employers who offer group health insurance.
Eligible employees	All insured employees are eligible.
Qualifying event	Involuntary termination of employment; death of employee; permanent reduction in workforce; employer's going out of business.
Length of coverage for employee	18 months (but not longer than continuous employment).
Length of coverage for dependents	18 months (but not longer than continuous employment).
Time employer has to notify employee of continuation rights	Employers must post a conspicuous notice of employee continuation rights.
Time employee has to apply	30 days from termination of coverage.
South Carolina	**S.C. Code Ann. § 38-71-770**
Employers affected	All employers who offer group health insurance.
Eligible employees	Employees continuously insured for previous 6 months.
Qualifying event	Any reason employee or dependent becomes ineligible for coverage.
Length of coverage for employee	6 months (in addition to part of month remaining at termination).
Length of coverage for dependents	6 months (in addition to part of month remaining at termination).
Time employer has to notify employee of continuation rights	At time of termination must clearly and meaningfully advise employee of continuation rights.
Special benefits	Excludes: accidental injury; specific diseases.
South Dakota	**S.D. Codified Laws Ann. §§ 58-18-7.5, 58-18-7.12; 58-18C-1**
Employers affected	All employers who offer group health insurance.
Eligible employees	Employees continuously insured for previous 6 months.

Qualifying event	Termination of employment; death of employee; divorce or legal separation; loss of dependent status; employee's eligibility for Medicare.
Length of coverage for employee	18 months. (29 months if disabled at termination or during first 60 days of continuation coverage.)
Length of coverage for dependents	18 months. (29 months if disabled at termination or during first 60 days of continuation coverage; 36 months upon death of employee, divorce or legal separation, loss of dependent status, employee's eligibility for Medicare.)
Special situations	Employer goes out of business: 12 months coverage for all employees. Employer must notify employees within 10 days of termination of benefits; employees must apply within 60 days of receipt of notice or within 90 days of termination of benefits if no notice given.
Tennessee	**Tenn. Code Ann. § 56-7-2312**
Employers affected	All employers who offer group health insurance.
Eligible employees	Employees continuously insured for previous 3 months.
Qualifying event	Termination of employment; death of employee; change in marital status.
Length of coverage for employee	3 months (in addition to part of month remaining at termination).
Length of coverage for dependents	3 months (in addition to part of month remaining at termination); 15 months upon death of employee or divorce.
Special situations	Employee or dependent who is pregnant at time of termination entitled to continuation benefits for 6 months following the end of pregnancy.
Texas	**Tex. Ins. Code Ann. §§ 3.51-6(d)(3), 3.51-8**
Employers affected	All employers who offer group health insurance.
Eligible employees	Employees continuously insured for previous 3 months.
Qualifying event	Termination of employment (except for cause); employee leaves for health reasons.
Length of coverage for employee	6 months.
Length of coverage for dependents	6 months.
Time employee has to apply	31 days from termination of coverage or receiving notice from employer, whichever is later.
Special situations	Layoff due to strike: employee entitled to continuation benefits for duration of strike, but no longer than 6 months.

Utah	Utah Code Ann. §§ 31A-22-703, 31A-22-714
Employers affected	All employers who offer group health insurance.
Eligible employees	Employees continuously insured for previous 6 months.
Qualifying event	Termination of employment.
Length of coverage for employee	6 months.
Length of coverage for dependents	6 months.
Time employer has to notify employee of continuation rights	In writing within 30 days of termination of coverage.
Time employee has to apply	Within 30 days of receiving notice.
Special benefits	Excludes: accidental injury; catastrophic benefits; dental care; specific diseases.

Vermont	Vt. Stat. Ann. tit. 8, § 4090a
Employers affected	All employers who offer group health insurance.
Eligible employees	Employees continuously insured for previous 3 months.
Qualifying event	Termination of employment; death of employee.
Length of coverage for employee	6 months.
Length of coverage for dependents	6 months.
Time employee has to apply	30 days from termination of employment.

Virginia	Va. Code Ann. §§ 38.2-3541; 38.2-3416
Employers affected	All employers who offer group health insurance.
Eligible employees	Employees continuously insured for previous 3 months.
Qualifying event	Any reason employee or dependent becomes ineligible for coverage.
Length of coverage for employee	90 days.
Length of coverage for dependents	90 days.
Time employee has to apply	Must pay 3 months' premium before termination.
Special situations	Employee may convert to an individual policy instead of group continuation coverage (must apply within 31 days of termination).

Washington	Wash. Rev. Code Ann. § 48.21.250
Employers affected	Optional for all employers who offer group health insurance (except during strike).
Eligible employees	All insured employees are eligible.
Qualifying event	Any reason employee or dependent becomes ineligible for coverage.
Length of coverage for employee	Term and rate of coverage agreed upon by employer and employee.

Length of coverage for dependents	Term and rate of coverage agreed upon by employer and employee.
Special situations	Layoff or termination due to strike: 6 months coverage (mandatory for all employers). In other situations: if continuation benefits are not offered, employee may convert to an individual policy (must apply within 31 days of termination of group coverage).
West Virginia	**W.Va. Code §§ 33-16-2, 33-16-3(e)**
Employers affected	Employers providing insurance for at least 10 employees.
Eligible employees	All insured employees are eligible.
Qualifying event	Involuntary layoff.
Length of coverage for employee	18 months.
Wisconsin	**Wis. Stat. Ann. § 632.897**
Employers affected	All employers who offer group health insurance.
Eligible employees	Employees continuously insured for previous 3 months.
Qualifying event	Any reason employee or dependent becomes ineligible for coverage.
Length of coverage for employee	18 months (or longer at insurer's option).
Length of coverage for dependents	18 months (or longer at insurer's option).
Time employer has to notify employee of continuation rights	5 days from termination of coverage.
Time employee has to apply	30 days after receiving notice.
Wyoming	**Wyo. Stat. § 26-19-113**
Employers affected	Employers not subject to federal COBRA laws.
Eligible employees	Employees continuously insured for previous 3 months.
Qualifying event	Termination of employment.
Length of coverage for employee	12 months.
Length of coverage for dependents	12 months.
Time employee has to apply	31 days from termination of coverage.
Special benefits	If dental, vision care or any benefits other than hospital, surgical or major medical were included in the group policy, they may be continued at employee or dependent's request.

Current as of February 28, 2002

G. Text of Sections of COBRA

U.S. Code
Title 29: Labor
Chapter 18: Employee Retirement Income Security Program
Subchapter I: Protection of Employee Benefit Rights
Subtitle B: Regulatory Provisions
Part 6: Continuation Coverage and Additional Standards for Group Health Plans

§ 1161. Plans must provide continuation coverage to certain individuals.
§ 1162. Continuation coverage.
§ 1163. Qualifying event.
§ 1164. Applicable premium.
§ 1165. Election.
§ 1166. Notice requirements.
§ 1167. Definitions and special rules.
§ 1168. Regulations.
§ 1169. Additional standards for group health plans.

§ 1161. Plans must provide continuation coverage to certain individuals

(a) In general

The plan sponsor of each group health plan shall provide, in accordance with this part, that each qualified beneficiary who would lose coverage under the plan as a result of a qualifying event is entitled, under the plan, to elect, within the election period, continuation coverage under the plan.

(b) Exception for certain plans

Subsection (a) of this section shall not apply to any group health plan for any calendar year if all employers maintaining such plan normally employed fewer than 20 employees on a typical business day during the preceding calendar year

§ 1162. Continuation coverage

For purposes of section 1161 of this title, the term "continuation coverage" means coverage under the plan which meets the following requirements:

(1) Type of benefit coverage

The coverage must consist of coverage which, as of the time the coverage is being provided, is identical to the coverage provided under the plan to similarly situated beneficiaries under the plan with respect to whom a qualifying event has not occurred. If coverage is modified under the plan for any group of similarly situated beneficiaries, such coverage shall also be modified in the same manner for all individuals who are qualified beneficiaries under the plan pursuant to this part in connection with such group.

(2) Period of coverage

The coverage must extend for at least the period beginning on the date of the qualifying event and ending not earlier than the earliest of the following:

  (A) Maximum required period

    (i) General rule for terminations and reduced hours

    In the case of a qualifying event described in section 1163(2) of this title, except as provided in clause (ii), the date which is 18 months after the date of the qualifying event.

    (ii) Special rule for multiple qualifying events

    If a qualifying event (other than a qualifying event described in section 1163(6) of this title) occurs during the 18 months after the date of a qualifying event described in section 1163(2) of this title, the date which is 36 months after the date of the qualifying event described in section 1163(2) of this title.

    (iii) Special rule for certain bankruptcy proceedings

    In the case of a qualifying event described in section 1163(6) of this title (relating to bankruptcy proceedings), the date of the death of the covered employee or qualified beneficiary (described in section 1167(3)(C)(iii) of this title), or in the case of the surviving spouse or dependent children of the covered employee, 36 months after the date of the death of the covered employee.

    (iv) General rule for other qualifying events

    In the case of a qualifying event not described in section 1163(2) or 1163(6) of this title, the date which is 36 months after the date of the qualifying event.

    (v) Medicare entitlement followed by qualifying event

    In the case of a qualifying event described in section 1163(2) of this title that occurs less than 18 months after the date the covered employee became entitled to benefits under title XVIII of the Social Security Act (42 U.S.C. 1395 et seq.), the period of coverage for qualified beneficiaries other than the covered employee shall not terminate under this subparagraph before the close of the 36-month period beginning on the date the covered employee became so entitled.

In the case of a qualified beneficiary who is determined, under title II or XVI of the Social Security Act (42 U.S.C. 401 et seq., 1381 et seq.), to have been disabled at any time during the first 60 days of continuation coverage under this part, any reference in clause (i) or (ii) to 18 months is deemed a reference to 29 months (with respect to all qualified beneficiaries), but only if the qualified beneficiary has provided notice of such determination under section 1166(3) [1] of this title before the end of such 18 months.

(B) End of plan

The date on which the employer ceases to provide any group health plan to any employee.

(C) Failure to pay premium

The date on which coverage ceases under the plan by reason of a failure to make timely payment of any premium required under the plan with respect to the qualified beneficiary. The payment of any premium (other than any payment referred to in the last sentence of paragraph (3)) shall be considered to be timely if made within 30 days after the date due or within such longer period as applies to or under the plan.

(D) Group health plan coverage or medicare entitlement

The date on which the qualified beneficiary first becomes, after the date of the election—

(i) covered under any other group health plan (as an employee or otherwise) which does not contain any exclusion or limitation with respect to any preexisting condition of such beneficiary (other than such an exclusion or limitation which does not apply to (or is satisfied by) such beneficiary by reason of chapter 100 of title 26, part 7 of this subtitle, or title XXVII of the Public Health Service Act (42 U.S.C. 300gg et seq.)), or

(ii) in the case of a qualified beneficiary other than a qualified beneficiary described in section 1167(3)(C) of this title, entitled to benefits under title XVIII of the Social Security Act (42 U.S.C. 1395 et seq.).

(E) Termination of extended coverage for disability

In the case of a qualified beneficiary who is disabled at any time during the first 60 days of continuation coverage under this part, the month that begins more than 30 days after the date of the final determination under title II or XVI of the Social Security Act (42 U.S.C. 401 et seq., 1381 et seq.) that the qualified beneficiary is no longer disabled.

(3) Premium requirements

The plan may require payment of a premium for any period of continuation coverage, except that such premium—

(A) shall not exceed 102 percent of the applicable premium for such period, and

(B) may, at the election of the payor, be made in monthly installments.

In no event may the plan require the payment of any premium before the day which is 45 days after the day on which the qualified beneficiary made the initial election for continuation coverage. In the case of an individual described in the last sentence of paragraph (2)(A), any reference in subparagraph (A) of this paragraph to "102 percent" is deemed a reference to "150 percent" for any month after the 18th month of continuation coverage described in clause (i) or (ii) of paragraph (2)(A).

(4) No requirement of insurability

The coverage may not be conditioned upon, or discriminate on the basis of lack of, evidence of insurability.

(5) Conversion option

In the case of a qualified beneficiary whose period of continuation coverage expires under paragraph (2)(A), the plan must, during the 180-day period ending on such expiration date, provide to the qualified beneficiary the option of enrollment under a conversion health plan otherwise generally available under the plan

§ 1163. Qualifying event

For purposes of this part, the term "qualifying event" means, with respect to any covered employee, any of the following events which, but for the continuation coverage required under this part, would result in the loss of coverage of a qualified beneficiary:

(1) The death of the covered employee.

(2) The termination (other than by reason of such employee's gross misconduct), or reduction of hours, of the covered employee's employment.

(3) The divorce or legal separation of the covered employee from the employee's spouse.

(4) The covered employee becoming entitled to benefits under title XVIII of the Social Security Act (42 U.S.C. 1395 et seq.).

(5) A dependent child ceasing to be a dependent child under the generally applicable requirements of the plan.

(6) A proceeding in a case under title 11, commencing on or after July 1, 1986, with respect to the employer from whose employment the covered employee retired at any time.

In the case of an event described in paragraph (6), a loss of coverage includes a substantial elimination of coverage with respect to a qualified beneficiary described in section 1167(3)(C) of this title within one year before or after the date of commencement of the proceeding

§ 1164. Applicable premium

For purposes of this part—

(1) In general

The term "applicable premium" means, with respect to any period of continuation coverage of qualified beneficiaries, the cost to the plan for such period of the coverage for similarly situated beneficiaries with respect to whom a qualifying event has not occurred (without regard to whether such cost is paid by the employer or employee).

(2) Special rule for self-insured plans

To the extent that a plan is a self-insured plan—

(A) In general

Except as provided in subparagraph (B), the applicable premium for any period of continuation coverage of qualified beneficiaries shall be equal to a reasonable estimate of the cost of providing coverage for such period for similarly situated beneficiaries which—

(i) is determined on an actuarial basis, and

(ii) takes into account such factors as the Secretary may prescribe in regulations.

(B) Determination on basis of past cost

If an administrator elects to have this subparagraph apply, the applicable premium for any period of continuation coverage of qualified beneficiaries shall be equal to—

(i) the cost to the plan for similarly situated beneficiaries for the same period occurring

during the preceding determination period under paragraph (3), adjusted by

(ii) the percentage increase or decrease in the implicit price deflator of the gross national product (calculated by the Department of Commerce and published in the Survey of Current Business) for the 12-month period ending on the last day of the sixth month of such preceding determination period.

(C) Subparagraph (B) not to apply where significant change

An administrator may not elect to have subparagraph (B) apply in any case in which there is any significant difference, between the determination period and the preceding determination period, in coverage under, or in employees covered by, the plan. The determination under the preceding sentence for any determination period shall be made at the same time as the determination under paragraph (3).

(3) Determination period

The determination of any applicable premium shall be made for a period of 12 months and shall be made before the beginning of such period

§ 1165. Election

For purposes of this part—

(1) Election period

The term "election period" means the period which—

(A) begins not later than the date on which coverage terminates under the plan by reason of a qualifying event,

(B) is of at least 60 days' duration, and

(C) ends not earlier than 60 days after the later of—

(i) the date described in subparagraph (A), or

(ii) in the case of any qualified beneficiary who receives notice under section 1166(4) [1] of this title, the date of such notice.

(2) Effect of election on other beneficiaries

Except as otherwise specified in an election, any election of continuation coverage by a qualified beneficiary described in subparagraph (A)(i) or (B) of section 1167(3) of this title shall be deemed to include an election of continuation coverage on behalf of any other qualified beneficiary who would lose coverage under the plan by reason of the qualifying event. If there is a choice among types of coverage under the plan, each qualified beneficiary is entitled to make a separate selection among such types of coverage

§ 1166. Notice requirements

(a) In general

In accordance with regulations prescribed by the Secretary—

(1) the group health plan shall provide, at the time of commencement of coverage under the plan, written notice to each covered employee and spouse of the employee (if any) of the rights provided under this subsection,

(2) the employer of an employee under a plan must notify the administrator of a qualifying event described in paragraph (1), (2), (4), or (6) of section 1163 of this title within 30 days (or, in the case of a group health plan which is a multiemployer plan, such longer period of time as may be provided in the terms of the plan) of the date of the qualifying event,

(3) each covered employee or qualified beneficiary is responsible for notifying the administrator of the occurrence of any qualifying event described in paragraph (3) or (5) of section 1163 of this title within 60 days after the date of the qualifying event and each qualified beneficiary who is determined, under title II or XVI of the Social Security Act (42 U.S.C. 401 et seq., 1381 et seq.), to have been disabled at any time during the first 60 days of continuation coverage under this part is responsible for notifying the plan administrator of such determination within 60 days after the date of the determination and for notifying the plan administrator within 30 days after the date of any final determination under such title or titles that the qualified beneficiary is no longer disabled, and

(4) the administrator shall notify—

(A) in the case of a qualifying event described in paragraph (1), (2), (4), or (6) of section 1163 of this title, any qualified beneficiary with respect to such event, and

(B) in the case of a qualifying event described in paragraph (3) or (5) of section 1163 of this title where the covered employee notifies the administrator under paragraph (3), any qualified beneficiary with respect to such event, of such beneficiary's rights under this subsection.

(b) Alternative means of compliance with requirements for notification of multiemployer plans by employers

The requirements of subsection (a)(2) of this section shall be considered satisfied in the case of a multiemployer plan in connection with a qualifying event described in paragraph (2) of section 1163 of this title if the plan provides that the determination of the occurrence of such qualifying event will be made by the plan administrator.

(c) Rules relating to notification of qualified beneficiaries by plan administrator

For purposes of subsection (a)(4) of this section, any notification shall be made within 14 days (or, in the case of a group health plan which is a multiemployer plan, such longer period of time as may be provided in the terms of the plan) of the date on which the administrator is notified under paragraph (2) or (3), whichever is applicable, and any such notification to an individual who is a qualified beneficiary as the spouse of the covered employee shall be treated as notification to all other qualified beneficiaries residing with such spouse at the time such notification is made

§ 1167. Definitions and special rules

For purposes of this part—

(1) Group health plan

The term "group health plan" means an employee welfare benefit plan providing medical care (as defined in section 213(d) of title 26) to participants or beneficiaries directly or through insurance, reimbursement, or otherwise. Such term shall not include any plan substantially all of the coverage under which is for qualified long-term care services (as defined in section 7702B(c) of title 26).

(2) Covered employee

The term "covered employee" means an individual who is (or was) provided coverage under a group health plan by virtue of the performance of services by the individual for 1 or more persons maintaining the plan (including as an employee defined in section 401(c)(1) of title 26).

(3) Qualified beneficiary

(A) In general

The term "qualified beneficiary" means, with respect to a covered employee under a group health plan, any other individual who, on the day before the qualifying event for that employee, is a beneficiary under the plan—

(i) as the spouse of the covered employee, or

(ii) as the dependent child of the employee.

Such term shall also include a child who is born to or placed for adoption with the covered employee during the period of continuation coverage under this part.

(B) Special rule for terminations and reduced employment

In the case of a qualifying event described in section 1163(2) of this title, the term "qualified beneficiary" includes the covered employee.

(C) Special rule for retirees and widows

In the case of a qualifying event described in section 1163(6) of this title, the term "qualified beneficiary" includes a covered employee who had retired on or before the date of substantial elimination of coverage and any other individual who, on the day before such qualifying event, is a beneficiary under the plan—

(i) as the spouse of the covered employee,

(ii) as the dependent child of the employee, or

(iii) as the surviving spouse of the covered employee.

(4) Employer

Subsection (n) (relating to leased employees) and subsection (t) (relating to application of controlled group rules to certain employee benefits) of section 414 of title 26 shall apply for purposes of this part in the same manner and to the same extent as such subsections apply for purposes of section 106 of title 26. Any regulations prescribed by the Secretary pursuant to the preceding sentence shall be consistent and coextensive with any regulations prescribed for similar purposes by the Secretary of the Treasury (or such Secretary's delegate) under such subsections.

(5) Optional extension of required periods

A group health plan shall not be treated as failing to meet the requirements of this part solely because the plan provides both—

(A) that the period of extended coverage referred to in section 1162(2) of this title commences with the date of the loss of coverage, and

(B) that the applicable notice period provided under section 1166(a)(2) of this title commences with the date of the loss of coverage.

§ 1168. Regulations

The Secretary may prescribe regulations to carry out the provisions of this part

§ 1169. Additional standards for group health plans

(a) Group health plan coverage pursuant to medical child support orders

(1) In general

Each group health plan shall provide benefits in accordance with the applicable requirements of any qualified medical child support order. A qualified

medical child support order with respect to any participant or beneficiary shall be deemed to apply to each group health plan which has received such order, from which the participant or beneficiary is eligible to receive benefits, and with respect to which the requirements of paragraph (4) are met.

(2) Definitions

For purposes of this subsection—

(A) Qualified medical child support order

The term "qualified medical child support order" means a medical child support order—

(i) which creates or recognizes the existence of an alternate recipient's right to, or assigns to an alternate recipient the right to, receive benefits for which a participant or beneficiary is eligible under a group health plan, and

(ii) with respect to which the requirements of paragraphs (3) and (4) are met.

(B) Medical child support order

The term "medical child support order" means any judgment, decree, or order (including approval of a settlement agreement) which—

(i) provides for child support with respect to a child of a participant under a group health plan or provides for health benefit coverage to such a child, is made pursuant to a State domestic relations law (including a community property law), and relates to benefits under such plan, or

(ii) is made pursuant to a law relating to medical child support described in section 1908 of the Social Security Act (42 U.S.C. 1396g-1) (as added by section 13822 [1] of the Omnibus Budget Reconciliation Act of 1993) with respect to a group health plan, if such judgment, decree, or order

(I) is issued by a court of competent jurisdiction or

(II) is issued through an administrative process established under State law and has the force and effect of law under applicable State law. For purposes of this subparagraph, an administrative notice which is issued pursuant to an administrative process referred to in subclause (II) of the preceding sentence and which has the effect of an order described in clause (i) or (ii) of the preceding sentence shall be treated as such an order.

(C) Alternate recipient

The term "alternate recipient" means any child of a participant who is recognized under a medical child support order as having a right to enrollment under a group health plan with respect to such participant.

(D) Child

The term "child" includes any child adopted by, or placed for adoption with, a participant of a group health plan.

(3) Information to be included in qualified order

A medical child support order meets the requirements of this paragraph only if such order clearly specifies—

(A) the name and the last known mailing address (if any) of the participant and the name and mailing address of each alternate recipient covered by the order, except that, to the extent provided in the order, the name and mailing address of an official of a State or a political subdivision thereof may be substituted for the mailing address of any such alternate recipient,

(B) a reasonable description of the type of coverage to be provided to each such alternate recipient, or the manner in which such type of coverage is to be determined, and

(C) the period to which such order applies.

(4) Restriction on new types or forms of benefits

A medical child support order meets the requirements of this paragraph only if such order does not require a plan to provide any type or form of benefit, or any option, not otherwise provided under the plan, except to the extent necessary to meet the requirements of a law relating to medical child support described in section 1908 of the Social Security Act (42 U.S.C. 1396g-1) (as added by section 13822 [1] of the Omnibus Budget Reconciliation Act of 1993).

(5) Procedural requirements

(A) Timely notifications and determinations

In the case of any medical child support order received by a group health plan—

(i) the plan administrator shall promptly notify the participant and each alternate recipient of the receipt of such order and the plan's procedures for determining whether medical child support orders are qualified medical child support orders, and

(ii) within a reasonable period after receipt of such order, the plan administrator shall determine whether such order is a qualified medical child support order and notify the participant and each alternate recipient of such determination.

(B) Establishment of procedures for determining qualified status of orders

Each group health plan shall establish reasonable procedures to determine whether medical child support orders are qualified medical child support orders and to administer the provision of benefits under such qualified orders. Such procedures—

(i) shall be in writing,

(ii) shall provide for the notification of each person specified in a medical child support order as eligible to receive benefits under the plan (at the address included in the medical child support order) of such procedures promptly upon receipt by the plan of the medical child support order, and

(iii) shall permit an alternate recipient to designate a representative for receipt of copies of notices that are sent to the alternate recipient with respect to a medical child support order.

(C) National Medical Support Notice deemed to be a qualified medical child support order

(i) In general

If the plan administrator of a group health plan which is maintained by the employer of a noncustodial parent of a child or to which such an employer contributes receives an appropriately completed National Medical Support Notice promulgated pursuant to section 401(b) of the Child Support Performance and Incentive Act of 1998 in the case of such child, and the Notice meets the requirements of paragraphs (3) and (4), the Notice shall be deemed to be a qualified medical child support order in the case of such child.

(ii) Enrollment of child in plan

In any case in which an appropriately completed National Medical Support Notice is issued in the case of a child of a participant under a group health plan who is a noncustodial parent of the child, and the Notice is deemed under clause (i) to be a qualified medical child support order, the plan administrator, within 40 business days after the date of the Notice, shall—

(I) notify the State agency issuing the Notice with respect to such child whether coverage of the child is available under the terms of the plan and, if so, whether such child is covered under the plan and either the effective date of the coverage or, if necessary, any steps to be taken by the custodial parent (or by the official of a

State or political subdivision thereof substituted for the name of such child pursuant to paragraph (3)(A)) to effectuate the coverage; and

(II) provide to the custodial parent (or such substituted official) a description of the coverage available and any forms or documents necessary to effectuate such coverage.

(iii) Rule of construction

Nothing in this subparagraph shall be construed as requiring a group health plan, upon receipt of a National Medical Support Notice, to provide benefits under the plan (or eligibility for such benefits) in addition to benefits (or eligibility for benefits) provided under the terms of the plan as of immediately before receipt of such Notice.

(6) Actions taken by fiduciaries

If a plan fiduciary acts in accordance with part 4 of this subtitle in treating a medical child support order as being (or not being) a qualified medical child support order, then the plan's obligation to the participant and each alternate recipient shall be discharged to the extent of any payment made pursuant to such act of the fiduciary.

(7) Treatment of alternate recipients

(A) Treatment as beneficiary generally

A person who is an alternate recipient under a qualified medical child support order shall be considered a beneficiary under the plan for purposes of any provision of this chapter.

(B) Treatment as participant for purposes of reporting and disclosure requirements

A person who is an alternate recipient under any medical child support order shall be considered a participant under the plan for purposes of the reporting and disclosure requirements of part 1 of this subtitle.

(8) Direct provision of benefits provided to alternate recipients

Any payment for benefits made by a group health plan pursuant to a medical child support order in reimbursement for expenses paid by an alternate recipient or an alternate recipient's custodial parent or legal guardian shall be made to the alternate recipient or the alternate recipient's custodial parent or legal guardian.

(9) Payment to State official treated as satisfaction of plan's obligation to make payment to alternate recipient

Payment of benefits by a group health plan to an official of a State or a political subdivision thereof

whose name and address have been substituted for the address of an alternate recipient in a qualified medical child support order, pursuant to paragraph (3)(A), shall be treated, for purposes of this subchapter, as payment of benefits to the alternate recipient.

(b) Rights of States with respect to group health plans where participants or beneficiaries thereunder are eligible for medicaid benefits

(1) Compliance by plans with assignment of rights

A group health plan shall provide that payment for benefits with respect to a participant under the plan will be made in accordance with any assignment of rights made by or on behalf of such participant or a beneficiary of the participant as required by a State plan for medical assistance approved under title XIX of the Social Security Act (42 U.S.C. 1396 et seq.) pursuant to section 1912(a)(1)(A) of such Act (42 U.S.C. 1396k(a)(1)(A)) (as in effect on August 10, 1993).

(2) Enrollment and provision of benefits without regard to medicaid eligibility

A group health plan shall provide that, in enrolling an individual as a participant or beneficiary or in determining or making any payments for benefits of an individual as a participant or beneficiary, the fact that the individual is eligible for or is provided medical assistance under a State plan for medical assistance approved under title XIX of the Social Security Act (42 U.S.C. 1396 et seq.) will not be taken into account.

(3) Acquisition by States of rights of third parties

A group health plan shall provide that, to the extent that payment has been made under a State plan for medical assistance approved under title XIX of the Social Security Act (42 U.S.C. 1396 et seq.) in any case in which a group health plan has a legal liability to make payment for items or services constituting such assistance, payment for benefits under the plan will be made in accordance with any State law which provides that the State has acquired the rights with respect to a participant to such payment for such items or services.

(c) Group health plan coverage of dependent children in cases of adoption

(1) Coverage effective upon placement for adoption

In any case in which a group health plan provides coverage for dependent children of participants or beneficiaries, such plan shall provide benefits to dependent children placed with participants or beneficiaries for adoption under the same terms and conditions as apply in the case of dependent children who are natural children of participants or beneficiaries under the plan, irrespective of whether the adoption has become final.

(2) Restrictions based on preexisting conditions at time of placement for adoption prohibited

A group health plan may not restrict coverage under the plan of any dependent child adopted by a participant or beneficiary, or placed with a participant or beneficiary for adoption, solely on the basis of a preexisting condition of such child at the time that such child would otherwise become eligible for coverage under the plan, if the adoption or placement for adoption occurs while the participant or beneficiary is eligible for coverage under the plan.

(3) Definitions

For purposes of this subsection—

(A) Child

The term "child" means, in connection with any adoption, or placement for adoption, of the child, an individual who has not attained age 18 as of the date of such adoption or placement for adoption.

(B) Placement for adoption

The term "placement", or being "placed", for adoption, in connection with any placement for adoption of a child with any person, means the assumption and retention by such person of a legal obligation for total or partial support of such child in anticipation of adoption of such child. The child's placement with such person terminates upon the termination of such legal obligation.

(d) Continued coverage of costs of a pediatric vaccine under group health plans

A group health plan may not reduce its coverage of the costs of pediatric vaccines (as defined under section 1928(h)(6) of the Social Security Act (42 U.S.C. 1396s(h)(6)) as amended by section 13830 [2] of the Omnibus Budget Reconciliation Act of 1993) below the coverage it provided as of May 1, 1993.

(e) Regulations

Any regulations prescribed under this section shall be prescribed by the Secretary of Labor, in consultation with the Secretary of Health and Human Services. ■

Chapter 5

Equal Pay Act (EPA)

Statute: 29 U.S.C. § 206(d)

http://www4.law.cornell.edu/uscode/29/206.html

Regulations: 29 C.F.R. §§ 516, 1620 & 1621

http://cfr.law.cornell.edu/cfr/cfr.php?title=29&type=part&value=516

http://cfr.law.cornell.edu/cfr/cfr.php?title=29&type=part&value=1620

http://cfr.law.cornell.edu/cfr/cfr.php?title=29&type=part&value=1621

Definitions

Competitive service

All civil service jobs in the executive branch of the federal government, except positions to which appointments are made by nomination for confirmation by the Senate and positions in the Senior Executive Service (positions classified above level GS-15 that carry substantial executive or supervisory responsibilities).

Effort

The amount of physical or mental exertion a job generally requires. In determining how much effort a job requires, courts will take into account aspects of the job that are particularly stressful or tiring, as well as job factors that alleviate fatigue. Two jobs may require equal effort even if they require different types of effort.

Establishment

A distinct physical place of business (such as a factory or office) rather than an employer's entire business or enterprise.

Responsibility

The level of accountability a job carries. In assessing responsibility, courts consider how important a particular task is to the employer, as well as how much time a worker spends on that task. Examples of job tasks that require significant responsibility include supervising other workers, generating substantial revenues or approving financial transactions.

Skill

The abilities or aptitudes required to perform a job. Skill is composed of experience, training, education and ability. In determining whether two jobs require equal skill, courts look only at the skills actually required to do the job, not any additional skills the employees may happen to possess.

Willful violation

An employer commits a willful violation of the EPA if it violates the law knowingly or with reckless disregard as to whether its conduct was illegal.

Working conditions

The environment in which a job must be performed. Working conditions include physical surroundings, such as temperature, ventilation and location, as well as hazards, like exposure to toxic chemicals or dangerous terrain.

A. Overview of the EPA

1. Summary

The Equal Pay Act (EPA) requires employers to give men and women equal pay when they do equal work. Congress passed the EPA to combat "the ancient but outmoded belief that a man, because of his role in society, should be paid more than a woman." *Corning Glass Works v. Brennan*, 417 U.S. 188, 195 (1974). Despite its gender-specific origins, however, the EPA protects both men and women from wage discrimination based on sex.

2. Regulated Employers

Most government and private employers must comply with the EPA.

Government Employers

All state and local governments must comply with the EPA.

Most, but not all, federal government agencies and departments must comply, including:

- Military departments that employ civilians (only the civilian employees are covered by the law—see Section A3, below).
- All executive agencies
- The United State Postal Service and Postal Rate Commission
- The Library of Congress
- Any unit of the judicial or legislative branch that has positions in the *competitive service* (only employees in these positions are covered by the law—see Section A3, below).

Private Employers

Not every private employer is subject to the EPA, although most are. Generally, a business is covered if it has $500,000 or more in annual sales. Businesses that generate lower sales will still be covered if they are involved in interstate commerce. Practically speaking, this means that most businesses are covered—any employer whose workers produce or buy goods that have come from or will be sent to another state, transport goods or services interstate and or sell products or services that have come from or will go to another state engages in interstate commerce.

Unions

The EPA prohibits unions from causing, or trying to cause, employers to violate the law's provisions. If, for example, a union seeks a collective bargaining agreement that sets higher pay scales for men than for women doing equal work, the union has violated the EPA.

3. Covered Workers

The EPA protects all employees who work for a regulated employer, as defined above, except:

- Uniformed service members are not covered, even if they are employed by a federal agency that also has civilian employees.
- Federal employees of the judicial or legislative branch of government are not covered unless they are in the *competitive service*.

4. What's Prohibited: Employers

Employers are prohibited from paying workers of one sex more than workers of the opposite sex to do equal work. See Section A5, below.

5. What's Required: Employers

Employers must give equal pay to men and women for doing equal work. However, the equal pay requirement applies only to those working in substantially similar jobs, as defined by the EPA. And the EPA requires only that workers performing equal work be paid at the same *pay rate*, not that workers receive the same total amount of pay.

Equal work

Male and female employees are entitled to equal pay even if their jobs are not absolutely identical. The equal pay requirement applies when the jobs are substantially equal—that is, they require substantially equal *skill, effort* and *responsibility*, and are performed under similar *working conditions* within the same *establishment*.

Two jobs may constitute equal work even if they require different types of skill, effort or responsibility. For example, if two employees work as salespeople in a retail establishment and each has some additional responsibilities—one to keep the financial books and the other to supervise temporary sales help—a court might find that their jobs require equal re-sponsibility, even though each has a different type of responsibility.

Generally, however, courts will find that two jobs constitute equal work only where they are quite similar. Although operating a jack hammer might require as much effort and skill as drafting detailed architectural designs, no court would find that these two jobs are equal work requiring equal pay.

Job titles do not determine whether two jobs are substantially equal. Courts will look at the tasks a worker actually has to perform, rather than the job description or designation. For example, an employer may not pay a male "administrative assistant" more than a female "secretary" if both do essentially the same tasks.

Equal Pay and Benefits

The EPA requires more than equal wages. If employees do equal work, they are also entitled to equal fringe benefits, such as insurance coverage, pensions and use of a company car. And the EPA applies to other forms of compensation, such as vacation time, profit sharing and bonuses.

However, the EPA requires only that employers pay workers at the same rate, not that they pay workers the same total amount. If an employer pays on commission or by the piece, for example, the employer must use the same formula—such as 10% of the company's gross profit per sale or $1.00 per unit produced—to calculate pay for men and women. If one worker earns more than another because of higher productivity (making more sales or turning out more units), that does not violate the EPA.

Financial incentives for good performance work the same way. An employer may not offer men the opportunity to earn a bonus for high sales volume or productivity while denying the same opportunity to women. However, if a bonus is offered on the same terms to all employees and the only workers who meet the criteria for the bonus are men, an employer may legally pay the bonus to those men only.

6. What's Required: Workers

The EPA imposes no obligations on workers.

7. Exceptions

There are four exceptions to the EPA. An employer may pay workers of one sex at a higher rate than workers of the opposite sex for doing equal work only if the difference is based on one of these factors:

- **Seniority:** An employer may pay more to workers who have been with the company longer, even if this results in workers of one sex getting paid more to do the same job.
- **Merit:** An employer may pay higher rates (by giving larger bonuses or a performance-based raises, for example) to workers whose performance is better, regardless of gender.
- **Quantity or quality of production:** An employer may pay a higher rate for better quality work or pay workers based on their productivity (by the piece or on commission, for example), as long

as both men and women have the opportunity to earn this higher rate.

- **Any factor other than sex:** This "catchall" exception is intended to encompass any legitimate reason why an employer might pay one worker more than another to do the same job—as long as that discrepancy isn't based on the workers' gender. It would not violate the EPA for an employer to pay a shift premium to all workers on the night shift or to pay workers a higher starting salary if they earned more at a previous job, for example, even if it turned out that more men than women worked the night shift or had a higher salary at a prior job.

B. How the EPA Is Enforced

1. Individual Complaints

An employee who wants to file a complaint against an employer for violating the EPA can file a charge (also called a complaint) of discrimination at the Equal Employment Opportunity Commission (EEOC) (see "Agency Enforcement," below).

However, an employee does not have to file a charge at the EEOC. Instead, the employee may bypass the agency and go straight to state or federal court to file a lawsuit.

The employee must file a lawsuit within two years after the employer violated the EPA. This time limit is extended to three years if the employer committed a *willful violation* of the law. These time limits can be extended if the employee did not know about the violation because the employer lied about or concealed it.

2. Agency Enforcement

The federal agency responsible for investigating EPA complaints is the EEOC. An employee usually initiates the process by filing a charge (complaint) of wage discrimination with the EEOC, although the agency can also act on its own initiative. The EEOC has the power to investigate, negotiate with employers and bring lawsuits against employers to stop discriminatory practices.

C. For Employers: Complying With the EPA

1. Reporting Requirements

There are no reporting requirements under the EPA.

2. Recordkeeping Requirements

The EPA requires employer to keep two types of records: basic wage and hour records, as required by the Fair Labor Standards Act; and records relating specifically to differences in pay between men and women.

Wage and Hour Records
The EPA is part of the Fair Labor Standards Act (FLSA). Employers subject to the EPA must comply with the FLSA's recordkeeping

requirements, described in detail in Section D of the chapter on the FLSA.

Records of Pay Differentials
In addition to general wage and hour records, employers subject to the EPA must also keep all records that (1) describe or explain the basis for any difference in wages between men and women, and (2) may help show whether that differential is based on a factor other than sex. Such records include documents regarding

- payment of wages
- wage rates
- job evaluations
- job descriptions
- merit systems
- seniority systems
- collective bargaining agreement
- pay practices.

You must keep these records for at least two years.

3. Practical Tips

Protect yourself from EPA trouble by following these tips:

- **Base pay scales on your workers' job duties, not their job titles.** If men's and women's job duties differ, you don't have to pay them equally. For example, if you have a male secretary and a female file clerk, you can pay them at different rates, as long as their job duties are not the same. However, if you have a male "sales assistant" and a female "customer service representative" who do basically the same work, they are entitled to equal pay—no matter what you call them.

- **Audit your pay practices.** On a regular basis (perhaps once a year), take a close look at what you pay your employees. If there is a disparity between what men and women earn, figure out why. Is there a legitimate reason—such as seniority, performance, differences in job duties or disparate working conditions—for the differential? If not, or if you find that you are not applying these criteria consistently, consider adjusting your pay scales.

- **Your good intentions don't matter.** An employee does not have to prove that you intended to discriminate to win an EPA lawsuit. If you pay men and women unequally and none of the EPA's exceptions apply, you have violated the statute —period. Keep track of what you pay your workers and why, to avoid inadvertent illegalities.

- **Keep good records.** If an employee can show that you paid more to a worker of the opposite sex to do the same job, you will have to prove that one of the EPA's exceptions applies. Your best defense is a well-organized and complete folder of documents, demonstrating that you had legitimate reasons for the difference in pay. You are legally required to keep certain documents for two years (see Section C2, above), but make sure to keep every document that might conceivably support your pay practices. If your workers' pay depends to any extent on seniority, productivity, merit or other demonstrable factors, you will need records showing how much each worker produced, how long each worker has been in your employ and so on.

- **Lift all the boats instead of draining the sea.** If a court finds that you have violated the EPA, you must remedy the violation by paying men and women equally. However, the law prohibits you from reducing any employee's pay to comply. Instead, you must bring everyone's pay up to the higher level.

4. Penalties

If a court finds that an employer has violated the EPA, the employer may be ordered to do any or all of the following:

- Pay back wages, equal to the difference between what the employee actually earned and what employees of the opposite sex earned for doing equal work. An employee can collect up to two years' worth of back pay, or three years if the employer committed a *willful violation* of the statute.
- Pay an additional penalty (called "liquidated damages") equal to the entire back pay award, unless the employer can demonstrate that it acted in good faith and had reasonable grounds to believe that its conduct did not violate the EPA.
- Pay the employee's court costs and attorney fees, and
- Change its pay policies to avoid further violations of the law. In making these changes, an employer may not reduce any employee's pay rate. Rather, the employer must raise the pay of employees who were underpaid.

D. For Workers: Asserting Rights Under the EPA

1. Where to Start

If you believe your employer has violated the EPA by paying you less than an employee of the opposite sex who does the same work, your first course of action should be to make an internal complaint. Follow your company's complaint policy or, if there is no policy, complain to a human resources representative or a member of management.

If you are a union member, talk to your shop steward or union representative.

If internal and union complaints don't work, you have two choices for further action. You may file a charge of discrimination at the EEOC or you may bypass the EEOC altogether and file a lawsuit in state or federal court. You can file a charge by mail or in person at your nearest EEOC office. To find the office closest to you, call 800-669-4000 or refer to the agency's website at http://www.eeoc.gov/teledir.html.

If you choose to file an EEOC charge, you must wait for the EEOC to issue you a "right to sue" letter before you can file a lawsuit.

2. Required Forms

If you decide to file a charge with the EEOC, you will have to use their charge form. This form is available at EEOC offices and through the EEOC's website. See Section E for agency information.

3. Practical Tips

Here are some tips to keep in mind:

- **Let the government work for you.** You don't have to file a charge of discrimination with the EEOC before you file a lawsuit based on wage discrimination. But you might as well—the EEOC will probably investigate your case, and may try to resolve the matter with your employer. If the agency thinks you have an especially strong claim, it might even file a lawsuit on your behalf (the EEOC has shown special interest of late in prosecuting wage discrimination claims). But even if the EEOC can't settle the case and decides not to represent you in court, you can use what it discovers in its investigation in your own lawsuit.

- **Get free help.** Many women's groups are particularly interested in claims of gender-based wage discrimination—especially if you work for a large employer. Some of these groups can offer free assistance, advice or even legal representation.

Look in your local phone book under Women's Organizations, Legal Clinics or Attorneys.

- **Don't forget other anti-discrimination laws.** Under the EPA, you have to prove that you were paid less than an employee of the opposite sex for doing the same work. If there are some differences between your job and the job held by a worker of the opposite sex, the EPA won't protect you. However, Title VII may—under Title VII, you can allege sex-based pay discrimination without having to show that someone else got paid more for doing the same job (for example, if your employer matches the salary newly hired men made at their last job but does not do so for women). And remember, the EPA only prohibits gender-based pay differences. If you believe that you have received lower wages for some other discriminatory reason—because of your age, race, religion or disability, for example—you cannot sue under the EPA.

E. Agency Charged With Enforcement & Compliance

Equal Employment Opportunity Commission
1801 L Street, NW
Washington, DC 20507
Phone: 202-663-4900
TTY: 202-663-4494
http://www.eeoc.gov

Agency Resources for Employers

(These can be obtained either at the Web addresses listed below or at the address and phone number listed above.)

- Tips on auditing pay practices for fairness

  Ten Steps to an Equal Pay Self-Audit for Employers

  http://www.dol.gov/dol/wb/10step71.htm

- Techniques employers can use to determine whether their pay practices are discriminatory

  Analyzing Compensation Data: A Guide to Three Approaches

  http://www.dol.gov/dol/esa/public/regs/compliance/ofccp/compdata.htm

- A list of the addresses and phone numbers of EEOC field offices throughout the United States

  Contacting the EEOC

  http://www.eeoc.gov/teledir.html

- A list and links to EEOC resources on the EPA

  Equal Pay and Compensation Discrimination

  http://www.eeoc.gov/epa/index.html

- A fact sheet on discrimination in pay, including EPA violations

  Facts About Compensation Discrimination

  http://www.eeoc.gov/facts/fs-epa.html

Agency Resources for Workers

(These can be obtained either at the Web addresses listed below or at the address and phone number listed above.)

- A list of the addresses and phone numbers of EEOC field offices throughout the United States

  Contacting the EEOC

  http://www.eeoc.gov/teledir.html

- A list and links to EEOC resources on the EPA

  Equal Pay and Compensation Discrimination

  http://www.eeoc.gov/epa/index.html

- A fact sheet on discrimination in pay, including EPA violations

  Facts About Compensation Discrimination

  http://www.eeoc.gov/facts/fs-epa.html

F. State Laws Relating to Equal Pay

Some states have their own equal pay laws. To find out whether your state has such a law, contact your state department of labor. A list of state labor departments can be found in the Appendix.

G. Full Text of the EPA

U.S. Code
Chapter 29: Labor
Chapter 8: Fair Labor Standards

§ 206. Minimum wage
(d) Prohibition of sex discrimination

(1) No employer having employees subject to any provisions of this section shall discriminate, within any establishment in which such employees are employed, between employees on the basis of sex by paying wages to employees in such establishment at a rate less than the rate at which he pays wages to employees of the opposite sex in such establishment for equal work on jobs the performance of which requires equal skill, effort, and responsibility, and

which are performed under similar working conditions, except where such payment is made pursuant to

(i) a seniority system;

(ii) a merit system;

(iii) a system which measures earnings by quantity or quality of production; or

(iv) a differential based on any other factor other than sex: Provided, That an employer who is paying a wage rate differential in violation of this subsection shall not, in order to comply with the provisions of this subsection, reduce the wage rate of any employee.

(2) No labor organization, or its agents, representing employees of an employer having employees subject to any provisions of this section shall cause or attempt to cause such an employer to discriminate against an employee in violation of paragraph (1) of this subsection.

(3) For purposes of administration and enforcement, any amounts owing to any employee which have been withheld in violation of this subsection shall be deemed to be unpaid minimum wages or unpaid overtime compensation under this chapter.

(4) As used in this subsection, the term "labor organization" means any organization of any kind, or any agency or employee representation committee or plan, in which employees participate and which exists for the purpose, in whole or in part, of dealing with employers concerning grievances, labor disputes, wages, rates of pay, hours of employment, or conditions of work.

Chapter 6

Employee Polygraph Protection Act (EPPA)

Statute: 29 U.S.C. §§ 2001–2009
http://www4.law.cornell.edu/uscode/29/ch22.html

Regulations: 29 C.F.R. § 801
http://cfr.law.cornell.edu/cfr/cfr.php?title=29&type=part&value=801

Definitions

Access

The opportunity to cause, or aid in causing, a specific economic loss or loss of a controlled substance. An employee need not have regular contact with property to have access to it. If the employee is able to get at the property (by working in its vicinity or knowing the combination to a safe where it is kept, for example), the employee has access—even if the employee's job does not require contact with or use of the property.

Adverse employment action

Firing, disciplining, discriminating against or refusing to hire or promote any applicant or current employee.

Counterintelligence

Information gathered and activities conducted to protect against espionage and other clandestine intelligence activities, sabotage, terrorism or assassinations conducted by or on behalf of foreign governments, foreign or domestic organizations or persons.

Currency, negotiable securities and precious commodities

Assets that are typically handled by, protected for and transported between commercial and financial institutions. Also includes cash assets handled by casinos, racetracks, lotteries and other businesses where cash constitutes the inventory or stock in trade; and gold, silver or diamonds.

Direct access

Contact with or responsibility for a controlled substance, as part of an employee's job responsibilities. An employee whose job requires dispensing, obtaining, manufacturing, storing, testing, distributing, packaging, transporting, taking inventory of, providing security for or prescribing controlled substances has direct access, as long as the employee's job duties include either physical contact with the substances or the opportunity to get possession of such substances.

Economic loss or injury to the employer's business

Financial harm to an employer's business. For example, loss due to theft, embezzlement, misappropriation of trade secrets or sabotage of an employer's property; use of an employer's business to commit a crime, such as money laundering or check kiting; or theft or harm to property belonging to a third party, if the employer is responsible for protecting that property. Examples of losses that would not qualify under this exception are theft of a client's property (unless the employer is responsible for that property), threatened or potential harm, losses caused by legal or unintentional conduct (for example, damages caused by a workplace accident) or theft of another employee's property.

Facilities, materials or operations having a significant impact on the national security of the United States or the health or safety of any state or political subdivision thereof

Those facilities, operations or materials that are targets of acts of sabotage, espionage, terrorism or other destructive or illegal acts, where the consequences could significantly affect the general public's safety or health or

Definitions (continued)

national security. Examples include government office buildings, prisons, facilities used for production or distribution of nuclear or electric power, the public water supply, shipment or storage of toxic waste, public transportation, public schools, military posts or laboratories, factories or plants used to produce, store or process products related to the national defense, factories or plants which produce hazardous chemicals, public and private energy supplies and reserves, the Federal Reserve System and hospitals.

Lie detector

Any mechanical or electrical device that is used, or the results of which are used, for the purpose of rendering a diagnostic opinion about whether a person is telling the truth. *Polygraph*s, deceptographs, voice stress analyzers and psychological stress evaluators all constitute lie detectors under the EPPA. However, medical tests to determine whether an employee has taken drugs or alcohol, written or oral honesty tests and handwriting tests are not considered *lie detector tests* and are not subject to the EPPA's restrictions.

Ongoing investigation

An existing investigation into a specific incident or activity. An employer may not request *polygraph* testing to determine whether any economic losses have been incurred—testing is allowed only in response to a specific, identifiable incident of loss. Nor may employers request *polygraph* testing to investigate a continuing loss—for example, regular inventory shortages that occur all the time in a ware-

house would not be a sufficiently specific incident to allow testing.

Polygraph

An instrument that (1) records continuously, visually, permanently and simultaneously any changes in cardiovascular, respiratory and electrodermal patterns, and (2) is used, or the results of which are used, for the purpose of rendering an opinion about whether a person is honest or dishonest.

Primary business purpose

For purposes of the security services exception (Section B1), an employer's primary business purpose is providing security services if at least 50% of its annual dollar volume of business derives from that activity.

Proprietary information

Business assets such as trade secrets, manufacturing processes, research and development data and cost or pricing data.

Reasonable suspicion

A demonstrable factual basis for believing that a particular employee was involved in, or responsible for, an economic loss or injury to the employer's business. In deciding whether an employer had a reasonable suspicion for testing, courts will consider all of the circumstances including reliable information from co-workers, an employee's demeanor or conduct, or inconsistencies between facts or statements that come up during the investigation. Generally, an employee's opportunity to cause the loss will not be enough, on its own, to create reasonable suspicion.

A. Overview of the EPPA

1. Summary

The Employee Polygraph Protection Act (EPPA) prohibits most private employers from requiring job applicants or current employees to take *lie detector test*s, except in very limited circumstances. In the few situations when an employer is legally allowed to use a *polygraph* test, the EPPA places strict limits on how the employer can use the results of the test.

The EPPA contains provisions on:

- **Polygraph use:** Employers generally may not ask or require workers to take a *polygraph* test, except in very limited circumstances.
- **Test results:** Employers may use the results of a *polygraph* against an employee only if additional evidence supports the decision.
- **Employees' rights:** Employees are entitled to certain information and protections before, during and after a *polygraph* test.
- **Polygraph examiners:** Those who administer the test must meet certain job qualifications and render their conclusions in a prescribed format.
- **Retaliation:** Employers may not take *adverse employment actions* against employees who exercise their rights under the law.

2. Regulated Employers

The EPPA does not apply to governmental employers, whether federal, state or local.

Private employers are subject to the EPPA if they are covered by the Fair Labor Standards Act (FLSA). For information on coverage, see the chapter on the FLSA.

Foreign employers are subject to the EPPA for any actions they take within the United States relating to the administration of *lie detector test*s. For example, if a foreign corporation has an office in the United States and prepares paperwork in that office relating to *polygraph* testing, the EPPA applies to that employer—even if the *polygraph* tests will be conducted in a foreign country.

The EPPA also applies to any person acting in an employer's interest in relation to an employee or applicant. For example, employment placement agencies, job recruiting firms and vocational trade schools may be subject to the EPPA for job applicants whom they refer to prospective employers. However, these referring organizations will be liable for violations of the EPPA only if they had reason to know that the prospective employer would require applicants to take a *polygraph* or otherwise act in violation of the law.

3. Covered Workers

The EPPA covers all employees who work for a regulated private employer. It does not cover federal, state or local government employees.

The EPPA also protects former employees from discrimination. For example, if an employee decides to quit rather than take a *polygraph*, an employer may not threaten or take negative action against that person (by attempting to prevent that person from getting another job, for example).

4. What's Prohibited: Employers

Employers are prohibited from requiring applicants or employees to take *lie detector tests*, except in very limited circumstances. Those employers who are legally allowed to conduct *polygraph* tests may not rely on the results to take an adverse employment action against an employee unless they have additional evidence of the employee's guilt. See Sections C1 and C2, below, for more information on these provisions.

5. What's Required: Employers

Employers who are legally allowed to administer *polygraph* tests must carefully observe the tested employee's rights throughout the process by, among other things, providing a written statement of the nature of and reasons for the test. Employers must use *polygraph* examiners who meet certain qualifications and requirements as spelled out in the law. See Sections B3 and B4, below, for more information on these provisions.

Employers are also required to post a notice in the workplace (prepared by the Department of Labor) describing the EPPA's provisions. See Section D2, below.

6. What's Required: Workers

The EPPA imposes no obligations on workers.

7. Exceptions

There are several exceptions to the EPPA's prohibition on private employers' use of *lie detector tests*. These exceptions are discussed in Section B1.

B. Major Provisions of the EPPA

1. Polygraph Use

In general, the EPPA prohibits private employers from requiring any applicant or current employee to take a *lie detector test*. The law also prohibits private employers from firing, disciplining, discriminating against or refusing to hire or promote any applicant or current employee for refusing to take a *lie detector test*.

However, the law includes several exceptions—circumstances in which certain private employers may require employees or applicants to take *polygraph tests*—explained below. In addition, the law allows certain public employers to administer *lie detector tests* to employees of private employers.

Regulated Employers

All employers must comply with this provision unless they fall within one of the law's exceptions.

Covered Workers

All employees of regulated employers are protected by this provision.

What's Prohibited: Employers

Unless they fall within one of the exceptions outlined below, employers may not, directly or indirectly, require, suggest, request or cause any applicant or current employee to take or submit to a *lie detector test*.

What's Required: Employers

An employer who falls within one of the law's exceptions and wishes to request or administer a *polygraph test* must generally meet the requirements set forth in sections B3 and B4.

What's Required: Workers

The law imposes no obligations on workers.

Exceptions—Public Employers Testing Private Employees

There are two circumstances in which federal, state or local authorities can require private employees to undertake *lie detector test*s. In these circumstances, the private employers for whom these employees work cannot be held liable for the testing under the EPPA.

Law Enforcement Exception

If a private employer reports a theft or other economic loss to law enforcement authorities, and those authorities deem it necessary, in the normal course of investigating the incident, to administer a *polygraph test* to a suspected employee, that testing is not prohibited by the EPPA. The employer may cooperate with law enforcement officials in the investigation— for example, by allowing the police to test a suspect on the employer's premises or letting the employee leave work early to take a *polygraph* test at the police station. However, if an employer participates actively in the testing, by administering the test itself or by reimbursing police for the costs of testing, the employer will be subject to the EPPA—and the employer will have violated the law unless one of the private employer exceptions (below) applies.

Federal Government Counterintelligence Exception

If a private employer does projects or work for the federal government, the government may, in the performance of its *counterintelligence* functions, require the private employees to take *lie detector tests*. This exception allows the government to require *lie detector tests* of:

- Any expert or consultant under contract to, or any employee of any contractor of, the Department of Defense
- Any expert or consultant under contract to or any employee of any contractor of, the Department of Energy in connection with its atomic energy defense activities
- Any individual assigned or detailed to, any expert or consultant under contract to, any employee of a contractor of or any person assigned to a space where sensitive cryptologic information is produced, processed or stored for, the National Security Agency, Defense Intelligence Agency, National Imagery and Mapping Agency or the Central Intelligence Agency

- Any expert or consultant under contract to or any employee of any contractor of, any department, agency or program of the federal government, if that person's duties involve access to information that has been classified as top secret or designated as being within a special access program
- Any employee of any contractor to the Federal Bureau of Investigation, if that employee actually performs any work under the contract.

Exceptions—Private Employers

There are three exceptions available to private employers. These exceptions apply only to *polygraph tests*. Therefore, private employers are always prohibited from administering *lie detector tests* other than *polygraph tests*, even if one of the exceptions applies.

Controlled Substances Exception

Employers who are authorized by the Drug Enforcement Administration (DEA) to manufacture, distribute or dispense specified controlled substances (those listed in Schedule I, II, III or IV of the Controlled Substances Act, 21 U.S.C. § 812) may require *polygraph* testing only of:

- **Job applicants** who would, if hired, have *direct access* to the manufacture, storage, distribution or sale of a controlled substance, and
- **Current employees** in connection with an *ongoing investigation* of criminal or other misconduct involving actual or potential loss or injury to the manufac-

ture, distribution or dispensing of a controlled substance, but only if the employee had *access* to the person or property that is the subject of the investigation.

This exception applies only to employers who have DEA authorization to deal in these controlled substances. It does not apply to other employers, even if their employees may come in contact with controlled substances as a normal part of their jobs, as might be true of truck drivers or warehouse employees.

The term "job applicants" as used in this exception might include current employees who apply for transfer or promotion to a different position. For example, if an employee who currently works in a position with no *direct access* to controlled substances applies for a position that provides such access, that employee can be required to take a *polygraph* test under the rule applicable to job applicants.

Security Services Exception

Certain private employers that provide security services may require job applicants to take a *polygraph* test. This exception applies only if:

- The employer's *primary business purpose* is providing armored car personnel, personnel who design, install and maintain security alarm systems or other uniformed or plainclothes security personnel
- The employer's function includes protecting (1) *facilities, materials or operations having a significant impact on the national security of the United States or the health or safety of any state or*

political subdivision thereof or (2) *currency, negotiable securities, precious commodities* or *proprietary information,* and

- The applicant tested would be employed to protect the facilities, materials, operations or assets listed above. An applicant for a position that would allow the opportunity to cause or participate in a security breach is covered by this requirement.

The term "job applicants" as used in this exception might include current employees who apply for transfer or promotion to a different position. For example, if an employee who currently provides security for an appliance store applies for a position guarding a nuclear facility, that employee can be required to take a *polygraph* test under the rule applicable to job applicants.

Ongoing Investigation Exception

A private employer may ask an employee to submit to a *polygraph* test if:

- The test is administered in connection with an *ongoing investigation* of economic loss or injury to the employer's business
- The employee had *access* to the property that is the subject of the investigation
- The employer has a *reasonable suspicion* that the employee was involved in the incident or activity under investigation, and
- The employer gives the employee a written statement, at least two working days before the test, that (1) describes

the specific incident or activity under investigation and the basis for testing the employee; (2) identifies the specific *economic loss or injury to the employer's business*; (3) states that the employee had *access* to the property that is the subject of the investigation; (4) describes the basis for the employer's *reasonable suspicion* of the employee; and (5) is signed by someone authorized to legally bind the employer, such as an officer or director of the company. This statement must be signed by the employee and must indicate the time and date when the employee received the statement.

2. Test Results

Unless one of the exceptions discussed in Section B1 applies, employers may not:

- Use, accept, refer to or inquire about the results of any *lie detector test* taken by an applicant or current employee
- Take any *adverse employment action* against an employee or applicant on the basis of the results of a *lie detector test* or the employee's or applicant's refusal to take a *lie detector test.*

If one of the exceptions applies, employers may use the results of a *polygraph* test—or an employee's refusal to take a properly supported *polygraph* test—as one basis for taking an *adverse employment action* against an employee. However, the employer must administer the test properly, by following the requirements set forth in sections B3 and B4.

And the employer may not rely solely on the results of the *polygraph* test or the employee's refusal to take it. An employer must have additional reasons for the decision; what's required depends on the exception that applies.

Ongoing Investigation Exception

An employer may not use the results of a *polygraph* test administered under the ongoing investigation exception or the employee's refusal to take such a test as the basis for an *adverse employment action* against an employee without additional supporting evidence. Such evidence might include:

- Evidence showing that the employee had *access* to the property that is the subject of the investigation, and
- Evidence creating a reasonable suspicion that the employee was involved in the incident or activity under investigation.

Admissions or statements made by the employee before, during or after the *polygraph* test may also create sufficient additional supporting evidence to act on the results of the test.

Controlled Substances and Security Services Exceptions

An employer may not use the results of a *polygraph* test administered under the controlled substances or security services exceptions or the employee's refusal to take such a test as the sole basis for an *adverse employment action* against an employee. An employer must have another reason for the decision, supported by evidence. Such a reason might include:

- Traditional factors on which employers rely to make job decisions, such as job performance or prior employment experience, or
- Admissions or statements made by the employee before, during or after a *polygraph* test.

3. Employees' Rights

Employers may rely on the results of a *polygraph* test only if they meet a long list of requirements designed to protect an employee's rights before, during and after a *polygraph* test. Some of these requirements (for example, those about the manner in which the test is conducted) rely on the cooperation of the *polygraph* examiner. In these cases, the employer is responsible for ensuring that the examiner does not violate the employee's rights.

Pretest Rights

The pretest phase of a *polygraph* test refers to the period of questioning and other methods of preparing the employee to take the test. During this phase, an employee must receive:

- Written notice, in a language the employee understands, of the date, time and location of the test, and the employee's right to consult with an attorney or an employee representative before each phase of the test. The notice must be signed by the employee and indicate the date and time the employee received it. The employee must receive this notice two working days before the test.

- Written and oral notice of the nature and characteristics of the *polygraph* instrument and examination, including an explanation of how the *polygraph* instrument works and the procedure to be used during the examination.
- Written notice, in a language the employee understands, indicating:
  (1) whether the testing area contains a two-way mirror, camera or other device to observe the employee;
  (2) whether any other device (such as a tape recorder or other monitoring instrument) will be used during the test;
  (3) that the employee has a right to record the test, if the employer is told of the recording;
  (4) that the employee may stop the test at any time;
  (5) that the employee has the right, and will be given an opportunity, to review all questions to be asked during the test;
  (6) that the employee may not be asked questions in a manner that is degrading or needlessly intrudes on the employee;
  (7) that the employee may not be asked any questions about religious beliefs or opinions, beliefs regarding racial matters, political beliefs or affiliations, matters of sexual behavior, or beliefs, affiliations, opinions or lawful activities relating to unions or labor organizations;
  (8) that the test may not be conducted if a physician provides sufficient written evidence that the employee suffers from a medical or psychological condition or is undergoing treatment that might cause abnormal responses during the test;
  (9) that the test cannot be required as a condition of employment;
  (10) that the employer may not take an *adverse employment action* against the employee based on the results of the test, or the employee's refusal to take the test, without additional evidence to support the action;
  (11) if the test is given under the ongoing investigation exception, that the additional evidence required to support the *adverse employment action* may include evidence that the employee had *access* to the property and evidence supporting the employer's *reasonable suspicion* that the employee was involved in the incident;
  (12) that any statements the employee makes before, during or after the test may provide additional evidence to support an *adverse employment action*;
  (13) that any admission of criminal conduct may be transmitted to an appropriate government law enforcement agency;
  (14) that information gained from the test may be disclosed by the examiner or

the employer only to the employee; any person whom the employee specifically authorizes, in writing, to receive the results; the employer; a court, governmental agency, arbitrator or mediator, pursuant to court order; an official of the U.S. Department of Labor, if the employee authorizes such disclosure in writing; or to an appropriate governmental law enforcement agency, if the information is an admission of criminal conduct;

(15) a description of the employee's legal rights if the employer violates the law;

(16) that the employee has the right to consult with legal counsel or another representative during every phase of the test, although that person may be excluded from the room when the test is actually conducted; and

(17) that the employee may not give up his rights under the EPPA, voluntarily or involuntarily, by contract or otherwise, except as part of a written settlement agreement. The employer must give the employee this notice and read the notice to the employee. The Department of Labor has prepared a standard form that the employer can use to fulfill this requirement. See "Agency Resources for Employers" in Section F for more information.

- The opportunity to review, in writing, all questions that the examiner will ask during the test.

Rights During the Test

During the *polygraph* test, the employee has the right:

- To end the test at any time
- Not to be asked questions in a manner designed to degrade or needlessly intrude on the employee
- Not to be asked any question about (1) religious beliefs or affiliations; (2) beliefs or opinions regarding racial matters; (3) political beliefs or affiliations; (4) any matter relating to sexual behavior; or (5) beliefs, affiliations, opinions or lawful activities regarding unions or labor organizations
- Not to be tested if a physician provides sufficient written evidence that the employee is suffering from a medical or psychological condition or is undergoing treatment that might cause abnormal responses to the test
- To be asked only questions that were presented to the employee for review, in writing, before the test, and
- To a test of no less than 90 minutes in length (unless the employee ends the test before it is complete).

Rights After the Test

Before taking any adverse employment action based on the results of a test, the employer must:

- Interview the employee further, based on the results of the test, and
- Provide the employee with (1) a written copy of any opinion or conclusion rendered as a result of the test; and (2)

a copy of the questions asked during the test and the corresponding charted responses (copies of the charts of the entire examination, showing the employee's physiological responses to each question).

Disclosure of Test Results

Although the employee who takes the test can disclose the results as he or she sees fits, the EPPA strictly limits the circumstances in which an employer or *polygraph* examiner may reveal test results. An examiner may disclose results only to:

- The employee or any other person whom the employee authorizes, in writing, to receive the results
- The employer that requested the test, or
- Any court, governmental agency, arbitrator or mediator, pursuant to a court order requiring such disclosure.

An employer may disclose *polygraph* results only to

- The employee or any other person whom the employee authorizes, in writing, to receive the results
- Any court, governmental agency, arbitrator or mediator, pursuant to a court order requiring such disclosure, or
- A governmental law enforcement agency, if the disclosed information is an admission of criminal conduct.

4. Polygraph Examiners

Even if an employer is entitled to request or conduct a *polygraph* test under one of the

exceptions listed in Section B1, that test will violate the EPPA unless the employer uses a *polygraph* examiner who meets certain qualifications and requirements. The examiner must:

- have a valid, current license, if required in the state where the *polygraph* will be conducted (over half the states require licenses)
- maintain a minimum $50,000 bond or an equivalent amount of professional liability coverage
- administer no more than five *polygraph* tests in any single day on which a test or tests subject to the EPPA is conducted (not including any tests terminated voluntarily by the employee), and
- administer no *polygraph* examination that is less than 90 minutes long (unless the test is terminated voluntarily by the employee).

In addition, if the examiner renders any opinion or conclusion regarding the employee's truthfulness or deception, the report must:

- be in writing
- be based solely on an analysis of *polygraph* test charts
- not contain information other than admissions, information, case facts and interpretation of the charts relevant to the purpose and stated objectives of the test, and
- not include any recommendation about the employment of the employee.

The examiner must also retain all opinions, reports, charts, written questions, lists and other records relating to the test (including written notices signed by the employee and electronic recordings of the test) for at least three years after the test is conducted.

5. Retaliation

An employer may not take or threaten to take an *adverse employment action* against an employee or job applicant for exercising rights granted by EPPA (by, for example, filing an administrative complaint or testifying in a lawsuit).

C. How the EPPA Is Enforced

1. Individual Complaints

An employee who wishes to file a complaint under the EPPA has two options. The employee may make a complaint to the Wage and Hour Division of the Department of Labor (DOL) (see Section C2, below). Or, the employee may bypass the DOL and file a lawsuit in state court or in federal district court. The employee must file this lawsuit within three years of the date the employer violated the law.

2. Agency Enforcement

If an employee files a complaint with the DOL, the agency may choose to investigate the employer—particularly if the employer conducts a lot of *polygraph* tests, raising the possibility that many employees' rights have been violated.

DOL investigations are similar to audits. An investigator may contact the employer ahead of time or may simply show up at the workplace. The investigator will examine the employer's records and interview employees who may have information about the complaint. Once the investigation is complete, the investigator will meet with the employer to try to resolve any problems the investigation uncovered. The investigator will tell the employer whether it has violated the law and how it can correct those violations—for example, by reinstating an employee who was fired illegally for refusing to take a *polygraph* or by immediately ceasing to require all applicants to take a *polygraph*.

If the employer refuses to comply, the Secretary of Labor can file a lawsuit in federal district court on behalf of the employees whose rights were violated. The Secretary may also impose civil penalties of up to $10,000 against the employer—these penalties are assessed in an administrative hearing process, not a lawsuit. However, if the employer objects to the penalties, it has the right to appeal to federal district court.

D. For Employers: Complying With the EPPA

1. Reporting Requirements

The EPPA imposes no reporting requirements.

2. Posting Requirements

Employers are required to post a notice (prepared by the DOL) in the workplace describing the EPPA's provisions. Employers must post this notice in a prominent location in every business location, where it can be easily seen and read by employees and job applicants. You can download the EPPA poster from the DOL's website at the address given in Section F.

3. Recordkeeping Requirements

Employers must keep the following records for at least three years from the date the *polygraph* test is conducted (or from the date the employer asks the employee to take the test, if no test is ever conducted):

- a copy of the employer's written notice to the *polygraph* examiner identifying the person(s) to be tested
- copies of all opinions, reports or other records that the *polygraph* examiner gives to the employer

- if the test is administered under the ongoing investigation exception, a copy of the statement to the employee setting forth the specific incident under investigation and the basis for testing that particular employee, and
- if the test is administered to a current employee under the controlled substances exception, records specifically identifying the loss or injury under investigation and the nature of the employee's *access* to the person or property investigated.

The employer must make these records available to the Secretary of Labor or an investigator from the DOL within 72 hours after they are requested.

4. Practical Tips

Here are some practical tips for complying with the EPPA:

- **Don't request polygraph tests unless it's absolutely necessary.** As you have probably concluded by now, the EPPA is a complicated law—and one that strongly discourages *polygraph* testing. If you want to administer a *polygraph*, make sure you fit within one of its very narrow exceptions. If you proceed, document the extensive requisite notices to the employee, find an examiner who meets the law's requirements—and even if the test indicates that the employee is not telling the truth, remember that you can't use the results without more evidence. In short, complying with this

law can be a time-consuming chore—
one you should take on only if you
really need to.

- **The jury's still out on polygraph test
  results.** Experts disagree—strongly—
  over whether and how well *polygraph*
  tests really measure truthfulness. Some
  claim the tests are highly accurate, if
  properly administered; others dismiss
  them as "junk science." This means that,
  if you get sued by an employee claiming that you improperly used the results
  of a *polygraph* against him, you should
  expect to hear expert witnesses arguing
  over the accuracy of *polygraph* tests.

- **Choose an experienced examiner.** If you
  decide to test, take the time to find a
  good examiner. After all, the results of
  the test are only as good as the person
  who interprets them. And an examiner
  familiar with the requirements of the
  EPPA will know how to conduct an
  examination that complies with the law,
  how to prepare the necessary paperwork and what records to keep for the
  DOL.

- **Keep all of your records.** The EPPA
  requires you to keep records documenting the notices you gave to the employee
  and the results of any test administered.
  But for the savvy employer, these records
  are only the beginning. You should
  keep copies of all records relating in any
  way to your decision to ask for a *polygraph* and your subsequent treatment of
  the employee. For example, you will
  want records of any investigation con-

ducted, inventory records showing
missing or stolen items, copies of any
relevant police reports, records of any
additional evidence you considered in
deciding whether to retain, hire or fire
the employee and so on. If you are investigated or sued, these documents will
help you prove that you followed the
law.

5. Penalties

Employers who violate the EPPA may be
required to:

- take action to remedy the violation,
  such as hiring, promoting or reinstating
  the worker who was wrongfully asked
  or required to take a *polygraph*, or who
  was improperly subjected to an *adverse
  employment action* in violation of the
  law

- pay the worker for any benefits or
  wages lost because of the employer's
  violation, and

- pay the worker's attorney fees and
  court costs.

E. For Workers: Asserting Rights Under the EPPA

1. Where to Start

If you believe that your employer or a prospective employer has violated the EPPA—by
asking or requiring you to take a *lie detector
test* in violation of the EPPA, violating your

rights when administering a test or illegally using the results of a test, for example—start by complaining internally to the company. If the company has a complaint policy, follow the designated procedures to file a complaint. If the company has no complaint policy, talk to a human resources representative or a member of management.

If you are a union member, talk to your shop steward or union representative.

If internal complaints and/or union complaints don't work, you can file a lawsuit or file a complaint with the DOL. For more on agency enforcement, see Section C2.

2. Required Forms

Contact your local office of the Wage and Hour Division of the DOL to find out if you have to use a particular form to file an administrative complaint. See Section F for contact information.

3. Practical Tips

Here are some practical tips on enforcing your rights under the EPPA:

- **Unless an exception applies, it's probably best to avoid the test.** It is legal for a private employer to request a *polygraph* test only if one of the exceptions, discussed above in Section B1, applies. If you are asked to take a *polygraph* illegally—as part of a random testing program, for example—consider just saying no. Because *polygraph*s are not always accurate, submitting to an illegal test can be risky. Be sure to tell your employer that you are aware of your rights—and that you will take action if you are retaliated against.

- **Review the questions in advance.** Under the EPPA, you have the right to see all questions you will be asked, in writing, before the test. Take advantage of this opportunity. Look through the questions carefully. Do any of them seem to dig into your private life or personal affairs? Do they include questions regarding racial matters or union affiliations? If you have any concerns about the list of questions, talk to an attorney or union representative before the test.

- **Do your homework before the test.** Before the test, your employer is required to tell you, among other things, what type of *polygraph* will be administered and how the machine functions. Read this material carefully. You can also find lots of information on the Internet about various types of *polygraph*s, how they work and what they measure.

- **If you are one of many, go to the DOL.** If your employer engages in wholesale violations of the EPPA—by forcing all applicants to take a *polygraph* or by conducting random *polygraph* testing, for example—get the government's help. The DOL will have a greater interest in pursuing your case if you are only the tip of the iceberg. The government will get the biggest bang for its buck if its enforcement efforts against one employer help many employees.

F. Agency Charged With Enforcement & Compliance

Employment Standards Administration, Wage and Hour Division, Department of Labor

200 Constitution Ave., NW

Washington, DC 20210

Phone: 866-4-USA-DOL

TTY: 877-889-5627

http://www.dol.gov

Agency Resources for Employers

(These can be obtained either at the Web addresses listed below or at the address and phone number listed above.)

- Download copies of the DOL's poster on the EPPA (in English or Spanish)

  Notice: Employee Polygraph Protection Act

  http://www.dol.gov/dol/esa/public/regs/compliance/posters/pdf/eppabw.pdf.

- A standard form employers can use to inform those asked to take a polygraph of their rights—the form appears as an appendix to Part 801 of Title 29 of the Code of Federal Regulations

  Notice to Examinee

  http://squid.law.cornell.edu/cgi-bin/get-cfr.cgi?TITLE=29&PART=801&SECTION=75&TYPE=TEXT

- A fact sheet on the law's provisions

  Employee Polygraph Protection Act of 1988

  http://www.dol.gov/dol/esa/public/regs/compliance/whd/whfs36.html

- A fact sheet explaining DOL audits

  Visits to Employers

  http://www.dol.gov/dol/esa/public/regs/compliance/whd/whdfs44.htm

- A list of the addresses and telephone numbers of local offices of the Wage and Hour Division

  Employment Standards Administration: Wage and Hour Division: District Office Locations

  http://www.dol.gov/dol/esa/public/contacts/whd/america2.htm

Agency Resources for Workers

(These can be obtained either at the Web addresses listed below or at the address and phone number listed above.)

- A fact sheet on the law's provisions
  Employee Polygraph Protection Act of 1988
  http://www.dol.gov/dol/esa/public/regs/compliance/whd/whfs36.html
- A list of the addresses and telephone numbers of local offices of the Wage and Hour Division
  Employment Standards Administration: Wage and Hour Division:
  District Office Locations
  http://www.dol.gov/dol/esa/public/contacts/whd/america2.htm

G. State Laws Relating to Polygraph Tests

Employee Polygraph Examination Laws

Most states have laws prohibiting employers from requiring employees or prospective employees to take a *polygraph* test as a condition of being hired, or continuing employment.

Some states go further and prohibit even the suggestion of such a test.

Still others prohibit the employer from using the results of any such examination in any employment-related decisions, regardless of how the test results were obtained.

Some states, however, allow employers to request and use the results of a test if the employee is first informed of his or her absolute right to refuse to take the test without penalty.

States not listed here have no statutes prohibiting the use of *lie detectors* on private sector employees.

Jurisdiction Citation	Employers Covered	What Employer Cannot Do As a Condition of Employment (with exceptions as noted)
Alaska Alaska Stat. § 23.10.037	All	Suggest, request, or require.
California Cal. Lab. Code § 432.2	All	Demand or require. However, may request if it first advises the subject, in writing, of their legal right to refuse.
Connecticut Conn. Gen. Stat. Ann. § 31-51(g)	All	Request or require.
Delaware Del. Code Ann. tit. 19, § 704(e)	All	Suggest, request or require.
District of Columbia D.C. Code Ann. § 32-901 and following	All	Administer, use or accept the results of any polygraph examination.
Hawaii Haw. Rev. Stat. § 378-26.5	All	Require. May request if subject is advised, orally and in writing, of right to refuse without adverse consequences.
Idaho Idaho Code § 44-903	All	Require.
Illinois 225 Ill. Comp. Stat. § 430/14.1	All	No lie detector examiner may inquire into any of the following areas during preemployment or periodic employment examinations, unless the area is directly related to employment: • religious beliefs or affiliations • beliefs or opinions regarding racial matters • political beliefs or affiliations • beliefs, affiliations or lawful activities regarding unions or labor organizations, or • sexual preferences or activity.
Iowa Iowa Code § 730.4	All	Request, require or administer.
Maine Me. Rev. Stat. Ann. tit. 32, § 7166	All	Request, require, suggest or administer. Employee can request a test but (1) the results cannot be used against employee (2) employer must give employee a copy of the law when employee requests test, and (3) test must be recorded or a witness of the employee's choice must be present or both, as the employee requests.
Maryland Md. Code Ann., [Lab. & Empl.] § 3-702	All	Require or demand. All employment applications must include specified language informing applicants that they cannot be required to take a lie detector test and must provide space for applicants to sign to acknowledge the notice.

Jurisdiction Citation	Employers Covered	What Employer Cannot Do As a Condition of Employment (with exceptions as noted)
Massachusetts Mass. Gen. Laws ch. 149, § 19B	All	Request, require or administer. All employment applications must include specified language informing applicants of this prohibition.
Michigan Mich. Comp. Laws § 37.201	All	Request, require or administer. Employer can administer test if requested by the employee, but (1) employer must give employee a copy of the law before the test (2) employer must use a licensed examiner to administer the test (3) examiner must follow specific procedures, including giving employee notice of rights, information about the questions to be asked and a copy of the completed test, and (4) examiner may not ask questions about employee's sexual practices, labor union, political or religious affiliations or marital relationship, unless such questions are relevant to the test.
Minnesota Minn. Stat. Ann. § 181.75	All	Directly or indirectly solicit or require. Employee can request a test, but the employer must inform the employee that the test is voluntary.
Montana Mont. Code Ann. § 39-2-304		Require.
Nebraska Neb. Rev. Stat. § 81-1932	All	Require. Employer may ask employee or applicant to take a test as long as they meet specified requirements. However, a test may be requested only in connection with a specific investigation, and may not inquire into the test taker's • sexual practices • labor union, political or religious affiliations, or • marital relationships.
Nevada Nev. Rev. Stat. Ann. § 613.480	All	Require. May ask employee to take test if given written and oral notice that test is voluntary and may be terminated at any time. However, test may be requested only (1) in connection with an ongoing investigation of economic loss to the employer (2) of applicants for certain security positions, or (3) of applicants who would deal with certain controlled substances (or of employees involved in investigation of misconduct relating to controlled substances).

Jurisdiction Citation	Employers Covered	What Employer Cannot Do As a Condition of Employment (with exceptions as noted)
New Jersey N.J. Stat. Ann. § 2C:40A-1	All employers except those that deal with controlled substances.	Influence, request or require.
New York N.Y. Lab. Law § 733	All	Require, request, suggest, permit or use the results of.
Oregon Or. Rev. Stat. § 659.225	All	Require. Individual may consent to test during the course of criminal or civil judicial proceedings in which the individual is a party or witness, or during the course of a criminal investigation conducted by a law enforcement agency, a district attorney or the Attorney General.
Pennsylvania 18 Pa. Cons. Stat. Ann. § 7321	All	Require, except that employer may require test for positions that dispense or have access to narcotics or dangerous drugs.
Rhode Island R.I. Gen. Laws § 28-6.1-1	All	Request, require or subject.
Tennessee Tenn. Code Ann. § 62-27-128	All	Take any personnel action based solely upon the results of a polygraph examination. May not ask about a list of topics, unless the examination is administered as a result of an investigation of illegal activity in the subject area and the inability to pose relevant questions in relation to the illegal activity would be detrimental to the investigation: • religious beliefs or affiliations • beliefs or opinions regarding racial matters; political beliefs or affiliations • beliefs, affiliations or lawful activities regarding unions or labor organizations • sexual preferences or activities • any disabilities covered by the Americans with Disabilities Act, or • activities that occurred more than five years before the examination, except for felony convictions and violations of the state drug control act. Each prospective examinee must be shown a list of the questions to be asked on an official form and a list of the areas that the examination will cover. Examinee must receive written notice of rights under the law. Also, the questions must be reviewed with the examinee before the examination.

Jurisdiction Citation	Employers Covered	What Employer Cannot Do As a Condition of Employment (with exceptions as noted)
Vermont Vt. Stat. Ann. tit. 21, § 494a-e	All except • employers whose primary business is sale of precious metals, gems or jewelry • employers whose business includes the manufacture or sale of regulated drugs, if the applicant's position would require contact with drugs, and • any employers authorized by federal law to require a test.	Request, require, or administer.
Virginia Va. Code Ann. § 40.1-51.4:3	All	Require an applicant to answer questions in a polygraph test concerning the individual's sexual activities, unless the sexual activity of the individual has resulted in a conviction for violation of a state law.
Washington Wash. Rev. Code Ann. § 49.44.120	All	Require, directly or indirectly, unless examinee would • manufacture, distribute or dispense controlled substances, or • work in a sensitive position directly involving national security.
West Virginia W. Va. Code § 21-5-5(b)	All employees except those authorized to manufacture, distribute or dispense controlled substances.	Require or request, either directly or indirectly, or knowingly use the results.
Wisconsin Wis. Stat. Ann. § 111.37	All	Directly or indirectly require, request, suggest or use the results of, unless test administered: (1) in connection with an ongoing investigation of economic loss to the employer (2) to applicants for certain security positions, or (3) to applicants who would deal with certain controlled substances.

H. Full Text of the EPPA

29 U.S.C. §§ 2001-2009
U.S. Code
Title 29: Labor
Chapter 22: Employee Polygraph Protection

§ 2001. Definitions
§ 2002. Prohibitions on lie detector use
§ 2003. Notice of protection
§ 2004. Authority of Secretary
§ 2005. Enforcement provisions
§ 2006. Exemptions
§ 2007. Restrictions on use of exemptions
§ 2008. Disclosure of information
§ 2009. Effect on other law and agreements

§ 2001. Definitions

As used in this chapter:

(1) Commerce

The term "commerce" has the meaning provided by section 203(b) of this title.

(2) Employer

The term "employer" includes any person acting directly or indirectly in the interest of an employer in relation to an employee or prospective employee.

(3) Lie detector

The term "lie detector" includes a polygraph, deceptograph, voice stress analyzer, psychological stress evaluator, or any other similar device (whether mechanical or electrical) that is used, or the results of which are used, for the purpose of rendering a diagnostic opinion regarding the honesty or dishonesty of an individual.

(4) Polygraph

The term "polygraph" means an instrument that—

(A) records continuously, visually, permanently, and simultaneously changes in cardiovascular, respiratory, and electrodermal patterns as minimum instrumentation standards; and

(B) is used, or the results of which are used, for the purpose of rendering a diagnostic opinion regarding the honesty or dishonesty of an individual.

(5) Secretary

The term "Secretary" means the Secretary of Labor.

§ 2002. Prohibitions on lie detector use

Except as provided in sections 2006 and 2007 of this title, it shall be unlawful for any employer engaged in or affecting commerce or in the production of goods for commerce—

(1) directly or indirectly, to require, request, suggest, or cause any employee or prospective employee to take or submit to any lie detector test;

(2) to use, accept, refer to, or inquire concerning the results of any lie detector test of any employee or prospective employee;

(3) to discharge, discipline, discriminate against in any manner, or deny employment or promotion to, or threaten to take any such action against—

(A) any employee or prospective employee who refuses, declines, or fails to take or submit to any lie detector test, or

(B) any employee or prospective employee on the basis of the results of any lie detector test; or

(4) to discharge, discipline, discriminate against in any manner, or deny employment or promotion to, or threaten to take any such action against, any employee or prospective employee because—

(A) such employee or prospective employee has filed any complaint or instituted or caused to be instituted any proceeding under or related to this chapter,

(B) such employee or prospective employee has testified or is about to testify in any such proceeding, or

(C) of the exercise by such employee or prospective employee, on behalf of such employee or another person, of any right afforded by this chapter

§ 2003. Notice of protection

The Secretary shall prepare, have printed, and distribute a notice setting forth excerpts from, or summaries of, the pertinent provisions of this chapter. Each employer shall post and maintain such notice in conspicuous places on its premises where notices to employees and applicants to employment are customarily posted

§ 2004. Authority of Secretary

(a) In general

The Secretary shall—

(1) issue such rules and regulations as may be necessary or appropriate to carry out this chapter;

(2) cooperate with regional, State, local, and other agencies, and cooperate with and furnish technical

assistance to employers, labor organizations, and employment agencies to aid in effectuating the purposes of this chapter; and

(3) make investigations and inspections and require the keeping of records necessary or appropriate for the administration of this chapter.

(b) Subpoena authority

For the purpose of any hearing or investigation under this chapter, the Secretary shall have the authority contained in sections 49 and 50 of title 15

§ 2005. Enforcement provisions

(a) Civil penalties

(1) In general

Subject to paragraph (2), any employer who violates any provision of this chapter may be assessed a civil penalty of not more than $10,000.

(2) Determination of amount

In determining the amount of any penalty under paragraph (1), the Secretary shall take into account the previous record of the person in terms of compliance with this chapter and the gravity of the violation.

(3) Collection

Any civil penalty assessed under this subsection shall be collected in the same manner as is required by subsections (b) through (e) of section 1853 of this title with respect to civil penalties assessed under subsection (a) of such section.

(b) Injunctive actions by Secretary

The Secretary may bring an action under this section to restrain violations of this chapter. The Solicitor of Labor may appear for and represent the Secretary in any litigation brought under this chapter. In any action brought under this section, the district courts of the United States shall have jurisdiction, for cause shown, to issue temporary or permanent restraining orders and injunctions to require compliance with this chapter, including such legal or equitable relief incident thereto as may be appropriate, including, but not limited to, employment, reinstatement, promotion, and the payment of lost wages and benefits.

(c) Private civil actions

(1) Liability

An employer who violates this chapter shall be liable to the employee or prospective employee affected by such violation. Such employer shall be liable for such legal or equitable relief as may be appropriate, including, but not limited to, employment, reinstatement, promotion, and the payment of lost wages and benefits.

(2) Court

An action to recover the liability prescribed in paragraph (1) may be maintained against the employer in any Federal or State court of competent jurisdiction by an employee or prospective employee for or on behalf of such employee, prospective employee, and other employees or prospective employees similarly situated. No such action may be commenced more than 3 years after the date of the alleged violation.

(3) Costs

The court, in its discretion, may allow the prevailing party (other than the United States) reasonable costs, including attorney's fees.

(d) Waiver of rights prohibited

The rights and procedures provided by this chapter may not be waived by contract or otherwise, unless such waiver is part of a written settlement agreed to and signed by the parties to the pending action or complaint under this chapter.

§ 2006. Exemptions

(a) No application to governmental employers

This chapter shall not apply with respect to the United States Government, any State or local government, or any political subdivision of a State or local government.

(b) National defense and security exemption

(1) National defense

Nothing in this chapter shall be construed to prohibit the administration, by the Federal Government, in the performance of any counterintelligence function, of any lie detector test to—

(A) any expert or consultant under contract to the Department of Defense or any employee of any contractor of such Department; or

(B) any expert or consultant under contract with the Department of Energy in connection with the atomic energy defense activities of such Department or any employee of any contractor of such Department in connection with such activities.

(2) Security

Nothing in this chapter shall be construed to prohibit the administration, by the Federal Government, in the performance of any intelligence or counterintelligence function, of any lie detector test to—

(A)

(i) any individual employed by, assigned to, or detailed to, the National Security Agency, the Defense Intelligence Agency, the National Imagery and Mapping Agency, or the Central Intelligence Agency,

(ii) any expert or consultant under contract to any such agency,

(iii) any employee of a contractor to any such agency,

(iv) any individual applying for a position in any such agency, or

(v) any individual assigned to a space where sensitive cryptologic information is produced, processed, or stored for any such agency; or

(B) any expert, or consultant (or employee of such expert or consultant) under contract with any Federal Government department, agency, or program whose duties involve access to information that has been classified at the level of top secret or designated as being within a special access program under section 4.2(a) of Executive Order 12356 (or a successor Executive order).

(c) FBI contractors exemption

Nothing in this chapter shall be construed to prohibit the administration, by the Federal Government, in the performance of any counterintelligence function, of any lie detector test to an employee of a contractor of the Federal Bureau of Investigation of the Department of Justice who is engaged in the performance of any work under the contract with such Bureau.

(d) Limited exemption for ongoing investigations

Subject to sections 2007 and 2009 of this title, this chapter shall not prohibit an employer from requesting an employee to submit to a polygraph test if—

(1) the test is administered in connection with an ongoing investigation involving economic loss or injury to the employer's business, such as theft, embezzlement, misappropriation, or an act of unlawful industrial espionage or sabotage;

(2) the employee had access to the property that is the subject of the investigation;

(3) the employer has a reasonable suspicion that the employee was involved in the incident or activity under investigation; and

(4) the employer executes a statement, provided to the examinee before the test, that—

(A) sets forth with particularity the specific incident or activity being investigated and the basis for testing particular employees,

(B) is signed by a person (other than a polygraph examiner) authorized to legally bind the employer,

(C) is retained by the employer for at least 3 years, and

(D) contains at a minimum—

(i) an identification of the specific economic loss or injury to the business of the employer,

(ii) a statement indicating that the employee had access to the property that is the subject of the investigation, and

(iii) a statement describing the basis of the employer's reasonable suspicion that the employee was involved in the incident or activity under investigation.

(e) Exemption for security services

(1) In general

Subject to paragraph (2) and sections 2007 and 2009 of this title, this chapter shall not prohibit the use of polygraph tests on prospective employees by any private employer whose primary business purpose consists of providing armored car personnel, personnel engaged in the design, installation, and maintenance of security alarm systems, or other uniformed or plainclothes security personnel and whose function includes protection of—

(A) facilities, materials, or operations having a significant impact on the health or safety of any State or political subdivision thereof, or the national security of the United States, as determined under rules and regulations issued by the Secretary within 90 days after June 27, 1988, including—

(i) facilities engaged in the production, transmission, or distribution of electric or nuclear power,

(ii) public water supply facilities,

(iii) shipments or storage of radioactive or other toxic waste materials, and

(iv) public transportation, or

(B) currency, negotiable securities, precious commodities or instruments, or proprietary information.

(2) Access

The exemption provided under this subsection shall not apply if the test is administered to a prospective employee who would not be employed to protect facilities, materials, operations, or assets referred to in paragraph (1).

(f) Exemption for drug security, drug theft, or drug diversion investigations

(1) In general

Subject to paragraph (2) and sections 2007 and 2009 of this title, this chapter shall not prohibit the use of a polygraph test by any employer authorized to manufacture, distribute, or dispense a controlled substance listed in schedule I, II, III, or IV of section 812 of title 21.

(2) Access

The exemption provided under this subsection shall apply—

(A) if the test is administered to a prospective employee who would have direct access to the manufacture, storage, distribution, or sale of any such controlled substance; or

(B) in the case of a test administered to a current employee, if—

(i) the test is administered in connection with an ongoing investigation of criminal or other misconduct involving, or potentially involving, loss or injury to the manufacture, distribution, or dispensing of any such controlled substance by such employer, and

(ii) the employee had access to the person or property that is the subject of the investigation.

§ 2007. Restrictions on use of exemptions

(a) Test as basis for adverse employment action

(1) Under ongoing investigations exemption

Except as provided in paragraph (2), the exemption under subsection (d) of section 2006 of this title shall not apply if an employee is discharged, disciplined, denied employment or promotion, or otherwise discriminated against in any manner on the basis of the analysis of a polygraph test chart or the refusal to take a polygraph test, without additional supporting evidence. The evidence required by such subsection may serve as additional supporting evidence.

(2) Under other exemptions

In the case of an exemption described in subsection (e) or (f) of such section, the exemption shall not apply if the results of an analysis of a polygraph test chart are used, or the refusal to take a polygraph test is used, as the sole basis upon which an adverse employment action described in paragraph (1) is taken against an employee or prospective employee.

(b) Rights of examinee

The exemptions provided under subsections (d), (e), and (f) of section 2006 of this title shall not apply unless the requirements described in the following paragraphs are met:

(1) All phases

Throughout all phases of the test—

(A) the examinee shall be permitted to terminate the test at any time;

(B) the examinee is not asked questions in a manner designed to degrade, or needlessly intrude on, such examinee;

(C) the examinee is not asked any question concerning—

(i) religious beliefs or affiliations,

(ii) beliefs or opinions regarding racial matters,

(iii) political beliefs or affiliations,

(iv) any matter relating to sexual behavior; and

(v) beliefs, affiliations, opinions, or lawful activities regarding unions or labor organizations; and

(D) the examiner does not conduct the test if there is sufficient written evidence by a physician that the examinee is suffering from a medical or psychological condition or undergoing treatment that might cause abnormal responses during the actual testing phase.

(2) Pretest phase

During the pretest phase, the prospective examinee—

(A) is provided with reasonable written notice of the date, time, and location of the test, and of such examinee's right to obtain and consult with legal counsel or an employee representative before each phase of the test;

(B) is informed in writing of the nature and characteristics of the tests and of the instruments involved;

(C) is informed, in writing—

(i) whether the testing area contains a two-way mirror, a camera, or any other device through which the test can be observed,

(ii) whether any other device, including any device for recording or monitoring the test, will be used, or

(iii) that the employer or the examinee may (with mutual knowledge) make a recording of the test;

(D) is read and signs a written notice informing such examinee—

(i) that the examinee cannot be required to take the test as a condition of employment,

(ii) that any statement made during the test may constitute additional supporting evidence for the purposes of an adverse employment action described in subsection (a) of this section,

(iii) of the limitations imposed under this section,

(iv) of the legal rights and remedies available to the examinee if the polygraph test is not conducted in accordance with this chapter, and

(v) of the legal rights and remedies of the employer under this chapter (including the rights of the employer under section 2008(c)(2) of this title); and

(E) is provided an opportunity to review all questions to be asked during the test and is informed of the right to terminate the test at any time.

(3) Actual testing phase

During the actual testing phase, the examiner does not ask such examinee any question relevant during the test that was not presented in writing for review to such examinee before the test.

(4) Post-test phase

Before any adverse employment action, the employer shall—

(A) further interview the examinee on the basis of the results of the test; and

(B) provide the examinee with—

(i) a written copy of any opinion or conclusion rendered as a result of the test, and

(ii) a copy of the questions asked during the test along with the corresponding charted responses.

(5) Maximum number and minimum duration of tests

The examiner shall not conduct and complete more than five polygraph tests on a calendar day on which the test is given, and shall not conduct any such test for less than a 90-minute duration.

(c) Qualifications and requirements of examiners

The exemptions provided under subsections (d), (e), and (f) of section 2006 of this title shall not apply unless the individual who conducts the polygraph test satisfies the requirements under the following paragraphs:

(1) Qualifications

The examiner—

(A) has a valid and current license granted by licensing and regulatory authorities in the State in which the test is to be conducted, if so required by the State; and

(B) maintains a minimum of a $50,000 bond or an equivalent amount of professional liability coverage.

(2) Requirements

The examiner—

(A) renders any opinion or conclusion regarding the test—

(i) in writing and solely on the basis of an analysis of polygraph test charts,

(ii) that does not contain information other than admissions, information, case facts, and interpretation of the charts relevant to the purpose and stated objectives of the test, and

(iii) that does not include any recommendation concerning the employment of the examinee; and

(B) maintains all opinions, reports, charts, written questions, lists, and other records relating to the test for a minimum period of 3 years after administration of the test.

§ 2008. Disclosure of information

(a) In general

A person, other than the examinee, may not disclose information obtained during a polygraph test, except as provided in this section.

(b) Permitted disclosures

A polygraph examiner may disclose information acquired from a polygraph test only to—

(1) the examinee or any other person specifically designated in writing by the examinee;

(2) the employer that requested the test; or

(3) any court, governmental agency, arbitrator, or mediator, in accordance with due process of law, pursuant to an order from a court of competent jurisdiction.

(c) Disclosure by employer

An employer (other than an employer described in subsection (a), (b), or (c) of section 2006 of this title) for whom a polygraph test is conducted may disclose information from the test only to—

(1) a person in accordance with subsection (b) of this section; or

(2) a governmental agency, but only insofar as the disclosed information is an admission of criminal conduct.

§ 2009. Effect on other law and agreements

Except as provided in subsections (a), (b), and (c) of section 2006 of this title, this chapter shall not preempt any provision of any State or local law or of any negotiated collective bargaining agreement that prohibits lie detector tests or is more restrictive with respect to lie detector tests than any provision of this chapter.

Chapter 7

Employee Retirement Income Security Act (ERISA)

Statute: 29 U.S.C. § 1001 and following
http://www4.law.cornell.edu/uscode/29/1001.html

Regulations: 29 C.F.R § 2509 and following
http://cfr.law.cornell.edu/cfr/cfr.php?title=29&type=part&value=2509

(There are parallel provisions in the Internal Revenue Code Regulations and the
Department of Treasury Regulations.)

Definitions

Beneficiary

A person who is entitled to benefits under an *employee benefit plan* because of a relationship with a *participant* in the plan. Examples of beneficiaries include spouses and dependent children.

Benefit accrual requirement

Determines the amount of benefit that a *plan participant* or *beneficiary* will receive from a plan. This term applies only in the context of *pension plans*.

Church plan

An *employee benefit plan* established and maintained by a church or an association or convention of churches that is tax exempt under Internal Revenue Code Section 501(a).

Defined benefit plan

A type of *pension plan* that guarantees that participants will receive a pension according to a set formula when they retire—for example, 1% of final average salary per year of service.

Defined contribution plan

A type of *pension plan* with no guaranteed benefit formula. Instead, each employee has an individual account consisting of contributions from the employer and/or employee, plus investment returns. The employee's pension is whatever amount happens to be in the account when the employee retires. A common example of a defined contribution plan is a 401(k) plan.

Employee benefit plan

A benefit program that an employer provides to an employee or group of employees.

Pension plans (for example, retirement plans) and *welfare plans* (for example, health insurance plans and long-term disability plans) are the two categories of employee benefit plans.

Employee organization

An organization of employees (such as a labor union) that bargains with an employer about an *employee benefit plan*.

Excess benefit plan

An *employee benefit plan* that an employer maintains to provide benefits in excess of the benefits permitted for *qualified plans* by the Internal Revenue Code. Many of these plans are referred to as "top hat" plans for a select group of highly compensated employees.

Fiduciary

An individual who has any discretionary authority or control over how a plan is managed or how the plan's assets are managed. Fiduciaries can include plan administrators, employers and paid investment advisors—if they have the requisite authority or control. For more on this, see Section B4.

Fiduciary obligations

The standards of conduct, prudence and loyalty that a *fiduciary* must follow. For more about this, see Section B4.

Multiemployer plan

An *employee benefit plan* established and maintained by one or more unions and more than one employer pursuant to a collective bargaining agreement.

Definitions (continued)

Participant

A current or former employee who is or may become eligible to receive benefits from an *employee benefit plan*.

Participation requirement

Determines when a *participant* or *beneficiary* is entitled to start participating in an *employee benefit plan*.

Pension plan

A type of *employee benefit plan* that accumulates money to pay for retirement income or other deferred income to *participants* and *beneficiaries* at some future date, generally a retirement age set by the plan.

Qualified plan

A *pension plan* that receives certain tax benefits because it satisfies the requirements of the Internal Revenue Code.

Summary plan description

A document that plan administrators must give to *participants* and *beneficiaries*. The document provides certain information about the plan, including people's rights, benefits and obligations under the plan. For more, see Section B1, below.

Vesting

A *participant* or *beneficiary* whose benefits become vested cannot lose those benefits, even if he or she leaves the employer sponsoring the plan. Although pension benefits begin to accrue as soon as an individual starts participating in the plan, the individual has no legal right to those benefits until the benefits vest. This term applies only in the context of *pension plans*.

Welfare plan

A type of *employee benefit plan* that provides *participants* and *beneficiaries* with benefits—other than retirement benefits—including health, medical, surgical, disability, death, accident, dependent day care, scholarship and prepaid legal benefits.

A. Overview of ERISA

1. Summary

Congress passed the Employee Retirement Income Security Act (ERISA) to ensure that employees receive the pension, health and other benefits promised to them by their employers. ERISA sets minimum standards for establishing, administering and maintaining two types of *employee benefit plans: pension plans* and *welfare plans*. Some of ERISA's provisions apply to both types of plans, and some provisions apply to only one.

ERISA and the Internal Revenue Code work hand in hand to govern *pension plans* and *welfare plans*. The Code gives tax breaks to employers who establish these plans, and ERISA sets standards for administering the plans. If employers do not follow ERISA or its parallel provisions in the Code, they lose those tax breaks—and face the possibility of paying back some of the tax benefits that they enjoyed over the years. This can turn into quite a hefty sum. In addition, employers and plan administrators who don't follow ERISA's rules face possible fines, civil liability and prison.

ERISA is a long and complicated law. Fortunately, the vast majority of employers do not have to learn the law's details, because plan administrators and other service providers usually handle the requirements themselves. Nonetheless, employers should have a general understanding of ERISA so they can intelligently oversee administrators and service providers. And, of course, employers who take on the administration responsibilities themselves have to follow ERISA to the letter.

The following discussion does not attempt to provide all of the information an employer or plan administrator needs to comply with ERISA on a day-to-day basis. It also does not contain a great deal of detailed information about employee rights and obligations under ERISA. Rather, the discussion provides a general overview. Employers, plan administrators, *participants* and *beneficiaries* who need more specific information should refer to the agency resources listed in Section F, visit their local law library or consult an attorney experienced in ERISA matters.

The following are ERISA's major provisions discussed in this chapter. In parenthesis are the types of plans to which the provisions apply:

- reporting, disclosure and notice rules (*pension plans* and *welfare plans*)
- *participation, vesting* and *benefit accrual* requirements (*pension plans*)
- minimum funding requirements (*defined benefit plans*)
- *fiduciary obligations* (*pension plans* and *welfare plans*)
- administration and enforcement (*pension plans* and *welfare plans*), and
- pension insurance (*defined benefit plans*).

In addition, ERISA has two provisions that specifically address health insurance issues. Those provisions are:

- the Health Insurance Portability and Accountability Act (HIPAA), which governs pre-existing conditions, among other things, and
- the Consolidated Omnibus Budget Reconciliation Act (COBRA), which governs health insurance continuation.

This book contains a separate chapter on COBRA. HIPAA is beyond the scope of this book because its rules apply mainly to plan administrators, not to employers.

This discussion limits itself to ERISA's coverage of single employer plans. We do not address ERISA rules as they apply to *multiemployer plans*.

2. Regulated Employers and Plans

All private employers—regardless of size—must comply with ERISA if they sponsor a *pension plan* or a *welfare plan*, unless the plan itself falls outside of ERISA's coverage (see immediately below). Unions and other types of *employee organizations* that offer covered plans must also comply with the law.

ERISA does not cover the following types of plans:

- *church plans* where the church organization has not asked for the plan to be covered by the Internal Revenue Code
- federal government plans, including plans established under the Railroad Retirement Security Act
- state and municipal government plans
- plans of fraternal or similar organizations where the plan does not receive any contributions from the employers of the participants
- plans that employers sponsor solely to comply with state laws on workers' compensation insurance, disability insurance or unemployment insurance
- plans maintained outside the United States primarily for the benefit of non-citizens.

3. Covered Workers

ERISA covers all *participants* in covered *pension plans* and covered *welfare plans*. ERISA also covers any *beneficiaries* of these plans.

B. Major Provisions of ERISA

1. Reporting, Disclosure and Notice

Congress passed ERISA to protect employee benefits from unwise or fraudulent management by employers. Congress believed that one way to protect benefits was to expose plan management and administration to review by *beneficiaries, participants, fiduciaries* and federal regulators. To that end, ERISA contains numerous reporting, disclosure and notice requirements. These requirements apply to both *pension plans* and *welfare plans*.

Regulated Employers and Plans
See Section A2, above.

Covered Workers
See Section A3, above.

What's Required: Employers and Plan Administrators
ERISA places the following reporting and disclosure obligations on plan administrators:

- The administrator must furnish *participants* and *beneficiaries* with a description of the plan (called a *summary plan description*). The administrator must make this description understandable to an average person (in other words, no legalese and no technical jargon), and the administrator must take into account the education level of employees. The description must explain people's rights, benefits and obligations under the plan, and it must give certain information about the plan.
- The administrator must inform *participants* and *beneficiaries* of any important changes to the plan or to the information in the *summary plan description*. The administrator must file a copy of this document with the U.S. Department of Labor.

- The administrator must give a summary annual report of pension benefits to *participants*.
- The administrator must inform *participants* if it intends to terminate a *pension plan*.
- The administrator must file various reports with the U.S. Internal Revenue Service, the U.S. Department of Labor and the Pension and Benefit Guaranty Corporation, including a Form 5500 annual report. Sometimes, the administrator must give copies of these reports to plan *participants* and *beneficiaries*.
- If a *pension plan* fails to meet minimum funding requirements (see Section B3, below), the administrator must notify *participants* and *beneficiaries*.
- If an administrator transfers excess pension assets into health benefit accounts, the administrator must notify *participants* and *beneficiaries*, the U.S. Department of Labor and the U.S. Treasury Department.
- If a *beneficiary* or *participant* requests it in writing, the plan administrator must provide a statement of the individual's total benefits *accrued* and any *vested* pension benefits *accrued*.

Employers and plan administrators must keep records that provide the basis and support for the information in the reports and the disclosures. The records must be sufficiently detailed to verify, clarify and explain the information. Administrators must keep these records for at least six years.

2. Participation, Vesting and Benefit Accrual

One of the goals of ERISA is to encourage the growth of private *pension plans*. Congress also wanted to protect *participants* from stingy plan rules that would keep them from obtaining their pension upon retirement. To accomplish these goals, Congress limited the types of *participation, vesting* and *benefit accrual* rules that plans could impose.

These requirements apply only to *pension plans*. They do not apply to *welfare plans*.

The Internal Revenue Code contains similar *participation, vesting* and *benefit accrual* requirements.

Regulated Employers and Plans
See Section A2, above.

Covered Workers
See Section A3, above.

What's Required: Employers and Plan Administrators
Most employers want to limit the number of employees who *participate* in a *pension plan* —the fewer employees who *participate*, the cheaper the plan. In addition, to entice good employees to stay with the company, employers limit *participation* to those who have been with the company for a minimum amount of time or longer. For similar reasons, employers often place limits on when employee benefits *vest* and *accrue*.

ERISA, however, limits how far employers can go in this area.

Participation Requirements

The following rules apply to *participation requirements*:

- The employer must allow employees to *participate* in the *pension plan* after they reach age 21 and have completed one year of work for the employer (as long as that year included at least 1,000 hours of work). This service requirement can be two years instead of one if the employee's benefits are 100% *vested* after the two years. This rule does not apply to plans benefiting employees of certain educational institutions.
- Employers cannot exclude employees from a *pension plan* because the employees are too old.

Vesting Requirements

The following rules apply to *vesting* requirements:

- Employee contributions to a plan are immediately 100% *vested*.
- At a minimum, employee rights to employer contributions to a plan must *vest* under one of two schedules set out in the law. The first, called "cliff vesting," provides for full *vesting* after no more than five years. The second, called "gradual vesting," calls for 20% *vesting* after three years and 20% *vesting* each subsequent year. Under gradual *vesting*, the benefits are fully *vested* after no more than seven years.
- Once employee rights are 100% *vested*, employees cannot lose their pension benefits, even if the employee leaves

the employer (either voluntarily or involuntarily) before retirement.

- All *pension plans* must contain certain provisions that protect the survivors of the plan *participants* who had *vested* benefits when the *participant* died.
- Employee rights will *vest* faster in so-called "top heavy plans." A top heavy plan is one that provides more than 60% of its benefits to certain key employees.
- If an employer terminates or partially terminates a plan, all benefits must *vest* immediately.

Benefit Accrual Requirements

In a *defined benefit plan*, participants and beneficiaries *accrue* a specific amount of money each year toward their retirement benefits. The amount *accrued* each year is based on a schedule set by the plan. ERISA establishes minimum standards for that schedule. Those standards are beyond the scope of this discussion.

Exceptions

This provision does not apply to:

- an unfunded plan whose sole purpose is to provide deferred compensation to a select group of management or highly compensated employees
- plans maintained by certain tax-exempt organizations (so long as the *participants* don't make any contributions to the plan) (see the Internal Revenue Code—26 U.S.C. § 501(c)(8) or (9)—for a description of these tax-exempt organizations)

- certain tax-exempt trusts (see the Internal Revenue Code—26 U.S.C. § 501(c)(18)—for a description of these tax-exempt trusts)
- plans maintained by tax-exempt labor organizations (so long as the employer does not make any contributions to the plan) (see the Internal Revenue Code—26 U.S.C. § 501(c)(5)—for a description of these tax-exempt labor organizations)
- any agreement providing payments to a retired partner or a deceased partner's beneficiary, as described in the Internal Revenue Code—26 U.S.C. § 736
- an individual retirement account or annuity (commonly known as an IRA) (see Internal Revenue Code—26 U.S.C. § 408—for a description)
- a retirement bond (see Internal Revenue Code—26 U.S.C. § 409—for a description)
- certain plans of employers whose stock is completely owned by employees, former employees and beneficiaries.

3. Funding

Another goal of ERISA is to protect the financial stability of *pension plans* so that employees get the funds promised them when they retire. To that end, ERISA requires that employers put a certain amount of money into the plan every year. This provision applies only to *defined benefit plans*.

Regulated Employers and Plans

See Section A2, above.

Covered Workers

See Section A3, above.

What's Required: Employers and Plan Administrators

Each year, employers must contribute enough money to the plan to fund a portion of the projected retirement benefits of plan *participants*. Calculating the required amount is very complicated and is done by an actuary.

4. Fiduciary Responsibility

To protect the interests of *participants* and *beneficiaries*, ERISA imposes strict standards of conduct, loyalty and prudence on the people who control the plans. These standards are called *fiduciary obligations*. The people who must follow the standards are called *fiduciaries*. *Fiduciary obligations* apply to *pension plans* and *welfare plans*. They are described below.

In addition to *fiduciary obligations*, ERISA's fiduciary provisions also impose certain requirements on the plan and prohibit certain transactions involving the plan. These provisions apply to *pension plans* and *welfare plans*. They are also described below.

Fiduciary Obligations

Fiduciaries must manage the plan solely in the interests of the plan *participants* and *beneficiaries*. Only *fiduciaries* are bound by this provision.

Who Is a Fiduciary

Not all people associated with a plan are *fiduciaries*. Only those individuals who have any discretionary authority or control over how the plan is managed or how the plan assets are managed are *fiduciaries*. Congress intended for this term to be broadly interpreted. Plan administrators can be *fiduciaries* if they exercise control, and so can paid investment advisors, consultants and bank trustees. The officers and directors of the employer or labor union are *fiduciaries* if they exercise any control over the plan, have the power to exercise any control over the plan, exercise any control over the people who control and manage the plan or select the plan's investment committee or the plan officers or directors.

What Fiduciaries Can and Cannot Do

Fiduciaries must:

- use the same care, skill and diligence in managing the plan that a prudent person would use in similar circumstances
- diversify plan investments to minimize the risk of large losses

- follow the plan documents and instruments, and
- act solely in the interests of *participants* and *beneficiaries*.

Fiduciaries may not:

- manage the plan assets for their own benefit
- receive compensation from any person in connection with any action involving plan assets
- act on behalf of a party whose interests are opposed to those of the *participants* and *beneficiaries*
- invest in assets—usually outside our borders—that cannot be sued in federal court (for example, a foreign company that has no ties with the United States and therefore cannot be sued here) or
- engage in a prohibited transaction (see below).

Prohibited Transactions

In addition to the *fiduciary obligations* described above, ERISA's fiduciary provision also prohibits certain transactions between a party in interest (see below) and the plan.

Who Are Parties in Interest

The following are all parties in interest who must follow the prohibited transaction rules:

- *fiduciaries*, counsel or employees of the plan
- people who provide services to the plan
- any employer who has employees covered by the plan
- any labor union who has members covered by the plan

- owners, direct or indirect, of 50% or more of the stock of a corporation or partnership
- people who are 10% shareholders or partners
- relatives of any of the people listed above.

What Parties in Interest Can't Do

Parties in interest cannot engage in any of the following activities with an *employee benefit plan:*

- selling, exchanging or leasing property
- lending money or extending credit
- furnishing goods, services or facilities
- using plan assets for the benefit of a party in interest
- acquiring qualifying employer securities and real property in excess of allowable limits.

Plan Requirements

ERISA's fiduciary provisions require that plans be established in writing and that the writing contain certain provisions. Plans must also establish a trust to hold the plan assets.

Regulated Employers and Plans

See Section A2, above.

Covered Workers

See Section A3, above.

Exceptions

There are a number of exceptions to the fiduciary provisions described above. They are quite complicated and narrow and are therefore beyond the scope of this discussion.

5. Administration and Enforcement

Most of ERISA's administration and enforcement provision concerns providing the government with a means to enforce ERISA's requirements and giving *participants, beneficiaries,* and *fiduciaries* avenues for asserting their rights. We discuss those issues in Sections C-E, below.

This provision also places some specific duties on employers and plan administrators, and it places certain prohibitions on them. We discuss those issues in this section.

This provision applies to *pension plans* and *welfare plans.*

Regulated Employers and Plans

See Section A2, above.

Covered Workers

See Section A3, above.

What's Prohibited: Employers and Plan Administrators

Employers may not retaliate against employees who assert their rights under ERISA. For example, employers may not fire, fine, suspend, demote, discipline or discriminate against employees for asserting their ERISA rights. Employers also may not interfere with the ERISA rights of any *participant* or *beneficiary* through fraud, force, violence, threats, intimidation or other means.

What's Required: Employers and Plan Administrators

Employee benefit plans must have internal claims procedures. A plan must:

- Provide written notice to a *participant* or *beneficiary* whose claim for benefits has been denied. The notice must give specific reasons for the denial and be easily understood.
- Give the *participant* or *beneficiary* a method for appealing the claims denial.

6. Plan Termination Insurance

Prior to ERISA, companies sometimes did not pay *vested* pension benefits if they merged with another company, went out of business or simply decided to terminate the plan. This left all of the employees—some of whom had given a lifetime of service—with nothing upon retirement.

To prevent this, ERISA requires companies that sponsor *defined benefit plans* to pay mandatory insurance premiums to the Pension and Benefit Guaranty Corporation, which will pay certain guaranteed retirement benefits if a plan terminates with insufficient assets.

This provision applies only to *defined benefit plans*.

Regulated Employers and Plans
See Section A2, above.

Covered Workers
See Section A3, above.

What's Required: Employers and Plan Administrators
Employers must pay an annual insurance premium to the PBGC. This premium is based on the number of *participants* in the plan.

C. How ERISA Is Enforced

1. Individual Complaints

Only *participants, beneficiaries* and *fiduciaries* can act to enforce ERISA. Depending on the provision involved, they can request the federal government to bring a lawsuit on their behalf, or they can file a lawsuit themselves.

Participants and *beneficiaries* can bring a civil action to:

- recover benefits that they should have received under the plan
- enforce rights under the terms of the plan
- clarify future rights to benefits
- seek redress for breaches of *fiduciary obligations*
- stop any actions that violate the plan or ERISA
- force the plan administrator to disclose information about the plan.

Fiduciaries can bring a civil action to:

- seek redress for breaches of *fiduciary obligations*
- stop any actions that violate the plan or ERISA.

2. Agency Enforcement

The Department of Labor and the Department of the Treasury share enforcement responsibilities. ERISA's enforcement provisions are quite complicated, and often one department can act only if it consults with the other. Although we summarize the division of enforcement responsibilities below, the reality is that this issue can be much more convoluted than it seems at first blush.

The Department of Labor issues regulations about and enforces the reporting and disclosure provisions, the fiduciary standards and the prohibited transaction rules.

Although the Department of the Treasury issues regulations about the funding, participation and *vesting* rules, the Department of Labor enforces those provisions.

A Note About the Internal Revenue Code

As mentioned at the beginning of this chapter, ERISA has many provisions that parallel provisions in the Internal Revenue Code. Although the provisions are identical, the consequences for violating them are quite different. An employer who violates ERISA faces—among other things—lawsuits from the Department of Labor, *participants*, *beneficiaries* and *fiduciaries*.

In contrast, an employer who violates the Internal Revenue Code provisions faces tax disqualification of the plan—no private lawsuits are allowed. The IRS can sue on its own initiative, however.

D. For Employers: Complying With ERISA

1. Reporting Requirements

ERISA's reporting requirements are fairly complicated and depend on the type of employer you are, the type of plan you are

sponsoring and the provision that is at issue. They are beyond the scope of this discussion.

2. Posting Requirements

ERISA imposes no posting requirements.

3. Recordkeeping Requirements

Similarly, ERISA has a number of recordkeeping requirements. They depend on the type of employer you are, the type of plan you are sponsoring and the provision that is at issue. They are beyond the scope of this discussion.

4. Practical Tips

If you have a plan administrator, you probably do not need to concern yourself with ERISA. Still, you should talk to the administrator and make sure that it is following ERISA's rules.

If you are administering a plan yourself, get professional help. ERISA is not a do-it-yourself law. Its complexities can trip up even the most sophisticated employer. Better to pay for expertise than to face fines and penalties and lawsuits.

5. Penalties

The penalties for violating ERISA are as complicated as ERISA itself. They vary widely depending on which provision has been violated and how. They include civil fines, criminal fines, restitution, lawsuits and imprisonment.

A defendant who loses a lawsuit may be ordered to pay the attorney's fees and costs of the people who filed the suit.

An employer or plan administrator suspected of violating ERISA will have to endure an investigation by the Department of Labor or the Department of the Treasury. Investigations can be quite expansive and can include inspecting records and accounts, subpoenaing documents and interviewing witnesses.

E. For Workers: Asserting Rights Under ERISA

1. Where to Start

If you think that your plan has unfairly denied your claim for benefits, start by following your plan's administrative claim procedures. Your plan administrator must tell you how to appeal the denial of your claim. If you can afford to, it's a good idea to hire an attorney for the administrative claim process. This is because if you lose the administrative review and want to assert your claim in a lawsuit in court, the judge will consider only the evidence produced at the review, no more. A lawyer is more likely than you to know which evidence will be helpful and how to present it—and how to keep damaging evidence out.

If you are not successful on your appeal, contact the Department of Labor for more assistance. Someone from the department may call your plan administrator and try to mediate a resolution to the problem.

If you still cannot resolve your problem to your satisfaction, consult with an attorney who specializes in ERISA matters. That attorney may file a lawsuit on your behalf.

2. Required Forms

Although there are no required government forms, your plan likely has specific forms that you must complete to receive benefits and to appeal a denial of a claim for benefits.

3. Practical Tips

Read your *summary plan description*, which is a document the plan administrator must give you that explains your rights and benefits under the plan.

If you want to file a claim for benefits, follow your plan's procedures to the letter. Similarly, if you want to appeal a denial of your claim, make sure you follow your plan's procedures. If you have to go to court to enforce your rights under the plan, you don't want to be at a disadvantage because you failed to follow some procedure or other.

Make sure you meet deadlines for filing claims and making appeals. These should be explained in the *summary plan description*.

If you decide to seek private legal assistance, be sure to go to an attorney who is experienced in ERISA matters. Non-specialists will lack the skill and knowledge needed to represent you fully and effectively. The earlier you can consult with an attorney, the better— before you begin your plan's administrative appeal process is ideal.

F. Agencies Charged With Enforcement & Compliance

Pension and Welfare Benefits Administration

U.S. Department of Labor
200 Constitution Ave., NW
Room N-5619
Washington, DC 20210
Phone: 202-219-8776
http://www.dol.gov/dol/pwba/welcome.html

The Department of Labor has local field offices that you can visit or call. To find a list of those field offices, refer to:
http://askpwba.dol.gov/contact_us_3.html#regional

Agency Resources for Employers and Plan Administrators

(These can be obtained either at the Web addresses listed below or at the address and phone number listed above.)

- Information about the computerized system that streamlines filing and processing of Form 5500. Includes filing instructions and frequently asked questions.
  EFAST Filing Acceptance System
  http://www.efast.dol.gov
- The manual that the PWBA uses in enforcing ERISA
  Enforcement Manual
  http://www.dol.gov/dol/pwba/public/programs/oemanual/cover.htm
- A guide that assists filers in preparing Form 5500
  Troubleshooter's Guide to Filing the ERISA Annual Report Form 5500
  http://www.dol.gov/dol/pwba/public/pubs/troubleg.pdf

Agency Resources for Workers

(These can be obtained either at the Web addresses listed below or at the address and phone number listed above.)

- A guide to filing a claim for benefits under any plan covered by ERISA
  How to File a Claim for Your Benefits
  http://www.dol.gov/dol/pwba/public/pubs/fileclaim/fileclam.htm

- A guide to obtaining information from the Department of Labor about any plan covered by ERISA
  How to Obtain Employee Benefit Documents from the Labor Department
  http://www.dol.gov/dol/pwba/public/pubs/howtob/howtobt.htm
- An explanation of what happens to pension and health benefits if you are affected by a plant closing or layoff
  Pension and Health Care Coverage ... Questions and Answers for Dislocated Workers
  http://www.dol.gov/dol/pwba/public/pubs/disloc1.htm
- Information about health benefits for retirees
  Can the Retiree Health Benefits Provided By Your Employer Be Cut?
  http://www.dol.gov/dol/pwba/public/pubs/brief1.htm
- An explanation of how to be proactive with your health benefits
  Top Ten Ways to Make Your Health Benefits Work for You
  http://www.dol.gov/dol/pwba/public/pubs/health/top10-text.html
- An explanation of what happens to benefits when an employer files for bankruptcy
  Fact Sheet: Your Employer's Bankruptcy: How Will It Affect Your Employee Benefits?
  http://www.dol.gov/dol/pwba/public/pubs/bkrupfs.htm

Internal Revenue Service

U.S. Treasury Department
1500 Pennsylvania Avenue, NW
Washington, DC 20220
Phone: 202-622-2000
http://www.irs.gov

The Internal Revenue Service has local field offices that you can visit or call. To find a list of those field offices, refer to:
http://www.irs.gov/where_file/index.html

Agency Resources for Employers and Plan Administrators
None.

Agency Resources for Workers
None.

G. State Laws Relating to Employee Benefit Plans

Although ERISA preempts most state laws that govern *employee benefit plans*, it does save from preemption state laws regulating insurance and a few other areas. Those state laws are beyond the scope of this discussion.

H. Outline of ERISA

29 U.S.C. § 1001 and following
U.S. Code
Title 29: Labor
Chapter 18:
Subchapter I: Protection of Employee Benefit Rights
Subtitle A: General Provisions

§ 1001. Congressional findings and declaration of policy
§ 1001a. Additional Congressional findings and declaration of policy
§ 1001b. Findings and declaration of policy
§ 1002. Definitions
§ 1003. Coverage

Subtitle B: Regulatory Provisions

Part 1: Reporting and Disclosure
§ 1021. Duty of disclosure and reporting
§ 1022. Summary plan description
§ 1023. Annual reports
§ 1024. Filing and furnishing of information
§ 1025. Reporting of participant's benefit rights
§ 1026. Reports made public information
§ 1027. Retention of records
§ 1028. Reliance on administrative interpretations
§ 1029. Forms
§ 1030. Alternative methods of compliance
§ 1031. Repeal and effective date

Part 2: Participation and Vesting
§ 1051. Coverage
§ 1052. Minimum participation standards
§ 1053. Minimum vesting standards
§ 1054. Benefit accrual requirements
§ 1055. Requirement of joint and survivor annuity and preretirement survivor annuity
§ 1056. Form and payment of benefits
§ 1057. Temporary variances from certain vesting requirements
§ 1058. Mergers and consolidations of plans or transfers of plan assets
§ 1059. Recordkeeping and reporting requirements
§ 1060. Multiple employer plans
§ 1061. Effective dates

Part 3: Funding
§ 1081. Coverage
§ 1082. Minimum funding standards
§ 1083. Variance from minimum funding standard
§ 1084. Extension of amortization periods
§ 1085. Alternative minimum funding standard
§ 1085a. Security for waivers of minimum funding standard and extensions of amortization period
§ 1085b. Security required upon adoption of plan amendment resulting in significant underfunding
§ 1086. Effective dates

Part 4: Fiduciary Responsibility
§ 1101. Coverage
§ 1102. Establishment of plan
§ 1103. Establishment of trust
§ 1104. Fiduciary duties
§ 1105. Liability for breach of co-fiduciary
§ 1106. Prohibited transactions
§ 1107. Limitation with respect to acquisition and holding of employer securities and employer real property by certain plans
§ 1108. Exemptions from prohibited transactions
§ 1109. Liability for breach of fiduciary duty
§ 1110. Exculpatory provisions; insurance
§ 1111. Persons prohibited from holding certain positions
§ 1112. Bonding
§ 1113. Limitation of actions
§ 1114. Effective date

Part 5: Administration and Enforcement

Part 6: Continuation Coverage and Additional Standards for Group Health Plans (COBRA)

Part 7: Group Health Plan Requirements

Subpart A: Requirements Relating to Portability, Access, and Renewability

Subpart B: Other Requirements

Subpart C: General Provisions

Space does not permit the reprinting of the entire text of ERISA. See the chapter on COBRA for the text of the sections in Part 6 of ERISA.

■

Chapter 8

Fair Credit Reporting Act (FCRA)

Statute: 15 U.S.C. § 1681 and following:
http://www.ftc.gov/os/statutes/fcrajump.htm

Regulations: 16 C.F.R. § 600.1 and following:
http://cfr.law.cornell.edu/cfr/cfr.php?title=16&type=part&value=600

Definitions

Adverse action

Any decision made by an employer for *employment purposes* that negatively affects the individual. Examples include refusing to hire the individual, refusing to promote the individual and firing the individual.

Consumer report

In the context of employment, a consumer report is written or oral information that (1) will be used for *employment purposes*, (2) comes from a *consumer reporting agency* and (3) relates to an individual's:

- creditworthiness
- credit standing
- credit capacity
- general reputation
- personal characteristics, or
- lifestyle.

Examples of consumer reports include criminal background checks, educational history checks and license checks. If the employer (rather than a *consumer reporting agency)* gathers the information itself, the information is not a consumer report and the employer does not have to follow the FCRA.

Consumer reporting agency

A person or entity that regularly provides *consumer reports* to third parties. Examples of consumer reporting agencies include credit bureaus, private investigators, records search firms, law firms and background checking services.

A state entity that is required to keep certain information as a matter of public record—for example, a court clerk—is not a consumer reporting agency, and any information it provides is not a *consumer report*.

Although the FCRA does not explicitly say so, some courts have held that federal agencies such as the Federal Bureau of Investigation are not consumer reporting agencies.

Employment purposes

Evaluating an individual for hiring, promotion, reassignment or termination. Although the term refers to employment, it extends to independent contractors.

Investigative consumer report

A *consumer report* based at least in part on personal interviews that go beyond simply verifying facts that the individual has provided to the employer. For example, if a *consumer reporting agency* phones a college to verify the degree the individual earned, a report of that phone call would not be an investigative consumer report. If, however, the agency phoned the individual's professors to get their opinions about the individual, a report of those phone calls would be an investigative consumer report.

Examples of investigative consumer reports include reference checks and investigations of workplace misconduct.

To qualify as an investigative consumer report, the information must have been gathered by a *consumer reporting agency*. For example, if an employer hires an attorney to investigate a complaint of sexual harassment in the workplace, the attorney's report of the investigation is an investigative consumer report. If the employer's human resources manager conducts the investigation, however, the report of the investigation is not an investigative consumer report and the employer does not have to follow the FCRA.

A. Overview of the FCRA

1. Summary

The Fair Credit Reporting Act has two goals: to protect the privacy of consumer credit information and to ensure the accuracy of that information. To those ends, it imposes legal obligations on employers who investigate prospective and current employees and independent contractors. Employers must notify individuals if they want to obtain a *consumer report* or an *investigative consumer report;* they must get authorization from individuals before seeking the report, and they must give the individuals certain information if they take an *adverse action* based on the report.

Although the Act also imposes a number of legal obligations on *consumer reporting agencies,* those obligations are beyond the scope of this discussion.

In the context of employment, the Act has two main provisions:

- **Notice, authorization and certification procedures:** Before seeking a *consumer report* or *investigative consumer report* for *employment purposes,* employers must notify individuals in writing that they want a report. In addition, they must obtain written authorization from the individuals before actually requesting the report. They must then verify to the *consumer reporting agency* that they have given the individual notice and received authorization.
- **Adverse action procedures:** Employers who take an *adverse action* because of

a *consumer report* or an *investigative consumer report* must provide individuals with specific types of information about both the report and the *consumer reporting agency* that provided it.

2. Regulated Employers

The Act covers all employers, including:
- the federal government and its agencies
- state governments and their agencies
- local and municipal governments
- private employers, regardless of size.

3. Covered Workers

The Act covers all individuals. This means that any time an employer seeks a *consumer report* or an *investigative consumer report* for *employment purposes*, the employer must comply with the Act.

B. Major Provisions of the FCRA

1. Notice, Authorization and Certification Procedures

Employers must follow the procedures described in this section before obtaining a *consumer report* or an *investigative consumer report.*

Regulated Employers
See Section A2, above.

Covered Workers
See Section A3, above.

What's Prohibited: Employers

Employers cannot request a *consumer report* or an *investigative consumer report* for any purpose other than *employment purposes*. For example, an employer that is fighting a union cannot request reports on employees who are organizing if the purpose of the reports is to gain information to hamper the organizing effort.

Employers cannot request a *consumer report* or an *investigative consumer report* without notifying the individual and receiving authorization from the individual. (For more on this, see "What's Required," immediately below.)

What's Required: Employers

Employers must do all of the following to obtain a *consumer report* or an *investigative consumer report*:

- Notify the individual in writing that they want to obtain a report about the individual. The employer cannot include any other information on this document—it must consist only of this notice.
- Obtain the individual's written authorization before asking a *consumer reporting agency* for a report.
- Verify to the *consumer reporting agency* that they have notified the individual and obtained written authorization.

Special Rules for Investigative Consumer Reports

In addition to following the rules described above, an employer that wants an *investigative consumer report* must give the following

information to the individual in writing after requesting the report:

- a statement that the requested report is an *investigative consumer report*
- a statement briefly identifying the type(s) of information the report will contain—such as information about the individual's character, general reputation, personal characteristics or way of life, and
- a statement that the individual has the right to submit a written request for complete and accurate information about the nature and scope of the investigation.

Exceptions

The Trucking Industry

Unlike other employers, which the law limits to using written documents, the trucking industry can meet the notice and authorization requirements by oral, written or electronic means. This exception applies only to applicants, and only when all of the interactions between the applicant and employer prior to obtaining the report are not in person—for example, by phone or email. If there is any in-person contact between the employer and the applicant, the exception does not apply. For example, it the applicant stops by the employer's office to pick up a job application, the employer must follow the standard written notice and authorization procedures.

Penalties

See Section D4, below.

2. Adverse Action Procedures

If the employer takes an *adverse action* against an individual as a result of learning information in the report, there are some additional steps the employer must take.

Regulated Employers

See Section A2, above.

Covered Workers

See Section A3, above.

What's Required: Employers

If an employer takes an *adverse action* against an individual based on information in a *consumer report* or an *investigative consumer report*, the employer must make certain disclosures to the individual both before and after the *adverse action*.

Before the Adverse Action

Prior to taking the *adverse action*, the employer must give the employee two documents:

- a copy of the report, and
- a copy of a document from the Federal Trade Commission called "Prescribed Summary of Consumer Rights." (To learn how to obtain this document from the FTC, see Section F, below.)

After the Adverse Action

After taking the *adverse action* against the individual, the employer must give the individual an "adverse action notice." This notice can be oral, in writing or electronic, and it must contain the following information:

- the name, address and phone number of the *consumer reporting agency* that supplied the report
- a statement that the *consumer reporting agency* did not make the decision to take the *adverse action* and cannot give the individual the specific reasons behind the *adverse action*
- a statement that the individual has a right to dispute the accuracy or completeness of the information in the report, and
- a statement that the individual has a right to request a free copy of the report from the *consumer reporting agency*.

Exceptions

There are two main exceptions to the *adverse actions* procedures: one for federal agencies and departments conducting national security investigations and the other for the trucking industry.

National Security Investigations

If a federal agency or department requests a *consumer report* or an *investigative consumer report* for *employment purposes*, it does not have to comply with the *adverse action* procedures if the head of the department or agency states in writing that:

- the report is part of a national security investigation
- the agency or department has jurisdiction over the investigation, and
- negative consequences—including danger to life or physical safety, destruction of evidence, flight from prosecution—

will result if the agency or department complies with the *adverse action* procedures.

The Trucking Industry

Because it is difficult to correspond with applicants who are on the road, trucking companies are allowed to take *adverse action* without prior notice as long as they give the applicant the required information within three days of the action.

Penalties

See Section D4, below.

C. How the FCRA Is Enforced

1. Individual Complaints

Individuals can sue in federal district court over violations of the FCRA. Individuals may also file a complaint with the Federal Trade Commission. (See Section F, below, for more about the FTC.)

2. Agency Enforcement

The Federal Trade Commission enforces the FCRA and can, on its own initiative, investigate and bring a civil action against anyone it suspects of violating the FCRA. (See Section F, below, for more about the FTC.)

The states and several federal agencies and departments also have the power to enforce this law. (See Section D4 below, for more about this issue.)

D. For Employers: Complying With the FCRA

1. Reporting Requirements

The FCRA imposes no reporting requirements.

2. Recordkeeping Requirements

The FCRA does not require recordkeeping.

3. Practical Tips

The FCRA's requirements are not terribly onerous, but the consequences of violating the Act are serious. The best thing you can do is simply follow the law to the letter every time you hire someone outside of your company to locate information about a prospective employee, current employee or independent contractor. If you get caught up in trying to decide whether the person you are hiring to locate information is technically a *consumer reporting agency* or whether the information you seek really fits the definition of a *consumer report*, you'll take the unnecessary risk of violating the law.

If you don't want to deal with the FCRA's requirements, there is an easy way around them: You or someone in your company can do all the investigating. Remember—information gathered about an applicant, employee or contractor is considered a *consumer report* or *investigative consumer report* only if someone *outside your company* collects the information.

A tricky situation arises when a company hires a lawyer to investigate allegations of workplace misconduct. According to the Federal Trade Commission, a lawyer's investigation in these circumstances fits within the FCRA, and you will have to comply with the Act's requirements. Be sure to discuss this issue with your lawyer before giving the go-ahead for the investigation.

4. Penalties

Penalties depend on who is bringing the lawsuit—an individual, a *consumer reporting agency*, the Federal Trade Commission, another federal agency or a state.

Liability to Individuals

If an individual sues an employer over violations of the FCRA, the employer faces the penalties described in this section. The penalties depend on whether the employer's actions were willful or negligent. A willful action occurs when the employer knowingly and intentionally violates the law. A negligent action occurs when the employer doesn't know that it is violating the law, but should know.

Willful Actions

If an employer is found guilty of willfully failing to comply with any of the provisions, it must:

- Pay the actual damages suffered by the individual. The payment must be at least $100 but not more than $1,000.
- Pay any punitive damages to the individual that the court might order.

- Pay for the costs of the action and the individual's attorney's fees.

Negligent Actions

If an employer is found guilty of negligently failing to comply with the Act, the employer will have to pay the individual actual damages, the costs of the action and attorney's fees.

Liability to Consumer Reporting Agencies

An employer that misleads a *consumer reporting agency* must pay to the agency either actual damages or $1,000, whichever is greater.

Liability to the Federal Trade Commission

If the Federal Trade Commission investigates an employer and finds that it has repeatedly and knowingly violated the Act, the employer must pay a penalty of not more than $2,500 per violation.

Liability to Others

Other federal agencies (including the Federal Deposit Insurance Commission and the National Credit Union Administration) and state governments may also investigate and penalize wrongdoers. Those penalties are beyond the scope of this section.

E. For Workers: Asserting Rights Under the FCRA

1. Where to Start

Individuals who think that an employer has violated the FCRA can sue the employer in federal district court within two years of the violation. If the employer gives false information to the individual about its obligations or actions under the FCRA, then the individual can bring the lawsuit within two years after discovering the false information.

Individuals may also file a complaint with the Federal Trade Commission (see Section F, below, for more about the FTC).

Exhaustion

The Act does not require individuals to file a complaint with the FTC before filing a lawsuit in federal district court.

2. Required Forms

Individuals who choose to complain to the Federal Trade Commission should use the FTC's complaint form. (See Section F, below, to find out how to obtain a copy of the form.)

3. Practical Tips

Although the FCRA gives you the right to sue an employer or *consumer reporting agency* that violates the statute, a victory in court may be cold comfort if your credit or reputation has been damaged in the meantime. The best way to protect yourself is by being vigilant about the information that is circulating about you:

- The FCRA requires that *consumer reporting agencies* and the entities that provide information to them correct inaccurate information. Therefore, if you see inaccurate, incorrect or misleading information on a *consumer report* or an *investigative consumer report*, notify the *consumer reporting agency* in writing right away. If you know where the agency got the incorrect information (for example, from a former employer) notify that entity in writing as well. *Consumer reporting agencies* must reinvestigate within 30 days the items you question. The *consumer reporting agency* must notify you in writing about the results of its reinvestigation. If the agency won't correct the disputed information, ask the agency to include your statement of the dispute in your file and in future reports.

- If you are thinking about applying for a job or a promotion, and if you are concerned that there might be some negative information about you lurking out there, find out for yourself. Contact the entity or agency that has the information and ask for whatever information they have on you. For example, if you think the negative information is at an old job, find out what information your former boss plans to give to reference seekers. And ask to see a copy of your personnel file. (Most state laws give you the right to view your personnel file even after you have left a job. Contact your state labor department for details.)

- Order a copy of your credit report. The three credit reporting companies are: Equifax, Inc. (800-685-1111), Experian (888-397-3742) and Trans Union LLC (800-888-4213).

F. Agency Charged With Enforcement & Compliance

Federal Trade Commission (FTC)
600 Pennsylvania Avenue
Washington, DC 20580
Phone: 1-877-FTC-HELP
http://www.ftc.gov

Agency Resources for Employers
(These can be obtained either at the Web addresses listed below or at the address and phone number listed above.)
- A guide for employers on how to follow the FCRA when doing background checks on employees
  Using Consumer Reports: What Every Employer Needs to Know
  http://www.ftc.gov/bcp/conline/pubs/buspubs/credempl.htm
- The document that employers must give to individuals about whom they seek a credit report
  Prescribed Summary of Consumer Rights
  http://www.ftc.gov/os/statutes/2summary.htm

Agency Resources for Workers
(These can be obtained either at the Web addresses listed below or at the address and phone number listed above.)
- Information for consumers about credit reports and credit reporting agencies
  Fair Credit Reporting
  http://www.ftc.gov/bcp/conline/pubs/credit/fcra.htm
- Online interactive complaint form
  FTC Consumer Complaint Form
  https://rn.ftc.gov/dod/wsolcq$.startup?Z_ORG_CODE=PU01

G. State Laws Relating to Credit

Some states have their own fair credit reporting laws. To find out about the laws of your state, contact the state agency that handles consumer issues (sometimes called the Department of Consumer Affairs or Consumer Protection Agency).

H. Selected Text of the FCRA

U.S. Code
Title 15: Commerce and Trade
Chapter 41: Consumer Credit Protection
Subchapter III: Credit Reporting
  Agencies

Full text is provided only for the following sections: 1681, 1681a, 1681b, 1681c, 1681k, 1681m, 1681n, 1681o, 1681p, 1681s.

§ 1681. Congressional findings and statement of purpose
§ 1681a. Definitions; rules of construction
§ 1681b. Permissible purposes of consumer reports
§ 1681c. Requirements relating to information contained in consumer reports
§ 1681d. Disclosure of investigative consumer reports
§ 1681e. Compliance procedures
§ 1681f. Disclosures to governmental agencies
§ 1681g. Disclosures to consumers
§ 1681h. Conditions and form of disclosure to consumers
§ 1681i. Procedure in case of disputed accuracy
§ 1681j. Charges for certain disclosures
§ 1681k. Public record information for employment purposes
§ 1681l. Restrictions on investigative consumer reports
§ 1681m. Requirements on users of consumer reports
§ 1681n. Civil liability for willful noncompliance
§ 1681o. Civil liability for negligent noncompliance
§ 1681p. Jurisdiction of courts; limitation of actions
§ 1681q. Obtaining information under false pretenses
§ 1681r. Unauthorized disclosures by officers or employees
§ 1681s. Administrative enforcement
§ 1681s-1. Information on overdue child support obligations
§ 1681s-2. Responsibilities of furnishers of information to consumer reporting agencies
§ 1681t. Relation to State laws
§ 1681u. Disclosures to FBI for counterintelligence purposes

§ 1681. Congressional findings and statement of purpose

(a) Accuracy and fairness of credit reporting
The Congress makes the following findings:

   (1) The banking system is dependent upon fair and accurate credit reporting. Inaccurate credit reports directly impair the efficiency of the banking system, and unfair credit reporting methods undermine the public confidence which is essential to the continued functioning of the banking system.

   (2) An elaborate mechanism has been developed for investigating and evaluating the credit worthiness, credit standing, credit capacity, character, and general reputation of consumers.

   (3) Consumer reporting agencies have assumed a vital role in assembling and evaluating consumer credit and other information on consumers.

   (4) There is a need to insure that consumer reporting agencies exercise their grave responsibilities with fairness, impartiality, and a respect for the consumer's right to privacy.

(b) Reasonable procedures
It is the purpose of this subchapter to require that consumer reporting agencies adopt reasonable procedures for meeting the needs of commerce for consumer credit, personnel, insurance, and other information in a manner which is fair and equitable to the consumer, with regard to the confidentiality, accuracy, relevancy, and proper utilization of such information in accordance with the requirements of this subchapter

§ 1681a. Definitions; rules of construction

(a) Definitions and rules of construction set forth in this section are applicable for the purposes of this subchapter.

(b) The term "person" means any individual, partnership, corporation, trust, estate, cooperative, association, government or governmental subdivision or agency, or other entity.

(c) The term "consumer" means an individual.

(d) Consumer Report.—

(1) In general.—

The term "consumer report" means any written, oral, or other communication of any information by a consumer reporting agency bearing on a consumer's credit worthiness, credit standing, credit capacity, character, general reputation, personal characteristics, or mode of living which is used or expected to be used or collected in whole or in part for the purpose of serving as a factor in establishing the consumer's eligibility for—

(A) credit or insurance to be used primarily for personal, family, or household purposes;

(B) employment purposes; or

(C) any other purpose authorized under section 1681b of this title.

(2) Exclusions.—

The term "consumer report" does not include—

(A) any—

(i) report containing information solely as to transactions or experiences between the consumer and the person making the report;

(ii) communication of that information among persons related by common ownership or affiliated by corporate control; or

(iii) communication of other information among persons related by common ownership or affiliated by corporate control, if it is clearly and conspicuously disclosed to the consumer that the information may be communicated among such persons and the consumer is given the opportunity, before the time that the information is initially communicated, to direct that such information not be communicated among such persons;

(B) any authorization or approval of a specific extension of credit directly or indirectly by the issuer of a credit card or similar device;

(C) any report in which a person who has been requested by a third party to make a specific extension of credit directly or indirectly to a consumer conveys his or her decision with respect to such request, if the third party advises the consumer of the name and address of the person to whom the request was made, and such person

makes the disclosures to the consumer required under section 1681m of this title; or

(D) a communication described in subsection (o) of this section.

(e) The term "investigative consumer report" means a consumer report or portion thereof in which information on a consumer's character, general reputation, personal characteristics, or mode of living is obtained through personal interviews with neighbors, friends, or associates of the consumer reported on or with others with whom he is acquainted or who may have knowledge concerning any such items of information. However, such information shall not include specific factual information on a consumer's credit record obtained directly from a creditor of the consumer or from a consumer reporting agency when such information was obtained directly from a creditor of the consumer or from the consumer.

(f) The term "consumer reporting agency" means any person which, for monetary fees, dues, or on a cooperative nonprofit basis, regularly engages in whole or in part in the practice of assembling or evaluating consumer credit information or other information on consumers for the purpose of furnishing consumer reports to third parties, and which uses any means or facility of interstate commerce for the purpose of preparing or furnishing consumer reports.

(g) The term "file", when used in connection with information on any consumer, means all of the information on that consumer recorded and retained by a consumer reporting agency regardless of how the information is stored.

(h) The term "employment purposes" when used in connection with a consumer report means a report used for the purpose of evaluating a consumer for employment, promotion, reassignment or retention as an employee.

(i) The term "medical information" means information or records obtained, with the consent of the individual to whom it relates, from licensed physicians or medical practitioners, hospitals, clinics, or other medical or medically related facilities.

(j) Definitions Relating to Child Support Obligations.—

(1) Overdue support.—

The term "overdue support" has the meaning given to such term in section 666(e) of title 42.

(2) State or local child support enforcement agency.—

The term "State or local child support enforcement agency" means a State or local agency which administers a State or local program for establishing and enforcing child support obligations.

(k) Adverse Action.—

(1) Actions included.—

The term "adverse action"—

(A) has the same meaning as in section 1691(d)(6) of this title; and

(B) means—

(i) a denial or cancellation of, an increase in any charge for, or a reduction or other adverse or unfavorable change in the terms of coverage or amount of, any insurance, existing or applied for, in connection with the underwriting of insurance;

(ii) a denial of employment or any other decision for employment purposes that adversely affects any current or prospective employee;

(iii) a denial or cancellation of, an increase in any charge for, or any other adverse or unfavorable change in the terms of, any license or benefit described in section 1681b(a)(3)(D) of this title; and

(iv) an action taken or determination that is—

(I) made in connection with an application that was made by, or a transaction that was initiated by, any consumer, or in connection with a review of an account under section 1681b(a)(3)(F)(ii) of this title; and

(II) adverse to the interests of the consumer.

(2) Applicable findings, decisions, commentary, and orders.—

For purposes of any determination of whether an action is an adverse action under paragraph (1)(A), all appropriate final findings, decisions, commentary, and orders issued under section 1691(d)(6) of this title by the Board of Governors of the Federal Reserve System or any court shall apply.

(l) Firm Offer of Credit or Insurance.—

The term "firm offer of credit or insurance" means any offer of credit or insurance to a consumer that will be honored if the consumer is determined, based on information in a consumer report on the consumer, to meet the specific criteria used to select the consumer for the offer, except that the offer may be further conditioned on one or more of the following:

(1) The consumer being determined, based on information in the consumer's application for the credit or insurance, to meet specific criteria bearing on credit worthiness or insurability, as applicable, that are established—

(A) before selection of the consumer for the offer; and

(B) for the purpose of determining whether to extend credit or insurance pursuant to the offer.

(2) Verification—

(A) that the consumer continues to meet the specific criteria used to select the consumer for the offer, by using information in a consumer report on the consumer, information in the consumer's application for the credit or insurance, or other information bearing on the credit worthiness or insurability of the consumer; or

(B) of the information in the consumer's application for the credit or insurance, to determine that the consumer meets the specific criteria bearing on credit worthiness or insurability.

(3) The consumer furnishing any collateral that is a requirement for the extension of the credit or insurance that was—

(A) established before selection of the consumer for the offer of credit or insurance; and

(B) disclosed to the consumer in the offer of credit or insurance.

(m) Credit or Insurance Transaction That Is Not Initiated by the Consumer.—

The term "credit or insurance transaction that is not initiated by the consumer" does not include the use of a consumer report by a person with which the consumer has an account or insurance policy, for purposes of—

(1) reviewing the account or insurance policy; or

(2) collecting the account.

(n) State.—

The term "State" means any State, the Commonwealth of Puerto Rico, the District of Columbia, and any territory or possession of the United States.

(o) Excluded Communications.—

A communication is described in this subsection if it is a communication—

(1) that, but for subsection (d)(2)(D) of this section, would be an investigative consumer report;

(2) that is made to a prospective employer for the purpose of—

(A) procuring an employee for the employer; or

(B) procuring an opportunity for a natural person to work for the employer;

(3) that is made by a person who regularly performs such procurement;

(4) that is not used by any person for any purpose other than a purpose described in subparagraph (A) or (B) of paragraph (2); and

(5) with respect to which—

(A) the consumer who is the subject of the communication—

(i) consents orally or in writing to the nature and scope of the communication, before the collection of any information for the purpose of making the communication;

(ii) consents orally or in writing to the making of the communication to a prospective employer, before the making of the communication; and

(iii) in the case of consent under clause (i) or (ii) given orally, is provided written confirmation of that consent by the person making the communication, not later than 3 business days after the receipt of the consent by that person;

(B) the person who makes the communication does not, for the purpose of making the communication, make any inquiry that if made by a prospective employer of the consumer who is the subject of the communication would violate any applicable Federal or State equal employment opportunity law or regulation; and

(C) the person who makes the communication—

(i) discloses in writing to the consumer who is the subject of the communication, not later than 5 business days after receiving any request from the consumer for such disclosure, the nature and substance of all information in the consumer's file at the time of the request, except that the sources of any information that is acquired solely for use in making the communication and is actually used for no other purpose, need not be disclosed other than under appropriate discovery procedures in any court of competent jurisdiction in which an action is brought; and

(ii) notifies the consumer who is the subject of the communication, in writing, of the consumer's right to request the information described in clause (i).

(p) Consumer Reporting Agency That Compiles and Maintains Files on Consumers on a Nationwide Basis.—
The term "consumer reporting agency that compiles and maintains files on consumers on a nationwide basis" means a consumer reporting agency that regularly engages in the practice of assembling or evaluating, and maintaining, for the purpose of furnishing consumer reports to third parties bearing on a consumer's credit worthiness, credit standing, or credit capacity, each of the following regarding consumers residing nationwide:

(1) Public record information.

(2) Credit account information from persons who furnish that information regularly and in the ordinary course of business.

§ 1681b. Permissible purposes of consumer reports

(a) In general

Subject to subsection (c) of this section, any consumer reporting agency may furnish a consumer report under the following circumstances and no other:

(1) In response to the order of a court having jurisdiction to issue such an order, or a subpoena issued in connection with proceedings before a Federal grand jury.

(2) In accordance with the written instructions of the consumer to whom it relates.

(3) To a person which it has reason to believe—

(A) intends to use the information in connection with a credit transaction involving the consumer on whom the information is to be furnished and involving the extension of credit to, or review or collection of an account of, the consumer; or

(B) intends to use the information for employment purposes; or

(C) intends to use the information in connection with the underwriting of insurance involving the consumer; or

(D) intends to use the information in connection with a determination of the consumer's eligibility for a license or other benefit granted by a governmental instrumentality required by law to consider an applicant's financial responsibility or status; or

(E) intends to use the information, as a potential investor or servicer, or current insurer, in connection with a valuation of, or an assessment of the credit or prepayment risks associated with, an existing credit obligation; or

(F) otherwise has a legitimate business need for the information—

(i) in connection with a business transaction that is initiated by the consumer; or

(ii) to review an account to determine whether the consumer continues to meet the terms of the account.

(4) In response to a request by the head of a State or local child support enforcement agency (or a State or local government official authorized by the head of such an agency), if the person making the request certifies to the consumer reporting agency that—

(A) the consumer report is needed for the purpose of establishing an individual's capacity to make child support payments or determining the appropriate level of such payments;

(B) the paternity of the consumer for the child to which the obligation relates has been established or acknowledged by the consumer in accordance with State laws under which the obligation arises (if required by those laws);

(C) the person has provided at least 10 days' prior notice to the consumer whose report is requested, by certified or registered mail to the last known address of the consumer, that the report will be requested; and

(D) the consumer report will be kept confidential, will be used solely for a purpose described in subparagraph (A), and will not be used in connection with any other civil, administrative, or criminal proceeding, or for any other purpose.

(5) To an agency administering a State plan under section 654 of title 42 for use to set an initial or modified child support award.

(b) Conditions for furnishing and using consumer reports for employment purposes

(1) Certification from user

A consumer reporting agency may furnish a consumer report for employment purposes only if—

(A) the person who obtains such report from the agency certifies to the agency that—

(i) the person has complied with paragraph (2) with respect to the consumer report, and the person will comply with paragraph (3) with respect to the consumer report if paragraph (3) becomes applicable; and

(ii) information from the consumer report will not be used in violation of any applicable Federal or State equal employment opportunity law or regulation; and

(B) the consumer reporting agency provides with the report, or has previously provided, a summary of the consumer's rights under this subchapter, as prescribed by the Federal Trade Commission under section 1681g(c)(3) of this title.

(2) Disclosure to consumer

(A) In general

Except as provided in subparagraph (B), a person may not procure a consumer report, or cause a consumer report to be procured, for employment purposes with respect to any consumer, unless—

(i) a clear and conspicuous disclosure has been made in writing to the consumer at any time before the report is procured or caused to be procured, in a document that consists solely of the disclosure, that a consumer report may be obtained for employment purposes; and

(ii) the consumer has authorized in writing (which authorization may be made on the document referred to in clause (i)) the procurement of the report by that person.

(B) Application by mail, telephone, computer, or other similar means

If a consumer described in subparagraph (C) applies for employment by mail, telephone, computer, or other similar means, at any time before a consumer report is procured or caused to be procured in connection with that application—

(i) the person who procures the consumer report on the consumer for employment purposes shall provide to the consumer, by oral, written, or electronic means, notice that a consumer report may be obtained for employment purposes, and a summary of the consumer's rights under section 1681m(a)(3) of this title; and

(ii) the consumer shall have consented, orally, in writing, or electronically to the procurement of the report by that person.

(C) Scope

Subparagraph (B) shall apply to a person procuring a consumer report on a consumer in connection with the consumer's application for employment only if—

(i) the consumer is applying for a position over which the Secretary of Transportation has the power to establish qualifications and maximum hours of service pursuant to the provisions of section 31502 of title 49, or a position subject to safety regulation by a State transportation agency; and

(ii) as of the time at which the person procures the report or causes the report to be procured the only interaction between the consumer and the person in connection with that employment application has been by mail, telephone, computer, or other similar means.

(3) Conditions on use for adverse actions

(A) In general

Except as provided in subparagraph (B), in using a consumer report for employment purposes, before taking any adverse action based in whole or in part on the report, the person intending to take such adverse action shall provide to the consumer to whom the report relates—

(i) a copy of the report; and

(ii) a description in writing of the rights of the consumer under this subchapter, as prescribed by the Federal Trade Commission under section 1681g(c)(3) of this title.

(B) Application by mail, telephone, computer, or other similar means

(i) If a consumer described in subparagraph (C) applies for employment by mail, telephone, computer, or other similar means, and if a person who has procured a consumer report on the consumer for employment purposes takes adverse action on the employment application based in whole or in part on the report, then the person must provide to the consumer to whom the report relates, in lieu of the notices required under subparagraph (A) of this section and under section 1681m(a) of this title, within 3 business days of taking such action, an oral, written or electronic notification—

(I) that adverse action has been taken based in whole or in part on a consumer report received from a consumer reporting agency;

(II) of the name, address and telephone number of the consumer reporting agency that furnished the consumer report (including a toll-free telephone number established by the agency if the agency compiles and maintains files on consumers on a nationwide basis);

(III) that the consumer reporting agency did not make the decision to take the adverse action and is unable to provide to the consumer the specific reasons why the adverse action was taken; and

(IV) that the consumer may, upon providing proper identification, request a free copy of a report and may dispute with the consumer reporting agency the accuracy or completeness of any information in a report.

(ii) If, under clause (B)(i)(IV), the consumer requests a copy of a consumer report from the person who procured the report, then, within 3 business days of receiving the consumer's request, together with proper identification, the person must send or provide to the consumer a copy of a report and a copy of the consumer's rights as prescribed by the Federal Trade

Commission under section 1681g(c)(3) of this title.

(C) Scope

Subparagraph (B) shall apply to a person procuring a consumer report on a consumer in connection with the consumer's application for employment only if—

(i) the consumer is applying for a position over which the Secretary of Transportation has the power to establish qualifications and maximum hours of service pursuant to the provisions of section 31502 of title 49, or a position subject to safety regulation by a State transportation agency; and

(ii) as of the time at which the person procures the report or causes the report to be procured the only interaction between the consumer and the person in connection with that employment application has been by mail, telephone, computer, or other similar means.

(4) Exception for national security investigations

(A) In general

In the case of an agency or department of the United States Government which seeks to obtain and use a consumer report for employment purposes, paragraph (3) shall not apply to any adverse action by such agency or department which is based in part on such consumer report, if the head of such agency or department makes a written finding that—

(i) the consumer report is relevant to a national security investigation of such agency or department;

(ii) the investigation is within the jurisdiction of such agency or department;

(iii) there is reason to believe that compliance with paragraph (3) will—

(I) endanger the life or physical safety of any person;

(II) result in flight from prosecution;

(III) result in the destruction of, or tampering with, evidence relevant to the investigation;

(IV) result in the intimidation of a potential witness relevant to the investigation;

(V) result in the compromise of classified information; or

(VI) otherwise seriously jeopardize or unduly delay the investigation or another official proceeding.

(B) Notification of consumer upon conclusion of investigation

Upon the conclusion of a national security investigation described in subparagraph (A), or upon the determination that the exception under subparagraph (A) is no longer required for the reasons set forth in such subparagraph, the official exercising the authority in such subparagraph shall provide to the consumer who is the subject of the consumer report with regard to which such finding was made—

(i) a copy of such consumer report with any classified information redacted as necessary;

(ii) notice of any adverse action which is based, in part, on the consumer report; and

(iii) the identification with reasonable specificity of the nature of the investigation for which the consumer report was sought.

(C) Delegation by head of agency or department

For purposes of subparagraphs (A) and (B), the head of any agency or department of the United States Government may delegate his or her authorities under this paragraph to an official of such agency or department who has personnel security responsibilities and is a member of the Senior Executive Service or equivalent civilian or military rank.

(D) Report to the Congress

Not later than January 31 of each year, the head of each agency and department of the United States Government that exercised authority under this paragraph during the preceding year shall submit a report to the Congress on the number of times the department or agency exercised such authority during the year.

(E) Definitions

For purposes of this paragraph, the following definitions shall apply:

(i) Classified information

The term "classified information" means information that is protected from unauthorized disclosure under Executive Order No. 12958 or successor orders.

(ii) National security investigation

The term "national security investigation" means any official inquiry by an agency or department of the United States Government to determine the eligibility of a consumer to receive access or continued access to classified information or to

determine whether classified information has been lost or compromised.

(c) Furnishing reports in connection with credit or insurance transactions that are not initiated by consumer

(1) In general

A consumer reporting agency may furnish a consumer report relating to any consumer pursuant to subparagraph (A) or (C) of subsection (a)(3) of this section in connection with any credit or insurance transaction that is not initiated by the consumer only if—

(A) the consumer authorizes the agency to provide such report to such person; or

(B)

(i) the transaction consists of a firm offer of credit or insurance;

(ii) the consumer reporting agency has complied with subsection (e) of this section; and

(iii) there is not in effect an election by the consumer, made in accordance with subsection (e) of this section, to have the consumer's name and address excluded from lists of names provided by the agency pursuant to this paragraph.

(2) Limits on information received under paragraph (1)(B)

A person may receive pursuant to paragraph (1)(B) only—

(A) the name and address of a consumer;

(B) an identifier that is not unique to the consumer and that is used by the person solely for the purpose of verifying the identity of the consumer; and

(C) other information pertaining to a consumer that does not identify the relationship or experience of the consumer with respect to a particular creditor or other entity.

(3) Information regarding inquiries

Except as provided in section 1681g(a)(5) of this title, a consumer reporting agency shall not furnish to any person a record of inquiries in connection with a credit or insurance transaction that is not initiated by a consumer.

(d) Reserved

(e) Election of consumer to be excluded from lists

(1) In general

A consumer may elect to have the consumer's name and address excluded from any list provided by a consumer reporting agency under subsection (c)(1)(B) of this section in connection with a credit or insurance transaction that is not initiated by the consumer, by notifying the agency in accordance with paragraph (2) that the consumer does not consent to any use of a consumer report relating to the consumer in connection with any credit or insurance transaction that is not initiated by the consumer.

(2) Manner of notification

A consumer shall notify a consumer reporting agency under paragraph (1)—

(A) through the notification system maintained by the agency under paragraph (5); or

(B) by submitting to the agency a signed notice of election form issued by the agency for purposes of this subparagraph.

(3) Response of agency after notification through system

Upon receipt of notification of the election of a consumer under paragraph (1) through the notification system maintained by the agency under paragraph (5), a consumer reporting agency shall—

(A) inform the consumer that the election is effective only for the 2-year period following the election if the consumer does not submit to the agency a signed notice of election form issued by the agency for purposes of paragraph (2)(B); and

(B) provide to the consumer a notice of election form, if requested by the consumer, not later than 5 business days after receipt of the notification of the election through the system established under paragraph (5), in the case of a request made at the time the consumer provides notification through the system.

(4) Effectiveness of election

An election of a consumer under paragraph (1)—

(A) shall be effective with respect to a consumer reporting agency beginning 5 business days after the date on which the consumer notifies the agency in accordance with paragraph (2);

(B) shall be effective with respect to a consumer reporting agency—

(i) subject to subparagraph (C), during the 2-year period beginning 5 business days after the date on which the consumer notifies the agency of the election, in the case of an election for which a consumer notifies the agency only in accordance with paragraph (2)(A); or

(ii) until the consumer notifies the agency under subparagraph (C), in the case of an election for which a consumer notifies the agency in accordance with paragraph (2)(B);

(C) shall not be effective after the date on which the consumer notifies the agency, through the notification system established by the agency under paragraph (5), that the election is no longer effective; and

(D) shall be effective with respect to each affiliate of the agency.

(5) Notification system

(A) In general

Each consumer reporting agency that, under subsection (c)(1)(B) of this section, furnishes a consumer report in connection with a credit or insurance transaction that is not initiated by a consumer, shall—

(i) establish and maintain a notification system, including a toll-free telephone number, which permits any consumer whose consumer report is maintained by the agency to notify the agency, with appropriate identification, of the consumer's election to have the consumer's name and address excluded from any such list of names and addresses provided by the agency for such a transaction; and

(ii) publish by not later than 365 days after September 30, 1996, and not less than annually thereafter, in a publication of general circulation in the area served by the agency—

(I) a notification that information in consumer files maintained by the agency may be used in connection with such transactions; and

(II) the address and toll-free telephone number for consumers to use to notify the agency of the consumer's election under clause (i).

(B) Establishment and maintenance as compliance

Establishment and maintenance of a notification system (including a toll-free telephone number) and publication by a consumer reporting agency on the agency's own behalf and on behalf of any of its affiliates in accordance with this paragraph is deemed to be compliance with this paragraph by each of those affiliates.

(6) Notification system by agencies that operate nationwide

Each consumer reporting agency that compiles and maintains files on consumers on a nationwide basis shall establish and maintain a notification system for purposes of paragraph (5) jointly with other such consumer reporting agencies.

(f) Certain use or obtaining of information prohibited

A person shall not use or obtain a consumer report for any purpose unless—

(1) the consumer report is obtained for a purpose for which the consumer report is authorized to be furnished under this section; and

(2) the purpose is certified in accordance with section 1681e of this title by a prospective user of the report through a general or specific certification.

(g) Furnishing reports containing medical information

A consumer reporting agency shall not furnish for employment purposes, or in connection with a credit or insurance transaction, a consumer report that contains medical information about a consumer, unless the consumer consents to the furnishing of the report.

§ 1681c. Requirements relating to information contained in consumer reports

(a) Information excluded from consumer reports

Except as authorized under subsection (b) of this section, no consumer reporting agency may make any consumer report containing any of the following items of information:

(1) cases under title 11 or under the Bankruptcy Act that, from the date of entry of the order for relief or the date of adjudication, as the case may be, antedate the report by more than 10 years.

(2) Civil suits, civil judgments, and records of arrest that, from date of entry, antedate the report by more than seven years or until the governing statute of limitations has expired, whichever is the longer period.

(3) Paid tax liens which, from date of payment, antedate the report by more than seven years.

(4) Accounts placed for collection or charged to profit and loss which antedate the report by more than seven years.

(5) Any other adverse item of information, other than records of convictions of crimes which antedates the report by more than seven years.

(b) Exempted cases

The provisions of subsection (a) of this section are not applicable in the case of any consumer credit report to be used in connection with—

(1) a credit transaction involving, or which may reasonably be expected to involve, a principal amount of $150,000 or more;

(2) the underwriting of life insurance involving, or which may reasonably be expected to involve, a face amount of $150,000 or more; or

(3) the employment of any individual at an annual salary which equals, or which may reasonably be expected to equal, $75,000, or more.

(c) Running of reporting period

(1) In general

The 7-year period referred to in paragraphs (4) and (6) of subsection (a) of this section shall begin, with respect to any delinquent account that is placed for collection (internally or by referral to a third party, whichever is earlier), charged to profit and loss, or subjected to any similar action, upon the expiration of the 180-day period beginning on the date of the commencement of the delinquency which immediately preceded the collection activity, charge to profit and loss, or similar action.

(2) Effective date

Paragraph (1) shall apply only to items of information added to the file of a consumer on or after the date that is 455 days after September 30, 1996.

(d) Information required to be disclosed

Any consumer reporting agency that furnishes a consumer report that contains information regarding any case involving the consumer that arises under title 11 shall include in the report an identification of the chapter of such title 11 under which such case arises if provided by the source of the information. If any case arising or filed under title 11 is withdrawn by the consumer before a final judgment, the consumer reporting agency shall include in the report that such case or filing was withdrawn upon receipt of documentation certifying such withdrawal.

(e) Indication of closure of account by consumer

If a consumer reporting agency is notified pursuant to section 1681s-2(a)(4) of this title that a credit account of a consumer was voluntarily closed by the consumer, the agency shall indicate that fact in any consumer report that includes information related to the account.

(f) Indication of dispute by consumer

If a consumer reporting agency is notified pursuant to section 1681s-2(a)(3) of this title that information regarding a consumer who was furnished to the agency is disputed by the consumer, the agency shall indicate that fact in each consumer report that includes the disputed information.

§ 1681d. Disclosure of investigative consumer reports

Not printed here.

§ 1681e. Compliance procedures

Not printed here.

§ 1681f. Disclosures to governmental agencies

Not printed here.

§ 1681g. Disclosures to consumers

Not printed here.

§ 1681h. Conditions and form of disclosure to consumers

Not printed here.

§ 1681i. Procedure in case of disputed accuracy

Not printed here.

§ 1681j. Charges for certain disclosures

Not printed here.

§ 1681k. Public record information for employment purposes

(a) In general

A consumer reporting agency which furnishes a consumer report for employment purposes and which for that purpose compiles and reports items of information on consumers which are matters of public record and are likely to have an adverse effect upon a consumer's ability to obtain employment shall—

(1) at the time such public record information is reported to the user of such consumer report, notify the consumer of the fact that public record information is being reported by the consumer reporting agency, together with the name and address of the person to whom such information is being reported; or

(2) maintain strict procedures designed to insure that whenever public record information which is likely to have an adverse effect on a consumer's ability to obtain employment is reported it is complete and up to date. For purposes of this paragraph, items of public record relating to arrests, indictments, convictions, suits, tax liens, and outstanding judgments shall be considered up to date if the current public record status of the item at the time of the report is reported.

(b) Exemption for national security investigations

Subsection (a) of this section does not apply in the case of an agency or department of the United States Government that seeks to obtain and use a consumer report for employment purposes, if the head of the agency or department makes a written finding as prescribed under section 1681b(b)(4)(A) of this title.

§ 1681l. Restrictions on investigative consumer reports

Not printed here.

§ 1681m. Requirements on users of consumer reports

(a) Duties of users taking adverse actions on basis of information contained in consumer reports

If any person takes any adverse action with respect to any consumer that is based in whole or in part on any information contained in a consumer report, the person shall—

(1) provide oral, written, or electronic notice of the adverse action to the consumer;

(2) provide to the consumer orally, in writing, or electronically—

(A) the name, address, and telephone number of the consumer reporting agency (including a toll-free telephone number established by the agency if the agency compiles and maintains files on consumers on a nationwide basis) that furnished the report to the person; and

(B) a statement that the consumer reporting agency did not make the decision to take the adverse action and is unable to provide the consumer the specific reasons why the adverse action was taken; and

(3) provide to the consumer an oral, written, or electronic notice of the consumer's right—

(A) to obtain, under section 1681j of this title, a free copy of a consumer report on the consumer from the consumer reporting agency referred to in paragraph (2), which notice shall include an indication of the 60-day period under that section for obtaining such a copy; and

(B) to dispute, under section 1681i of this title, with a consumer reporting agency the accuracy or completeness of any information in a consumer report furnished by the agency.

(b) Adverse action based on information obtained from third parties other than consumer reporting agencies

(1) In general

Whenever credit for personal, family, or household purposes involving a consumer is denied or the charge for such credit is increased either wholly or partly because of information obtained from a person other than a consumer reporting agency bearing upon the consumer's credit worthiness, credit standing, credit capacity, character, general reputation, personal characteristics, or mode of living, the user of such information shall, within a reasonable period of time, upon the consumer's written request for the reasons for such adverse action received within sixty days after learning of such adverse action, disclose the nature of the information to the consumer. The user of such information shall clearly and accurately disclose to the consumer his right to make such written request at the time such adverse action is communicated to the consumer.

(2) Duties of person taking certain actions based on information provided by affiliate

(A) Duties, generally

If a person takes an action described in subparagraph (B) with respect to a consumer, based in whole or in part on information described in subparagraph (C), the person shall—

(i) notify the consumer of the action, including a statement that the consumer may obtain the information in accordance with clause (ii); and

(ii) upon a written request from the consumer received within 60 days after transmittal of the notice required by clause (i), disclose to the consumer the nature of the information upon which the action is based by not later than 30 days after receipt of the request.

(B) Action described

An action referred to in subparagraph (A) is an adverse action described in section 1681a(k)(1)(A) of this title, taken in connection with a transaction initiated by the consumer, or any adverse action described in clause (i) or (ii) of section 1681a(k)(1)(B) of this title.

(C) Information described

Information referred to in subparagraph (A)—

(i) except as provided in clause (ii), is information that—

(I) is furnished to the person taking the action by a person related by common ownership or affiliated by common corporate control to the person taking the action; and

(II) bears on the credit worthiness, credit standing, credit capacity, character, general reputation, personal characteristics, or mode of living of the consumer; and

(ii) does not include—

(I) information solely as to transactions or experiences between the consumer and the person furnishing the information; or

(II) information in a consumer report.

(c) Reasonable procedures to assure compliance

No person shall be held liable for any violation of this section if he shows by a preponderance of the evidence that at the time of the alleged violation he maintained reasonable procedures to assure compliance with the provisions of this section.

(d) Duties of users making written credit or insurance solicitations on basis of information contained in consumer files

(1) In general

Any person who uses a consumer report on any consumer in connection with any credit or insurance transaction that is not initiated by the consumer, that is provided to that person under section 1681b(c)(1)(B) of this title, shall provide with each written solicitation made to the consumer regarding the transaction a clear and conspicuous statement that—

(A) information contained in the consumer's consumer report was used in connection with the transaction;

(B) the consumer received the offer of credit or insurance because the consumer satisfied the criteria for credit worthiness or insurability under which the consumer was selected for the offer;

(C) if applicable, the credit or insurance may not be extended if, after the consumer responds to the offer, the consumer does not meet the criteria used to select the consumer for the offer or any applicable criteria bearing on credit worthiness or insurability or does not furnish any required collateral;

(D) the consumer has a right to prohibit information contained in the consumer's file with any consumer reporting agency from being used in connection with any credit or insurance transaction that is not initiated by the consumer; and

(E) the consumer may exercise the right referred to in subparagraph (D) by notifying a notification system established under section 1681b(e) of this title.

(2) Disclosure of address and telephone number

A statement under paragraph (1) shall include the address and toll-free telephone number of the appropriate notification system established under section 1681b(e) of this title.

(3) Maintaining criteria on file

A person who makes an offer of credit or insurance to a consumer under a credit or insurance transaction described in paragraph (1) shall maintain on file the criteria used to select the consumer to receive the offer, all criteria bearing on credit worthiness or insurability, as applicable, that are the basis for determining whether or not to extend credit or insurance pursuant to the offer, and any requirement for the furnishing of collateral as a condition of the extension of credit or insurance, until the expiration of the 3-year period beginning on the date on which the offer is made to the consumer.

(4) Authority of Federal agencies regarding unfair or deceptive acts or practices not affected

This section is not intended to affect the authority of any Federal or State agency to enforce a prohibition against unfair or deceptive acts or practices, including the making of false or misleading statements in connection with a credit or insurance transaction that is not initiated by the consumer.

§ 1681n. Civil liability for willful noncompliance

(a) In general

Any person who willfully fails to comply with any requirement imposed under this subchapter with respect to any consumer is liable to that consumer in an amount equal to the sum of—

(1)

(A) any actual damages sustained by the consumer as a result of the failure or damages of not less than $100 and not more than $1,000; or

(B) in the case of liability of a natural person for obtaining a consumer report under false pretenses or knowingly without a permissible purpose, actual damages sustained by the consumer as a result of the failure or $1,000, whichever is greater;

(2) such amount of punitive damages as the court may allow; and

(3) in the case of any successful action to enforce any liability under this section, the costs of the action together with reasonable attorney's fees as determined by the court.

(b) Civil liability for knowing noncompliance

Any person who obtains a consumer report from a consumer reporting agency under false pretenses or knowingly without a permissible purpose shall be liable to the consumer reporting agency for actual damages

sustained by the consumer reporting agency or $1,000, whichever is greater.

(c) Attorney's fees

Upon a finding by the court that an unsuccessful pleading, motion, or other paper filed in connection with an action under this section was filed in bad faith or for purposes of harassment, the court shall award to the prevailing party attorney's fees reasonable in relation to the work expended in responding to the pleading, motion, or other paper.

§ 1681o. Civil liability for negligent noncompliance

(a) In general

Any person who is negligent in failing to comply with any requirement imposed under this subchapter with respect to any consumer is liable to that consumer in an amount equal to the sum of—

(1) any actual damages sustained by the consumer as a result of the failure;

(2) in the case of any successful action to enforce any liability under this section, the costs of the action together with reasonable attorney's fees as determined by the court.

(b) Attorney's fees

On a finding by the court that an unsuccessful pleading, motion, or other paper filed in connection with an action under this section was filed in bad faith or for purposes of harassment, the court shall award to the prevailing party attorney's fees reasonable in relation to the work expended in responding to the pleading, motion, or other paper.

§ 1681p. Jurisdiction of courts; limitation of actions

An action to enforce any liability created under this subchapter may be brought in any appropriate United States district court without regard to the amount in controversy, or in any other court of competent jurisdiction, within two years from the date on which the liability arises, except that where a defendant has materially and willfully misrepresented any information required under this subchapter to be disclosed to an individual and the information so misrepresented is material to the establishment of the defendant's liability to that individual under this subchapter, the action may be brought at any time within two years after discovery by the individual of the misrepresentation.

§ 1681q. Obtaining information under false pretenses

Not printed here.

§ 1681r. Unauthorized disclosures by officers or employees

Not printed here.

§ 1681s. Administrative enforcement

(a) Enforcement by Federal Trade Commission

(1) Compliance with the requirements imposed under this subchapter shall be enforced under the Federal Trade Commission Act (15 U.S.C. 41 et seq.) by the Federal Trade Commission with respect to consumer reporting agencies and all other persons subject thereto, except to the extent that enforcement of the requirements imposed under this subchapter is specifically committed to some other government agency under subsection (b) hereof. For the purpose of the exercise by the Federal Trade Commission of its functions and powers under the Federal Trade Commission Act, a violation of any requirement or prohibition imposed under this subchapter shall constitute an unfair or deceptive act or practice in commerce in violation of section 5(a) of the Federal Trade Commission Act (15 U.S.C. 45(a)) and shall be subject to enforcement by the Federal Trade Commission under section 5(b) thereof (15 U.S.C. 45(b)) with respect to any consumer reporting agency or person subject to enforcement by the Federal Trade Commission pursuant to this subsection, irrespective of whether that person is engaged in commerce or meets any other jurisdictional tests in the Federal Trade Commission Act. The Federal Trade Commission shall have such procedural, investigative, and enforcement powers, including the power to issue procedural rules in enforcing compliance with the requirements imposed under this subchapter and to require the filing of reports, the production of documents, and the appearance of witnesses as though the applicable terms and conditions of the Federal Trade Commission Act were part of this subchapter. Any person violating any of the provisions of this subchapter shall be subject to the penalties and entitled to the privileges and immunities provided in the Federal Trade Commission Act as though the applicable terms and provisions thereof were part of this subchapter.

(2)

(A) In the event of a knowing violation, which constitutes a pattern or practice of violations of this subchapter, the Commission may commence a civil action to recover a civil penalty in a district court of the United States against any person that violates this subchapter. In such action, such person shall be liable for a civil penalty of not more than $2,500 per violation.

(B) In determining the amount of a civil penalty under subparagraph (A), the court shall take into account the degree of culpability, any history of prior such conduct, ability to pay, effect on ability to continue to do business, and such other matters as justice may require.

(3) Notwithstanding paragraph (2), a court may not impose any civil penalty on a person for a violation of section 1681s-2(a)(1) of this title unless the person has been enjoined from committing the violation, or ordered not to commit the violation, in an action or proceeding brought by or on behalf of the Federal Trade Commission, and has violated the injunction or order, and the court may not impose any civil penalty for any violation occurring before the date of the violation of the injunction or order.

(b) Enforcement by other agencies

Compliance with the requirements imposed under this subchapter with respect to consumer reporting agencies, persons who use consumer reports from such agencies, persons who furnish information to such agencies, and users of information that are subject to subsection (d) of section 1681m of this title shall be enforced under—

(1) section 8 of the Federal Deposit Insurance Act (12 U.S.C. 1818), in the case of—

(A) national banks, and Federal branches and Federal agencies of foreign banks, by the Office of the Comptroller of the Currency;

(B) member banks of the Federal Reserve System (other than national banks), branches and agencies of foreign banks (other than Federal branches, Federal agencies, and insured State branches of foreign banks), commercial lending companies owned or controlled by foreign banks, and organizations operating under section 25 or 25(a) of the Federal Reserve Act (12 U.S.C. 601 et seq., 611 et seq.), by the Board of Governors of the Federal Reserve System; and

(C) banks insured by the Federal Deposit Insurance Corporation (other than members of the Federal Reserve System) and insured State branches of foreign banks, by the Board of Directors of the Federal Deposit Insurance Corporation;

(2) section 8 of the Federal Deposit Insurance Act (12 U.S.C. 1818), by the Director of the Office of Thrift

Supervision, in the case of a savings association the deposits of which are insured by the Federal Deposit Insurance Corporation;

(3) the Federal Credit Union Act (12 U.S.C. 1751 et seq.), by the Administrator of the National Credit Union Administration with respect to any Federal credit union;

(4) subtitle IV of title 49, by the Secretary of Transportation, with respect to all carriers subject to the jurisdiction of the Surface Transportation Board;

(5) part A of subtitle VII of title 49, by the Secretary of Transportation with respect to any air carrier or foreign air carrier subject to that part; and

(6) the Packers and Stockyards Act, 1921 (7 U.S.C. 181 et seq.) (except as provided in section 406 of that Act (7 U.S.C. 226, 227)), by the Secretary of Agriculture with respect to any activities subject to that Act.

The terms used in paragraph (1) that are not defined in this subchapter or otherwise defined in section 3(s) of the Federal Deposit Insurance Act (12 U.S.C. 1813(s)) shall have the meaning given to them in section 1(b) of the International Banking Act of 1978 (12 U.S.C. 3101).

(c) State action for violations

(1) Authority of States

In addition to such other remedies as are provided under State law, if the chief law enforcement officer of a State, or an official or agency designated by a State, has reason to believe that any person has violated or is violating this subchapter, the State—

(A) may bring an action to enjoin such violation in any appropriate United States district court or in any other court of competent jurisdiction;

(B) subject to paragraph (5), may bring an action on behalf of the residents of the State to recover—

(i) damages for which the person is liable to such residents under sections 1681n and 1681o of this title as a result of the violation;

(ii) in the case of a violation of section 1681s-2(a) of this title, damages for which the person would, but for section 1681s-2(c) of this title, be liable to such residents as a result of the violation; or

(iii) damages of not more than $1,000 for each willful or negligent violation; and

(C) in the case of any successful action under subparagraph (A) or (B), shall be awarded the costs of the action and reasonable attorney fees as determined by the court.

(2) Rights of Federal regulators

The State shall serve prior written notice of any action under paragraph (1) upon the Federal Trade Commission or the appropriate Federal regulator determined under subsection (b) of this section and provide the Commission or appropriate Federal regulator with a copy of its complaint, except in any case in which such prior notice is not feasible, in which case the State shall serve such notice immediately upon instituting such action. The Federal Trade Commission or appropriate Federal regulator shall have the right—

(A) to intervene in the action;

(B) upon so intervening, to be heard on all matters arising therein;

(C) to remove the action to the appropriate United States district court; and

(D) to file petitions for appeal.

(3) Investigatory powers

For purposes of bringing any action under this subsection, nothing in this subsection shall prevent the chief law enforcement officer, or an official or agency designated by a State, from exercising the powers conferred on the chief law enforcement officer or such official by the laws of such State to conduct investigations or to administer oaths or affirmations or to compel the attendance of witnesses or the production of documentary and other evidence.

(4) Limitation on State action while Federal action pending

If the Federal Trade Commission or the appropriate Federal regulator has instituted a civil action or an administrative action under section 8 of the Federal Deposit Insurance Act (12 U.S.C. 1818) for a violation of this subchapter, no State may, during the pendency of such action, bring an action under this section against any defendant named in the complaint of the Commission or the appropriate Federal regulator for any violation of this subchapter that is alleged in that complaint.

(5) Limitations on State actions for violation of section 1681s-2(a)(1)

(A) Violation of injunction required

A State may not bring an action against a person under paragraph (1)(B) for a violation of section 1681s-2(a)(1) of this title, unless—

(i) the person has been enjoined from committing the violation, in an action brought by the State under paragraph (1)(A); and

(ii) the person has violated the injunction.

(B) Limitation on damages recoverable

In an action against a person under paragraph (1)(B) for a violation of section 1681s-2(a)(1) of this title, a State may not recover any damages incurred before the date of the violation of an injunction on which the action is based.

(d) Enforcement under other authority

For the purpose of the exercise by any agency referred to in subsection (b) of this section of its powers under any Act referred to in that subsection, a violation of any requirement imposed under this subchapter shall be deemed to be a violation of a requirement imposed under that Act. In addition to its powers under any provision of law specifically referred to in subsection (b) of this section, each of the agencies referred to in that subsection may exercise, for the purpose of enforcing compliance with any requirement imposed under this subchapter any other authority conferred on it by law.

(e) Regulatory authority

(1) The Federal banking agencies referred to in paragraphs (1) and (2) of subsection (b) of this section shall jointly prescribe such regulations as necessary to carry out the purposes of this subchapter with respect to any persons identified under paragraphs (1) and (2) of subsection (b) of this section, and the Board of Governors of the Federal Reserve System shall have authority to prescribe regulations consistent with such joint regulations with respect to bank holding companies and affiliates (other than depository institutions and consumer reporting agencies) of such holding companies.

(2) The Board of the National Credit Union Administration shall prescribe such regulations as necessary to carry out the purposes of this subchapter with respect to any persons identified under paragraph (3) of subsection (b) of this section.

§ 1681s-1. Information on overdue child support obligations

Notwithstanding any other provision of this subchapter, a consumer reporting agency shall include in any consumer report furnished by the agency in accordance with section 1681b of this title, any information on the failure of the consumer to pay overdue support which—

(1) is provided—

(A) to the consumer reporting agency by a State or local child support enforcement agency; or

(B) to the consumer reporting agency and verified by any local, State, or Federal Government agency; and

(2) antedates the report by 7 years or less.

§ 1681s-2. Responsibilities of furnishers of information to consumer reporting agencies

(a) Duty of furnishers of information to provide accurate information

(1) Prohibition

(A) Reporting information with actual knowledge of errors

A person shall not furnish any information relating to a consumer to any consumer reporting agency if the person knows or consciously avoids knowing that the information is inaccurate.

(B) Reporting information after notice and confirmation of errors

A person shall not furnish information relating to a consumer to any consumer reporting agency if—

(i) the person has been notified by the consumer, at the address specified by the person for such notices, that specific information is inaccurate; and

(ii) the information is, in fact, inaccurate.

(C) No address requirement

A person who clearly and conspicuously specifies to the consumer an address for notices referred to in subparagraph (B) shall not be subject to subparagraph (A); however, nothing in subparagraph (B) shall require a person to specify such an address.

(2) Duty to correct and update information

A person who—

(A) regularly and in the ordinary course of business furnishes information to one or more consumer reporting agencies about the person's transactions or experiences with any consumer; and

(B) has furnished to a consumer reporting agency information that the person determines is not complete or accurate,

shall promptly notify the consumer reporting agency of that determination and provide to the agency any corrections to that information, or any additional information, that is necessary to make the information provided by the person to the agency complete and accurate, and shall not thereafter furnish to the agency any of the information that remains not complete or accurate.

(3) Duty to provide notice of dispute

If the completeness or accuracy of any information furnished by any person to any consumer reporting agency is disputed to such person by a consumer, the person may not furnish the information to any consumer reporting agency without notice that such information is disputed by the consumer.

(4) Duty to provide notice of closed accounts

A person who regularly and in the ordinary course of business furnishes information to a consumer reporting agency regarding a consumer who has a credit account with that person shall notify the agency of the voluntary closure of the account by the consumer, in information regularly furnished for the period in which the account is closed.

(5) Duty to provide notice of delinquency of accounts

A person who furnishes information to a consumer reporting agency regarding a delinquent account being placed for collection, charged to profit or loss, or subjected to any similar action shall, not later than 90 days after furnishing the information, notify the agency of the month and year of the commencement of the delinquency that immediately preceded the action.

(b) Duties of furnishers of information upon notice of dispute

(1) In general

After receiving notice pursuant to section 1681i(a)(2) of this title of a dispute with regard to the completeness or accuracy of any information provided by a person to a consumer reporting agency, the person shall—

(A) conduct an investigation with respect to the disputed information;

(B) review all relevant information provided by the consumer reporting agency pursuant to section 1681i(a)(2) of this title;

(C) report the results of the investigation to the consumer reporting agency; and

(D) if the investigation finds that the information is incomplete or inaccurate, report those results to all other consumer reporting agencies to which the person furnished the information and that compile and maintain files on consumers on a nationwide basis.

(2) Deadline

A person shall complete all investigations, reviews, and reports required under paragraph (1) regarding information provided by the person to a consumer reporting agency, before the expiration of the period under section 1681i(a)(1) of this title within which the consumer reporting agency is required to complete actions required by that section regarding that information.

(c) Limitation on liability

Sections 1681n and 1681o of this title do not apply to any failure to comply with subsection (a) of this section, except as provided in section 1681s(c)(1)(B) of this title.

(d) Limitation on enforcement

Subsection (a) of this section shall be enforced exclusively under section 1681s of this title by the Federal agencies and officials and the State officials identified in that section.

§ 1681t. Relation to State laws

Not printed here.

§ 1681u. Disclosures to FBI for counterintelligence purposes

Not printed here.

Chapter 9

Fair Labor Standards Act (FLSA)

Statute: 29 U.S.C. §§ 201–219

http://www4.law.cornell.edu/uscode/29/ch8.html

Regulations: 29 C.F.R. §§ 541 and following

http://cfr.law.cornell.edu/cfr/cfr.php?title=29&type=part&value=541

Definitions

Independent contractors

An independent contractor performs services for another person or business under contract. In determining whether a worker is an independent contractor rather than an employee, courts consider whether the worker has the right to control how to do his job, whether the worker has an opportunity for profit or loss depending on the worker's skill, whether the worker has invested in equipment or material or hired helpers, whether the worker's job requires special skills, the permanence of the work relationship and whether the worker's job constitutes an essential part of the employer's business.

Outside salespeople

Employees who customarily and regularly work away from the employer's business, selling or taking orders to sell goods and services.

Willful violation

An employer commits a willful violation of the FLSA if it knew that its conduct was illegal or showed reckless disregard as to whether its conduct violated the law.

A. Overview of the FLSA

1. Summary

The Fair Labor Standards Act (FLSA) regulates wages and hours—how much workers must be paid, how many hours they can be required to work and the special rules that apply to younger workers. The FLSA became law in 1938, as part of President Roosevelt's New Deal, to respond to growing concerns about poor working conditions in many industries.

The law includes provisions on:

- minimum wage
- hours worked
- overtime, and
- child labor.

2. Regulated Employers

The FLSA applies to most employers, including:

- the federal government
- state and local governments
- private employers who have annual gross sales of at least $500,000
- private employers who are engaged in commerce or the production of goods for commerce—that is, whose employees handle, sell, produce or otherwise work on goods or materials that have come from or will go to another state; or whose employees use the mail, telephone or equipment to communicate across state lines

- private employers who are primarily engaged in institutional care of the sick, aged or mentally ill
- preschools, elementary schools, secondary schools and schools for mentally or physically disabled or gifted children.

3. Covered Workers

The FLSA applies to all employees of regulated employers, set forth above. In addition, the FLSA applies to any employee who is engaged in commerce or the production of goods for commerce. Even if an employer is not covered by the FLSA, some of its employees may be protected under this test. However, many workers (called "exempt employees"—see below) are not entitled to minimum wage or overtime under the FLSA, although they are covered by the law.

Exempt Employees

The minimum wage and overtime requirements of the FLSA do not apply to every worker whom the law covers. Some workers, called exempt employees, are not entitled to minimum wage or overtime—although they are still protected by the rest of the FLSA's provisions.

Employers of exempt workers remain covered by the FLSA as far as the rest of their workforce is concerned—they have to pay minimum wage and overtime to their nonexempt employees (those who do not fall within one of the exceptions listed below). They also have to follow the FLSA's recordkeeping and child labor requirements.

The following workers are exempt—that is, the minimum wage and overtime requirements of the FLSA do not apply to them:

- executive, administrative and professional employees who are paid on a salary basis (see "Salaried Executive, Administrative and Professional Employees," below)
- *independent contractors*
- volunteer workers
- *outside salespeople*
- certain computer specialists—systems analysts, programmers and software engineers who earn at least $27.63 an hour
- employees of seasonal amusement or recreational businesses, like ski resorts or county fairs
- employees of organized camps or religious and nonprofit educational conference centers that operate fewer than seven months a year
- employees of certain small newspapers and newspaper deliverers
- workers engaged in fishing operations
- seamen
- employees who work on small farms
- certain switchboard operators
- criminal investigators
- casual domestic baby sitters and persons who provide companionship to those who are unable to care for themselves—this exception does not apply to those who provide nursing care or personal and home care aides who perform a variety of domestic services.

In addition, certain workers are exempt from the FLSA's overtime provisions only. See Section B3 for details.

Salaried Executive, Administrative and Professional Employees

Probably the most commonly used—and most confusing— exemptions to the FLSA's overtime and minimum wage requirements are for "white collar workers"—executive, administrative and professional employees who are paid on a salary basis. For each of these exemptions, the employee must meet two tests: a salary test and a job duties test.

Salary Test

A worker is exempt as an administrative, executive or professional employee only if paid on a salary (rather than hourly) basis. Workers are paid on a salary basis if they receive their full salary for any week in which they perform any work, regardless of the number of hours worked. If an employer docks a worker's pay for absences of less than a full day, or for absences of less than one full week for jury duty, service as a witness or military leave, that worker is no longer paid on a salary basis—and is not exempt under the FLSA.

Exempt workers must also earn a minimum weekly salary. However, because the minimum currently ranges from $155 to $170 per week, very few employees will fail this part of the test.

Job Duties Test

An employee must perform certain job duties to qualify as an administrator, executive or professional. The job duties required depend on the exemption and on how much the worker makes. Workers who earn at least $250 per week (a category that likely includes virtually all exempt workers) must meet the requirements of a "short test"—so named to distinguish it from the "long test" that applies to workers who earn less than $250 per week. The long test for each exemption is harder to satisfy—we give both tests below.

Administrative Employees:

Regardless of which test applies, an administrative employee must either (1) regularly and directly assist the owner of a business or another executive or administrative employee, (2) perform specialized or technical work under only general supervision, or (3) perform special assignments under only general supervision. In addition, the employee must meet one of these tests, depending on the employee's salary

- **Short Test** (for workers who earn at least $250 per week in salary):

   (1) the employee's primary duty must be either

   (a) performing either office or non-manual work directly related to management policies or the general business operations of the employer or its customers, or

   (b) duties relating to administration of a school system or educational institution, in work directly related to academic training or instruction, and

(2) the employee's primary duties include work requiring the exercise of discretion and independent judgment.

- **Long Test** (for employees who earn between $155 and $250 per week in salary):

    (1) the employee must meet the first requirement of the short test, and

    (2) the employee must customarily and regularly exercise discretion and independent judgment (this requires more independence that the second requirement of the short test, above)

    (3) the employee may not spend more than 20% of working hours (or 40%, for retail or service workers) on activities that are not closely related to the first two requirements of the test.

Executive Employees:

- **Short Test** (for employees who earn at least $250 per week in salary):

    (1) the employee's primary duty is managing an enterprise or one of its subdivisions, and

    (2) the employee regularly and customarily directs the work of two or more employees within that enterprise or subdivision.

- **Long Test** (for employees who earn between $155 and $250 per week in salary):

    (1) the employee meets both requirements of the short test

    (2) the employee has hiring and firing authority, or the employee's recom-

mendations on hiring and firing are given particular weight

(3) the employee customarily and regularly exercises discretion, and

(4) the employee spends no more than 20% of work hours (or 40%, for retail or service employees) on activities that are not directly and closely related to the factors listed above.

Professional Employees:

- **Short Test** (for employees who earn at least $250 per week in salary):

    (1) the employee's work requires advanced knowledge and education

    (2) the employee's work requires invention, imagination or talent in a recognized artistic field, or

    (3) the employee works as a teacher.

- **Long Test** (for employees who earn between $170 and $250 per week in salary):

    (1) the employee meets the above requirement of the short test

    (2) the employee's work is predominantly intellectual and varied in character (rather than routine mental or manual work), the accomplishment of which cannot be standardized as to time

    (3) the employee's work requires the consistent exercise of discretion and judgment, and

    (4) the employee spends no more than 20% of work time on activities that are not an essential part, or necessarily incidental to, the work described above.

B. Major Provisions of the FLSA

1. Minimum Wage

The FLSA sets the minimum wage for all covered employees. It includes special rules for employees who receive tips, younger workers and workers who can be paid less than the minimum wage pursuant to certificates issued by the Department of Labor.

Regulated Employers

All employers regulated by the FLSA must comply with its minimum wage provisions for covered workers.

Covered Workers

All covered non-exempt workers are entitled to the minimum wage.

What's Required: Employers

Basic Minimum Wage Requirement

Employers must pay covered employees at least the minimum wage— $5.15 per hour, as of September 1, 1997. Employers are not required to pay employees by the hour, however. Employers may pay a salary, commission or piece rate, for example, as long as the total amount paid divided by the total number of hours worked is equal to the minimum wage.

Each state is free to impose a higher minimum wage requirement, and many have chosen to do so. The employer must pay whichever amount is higher—the federal minimum wage or the state minimum wage.

Youth Minimum Wage

Employers may pay workers under the age of 20 a lower minimum wage for a few months. Employers must pay youth workers at least $4.25 an hour for the first 90 calendar days of their employment. Once the worker reaches the age of 20, the employer must pay that worker the regular minimum wage of $5.15 an hour—even if the worker has not yet worked 90 days for the employer.

Some states do not recognize or allow a separate minimum wage for younger workers. Employers doing business in such states must pay younger workers the same minimum wage as everyone else. See Section G, "State Laws Relating to Wages and Hours," for information on state minimum wage laws.

Subminimum Wage Certificates

Employers may apply to the Department of Labor (DOL) for a certificate allowing them to pay certain workers a subminimum wage. The DOL can issue such a certificate only if necessary to prevent the curtailment of employment opportunities for these workers. Employers can apply for a certificate for the following employees:

- Messengers: those employed primarily in delivering letters and messages
- Apprentices: employees who are at least 16 years old and are employed to learn a skilled trade
- Full-time students: students who are employed in retail, service industry or agriculture, or who work for the institution in which they are enrolled, as long as the total hours of all students

employed at subminimum wage by a retail or service establishment don't exceed 10% of the total hours worked by all employees at the establishment

- Student learners: students who are receiving instruction in an accredited school and working part time in a vocational training program, as long as the student spends no more than 40 hours on school and training work combined
- Learners: in certain industries, employees who have worked fewer than a specified number of hours (determined on an industry by industry basis) in the previous three years
- Disabled employees: workers whose earning or productive capacity is impaired by a physical or mental disability (for more on disability, see the Chapter on the ADA).

Tipped Employees

If an employee makes at least $30 per month in tips, the employer has to pay that employee only half of the minimum wage. However, if the employee's wage plus the tips the employee actually earns do not add up to the minimum wage in any pay period, the employer must pay the difference.

Some states do not allow employers to pay tipped employees a lower minimum wage. Employers doing business in such states must pay tipped employees the same minimum wage as everyone else. See Section G, "State Laws Relating to Wages and Hours," for information on state laws regarding tips.

Deductions

The FLSA allows employers to withhold money from a worker's paycheck to satisfy a debt the worker owes the employer or to cover the cost of certain employment expenses (such as uniforms or tools). However, the employer may not deduct so much that the employee's earnings for the pay period drop below the minimum wage.

The FLSA makes an exception for deductions for room and board. An employer may deduct the reasonable cost of meals and housing provided to a worker, even if these deductions cause the worker's pay to fall below minimum wage. However, the employer can make such deductions only if all of the following requirements are met:

- the employer customarily paid the expenses
- the items were provided for the benefit of the employee
- the employee was told, in advance, about the deductions, and
- the employee voluntarily agreed to accept less than the minimum wage in exchange for the food and lodging provided.

Some states do not allow employers to charge employees for certain expenses.

2. Hours Worked

For purposes of the minimum wage and overtime rules, the FLSA requires employers to pay employees for any of their time that benefits the employer and that the employer controls. The rules for several common situations are set forth below, in "What's Required: Employers."

Regulated Employers

All employers regulated by the FLSA must comply with these rules.

Covered Workers

All covered nonexempt workers are entitled to these protections.

What's Required: Employers

Employers must pay employees for time that the employer controls. Conversely, employees are not entitled to be paid for time that they can spend as they wish. The FLSA does not provide much guidance on what constitutes work time, but the Department of Labor and the courts have addressed some of the most common questions.

On-Call Time

Employers must pay employees for all of the time they spend on site waiting for work, even if they do not spend that time actually working. If an employee is on call elsewhere, an employer must pay for those hours over which the employees have little or no control and which they cannot spend as they wish. The more restrictions an employer places on an employee on call, the more likely that employee is entitled to be paid. Courts will consider a number of factors to determine whether on-call time should be paid, including:

- whether the employee was restricted to a limited geographical area (for example, if the employer required the employee to stay within one mile of the work site)

- how many calls the employee received while on call
- how long the employee was given to respond to calls
- how the employee actually spent on-call time (that is, could the employee spend this time on personal pursuits or were the employer's rules so restrictive that the employee couldn't do much of anything).

Meals and Breaks

Employers are not required to pay employees for time spent on a meal or rest break during the work day, as long as the employee is relieved of all work duties during the break. If the employee has to do some work while on break, that time must be paid.

Many states require employers to provide workers with specified breaks for meals or rest during the workday—and some states require that this time be paid. For more information, see Section G, "State Laws Relating to Wages and Hours."

Sleeping Breaks

Employers must pay employees for any time during which they are allowed to sleep during a shift. However, if an employee has to be on duty for more than 24 hours at a time, the employer and employee may agree that eight of those hours will be for meals and sleep periods and will not be paid. If the employee has to actually work during that period, or is unable to get at least five hours of sleep because of work conditions, the eight hours must be paid.

Travel and Commuting

Commuting time—the time it takes a worker to get from home to the workplace—does not count as work time. However, an employer must pay employees for travel time if travel is part of the job—for example, if employees are required to go out on service or sales calls or have to drive from one work site to another during the workday.

3. Overtime

Certain employees are entitled to overtime pay—time and a half for each additional hour worked—if they work more than 40 hours a week.

Regulated Employers

All employers regulated by the FLSA must comply with these rules.

Covered Workers

All covered nonexempt workers are entitled to these protections, with the following exceptions:

- Rail, air and motor carrier employees
- Employees who buy poultry, eggs, cream or milk in their unprocessed state
- Those who sell cars, trucks, farm implements, trailers, boats or aircraft
- Mechanics or parts-persons who service cars, trucks or farm implements
- Announcers, news editors and chief engineers of certain broadcasting stations
- Local delivery drivers or drivers' helpers who are compensated on a trip rate plan
- Agricultural workers

- Taxi drivers
- Domestic service workers who live in the employer's home
- Movie theater employees.

What's Required: Employers

Employers must pay an overtime premium to covered employees who work more than a certain number of hours during a work period. The FLSA uses 40 hours per week as the standard—any employee who works more than 40 hours in a week is entitled to an overtime premium for the extra hours worked. Some states have a daily overtime standard—see Section G, "State Laws Relating to Wages and Hours" for more information.

The overtime premium is 50% of the employee's hourly wage. An employee who works overtime must be paid his usual hourly wage plus the 50% overtime premium—called "time and a half"—for every overtime hour worked.

Compensatory Time

Employers may not give their employees straight compensatory time—one hour off for every overtime hour worked—instead of overtime. However, employers may allow employees to take 1½ hours off for each hour of overtime worked, as long as the employee takes the time off during the same pay period as the overtime work.

4. Child Labor

The FLSA regulates the employment of workers under the age of 18 by limiting the types of work they are legally allowed to do and the hours during which they can work.

Regulated Employers

All employers regulated by the FLSA must comply with these rules.

Covered Workers

All covered workers are entitled to these protections.

What's Prohibited: Employers

The FLSA limits the types of jobs younger workers can do. These restrictions differ depending on whether the work is hazardous and whether the work is agricultural.

Hazardous Work

The Secretary of Labor has the authority to designate certain occupations as hazardous for minors. These occupations include:

- mining
- driving or being an outside helper on a motor vehicle
- working with explosives
- logging and sawmilling
- working with radioactive substances
- working with power-driven wood-working or paper products machines
- working with power-driven hoisting equipment
- working with power-driven metal-forming, punching and shearing machines
- slaughtering and meat packing
- manufacturing tile and brick
- working with power-driven bakery machines

- working with power-driven circular saws, band saws and guillotine shears
- wrecking, demolition and ship-breaking operations
- roofing and excavation operations.

Agricultural Work

Employers who own or operate a farm or other agricultural business must follow these rules:

- Children aged 16 and older may be hired to do any type of work, for unlimited hours.
- Children aged 14 or 15 may be hired to do any nonhazardous work, outside of school hours.
- Children aged 12 or 13 may be hired to do any nonhazardous work outside of school hours, but only if the child's parents work on the same farm or have consented, in writing, to the arrangement.
- Children aged ten or 11 may be hired to harvest crops by hand for no more than eight weeks per calendar year, but only if the Department of Labor has granted the employer a waiver.
- Children of any age may be hired by their own parents to do any type of work, if the parents own or operate the business.

Nonagricultural Work

Employers seeking younger workers for nonagricultural work must follow these rules:

- Children aged 16 and 17 may be hired to do any nonhazardous work, for unlimited hours.

- Workers aged 14 and 15 may be hired to do certain retail, food service and service station jobs. However, they may not work more than three hours per school day, 18 hours per school week, eight hours on a non-school day or 40 hours in a non-school week. Also, they cannot begin work before 7 a.m. or end after 7 p.m. (except during the summer, when they can work until 9 p.m.).

Exceptions

Exempt Professions

Certain minor employees are not covered by the child labor laws. Such workers include:

- Child actors or performers
- Newspaper carriers
- Children under the age of 16 who are employed by their parents in an occupation other than mining, manufacturing or other hazardous job
- Children under the age of 16 who are engaged in certain training and apprenticeship programs.

C. How the FLSA Is Enforced

1. Individual Complaints

An employee who wishes to file a complaint regarding the FLSA's minimum wage and overtime requirements has two choices. The employee may make a complaint to the Wage and Hour Division of the Department of Labor (DOL) (see Section C2, below). An employee does not have to complain to a government agency, however. The employee may choose, instead, to file a lawsuit in state court or in federal district court. The employee must file this lawsuit within two years of the date the employer violated the law, or within three years, if the employer committed a *willful violation*.

Only the DOL may enforce the FLSA's restrictions on child labor. This means that individual employees do not have the right to file a lawsuit alleging child labor violations.

2. Agency Enforcement

If an employee files a complaint with the DOL, the agency may choose to investigate the employer.

DOL investigations are similar to audits. An investigator may contact the employer ahead of time or may simply show up at the workplace. The investigator will examine the employer's records and interview employees who may have information about the complaint. Once the investigation is complete, the investigator will meet with the employer to try to resolve any problems the investigation uncovered. The investigator will tell the employer whether it has violated the law, and how it can correct those violations—for example, by paying overdue wages to its workers.

If the employer refuses to comply, the Secretary of Labor can file a lawsuit in federal district court on behalf of the employees whose rights were violated. However, if the Secretary files a lawsuit on behalf of one or more employees, the employee no longer has the right to sue the employer on his or her own. The Secretary may also impose civil penalties of up to $1,000 against the employer—these penalties are assessed in an administrative hearing process, not a lawsuit (and they are paid to the government, not to the employee).

D. For Employers: Complying With the FLSA

1. Reporting Requirements

The FLSA has no general reporting requirements. However, employers who apply for a subminimum wage certificate (see Section B1), or a waiver from the child labor laws (see Section B4), may have to provide certain information to the DOL.

2. Posting Requirements

All employers subject to the FLSA are required to post a notice (created by the DOL) describing the law's provisions. A copy of the notice must be posted conspicuously in every establishment, where every employee can readily see it. You can print out this notice by going to the link provided in Section F, below.

Employers who hire disabled workers at subminimum wage pursuant to a certificate issued by the DOL (see Section B1, above) must post an official DOL notice about this program. You can print out this notice by going to the link provided in Section F, below.

3. Recordkeeping Requirements

Employers must keep specified wage and hour records on each worker. You do not have to create or keep the records in any particular format—and you do not have to require your workers to punch a time clock or fill in time cards.

These records must be kept for three years:

- payroll records showing each employee's name, address, occupation, sex, birth date (if the worker is under the age of 19), hour and day when the workweek begins, total hours worked each day and week, total daily or weekly earnings, regular hourly pay rate in any week when the employee works overtime, total overtime pay for each week, any deductions from or additions to pay for each pay period, total wages paid each pay period and the date of the payment for each pay period
- plans, trusts, collective bargaining agreements and individual employment contracts
- all certificates or notices required by the FLSA, and
- records showing the total dollar volume of the business and the total volume of goods purchased or received.

These additional records must be kept for two years:

- time cards or other records showing workers' daily stop and start time
- records showing the amount of work accomplished by individual employees on a daily, weekly or pay period basis, if those amounts affect the employees' wages (for example, if they are paid on commission or by the piece)
- wage rate tables or other documents that show the rates used to compute piece work pay, straight time earnings wages, salary or overtime pay
- order, shipping and billing records
- records of additions to, or deductions from, wages paid, including records used by the employer to determine the original cost, operating cost, maintenance cost, depreciation and interest charges, if these amounts are used to determine additions to or deductions from wages.

The regulations require employers to keep different types of records or additional records for certain types of employees, such as local delivery workers, seamen and tipped employees. For more information on these requirements, see 29 C.F.R. § 516, which sets forth the FLSA's recordkeeping requirements in detail.

4. Practical Tips

Here are some tips for complying with the FLSA:

- **Check your state and local laws.** Many states have passed laws that provide more protections to workers—a higher minimum wage or stricter requirements for overtime, for example. And some local governments have also gotten in on the act, passing living wage laws that require certain employers to pay a minimum wage much higher than the federal standard. As an employer, you have to follow whichever law is most beneficial to your workers in a given situation—for example, you may have to pay your employees the state minimum wage (if it's higher than the federal requirement) while honoring the FLSA's restrictions on child labor. So make sure to find out what your state and local laws require.

- **Don't misclassify your employees as executive, administrative or professional.** Many employers routinely classify lower-level workers as assistant managers, in the hopes that this will get them out of having to pay overtime. This is illegal—only true managers who spend most of their time supervising other workers are exempt under the FLSA, no matter what their job title. And if you get caught misclassifying large numbers of workers, you will have to pay dearly for it.

- **Don't treat an exempt employee like an hourly worker.** Even if an employee meets all the tests for the executive, administrative or professional exemption, you can undo the exemption by docking that worker's pay for absences of less than a day, tardiness or minor rule infractions.

- **Deduct with care.** If some of your workers earn barely more than the minimum wage, be careful when taking deductions from their paychecks for tools, uniforms, advances and so on. If you deduct so much that you leave the worker with less than the minimum wage, you have violated the FLSA. If a worker owes you a larger debt, deduct it in installments.

- **Get your records in order.** The record-keeping requirements of the FLSA can be very tough to meet, particularly for smaller employers and employers who don't usually keep a lot of paperwork. You can save time and money in the long run by creating a system that requires you to make and keep the records you need. If you don't want to generate your own forms and filing systems, there are a number of decent products on the market, both in software and documentary form, that can help you do the job. Contact a local human resources professional group for more information on these products.

5. Penalties

If a court finds that an employer has violated the FLSA, it may order the employer to:

- pay back wages, equal to the difference between what the employee actually earned and what the employee should have earned if the employer had followed the law, plus interest. An employee can collect up to two years' worth of back pay, or three years if the employer committed a *willful violation* of the statute.

- pay an additional penalty (known as "liquidated damages"), equal to the entire back pay award, if the employer willfully violated the statute.

- pay the employee's court costs and attorney fees.

E. For Workers: Asserting Rights Under the FLSA

1. Where to Start

If you believe that your employer has violated the FLSA, start by complaining internally to the company. If the company has a complaint policy, follow the designated procedures to file a complaint. If the company has no complaint policy, talk to a human resources representative or a member of management.

If you are a union member, talk to your shop steward or union representative.

If internal complaints and/or union complaints don't work, you can file a lawsuit or file a complaint with the DOL. For more on agency enforcement, see Section C2.

2. Required Forms

Contact your local office of the Wage and Hour Division of the DOL to find out if you have to use a particular form to file an administrative complaint. See Section F for contact information.

3. Practical Tips

Here are some tips for asserting your rights under the FLSA:

- **Check state and local laws.** Many states and local governments have passed wage and hour laws that give workers more rights than the FLSA —and your employer has to follow whichever law is most beneficial to you in any given situation. Find out whether your state and local laws give you more protection than the FLSA. If they do, you might want to pursue your claims through your state labor department rather than the DOL.

- **Don't settle for a fancy job title.** One of the most common ways employers violate the FLSA is by claiming that their low-level employees are exempt—and giving those employees job titles that make it sound as if they are executives in the company. Even if you are an Assistant Manager or Executive Administrator, you are entitled to overtime and minimum wage payments if you spend more than a small percentage of your time doing routine or manual work.

- **Present your complaints together.** If you are one of many workers who is paid less than minimum wage, is not paid for hours that should count as work time or has been improperly denied overtime compensation, try to get your coworkers to complain with you. Your employer will be more likely to take your complaint seriously if a number of employees come forward. And the DOL will be more likely to investigate and go after your employer if a large group goes to the agency together. If you can't convince your coworkers to go with you to complain, be sure to tell the DOL that many other workers' rights have been violated.

F. Agency Charged With Enforcement & Compliance

Employment Standards Administration
Wage and Hour Division
Department of Labor
200 Constitution Ave., NW
Washington, DC 20210
Phone: 866-4-USA-DOL
TTY: 877-889-5627.
http://www.dol.gov

Agency Resources for Employers and Workers
(These can be obtained either at the Web addresses listed below or at the address and phone numbers listed above.)

- A guide to the FLSA's requirements for employers and employees
  Fair Labor Standards Act: Employee/Employer Advisor
  http://www.dol.gov/elaws/flsa.htm
- The rules on employing minors in nonagricultural jobs
  Child Labor Bulletin 101
  http://www.dol.gov/dol/esa/public/regs/compliance/whd/childlabor101.pdf
- A fact sheet on calculating overtime pay
  Overtime Pay Requirements of the Fair Labor Standards Act
  http://www.dol.gov/dol/esa/public/regs/compliance/whd/whdfs23.htm
- A fact sheet on what types of activities count as work
  Hours Worked Under the Fair Labor Standards Act
  http://www.dol.gov/dol/esa/public/regs/compliance/whd/whdfs22.htm
- A fact sheet on employees exempt from overtime and minimum wage laws
  Exemption for Executive, Administrative, Professional and Outside Sales Employees under the Fair Labor Standards Act
  http://www.dol.gov/dol/esa/public/regs/compliance/whd/whdfs17.htm
- A fact sheet guide to the FLSA's recordkeeping rules
  Record Keeping Requirements under the Fair Labor Standards Act
  http://www.dol.gov/dol/esa/public/regs/compliance/whd/whdfs21.htm
- Poster employers are required to display regarding FLSA
  Your Rights Under the Fair Labor Standards Act
  http://www.dol.gov/dol/esa/public/regs/compliance/posters/pdf/minwagebwP.pdf

- Poster employers must display if they employ disabled workers at sub-minimum wage
  Notice to Workers With Disabilities Paid at Special Minimum Wages
  http://www.dol.gov/dol/esa/public/regs/compliance/posters/pdf/disabc.pdf
- A list of the addresses and telephone numbers of local offices of the Wage and Hour Division
  Employment Standards Administration: Wage and Hour Division: District Office Locations
  http://www.dol.gov/dol/esa/public/contacts/whd/america2.htm

G. State Laws Relating to Wages and Hours

Most states have their own wage and hour laws—and some of them are almost as extensive as the FLSA. Here, you'll find the state rules on minimum wage, overtime and meal and rest breaks. However, to find out whether your state has rules on hours worked, child labor, exempt vs. non-exempt employees or other wage and hour issues, contact your state labor department.

1. Minimum Wage Laws for Regular and Tipped Employees

"Maximum tip credit" means the maximum amount of actual tips that an employer can credit against the employee's hourly wage rate. That is, the employer can subtract the tip credit from the minimum wage, and only pay the employee the difference. Where the tip credit is a percentage, it means that up to that percent of the basic minimum hourly rate may be deducted as a tip credit for tipped employees. In no case may the total amount of employee's wages plus tips equal less than the basic minimum wage rate. If an employee's tips exceed the maximum tip credit, the employee gets to keep the extra amount.

"Minimum Cash Wage" is what the employer must actually pay a tipped employee per hour. It's equal to the regular minimum wage less the tip credit.

Jurisdiction	Citation & Notes	Basic Minimum Hourly Rate (*=Tied to Federal rate)	Maximum Tip Credit (tips only, not food and lodging unless specified)	Minimum Cash Wage for Tipped Employee	Definition of Tipped Employee by Minimum Tips Received (monthly unless otherwise specified)
United States	29 U.S.C. § 206	$5.15	$3.02	$2.13	More than $30
Alabama	No minimum wage law				
Alaska	Alaska Stat. § 23.10.065; 8 AAC 15.120	$5.65* $0.50 above FLSA rate	$0	$5.65	N/A
Arizona	No minimum wage law				
Arkansas	Ark. Code Ann. § 11-4-210 4 or more employees	$5.15	50%	$2.575	Not specified
California	8 Cal. Admin. Code § 11000	$6.75	$0	$6.75	
Colorado	Colo. Rev. Stat. § 8-6-109 Minimum wage applies to these industries: retail and service, commercial support service, food and beverage and health and medical.	$5.15	$3.02	$2.13	More than $30
Connecticut	Conn. Gen. Stat. Ann. § 31-58(j)	$6.70 or 0.5% above FLSA minimum if higher	Generally, $0.35	$6.35	Not specified
	Hotel, restaurant		29.3%	$4.74	At least $10 weekly for full-time employees or $2.00 daily for part-time
	Bartenders		8.2%	$6.15	Not specified
	Beauty shop		none	$6.70	Not specified
Delaware	Del. Code Ann. tit. 19, § 902(a)	$6.15 or FLSA rate if higher	$3.92	$2.23	More than $30
District of Columbia	D.C. Code Ann. § 32-1003(1)	$6.15* $1 above FLSA rate	55%	$2.77	Not specified
Florida	No minimum wage law				

Jurisdiction	Citation & Notes	Basic Minimum Hourly Rate (*=Tied to Federal rate)	Maximum Tip Credit (tips only, not food and lodging unless specified)	Minimum Cash Wage for Tipped Employee	Definition of Tipped Employee by Minimum Tips Received (monthly unless otherwise specified)
Georgia	Ga. Code Ann. § 34-4-3(a) 6 employees or more and sales of more than $40K per year.	$5.15	Minimum wage does not apply to those who receive tips.	N/A	
Hawaii	Haw. Rev. Stat. § 387-1 to 2	$5.75	$0.25	$5.50	More than $20, and employee's cash wage plus tips must be at least $.50 higher than the minimum wage
		$6.25 as of 2003	$0.25	$6.50	More than $20, and employee's cash wage plus tips must be at least $.50 higher than the minimum wage
Idaho	Idaho Code § 44-1502 For employees under 20 years old, $4.25 for first consecutive 90 days.	$5.15	35%	$3.35	More than $30
Illinois	820 Ill. Comp. Stat. § 105/4 4 or more employees	$5.15*	$2.06	$3.09	$20
Indiana	Ind. Code Ann. § 22-2-2-4 2 or more employees Under the age of 20, minimum wage is $4.25 for first consecutive 90 days.	$5.15	$3.02	$2.13	Not specified
Iowa	Iowa Code § 91D.1	$5.15* (doesn't apply to first 90 calendar days of emloyment)	40%	$3.09	More than $30
Kansas	Kan. Stat. Ann. § 44-1203 Employers not covered by the FLSA	$2.65	40%	$1.59	Not specified
Kentucky	Ky. Rev. Stat. Ann. § 337.275	$5.15*	$3.02	$2.13	More than $30
Louisiana	No minimum wage law				

Jurisdiction	Citation & Notes	Basic Minimum Hourly Rate (*=Tied to Federal rate)	Maximum Tip Credit (tips only, not food and lodging unless specified)	Minimum Cash Wage for Tipped Employee	Definition of Tipped Employee by Minimum Tips Received (monthly unless otherwise specified)
Maine	Me. Rev. Stat. Ann. tit. 26, § 664	$5.75 or FLSA rate if higher	50%	$2.88	More than $20
		$6.25 in 2003 or FLSA rate if higer	50%	$3.13	More than $20
Maryland	Md. Code Ann., [Lab. & Empl.] § 3-413	$5.15*	$2.77	$2.38	More than $30
Massachusetts	Mass. Gen. Laws ch. 151, § 1	$6.75 or $0.10 above FLSA rate if higher	$4.12	$2.63	More than $20
Michigan	Mich. Comp. Laws § 408.384 2 or more employees Excludes all employers subject to FLSA, unless state minimum wage is higher than federal.	$5.15	$2.50	$2.65	Not specified
Minnesota	Minn. Stat. Ann. § 177.24 Large employer (enterprise with annual receipts of $500,000 or more)	$5.15	None	$5.15	
	Small employer (enterprise with annual receipts of less than $500,000)	$4.90	None	$4.90	
Mississippi	No minimum wage law				
Missouri	Mo. Rev. Stat. § 290.502	$5.15*	Up to 50%	$2.575	
Montana	Mont. Code Ann. § 39-3-404 Businesses with gross annual sales of more than $110,000	$5.15*	None	$5.15*	
	Mont. Code Ann. § 39-3-409 Businesses with gross annual sales of $110,000 or less	$4.00	None	$4.00	

Jurisdiction	Citation & Notes	Basic Minimum Hourly Rate (*=Tied to Federal rate)	Maximum Tip Credit (tips only, not food and lodging unless specified)	Minimum Cash Wage for Tipped Employee	Definition of Tipped Employee by Minimum Tips Received (monthly unless otherwise specified)
Nebraska	Neb. Rev. Stat. § 48-1203 4 or more employees	$5.15	$3.02	$2.13	Not specified
Nevada	Nev. Rev. Stat. Ann. § 608.250	$5.15*	None	$5.15	
New Hampshire	N.H. Rev. Stat. Ann. § 279: 21	$5.15*	$2.57	$2.38	More than $20
New Jersey	N.J. Stat. Ann. §§ 34:11-56a4; 34:11-57 Rules may vary depending on occupation.	$5.15*	$2.13	$3.02	Not specified
New Mexico	N.M. Stat. Ann. § 50-4-22	$4.25.	$2.125	$2.125	More than $30
New York	N.Y. Lab. Law § 652	$5.15*	Tip credit varies from $.80 to $2.05, depending on occupation.		Not specified
North Carolina	N.C. Gen. Stat. § 95-25.3	$5.15*	$3.02	$2.13	More than $20
North Dakota	N.D. Cent. Code § 34-06-03	$5.15	33%	$3.45	More than $30
Ohio	Ohio Rev. Code Ann. § 4111.02 Employers with gross annual sales over $500K	$4.25 $2.80	50%	$2.125	More than $30
	Employers with gross annual sales from $150K to $500K	$3.35	50%		More than $30
	Employers with gross annual sales less than $150K	$2.80	50%		More than $30
Oklahoma	Okla. Stat. Ann. tit. 40, § 197.2 10 or more full time employees OR gross annual sales more than $100K	$5.15*	50% For tips, food and lodging combined.	$2.58	Not specified
	All other employers who are not subject to the FLSA	$2.00			Not specified

Jurisdiction	Citation & Notes	Basic Minimum Hourly Rate (*=Tied to Federal rate)	Maximum Tip Credit (tips only, not food and lodging unless specified)	Minimum Cash Wage for Tipped Employee	Definition of Tipped Employee by Minimum Tips Received (monthly unless otherwise specified)
Oregon	Or. Rev. Stat. § 653.025	$6.50	None	$6.50	
Pennsylvania	43 Pa. Cons. Stat. Ann. § 333.104	$5.15*	$2.32	$2.83	More than $30
Rhode Island	R.I. Gen. Laws § 28-12-3	$6.15	$3.26	$2.89	Not specified
South Carolina	No minimum wage law				
South Dakota	S.D. Codified Laws Ann. § 60-11-3 to 3.1	$5.15	$3.02	$2.13	More than $35
Tennessee	No minimum wage law				
Texas	Tex. Lab. Code Ann. § 62.051 Employers not covered by FLSA	$5.15*	$3.02	$2.13	More than $20
Utah	Utah Code Ann. § 34-40-103 Those not covered by the FLSA	$5.15*	$3.02	$2.13	More than $30
Vermont	Vt. Stat. Ann. tit. 21, § 384(a) 2 or more employees	$6.25 or FLSA rate if higher	45%	$3.44	More than $30
Virginia	Va. Code Ann. § 40.1-28.10 4 or more employees	5.15*	Actual amount received		Not specified
Washington	Wash. Rev. Code Ann. § 49.46.020 Adjusted annually for inflation	$6.90 in 2002	None	$6.90	
West Virginia	W. Va. Code § 21-5C-2a 6 or more employees at one location Only employers who are not covered by the FLSA	$5.15	20%	$4.12	Not specified
Wisconsin	Wis. Stat. Ann. § 104.02	$5.15	$2.42	$2.33	Not specified
Wyoming	Wyo. Stat. § 27-4-202	$5.15	$3.02	$2.13	More than $30

2. State Overtime Rules

Overtime rules summarized in this chart are not applicable to all employers or all employees.

State	Time and a half after x hours per		Citation and Notes
	DAY	WEEK	
Alabama			No overtime limits for private sector employers
Alaska	8	40	Alaska Stat. §§ 23.10.055; 23.10.060; 23.10.410 Applicable to employers of 4 or more employees. Under a voluntary flexible work hour plan approved by the Alaska Department of Labor, a 10-hour day, 40-hour workweek may be instituted with premium pay after 10 hours a day instead of after 8 hours.
Arizona			No overtime limits for private sector employers
Arkansas		40	Ark. Code Ann. §§ 11-4-211; 11-4-203 Applicable to employers of 4 or more employees, but excludes employment that is subject to the FLSA.
California	8 Over 12 (double time)	40 7th day: First 8 hours (time and half) Over 8 hours (double time)	Cal. Lab. Code §§ 510, 511 and Orders of the Industrial Welfare Commission, 8 Cal. Admin. Code § 11010 and following. Overtime is due after 8 hours per day or 40 hours per week unless an alternative workweek of no more than 4 days of 10 hours was established prior to 7/1/99. Premium pay on 7th day not required for employee whose total weekly work-hours do not exceed 30 and whose total hours in any one workday thereof do not exceed 6, in specific wage and hour orders.
Colorado	12	40	Colo. Rev. Stat. § 8-12-101 and following, Wage Order No. 222 Applies only to employees in retail and service, food and medical, and commercial support service industries.
Connecticut		40	Conn. Gen. Stat. Ann. §§ 31-58 and following; Conn. Admin. Code §§ 31-60-1 and following In restaurants and hotel restaurants, for the 7th consecutive day of work, premium pay is required at time and one-half the minimum rate.
Delaware			No overtime provisions
District of Columbia		40	D.C. Code Ann. § 32-1003
Florida			No overtime provisions
Georgia			No overtime provisions
Hawaii		40	Haw. Rev. Stat. § 387-3 In some seasonal jobs, 48 hours per week
Idaho			No overtime provisions
Illinois		40	820 Ill. Comp. Stat. § 105/4a Applicable to employers of 4 or more employees.

State	Time and a half after x hours per		Citation and Notes
	DAY	WEEK	
Indiana		40	Ind. Code Ann. § 22-2-2-4(j)
			Applicable to employers of 2 or more employees, but excludes employment that is subject to the FLSA.
Iowa			No overtime provisions
Kansas		46	Kan. Stat. Ann. § 44-1204
			Not applicable to employment that is subject to the FLSA.
Kentucky		40	Ky. Rev. Stat. Ann. §§ 337.050; 337.285
		7th Day	Premium pay required for employees who have to work a 7th day, if they have already worked 40 hours in the previous six days.
Louisiana			No overtime provisions
Maine		40	Me. Rev. Stat. Ann. tit. 26, § 664
Maryland		40	Md. Code Ann., [Lab. & Empl.] § 3-420
			Time and a half is required after 48 hours in bowling alleys and for residential employees of institutions (other than a hospital) primarily engaged in the care of the sick, aged or mentally ill.
Massachusetts		40	Mass. Gen. Laws ch. 151, § 1A
Michigan		40	Mich. Comp. Laws § 408.384a
			Applicable to employers of 2 or more employees, but excludes employment that is subject to the FLSA if federal rate is higher than the state rate.
Minnesota		48	Minn. Stat. Ann. § 177.25
Mississippi			No overtime provisions
Missouri		40	Mo. Rev. Stat. §§ 290.500 and following
			Not applicable to employment that is subject to the FLSA.
			In addition, the law exempts, among others, employees of a retail or service business with gross annual sales or business done of less than $500,000.
			Premium pay required after 52 hours in seasonal amusement or recreation businesses.
Montana		40	Mont. Code Ann. § 39-3-405
Nebraska			No overtime provisions
Nevada	8	40	Nev. Rev. Stat. Ann. § 608.018
			By mutual employer/employee agreement, a scheduled 10-hour day for 4 days a week may be worked without premium pay after 8 hours.
			Law does not apply to employees who are paid at least one and one-half times the minimum rate or to employees of enterprises with a gross annual sales volume of less than $250,000.
New Hampshire		40	N.H. Rev. Stat. Ann. § 279:21
			Doesn't apply to employees of employers covered by the FLSA.
New Jersey		40	N.J. Stat. Ann. § 34:11-56a4

| State | Time and a half after x hours per | | Citation and Notes |
	DAY	WEEK	
New Mexico		40	N.M. Stat. Ann. § 50-4-22
New York		40	N.Y. Lab. Law § 651
North Carolina		40	N.C. Gen. Stat. § 95-25.4 Premium pay is required after 45 hours a week in seasonal amusements or recreational establishments. Excludes employment that is subject to the FLSA.
North Dakota		40	N.D. Admin. Code 46-02-07-02
Ohio		40	Ohio Rev. Code Ann. § 4111.03
Oklahoma			No overtime provisions
Oregon		40	Or. Rev. Stat. §§ 653.261, 653.265 Premium pay required after 10 hours a day in nonfarm canneries, driers or packing plants and in mills, factories or manufacturing establishments (excluding sawmills, planing mills, shingle mills and logging camps).
Pennsylvania		40	43 Pa. Cons. Stat. Ann. § 333.104(c)
Rhode Island		40	R.I. Gen. Laws §§ 28-12-4.1; 5-23-2 Time and one-half premium pay for work on Sundays and holidays in retail and certain other business is required.
South Carolina			No overtime provisions
South Dakota			No overtime provisions
Tennessee			No overtime provisions
Texas			No overtime provisions
Utah			No overtime provisions
Vermont		40	Vt. Stat. Ann. tit. 21, § 384 Applicable to employers of two or more employees. The state overtime pay provision has very limited application because it exempts numerous types of establishments, such as retail and service; seasonal amusement/recreation; hotels, motels, restaurants; and transportation employees to whom the federal (FLSA) overtime provision does not apply.
Virginia			No overtime provisions
Washington		40	Wash. Rev. Code Ann. § 49.46.130 Premium pay not applicable to employees who request compensating time off in lieu of premium pay.
West Virginia		40	W. Va. Code § 21-5c-3 Applicable to employers of 6 or more employees at one location, but excludes employment that is subject to the FLSA.
Wisconsin		40	Wis. Stat. Ann. § 104.02
Wyoming			No overtime provisions

3. Meal and Rest Break Laws

California	Cal. Lab. Code § 512
Applies To	Employers in most industries.
Exceptions	Excludes professional actors, sheepherders under Agricultural Occupations Order and personal attendants under Household Occupations Order.
	Meal break does not apply to motion picture, agricultural & household occupations.
Meal Break	30 minutes, after 5 hours, except when workday will be completed in 6 hours or less and there is mutual employer/employee consent to waive meal period.
	On-duty meal period counted as time worked and permitted only when nature of work prevents relief from all duties and there is written agreement between parties.
Rest Break	Paid 10-minute rest period for each 4 hours worked or major fraction thereof; as practicable, in middle of each work period. Not required for employees whose total daily work time is less than $3\frac{1}{2}$ hours.
Applies To	Broadcasting industry and motion picture industry.
Meal Break	$\frac{1}{2}$ hour, to not more than 1 hour, after 6 hours, with subsequent meal periods required 6 hours after termination of preceding meal period. On-duty meal period counted as time worked and permitted only when nature of work prevents relief from all duties and there is written agreement between parties.
Colorado	Wage Order # 22
Applies To	Retail trade, food and beverage, public housekeeping, medical profession, beauty service, laundry and dry cleaning and janitorial service industries.
Exceptions	Excludes certain occupations, such as teacher, nurse and other medical professionals.
Meal Break	30 minutes after 5 hours of work. On-duty meal period permitted when nature of work prevents relief from all duties; such meal period must be paid.
Rest Break	Paid 10-minute rest period for each 4-hour work period or major fraction thereof; as practicable, in middle of each work period.
Connecticut	Conn. Gen. Stat. Ann. § 31-51ii
Applies To	All employers, except as noted.
Exceptions	Does not apply to employers who provide 30 or more minutes of paid or meal periods within each $7\frac{1}{2}$ hour work period.

	Does not apply if collective bargaining agreement in effect on 7/1/90 or written agreement between employer and employee provides for different breaks.
	Labor Commissioner is directed to exempt by regulation any employer on a finding that compliance would be adverse to public safety, or that duties of a position can be performed only by one employee, or in continuous operations under specified conditions, or that employer employs less than 5 employees on a shift at a single place of business provided the exemption applies only to employees on such shift.
Meal Break	30 minutes after first 2 hours and before last 2 hours for employees who work 7½ consecutive hours or more.
Delaware	Del. Code Ann. tit. 19, § 707
Applies To	All employers, except as noted.
Exceptions	Excludes teachers and workplaces covered by a collective bargaining agreement or other written employer/employee agreement providing otherwise.
	Exemptions may also be granted where compliance would adversely affect public safety; only one employee may perform the duties of a position; an employer has fewer than five employees on a shift at a single place of business; or where the continuous nature of an employer's operations requires employees to respond to urgent or unusual conditions at all times and the employees are compensated for their meal break periods.
Meal Break	30 minutes after first 2 hours and before the last 2 hours, for employees who work 7½ consecutive hours or more.
Illinois	820 Ill. Comp. Stat. § 140/3
Applies To	All employers.
Exceptions	Employees whose meal periods are established by collective bargaining agreement.
	Employees who monitor individuals with developmental disabilities or mental illness, or both, and who are required to be on call during an entire 8-hour work period; these employees must be allowed to eat a meal while working.
Meal Break	20 minutes, after 5 hours, for employees who work 7½ continuous hours or more.
Kentucky	Ky. Rev. Stat. Ann. §§ 337.355, 337.365
Applies To	All employers, except as noted.
Exceptions	Excludes employers subject to Federal Railway Labor Act.

Meal Break	Reasonable off-duty period (ordinarily 30 minutes but a shorter period may be permitted under special conditions) between 3rd and 5th hour of work. Coffee breaks and snack time may not be included in meal period.
	Employee may be entitled to different meal period, pursuant to collective bargaining agreement or mutual agreement between employer and employee.
Rest Break	Paid 10-minute rest period for each 4-hour work period.
	Rest period must be in addition to regularly scheduled meal period.

Maine	Me. Rev. Stat. Ann. tit. 26, § 601
Applies To	Places of employment where 3 or more employees are on duty at one time and the nature of their work allows them to take frequent breaks during the workday.
Exceptions	General rule not applicable if collective bargaining or other written employer-employee agreement provides otherwise.
Meal Break	30 minutes after 6 consecutive hours of work, except in cases of emergency.

Massachusetts	Mass. Gen. Laws ch. 149, § 100
Applies To	All employers, except as noted.
Exceptions	Excludes iron works, glass works, paper mills, letterpress establishments, print works and bleaching or dyeing works.
Meal Break	30 minutes, if work is for more than 6 hours.

Minnesota	Minn. Stat. Ann. §§ 177.253, 177.254
Applies To	All employers.
Exceptions	Excludes certain agricultural and seasonal employees.
	Different rest and meal breaks are permitted pursuant to a collective bargaining agreement.
Meal Break	Sufficient unpaid time for employees who work 8 consecutive hours or more.
Rest Break	Paid adequate rest period within each 4 consecutive hours of work, to utilize nearest convenient restroom.

Nebraska	Neb. Rev. Stat. § 48-212
Applies To	Assembly plant, workshop or mechanical establishment, unless establishment operates three 8-hour shifts daily.
Meal Break	30 minutes off premises, between 12 noon and 1 p.m. or at other suitable lunch time.

Nevada	Nev. Rev. Stat. Ann. § 608.019
Applies To	Employers of two or more employees.
Exceptions	Employees covered by collective bargaining agreement.
Meal Break	30 minutes, if work is for 8 continuous hours.
Rest Break	Paid 10-minute rest period for each 4 hours worked or major fraction thereof; as practicable, in middle of each work period. Not required for employees whose total daily work time is less than $3^{1}/_{2}$ hours.

New Hampshire	N.H. Rev. Stat. Ann. § 275:30-a
Applies To	All employers.
Meal Break	30 minutes after 5 consecutive hours, unless the employer allows the employee to eat while working and it is feasible for the employee to do so.

New York	N.Y. Lab. Law § 162
Applies To	Factories.
Meal Break	1 hour noonday period.
	Labor Commissioner may give written permission for shorter meal period.
Applies To	All other establishments and occupations covered by the Labor Law.
Meal Break	30 minute noonday period for employees who work shifts of more than 6 hours that extend over the noonday meal period.
	45 minutes for employees who workshifts of more than 6 hours, if their shift starts between 1 p.m. and 6 a.m.
	Labor Commissioner may give written permission for shorter meal period.
Applies To	All industries and occupations.
Meal Break	An additional 20 minutes between 5 p.m. and 7 p.m. for those employed on a shift starting before 11 a.m. and continuing after 7 p.m.
	Labor Commissioner may give written permission for shorter meal period.
Applies To	All industries and occupations.
Meal Break	1 hour in factories, 30 minutes in other establishments, midway in shift, for those employed more than a 6-hour period starting between 1 p.m. and 6 a.m.
	Labor Commissioner may give written permission for shorter meal period.

North Dakota	N.D. Admin. Code § 46-02-07-02
Applies To	Applicable when two or more employees are on duty.

Exceptions	Collective bargaining agreement takes precedence over meal period requirement.
Meal Break	30-minutes, if employee desires, on each shift exceeding 5 hours.
	Employees who are completely relieved of their duties but required to remain on site do not have to be paid.

Oregon	Or. Admin. R. § 839-020-0050
Applies To	All employers except as noted.
Exceptions	Agricultural employees.
	Employees covered by a collective bargaining agreement.
Meal Break	30-minute break for each work period of 6 to 8 hours, between 2nd and 5th hour for work period of 7 hours or less and between 3rd and 6th hour for work period over 7 hours; or at least 20-minute paid break, where employer can show that such a paid meal period is industry practice or custom; or, where employer can show that nature of work prevents relief from all duty, an eating period with pay while on duty for each period of 6 to 8 hours.
Rest Break	Paid 15-minute rest period for every 4-hour segment or major portion thereof in one work period; as feasible, approximately in middle of each segment of work period.
	Rest period must be in addition to usual meal period and taken separately; not to be added to usual meal period or deducted from beginning or end of work period to reduce overall length of total work period.
	Rest period is not required for employees age 18 or older who work alone in a retail or service establishment serving the general public and who work less than 5 hours in a period of 16 continuous hours, as long as employee has opportunity to use rest room.

Rhode Island	R.I. Gen. Laws § 28-3-14
Applies To	Factory, workshop and mechanical or mercantile establishments.
Exceptions	Certain nighttime switchboard operators.
Meal Break	20 minutes after 6 hours of work.
	Employees are not entitled to a break if their shift lasts for $6^{1}/_{2}$ hours or less and ends by 1 p.m.; or if their shift lasts for $7^{1}/_{2}$ hours or less and ends by 2 p.m., as long as employee has opportunity to eat during employment.

Tennessee	Tenn. Code Ann. §§ 50-2-103(d), 50-1-305
Applies To	All employers.

Meal Break	30 minutes for employees scheduled to work 6 consecutive hours or more. Also must provide break for mothers to express breast milk for infants.
Vermont	Vt. Stat. Ann. tit. 21, § 304
Applies To	All employers.
Meal Break	Employees must be afforded a reasonable opportunity to eat and use toilet facilities during work periods.
Washington	Wash. Admin. Code § 296-126-092
Applies To	All employers except as noted.
Exceptions	Excludes newspaper vendor or carrier, domestic or casual labor around private residence, sheltered workshop and agricultural labor.
Meal Break	30-minute break, if work period is more than 5 consecutive hours, to be given not less than 2 hours nor more than 5 hours from beginning of shift. Employees who work 3 or more hours longer than regular workday are entitled to an additional ½ hour, before or during overtime.
Rest Break	Paid 10-minute rest period for each 4-hour work period, scheduled as near as possible to midpoint of each work period. Employee may not be required to work more than 3 hours without a rest period.
	Scheduled rest periods not required where nature of work allows employee to take intermittent rest periods equivalent to required standard.
	Although agricultural workers are excluded from the general rest requirement, a separate regulation requires a paid 10-minute rest period in each 4-hour period of agricultural work.
West Virginia	W.Va. Code § 21-3-10a
Applies To	All employers.
Meal Break	20-minute break for each 6 consecutive hours worked, where employees are not allowed to take breaks as needed and/or permitted to eat lunch while working.
Rest Break	Rest breaks of 20 minutes or less must be counted as paid work time.
Wisconsin	Wis. Admin. Code § DWD 274.02
Applies To	All employers.
Meal Break	30 minutes close to usual meal time or near middle of shift is recommended but not required. Shifts of more than six hours without a meal break should be avoided.

H. Text of the FSLA

29 U.S.C §§ 201-219
U.S. Code
Title 29: Labor
Chapter 8: Fair Labor Standards

Italicized provisions are not printed below.

§ 201. Short title

§ 202. Congressional finding and declaration of policy

§ 203. Definitions

§ 204. Administration

§ 205. Special industry committees for American Samoa

§ 206. Minimum wage

§ 207. Maximum hours

§ 208. Wage orders in American Samoa

§ 209. Attendance of witnesses

§ 210. Court review of wage orders in Puerto Rico and the Virgin Islands

§ 211. Collection of data

§ 212. Child labor provisions

§ 213. Exemptions

§ 214. Employment under special certificates

§ 215. Prohibited acts; prima facie evidence

§ 216. Penalties

§ 216a. Repealed. Oct. 26, 1949, ch. 736, § 16f, 63 Stat. 920

§ 216b. Liability for overtime work performed prior to July 20, 1949

§ 217. Injunction proceedings

§ 218. Relation to other laws

§ 219. Separability

§ 201.—Short title

This chapter may be cited as the "Fair Labor Standards Act of 1938".

§ 202. Congressional finding and declaration of policy

(a) The Congress finds that the existence, in industries engaged in commerce or in the production of goods for commerce, of labor conditions detrimental to the maintenance of the minimum standard of living necessary for health, efficiency, and general well-being of workers

(1) causes commerce and the channels and instrumentalities of commerce to be used to spread and perpetuate such labor conditions among the workers of the several States;

(2) burdens commerce and the free flow of goods in commerce;

(3) constitutes an unfair method of competition in commerce;

(4) leads to labor disputes burdening and obstructing commerce and the free flow of goods in commerce; and

(5) interferes with the orderly and fair marketing of goods in commerce. That Congress further finds that the employment of persons in domestic service in households affects commerce.

(b) It is declared to be the policy of this chapter, through the exercise by Congress of its power to regulate commerce among the several States and with foreign nations, to correct and as rapidly as practicable to eliminate the conditions above referred to in such industries without substantially curtailing employment or earning power.

§ 203. Definitions

As used in this chapter—

(a) "Person" means an individual, partnership, association, corporation, business trust, legal representative, or any organized group of persons.

(b) "Commerce" means trade, commerce, transportation, transmission, or communication among the several States or between any State and any place outside thereof.

(c) "State" means any State of the United States or the District of Columbia or any Territory or possession of the United States.

(d) "Employer" includes any person acting directly or indirectly in the interest of an employer in relation to an employee and includes a public agency, but does not include any labor organization (other than when acting as an employer) or anyone acting in the capacity of officer or agent of such labor organization.

(e)

(1) Except as provided in paragraphs (2), (3), and (4), the term "employee" means any individual employed by an employer.

(2) In the case of an individual employed by a public agency, such term means—

(a) any individual employed by the Government of the United States—

(i) as a civilian in the military departments (as defined in section 102 of title 5),

(ii) in any executive agency (as defined in section 105 of such title),

(iii) in any unit of the judicial branch of the Government which has positions in the competitive service,

(iv) in a nonappropriated fund instrumentality under the jurisdiction of the Armed Forces,

(v) in the Library of Congress, or

(vi) the [1] Government Printing Office; "in".

(b) any individual employed by the United States Postal Service or the Postal Rate Commission; and

(c) any individual employed by a State, political subdivision of a State, or an interstate governmental agency, other than such an individual—

(i) who is not subject to the civil service laws of the State, political subdivision, or agency which employes him; and

(ii) who—

(i) holds a public elective office of that State, political subdivision, or agency,

(ii) is selected by the holder of such an office to be a member of his personal staff,

(iii) is appointed by such an officeholder to serve on a policymaking level,

(iv) is an immediate adviser to such an officeholder with respect to the constitutional or legal powers of his office, or

(v) is an employee in the legislative branch or legislative body of that State, political subdivision, or agency and is not employed by the legislative library of such State, political subdivision, or agency.

(3) For purposes of subsection (u) of this section, such term does not include any individual employed by an employer engaged in agriculture if such individual is the parent, spouse, child, or other member of the employer's immediate family.

(4)

(a) The term "employee" does not include any individual who volunteers to perform services for a public agency which is a State, a political sub-division of a State, or an interstate governmental agency, if—

(i) the individual receives no compensation or is paid expenses, reasonable benefits, or a nominal fee to perform the services for which the individual volunteered; and

(ii) such services are not the same type of services which the individual is employed to perform for such public agency.

(b) An employee of a public agency which is a State, political subdivision of a State, or an interstate governmental agency may volunteer to perform services for any other State, political subdivision, or interstate governmental agency, including a State, political subdivision or agency with which the employing State, political subdivision, or agency has a mutual aid agreement.

(5) The term "employee" does not include individuals who volunteer their services solely for humanitarian purposes to private non-profit food banks and who receive from the food banks groceries.

(f) "Agriculture" includes farming in all its branches and among other things includes the cultivation and tillage of the soil, dairying, the production, cultivation, growing, and harvesting of any agricultural or horticultural commodities (including commodities defined as agricultural commodities in section 1141j(g) of title 12), the raising of livestock, bees, fur-bearing animals, or poultry, and any practices (including any forestry or lumbering operations) performed by a farmer or on a farm as an incident to or in conjunction with such farming operations, including preparation for market, delivery to storage or to market or to carriers for transportation to market.

(g) "Employ" includes to suffer or permit to work.

(h) "Industry" means a trade, business, industry, or other activity, or branch or group thereof, in which individuals are gainfully employed.

(i) "Goods" means goods (including ships and marine equipment), wares, products, commodities, merchandise, or articles or subjects of commerce of any character, or any part or ingredient thereof, but does not include goods after their delivery into the actual physical possession of the ultimate consumer thereof other than a producer, manufacturer, or processor thereof.

(j) "Produced" means produced, manufactured, mined, handled, or in any other manner worked on in any State; and for the purposes of this chapter an employee shall be deemed to have been engaged in the production of goods if such employee was employed in producing, manufacturing, mining, handling, transporting, or in any other manner working on such goods, or in any closely related process or occupation directly essential to the production thereof, in any State,

(k) "Sale" or "sell" includes any sale, exchange, contract to sell, consignment for sale, shipment for sale, or other disposition.

(l) "Oppressive child labor" means a condition of employment under which

(1) any employee under the age of sixteen years is employed by an employer (other than a parent or a person standing in place of a parent employing his own child or a child in his custody under the age of sixteen years in an occupation other than manufacturing or mining or an occupation found by the Secretary of Labor to be particularly hazardous for the employment of children between the ages of sixteen and eighteen years or detrimental to their health or well-being) in any occupation, or

(2) any employee between the ages of sixteen and eighteen years is employed by an employer in any occupation which the Secretary of Labor shall find and by order declare to be particularly hazardous for the employment of children between such ages or detrimental to their health or well-being; but oppressive child labor shall not be deemed to exist by virtue of the employment in any occupation of any person with respect to whom the employer shall have on file an unexpired certificate issued and held pursuant to regulations of the Secretary of Labor certifying that such person is above the oppressive child-labor age. The Secretary of Labor shall provide by regulation or by order that the employment of employees between the ages of fourteen and sixteen years in occupations other than manufacturing and mining shall not be deemed to constitute oppressive child labor if and to the extent that the Secretary of Labor determines that such employment is confined to periods which will not interfere with their schooling and to conditions which will not interfere with their health and well-being.

(m) "Wage" paid to any employee includes the reasonable cost, as determined by the Administrator, to the employer of furnishing such employee with board, lodging, or other facilities, if such board, lodging or other facilities are customarily furnished by such employer to his employees: Provided, That the cost of board, lodging, or other facilities shall not be included as a part of the wage paid to any employee to the extent it is excluded therefrom under the terms of a bona fide collective-bargaining agreement applicable to the particular employee: Provided further, That the Secretary is authorized to determine the fair value of such board, lodging, or other facilities for defined classes of employees and in defined areas, based on average cost to the employer or to groups of employers similarly situated, or average value to groups of employees, or other appropriate measures of fair value. Such

evaluations, where applicable and pertinent, shall be used in lieu of actual measure of cost in determining the wage paid to any employee. In determining the wage an employer is required to pay a tipped employee, the amount paid such employee by the employee's employer shall be an amount equal to—

(1) the cash wage paid such employee which for purposes of such determination shall be not less than the cash wage required to be paid such an employee on August 20, 1996; and

(2) an additional amount on account of the tips received by such employee which amount is equal to the difference between the wage specified in paragraph (1) and the wage in effect under section 206(a)(1) of this title.

The additional amount on account of tips may not exceed the value of the tips actually received by an employee. The preceding 2 sentences shall not apply with respect to any tipped employee unless such employee has been informed by the employer of the provisions of this subsection, and all tips received by such employee have been retained by the employee, except that this subsection shall not be construed to prohibit the pooling of tips among employees who customarily and regularly receive tips.

(n) "Resale" shall not include the sale of goods to be used in residential or farm building construction, repair, or maintenance: Provided, That the sale is recognized as a bona fide retail sale in the industry.

(o) Hours Worked.—

In determining for the purposes of sections 206 and 207 of this title the hours for which an employee is employed, there shall be excluded any time spent in changing clothes or washing at the beginning or end of each workday which was excluded from measured working time during the week involved by the express terms of or by custom or practice under a bona fide collective-bargaining agreement applicable to the particular employee.

(p) "American vessel" includes any vessel which is documented or numbered under the laws of the United States.

(q) "Secretary" means the Secretary of Labor.

(r)

(1) "Enterprise" means the related activities performed (either through unified operation or common control) by any person or persons for a common business purpose, and includes all such activities whether performed in one or more establishments or by one or more corporate or other organizational units

including departments of an establishment operated through leasing arrangements, but shall not include the related activities performed for such enterprise by an independent contractor. Within the meaning of this subsection, a retail or service establishment which is under independent ownership shall not be deemed to be so operated or controlled as to be other than a separate and distinct enterprise by reason of any arrangement, which includes, but is not necessarily limited to, an agreement,

(a) that it will sell, or sell only, certain goods specified by a particular manufacturer, distributor, or advertiser, or

(b) that it will join with other such establishments in the same industry for the purpose of collective purchasing, or

(c) that it will have the exclusive right to sell the goods or use the brand name of a manufacturer, distributor, or advertiser within a specified area, or by reason of the fact that it occupies premises leased to it by a person who also leases premises to other retail or service establishments.

(2) For purposes of paragraph (1), the activities performed by any person or persons—

(a) in connection with the operation of a hospital, an institution primarily engaged in the care of the sick, the aged, the mentally ill or defective who reside on the premises of such institution, a school for mentally or physically handicapped or gifted children, a preschool, elementary or secondary school, or an institution of higher education (regardless of whether or not such hospital, institution, or school is operated for profit or not for profit), or

(b) in connection with the operation of a street, suburban or interurban electric railway, or local trolley or motorbus carrier, if the rates and services of such railway or carrier are subject to regulation by a State or local agency (regardless of whether or not such railway or carrier is public or private or operated for profit or not for profit), or

(c) in connection with the activities of a public agency,

shall be deemed to be activities performed for a business purpose.

(s)

(1) "Enterprise engaged in commerce or in the production of goods for commerce" means an enterprise that—

(a)

(i) has employees engaged in commerce or in the production of goods for commerce, or that has employees handling, selling, or otherwise working on goods or materials that have been moved in or produced for commerce by any person; and

(ii) is an enterprise whose annual gross volume of sales made or business done is not less than $500,000 (exclusive of excise taxes at the retail level that are separately stated);

(b) is engaged in the operation of a hospital, an institution primarily engaged in the care of the sick, the aged, or the mentally ill or defective who reside on the premises of such institution, a school for mentally or physically handicapped or gifted children, a preschool, elementary or secondary school, or an institution of higher education (regardless of whether or not such hospital, institution, or school is public or private or operated for profit or not for profit); or

(c) is an activity of a public agency.

(2) Any establishment that has as its only regular employees the owner thereof or the parent, spouse, child, or other member of the immediate family of such owner shall not be considered to be an enterprise engaged in commerce or in the production of goods for commerce or a part of such an enterprise. The sales of such an establishment shall not be included for the purpose of determining the annual gross volume of sales of any enterprise for the purpose of this subsection.

(t) "Tipped employee" means any employee engaged in an occupation in which he customarily and regularly receives more than $30 a month in tips.

(v) "Elementary school" means a day or residential school which provides elementary education, as determined under State law.

(u) "Man-day" means any day during which an employee performs any agricultural labor for not less than one hour.

(w) "Secondary school" means a day or residential school which provides secondary education, as determined under State law.

(x) "Public agency" means the Government of the United States; the government of a State or political subdivision thereof; any agency of the United States (including the United States Postal Service and Postal Rate Commission), a State, or a political subdivision of a State; or any interstate governmental agency.

(y) "Employee in fire protection activities" means an employee, including a firefighter, paramedic, emergency medical technician, rescue worker, ambulance personnel, or hazardous materials worker, who—

(1) is trained in fire suppression, has the legal authority and responsibility to engage in fire suppression, and is employed by a fire department of a municipality, county, fire district, or State; and

(2) is engaged in the prevention, control, and extinguishment of fires or response to emergency situations where life, property, or the environment is at risk.

§ 204. Administration

(a) Creation of Wage and Hour Division in Department of Labor; Administrator

There is created in the Department of Labor a Wage and Hour Division which shall be under the direction of an Administrator, to be known as the Administrator of the Wage and Hour Division (in this chapter referred to as the "Administrator"). The Administrator shall be appointed by the President, by and with the advice and consent of the Senate.

(b) Appointment, selection, classification, and promotion of employees by Administrator

The Administrator may, subject to the civil-service laws, appoint such employees as he deems necessary to carry out his functions and duties under this chapter and shall fix their compensation in accordance with chapter 51 and subchapter III of chapter 53 of title 5. The Administrator may establish and utilize such regional, local, or other agencies, and utilize such voluntary and uncompensated services, as may from time to time be needed. Attorneys appointed under this section may appear for and represent the Administrator in any litigation, but all such litigation shall be subject to the direction and control of the Attorney General. In the appointment, selection, classification, and promotion of officers and employees of the Administrator, no political test or qualification shall be permitted or given consideration, but all such appointments and promotions shall be given and made on the basis of merit and efficiency.

(c) Principal office of Administrator; jurisdiction

The principal office of the Administrator shall be in the District of Columbia, but he or his duly authorized representative may exercise any or all of his powers in any place.

(d) Biennial report to Congress; studies of exemptions to hour and wage provisions and means to prevent curtailment of employment opportunities

(1) The Secretary shall submit biennially in January a report to the Congress covering his activities for the preceding two years and including such information,

data, and recommendations for further legislation in connection with the matters covered by this chapter as he may find advisable. Such report shall contain an evaluation and appraisal by the Secretary of the minimum wages and overtime coverage established by this chapter, together with his recommendations to the Congress. In making such evaluation and appraisal, the Secretary shall take into consideration any changes which may have occurred in the cost of living and in productivity and the level of wages in manufacturing, the ability of employers to absorb wage increases, and such other factors as he may deem pertinent. Such report shall also include a summary of the special certificates issued under section 214(b) of this title.

(2) The Secretary shall conduct studies on the justification or lack thereof for each of the special exemptions set forth in section 213 of this title, and the extent to which such exemptions apply to employees of establishments described in subsection (g) of such section and the economic effects of the application of such exemptions to such employees. The Secretary shall submit a report of his findings and recommendations to the Congress with respect to the studies conducted under this paragraph not later than January 1, 1976.

(3) The Secretary shall conduct a continuing study on means to prevent curtailment of employment opportunities for manpower groups which have had historically high incidences of unemployment (such as disadvantaged minorities, youth, elderly, and such other groups as the Secretary may designate). The first report of the results of such study shall be transmitted to the Congress not later than one year after the effective date of the Fair Labor Standards Amendments of 1974. Subsequent reports on such study shall be transmitted to the Congress at two-year intervals after such effective date. Each such report shall include suggestions respecting the Secretary's authority under section 214 of this title.

(e) Study of effects of foreign production on unemployment; report to President and Congress

Whenever the Secretary has reason to believe that in any industry under this chapter the competition of foreign producers in United States markets or in markets abroad, or both, has resulted, or is likely to result, in increased unemployment in the United States, he shall undertake an investigation to gain full information with respect to the matter. If he determines such increased unemployment has in fact resulted, or is in fact likely to result, from such competition, he shall make a full and complete report of his findings and determinations to the President and to the Congress: Provided, That he may also include in such report information on the increased employment resulting from additional exports in any industry under this chapter as he may determine to be pertinent to such report.

(f) Employees of Library of Congress; administration of provisions by Office of Personnel Management

The Secretary is authorized to enter into an agreement with the Librarian of Congress with respect to individuals employed in the Library of Congress to provide for the carrying out of the Secretary's functions under this chapter with respect to such individuals.

Notwithstanding any other provision of this chapter, or any other law, the Director of the Office of Personnel Management is authorized to administer the provisions of this chapter with respect to any individual employed by the United States (other than an individual employed in the Library of Congress, United States Postal Service, Postal Rate Commission, or the Tennessee Valley Authority). Nothing in this subsection shall be construed to affect the right of an employee to bring an action for unpaid minimum wages, or unpaid overtime compensation, and liquidated damages under section 216(b) of this title.

§ 205. Special industry committees for American Samoa

(Not printed here.)

§ 206. Minimum wage

(a) Employees engaged in commerce; home workers in Puerto Rico and Virgin Islands; employees in American Samoa; seamen on American vessels; agricultural employees.

Every employer shall pay to each of his employees who in any workweek is engaged in commerce or in the production of goods for commerce, or is employed in an enterprise engaged in commerce or in the production of goods for commerce, wages at the following rates:

(1) except as otherwise provided in this section, not less than $4.25 an hour during the period ending on September 30, 1996, not less than $4.75 an hour during the year beginning on October 1, 1996, and not less than $5.15 an hour beginning September 1, 1997;

(2) if such employee is a home worker in Puerto Rico or the Virgin Islands, not less than the minimum piece rate prescribed by regulation or order; or, if no such minimum piece rate is in effect, any piece rate adopted by such employer which shall yield, to the proportion

or class of employees prescribed by regulation or order, not less than the applicable minimum hourly wage rate. Such minimum piece rates or employer piece rates shall be commensurate with, and shall be paid in lieu of, the minimum hourly wage rate applicable under the provisions of this section. The Administrator, or his authorized representative, shall have power to make such regulations or orders as are necessary or appropriate to carry out any of the provisions of this paragraph, including the power without limiting the generality of the foregoing, to define any operation or occupation which is performed by such home work employees in Puerto Rico or the Virgin Islands; to establish minimum piece rates for any operation or occupation so defined; to prescribe the method and procedure for ascertaining and promulgating minimum piece rates; to prescribe standards for employer piece rates, including the proportion or class of employees who shall receive not less than the minimum hourly wage rate; to define the term "home worker"; and to prescribe the conditions under which employers, agents, contractors, and subcontractors shall cause goods to be produced by home workers;

(3) if such employee is employed in American Samoa, in lieu of the rate or rates provided by this subsection or subsection (b) of this section, not less than the applicable rate established by the Secretary of Labor in accordance with recommendations of a special industry committee or committees which he shall appoint pursuant to sections 205 and 208 of this title. The minimum wage rate thus established shall not exceed the rate prescribed in paragraph (1) of this subsection;

(4) if such employee is employed as a seaman on an American vessel, not less than the rate which will provide to the employee, for the period covered by the wage payment, wages equal to compensation at the hourly rate prescribed by paragraph (1) of this subsection for all hours during such period when he was actually on duty (including periods aboard ship when the employee was on watch or was, at the direction of a superior officer, performing work or standing by, but not including off-duty periods which are provided pursuant to the employment agreement); or

(5) if such employee is employed in agriculture, not less than the minimum wage rate in effect under paragraph (1) after December 31, 1977.

(b) Additional applicability to employees pursuant to subsequent amendatory provisions

Every employer shall pay to each of his employees (other than an employee to whom subsection (a)(5) of this section applies) who in any workweek is engaged in commerce or in the production of goods for commerce, or is employed in an enterprise engaged in commerce or in the production of goods for commerce, and who in such workweek is brought within the purview of this section by the amendments made to this chapter by the Fair Labor Standards Amendments of 1966; title IX of the Education Amendments of 1972 (20 U.S.C. 1681 et seq.), or the Fair Labor Standards Amendments of 1974, wages at the following rate: Effective after December 31, 1977, not less than the minimum wage rate in effect under subsection (a)(1) of this section.

(c) Repealed. Pub. L. 104-188, (title II), § 2104(c), Aug. 20, 1996, 110 Stat. 1929

(d) Prohibition of sex discrimination

(1) No employer having employees subject to any provisions of this section shall discriminate, within any establishment in which such employees are employed, between employees on the basis of sex by paying wages to employees in such establishment at a rate less than the rate at which he pays wages to employees of the opposite sex in such establishment for equal work on jobs the performance of which requires equal skill, effort, and responsibility, and which are performed under similar working conditions, except where such payment is made pursuant to

(i) a seniority system;

(ii) a merit system;

(iii) a system which measures earnings by quantity or quality of production; or

(iv) a differential based on any other factor other than sex: Provided, That an employer who is paying a wage rate differential in violation of this subsection shall not, in order to comply with the provisions of this subsection, reduce the wage rate of any employee.

(2) No labor organization, or its agents, representing employees of an employer having employees subject to any provisions of this section shall cause or attempt to cause such an employer to discriminate against an employee in violation of paragraph (1) of this subsection.

(3) For purposes of administration and enforcement, any amounts owing to any employee which have been withheld in violation of this subsection shall be deemed to be unpaid minimum wages or unpaid overtime compensation under this chapter.

(4) As used in this subsection, the term "labor organization" means any organization of any kind, or any agency or employee representation committee or plan, in which employees participate and which exists for the purpose, in whole or in part, of dealing with employers concerning grievances, labor disputes, wages, rates of pay, hours of employment, or conditions of work.

(e) Employees of employers providing contract services to United States

(1) Notwithstanding the provisions of section 213 of this title (except subsections (a)(1) and (f) thereof), every employer providing any contract services (other than linen supply services) under a contract with the United States or any subcontract thereunder shall pay to each of his employees whose rate of pay is not governed by the Service Contract Act of 1965 (41 U.S.C. 351-357) or to whom subsection (a)(1) of this section is not applicable, wages at rates not less than the rates provided for in subsection (b) of this section.

(2) Notwithstanding the provisions of section 213 of this title (except subsections (a)(1) and (f) thereof) and the provisions of the Service Contract Act of 1965 (41 U.S.C. 351 et seq.) every employer in an establishment providing linen supply services to the United States under a contract with the United States or any subcontract thereunder shall pay to each of his employees in such establishment wages at rates not less than those prescribed in subsection (b) of this section, except that if more than 50 per centum of the gross annual dollar volume of sales made or business done by such establishment is derived from providing such linen supply services under any such contracts or subcontracts, such employer shall pay to each of his employees in such establishment wages at rates not less than those prescribed in subsection (a)(1) of this section.

(f) Employees in domestic service

Any employee—

(1) who in any workweek is employed in domestic service in a household shall be paid wages at a rate not less than the wage rate in effect under subsection (b) of this section unless such employee's compensation for such service would not because of section 209(a)(6) of the Social Security Act (42 U.S.C. 409(a)(6)) constitute wages for the purposes of title II of such Act (42 U.S.C. 401 et seq.), or

(2) who in any workweek—

(a) is employed in domestic service in one or more households, and

(b) is so employed for more than 8 hours in the aggregate, shall be paid wages for such employment in such workweek at a rate not less than the wage rate in effect under subsection (b) of this section.

(g) Newly hired employees who are less than 20 years old

(1) In lieu of the rate prescribed by subsection (a)(1) of this section, any employer may pay any employee of such employer, during the first 90 consecutive calendar days after such employee is initially employed by such employer, a wage which is not less than $4.25 an hour.

(2) No employer may take any action to displace employees (including partial displacements such as reduction in hours, wages, or employment benefits) for purposes of hiring individuals at the wage authorized in paragraph (1).

(3) Any employer who violates this subsection shall be considered to have violated section 215(a)(3) of this title.

(4) This subsection shall only apply to an employee who has not attained the age of 20 years.

§ 207. Maximum hours

(a) Employees engaged in interstate commerce; additional applicability to employees pursuant to subsequent amendatory provisions

(1) Except as otherwise provided in this section, no employer shall employ any of his employees who in any workweek is engaged in commerce or in the production of goods for commerce, or is employed in an enterprise engaged in commerce or in the production of goods for commerce, for a workweek longer than forty hours unless such employee receives compensation for his employment in excess of the hours above specified at a rate not less than one and one-half times the regular rate at which he is employed.

(2) No employer shall employ any of his employees who in any workweek is engaged in commerce or in the production of goods for commerce, or is employed in an enterprise engaged in commerce or in the production of goods for commerce, and who in such workweek is brought within the purview of this subsection by the amendments made to this chapter by the Fair Labor Standards Amendments of 1966—

(a) for a workweek longer than forty-four hours during the first year from the effective date of the Fair Labor Standards Amendments of 1966,

(b) for a workweek longer than forty-two hours during the second year from such date, or

(c) for a workweek longer than forty hours after the expiration of the second year from such date,

unless such employee receives compensation for his employment in excess of the hours above specified at a rate not less than one and one-half times the regular rate at which he is employed.

(b) Employment pursuant to collective bargaining agreement; employment by independently owned and controlled local enterprise engaged in distribution of petroleum products

No employer shall be deemed to have violated subsection (a) of this section by employing any employee for a workweek in excess of that specified in such subsection without paying the compensation for overtime employment prescribed therein if such employee is so employed—

(1) in pursuance of an agreement, made as a result of collective bargaining by representatives of employees certified as bona fide by the National Labor Relations Board, which provides that no employee shall be employed more than one thousand and forty hours during any period of twenty-six consecutive weeks; or

(2) in pursuance of an agreement, made as a result of collective bargaining by representatives of employees certified as bona fide by the National Labor Relations Board, which provides that during a specified period of fifty-two consecutive weeks the employee shall be employed not more than two thousand two hundred and forty hours and shall be guaranteed not less than one thousand eight hundred and forty-hours (or not less than forty-six weeks at the normal number of hours worked per week, but not less than thirty hours per week) and not more than two thousand and eighty hours of employment for which he shall receive compensation for all hours guaranteed or worked at rates not less than those applicable under the agreement to the work performed and for all hours in excess of the guaranty which are also in excess of the maximum workweek applicable to such employee under subsection (a) of this section or two thousand and eighty in such period at rates not less than one and one-half times the regular rate at which he is employed; or

(3) by an independently owned and controlled local enterprise (including an enterprise with more than one bulk storage establishment) engaged in the wholesale or bulk distribution of petroleum products if—

(a) the annual gross volume of sales of such enterprise is less than $1,000,000 exclusive of excise taxes,

(b) more than 75 per centum of such enterprise's annual dollar volume of sales is made within the State in which such enterprise is located, and

(c) not more than 25 per centum of the annual dollar volume of sales of such enterprise is to customers who are engaged in the bulk distribution of such products for resale,

and such employee receives compensation for employment in excess of forty hours in any workweek at a rate not less than one and one-half times the minimum wage rate applicable to him under section 206 of this title, and if such employee receives compensation for employment in excess of twelve hours in any workday, or for employment in excess of fifty-six hours in any workweek, as the case may be, at a rate not less than one and one-half times the regular rate at which he is employed.

(c), (d), (e) Repealed. Pub. L. 93-259, § 1, Apr. 8, 1974, 88 Stat. 66

(e) "Regular rate" defined

As used in this section the "regular rate" at which an employee is employed shall be deemed to include all remuneration for employment paid to, or on behalf of, the employee, but shall not be deemed to include—

(1) sums paid as gifts; payments in the nature of gifts made at Christmas time or on other special occasions, as a reward for service, the amounts of which are not measured by or dependent on hours worked, production, or efficiency;

(2) payments made for occasional periods when no work is performed due to vacation, holiday, illness, failure of the employer to provide sufficient work, or other similar cause; reasonable payments for traveling expenses, or other expenses, incurred by an employee in the furtherance of his employer's interests and properly reimbursable by the employer; and other similar payments to an employee which are not made as compensation for his hours of employment;

(3) Sums [1] paid in recognition of services performed during a given period if either,

(a) both the fact that payment is to be made and the amount of the payment are determined at the sole discretion of the employer at or near the end of the period and not pursuant to any prior contract, agreement, or promise causing the employee to expect such payments regularly; or

(b) the payments are made pursuant to a bona fide profit-sharing plan or trust or bona fide thrift or savings plan, meeting the requirements of the Administrator set forth in appropriate regulations

which he shall issue, having due regard among other relevant factors, to the extent to which the amounts paid to the employee are determined without regard to hours of work, production, or efficiency; or

(c) the payments are talent fees (as such talent fees are defined and delimited by regulations of the Administrator) paid to performers, including announcers, on radio and television programs;

(4) contributions irrevocably made by an employer to a trustee or third person pursuant to a bona fide plan for providing old-age, retirement, life, accident, or health insurance or similar benefits for employees;

(5) extra compensation provided by a premium rate paid for certain hours worked by the employee in any day of workweek because such hours are hours worked in excess of eight in a day or in excess of the maximum workweek applicable to such employee under subsection (a) of this section or in excess of the employee's normal working hours or regular working hours, as the case may be;

(6) extra compensation provided by a premium rate paid for work by the employee on Saturdays, Sundays, holidays, or regular days of rest, or on the sixth or seventh day of the workweek, where such premium rate is not less than one and one-half times the rate established in good faith for like work performed in nonovertime hours on other days;

(7) extra compensation provided by a premium rate paid to the employee, in pursuance of an applicable employment contract or collective-bargaining agreement, for work outside of the hours established in good faith by the contract or agreement as the basic, normal, or regular workday (not exceeding eight hours) or workweek (not exceeding the maximum workweek applicable to such employee under subsection (a) of this section, [2] where such premium rate is not less than one and one-half times the rate established in good faith by the contract or agreement for like work performed during such workday or workweek; or

(8) any value or income derived from employer-provided grants or rights provided pursuant to a stock option, stock appreciation right, or bona fide employee stock purchase program which is not otherwise excludable under any of paragraphs (1) through (7) if—

(a) grants are made pursuant to a program, the terms and conditions of which are communicated to participating employees either at the beginning of the employee's participation in the program or at the time of the grant;

(b) in the case of stock options and stock appreciation rights, the grant or right cannot be exercisable for a period of at least 6 months after the time of grant (except that grants or rights may become exercisable because of an employee's death, disability, retirement, or a change in corporate ownership, or other circumstances permitted by regulation), and the exercise price is at least 85 percent of the fair market value of the stock at the time of grant;

(c) exercise of any grant or right is voluntary; and

(d) any determinations regarding the award of, and the amount of, employer-provided grants or rights that are based on performance are—

(i) made based upon meeting previously established performance criteria (which may include hours of work, efficiency, or productivity) of any business unit consisting of at least 10 employees or of a facility, except that, any determinations may be based on length of service or minimum schedule of hours or days of work; or

(ii) made based upon the past performance (which may include any criteria) of one or more employees in a given period so long as the determination is in the sole discretion of the employer and not pursuant to any prior contract.

(f) Employment necessitating irregular hours of work

No employer shall be deemed to have violated subsection (a) of this section by employing any employee for a workweek in excess of the maximum workweek applicable to such employee under subsection (a) of this section if such employee is employed pursuant to a bona fide individual contract, or pursuant to an agreement made as a result of collective bargaining by representatives of employees, if the duties of such employee necessitate irregular hours of work, and the contract or agreement

(1) specifies a regular rate of pay of not less than the minimum hourly rate provided in subsection (a) or (b) of section 206 of this title (whichever may be applicable) and compensation at not less than one and one-half times such rate for all hours worked in excess of such maximum workweek, and

(2) provides a weekly guaranty of pay for not more than sixty hours based on the rates so specified.

(g) Employment at piece rates

No employer shall be deemed to have violated subsection (a) of this section by employing any employee for a workweek in excess of the maximum workweek applicable to such employee under such subsection if, pursuant to an agreement or understanding arrived at between the employer and the employee before performance of the work, the amount paid to the employee for the number of hours worked by him in such workweek in excess of the maximum workweek applicable to such employee under such subsection—

(1) in the case of an employee employed at piece rates, is computed at piece rates not less than one and one-half times the bona fide piece rates applicable to the same work when performed during nonovertime hours; or

(2) in the case of an employee performing two or more kinds of work for which different hourly or piece rates have been established, is computed at rates not less than one and one-half times such bona fide rates applicable to the same work when performed during nonovertime hours; or

(3) is computed at a rate not less than one and one-half times the rate established by such agreement or understanding as the basic rate to be used in computing overtime compensation thereunder: Provided, That the rate so established shall be authorized by regulation by the Administrator as being substantially equivalent to the average hourly earnings of the employee, exclusive of overtime premiums, in the particular work over a representative period of time; and if

(i) the employee's average hourly earnings for the workweek exclusive of payments described in paragraphs (1) through (7) of subsection (e) of this section are not less than the minimum hourly rate required by applicable law, and

(ii) extra overtime compensation is properly computed and paid on other forms of additional pay required to be included in computing the regular rate.

(h) Credit toward minimum wage or overtime compensation of amounts excluded from regular rate

(1) Except as provided in paragraph (2), sums excluded from the regular rate pursuant to subsection (e) of this section shall not be creditable toward wages required under section 206 of this title or overtime compensation required under this section.

(2) Extra compensation paid as described in paragraphs (5), (6), and (7) of subsection (e) of this section shall be creditable toward overtime compensation payable pursuant to this section.

(i) Employment by retail or service establishment

No employer shall be deemed to have violated subsection (a) of this section by employing any employee of a retail or service establishment for a workweek in excess of the applicable workweek specified therein, if

(1) the regular rate of pay of such employee is in excess of one and one-half times the minimum hourly rate applicable to him under section 206 of this title, and

(2) more than half his compensation for a representative period (not less than one month) represents commissions on goods or services. In determining the proportion of compensation representing commissions, all earnings resulting from the application of a bona fide commission rate shall be deemed commissions on goods or services without regard to whether the computed commissions exceed the draw or guarantee.

(j) Employment in hospital or establishment engaged in care of sick, aged, or mentally ill

No employer engaged in the operation of a hospital or an establishment which is an institution primarily engaged in the care of the sick, the aged, or the mentally ill or defective who reside on the premises shall be deemed to have violated subsection (a) of this section if, pursuant to an agreement or understanding arrived at between the employer and the employee before performance of the work, a work period of fourteen consecutive days is accepted in lieu of the workweek of seven consecutive days for purposes of overtime computation and if, for his employment in excess of eight hours in any workday and in excess of eighty hours in such fourteen-day period, the employee receives compensation at a rate not less than one and one-half times the regular rate at which he is employed.

(k) Employment by public agency engaged in fire protection or law enforcement activities

No public agency shall be deemed to have violated subsection (a) of this section with respect to the employment of any employee in fire protection activities or any employee in law enforcement activities (including security personnel in correctional institutions) if—

(1) in a work period of 28 consecutive days the employee receives for tours of duty which in the aggregate exceed the lesser of

(a) 216 hours, or

(b) the average number of hours (as determined by the Secretary pursuant to section 6(c)(3) of the Fair Labor Standards Amendments of 1974) in tours of duty of employees engaged in such activities in work periods of 28 consecutive days in calendar year 1975; or

(2) in the case of such an employee to whom a work period of at least 7 but less than 28 days applies, in his work period the employee receives for tours of duty which in the aggregate exceed a number of hours which bears the same ratio to the number of consecutive days in his work period as 216 hours (or if lower, the number of hours referred to in clause (B) of paragraph (1)) bears to 28 days,

compensation at a rate not less than one and one-half times the regular rate at which he is employed.

(l) Employment in domestic service in one or more households

No employer shall employ any employee in domestic service in one or more households for a workweek longer than forty hours unless such employee receives compensation for such employment in accordance with subsection (a) of this section.

(m) Employment in tobacco industry

For a period or periods of not more than fourteen workweeks in the aggregate in any calendar year, any employer may employ any employee for a workweek in excess of that specified in subsection (a) of this section without paying the compensation for overtime employment prescribed in such subsection, if such employee—

(1) is employed by such employer—

(a) to provide services (including stripping and grading) necessary and incidental to the sale at auction of green leaf tobacco of type 11, 12, 13, 14, 21, 22, 23, 24, 31, 35, 36, or 37 (as such types are defined by the Secretary of Agriculture), or in auction sale, buying, handling, stemming, redrying, packing, and storing of such tobacco,

(b) in auction sale, buying, handling, sorting, grading, packing, or storing green leaf tobacco of type 32 (as such type is defined by the Secretary of Agriculture), or

(c) in auction sale, buying, handling, stripping, sorting, grading, sizing, packing, or stemming prior to packing, of perishable cigar leaf tobacco of type 41, 42, 43, 44, 45, 46, 51, 52, 53, 54, 55, 61, or 62 (as such types are defined by the Secretary of Agriculture); and

(2) receives for—

(a) such employment by such employer which is in excess of ten hours in any workday, and

(b) such employment by such employer which is in excess of forty-eight hours in any workweek,

compensation at a rate not less than one and one-half times the regular rate at which he is employed.

An employer who receives an exemption under this subsection shall not be eligible for any other exemption under this section.

(n) Employment by street, suburban, or interurban electric railway, or local trolley or motorbus carrier

In the case of an employee of an employer engaged in the business of operating a street, suburban or interurban electric railway, or local trolley or motorbus carrier (regardless of whether or not such railway or carrier is public or private or operated for profit or not for profit), in determining the hours of employment of such an employee to which the rate prescribed by subsection (a) of this section applies there shall be excluded the hours such employee was employed in charter activities by such employer if

(1) the employee's employment in such activities was pursuant to an agreement or understanding with his employer arrived at before engaging in such employment, and

(2) if employment in such activities is not part of such employee's regular employment.

(o) Compensatory time

(1) Employees of a public agency which is a State, a political subdivision of a State, or an interstate governmental agency may receive, in accordance with this subsection and in lieu of overtime compensation, compensatory time off at a rate not less than one and one-half hours for each hour of employment for which overtime compensation is required by this section.

(2) A public agency may provide compensatory time under paragraph (1) only—

(a) pursuant to—

(i) applicable provisions of a collective bargaining agreement, memorandum of understanding, or any other agreement between the public agency and representatives of such employees; or

(ii) in the case of employees not covered by subclause (i), an agreement or understanding arrived at between the employer and employee before the performance of the work; and

(b) if the employee has not accrued compensatory time in excess of the limit applicable to the employee prescribed by paragraph (3).

In the case of employees described in clause (A)(ii) hired prior to April 15, 1986, the regular practice in effect on April 15, 1986, with respect to compensatory time off for such employees in lieu of the receipt of overtime compensation, shall constitute an agreement or understanding under such clause (A)(ii). Except as provided in the previous sentence, the provision of compensatory time off to such employees for hours worked after April 14, 1986, shall be in accordance with this subsection.

(3)

(a) If the work of an employee for which compensatory time may be provided included work in a public safety activity, an emergency response activity, or a seasonal activity, the employee engaged in such work may accrue not more than 480 hours of compensatory time for hours worked after April 15, 1986. If such work was any other work, the employee engaged in such work may accrue not more than 240 hours of compensatory time for hours worked after April 15, 1986. Any such employee who, after April 15, 1986, has accrued 480 or 240 hours, as the case may be, of compensatory time off shall, for additional overtime hours of work, be paid overtime compensation.

(b) If compensation is paid to an employee for accrued compensatory time off, such compensation shall be paid at the regular rate earned by the employee at the time the employee receives such payment.

(4) An employee who has accrued compensatory time off authorized to be provided under paragraph (1) shall, upon termination of employment, be paid for the unused compensatory time at a rate of compensation not less than—

(a) the average regular rate received by such employee during the last 3 years of the employee's employment, or

(b) the final regular rate received by such employee,

whichever is higher [3].

(5) An employee of a public agency which is a State, political subdivision of a State, or an interstate governmental agency—

(a) who has accrued compensatory time off authorized to be provided under paragraph (1), and

(b) who has requested the use of such compensatory time,

shall be permitted by the employee's employer to use such time within a reasonable period after making the request if the use of the compensatory time does not unduly disrupt the operations of the public agency.

(6) The hours an employee of a public agency performs court reporting transcript preparation duties shall not be considered as hours worked for the purposes of subsection (a) of this section if—

(a) such employee is paid at a per-page rate which is not less than—

(i) the maximum rate established by State law or local ordinance for the jurisdiction of such public agency,

(ii) the maximum rate otherwise established by a judicial or administrative officer and in effect on July 1, 1995, or

(iii) the rate freely negotiated between the employee and the party requesting the transcript, other than the judge who presided over the proceedings being transcribed, and

(b) the hours spent performing such duties are outside of the hours such employee performs other work (including hours for which the agency requires the employee's attendance) pursuant to the employment relationship with such public agency.

For purposes of this section, the amount paid such employee in accordance with subparagraph (A) for the performance of court reporting transcript preparation duties, shall not be considered in the calculation of the regular rate at which such employee is employed.

(7) For purposes of this subsection—

(a) the term "overtime compensation" means the compensation required by subsection (a), and

(b) the terms "compensatory time" and "compensatory time off" mean hours during which an employee is not working, which are not counted as hours worked during the applicable workweek or other work period for purposes of overtime compensation, and for which the employee is compensated at the employee's regular rate.

(p) Special detail work for fire protection and law enforcement employees; occasional or sporadic employment; substitution

(1) If an individual who is employed by a State, political subdivision of a State, or an interstate governmental agency in fire protection or law enforcement activities (including activities of security personnel in correctional institutions) and who, solely at such individual's option, agrees to be employed on a special detail by a separate or independent employer in fire protection, law enforcement, or related activities, the hours such individual was employed by such separate and independent employer shall be excluded by the public agency employing such individual in the calculation of the

hours for which the employee is entitled to overtime compensation under this section if the public agency—

(a) requires that its employees engaged in fire protection, law enforcement, or security activities be hired by a separate and independent employer to perform the special detail,

(b) facilitates the employment of such employees by a separate and independent employer, or

(c) otherwise affects the condition of employment of such employees by a separate and independent employer.

(2) If an employee of a public agency which is a State, political subdivision of a State, or an interstate governmental agency undertakes, on an occasional or sporadic basis and solely at the employee's option, part-time employment for the public agency which is in a different capacity from any capacity in which the employee is regularly employed with the public agency, the hours such employee was employed in performing the different employment shall be excluded by the public agency in the calculation of the hours for which the employee is entitled to overtime compensation under this section.

(3) If an individual who is employed in any capacity by a public agency which is a State, political subdivision of a State, or an interstate governmental agency, agrees, with the approval of the public agency and solely at the option of such individual, to substitute during scheduled work hours for another individual who is employed by such agency in the same capacity, the hours such employee worked as a substitute shall be excluded by the public agency in the calculation of the hours for which the employee is entitled to overtime compensation under this section.

(q) Maximum hour exemption for employees receiving remedial education

Any employer may employ any employee for a period or periods of not more than 10 hours in the aggregate in any workweek in excess of the maximum workweek specified in subsection (a) of this section without paying the compensation for overtime employment prescribed in such subsection, if during such period or periods the employee is receiving remedial education that is—

(1) provided to employees who lack a high school diploma or educational attainment at the eighth grade level;

(2) designed to provide reading and other basic skills at an eighth grade level or below; and

(3) does not include job specific training.

§ 208. Wage orders in American Samoa

(Not printed here.)

§ 209. Attendance of witnesses

For the purpose of any hearing or investigation provided for in this chapter, the provisions of sections 49 and 50 of title 15 (relating to the attendance of witnesses and the production of books, papers, and documents), are made applicable to the jurisdiction, powers, and duties of the Administrator, the Secretary of Labor, and the industry committees.

§ 210. Court review of wage orders in Puerto Rico and the Virgin Islands

(Not printed here.)

§ 211. Collection of data

(a) Investigations and inspections

The Administrator or his designated representatives may investigate and gather data regarding the wages, hours, and other conditions and practices of employment in any industry subject to this chapter, and may enter and inspect such places and such records (and make such transcriptions thereof), question such employees, and investigate such facts, conditions, practices, or matters as he may deem necessary or appropriate to determine whether any person has violated any provision of this chapter, or which may aid in the enforcement of the provisions of this chapter. Except as provided in section 212 of this title and in subsection (b) of this section, the Administrator shall utilize the bureaus and divisions of the Department of Labor for all the investigations and inspections necessary under this section. Except as provided in section 212 of this title, the Administrator shall bring all actions under section 217 of this title to restrain violations of this chapter.

(b) State and local agencies and employees

With the consent and cooperation of State agencies charged with the administration of State labor laws, the Administrator and the Secretary of Labor may, for the purpose of carrying out their respective functions and duties under this chapter, utilize the services of State and local agencies and their employees and, notwithstanding any other provision of law, may reimburse such State and local agencies and their employees for services rendered for such purposes.

(c) Records

Every employer subject to any provision of this chapter or of any order issued under this chapter shall make, keep, and preserve such records of the persons employed by him and of the wages, hours, and other conditions and practices of employment maintained by him, and shall preserve such records for such periods of time, and shall make such reports therefrom to the Administrator as he shall prescribe by regulation or order as necessary or appropriate for the enforcement of the provisions of this chapter or the regulations or orders thereunder. The employer of an employee who performs substitute work described in section 207(p)(3) of this title may not be required under this subsection to keep a record of the hours of the substitute work.

(d) Homework regulations

The Administrator is authorized to make such regulations and orders regulating, restricting, or prohibiting industrial homework as are necessary or appropriate to prevent the circumvention or evasion of and to safeguard the minimum wage rate prescribed in this chapter, and all existing regulations or orders of the Administrator relating to industrial homework are continued in full force and effect.

§ 212. Child labor provisions

(a) Restrictions on shipment of goods; prosecution; conviction

No producer, manufacturer, or dealer shall ship or deliver for shipment in commerce any goods produced in an establishment situated in the United States in or about which within thirty days prior to the removal of such goods therefrom any oppressive child labor has been employed: Provided, That any such shipment or delivery for shipment of such goods by a purchaser who acquired them in good faith in reliance on written assurance from the producer, manufacturer, or dealer that the goods were produced in compliance with the requirements of this section, and who acquired such goods for value without notice of any such violation, shall not be deemed prohibited by this subsection: And provided further, That a prosecution and conviction of a defendant for the shipment or delivery for shipment of any goods under the conditions herein prohibited shall be a bar to any further prosecution against the same defendant for shipments or deliveries for shipment of any such goods before the beginning of said prosecution.

(b) Investigations and inspections

The Secretary of Labor or any of his authorized representatives, shall make all investigations and inspections under section 211(a) of this title with respect to the employment of minors, and, subject to the direction and control of the Attorney General, shall bring all actions under section 217 of this title to enjoin any act or practice which is unlawful by reason of the existence of oppressive child labor, and shall administer all other provisions of this chapter relating to oppressive child labor.

(c) Oppressive child labor

No employer shall employ any oppressive child labor in commerce or in the production of goods for commerce or in any enterprise engaged in commerce or in the production of goods for commerce.

(d) Proof of age

In order to carry out the objectives of this section, the Secretary may by regulation require employers to obtain from any employee proof of age.

§ 213. Exemptions

(a) Minimum wage and maximum hour requirements

The provisions of sections 206 (except subsection (d) in the case of paragraph (1) of this subsection) and section 207 of this title shall not apply with respect to—

(1) any employee employed in a bona fide executive, administrative, or professional capacity (including any employee employed in the capacity of academic administrative personnel or teacher in elementary or secondary schools), or in the capacity of outside salesman (as such terms are defined and delimited from time to time by regulations of the Secretary, subject to the provisions of subchapter II of chapter 5 of title 5, except that an employee of a retail or service establishment shall not be excluded from the definition of employee employed in a bona fide executive or administrative capacity because of the number of hours in his workweek which he devotes to activities not directly or closely related to the performance of executive or administrative activities, if less than 40 per centum of his hours worked in the workweek are devoted to such activities); or

(2) Repealed. Pub. L. 101-157, § 3(c)(1), Nov. 17, 1989, 103 Stat. 939

(3) any employee employed by an establishment which is an amusement or recreational establishment organized camp, or religious or non-profit educational conference center, if

(a) it does not operate for more than seven months in any calendar year, or

(b) during the preceding calendar year, its average receipts for any six months of such year were not more than 33 1/3 per centum of its average receipts for the other six months of such year, except that the exemption from sections 206 and 207 of this title provided by this paragraph does not apply with respect to any employee of a private entity

engaged in providing services or facilities (other than, in the case of the exemption from section 206 of this title, a private entity engaged in providing services and facilities directly related to skiing) in a national park or a national forest, or on land in the National Wildlife Refuge System, under a contract with the Secretary of the Interior or the Secretary of Agriculture; or

(4) Repealed. Pub. L. 101-157, § 3(c)(1), Nov. 17, 1989, 103 Stat. 939

(5) any employee employed in the catching, taking, propagating, harvesting, cultivating, or farming of any kind of fish, shellfish, crustacea, sponges, seaweeds, or other aquatic forms of animal and vegetable life, or in the first processing, canning or packing such marine products at sea as an incident to, or in conjunction with, such fishing operations, including the going to and returning from work and loading and unloading when performed by any such employee; or

(6) any employee employed in agriculture

(a) if such employee is employed by an employer who did not, during any calendar quarter during the preceding calendar year, use more than five hundred man-days of agricultural labor,

(b) if such employee is the parent, spouse, child, or other member of his employer's immediate family,

(c) if such employee

(i) is employed as a hand harvest laborer and is paid on a piece rate basis in an operation which has been, and is customarily and generally recognized as having been, paid on a piece rate basis in the region of employment,

(ii) commutes daily from his permanent residence to the farm on which he is so employed, and

(iii) has been employed in agriculture less than thirteen weeks during the preceding calendar year,

(d) if such employee (other than an employee described in clause (C) of this subsection)

(i) is sixteen years of age or under and is employed as a hand harvest laborer, is paid on a piece rate basis in an operation which has been, and is customarily and generally recognized as having been, paid on a piece rate basis in the region of employment,

(ii) is employed on the same farm as his parent or person standing in the place of his parent, and

(iii) is paid at the same piece rate as employees over age sixteen are paid on the same farm, or

(e) if such employee is principally engaged in the range production of livestock; or

(7) any employee to the extent that such employee is exempted by regulations, order, or certificate of the Secretary issued under section 214 of this title; or

(8) any employee employed in connection with the publication of any weekly, semiweekly, or daily newspaper with a circulation of less than four thousand the major part of which circulation is within the county where published or counties contiguous thereto; or

(9) Repealed. Pub. L. 93-259, § 23(a)(1), Apr. 8, 1974, 88 Stat. 69.

(10) any switchboard operator employed by an independently owned public telephone company which has not more than seven hundred and fifty stations; or

(11) Repealed. Pub. L. 93-259, § 10(a), Apr. 8, 1974, 88 Stat. 63

(12) any employee employed as a seaman on a vessel other than an American vessel; or

(13), (14) Repealed. Pub. L. 93-259, § 9(b)(1), 23(b)(1), Apr. 8, 1974, 88 Stat. 63, 69

(15) any employee employed on a casual basis in domestic service employment to provide babysitting services or any employee employed in domestic service employment to provide companionship services for individuals who (because of age or infirmity) are unable to care for themselves (as such terms are defined and delimited by regulations of the Secretary); or

(16) a criminal investigator who is paid availability pay under section 5545a of title 5; or

(17) any employee who is a computer systems analyst, computer programmer, software engineer, or other similarly skilled worker, whose primary duty is—

(a) the application of systems analysis techniques and procedures, including consulting with users, to determine hardware, software, or system functional specifications;

(b) the design, development, documentation, analysis, creation, testing, or modification of computer systems or programs, including prototypes, based on and related to user or system design specifications;

(c) the design, documentation, testing, creation, or modification of computer programs related to machine operating systems; or

(d) a combination of duties described in subparagraphs (A), (B), and (C) the performance of which requires the same level of skills, and who, in the case of an employee who is compensated on an hourly basis, is compensated at a rate of not less than $27.63 an hour.

(b) Maximum hour requirements

The provisions of section 207 of this title shall not apply with respect to—

(1) any employee with respect to whom the Secretary of Transportation has power to establish qualifications and maximum hours of service pursuant to the provisions of section 31502 of title 49; or

(2) any employee of an employer engaged in the operation of a rail carrier subject to part A of subtitle IV of title 49; or

(3) any employee of a carrier by air subject to the provisions of title II of the Railway Labor Act (45 U.S.C. 181 et seq.); or

(4) Repealed. Pub. L. 93-259, § 11(c), Apr. 8, 1974, 88 Stat. 64

(5) any individual employed as an outside buyer of poultry, eggs, cream, or milk, in their raw or natural state; or

(6) any employee employed as a seaman; or

(7) Repealed. Pub. L. 93-259, § 21(b)(3), Apr. 8, 1974, 88 Stat. 68

(8) Repealed. Pub. L. 95-151, § 14(b), Nov. 1, 1977, 91 Stat. 1252

(9) any employee employed as an announcer, news editor, or chief engineer by a radio or television station the major studio of which is located

(a) in a city or town of one hundred thousand population or less, according to the latest available decennial census figures as compiled by the Bureau of the Census, except where such city or town is part of a standard metropolitan statistical area, as defined and designated by the Office of Management and Budget, which has a total population in excess of one hundred thousand, or

(b) in a city or town of twenty-five thousand population or less, which is part of such an area but is at least 40 airline miles from the principal city in such area; or

(10)

(a) any salesman, partsman, or mechanic primarily engaged in selling or servicing automobiles, trucks, or farm implements, if he is employed by a non-manufacturing establishment primarily engaged in the business of selling such vehicles or implements to ultimate purchasers; or

(b) any salesman primarily engaged in selling trailers, boats, or aircraft, if he is employed by a nonmanufacturing establishment primarily engaged in the business of selling trailers, boats, or aircraft to ultimate purchasers; or

(11) any employee employed as a driver or driver's helper making local deliveries, who is compensated for such employment on the basis of trip rates, or other delivery payment plan, if the Secretary shall find that such plan has the general purpose and effect of reducing hours worked by such employees to, or below, the maximum workweek applicable to them under section 207(a) of this title; or

(12) any employee employed in agriculture or in connection with the operation or maintenance of ditches, canals, reservoirs, or waterways, not owned or operated for profit, or operated on a sharecrop basis, and which are used exclusively for supply and storing of water, at least 90 percent of which was ultimately delivered for agricultural purposes during the preceding calendar year; or

(13) any employee with respect to his employment in agriculture by a farmer, notwithstanding other employment of such employee in connection with livestock auction operations in which such farmer is engaged as an adjunct to the raising of livestock, either on his own account or in conjunction with other farmers, if such employee

(a) is primarily employed during his workweek in agriculture by such farmer, and

(b) is paid for his employment in connection with such livestock auction operations at a wage rate not less than that prescribed by section 206(a)(1) of this title; or

(14) any employee employed within the area of production (as defined by the Secretary) by an establishment commonly recognized as a country elevator, including such an establishment which sells products and services used in the operation of a farm, if no more than five employees are employed in the establishment in such operations; or

(15) any employee engaged in the processing of maple sap into sugar (other than refined sugar) or syrup; or

(16) any employee engaged

(a) in the transportation and preparation for transportation of fruits or vegetables, whether or not performed by the farmer, from the farm to a place of first processing or first marketing within the same State, or

(b) in transportation, whether or not performed by the farmer, between the farm and any point within the same State of persons employed or to be employed in the harvesting of fruits or vegetables; or

(17) any driver employed by an employer engaged in the business of operating taxicabs; or

(18), (19) Repealed. Pub. L. 93-259, § 15(c), 16(b), Apr. 8, 1974, 88 Stat. 65

(20) any employee of a public agency who in any workweek is employed in fire protection activities or any employee of a public agency who in any workweek is employed in law enforcement activities (including security personnel in correctional institutions), if the public agency employs during the workweek less than 5 employees in fire protection or law enforcement activities, as the case may be; or

(21) any employee who is employed in domestic service in a household and who resides in such household; or

(22) Repealed. Pub. L. 95-151, § 5, Nov. 1, 1977, 91 Stat. 1249

(23) Repealed. Pub. L. 93-259, § 10(b)(3), Apr. 8, 1974, 88 Stat. 64

(24) any employee who is employed with his spouse by a nonprofit educational institution to serve as the parents of children—

(a) who are orphans or one of whose natural parents is deceased, or

(b) who are enrolled in such institution and reside in residential facilities of the institution,

while such children are in residence at such institution, if such employee and his spouse reside in such facilities, receive, without cost, board and lodging from such institution, and are together compensated, on a cash basis, at an annual rate of not less than $10,000; or

(25), (26) Repealed. Pub. L. 95-151, § 6(a), 7(a), Nov. 1, 1977, 91 Stat. 1249, 1250

(27) any employee employed by an establishment which is a motion picture theater; or

(28) any employee employed in planting or tending trees, cruising, surveying, or felling timber, or in preparing or transporting logs or other forestry products to the mill, processing plant, railroad, or other transportation terminal, if the number of employees employed by his employer in such forestry or lumbering operations does not exceed eight;

(29) any employee of an amusement or recreational establishment located in a national park or national forest or on land in the National Wildlife Refuge System if such employee

(a) is an employee of a private entity engaged in providing services or facilities in a national park or national forest, or on land in the National Wildlife Refuge System, under a contract with the Secretary of the Interior or the Secretary of Agriculture, and

(b) receives compensation for employment in excess of fifty-six hours in any workweek at a rate not less than one and one-half times the regular rate at which he is employed; or

(30) a criminal investigator who is paid availability pay under section 5545a of title 5.

(c) Child labor requirements

(1) Except as provided in paragraph (2) or (4), the provisions of section 212 of this title relating to child labor shall not apply to any employee employed in agriculture outside of school hours for the school district where such employee is living while he is so employed, if such employee—

(a) is less than twelve years of age and

(i) is employed by his parent, or by a person standing in the place of his parent, on a farm owned or operated by such parent or person, or

(ii) is employed, with the consent of his parent or person standing in the place of his parent, on a farm, none of the employees of which are (because of subsection (a)(6)(A) of this section) required to be paid at the wage rate prescribed by section 206(a)(5) of this title,

(b) is twelve years or thirteen years of age and

(i) such employment is with the consent of his parent or person standing in the place of his parent, or

(ii) his parent or such person is employed on the same farm as such employee, or

(c) is fourteen years of age or older.

(2) The provisions of section 212 of this title relating to child labor shall apply to an employee below the age of sixteen employed in agriculture in an occupation that the Secretary of Labor finds and declares to be particularly hazardous for the employment of children below the age of sixteen, except where such employee is employed by his parent or by a person standing in the place of his parent on a farm owned or operated by such parent or person.

(3) The provisions of section 212 of this title relating to child labor shall not apply to any child employed as an actor or performer in motion pictures or theatrical productions, or in radio or television productions.

(4)

(a) An employer or group of employers may apply to the Secretary for a waiver of the application of section 212 of this title to the employment for not more than eight weeks in any calendar year of individuals who are less than twelve years of age, but not less than ten years of age, as hand harvest laborers in an agricultural operation which has been, and is customarily and generally recognized as being, paid on a piece rate basis in the region in which such individuals would be employed. The Secretary may not grant such a waiver unless he finds, based on objective data submitted by the applicant, that—

(i) the crop to be harvested is one with a particularly short harvesting season and the application of section 212 of this title would cause severe economic disruption in the industry of the employer or group of employers applying for the waiver;

(ii) the employment of the individuals to whom the waiver would apply would not be deleterious to their health or well-being;

(iii) the level and type of pesticides and other chemicals used would not have an adverse effect on the health or well-being of the individuals to whom the waiver would apply;

(iv) individuals age twelve and above are not available for such employment; and

(v) the industry of such employer or group of employers has traditionally and substantially employed individuals under twelve years of age without displacing substantial job opportunities for individuals over sixteen years of age.

(b) Any waiver granted by the Secretary under subparagraph (A) shall require that—

(i) the individuals employed under such waiver be employed outside of school hours for the school district where they are living while so employed;

(ii) such individuals while so employed commute daily from their permanent residence to the farm on which they are so employed; and

(iii) such individuals be employed under such waiver

(i) for not more than eight weeks between June 1 and October 15 of any calendar year, and

(ii) in accordance with such other terms and conditions as the Secretary shall prescribe for such individuals' protection.

(5)

(a) In the administration and enforcement of the child labor provisions of this chapter, employees who are 16 and 17 years of age shall be permitted to load materials into, but not operate or unload materials from, scrap paper balers and paper box compactors—

(i) that are safe for 16- and 17-year-old employees loading the scrap paper balers or paper box compactors; and

(ii) that cannot be operated while being loaded.

(b) For purposes of subparagraph (A), scrap paper balers and paper box compactors shall be considered safe for 16- or 17-year-old employees to load only if—

(i)

(i) the scrap paper balers and paper box compactors meet the American National Standards Institute's Standard ANSI Z245.5-1990 for scrap paper balers and Standard ANSI Z245.2-1992 for paper box compactors; or

(ii) the scrap paper balers and paper box compactors meet an applicable standard that is adopted by the American National Standards Institute after August 6, 1996, and that is certified by the Secretary to be at least as protective of the safety of minors as the standard described in subclause (i);

(ii) the scrap paper balers and paper box compactors include an on-off switch incorporating a key-lock or other system and the control of the system is maintained in the custody of employees who are 18 years of age or older;

(iii) the on-off switch of the scrap paper balers and paper box compactors is maintained in an off position when the scrap paper balers and paper box compactors are not in operation; and

(iv) the employer of 16- and 17-year-old employees provides notice, and posts a notice, on the scrap paper balers and paper box compactors stating that—

(i) the scrap paper balers and paper box compactors meet the applicable standard described in clause (i);

(ii) 16- and 17-year-old employees may only load the scrap paper balers and paper box compactors; and

(iii) any employee under the age of 18 may not operate or unload the scrap paper balers and paper box compactors.

The Secretary shall publish in the Federal Register a standard that is adopted by the American National Standards Institute for scrap paper balers or paper box compactors and certified by the Secretary to be protective of the safety of minors under clause (i)(ii).

(c)

(i) Employers shall prepare and submit to the Secretary reports—

(i) on any injury to an employee under the age of 18 that requires medical treatment (other than first aid) resulting from the employee's contact with a scrap paper baler or paper box compactor during the loading, operation, or unloading of the baler or compactor; and

(ii) on any fatality of an employee under the age of 18 resulting from the employee's contact with a scrap paper baler or paper box compactor during the loading, operation, or unloading of the baler or compactor.

(ii) The reports described in clause (i) shall be used by the Secretary to determine whether or not the implementation of subparagraph (A) has had any effect on the safety of children.

(iii) The reports described in clause (i) shall provide—

(i) the name, telephone number, and address of the employer and the address of the place of employment where the incident occurred;

(ii) the name, telephone number, and address of the employee who suffered an injury or death as a result of the incident;

(iii) the date of the incident;

(iv) a description of the injury and a narrative describing how the incident occurred; and

(v) the name of the manufacturer and the model number of the scrap paper baler or paper box compactor involved in the incident.

(iv) The reports described in clause (i) shall be submitted to the Secretary promptly, but not later than 10 days after the date on which an incident relating to an injury or death occurred.

(v) The Secretary may not rely solely on the reports described in clause (i) as the basis for making a determination that any of the employers described in clause (i) has violated a provision of section 212 of this title relating to oppressive child labor or a regulation or order issued pursuant to section 212 of this title. The Secretary shall, prior to making such a determination, conduct an investigation and inspection in accordance with section 212(b) of this title.

(vi) The reporting requirements of this subparagraph shall expire 2 years after August 6, 1996.

(6) In the administration and enforcement of the child labor provisions of this chapter, employees who are under 17 years of age may not drive automobiles or trucks on public roadways. Employees who are 17 years of age may drive automobiles or trucks on public roadways only if—

(a) such driving is restricted to daylight hours;

(b) the employee holds a State license valid for the type of driving involved in the job performed and has no records of any moving violation at the time of hire;

(c) the employee has successfully completed a State approved driver education course;

(d) the automobile or truck is equipped with a seat belt for the driver and any passengers and the employee's employer has instructed the employee that the seat belts must be used when driving the automobile or truck;

(e) the automobile or truck does not exceed 6,000 pounds of gross vehicle weight;

(f) such driving does not involve—

(i) the towing of vehicles;

(ii) route deliveries or route sales;

(iii) the transportation for hire of property, goods, or passengers;

(iv) urgent, time-sensitive deliveries;

(v) more than two trips away from the primary place of employment in any single day for the purpose of delivering goods of the employee's employer to a customer (other than urgent, time-sensitive deliveries);

(vi) more than two trips away from the primary place of employment in any single day for the purpose of transporting passengers (other than employees of the employer);

(vii) transporting more than three passengers (including employees of the employer); or

(viii) driving beyond a 30-mile radius from the employee's place of employment; and

(g) such driving is only occasional and incidental to the employee's employment.

For purposes of subparagraph (g), the term "occasional and incidental" is no more than one-third of an employee's worktime in any workday and no more than 20 percent of an employee's worktime in any workweek.

(d) Delivery of newspapers and wreathmaking

The provisions of sections 206, 207, and 212 of this title shall not apply with respect to any employee engaged in the delivery of newspapers to the consumer or to any homeworker engaged in the making of wreaths composed principally of natural holly, pine, cedar, or other evergreens (including the harvesting of the evergreens or other forest products used in making such wreaths).

(e) Maximum hour requirements and minimum wage employees

The provisions of section 207 of this title shall not apply with respect to employees for whom the Secretary of Labor is authorized to establish minimum wage rates as provided in section 206(a)(3) of this title, except with respect to employees for whom such rates are in effect; and with respect to such employees the Secretary may make rules and regulations providing reasonable limitations and allowing reasonable variations, tolerances, and exemptions to and from any or all of the provisions of section 207 of this title if he shall find, after a public hearing on the matter, and taking into account the factors set forth in section 206(a)(3) of this title, that economic conditions warrant such action.

(f) Employment in foreign countries and certain United States territories

The provisions of sections 206, 207, 211, and 212 of this title shall not apply with respect to any employee whose services during the workweek are performed in a workplace within a foreign country or within territory under the jurisdiction of the United States other than the following: a State of the United States; the District of Columbia; Puerto Rico; the Virgin Islands; outer Continental Shelf lands defined in the Outer Continental Shelf Lands Act (ch. 345, 67 Stat. 462) (43 U.S.C. 1331 et seq.); American Samoa; Guam; Wake Island; Eniwetok Atoll; Kwajalein Atoll; and Johnston Island.

(g) Certain employment in retail or service establishments, agriculture

The exemption from section 206 of this title provided by paragraph (6) of subsection (a) of this section shall not apply with respect to any employee employed by an establishment

(1) which controls, is controlled by, or is under common control with, another establishment the activities of which are not related for a common business purpose to, but materially support the activities of the establishment employing such employee; and

(2) whose annual gross volume of sales made or business done, when combined with the annual gross volume of sales made or business done by each establishment which controls, is controlled by, or is under common control with, the establishment employing such employee, exceeds $10,000,000 (exclusive of excise taxes at the retail level which are separately stated).

(h) Maximum hour requirement: fourteen workweek limitation

The provisions of section 207 of this title shall not apply for a period or periods of not more than fourteen workweeks in the aggregate in any calendar year to any employee who—

(1) is employed by such employer—

(a) exclusively to provide services necessary and incidental to the ginning of cotton in an establishment primarily engaged in the ginning of cotton;

(b) exclusively to provide services necessary and incidental to the receiving, handling, and storing of raw cotton and the compressing of raw cotton when performed at a cotton warehouse or compress-warehouse facility, other than one operated in conjunction with a cotton mill, primarily engaged in storing and compressing;

(c) exclusively to provide services necessary and incidental to the receiving, handling, storing, and processing of cottonseed in an establishment primarily engaged in the receiving, handling, storing, and processing of cottonseed; or

(d) exclusively to provide services necessary and incidental to the processing of sugar cane or sugar beets in an establishment primarily engaged in the processing of sugar cane or sugar beets; and

(2) receives for—

(a) such employment by such employer which is in excess of ten hours in any workday, and

(b) such employment by such employer which is in excess of forty-eight hours in any workweek,

compensation at a rate not less than one and one-half times the regular rate at which he is employed.

Any employer who receives an exemption under this subsection shall not be eligible for any other exemption under this section or section 207 of this title.

(i) Cotton ginning

The provisions of section 207 of this title shall not apply for a period or periods of not more than fourteen workweeks in the aggregate in any period of fifty-two consecutive weeks to any employee who—

(1) is engaged in the ginning of cotton for market in any place of employment located in a county where cotton is grown in commercial quantities; and

(2) receives for any such employment during such workweeks—

(a) in excess of ten hours in any workday, and

(b) in excess of forty-eight hours in any workweek,

compensation at a rate not less than one and one-half times the regular rate at which he is employed. No week included in any fifty-two week period for purposes of the preceding sentence may be included for such purposes in any other fifty-two week period.

(j) Processing of sugar beets, sugar beet molasses, or sugar cane

The provisions of section 207 of this title shall not apply for a period or periods of not more than fourteen workweeks in the aggregate in any period of fifty-two consecutive weeks to any employee who—

(1) is engaged in the processing of sugar beets, sugar beet molasses, or sugar cane into sugar (other than refined sugar) or syrup; and

(2) receives for any such employment during such workweeks—

(a) in excess of ten hours in any workday, and

(b) in excess of forty-eight hours in any workweek,

compensation at a rate not less than one and one-half times the regular rate at which he is employed. No week included in any fifty-two week period for purposes of the preceding sentence may be included for such purposes in any other fifty-two week period.

§ 214. Employment under special certificates

(a) Learners, apprentices, messengers

The Secretary, to the extent necessary in order to prevent curtailment of opportunities for employment, shall by regulations or by orders provide for the employment of learners, of apprentices, and of messengers employed primarily in delivering letters and messages, under special certificates issued pursuant to regulations of the Secretary, at such wages lower than the minimum wage applicable under section 206 of this title and subject to such limitations as to time, number, proportion, and length of service as the Secretary shall prescribe.

(b) Students

(1)

(a) The Secretary, to the extent necessary in order to prevent curtailment of opportunities for employment, shall by special certificate issued under a regulation or order provide, in accordance with subparagraph (b), for the employment, at a wage rate not less than 85 per centum of the otherwise applicable wage rate in effect under section 206 of this title or not less than $1.60 an hour, whichever is the higher, of full-time students (regardless of age but in compliance with applicable child labor laws) in retail or service establishments.

(b) Except as provided in paragraph (4)(b), during any month in which full-time students are to be employed in any retail or service establishment under certificates issued under this subsection the proportion of student hours of employment to the total hours of employment of all employees in such establishment may not exceed—

(i) in the case of a retail or service establishment whose employees (other than employees engaged in commerce or in the production of goods for commerce) were covered by this chapter before the effective date of the Fair Labor Standards Amendments of 1974—

(i) the proportion of student hours of employment to the total hours of employment of all employees in such establishment for the corresponding month of the immediately preceding twelve-month period,

(ii) the maximum proportion for any corresponding month of student hours of employment to the total hours of employment of all employees in such establishment applicable to the issuance of certificates under this section at any time before the effective date of the Fair Labor Standards Amendments of 1974 for the employment of students by such employer, or

(iii) a proportion equal to one-tenth of the total hours of employment of all employees in such establishment,

whichever is greater;

(ii) in the case of retail or service establishment whose employees (other than employees engaged in commerce or in the production of goods for commerce) are covered for the first time on or after the effective date of the Fair Labor Standards Amendments of 1974—

(i) the proportion of hours of employment of students in such establishment to the total hours of employment of all employees in such establishment for the corresponding month of the twelve-month period immediately prior to the effective date of such Amendments,

(ii) the proportion of student hours of employment to the total hours of employment of all employees in such establishment for the corresponding month of the immediately preceding twelve-month period, or

(iii) a proportion equal to one-tenth of the total hours of employment of all employees in such establishment, whichever is greater; or

(iii) in the case of a retail or service establishment for which records of student hours worked are not available, the proportion of student hours of employment to the total hours of employment of all employees based on the practice during the immediately preceding twelve-month period in

(i) similar establishments of the same employer in the same general metropolitan area in which such establishment is located,

(ii) similar establishments of the same or nearby communities if such establishment is not in a metropolitan area, or

(iii) other establishments of the same general character operating in the community or the nearest comparable community.

For purpose of clauses (i), (ii), and (iii) of this subparagraph, the term "student hours of employment" means hours during which students are employed in a retail or service establishment under certificates issued under this subsection.

(2) The Secretary, to the extent necessary in order to prevent curtailment of opportunities for employment, shall by special certificate issued under a regulation or order provide for the employment, at a wage rate not less than 85 per centum of the wage rate in effect under section 206(a)(5) of this title or not less than $1.30 an hour, whichever is the higher, of full-time students (regardless of age but in compliance with applicable child labor laws) in any occupation in agriculture.

(3) The Secretary, to the extent necessary in order to prevent curtailment of opportunities for employment, shall by special certificate issued under a regulation or order provide for the employment by an institution of higher education, at a wage rate not less than 85 per centum of the otherwise applicable wage rate in effect under section 206 of this title or not less than $1.60 an hour, whichever is the higher, of full-time students (regardless of age but in compliance with applicable child labor laws) who are enrolled in such institution. The Secretary shall by regulation prescribe standards and requirements to insure that this paragraph will not create a substantial probability of reducing the full-time employment opportunities of persons other than those to whom the minimum wage rate authorized by this paragraph is applicable.

(4)

(a) A special certificate issued under paragraph (1), (2), or (3) shall provide that the student or students for whom it is issued shall, except during vacation periods, be employed on a part-time basis and not in excess of twenty hours in any workweek.

(b) If the issuance of a special certificate under paragraph (1) or (2) for an employer will cause the number of students employed by such employer under special certificates issued under this sub-section to exceed six, the Secretary may not issue such a special certificate for the employment of a student by such employer unless the Secretary finds employment of such student will not create a substantial probability of reducing the full-time employment opportunities of persons other than those employed under special certificates issued under this subsection. If the issuance of a special certificate under paragraph (1) or (2) for an employer will not cause the number of students employed by such employer under special certificates issued under this subsection to exceed six—

(i) the Secretary may issue a special certificate under paragraph (1) or (2) for the employment of a student by such employer if such employer certifies to the Secretary that the employment of such student will not reduce the full-time employment opportunities of persons other than those employed under special certificates issued under this subsection, and

(ii) in the case of an employer which is a retail or service establishment, subparagraph (b) of paragraph (1) shall not apply with respect to the issuance of special certificates for such employer under such paragraph.

The requirement of this subparagraph shall not apply in the case of the issuance of special certificates under paragraph (3) for the employment of full-time students by institutions of higher education; except that if the Secretary determines that an institution of higher education is employing students under certificates issued under paragraph (3) but in violation of the requirements of that paragraph or of regulations issued thereunder, the requirements of this subparagraph shall apply with respect to the issuance of special certificates under paragraph (3) for the employment of students by such institution.

(c) No special certificate may be issued under this subsection unless the employer for whom the certificate is to be issued provides evidence satisfactory to the Secretary of the student status of the employees to be employed under such special certificate.

(d) To minimize paperwork for, and to encourage, small businesses to employ students under special certificates issued under paragraphs (1) and (2), the Secretary shall, by regulation or order, prescribe a simplified application form to be used by employers in applying for such a certificate for the employment of not more than six full-time students. Such an application shall require only—

(i) a listing of the name, address, and business of the applicant employer,

(ii) a listing of the date the applicant began business, and

(iii) the certification that the employment of such full-time students will not reduce the full-time employment opportunities of persons other than persons employed under special certificates.

(c) Handicapped workers

(1) The Secretary, to the extent necessary to prevent curtailment of opportunities for employment, shall by regulation or order provide for the employment, under special certificates, of individuals (including individuals employed in agriculture) whose earning or productive capacity is impaired by age, physical or mental deficiency, or injury, at wages which are—

(a) lower than the minimum wage applicable under section 206 of this title,

(b) commensurate with those paid to nonhandi-capped workers, employed in the vicinity in which the individuals under the certificates are employed, for essentially the same type, quality, and quantity of work, and

(c) related to the individual's productivity.

(2) The Secretary shall not issue a certificate under paragraph (1) unless the employer provides written assurances to the Secretary that—

(a) in the case of individuals paid on an hourly rate basis, wages paid in accordance with paragraph (1) will be reviewed by the employer at periodic intervals at least once every six months, and

(b) wages paid in accordance with paragraph (1) will be adjusted by the employer at periodic intervals, at least once each year, to reflect changes in the prevailing wage paid to experienced nonhandicapped individuals employed in the locality for essentially the same type of work.

(3) Notwithstanding paragraph (1), no employer shall be permitted to reduce the hourly wage rate prescribed by certificate under this subsection in effect on June 1, 1986, of any handicapped individual for a period of two years from such date without prior authorization of the Secretary.

(4) Nothing in this subsection shall be construed to prohibit an employer from maintaining or establishing work activities centers to provide therapeutic activities for handicapped clients.

(5)

(a) Notwithstanding any other provision of this subsection, any employee receiving a special minimum wage at a rate specified pursuant to this subsection or the parent or guardian of such an employee may petition the Secretary to obtain a review of such special minimum wage rate. An employee or the employee's parent or guardian may file such a petition for and in behalf of the employee or in behalf of the employee and other employees similarly situated. No employee may be a party to any such action unless the employee or the employee's parent or guardian gives consent in writing to become such a party and such consent is filed with the Secretary.

(b) Upon receipt of a petition filed in accordance with subparagraph (a), the Secretary within ten days shall assign the petition to an administrative law judge appointed pursuant to section 3105 of title 5. The administrative law judge shall conduct a hearing on the record in accordance with section 554 of title 5 with respect to such petition within thirty days after assignment.

(c) In any such proceeding, the employer shall have the burden of demonstrating that the special minimum wage rate is justified as necessary in order to prevent curtailment of opportunities for employment.

(d) In determining whether any special minimum wage rate is justified pursuant to subparagraph (c), the administrative law judge shall consider—

(i) the productivity of the employee or employees identified in the petition and the conditions under which such productivity was measured; and

(ii) the productivity of other employees performing work of essentially the same type and quality for other employers in the same vicinity.

(e) The administrative law judge shall issue a decision within thirty days after the hearing provided for in subparagraph (b). Such action shall be deemed to be a final agency action unless within thirty days the Secretary grants a request to review the decision of the administrative law judge. Either the petitioner or the employer may request review by the Secretary within fifteen days of the date of issuance of the decision by the administrative law judge.

(f) The Secretary, within thirty days after receiving a request for review, shall review the record and either adopt the decision of the administrative law judge or issue exceptions. The decision of the administrative law judge, together with any exceptions, shall be deemed to be a final agency action.

(g) A final agency action shall be subject to judicial review pursuant to chapter 7 of title 5. An action seeking such review shall be brought within thirty days of a final agency action described in subparagraph (f).

(d) Employment by schools

The Secretary may by regulation or order provide that sections 206 and 207 of this title shall not apply with respect to the employment by any elementary or secondary school of its students if such employment constitutes, as determined under regulations prescribed by the Secretary, an integral part of the regular education program provided by such school and such employment is in accordance with applicable child labor laws

§ 215. Prohibited acts; prima facie evidence

(a) After the expiration of one hundred and twenty days from June 25, 1938, it shall be unlawful for any person—

(1) to transport, offer for transportation, ship, deliver, or sell in commerce, or to ship, deliver, or sell with knowledge that shipment or delivery or sale thereof in commerce is intended, any goods in the production of which any employee was employed in violation of section 206 or section 207 of this title, or in violation of any regulation or order of the Secretary issued under section 214 of this title; except that no provision of this chapter shall impose any liability upon any common carrier for the transportation in commerce in the regular course of its business of any goods not produced by such common carrier, and no provision of this chapter shall excuse any common carrier from its obligation to accept any goods for transportation; and except that any such transportation, offer, shipment, delivery, or sale of such goods by a purchaser who acquired them in good faith in reliance on written assurance from the producer that the goods were produced in compliance with the requirements of this chapter, and who acquired such goods for value without notice of any such violation, shall not be deemed unlawful;

(2) to violate any of the provisions of section 206 or section 207 of this title, or any of the provisions of any regulation or order of the Secretary issued under section 214 of this title;

(3) to discharge or in any other manner discriminate against any employee because such employee has filed any complaint or instituted or caused to be instituted any proceeding under or related to this chapter, or has testified or is about to testify in any such proceeding, or has served or is about to serve on an industry committee;

(4) to violate any of the provisions of section 212 of this title;

(5) to violate any of the provisions of section 211(c) of this title, or any regulation or order made or continued in effect under the provisions of section 211(d) of this title, or to make any statement, report, or record filed or kept pursuant to the provisions of such section or of any regulation or order thereunder, knowing such statement, report, or record to be false in a material respect.

(b) For the purposes of subsection (a)(1) of this section proof that any employee was employed in any place of employment where goods shipped or sold in commerce were produced, within ninety days prior to the removal of the goods from such place of employment, shall be prima facie evidence that such employee was engaged in the production of such goods.

§ 216. Penalties

(a) Fines and imprisonment

Any person who willfully violates any of the provisions of section 215 of this title shall upon conviction thereof be subject to a fine of not more than $10,000, or to imprisonment for not more than six months, or both. No person shall be imprisoned under this subsection except for an offense committed after the conviction of such person for a prior offense under this subsection.

(b) Damages; right of action; attorney's fees and costs; termination of right of action

Any employer who violates the provisions of section 206 or section 207 of this title shall be liable to the employee or employees affected in the amount of their unpaid minimum wages, or their unpaid overtime compensation, as the case may be, and in an additional equal amount as liquidated damages. Any employer who violates the provisions of section 215(a)(3) of this title shall be liable for such legal or equitable relief as may be appropriate to effectuate the purposes of section 215(a)(3) of this title, including without limitation employment, reinstatement, promotion, and the payment of wages lost and an additional equal amount as liquidated damages. An action to recover the liability prescribed in either of the preceding sentences may be maintained against any employer (including a public agency) in any Federal or State court of competent jurisdiction by any one or more employees for and in behalf of himself or themselves and other employees similarly situated. No employee shall be a party plaintiff to any such action unless he gives his consent in writing to become such a party and such consent is filed in the court in which such action is brought. The court in such action shall, in addition to any judgment awarded to the plaintiff or plaintiffs, allow a reasonable attorney's fee to be paid by the defendant, and costs of the action. The right provided by this subsection to bring an action by or on behalf of any employee, and the right of any employee to become a party plaintiff to any such action, shall terminate upon the filing of a complaint by the Secretary of Labor in an action under section 217 of this title in which

(1) restraint is sought of any further delay in the payment of unpaid minimum wages, or the amount of unpaid overtime compensation, as the case may be, owing to such employee under section 206 or section 207 of this title by an employer liable therefor under the provisions of this subsection or

(2) legal or equitable relief is sought as a result of alleged violations of section 215(a)(3) of this title.

(c) Payment of wages and compensation; waiver of claims; actions by the Secretary; limitation of actions

The Secretary is authorized to supervise the payment of the unpaid minimum wages or the unpaid overtime compensation owing to any employee or employees under section 206 or section 207 of this title, and the agreement of any employee to accept such payment shall upon payment in full constitute a waiver by such employee of any right he may have under subsection (b) of this section to such unpaid minimum wages or unpaid overtime compensation and an additional equal amount as liquidated damages. The Secretary may bring an action in any court of competent jurisdiction to recover the amount of unpaid minimum wages or overtime compensation and an equal amount as liquidated damages. The right provided by subsection (b) of this section to bring an action by or on behalf of any employee to recover the liability specified in the first sentence of such subsection and of any employee to become a party plaintiff to any such action shall terminate upon the filing of a complaint by the Secretary in an action under this subsection in which a recovery is sought of unpaid minimum wages or unpaid overtime compensation under sections 206 and 207 of this title or liquidated or other damages provided by this subsection owing to such employee by an employer liable under the provisions of subsection (b) of this section, unless such action is dismissed without prejudice on motion of the Secretary. Any sums thus recovered by the Secretary of Labor on behalf of an employee pursuant to this subsection shall be held in a special deposit account and shall be paid, on order of the Secretary of Labor, directly to the employee or employees affected. Any such sums not paid to an employee because of inability to do so within a period of three years shall be covered into the Treasury of the United States as miscellaneous receipts. In determining when an action is commenced by the Secretary of Labor under this subsection for the purposes of the statutes of limitations provided in section 255(a) of this title, it shall be considered to be commenced in the case of any individual claimant on the date when the complaint is filed if he is specifically named as a party plaintiff in the complaint, or if his name did not so appear, on the subsequent date on which his name is added as a party plaintiff in such action.

(d) Savings provisions

In any action or proceeding commenced prior to, on, or after August 8, 1956, no employer shall be subject to any liability or punishment under this chapter or the Portal-to-Portal Act of 1947 (29 U.S.C. 251 et seq.) on account of his failure to comply with any provision or provisions of this chapter or such Act

(1) with respect to work heretofore or hereafter performed in a workplace to which the exemption in section 213(f) of this title is applicable,

(2) with respect to work performed in Guam, the Canal Zone or Wake Island before the effective date of this amendment of subsection (d), or (3) with respect to work performed in a possession named in section 206(a)(3) of this title at any time prior to the establishment by the Secretary, as provided therein, of a minimum wage rate applicable to such work.

(e) Civil penalties for child labor violations

Any person who violates the provisions of section 212 of this title or section 213(c)(5) of this title, relating to child labor, or any regulation issued under section 212 of this title or section 213(c)(5) of this title, shall be subject to a civil penalty of not to exceed $10,000 for each employee who was the subject of such a violation. Any person who repeatedly or willfully violates section 206 or 207 of this title shall be subject to a civil penalty of not to exceed $1,000 for each such violation. In determining the amount of any penalty under this subsection, the appropriateness of such penalty to the size of the business of the person charged and the gravity of the violation shall be considered. The amount of any penalty under this subsection, when finally determined, may be—

(1) deducted from any sums owing by the United States to the person charged;

(2) recovered in a civil action brought by the Secretary in any court of competent jurisdiction, in which litigation the Secretary shall be represented by the Solicitor of Labor; or

(3) ordered by the court, in an action brought for a violation of section 215(a)(4) of this title or a repeated or willful violation of section 215(a)(2) of this title, to be paid to the Secretary.

Any administrative determination by the Secretary of the amount of any penalty under this subsection shall be final, unless within fifteen days after receipt of notice thereof by certified mail the person charged with the violation takes exception to the determination that the violations for which the penalty is imposed occurred, in which event final determination of the penalty shall be made in an administrative proceeding after opportunity for hearing in accordance with section 554 of title 5, and regulations to be promulgated by the Secretary. Except for civil penalties collected for violations of section 212 of this title, sums collected as penalties pursuant to this section shall be applied toward reimbursement of the costs of determining the violations and assessing and collecting such penalties, in accordance with the provisions of section 9a of this title. Civil penalties collected for violations of section 212 of this title shall be deposited in the general fund of the Treasury

§ 216a.

Repealed. Oct. 26, 1949.

§ 216b. Liability for overtime work performed prior to July 20, 1949

(Not printed here.)

§ 217. Injunction proceedings

The district courts, together with the United States District Court for the District of the Canal Zone, the District Court of the Virgin Islands, and the District Court of Guam shall have jurisdiction, for cause shown, to restrain violations of section 215 of this title, including in the case of violations of section 215(a)(2) of this title the restraint of any withholding of payment of minimum wages or overtime compensation found by the court to be due to employees under this chapter (except sums which employees are barred from recovering, at the time of the commencement of the action to restrain the violations, by virtue of the provisions of section 255 of this title).

§ 218. Relation to other laws

(a) No provision of this chapter or of any order thereunder shall excuse noncompliance with any Federal or State law or municipal ordinance establishing a minimum wage higher than the minimum wage established under this chapter or a maximum work week lower than the maximum workweek established under this chapter, and no provision of this chapter relating to the employment of child labor shall justify noncompliance with any Federal or State law or municipal ordinance establishing a higher standard than the standard established under this chapter. No provision of this chapter shall justify any employer in reducing a wage paid by him which is in excess of the applicable minimum wage under this chapter, or justify any employer in increasing hours of employment maintained by him which are shorter than the maximum hours applicable under this chapter.

(b) Notwithstanding any other provision of this chapter (other than section 213(f) of this title) or any other law—

(1) any Federal employee in the Canal Zone engaged in employment of the kind described in section 5102(c)(7) of title 5, or

(2) any employee employed in a nonappropriated fund instrumentality under the jurisdiction of the Armed Forces,

shall have his basic compensation fixed or adjusted at a wage rate that is not less than the appropriate wage rate provided for in section 206(a)(1) of this title (except that the wage rate provided for in section 206(b) of this title shall apply to any employee who performed services during the workweek in a work place within the Canal Zone), and shall have his overtime compensation set at an hourly rate not less than the overtime rate provided for in section 207(a)(1) of this title

§ 219. Separability

If any provision of this chapter or the application of such provision to any person or circumstance is held invalid, the remainder of this chapter and the application of such provision to other persons or circumstances shall not be affected thereby. ■

Chapter 10

Family and Medical Leave Act (FMLA)

Statute: 29 U.S.C. § 2601 and following
http://www4.law.cornell.edu/uscode/29/ch28.html

Regulations: 29 C.F.R. § 825.100 and following
http://cfr.law.cornell.edu/cfr/cfr.php?title=29&type=part&value=825

Definitions

Certification

A document that employees must give to their employer when they want to take leave for their own *serious health condition* or for a family member's *serious health condition*. A healthcare provider writes the certification after verifying that the *serious health condition* exists. For more about certification, see Section A5.

Eligible employee

An employee who is covered by the FMLA. To learn more about what makes an employee eligible to take FMLA leave, see Section A3.

Essential duties

The fundamental, not marginal, duties of a job. For more, see "For Employee's Own Health Problem" in Section A5.

Family member

A parent, spouse, son or daughter. Usually does not include in-laws, aunts, uncles or cousins. To learn more about who is and is not a family member, see "For a Family Member With a Health Problem" in Section A5.

Fitness for duty report

Employees who take FMLA leave for their own *serious health condition* provide this report before returning to work. A healthcare provider writes the report after verifying that the employee is healthy enough to return to work. For more, see Section A5.

Foster care

The 24-hour care for children in substitution of, and away from, their own parents or guardians. Informal care arrangements don't constitute foster care, which arises only when the state is involved in taking children away from their own family and placing them in another's home.

Intermittent schedule

A way to take family or medical leave, when an employee doesn't take all 12 weeks of leave at once for the same problem, but instead works a reduced schedule, taking the leave piecemeal over time (for example, working four days a week and taking leave one day a week).

Key employee

A salaried *eligible employee* who is among the highest paid 10% of the employer's employees within a 75-mile radius of the site where the employee works.

Serious health condition

An illness, injury, impairment, physical condition or mental condition that involves inpatient care (an overnight stay) in a medical facility, continuing treatment by a healthcare provider or a period of incapacity. It can include pregnancy and prenatal care. Cosmetic treatments (such as a face-lift) do not count, nor do common sicknesses such as a cold, the flu, earaches, upset stomach, headaches (other than migraines), minor ulcers or routine dental problems—unless complications arise. The term also includes a substance abuse problem that requires treatment.

A. Overview of the FMLA

1. Summary

The Family and Medical Leave Act (FMLA) requires covered employers to allow *eligible employees* to take up to 12 weeks of unpaid leave per 12-month period in the following circumstances:

- for the arrival of a new child—through birth, adoption or *foster care*
- to care for a *family member* who is suffering from a *serious health condition*
- because the employee's own *serious health condition* makes it impossible for the employee to work.

While employees are on FMLA leave, they are entitled to receive the same health benefits that they would have received had they not taken leave.

When employees return to work after FMLA leave, the employer must allow them to return to either the same position or to a position that is equal in pay, benefits and other terms and conditions of employment.

The FMLA has special rules for the employees of public and private schools. Those rules are beyond the scope of this discussion.

2. Regulated Employers

The following employers must adhere to the FMLA:

- private employers who employ 50 or more employees
- the federal government, its agencies and political subdivisions

- state and municipal governments, their agencies and political subdivisions
- public and private elementary schools and secondary schools.

3. Covered Workers

To be eligible to take FMLA leave, an employee must:

- have worked for a covered employer for at least 12 months (these months do not have to be consecutive)
- have worked at least 1,250 hours for the employer in those 12 months
- work at a location with 50 or more employees employed by the same employer or work within a 75-mile radius of 50 or more employees employed by the same employer.

4. What's Prohibited: Employers

Employers may not prevent employees from exercising their FMLA rights, nor may they discriminate against employees for exercising their FMLA rights. Employers cannot fire or otherwise retaliate against employees for properly taking FMLA leave.

Employers may not interfere with court proceedings or investigations pertaining to the FMLA. Prohibited interference includes firing or discriminating against someone who plans to testify or give information.

5. What's Required: Employers

Employers must grant leave to *eligible employees* in the following circumstances:

- to care for a newborn child (see "For a New Child," below)
- to care for a new child placed with the employee for adoption or *foster care* (see "For a New Child," below)
- to care for a *family member* with a *serious health condition* (see "For a Family Member With a Health Problem," below)
- because the employee is suffering from a *serious health condition* that makes it impossible for the employee to perform his or her job (see "For Employee's Own Health Problem," below).

Amount of Leave

Generally speaking, *eligible employees* can receive up to 12 workweeks of unpaid leave per 12-month period. When the employee takes leave to care for a new child, the 12-month period starts on the day of the birth or placement for adoption or *foster care*.

An employer can choose any one of the following methods for determining when the 12-month period begins and ends:

- the calendar year
- any fixed 12-month leave year, such as a fiscal year, a year required by state law or a year starting on an employee's anniversary date
- a 12-month period that begins on the date the employee first takes FMLA leave
- a 12-month period measured backward from the date the employee uses any FMLA leave.

The employer must use the same method of measuring the 12-month period for all employees.

Paid or Unpaid Leave

Generally speaking, FMLA leave is unpaid. However, employers have the option of forcing employees to use accrued paid leave as part of their FMLA leave. For example, if a female employee has three weeks of accrued vacation, the employer may require her to take that as part of the FMLA leave, which would leave her with nine weeks of unpaid FMLA leave.

The employee also has the option of choosing to substitute accrued paid leave for FMLA leave.

When an employee uses paid leave in the place of FMLA leave, the employee must follow the employer's leave policies.

Benefits While on Leave

Employees may keep their health benefits while on FMLA leave, and employers must continue to pay whatever premiums the employer would pay if the employee were not on leave. If the employee doesn't return from leave, the employee could be responsible for paying the cost of these premiums back to the employer, unless the employee fails to return for reasons beyond the employee's control (for example, a *serious health condition* that does not improve so that the employee can return to work).

For earned benefits, such as seniority or paid leave, the employee does not accrue those benefits while on FMLA leave so long as employees generally are not allowed to accrue these benefits while on other types of unpaid leave.

Reasons Employees May Take Leave

For a New Child

Mothers and fathers have an equal right to take FMLA leave to care for a new child—whether the new child comes by way of birth, adoption or *foster care.*

If a mother is unable to work because of pregnancy, she may take FMLA leave before the child is born. However, she still gets only 12 weeks of FMLA leave for that 12-month period, so the amount of time she takes before the birth will count against the amount of time she takes after the birth if both occur within the same 12-month period.

Mothers and fathers who are expecting a child through adoption or *foster care* may take some FMLA leave before the child arrives if the leave is needed to arrange for the child's placement. For example, some courts order parents to undergo counseling before receiving a foster child. The FMLA would cover time off from work for that counseling.

Parents can take leave on an *intermittent schedule* for the arrival of a new child only if the employer agrees.

For a Family Member With a Health Problem

Employees may take FMLA leave to care for a *family member* who is suffering from a *serious health condition.* The employee may take the leave only if he or she is needed. What constitutes being needed? The *family member* must be unable to care for his or her own basic medical, hygienic or nutritional needs or safety. Or, the *family member* must be unable to transport himself or herself to the doctor or other healthcare providers. Being needed also includes providing psychological comfort and support to a *family member* who is receiving inpatient or home care. It also includes filling in for other family members who are providing care, and it includes making arrangements for changes in care, such as a transfer to a nursing home.

Employers may ask employees to provide a *certification* from a healthcare provider that the *family member* is suffering from a *serious health condition.* For more information, see "Certification," below.

If an employee wants to take leave to care for a sick *family member*, the employee may do so on an *intermittent schedule.* The employee can take the intermittent leave both when the family member's health condition is intermittent and when the need for the employee is intermittent (for example, the employee shares care responsibilities with other people and is needed only one day a week). The employer may temporarily assign the employee to a different position with equal pay and benefits to accommodate the *intermittent schedule*.

Not all members of an employee's family are *family members* for purposes of the FMLA. *Family members* consist of sons, daughters, parents and spouses:

- A spouse must be someone whom state law recognizes as being married to the employee. For example, in states that do not recognize marriage between homosexuals, gay partners are not spouses under the law, even if they have had a commitment ceremony.

- A parent must be a biological, adopted or foster parent, or an individual who acted as a parent (that is, someone who had the day-to-day responsibility of caring for and financially supporting the employee as a child). Thus, a mother-in-law is not a parent, but an aunt who took day-to-day care of the orphaned employee from age two to 18 might be.

- A son or daughter is a biological child, adopted child, foster child, stepchild, legal ward or a child for whom the employee acts as a parent (that is, a child for whom the employee takes day-to-day responsibility for care and financial support).

For Employee's Own Health Problem

To take FMLA leave for their own health problem, employees must:

- be suffering from a *serious health condition*, and
- be unable to perform the *essential duties* of their job.

The term *essential duties* refers to the fundamental, as opposed to marginal, duties of a job. A job duty is an *essential duty* if:

- the reason the job exists is to perform that function (for example, an *essential duty* of a pilot is to fly the plane)
- only a few employees can perform the function, or
- the function is so highly specialized that the employer hires people into the position specifically because of their expertise in performing that function.

The following types of information are relevant to determining whether a job duty is an *essential duty*:

- written job descriptions prepared before advertising or interviewing for a position
- the employer's opinion
- the amount of time that people who hold that job have to spend performing that duty
- the consequences of someone holding the job who could not perform that duty
- the terms of a collective bargaining agreement
- the work experience of people who have held the job in the past
- the work experience of people who are currently holding the job.

Although this analysis might seem very complicated, it is rooted in common sense. A good question to ask when trying to determine whether a job duty is an *essential duty* is whether removing that job duty would fundamentally alter the job.

An employer may request that the employee provide *certification* from a healthcare provider that the employee is indeed unable to perform the *essential duties* of the job. For more, see "Certification," below.

Under certain circumstances, employees may take FMLA leave to treat their substance abuse problem.

If medically necessary, an employee may take the leave on an *intermittent schedule*. The employee must try to accommodate the employer's schedule and needs. The employer may temporarily assign the employee to a different position with equal pay and benefits to accommodate the *intermittent schedule*.

Certification

If an employee requests FMLA leave for his or her own *serious health condition* or for a *family member's serious health condition*, the employer has the right to request the employee provide a document from a healthcare provider certifying the existence of the *serious health condition*.

At the same time that the employer requests the *certification*, the employer must tell the employee what the consequences will be if the employee fails to provide *certification*.

When an employee provides *certification*, the employer must tell the employee if it thinks the *certification* is incomplete.

If the employer's policies generally impose *certification* requirements that are less stringent than the FMLA, then the employee needs to meet only the less stringent requirements.

Certifications must contain very specific and detailed information. The Department of Labor provides a form that employees can use when obtaining *certifications*. Although this form is optional, it is quite helpful to employers and medical providers because it requests the specific information that the FMLA requires. For more information about this form, see Section E, below.

After receiving a certification, an employer is not allowed to contact the employee's healthcare provider for more information. However, a healthcare provider hired by the employer can call the employee's healthcare provider for clarification or authentication.

If an employer doubts the validity of a *certification*, the employer can request a second opinion at the employer's expense. Although the employer can choose the second healthcare provider, that person may not be someone who works for the employer on a regular basis.

If the first and second opinions differ, the employer can request a third certification—again at the employer's expense. This third healthcare provider must be someone whom both the employer and the employee agree upon. This third opinion is final and binding.

Required Notice From the Employer

Employers must post a notice in their workplace explaining the FMLA. Employers can obtain this notice from the U.S. Department of Labor (see Section E for details).

If an employer has any written materials—such as an employee handbook—that explain employee benefits, the employer must include information about the FMLA. The information must explain employee rights and responsibilities under the law.

If an employer does not have written materials that explain employee benefits, the employer must give general written guidance about FMLA rights and obligations to employees who request leave. An employer will satisfy this requirement if it gives Department of Labor Fact Sheet No. 28 to employees (see Section E, below).

In addition, employers must give employees who take leave a written notice that describes the leave and details the employee's obligations. The employer must provide this notice within two business days after learning of the employee's intent to use FMLA leave. The employer may use the Department of Labor's "Employer Response to Employee Request for Family or Medical Leave" (Form WH-381) to fulfill this requirement (see Section E, below). For employers who don't use the form, the notice must include a statement that the FMLA covers the employee's leave and information on:

- whether the employer will require the employee to provide *certification* of a *serious health condition* (and the consequences of failing to provide the *certification*)
- the employee's right to substitute paid leave for the FMLA leave

- whether the employer will require the employee to substitute paid leave for the FMLA leave
- how health benefit premiums will be paid
- whether the employer will require the employee to provide a *fitness for duty report*
- whether the employee is a *key employee* and the consequences of that classification (see Section A7, below, for more about the *key employee* exception)
- the employee's right to the same or equivalent job upon return from leave
- the employee's potential liability for any health insurance premiums that the employer pays while the employee was on FMLA leave, which will arise if the employee fails to return to work from FMLA leave.

Required Notice From the Employee

To obtain FMLA leave, the employee must provide notice (at least 30 days when possible) to the employer. For more, see "Notice" in Section A6, below.

In addition to that initial notice, the employer can require an employee who is on FMLA leave to check in periodically and report on health status and intent to return to work.

Fitness for Duty Report

If an employee takes FMLA leave for his or her own *serious health condition*, the employer can require the employee to provide a *fitness for duty report* from his or her doctor before returning to work.

This report is much simpler than a *certification*. All it needs to say is that the employee is healthy enough to return to work.

An employer may not request a *fitness for duty report* if the employee is on an *intermittent schedule*.

Reasons to Delay Leave

An employer can delay an eligible employee's leave in the following circumstances:

- If an employee could have given 30 days notice but failed to do so, the employer can delay the leave until 30 days have passed from the date the employee told the employer about the leave.
- If an employee doesn't provide a *certification*, the employer can delay the leave until the employee does provide a *certification*.

Reasons to Delay or Deny Reinstatement

An employer can delay or deny an employee's return to work in the following circumstances:

- The employer can delay reinstatement until the employee provides a *fitness for duty report*.
- If the employee would have been fired or laid off while not on leave, it is OK for an employer to fire or lay off the employee while on leave. In such a situation, the employee has no right to reinstatement, continued leave or continued benefits. For example, suppose an employee who works in an accounting department goes on FMLA leave for the birth of a baby. While the employee is on leave, the employer lays off the entire accounting department. Because the employee's job no longer exists, the employee does not have a right to reinstatement.

- If an employee tells the employer that he or she does not intend to return to work, the employee has no right to reinstatement, continued leave or continued health benefits.
- If an employee is a *key employee*, the employer may deny reinstatement in certain circumstances. See Section A7, below, for more about the *key employee* exception.
- If an employee fraudulently obtains FMLA leave, the employee has no right to leave, reinstatement or continued benefits.

6. What's Required: Workers

Employees have two duties under the FMLA: notice and certification.

Notice

When possible, employees must give the employer 30 days notice of their desire to take FMLA leave. For example, if an employee is pregnant and knows her due date, she can give the employer the 30 days notice.

In cases where 30 days notice is not possible, employees must give whatever notice they can. For example, if an employee is diagnosed with cancer and must have surgery the following week, the most notice the employee can give is a week's notice.

When planning medical treatment, employees must make reasonable efforts to accommodate employer needs. This means employees should consult with employers before scheduling treatments if possible.

If an employee fails to give 30 days notice when he or she could have, the employer has the right to delay the employee's FMLA leave until 30 days after the date the employee finally provided notice. The employer can do this if only the employee knew of the notice requirement.

If the employee took leave but did not inform the employer that the leave was FMLA leave, the employee must notify the employer that the leave was FMLA leave within two business days of returning to work.

Certification

If the employer asks for it, the employee must submit a *certification* from a healthcare provider that the employee or the employee's *family member* (as the case may be) is actually suffering from a *serious health condition*. For more about *certification*, see Section A5.

7. Exceptions

Husband and Wife

If a husband and wife work for the same employer, the employer has the right to limit the amount of leave that the couple takes for the arrival of a new child or for the care of an employee's parent with a *serious health condition*. In those two circumstances, the employer can limit the employees to a combined total of 12 workweeks of unpaid leave during a 12-month period. For example, if the husband took four weeks to care for a new child, then the employer could limit the wife to eight weeks to care for the new child.

This limitation does not apply when the employees take leave for their own *serious health condition* or for the *serious health condition* of a *family member* other than a parent. Thus, if the husband took four weeks to care for the new daughter, he could still take eight weeks for his own *serious health condition*. Similar, if his wife took eight weeks to care for the new daughter, she could still take four weeks to care for the couple's son who suffers from a *serious health condition*.

Key Employees

If an employee is a *key employee*, the employer may refuse to allow the employee to return to work if the employee's return would cause severe economic injury to the employer.

B. How the FMLA Is Enforced

1. Individual Complaints

Employees who feel their employer has violated their FMLA rights can file a complaint with the Department of Labor, or they can file a private lawsuit.

2. Agency Enforcement

The Wage and Hour Division of the U.S. Department of Labor investigates complaints.

The Department can also file lawsuits in court to compel compliance.

C. For Employers: Complying With the FMLA

1. Reporting Requirements

The FMLA imposes no reporting requirements.

2. Posting Requirements

All covered employers must post a notice approved by the Department of Labor that explains employee rights and responsibilities under the FMLA. To find out how to obtain a copy of that notice, see Section E, below.

3. Recordkeeping Requirements

Employers must keep records pertaining to their FMLA obligations. These records include:

- payroll information for each employee, including name, address, job title, rate or basis of pay, terms of compensation, daily and weekly hours worked per pay period, additions to wages, deductions from wages and total compensation paid (unless the employee is exempt from the Fair Labor Standards Act's recordkeeping requirements) (see chapter on FLSA)
- dates the employee has taken FMLA leave

- if the employee has take less than a day of FMLA leave, the number of hours of leave taken
- copies of any written notices the employee has given the employer about FMLA leave
- copies of general and specific written notices that the employer has given to the employee about FMLA leave
- documents describing employee benefits
- documents describing employer policies regarding paid and unpaid leave
- premium payments of employee benefits
- records of any disputes between the employer and the employee regarding FMLA leave.

4. Practical Tips

One of the easiest FMLA requirements to comply with—giving notice to employees—is also the one that employers mess up the most. Perhaps this is because employees don't have to use the magic letters "F-M-L-A" when requesting leave. Any time an employee requests leave that looks anything like family or medical leave, a prudent employer should give the employee a document explaining the employee's FMLA rights and obligations. (See Section A5, above, for more about what information this document must contain.)

The Department of Labor has created several documents that automatically comply with the FMLA, so don't waste time (and don't risk failure) trying to write these notices yourself. For links to those documents, see Section E.

Develop a leave policy and stick with it. Always ask for *certifications* in similar circumstances. Always ask for *fitness for duty reports* in the same circumstances. Treat everyone who requests leave in the same way. This will help you avoid claims of discrimination.

The FMLA is not the only law that grants employees leave to deal with their own health problems. The federal Americans With Disabilities Act (ADA) also grants employees the right to leave under certain circumstances, as do state workers' compensation statutes. The intersection of these laws can be quite confusing. Sometimes, an employee might be covered by all three laws at the same time; other times, an employee might only be covered by one or two. The Equal Employment Opportunity Commission, which is the federal agency that enforces the ADA, has a document that attempts to guide employers through this difficult issue. You can find it at http://www.eeoc.gov/docs/fmlaada.html. If you think that you have an employee who might be covered under more than one law, be sure to review this document. You might also consider consulting with an attorney. (See the chapter on the ADA for more information.)

5. Penalties

If an employee prevails in a lawsuit against you, the employee might be entitled to one or all of the following remedies: lost wages, lost employment benefits, cost of providing care, interest on damages, money damages set by the statute (called liquidated damages), reinstatement, promotion, attorney's fees and costs.

If you fail to post required notices, the Department of Labor can impose a civil fine against you.

D. For Workers: Asserting Rights Under the FMLA

1. Where to Start

If you think your employer has violated your FMLA rights, try talking to someone at work who has some authority: a manager, a supervisor or someone in the human resources department. Keep a journal of your conversations about your leave. If your employer has an internal complaint procedure—and if there is time—use that.

If working within your company proves to be fruitless, contact your local office of the Wage and Hour Division and explain your situation. They will give you information about your rights and options. You can file a complaint with them, and they will conduct an investigation.

Depending on what happens at the Wage and Hour Division, your next step may be to talk to an employment lawyer about filing a lawsuit.

Whichever path you choose, be very mindful of time. For ordinary violations of the FMLA, you have two years from the date of the violation to file a lawsuit. If the employer's violation was knowing and willful, you get three years to file the lawsuit.

2. Required Forms

No particular form is required to file a complaint.

3. Practical Tips

Tell your employer as soon as you know that you will need to take some leave—even if the leave is more than 30 days away. The more notice you give your employer, the easier it will be for your employer to make arrangements to accommodate your leave.

When you request leave, do it in writing, explaining why you need the leave and how long you need to be away from work. Keep copies of this notice and of everything else you give your employer pertaining to your leave. Also keep copies of all documents that your employer gives to you.

If you are seeking leave for your own *serious health condition*, you may also qualify for protection under the Americans With Disabilities Act (ADA) if your condition is also a disability within the meaning of that law. Talk to your employer about this issue, because the ADA might allow you to obtain more than 12 weeks of leave, and it also provides for other types of accommodations. (See the Chapter on the ADA for more information.)

E. Agency Charged With Enforcement & Compliance

Wage and Hour Division
Department of Labor
Employment Standards Administration
200 Constitution Ave., NW
Room N-5619
Washington, DC 20210
Phone: 202-219-8776
http://www.dol.gov/dol/esa/public/whd_org.htm

The Wage and Hour Division has local field offices that you can visit or call. To find a list of those field offices, refer to:
http://www.dol.gov/dol/esa/public/contacts/whd/america2.htm

Agency Resources for Employers

(These can be obtained either at the Web addresses listed below or at the address and phone number listed above.)

- A guide for employers on how to comply with the FMLA
  FMLA Compliance Guide
  http://www.dol.gov/dol/esa/public/regs/compliance/whd/1421.htm
- Answers to frequently asked questions about the FMLA
  Family and Medical Leave Act: Employee/Employer Advisor
  http://www.dol.gov/elaws/fmla.htm
- General information about the FMLA
  FMLA Fact Sheet No. 28
  http://www.dol.gov/dol/esa/public/regs/compliance/whd/whdfs28.htm
- An optional form that an employer may use to respond to an employee's request for leave
  Prototype Notice, Form WH-381
  http://www.dol.gov/dol/esa/public/regs/compliance/whd/fmla/wh381.pdf
- An optional form that employees may use to obtain a medical certification from a healthcare provider
  Medical Certificate, Form WH-380
  http://www.dol.gov/dol/esa/public/regs/compliance/whd/fmla/wh380.pdf
- The poster that employers must display alerting employees to their FMLA rights and obligations
  Family and Medical Leave Act (FMLA) Poster
  http://www.dol.gov/dol/osbp/public/sbrefa/poster/main.htm

Agency Resources for Workers

(These can be obtained either at the Web addresses listed below or at the address and phone number listed above.)

- Answers to frequently asked questions about the FMLA
  Family and Medical Leave Act: Employee/Employer Advisor
  http://www.dol.gov/elaws/fmla.htm
- An optional form that may be used to obtain a medical certification from a healthcare provider
  Medical Certificate, Form WH-380
  http://www.dol.gov/dol/esa/public/regs/compliance/whd/fmla/wh380.pdf

F. State Laws Relating to Family and Medical Leave

States are free to require more family and medical leave rights than those granted by the FMLA. If a state grants fewer leave rights, however, covered employers must follow the FMLA, not the state law.

States that are not listed do not have medical leave laws or have laws that offer less than the FMLA.

State Citations Main Differences From FMLA	Employers Covered	Eligible Employees	Type and Amount of Leave for various kinds of family & medical leave
California Cal. Gov't. Code § 12945; Cal. Lab. Code § 230 and following Pregnancy-related disability leave extended to employers and employees not covered by FMLA.	5 or more employees —must offer pregnancy leave 25 or more employees —must offer domestic violence leave and school activity leave	All	**Pregnancy:** up to 4 months for disability related to pregnancy **Domestic violence issues:** Reasonable time for issues dealing with domestic violence, including health, counseling and safety measures 40 hours per year for **School activities**
Colorado Colo. Rev. Stat. § 19-5-211	All employers who offer leave for birth of a child	Adoptive parents	**Adoption:** Must allow same leave as for childbirth
Connecticut Conn. Gen. Stat. Ann. §§ 31-51kk and following; § 46a-51(10); § 46a-60(7) Includes parents-in-law under parent definition. Covers employees who've worked less than 1,250 hours Allows more than 12 weeks leave in a particular year.	75 employees for FML 3 employees for maternity disability	1 year and at least 1,000 hours for employer in past 12 months	16 weeks per any 24-month period for: **Childbirth** **Adoption** **Sickness of "family member"** AND 16 hours of unpaid leave during any 24-month period for **Own serious health condition** "Reasonable" amount for **Pregnancy/Maternity**
District of Columbia D.C. Code Ann. §§ 32-501 and following; 32-1202 Definition of family member includes persons sharing employee's residence and with whom employee has a committed relationship. Allows more than 12 weeks leave in a particular year.	At least 20 employees	Worked at company for at least one year, and who has worked at least 1,000 hours during the previous 12-month period	16 weeks of unpaid leave during any 24-month period for **Childbirth** **Adoption** **Pregnancy/Maternity** **Sickness of "family member"** 24 hours per year for **School activities**

State Citations Main Differences From FMLA	Employers Covered	Eligible Employees	Type and Amount of Leave for various kinds of family & medical leave
Hawaii Haw. Rev. Stat. §§ 398-1 and following; 378-1 Covers employees who have worked less than FMLA requires. Family members include parents-in-law, stepparents, grandparents, grandparents-in-law. Leave to care for ill family member does not include employees own serious health condition.	100 employees or more for FML leave All employers for pregnancy leave	6 months of service for FML benefits No minimum for pregnancy leave	4 weeks per calendar year for **Childbirth** **Adoption** **Sickness of "family member"** "Reasonable period" for Pregnancy/Maternity (required by statute and case law)
Illinois 820 Ill. Comp. Stat. § 147/15	All	6 months, at least half-time	8 hours per year for **School activities**
Iowa Iowa Code § 216.6	4 or more employees	All	Up to 8 weeks for **Disability due to pregnancy**
Kentucky Ky. Rev. Stat. Ann. § 337.015 Age of child.	All	Adoptive parents No hour requirements	Up to 6 weeks for **Adoption** of a child under 7 years old
Louisiana La. Rev. Stat. Ann. §§ 23:341-342; 23:1015 and following; 40:1299.124 Extends pregnancy leave to employers with less than 50 employees, and those who have worked less than 1,250 hours.	At least 25 employees in the state for pregnancy/maternity All employers for school activities 20 or more workers for bone marrow provisions	Any employee for school activities or pregnancy Those who work 20 or more hours per week for bone marrow donor	A "reasonable period of time" not to exceed four months, if necessary for: **Pregnancy** 16 hours per year for **School activities** 40 hours of paid leave to **Donate bone marrow**
Maine Me. Rev. Stat. Ann. tit. 26, § 843 and following Covers employers in the 15-49 employee range. Age of adopted child.	At least 15 workers in Maine	At least one year of service	10 weeks in any two-year period for **Childbirth** **Adoption** (age 16 or younger) **Sickness of family member**
Massachusetts Mass. Gen. Laws ch. 149, §§ 52D; 105A and following; Ch. 151B, § 1	At least 6 employees for maternity leave All employers for school activities	For childbirth and adoption leave: Full-time female employees who have completed probationary period or 3 months of service if no set probationary period	8 weeks for: **Childbirth** **Adoption** (for child under 18, or under 23 if disabled)

State Citations Main Differences From FMLA	Employers Covered	Eligible Employees	Type and Amount of Leave for various kinds of family & medical leave
Massachusetts (continued) Extends maternity leave requirement to employers of 6 to 49 employees. Adds "small necessities" leave to employees covered by FMLA.		For other leave, all employees covered by the FMLA	24 hours per year, total for **School activities** or Events directly related to **medical or dental care of a minor child or elderly relative**
Minnesota Minn. Stat. Ann. § 181.940 and following Extends maternity leave requirement to employers of 21 to 49 employees.	21 or more workers for maternity leave All employers for school activities At least 20 employees for bone marrow donation	At least one year, at least half-time for maternity leave At least one year for school activities At least 20 hours per week for bone marrow donation	6 weeks for **Childbirth** **Adoption** Can use own accrued sick leave for **Care of sick or injured child** 16 hours in 12-month period for **School activities** (includes activities related to child care, preschool, or special education) Up to 40 hours paid leave per year for **Bone marrow donation**
Montana Mont. Code Ann. § 49-2-310 & 311 Extends pregnancy leave mandate to employers of less than 50 employees and covers workers who have not worked 1,250 hours.	All employers	All	"Reasonable period of time" for **Childbirth** **Pregnancy**
Nebraska Neb. Rev. Stat. § 48-234	Employers that allow workers to take leave for the birth of a child	Adoptive parents	**Adoption:** Same amount of leave as is afforded biological parents for the birth of a child, to adopt a child under the age of 9 or a special needs child under the age of 19
Nevada Nev. Rev. Stat. Ann. § 392.920	All	Parent, guardian or custodian of a child	**School activities:** Employers may not fire or threaten to fire a parent, guardian or custodian for attending a school conference or responding to a child's emergency
New Jersey N.J. Stat. Ann. § 34:11B-1 to B-16 Family member includes parents-in-law	At least 50 employees		12 weeks of unpaid leave in any 24-month period for **Childbirth** **Adoption** **Sickness of family member**

State Citations Main Differences From FMLA	Employers Covered	Eligible Employees	Type and Amount of Leave for various kinds of family & medical leave
New Hampshire N.H. Rev. Stat. § 354-A:7	At least 6 employees	All	Leave for temporary disability due to **Pregnancy/Childbirth**
New York N.Y. Lab. Law §§ 201-c; 202-a	Employers that allow workers to take leave for the birth of a child for adoption At least 20 employees for bone marrow donation	Adoptive parents of preschool age children and disabled children under 18 At least 20 hours of work per week for bone marrow donation	**Adoption:** Same amount of leave as is afforded biological parents for the birth of a child Up to 24 hours of leave for **Bone marrow donation**
North Carolina N.C. Gen. Stat. § 95-28.3	All employers	Parents and guardians of children in school	4 hours of leave per year to participate in child's **School activities**
Oregon Or. Rev. Stat. §§ 659A.150-186; 69A.312 Extends FMLA-style benefits to employers of 24 to 49 employees and covers workers who have worked less than 1,250 hours.	At least 25 workers for FML leave All employers for bone marrow donation	At least 180 days, at least 25 hours per week, for FML leave At least 20 hours per week for bone marrow donation	12 weeks per year for **Pregnancy/Maternity** **Childbirth** **Adoption** **Sickness of family member** **Own serious health condition** **EXCEPT** (1) employee may take 12 weeks for pregnancy plus 12 weeks for maternity, sickness of family member or own serious health condition (2) employee may take 12 weeks for maternity or adoption plus 12 weeks to care for sick child Up to 40 hours or amount of accrued paid leave (whichever is less) for **Bone marrow donation**
Rhode Island R.I. Gen. Laws § 28-48-2 and 3 No allowance for intermittent leave; parents-in-law included in family definition.	Employers with 50 or more employees	Those who have worked 30 or more hours per week for employer for at least 12 consecutive months.	Up to 13 weeks in any two calendar years for **Childbirth** **Adoption** **Sickness of family member**
South Carolina S.C. Code Ann. § 44-43-80	At least 20 workers at one site	At least 20 hours per week	**Bone marrow donation:** cannot retaliate against workers who use up to 40 hours to donate bone marrow

State Citations Main Differences From FMLA	Employers Covered	Eligible Employees	Type and Amount of Leave for various kinds of family & medical leave
Tennessee Tenn. Code Ann. § 4-21-408 Maternity leave only	Employers of 100 or more	All female employees who have worked 12 consecutive months	**Pregnancy/Maternity disability:** Up to 4 months leave with 3 months advance notice, unless a medical emergency requires the leave to begin sooner
Vermont Vt. Stat. Ann. tit. 21, §§ 471 and following Family member includes parent-in-law; stepchild. Serious health condition is more narrowly defined than under FMLA.	Employers of 10 or more workers must provide parental leave Employers of 15 or more workers must provide family leave	At least one year, at least 30 hours per week	12 weeks per year **Childbirth** **Adoption (age 16 or under)** **Sickness of family member** Up to 4 hours of unpaid leave in a 30-day period (but not more than 24 hours per year) To participate in child's **school activities** or To **take a family member to a medical or professional appointment** or To respond to a **family member's medical emergency**
Washington Wash. Rev. Code Ann. §§ 49.12.350 and 360	At least 100 employees	At least one year, at least 35 hours per week	**Adoption:** must provide the same leave as childbirth to adoptive parents and stepparents of children under the age of six **Sickness of family member:** can use accrued sick leave to care for sick child
Wisconsin Wis. Stat. Ann. § 103.10 Extends FMLA-type benefits to persons not meeting the 1,250 hours requirement	At least 50 employees	Worked at company for at least one year, and has worked at least 1,000 hours during the previous 12-month period	8 weeks total per year: 6 weeks for **Childbirth** **Adoption** PLUS 2 weeks for **Sickness of family member** PLUS 2 weeks for **Own serious health condition**

G. Text of the FMLA

U.S. Code
Title 29: Labor
Chapter 28: Family and Medical Leave

§ 2601. Findings and purposes

§ 2611. Definitions

§ 2612. Leave requirement

§ 2613. Certification

§ 2614. Employment and benefits protection

§ 2615. Prohibited acts

§ 2616. Investigative authority

§ 2617. Enforcement

§ 2618. Special rules concerning employees of local educational agencies

§ 2619. Notice

§ 2631. Establishment

§ 2632. Duties

§ 2633. Membership

§ 2634. Compensation

§ 2635. Powers

§ 2636. Termination

§ 2651. Effect on other laws

§ 2652. Effect on existing employment benefits

§ 2653. Encouragement of more generous leave policies

§ 2654. Regulations

§ 2601. Findings and purposes

(a) Findings

Congress finds that—

(1) the number of single-parent households and two-parent households in which the single parent or both parents work is increasing significantly;

(2) it is important for the development of children and the family unit that fathers and mothers be able to participate in early childrearing and the care of family members who have serious health conditions;

(3) the lack of employment policies to accommodate working parents can force individuals to choose between job security and parenting;

(4) there is inadequate job security for employees who have serious health conditions that prevent them from working for temporary periods;

(5) due to the nature of the roles of men and women in our society, the primary responsibility for family caretaking often falls on women, and such responsibility affects the working lives of women more than it affects the working lives of men; and

(6) employment standards that apply to one gender only have serious potential for encouraging employers to discriminate against employees and applicants for employment who are of that gender.

(b) Purposes

It is the purpose of this Act—

(1) to balance the demands of the workplace with the needs of families, to promote the stability and economic security of families, and to promote national interests in preserving family integrity;

(2) to entitle employees to take reasonable leave for medical reasons, for the birth or adoption of a child, and for the care of a child, spouse, or parent who has a serious health condition;

(3) to accomplish the purposes described in paragraphs (1) and (2) in a manner that accommodates the legitimate interests of employers;

(4) to accomplish the purposes described in paragraphs (1) and (2) in a manner that, consistent with the Equal Protection Clause of the Fourteenth Amendment, minimizes the potential for employment discrimination on the basis of sex by ensuring generally that leave is available for eligible medical reasons (including maternity-related disability) and for compelling family reasons, on a gender-neutral basis; and

(5) to promote the goal of equal employment opportunity for women and men, pursuant to such clause.

§ 2611. Definitions

As used in this subchapter:

(1) Commerce

The terms "commerce" and "industry or activity affecting commerce" mean any activity, business, or industry in commerce or in which a labor dispute would hinder or obstruct commerce or the free flow of commerce, and include "commerce" and any "industry affecting commerce", as defined in paragraphs (1) and (3) of section 142 of this title.

(2) Eligible employee

(A) In general

The term "eligible employee" means an employee who has been employed—

(i) for at least 12 months by the employer with respect to whom leave is requested under section 2612 of this title; and

(ii) for at least 1,250 hours of service with such employer during the previous 12-month period.

(B) Exclusions

The term "eligible employee" does not include—

(i) any Federal officer or employee covered under subchapter V of chapter 63 of title 5; or

(ii) any employee of an employer who is employed at a worksite at which such employer employs less than 50 employees if the total number of employees employed by that employer within 75 miles of that worksite is less than 50.

(C) Determination

For purposes of determining whether an employee meets the hours of service requirement specified in subparagraph (A)(ii), the legal standards established under section 207 of this title shall apply.

(3) Employ; employee; State

The terms "employ", "employee", and "State" have the same meanings given such terms in subsections (c), (e), and (g) of section 203 of this title.

(4) Employer

(A) In general

The term "employer"—

(i) means any person engaged in commerce or in any industry or activity affecting commerce who employs 50 or more employees for each working day during each of 20 or more calendar workweeks in the current or preceding calendar year;

(ii) includes—

(I) any person who acts, directly or indirectly, in the interest of an employer to any of the employees of such employer; and

(II) any successor in interest of an employer; and

(iii) includes any "public agency", as defined in section 203(x) of this title.

(B) Public agency

For purposes of subparagraph (A)(iii), a public agency shall be considered to be a person engaged in commerce or in an industry or activity affecting commerce.

(5) Employment benefits

The term "employment benefits" means all benefits provided or made available to employees by an employer, including group life insurance, health insurance, disability insurance, sick leave, annual leave, educational benefits, and pensions, regardless of whether such benefits are provided by a practice or written policy of an employer or through an "employee benefit plan", as defined in section 1002(3) of this title.

(6) Healthcare provider

The term "healthcare provider" means—

(A) a doctor of medicine or osteopathy who is authorized to practice medicine or surgery (as appropriate) by the State in which the doctor practices; or

(B) any other person determined by the Secretary to be capable of providing healthcare services.

(7) Parent

The term "parent" means the biological parent of an employee or an individual who stood in loco parentis to an employee when the employee was a son or daughter.

(8) Person

The term "person" has the same meaning given such term in section 203(a) of this title.

(9) Reduced leave schedule

The term "reduced leave schedule" means a leave schedule that reduces the usual number of hours per workweek, or hours per workday, of an employee.

(10) Secretary

The term "Secretary" means the Secretary of Labor.

(11) Serious health condition

The term "serious health condition" means an illness, injury, impairment, or physical or mental condition that involves—

(A) inpatient care in a hospital, hospice, or residential medical care facility; or

(B) continuing treatment by a healthcare provider.

(12) Son or daughter

The term "son or daughter" means a biological, adopted, or foster child, a stepchild, a legal ward, or a child of a person standing in loco parentis, who is—

(A) under 18 years of age; or

(B) 18 years of age or older and incapable of self-care because of a mental or physical disability.

(13) Spouse

The term "spouse" means a husband or wife, as the case may be.

§ 2612. Leave requirement

(a) In general

(1) Entitlement to leave

Subject to section 2613 of this title, an eligible employee shall be entitled to a total of 12 workweeks of leave during any 12-month period for one or more of the following:

(A) Because of the birth of a son or daughter of the employee and in order to care for such son or daughter.

(B) Because of the placement of a son or daughter with the employee for adoption or foster care.

(C) In order to care for the spouse, or a son, daughter, or parent, of the employee, if such spouse, son, daughter, or parent has a serious health condition.

(D) Because of a serious health condition that makes the employee unable to perform the functions of the position of such employee.

(2) Expiration of entitlement

The entitlement to leave under subparagraphs (A) and (B) of paragraph (1) for a birth or placement of a son or daughter shall expire at the end of the 12-month period beginning on the date of such birth or placement.

(b) Leave taken intermittently or on reduced leave schedule

(1) In general

Leave under subparagraph (A) or (B) of subsection (a)(1) of this section shall not be taken by an employee intermittently or on a reduced leave schedule unless the employee and the employer of the employee agree otherwise. Subject to paragraph (2), subsection (e)(2) of this section, and section 2613(b)(5) of this title, leave under subparagraph (C) or (D) of subsection (a)(1) of this section may be taken intermittently or on a reduced leave schedule when medically necessary. The taking of leave intermittently or on a reduced leave schedule pursuant to this paragraph shall not result in a reduction in the total amount of leave to which the employee is entitled under subsection (a) of this Section beyond the amount of leave actually taken.

(2) Alternative position

If an employee requests intermittent leave, or leave on a reduced leave schedule, under subparagraph (C) or (D) of subsection (a)(1) of this section, that is foreseeable based on planned medical treatment, the employer may require such employee to transfer temporarily to an available alternative position offered by the employer for which the employee is qualified and that—

(A) has equivalent pay and benefits; and

(B) better accommodates recurring periods of leave than the regular employment position of the employee.

(c) Unpaid leave permitted

Except as provided in subsection (d) of this section, leave granted under subsection (a) may consist of unpaid leave. Where an employee is otherwise exempt under regulations issued by the Secretary pursuant to section 213(a)(1) of this title, the compliance of an employer with this subchapter by providing unpaid leave shall not affect the exempt status of the employee under such section.

(d) Relationship to paid leave

(1) Unpaid leave

If an employer provides paid leave for fewer than 12 workweeks, the additional weeks of leave necessary to attain the 12 workweeks of leave required under this subchapter may be provided without compensation.

(2) Substitution of paid leave

(A) In general

An eligible employee may elect, or an employer may require the employee, to substitute any of the accrued paid vacation leave, personal leave, or family leave of the employee for leave provided under subparagraph (A), (B), or (C) of subsection (a)(1) of this Section for any part of the 12-week period of such leave under such subsection.

(B) Serious health condition

An eligible employee may elect, or an employer may require the employee, to substitute any of the accrued paid vacation leave, personal leave, or medical or sick leave of the employee for leave provided under subparagraph (C) or (D) of subsection (a)(1) of this Section for any part of the 12-week period of such leave under such subsection, except that nothing in this subchapter shall require an employer to provide paid sick leave or paid medical leave in any situation in which such employer would not normally provide any such paid leave.

(e) Foreseeable leave

(1) Requirement of notice

In any case in which the necessity for leave under subparagraph (A) or (B) of subsection (a)(1) of this section is foreseeable based on an expected birth or placement, the employee shall provide the employer with not less than 30 days' notice, before the date the leave is to begin, of the employee's intention to take leave under such subparagraph, except that if the date of the birth or placement requires leave to begin in less than 30 days, the employee shall provide such notice as is practicable.

(2) Duties of employee

In any case in which the necessity for leave under subparagraph (C) or (D) of subsection (a)(1) of this section is foreseeable based on planned medical treatment, the employee—

(A) shall make a reasonable effort to schedule the treatment so as not to disrupt unduly the operations of the employer, subject to the approval of the healthcare provider of the employee or the healthcare provider of the son, daughter, spouse, or parent of the employee, as appropriate; and

(B) shall provide the employer with not less than 30 days' notice, before the date the leave is to begin, of the employee's intention to take leave under such subparagraph, except that if the date of the treatment requires leave to begin in less than 30 days, the employee shall provide such notice as is practicable.

(f) Spouses employed by same employer

In any case in which a husband and wife entitled to leave under subsection (a) of this section are employed by the same employer, the aggregate number of work-weeks of leave to which both may be entitled may be limited to 12 workweeks during any 12-month period, if such leave is taken—

(1) under subparagraph (A) or (B) of subsection (a)(1) of this section; or

(2) to care for a sick parent under subparagraph (C) of such subsection.

§ 2613. Certification

(a) In general

An employer may require that a request for leave under subparagraph (C) or (D) of section 2612(a)(1) of this title be supported by a certification issued by the healthcare provider of the eligible employee or of the son, daughter, spouse, or parent of the employee, as appropriate. The employee shall provide, in a timely manner, a copy of such certification to the employer.

(b) Sufficient certification

Certification provided under subsection (a) of this section shall be sufficient if it states—

(1) the date on which the serious health condition commenced;

(2) the probable duration of the condition;

(3) the appropriate medical facts within the knowledge of the healthcare provider regarding the condition;

(4)

(A) for purposes of leave under section 2612(a)(1)(C) of this title, a statement that the eligible employee is needed to care for the son,

daughter, spouse, or parent and an estimate of the amount of time that such employee is needed to care for the son, daughter, spouse, or parent; and

(B) for purposes of leave under section 2612(a)(1)(D) of this title, a statement that the employee is unable to perform the functions of the position of the employee;

(5) in the case of certification for intermittent leave, or leave on a reduced leave schedule, for planned medical treatment, the dates on which such treatment is expected to be given and the duration of such treatment;

(6) in the case of certification for intermittent leave, or leave on a reduced leave schedule, under section 2612(a)(1)(D) of this title, a statement of the medical necessity for the intermittent leave or leave on a reduced leave schedule, and the expected duration of the intermittent leave or reduced leave schedule; and

(7) in the case of certification for intermittent leave, or leave on a reduced leave schedule, under section 2612(a)(1)(C) of this title, a statement that the employee's intermittent leave or leave on a reduced leave schedule is necessary for the care of the son, daughter, parent, or spouse who has a serious health condition, or will assist in their recovery, and the expected duration and schedule of the intermittent leave or reduced leave schedule.

(c) Second opinion

(1) In general

In any case in which the employer has reason to doubt the validity of the certification provided under subsection (a) of this Section for leave under sub-paragraph (C) or (D) of section 2612(a)(1) of this title, the employer may require, at the expense of the employer, that the eligible employee obtain the opinion of a second healthcare provider designated or approved by the employer concerning any information certified under subsection (b) of this Section f for such leave.

(2) Limitation

A healthcare provider designated or approved under paragraph (1) shall not be employed on a regular basis by the employer.

(d) Resolution of conflicting opinions

(1) In general

In any case in which the second opinion described in subsection (c) of this Section differs from the opinion in the original certification provided under subsection (a) of this section, the employer may require, at the expense of the employer, that the employee obtain the opinion of a third healthcare provider designated or approved jointly by the employer and the employee concerning the information certified under subsection (b) of this section.

(2) Finality

The opinion of the third healthcare provider concerning the information certified under subsection (b) of this section shall be considered to be final and shall be binding on the employer and the employee.

(e) Subsequent recertification

The employer may require that the eligible employee obtain subsequent recertifications on a reasonable basis.

§ 2614. Employment and benefits protection

(a) Restoration to position

(1) In general

Except as provided in subsection (b) of this section, any eligible employee who takes leave under section 2612 of this title for the intended purpose of the leave shall be entitled, on return from such leave—

(A) to be restored by the employer to the position of employment held by the employee when the leave commenced; or

(B) to be restored to an equivalent position with equivalent employment benefits, pay, and other terms and conditions of employment.

(2) Loss of benefits

The taking of leave under section 2612 of this title shall not result in the loss of any employment benefit accrued prior to the date on which the leave commenced.

(3) Limitations

Nothing in this section shall be construed to entitle any restored employee to—

(A) the accrual of any seniority or employment benefits during any period of leave; or

(B) any right, benefit, or position of employment other than any right, benefit, or position to which the employee would have been entitled had the employee not taken the leave.

(4) Certification

As a condition of restoration under paragraph (1) for an employee who has taken leave under section 2612(a)(1)(D) of this title, the employer may have a uniformly applied practice or policy that requires each such employee to receive certification from the healthcare provider of the employee that the employee is able to resume work, except that nothing in this paragraph shall supersede a valid State or local law or a collective bargaining agreement that governs the return to work of such employees.

(5) Construction

Nothing in this subsection shall be construed to prohibit an employer from requiring an employee on leave under section 2612 of this title to report periodically to the employer on the status and intention of the employee to return to work.

(b) Exemption concerning certain highly compensated employees

(1) Denial of restoration

An employer may deny restoration under subsection (a) of this section to any eligible employee described in paragraph (2) if—

(A) such denial is necessary to prevent substantial and grievous economic injury to the operations of the employer;

(B) the employer notifies the employee of the intent of the employer to deny restoration on such basis at the time the employer determines that such injury would occur; and

(C) in any case in which the leave has commenced, the employee elects not to return to employment after receiving such notice.

(2) Affected employees

An eligible employee described in paragraph (1) is a salaried eligible employee who is among the highest paid 10 percent of the employees employed by the employer within 75 miles of the facility at which the employee is employed.

(c) Maintenance of health benefits

(1) Coverage

Except as provided in paragraph (2), during any period that an eligible employee takes leave under section 2612 of this title, the employer shall maintain coverage under any "group health plan" (as defined in section 5000(b)(1) of title 26) for the duration of such leave at the level and under the conditions coverage would have been provided if the employee had continued in employment continuously for the duration of such leave.

(2) Failure to return from leave

The employer may recover the premium that the employer paid for maintaining coverage for the employee under such group health plan during any period of unpaid leave under section 2612 of this title if—

(A) the employee fails to return from leave under section 2612 of this title after the period of leave to which the employee is entitled has expired; and

(B) the employee fails to return to work for a reason other than—

(i) the continuation, recurrence, or onset of a serious health condition that entitles the employee to leave under subparagraph (C) or (D) of section 2612(a)(1) of this title; or

(ii) other circumstances beyond the control of the employee.

(3) Certification

(A) Issuance

An employer may require that a claim that an employee is unable to return to work because of the continuation, recurrence, or onset of the serious health condition described in paragraph (2)(B)(i) be supported by—

(i) a certification issued by the healthcare provider of the son, daughter, spouse, or parent of the employee, as appropriate, in the case of an employee unable to return to work because of a condition specified in section 2612(a)(1)(C) of this title; or

(ii) a certification issued by the healthcare provider of the eligible employee, in the case of an employee unable to return to work because of a condition specified in section 2612(a)(1)(D) of this title.

(B) Copy

The employee shall provide, in a timely manner, a copy of such certification to the employer.

(C) Sufficiency of certification

(i) Leave due to serious health condition of employee

The certification described in subparagraph (A)(ii) shall be sufficient if the certification states that a serious health condition prevented the employee from being able to perform the functions of the position of the employee on the date that the leave of the employee expired.

(ii) Leave due to serious health condition of family member

The certification described in subparagraph (A)(i) shall be sufficient if the certification states that the employee is needed to care for the son, daughter, spouse, or parent who has a serious health condition on the date that the leave of the employee expired.

§ 2615. Prohibited acts

(a) Interference with rights

(1) Exercise of rights

It shall be unlawful for any employer to interfere with, restrain, or deny the exercise of or the attempt to exercise, any right provided under this subchapter.

(2) Discrimination

It shall be unlawful for any employer to discharge or in any other manner discriminate against any individual for opposing any practice made unlawful by this subchapter.

(b) Interference with proceedings or inquiries

It shall be unlawful for any person to discharge or in any other manner discriminate against any individual because such individual—

(1) has filed any charge, or has instituted or caused to be instituted any proceeding, under or related to this subchapter;

(2) has given, or is about to give, any information in connection with any inquiry or proceeding relating to any right provided under this subchapter; or

(3) has testified, or is about to testify, in any inquiry or proceeding relating to any right provided under this subchapter.

§ 2616. Investigative authority

(a) In general

To ensure compliance with the provisions of this subchapter, or any regulation or order issued under this subchapter, the Secretary shall have, subject to subsection (c) of this section, the investigative authority provided under section 211(a) of this title.

(b) Obligation to keep and preserve records

Any employer shall make, keep, and preserve records pertaining to compliance with this subchapter in accordance with section 211(c) of this title and in accordance with regulations issued by the Secretary.

(c) Required submissions generally limited to annual basis

The Secretary shall not under the authority of this section require any employer or any plan, fund, or program to submit to the Secretary any books or records more than once during any 12-month period, unless the Secretary has reasonable cause to believe there may exist a violation of this subchapter or any regulation or order issued pursuant to this subchapter, or is investigating a charge pursuant to section 2617(b) of this title.

(d) Subpoena powers

For the purposes of any investigation provided for in this section, the Secretary shall have the subpoena authority provided for under section 209 of this title.

§ 2617. Enforcement

(a) Civil action by employees

(1) Liability

Any employer who violates section 2615 of this title shall be liable to any eligible employee affected—

  (A) for damages equal to—

    (i) the amount of—

      (I) any wages, salary, employment benefits, or other compensation denied or lost to such employee by reason of the violation; or

      (II) in a case in which wages, salary, employment benefits, or other compensation have not been denied or lost to the employee, any actual monetary losses sustained by the employee as a direct result of the violation, such as the cost of providing care, up to a sum equal to 12 weeks of wages or salary for the employee;

    (ii) the interest on the amount described in clause (i) calculated at the prevailing rate; and

    (iii) an additional amount as liquidated damages equal to the sum of the amount described in clause (i) and the interest described in clause (ii), except that if an employer who has violated section 2615 of this title proves to the satisfaction of the court that the act or omission which violated section 2615 of this title was in good faith and that the employer had reasonable grounds for believing that the act or omission was not a violation of section 2615 of this title, such court may, in the discretion of the court, reduce the amount of the liability to the amount and interest determined under clauses (i) and (ii), respectively; and

  (B) for such equitable relief as may be appropriate, including employment, reinstatement, and promotion.

(2) Right of action

An action to recover the damages or equitable relief prescribed in paragraph (1) may be maintained against any employer (including a public agency) in any Federal or State court of competent jurisdiction by any one or more employees for and in behalf of—

  (A) the employees; or

  (B) the employees and other employees similarly situated.

(3) Fees and costs

The court in such an action shall, in addition to any judgment awarded to the plaintiff, allow a reasonable attorney's fee, reasonable expert witness fees, and other costs of the action to be paid by the defendant.

(4) Limitations

The right provided by paragraph (2) to bring an action by or on behalf of any employee shall terminate—

  (A) on the filing of a complaint by the Secretary in an action under subsection (d) of this section in which restraint is sought of any further delay in the payment of the amount described in paragraph (1)(A) to such employee by an employer responsible under paragraph (1) for the payment; or

  (B) on the filing of a complaint by the Secretary in an action under subsection (b) of this section in which a recovery is sought of the damages described in paragraph (1)(A) owing to an eligible employee by an employer liable under paragraph (1),

unless the action described in subparagraph (A) or (B) is dismissed without prejudice on motion of the Secretary.

(b) Action by Secretary

(1) Administrative action

The Secretary shall receive, investigate, and attempt to resolve complaints of violations of section 2615 of this title in the same manner that the Secretary receives, investigates, and attempts to resolve complaints of violations of sections 206 and 207 of this title.

(2) Civil action

The Secretary may bring an action in any court of competent jurisdiction to recover the damages described in subsection (a)(1)(A) of this section.

(3) Sums recovered

Any sums recovered by the Secretary pursuant to paragraph (2) shall be held in a special deposit account and shall be paid, on order of the Secretary, directly to each employee affected. Any such sums not paid to an employee because of inability to do so within a period of 3 years shall be deposited into the Treasury of the United States as miscellaneous receipts.

(c) Limitation

(1) In general

Except as provided in paragraph (2), an action may be brought under this section not later than 2 years after the date of the last event constituting the alleged violation for which the action is brought.

(2) Willful violation

In the case of such action brought for a willful violation of section 2615 of this title, such action may be brought within 3 years of the date of the last event constituting the alleged violation for which such action is brought.

(3) Commencement

In determining when an action is commenced by the Secretary under this Section f for the purposes of this subsection, it shall be considered to be commenced on the date when the complaint is filed.

(d) Action for injunction by Secretary

The district courts of the United States shall have jurisdiction, for cause shown, in an action brought by the Secretary—

(1) to restrain violations of section 2615 of this title, including the restraint of any withholding of payment of wages, salary, employment benefits, or other compensation, plus interest, found by the court to be due to eligible employees; or

(2) to award such other equitable relief as may be appropriate, including employment, reinstatement, and promotion.

(e) Solicitor of Labor

The Solicitor of Labor may appear for and represent the Secretary on any litigation brought under this section.

§ 2618. Special rules concerning employees of local educational agencies

(a) Application

(1) In general

Except as otherwise provided in this section, the rights (including the rights under section 2614 of this title, which shall extend throughout the period of leave of any employee under this section), remedies, and procedures under this subchapter shall apply to—

(A) any "local educational agency" (as defined in section 8801 of title 20) and an eligible employee of the agency; and

(B) any private elementary or secondary school and an eligible employee of the school.

(2) Definitions

For purposes of the application described in paragraph (1):

(A) Eligible employee

The term "eligible employee" means an eligible employee of an agency or school described in paragraph (1).

(B) Employer

The term "employer" means an agency or school described in paragraph (1).

(b) Leave does not violate certain other Federal laws

A local educational agency and a private elementary or secondary school shall not be in violation of the Individuals With Disabilities Education Act (20 U.S.C. 1400 et seq., section 794 of this title), or title VI of the Civil Rights Act of 1964 (42 U.S.C. 2000d et seq.), solely as a result of an eligible employee of such agency or school exercising the rights of such employee under this subchapter.

(c) Intermittent leave or leave on reduced schedule for instructional employees

(1) In general

Subject to paragraph (2), in any case in which an eligible employee employed principally in an instructional capacity by any such educational agency or school requests leave under subparagraph (C) or (D) of section 2612(a)(1) of this title that is foreseeable based on planned medical treatment and the employee would be on leave for greater than 20 percent of the total number of working days in the period during which the leave would extend, the agency or school may require that such employee elect either—

(A) to take leave for periods of a particular duration, not to exceed the duration of the planned medical treatment; or

(B) to transfer temporarily to an available alternative position offered by the employer for which the employee is qualified, and that—

(i) has equivalent pay and benefits; and

(ii) better accommodates recurring periods of leave than the regular employment position of the employee.

(2) Application

The elections described in subparagraphs (A) and (B) of paragraph (1) shall apply only with respect to an eligible employee who complies with section 2612(e)(2) of this title.

(d) Rules applicable to periods near conclusion of academic term

The following rules shall apply with respect to periods of leave near the conclusion of an academic term in the case of any eligible employee employed principally in an instructional capacity by any such educational agency or school:

(1) Leave more than 5 weeks prior to end of term

If the eligible employee begins leave under section 2612 of this title more than 5 weeks prior to the end of the academic term, the agency or school may require the employee to continue taking leave until the end of such term, if—

    (A) the leave is of at least 3 weeks duration; and

    (B) the return to employment would occur during the 3-week period before the end of such term.

(2) Leave less than 5 weeks prior to end of term

If the eligible employee begins leave under subparagraph (A), (B), or (C) of section 2612(a)(1) of this title during the period that commences 5 weeks prior to the end of the academic term, the agency or school may require the employee to continue taking leave until the end of such term, if—

    (A) the leave is of greater than 2 weeks duration; and

    (B) the return to employment would occur during the 2-week period before the end of such term.

(3) Leave less than 3 weeks prior to end of term

If the eligible employee begins leave under sub-paragraph (A), (B), or (C) of section 2612(a)(1) of this title during the period that commences 3 weeks prior to the end of the academic term and the duration of the leave is greater than 5 working days, the agency or school may require the employee to continue to take leave until the end of such term.

(e) Restoration to equivalent employment position

For purposes of determinations under section 2614(a)(1)(B) of this title (relating to the restoration of an eligible employee to an equivalent position), in the case of a local educational agency or a private elementary or secondary school, such determination shall be made on the basis of established school board policies and practices, private school policies and practices, and collective bargaining agreements.

(f) Reduction of amount of liability

If a local educational agency or a private elementary or secondary school that has violated this subchapter proves to the satisfaction of the court that the agency, school, or department had reasonable grounds for believing that the underlying act or omission was not a violation of this subchapter, such court may, in the discretion of the court, reduce the amount of the liability provided for under section 2617(a)(1)(A) of this title to the amount and interest determined under clauses (i) and (ii), respectively, of such section.

§ 2619. Notice

(a) In general

Each employer shall post and keep posted, in conspicuous places on the premises of the employer where notices to employees and applicants for employ-

ment are customarily posted, a notice, to be prepared or approved by the Secretary, setting forth excerpts from, or summaries of, the pertinent provisions of this subchapter and information pertaining to the filing of a charge.

(b) Penalty

Any employer that willfully violates this section may be assessed a civil money penalty not to exceed $100 for each separate offense.

§ 2631. Establishment

There is established a commission to be known as the Commission on Leave (referred to in this subchapter as the "Commission").

§ 2632. Duties

The Commission shall—

    (1) conduct a comprehensive study of—

        (A) existing and proposed mandatory and voluntary policies relating to family and temporary medical leave, including policies provided by employers not covered under this Act;

        (B) the potential costs, benefits, and impact on productivity, job creation and business growth of such policies on employers and employees;

        (C) possible differences in costs, benefits, and impact on productivity, job creation and business growth of such policies on employers based on business type and size;

        (D) the impact of family and medical leave policies on the availability of employee benefits provided by employers, including employers not covered under this Act;

        (E) alternate and equivalent State enforcement of subchapter I of this chapter with respect to employees described in section 2618(a) of this title;

        (F) methods used by employers to reduce administrative costs of implementing family and medical leave policies;

        (G) the ability of the employers to recover, under section 2614(c)(2) of this title, the premiums described in such section; and

        (H) the impact on employers and employees of policies that provide temporary wage replacement during periods of family and medical leave.

    (2) not later than 2 years after the date on which the Commission first meets, prepare and submit, to the appropriate Committees of Congress, a report concerning the subjects listed in paragraph (1).

§ 2633. Membership

(a) Composition

(1) Appointments

The Commission shall be composed of 12 voting members and 4 ex officio members to be appointed not later than 60 days after February 5, 1993, as follows:

(A) Senators

One Senator shall be appointed by the Majority Leader of the Senate, and one Senator shall be appointed by the Minority Leader of the Senate.

(B) Members of House of Representatives

One Member of the House of Representatives shall be appointed by the Speaker of the House of Representatives, and one Member of the House of Representatives shall be appointed by the Minority Leader of the House of Representatives.

(C) Additional members

(i) Appointment

Two members each shall be appointed by—

(I) the Speaker of the House of Representatives;

(II) the Majority Leader of the Senate;

(III) the Minority Leader of the House of Representatives; and

(IV) the Minority Leader of the Senate.

(ii) Expertise

Such members shall be appointed by virtue of demonstrated expertise in relevant family, temporary disability, and labor management issues. Such members shall include representatives of employers, including employers from large businesses and from small businesses.

(2) Ex officio members

The Secretary of Health and Human Services, the Secretary of Labor, the Secretary of Commerce, and the Administrator of the Small Business Administration shall serve on the Commission as nonvoting ex officio members.

(b) Vacancies

Any vacancy on the Commission shall be filled in the manner in which the original appointment was made. The vacancy shall not affect the power of the remaining members to execute the duties of the Commission.

(c) Chairperson and vice chairperson

The Commission shall elect a chairperson and a vice chairperson from among the members of the Commission.

(d) Quorum

Eight members of the Commission shall constitute a quorum for all purposes, except that a lesser number may constitute a quorum for the purpose of holding hearings.

§ 2634. Compensation

(a) Pay

Members of the Commission shall serve without compensation.

(b) Travel expenses

Members of the Commission shall be allowed reasonable travel expenses, including a per diem allowance, in accordance with section 5703 of title 5 when performing duties of the Commission.

§ 2635. Powers

(a) Meetings

The Commission shall first meet not later than 30 days after the date on which all members are appointed, and the Commission shall meet thereafter on the call of the chairperson or a majority of the members.

(b) Hearings and sessions

The Commission may hold such hearings, sit and act at such times and places, take such testimony, and receive such evidence as the Commission considers appropriate. The Commission may administer oaths or affirmations to witnesses appearing before it.

(c) Access to information

The Commission may secure directly from any Federal agency information necessary to enable it to carry out this subchapter, if the information may be disclosed under section 552 of title 5. Subject to the previous sentence, on the request of the chairperson or vice chairperson of the Commission, the head of such agency shall furnish such information to the Commission.

(d) Use of facilities and services

Upon the request of the Commission, the head of any Federal agency may make available to the Commission any of the facilities and services of such agency.

(e) Personnel from other agencies

On the request of the Commission, the head of any Federal agency may detail any of the personnel of such agency to serve as an Executive Director of the Commission or assist the Commission in carrying out the duties of the Commission. Any detail shall not interrupt or otherwise affect the civil service status or privileges of the Federal employee.

(f) Voluntary service

Notwithstanding section 1342 of title 31, the chairperson of the Commission may accept for the Commission voluntary services provided by a member of the Commission.

§ 2636. Termination

The Commission shall terminate 30 days after the date of the submission of the report of the Commission to Congress.

§ 2651. Effect on other laws

(a) Federal and State antidiscrimination laws

Nothing in this Act or any amendment made by this Act shall be construed to modify or affect any Federal or State law prohibiting discrimination on the basis of race, religion, color, national origin, sex, age, or disability.

(b) State and local laws

Nothing in this Act or any amendment made by this Act shall be construed to supersede any provision of any State or local law that provides greater family or medical leave rights than the rights established under this Act or any amendment made by this Act.

§ 2652. Effect on existing employment benefits

(a) More protective

Nothing in this Act or any amendment made by this Act shall be construed to diminish the obligation of an employer to comply with any collective bargaining agreement or any employment benefit program or plan

that provides greater family or medical leave rights to employees than the rights established under this Act or any amendment made by this Act.

(b) Less protective

The rights established for employees under this Act or any amendment made by this Act shall not be diminished by any collective bargaining agreement or any employment benefit program or plan.

§ 2653. Encouragement of more generous leave policies

Nothing in this Act or any amendment made by this Act shall be construed to discourage employers from adopting or retaining leave policies more generous than any policies that comply with the requirements under this Act or any amendment made by this Act.

§ 2654. Regulations

The Secretary of Labor shall prescribe such regulations as are necessary to carry out subchapter I of this chapter and this subchapter not later than 120 days after February 5, 1993. The provisions of the law are subject to interpretation and court precedent. More detailed information and the meaning of the Family and Medical Leave Act (FMLA) and its Provisions should be obtained from a qualified attorney.

■

Chapter 11

The Immigration Reform and Control Act of 1986 (IRCA)

Statute: 8 U.S.C. § 1324a, § 1324b

http://www.law.cornell.edu/uscode/8/1324a.html

Regulations: 8 C.F.R. § 274a

http://cfr.law.cornell.edu/cfr/cfr.php?title=8&type=part&value=274a

Definitions

Date of hire
The date of hire is when the employee actually starts working for wages or other remuneration. The date of hire does not commence on the date a job offer is made or accepted.

Unauthorized alien
An individual who is not a United States citizen and who is neither (1) an alien lawfully admitted into the United States for permanent residence, nor (2) an alien authorized by the

INS or the U.S. Attorney General to be employed in the United States.

Independent contractor
Someone who carries on an independent business, contracts to do a piece of work according to his or her own means or methods and is subject to control only as to results. Other federal and state laws have somewhat different definitions, but these are not relevant here.

A. Overview of IRCA

1. Summary

When IRCA was passed in 1986, it was the most sweeping immigration law passed by Congress in more than 35 years. It addresses many immigration issues, but this discussion examines only the law's regulation of certain aspects of the employment relationship. In addition, this discussion does not cover the law's regulation of agricultural workers.

The IRCA has three major provisions affecting non-agricultural employment:

- **Verification:** Employers must verify that all employees are legally authorized to work in the United States. IRCA makes it illegal for an employer to knowingly hire, recruit or refer for employment an *unauthorized alien.*

- **Recordkeeping:** Employers must maintain forms verifying that employees are legally authorized to work in the United States.
- **Anti-discrimination:** Employers may not discriminate based on citizenship status or national origin.

2. Exceptions

IRCA does not cover the following workers:

- *Independent contractors.*
- Individuals who provide domestic service (for example, baby-sitting or housecleaning) in a private home and whose service is sporadic, irregular or intermittent. If the individual's service is regular (say, once a week or twice a month), then the individual falls within IRCA.

- aliens granted asylum (but only for the specified period)
- aliens admitted into the United States as nonimmigrant fiancées and fiancees (but only for the specified period)
- citizens of Micronesia and the Marshall Islands
- aliens granted suspension of deportation
- aliens granted extended voluntary departure as members of certain nationality groups, by request of the Secretary of State.

What's Required: Workers

Within one business day of the *date of hire,* covered workers must complete their portion of the INS Form I-9, which is the form that employers must use to comply with IRCA.

Penalties

Employers who knowingly hire an unauthorized alien, or who knowingly continue to employ an unauthorized alien, face both criminal and civil penalties:

- **Criminal penalties:** Employers can be fined up to $3,000 for each *unauthorized alien* or be imprisoned for up to six months or both.
- **Civil penalties:** Employers can be ordered to cease from violating the law and to pay a fine according to the following schedule:
- **First offense:** $275 to $2,200 for each *unauthorized alien.*
- **Second offense:** $2,200 to $5,500 for each *unauthorized alien.*

- **More than two offenses:** $3,300 to $11,000 for each *unauthorized alien.*

Employers who fail to comply with the verification requirements must pay a fine of $110 to $1,100 for each individual.

2. Recordkeeping

Employers must keep records to prove that they verified the legality of their workers.

Regulated Employers

IRCA's recordkeeping provision applies to all employers regardless of size, including:

- all private employers
- the federal government
- state governments
- local governments, and
- persons or entities who refer individuals for a fee.

Covered Workers

IRCA's recordkeeping provision covers the following employees:

- United States citizens and nationals, and
- aliens who are legally authorized to work in the United States.

It does not cover *independent contractors* or certain domestic workers (see Section A2, above).

What's Prohibited: Employers

Covered employers may not do the following:

- If the individual presents documents sufficient to verify both identification and authorization, the employer may

B. Major Provisions of IRCA

1. Verification

Employers must verify that the people who work for them are legally authorized to work in the United States.

Regulated Employers

The verification provision of IRCA covers all employers regardless of size, including the following:

- all private employers
- the federal government
- state governments
- local governments, and
- persons or entities who refer individuals for a fee.

Covered Workers

The verification provision of IRCA covers all employees, including the following:

- United States citizens and nationals, and
- aliens who are legally authorized to work in the United States.

It does not cover *independent contractors* or certain domestic workers (see Section A2, above).

What's Prohibited: Employers

Covered employers may not do either of the following:

- knowingly hire, recruit or refer for a fee an *unauthorized alien* for employment in the United States, or
- continue to employ an individual after discovering that he or she is an *unauthorized alien.*

What's Required: Employers

Covered employers must do all of the following:

- Within three business days of the employee's *date of hire,* physically examine documents presented by the employee to establish the employee's identity and employment authorization. (See Section B2, below, for a list of acceptable documents that establish identity and authorization.)
- If the employer is hiring the employee for fewer than three days total, the employer must examine the documents before the end of the employee's first working day.

Individuals Authorized to Work in the United States

The following individuals are authorized to work in the United States:

- U.S. citizens
- lawful permanent resident aliens
- lawful temporary resident aliens
- aliens paroled into the United States as refugees (but only for the specified period)

not ask for additional documents. If an employer suspects that the employee has given the employer fraudulent documents, then the employer should contact the Immigration and Naturalization Service rather than insist on more documents. (See Section F, below, for more about the INS.)

- Employers may copy any of the documents presented by the individual for verification purposes, but only if the copy is kept with the INS Form I-9, which is the document that employers must complete to verify that they have checked the legality of their workers. (See "What's Required: Employers," immediately below, for more about INS Form I-9.) Employers may not use the document for any purpose other than complying with the IRCA.

What's Required: Employers

Covered employers must do all of the following:

- Within three business days of the *date of hire* verify under penalty of perjury that the employee is a United States citizen or authorized alien by completing INS Form I-9. Employers must do this for all employees, including family members, relatives and personal acquaintances.
- If the employer is hiring the employee for fewer than three days total, then the employer must complete INS Form I-9 before the end of the employee's first working day.

- Ensure that the employee completes his or her portion of the INS Form I-9 within one day of the *date of hire*.
- Employers must keep the INS Form I-9 for three years after the *date of hire* or one year after the date of termination.
- Employers must make all I-9 forms available for inspection by the INS or the U.S. Department of Labor. The employer will be given written notice of the inspection, and the employer will have at least three days advance notice.

Acceptable Documents

To satisfy the law's verification and record-keeping requirements, employers may view one document or a combination of documents, depending on the nature of the document.

Documents that are acceptable under the law fall into one of three categories:

- those that verify both identity and authorization to work in the United States (see List A, below)
- those that verify only identity (see List B, below), and
- those that verify only employment authorization (see List C, below).

If an employee submits a document from List A, no other documents are necessary. Otherwise, an employee must submit a document from BOTH List B and List C.

List A

The following documents establish both identity and employment authorization:

- U.S. passport (either expired or unexpired)

- unexpired foreign passport with an I-551 stamp or with an attached INS Form I-94 indicating unexpired employment authorization
- alien registration receipt card with photograph
- unexpired temporary card (INS Form I-689)
- unexpired temporary authorization card (INS Form I-688A)
- unexpired employment authorization document issued by the INS with photograph (INS Form I-688B), or
- unexpired employment authorization document issued by the INS (INS Form I-766).

If you have a copy of INS Form I-9, you may notice that the list above does not match the list of acceptable documents delineated on the I-9 itself. This is because the INS has revised the list, but has not yet revised the I-9 form. To get the most up-to-date information regarding acceptable documents, refer to the INS website at http://www.ins.gov.

List B
The following documents establish identity only:

- driver's license or identification card issued by a state or outlying possession of the United States, provided it contains a photograph or identifying information such as name, date of birth, sex, height, eye color and address
- identification card issued by federal, state or local government agencies or entities, provided it contains a photo-graph or identifying information such as name, date of birth, sex, height, eye color and address
- school identification card with a photograph
- voter's registration card
- U.S. military card or draft record
- military dependent's identification card
- U.S. Coast Guard Merchant Marine card
- Native American tribal document
- driver's license issued by a Canadian government authority
- school report or report card (for someone younger than 18)
- clinic, doctor or hospital record (for someone younger than 18), or
- day-care or nursery school record (for someone younger than 18).

List C
The following documents establish authorization only:

- U.S. Social Security card issued by the Social Security Administration (other than a card stating that it is not valid for employment)
- certification of birth abroad issued by the Department of State (Form FS-545 or Form DS-1350)
- original or certified copy of a birth certificate issued by a state, county, municipal authority or outlying possession of the United States bearing an official seal
- Native American tribal document
- U.S. citizen identification card (INS Form I-197)

- identification card of a resident citizen in the United States (INS Form I-179), or
- unexpired employment authorization document issued by the INS (other than those listed under List A, above).

Receipts Instead of Acceptable Documents

An employer may accept a document called a "receipt" in place of one of the acceptable documents listed above in one of the following instances:

- when the individual presents a receipt showing application for a replacement document
- when the individual presents the arrival portion of Form I-94, on which the INS has placed a temporary I-551 stamp (indicating lawful permanent residence) or the individual's picture, or
- when the individual presents the departure portion of Form I-94 that the INS has marked with a refugee admission stamp.

A receipt is a temporary replacement for an acceptable document. In the case of the I-551 stamp, the individual must present the stamp prior to the expiration date on the stamp. Once the stamp expires, the individual must present one or two acceptable documents listed above.

In the case of the I-94 form, the individual must present Form I-766, Form I-688B or an unrestricted Social Security account number card (accompanied by a List B document) within 90 days of the *date of hire* or by the date that the employment authorization expires.

What's Required: Workers

Within one business day of the *date of hire,* covered workers must complete their portion of the INS Form I-9.

Penalties

Employers who fail to inspect documents face the penalties described in Section B1, above.

Employers who refuse to honor acceptable documents presented to them, or who ask for more documents than necessary to follow the law, must pay a civil penalty of between $100 and $1,000 for each individual.

3. Discrimination

IRCA protects certain workers from discrimination based on citizenship or national origin.

Regulated Employers

The following employers must comply with IRCA's anti-discrimination provision:

- private employers with four or more employees
- the federal government
- state governments, and
- local governments.

Covered Workers

The following individuals are protected by IRCA's anti-discrimination provision:

- a citizen or national of the United States
- an alien lawfully admitted for permanent residence
- an alien lawfully admitted for temporary residence

- an alien admitted as a refugee, and
- an alien granted asylum.

What's Prohibited: Employers

Covered employers may not discriminate against covered employees on the basis of citizenship status or national origin unless a federal law explicitly allows them to do so. This prohibition applies to all phases of the employment relationship, including hiring, promotion, pay, job assignment, discipline and termination.

Employers may not retaliate against workers for asserting their rights under the law.

Exceptions

IRCA does not protect the following types of aliens:

- an alien who fails to apply for naturalization within six months of the date he or she first becomes eligible to apply for naturalization or,
- an alien who has applied on a timely basis, but who has not been naturalized as a citizen within two years after the date of the application, unless the alien can establish that he or she is actively pursuing naturalization. (Note: the time consumed by the INS processing the application does not count against the two years.)

IRCA also does not protect *independent contractors* or certain domestic workers (see Section A2, above).

If two individuals are equally qualified for a position, an employer may give preference to a citizen or national of the United States.

Penalties

Employers who discriminate on the basis of national origin or citizenship status face investigation by the Office of the Special Counsel for Immigration Related Unfair Employment (the OSC) and the EEOC, depending on the size of the employer and the nature of the discrimination. (See Section F, below, for more about the OSC.) (For more about the EEOC and national origin discrimination by employers with more than 14 employees, see the chapter on Title VII.)

Employers also face a hearing in front of an administrative law judge or a civil trial in federal court.

Employers who are found guilty of discrimination face the following penalties under IRCA:

- an order to reinstate the aggrieved individual(s) with or without back pay
- if the employer has never been found guilty before, a civil fine of between $250 and $2,000 for each aggrieved individual
- if the employer has been found guilty once before, a civil fine of between $2,000 and $5,000 for each aggrieved individual
- if the employer has previously been found guilty two or more times, a civil fine of between $3,000 and $10,000 for each aggrieved individual, and
- an order to pay the attorney's fees of the individual(s) who brought suit.

Employers who have more than 14 employees and have been found guilty of national origin discrimination also face penalties under Title VII. (For more, see the chapter on Title VII.)

C. How IRCA Is Enforced

1. Individual Complaints

Anyone may file a complaint with the INS if he or she thinks an employer is violating the recordkeeping or verification provisions of the law. (See Section F, below, for more about the INS.)

Employees who want to complain about discrimination can complain to either the OSC or the EEOC, depending on the type of discrimination and the size of the employer:

- Employees who think that they are being discriminated against on the basis of citizenship status—and who work for an employer with four or more employees—can file a charge with the OSC. (See Section F, below, for more about the OSC.)
- Employees who think that they are being discriminated against on the basis of national origin in violation of the law—and who work for an employer with between four and 14 employees—can file a charge with the OSC.
- Employees who think that they are being discriminated against on the basis of national origin—and who work for an employer with more than 14 employees—can file a charge with the U.S. Equal Employment Opportunity Commission. (For more about the EEOC

and national origin discrimination, see the chapter on Title VII.)

2. Agency Enforcement

The INS has the authority to conduct investigations of complaints and to inspect an employer's I-9 forms.

The OSC has the authority to conduct investigations of charges and to file a complaint against the employer before an administrative law judge. The OSC also has the power to act on its own initiative.

The EEOC has the authority to conduct investigations of charges and to file a complaint against the employer in a court of law. The EEOC also has the power to act on its own initiative.

D. For Employers: Complying With IRCA

1. Reporting Requirements

IRCA imposes no reporting requirements.

2. Recordkeeping Requirements

See Section B, above.

3. Practical Tips

The following are some tips for complying with IRCA:

- If possible, designate one person at your company to be in charge of I-9 compliance. Make sure this person knows IRCA's rules, and inform this person of all new hires.

- Do not keep an employee's I-9 form in his or her personnel file. Because the INS has the right to inspect I-9 forms, keeping the form in a file separate from the employee's other records protects the employee's privacy. In addition, keeping the I-9 separate means that supervisors and managers will not be privy to the employee's nationality and citizenship status—something that could help defeat claims of discrimination.
- Carry out your obligations under IRCA in the same manner for all employees. Otherwise, you leave yourself vulnerable to claims of discrimination.
- Keep I-9 forms as private as possible and allow them to be viewed on a need-to-know basis only. This will help prevent claims of discrimination.

4. Penalties

The penalties for violating IRCA depend on the provision violated—see Section B, above.

E. For Workers: Asserting Rights Under IRCA

1. Where to Start

If you believe you are being discriminated against because you are an immigrant worker, or because of your national origin or because of your citizenship status, start by complaining internally at your company. If you have an employee handbook, follow the complaint procedures set forth there. If there are no complaint procedures, complain to any member of management or to the human resources department.

If you are in a union, talk to your shop steward or union representative.

If complaining through your company or your union does not work, the next step is to file a complaint with a government agency. In doing this, *you must act quickly*. This is because you only get 180 days from the day of the discriminatory conduct to file a complaint.

To know where to file your complaint, you must know what type of discrimination you are suffering from and how large your employer is:

- If you think you are being discriminated against based on your citizenship status, you can file a charge form with the OSC (see Section F, below, for more about the OSC). To learn more, call the OSC's hotline at 800-255-7688.
- If you think you are being discriminated against based on your national origin, and if you work for a company with between four and 14 employees, you can file a charge form with the OSC.
- If you think you are being discriminated against based on your national origin, and if you work for a company with more than 14 employees, you can file a charge with the EEOC. (For more about the EEOC and national origin discrimi-

nation, see the chapter on Title VII.) To learn more, call the EEOC's hotline at 800-669-4000.

If you file a charge with the OSC, it will investigate the charge and, within 120 days, decide whether or not to bring a complaint before an administrative law judge. If the OSC does not bring a complaint before an administrative law judge within 120 days, it will notify you, and you will have the right to bring a complaint before the judge yourself within 90 days after receiving the notice from the OSC.

If you file a charge with the EEOC, it will investigate your complaint. The EEOC may try to negotiate a settlement on your behalf, file a civil suit on your behalf or give you a right-to-sue letter than permits you to file a civil suit on your own behalf.

2. Required Forms

Both the OSC and the EEOC have charge forms that you must complete to complain about discrimination. You can obtain those charge forms on the Internet or by contacting the agency by phone. See Section E1, above, for contact information.

3. Practical Tips

If you feel you are being treated differently because you are an immigrant, because of your national origin or because of your citizenship status, you can take action to protect yourself:

- **Complain soon and often.** As soon as you begin to suspect discrimination, follow your company's internal complaint procedures. Complain to managers or human resources. Be assertive. You may lose your rights if you passively sit back and expect someone else to deal with the problem for you.

- **Take notes.** Complaining about discrimination won't mean much if you can't prove what happened. Keep a journal or log of everything that happens to you that feels discriminatory. Keep notes of every conversation you have with anyone about the discriminatory conduct. Be extra sure to summarize instances when you complained to a manager or to human resources about discrimination. Be sure to date all of your notes and keep them in a safe place.

- **Act fast.** Don't let your company string you along for too long. You have only 180 days to complain to a government agency. And don't wait until the 179th day before complaining. You'll be surprised by how time-consuming the complaint process can be. Give yourself plenty of time to work through the government red tape.

- **Keep copies of every document that you mail to a government agency.** Keep everything that the agency sends to you. Use a journal to record all of your contacts with the government agency.

F. Agency Charged With Enforcement & Compliance

Department of Justice
U.S. Department of Justice
950 Pennsylvania Avenue, NW
Washington, DC 20530-0001
Phone: 800-375-5283
http://www.usdoj.gov

The Immigration and Naturalization Service (INS) division of the Department of Justice enforces IRCA's verification and recordkeeping provisions. The INS can be found on the Internet at: http://www.ins.gov

The Office of the Special Counsel for Immigration Related Unfair Employment Practices (OSC) in the department's Civil Rights Division enforces IRCA's anti-discrimination provisions. The OSC can be reached on the Internet at: http://www.usdoj.gov/crt/osc

Agency Resources for Employers
(These can be obtained either at the Web addresses listed below or at the address and phone number listed above.)
- *Handbook for Employers*
  http://www.ins.gov/graphics/lawsregs/handbook/hnmanual.htm
- *INS Form I-9*
  http://www.ins.gov/graphics/formsfee/forms/index.htm
- *Employer Guide*
  http://www.usdoj.gov/crt/osc/tools/index.html

Agency Resources for Workers
(These can be obtained either at the Web addresses listed below or at the address and phone number listed above.)
- *Worker Brochure*
  http://www.usdoj.gov/crt/osc/tools/index.html
- *Charge Form*
  http://www.usdoj.gov/crt/osc/facts/index.html
- *Federal Laws Prohibiting Job Discrimination, Q&A*
  http://www.eeoc.gov/facts/qanda.html
- *How to File a Charge*
  http://www.eeoc.gov/facts/howtofil.html

G. State Laws Relating to Immigration

To find out if your state has a law relating to immigration, contact your state labor department (see the Appendix for contact details).

H. Full Text of IRCA

Title 8—Aliens and Nationality
Chapter 12—Immigration and Nationality
Subchapter II—Immigration
Part VIII—General Penalty Provisions

...

§ 1324a. Unlawful employment of aliens

§ 1324b. Unfair immigration-related employment practices

...

§ 1324a.—Unlawful employment of aliens

(a) Making employment of unauthorized aliens unlawful

(1) In general

It is unlawful for a person or other entity—

(A) to hire, or to recruit or refer for a fee, for employment in the United States an alien knowing the alien is an unauthorized alien (as defined in subsection (h)(3) of this section) with respect to such employment, or

(B) (i) to hire for employment in the United States an individual without complying with the requirements of subsection (b) of this section or (ii) if the person or entity is an agricultural association, agricultural employer, or farm labor contractor (as defined in section 1802 of Title 29) to hire, or to recruit or refer for a fee, for employment in the United States an individual without complying with the requirements of subsection (b) of this section.

(2) Continuing employment

It is unlawful for a person or other entity, after hiring an alien for employment in accordance with paragraph (1), to continue to employ the alien in the United States knowing the alien is (or has become) an unauthorized alien with respect to such employment.

(3) Defense

A person or entity that establishes that it has complied in good faith with the requirements of subsection (b) of this section with respect to the hiring, recruiting, or referral for employment of an alien in the United States has established an affirmative defense that the person or entity has not violated paragraph (1)(A) with respect to such hiring, recruiting, or referral.

(4) Use of labor through contract

For purposes of this section, a person or other entity who uses a contract, subcontract, or exchange, entered into, renegotiated, or extended after the date of the enactment of this section [November 6, 1986], to obtain the labor of an alien in the United States knowing that the alien is an unauthorized alien (as defined in subsection (h)(3) of this section) with respect to performing such labor, shall be considered to have hired the alien for employment in the United States in violation of paragraph (1)(A).

(5) Use of State employment agency documentation

For purposes of paragraphs (1)(B) and (3), a person or entity shall be deemed to have complied with the requirements of subsection (b) of this section with respect to the hiring of an individual who was referred for such employment by a State employment agency (as defined by the Attorney General), if the person or entity has and retains (for the period and in the manner described in subsection (b)(3)) appropriate documentation of such referral by that agency, which documentation certifies that the agency has complied with the procedures specified in subsection (b) of this section with respect to the individual's referral.

(6) Treatment of documentation for certain employees

(A) In general

For purposes of this section, if—

(i) an individual is a member of a collective-bargaining unit and is employed, under a collective bargaining agreement entered into between one or more employee organizations and an association of two or more employers, by an employer that is a member of such association, and

(ii) within the period specified in subparagraph (B), another employer that is a member of the association (or an agent of such association on behalf of the employer) has complied with the requirements of subsection (b) of this section with respect to the employment of the individual,

the subsequent employer shall be deemed to have complied with the requirements of subsection (b) of this section with respect to the hiring of the employee and shall not be liable for civil penalties described in subsection (e)(5) of this section.

(B) Period

The period described in this subparagraph is 3 years, or, if less, the period of time that the individual is authorized to be employed in the United States.

(C) Liability

(i) In general

If any employer that is a member of an association hires for employment in the United States an individual and relies upon the provisions of subparagraph (A) to comply with the requirements of subsection (b) of this section and the individual is an alien not authorized to work in the United States, then for the purposes of paragraph (1)(A), subject to clause (ii), the employer shall be presumed to have known at the time of hiring or afterward that the individual was an alien not authorized to work in the United States.

(ii) Rebuttal of presumption

The presumption established by clause (i) may be rebutted by the employer only through the presentation of clear and convincing evidence that the employer did not know (and could not reasonably have known) that the individual at the time of hiring or afterward was an alien not authorized to work in the United States.

(iii) Exception

Clause (i) shall not apply in any prosecution under subsection (f)(1) of this section.

(7) Application to Federal Government

For purposes of this section, the term "entity" includes an entity in any branch of the Federal Government.

(b) Employment verification system

The requirements referred to in paragraphs (1)(B) and (3) of subsection (a) of this section are, in the case of a person or other entity hiring, recruiting, or referring an individual for employment in the United States, the requirements specified in the following three paragraphs:

(1) Attestation after examination of documentation

(A) In general

The person or entity must attest, under penalty of perjury and on a form designated or established by the Attorney General by regulation, that it has verified that the individual is not an unauthorized alien by examining—

(i) a document described in subparagraph (B), or

(ii) a document described in subparagraph (C) and a document described in subparagraph (D).

A person or entity has complied with the requirement of this paragraph with respect to examination of a document if the document reasonably appears on its face to be genuine. If an individual provides a document or combination of documents that reasonably appears on its face to be genuine and that is sufficient to meet the requirements of the first sentence of this paragraph, nothing in this paragraph shall be construed as requiring the person or entity to solicit the production of any other document or as requiring the individual to produce such another document.

(B) Documents establishing both employment authorization and identity

A document described in this subparagraph is an individual's—

(i) United States passport;

(ii) resident alien card, alien registration card, or other document designated by the Attorney General, if the document—

(I) contains a photograph of the individual and such other personal identifying information relating to the individual as the Attorney General finds, by regulation, sufficient for purposes of this subsection,

(II) is evidence of authorization of employment in the United States, and

(III) contains security features to make it resistant to tampering, counterfeiting, and fraudulent use.

(C) Documents evidencing employment authorization

A document described in this subparagraph is an individual's—

(i) social security account number card (other than such a card which specifies on the face that the issuance of the card does not authorize employment in the United States); or

(ii) other documentation evidencing authorization of employment in the United States which the Attorney General finds, by regulation, to be acceptable for purposes of this section.

(D) Documents establishing identity of individual

A document described in this subparagraph is an individual's—

(i) driver's license or similar document issued for the purpose of identification by a State, if it contains a photograph of the individual or such other personal identifying information relating to the individual as the Attorney General finds, by regulation, sufficient for purposes of this section; or

(ii) in the case of individuals under 16 years of age or in a State which does not provide for issuance of an identification document (other than a driver's license) referred to in clause (i), documentation of personal identity of such other type as the Attorney General finds, by regulation, provides a reliable means of identification.

(E) Authority to prohibit use of certain documents

If the Attorney General finds, by regulation, that any document described in subparagraph (B), (C), or (D) as establishing employment authorization or identity does not reliably establish such authorization or identity or is being used fraudulently to an unacceptable degree, the Attorney General may prohibit or place conditions on its use for purposes of this subsection.

(2) Individual attestation of employment authorization

The individual must attest, under penalty of perjury on the form designated or established for purposes of paragraph (1), that the individual is a citizen or national of the United States, an alien lawfully admitted for permanent residence, or an alien who is authorized under this chapter or by the Attorney General to be hired, recruited, or referred for such employment.

(3) Retention of verification form

After completion of such form in accordance with paragraphs (1) and (2), the person or entity must retain the form and make it available for inspection by officers of the Service, the Special Counsel for Immigration-Related Unfair Employment Practices, or the Department of Labor during a period beginning on the date of the hiring, recruiting, or referral of the individual and ending—

(A) in the case of the recruiting or referral for a fee (without hiring) of an individual, three years after the date of the recruiting or referral, and

(B) in the case of the hiring of an individual—

(i) three years after the date of such hiring, or

(ii) one year after the date the individual's employment is terminated,

whichever is later.

(4) Copying of documentation permitted

Notwithstanding any other provision of law, the person or entity may copy a document presented by an individual pursuant to this subsection and may retain the copy, but only (except as otherwise permitted under law) for the purpose of complying with the requirements of this subsection.

(5) Limitation on use of attestation form

A form designated or established by the Attorney General under this subsection and any information contained in or appended to such form, may not be used for purposes other than for enforcement of this chapter and sections 1001, 1028, 1546, and 1621 of Title 18.

(6) Good faith compliance

(A) In general

Except as provided in subparagraphs (B) and (C), a person or entity is considered to have complied with a requirement of this subsection notwithstanding a technical or procedural failure to meet such requirement if there was a good faith attempt to comply with the requirement.

(B) Exception if failure to correct after notice

Subparagraph (A) shall not apply if—

(i) the Service (or another enforcement agency) has explained to the person or entity the basis for the failure,

(ii) the person or entity has been provided a period of not less than 10 business days (beginning after the date of the explanation) within which to correct the failure, and

(iii) the person or entity has not corrected the failure voluntarily within such period.

(C) Exception for pattern or practice violators

Subparagraph (A) shall not apply to a person or entity that has or is engaging in a pattern or practice of violations of subsection (a)(1)(A) or (a)(2) of this section.

(c) No authorization of national identification cards

Nothing in this section shall be construed to authorize, directly or indirectly, the issuance or use of national identification cards or the establishment of a national identification card.

(d) Evaluation and changes in employment verification system

(1) Presidential monitoring and improvements in system

(A) Monitoring

The President shall provide for the monitoring and evaluation of the degree to which the employment verification system established under subsection (b) of this section provides a secure system to determine employment eligibility in the United States and shall examine the suitability of existing Federal and State identification systems for use for this purpose.

(B) Improvements to establish secure system

To the extent that the system established under subsection (b) of this section is found not to be a secure system to determine employment eligibility in the United States, the President shall, subject to paragraph (3) and taking into account the results of any demonstration projects conducted under paragraph (4), implement such changes in (including additions to) the requirements of subsection (b) of this section as may be necessary to establish a secure system to determine employment eligibility in the United States. Such changes in the system may be implemented only if the changes conform to the requirements of paragraph (2).

(2) Restrictions on changes in system

Any change the President proposes to implement under paragraph (1) in the verification system must be designed in a manner so the verification system, as so changed, meets the following requirements:

(A) Reliable determination of identity

The system must be capable of reliably determining whether—

(i) a person with the identity claimed by an employee or prospective employee is eligible to work, and

(ii) the employee or prospective employee is claiming the identity of another individual.

(B) Using of counterfeit-resistant documents

If the system requires that a document be presented to or examined by an employer, the document must be in a form which is resistant to counterfeiting and tampering.

(C) Limited use of system

Any personal information utilized by the system may not be made available to Government agencies, employers, and other persons except to the extent necessary to verify that an individual is not an unauthorized alien.

(D) Privacy of information

The system must protect the privacy and security of personal information and identifiers utilized in the system.

(E) Limited denial of verification

A verification that an employee or prospective employee is eligible to be employed in the United States may not be withheld or revoked under the system for any reason other than that the employee or prospective employee is an unauthorized alien.

(F) Limited use for law enforcement purposes

The system may not be used for law enforcement purposes, other than for enforcement of this chapter or sections 1001, 1028, 1546, and 1621 of Title 18.

(G) Restriction on use of new documents

If the system requires individuals to present a new card or other document (designed specifically for use for this purpose) at the time of hiring, recruitment, or referral, then such document may not be required to be presented for any purpose other than under this chapter (or enforcement of sections 1001, 1028, 1546, and 1621 of Title 18) nor to be carried on one's person.

(3) Notice to Congress before implementing changes

(A) In general

The President may not implement any change under paragraph (1) unless at least—

(i) 60 days,

(ii) one year, in the case of a major change described in subparagraph (D)(iii), or

(iii) two years, in the case of a major change described in clause (i) or (ii) of subparagraph (D),

before the date of implementation of the change, the President has prepared and transmitted to the Committee on the Judiciary of the House of Representatives and to the Committee on the Judiciary of the Senate a written report setting forth the proposed change. If the President proposes to make any change regarding social security account number cards, the President shall transmit to the Committee on Ways and Means of the House of Representatives and to the Committee on Finance of the Senate a written report setting forth the proposed change. The President promptly shall cause to have printed in the Federal Register the substance of any major change (described in subparagraph (D)) proposed and reported to Congress.

(B) Contents of report

In any report under subparagraph (A) the President shall include recommendations for the establishment of civil and criminal sanctions for unauthorized use or disclosure of the information or identifiers contained in such system.

(C) Congressional review of major changes

(i) Hearings and review

The Committees on the Judiciary of the House of Representatives and of the Senate shall cause to have printed in the Congressional Record the substance of any major change described in subparagraph (D), shall hold hearings respecting the feasibility and desirability of implementing such a change, and, within the two-year period before implementation, shall report to their respective Houses findings on whether or not such a change should be implemented.

(ii) Congressional action

No major change may be implemented unless the Congress specifically provides, in an appropriations or other Act, for funds for implementation of the change.

(D) Major changes defined

As used in this paragraph, the term "major change" means a change which would—

(i) require an individual to present a new card or other document (designed specifically for use for this purpose) at the time of hiring, recruitment, or referral,

(ii) provide for a telephone verification system under which an employer, recruiter, or referrer must transmit to a Federal official information concerning the immigration status of prospective employees and the official transmits to the person, and the person must record, a verification code, or

(iii) require any change in any card used for accounting purposes under the Social Security Act [42 U.S.C.A. § 301 et seq.]; including any change requiring that the only social security account number cards which may be presented in order to comply with subsection (b)(1)(C)(i) of this section are such cards as are in a counterfeit-resistant form consistent with the second sentence of section 205(c)(2)(D) of the Social Security Act [42 U.S.C.A. § 405(c)(2)(D)].

(E) General revenue funding of social security card changes

Any costs incurred in developing and implementing any change described in subparagraph (D)(iii) for purposes of this subsection shall not be paid for out of any trust fund established under the Social Security Act [42 U.S.C.A. § 301 et seq.].

(4) Demonstration projects

(A) Authority

The President may undertake demonstration projects (consistent with paragraph (2)) of different changes in the requirements of subsection (b) of this section. No such project may extend over a period of longer than five years.

(B) Reports on projects

The President shall report to the Congress on the results of demonstration projects conducted under this paragraph.

(e) Compliance

(1) Complaints and investigations

The Attorney General shall establish procedures—

(A) for individuals and entities to file written, signed complaints respecting potential violations of subsection (a) or (g)(1) of this section,

(B) for the investigation of those complaints which, on their face, have a substantial probability of validity,

(C) for the investigation of such other violations of subsection (a) or (g)(1) of this section as the Attorney General determines to be appropriate, and

(D) for the designation in the Service of a unit which has, as its primary duty, the prosecution of cases of violations of subsection (a) or (g)(1) of this section under this subsection.

(2) Authority in investigations

In conducting investigations and hearings under this subsection—

(A) immigration officers and administrative law judges shall have reasonable access to examine evidence of any person or entity being investigated,

(B) administrative law judges may, if necessary, compel by subpoena the attendance of witnesses and the production of evidence at any designated place or hearing, and

(C) immigration officers designated by the Commissioner may compel by subpoena the attendance of witnesses and the production of evidence at any designated place prior to the filing of a complaint in a case under paragraph (2).

In case of contumacy or refusal to obey a subpoena lawfully issued under this paragraph and upon application of the Attorney General, an appropriate district court of the United States may issue an order requiring compliance with such subpoena and any failure to obey such order may be punished by such court as a contempt thereof.

(3) Hearing

(A) In general

Before imposing an order described in paragraph (4), (5), or (6) against a person or entity under this subsection for a violation of subsection (a) or (g)(1) of this section, the Attorney General shall provide the person or entity with notice and, upon request made within a reasonable time (of not less than 30 days, as established by the Attorney General) of the date of the notice, a hearing respecting the violation.

(B) Conduct of hearing

Any hearing so requested shall be conducted before an administrative law judge. The hearing shall be conducted in accordance with the requirements of section 554 of Title 5. The hearing shall be held at the nearest practicable place to the place where the person or entity resides or of the place where the alleged violation occurred. If no hearing is so requested, the Attorney General's imposition of the order shall constitute a final and unappealable order.

(C) Issuance of orders

If the administrative law judge determines, upon the preponderance of the evidence received, that a person or entity named in the complaint has violated subsection (a) or (g)(1) of this section, the administrative law judge shall state his findings of fact and issue and cause to be served on such person or entity an order described in paragraph (4), (5), or (6).

(4) Cease and desist order with civil money penalty for hiring, recruiting, and referral violations

With respect to a violation of subsection (a)(1)(A) or (a)(2) of this section, the order under this subsection—

(A) shall require the person or entity to cease and desist from such violations and to pay a civil penalty in an amount of—

(i) not less than $250 and not more than $2,000 for each unauthorized alien with respect to whom a violation of either such subsection occurred.

(ii) not less than $2,000 and not more than $5,000 for each such alien in the case of a person or entity previously subject to one order under this paragraph, or

(iii) not less than $3,000 and not more than $10,000 for each such alien in the case of a person or entity previously subject to more than one order under this paragraph; and

(B) may require the person or entity—

(i) to comply with the requirements of subsection (b) (or subsection (d) of this section if applicable) with respect to individuals hired (or recruited or referred for employment for a fee) during a period of up to three years, and

(ii) to take such other remedial action as is appropriate.

In applying this subsection in the case of a person or entity composed of distinct, physically separate subdivisions each of which provides separately for the hiring, recruiting, or referring for employment, without reference to the practices of, and not under the control of or common control with, another subdivision, each such subdivision shall be considered a separate person or entity.

(5) Order for civil money penalty for paperwork violations

With respect to a violation of subsection (a)(1)(B) of this section, the order under this subsection shall require the person or entity to pay a civil penalty in an amount of not less than $100 and not more than $1,000 for each individual with respect to whom such violation occurred. In determining the amount of the penalty, due consideration shall be given to the size of the business of the employer being charged, the good faith of the employer, the seriousness of the violation, whether or not the individual was an unauthorized alien, and the history of previous violations.

(6) Order for prohibited indemnity bonds

With respect to a violation of subsection (g)(1) of this section, the order under this subsection may provide for the remedy described in subsection (g)(2) of this section.

(7) Administrative appellate review

The decision and order of an administrative law judge shall become the final agency decision and order of the Attorney General unless either (A) within 30 days, an official delegated by regulation to exercise review authority over the decision and order modifies or vacates the decision and order, or (B) within 30 days of the date of such a modification or vacation (or within 60 days of the date of decision and order of an administrative law judge if not so modified or vacated) the decision and order is referred to the Attorney General pursuant to regulations, in which case the decision and order of the Attorney General shall become the final agency decision and order under this subsection. The Attorney General may not delegate the Attorney General's authority under this paragraph to any entity which has review authority over immigration-related matters.

(8) Judicial review

A person or entity adversely affected by a final order respecting an assessment may, within 45 days after the date the final order is issued, file a petition in the Court of Appeals for the appropriate circuit for review of the order.

(9) Enforcement of orders

If a person or entity fails to comply with a final order issued under this subsection against the person or entity, the Attorney General shall file a suit to seek compliance with the order in any appropriate district court of the United States. In any such suit, the validity and appropriateness of the final order shall not be subject to review.

(f) Criminal penalties and injunctions for pattern or practice violations

(1) Criminal penalty

Any person or entity which engages in a pattern or practice of violations of subsection (a)(1)(A) or (a)(2) of this section shall be fined not more than $3,000 for each unauthorized alien with respect to whom such a violation occurs, imprisoned for not more than six months for the entire pattern or practice, or both, notwithstanding the provisions of any other Federal law relating to fine levels.

(2) Enjoining of pattern or practice violations

Whenever the Attorney General has reasonable cause to believe that a person or entity is engaged in a pattern or practice of employment, recruitment, or referral in violation of paragraph (1)(A) or (2) of subsection (a) of this section, the Attorney General may bring a civil action in the appropriate district court of the United States requesting such relief, including a permanent or temporary injunction, restraining order, or other order against the person or entity, as the Attorney General deems necessary.

(g) Prohibition of indemnity bonds

(1) Prohibition

It is unlawful for a person or other entity, in the hiring, recruiting, or referring for employment of any individual, to require the individual to post a bond or security, to pay or agree to pay an amount, or other-wise to provide a financial guarantee or indemnity, against any potential liability arising under this section relating to such hiring, recruiting, or referring of the individual.

(2) Civil penalty

Any person or entity which is determined, after notice and opportunity for an administrative hearing under subsection (e) of this section, to have violated paragraph (1) shall be subject to a civil penalty of $1,000 for each violation and to an administrative order requiring the return of any amounts received in violation of such paragraph to the employee or, if the employee cannot be located, to the general fund of the Treasury.

(h) Miscellaneous provisions

(1) Documentation

In providing documentation or endorsement of authorization of aliens (other than aliens lawfully admitted for permanent residence) authorized to be employed in the United States, the Attorney General shall provide that any limitations with respect to the period or type of employment or employer shall be conspicuously stated on the documentation or endorsement.

(2) Preemption

The provisions of this section preempt any State or local law imposing civil or criminal sanctions (other than through licensing and similar laws) upon those who employ, or recruit or refer for a fee for employment, unauthorized aliens.

(3) Definition of unauthorized alien

As used in this section, the term "unauthorized alien" means, with respect to the employment of an alien at a particular time, that the alien is not at that time either (A) an alien lawfully admitted for permanent residence, or (B) authorized to be so employed by this chapter or by the Attorney General.

§ 1324b. Unfair immigration-related employment practices

(a) Prohibition of discrimination based on national origin or citizenship status

(1) General rule

It is an unfair immigration-related employment practice for a person or other entity to discriminate against any individual (other than an unauthorized alien, as defined in section 1324a(h)(3) of this title) with respect to the hiring, or recruitment or referral for a fee, of the individual for employment or the discharging of the individual from employment—

(A) because of such individual's national origin, or

(B) in the case of a protected individual (as defined in paragraph (3)), because of such individual's citizenship status.

(2) Exceptions

Paragraph (1) shall not apply to—

(A) a person or other entity that employs three or fewer employees,

(B) a person's or entity's discrimination because of an individual's national origin if the discrimination with respect to that person or entity and that individual is covered under section 703 of the Civil Rights Act of 1964 [42 U.S.C.A. § 2000e-2], or

(C) discrimination because of citizenship status which is otherwise required in order to comply with law, regulation, or executive order, or required by Federal, State, or local government contract, or which the Attorney General determines to be essential for an employer to do business with an agency or department of the Federal, State, or local government.

(3) Definition of protected individual

As used in paragraph (1), the term "protected individual" means an individual who—

(A) is a citizen or national of the United States, or

(B) is an alien who is lawfully admitted for permanent residence, is granted the status of an alien lawfully admitted for temporary residence under section 1160(a) or 1255a(a)(1) of this title, is admitted as a refugee under section 1157 of this title, or is granted asylum under section 1158 of this title; but does not include (i) an alien who fails to apply for naturalization within six months of the date the alien first becomes eligible (by virtue of period of lawful permanent residence) to apply for naturalization or, if later, within six months after November 6, 1986; and (ii) an alien who has applied on a timely basis, but has not been naturalized as a citizen within 2 years after the date of the application, unless the alien can establish that the alien is actively pursuing naturalization, except that time consumed in the Service's processing the application shall not be counted toward the 2-year period.

(4) Additional exception providing right to prefer equally qualified citizens

Notwithstanding any other provision of this section, it is not an unfair immigration-related employment practice for a person or other entity to prefer to hire, recruit, or refer an individual who is a citizen or national of the United States over another individual who is an alien if the two individuals are equally qualified.

(5) Prohibition of intimidation or retaliation

It is also an unfair immigration-related employment practice for a person or other entity to intimidate, threaten, coerce, or retaliate against any individual for the purpose of interfering with any right or privilege secured under this section or because the individual intends to file or has filed a charge or a complaint, testified, assisted, or participated in any manner in an investigation, proceeding, or hearing under this section. An individual so intimidated, threatened, coerced, or retaliated against shall be considered, for purposes of subsections (d) and (g) of this section, to have been discriminated against.

(6) Treatment of certain documentary practices as employment practices

A person's or other entity's request, for purposes of satisfying the requirements of section 1324a(b) of this title, for more or different documents than are required under such section or refusing to honor documents tendered that on their face reasonably appear to be genuine shall be treated as an unfair immigration-related employment practice if made for the purpose or with the intent of discriminating against an individual in violation of paragraph (1).

(b) Charges of violations

(1) In general

Except as provided in paragraph (2), any person alleging that the person is adversely affected directly by an unfair immigration-related employment practice (or a person on that person's behalf) or an officer of the Service alleging that an unfair immigration-related employment practice has occurred or is occurring may file a charge respecting such practice or violation with the Special Counsel (appointed under subsection (c) of this section). Charges shall be in writing under oath or affirmation and shall contain such information as the Attorney General requires. The Special Counsel by certified mail shall serve a notice of the charge (including the date, place, and circumstances of the alleged unfair immigration-related employment practice) on the person or entity involved within 10 days.

(2) No overlap with EEOC complaints

No charge may be filed respecting an unfair immigration-related employment practice described in subsection (a)(1)(A) of this section if a charge with respect to that practice based on the same set of facts has been filed with the Equal Employment Opportunity Commission under title VII of the Civil Rights Act of 1964 [42 U.S.C.A. § 2000e et seq.], unless the charge is dismissed as being outside the scope of such title. No charge respecting an employment practice may be filed with the Equal Employment Opportunity Commission under such title if a charge with respect to such practice based on the same set of facts has been filed under this subsection, unless the charge is dismissed under this section as being outside the scope of this section.

(c) Special Counsel

(1) Appointment

The President shall appoint, by and with the advice and consent of the Senate, a Special Counsel for Immigration-Related Unfair Employment Practices (hereinafter in this section referred to as the "Special Counsel") within the Department of Justice to serve for a term of four years. In the case of a vacancy in the office of the Special Counsel the President may designate the officer or employee who shall act as Special Counsel during such vacancy.

(2) Duties

The Special Counsel shall be responsible for investigation of charges and issuance of complaints under this section and in respect of the prosecution of all such complaints before administrative law judges and the exercise of certain functions under subsection (j)(1) of this section.

(3) Compensation

The Special Counsel is entitled to receive compensation at a rate not to exceed the rate now or hereafter provided for grade GS-17 of the General Schedule, under section 5332 of Title 5.

(4) Regional offices

The Special Counsel, in accordance with regulations of the Attorney General, shall establish such regional offices as may be necessary to carry out his duties.

(d) Investigation of charges

(1) By Special Counsel

The Special Counsel shall investigate each charge received and, within 120 days of the date of the receipt of the charge, determine whether or not there is reasonable cause to believe that the charge is true and whether nor not to bring a complaint with respect to the charge before an administrative law judge. The Special Counsel may, on his own initiative, conduct investigations respecting unfair immigration-related employment practices and, based on such an investigation and subject to paragraph (3), file a complaint before such a judge.

(2) Private actions

If the Special Counsel, after receiving such a charge respecting an unfair immigration-related employment practice which alleges knowing and intentional discriminatory activity or a pattern or practice of discriminatory activity, has not filed a complaint before an administrative law judge with respect to such charge within such 120-day period, the Special Counsel shall notify the person making the charge of the determination not to file such a complaint during such period and the person making the charge may (subject to paragraph (3)) file a complaint directly before such a judge within 90 days after the date of receipt of the notice. The Special Counsel's failure to file such a complaint within such 120-day period shall not affect the right of the Special Counsel to investigate the charge or to bring a complaint before an administrative law judge during such 90-day period.

(3) Time limitations on complaints

No complaint may be filed respecting any unfair immigration-related employment practice occurring more than 180 days prior to the date of the filing of the charge with the Special Counsel. This subparagraph shall not prevent the subsequent amending of a charge or complaint under subsection (e)(1) of this section.

(e) Hearings

(1) Notice

Whenever a complaint is made that a person or entity has engaged in or is engaging in any such unfair immigration-related employment practice, an administrative law judge shall have power to issue and cause to be served upon such person or entity a copy of the complaint and a notice of hearing before the judge at a place therein fixed, not less than five days after the serving of the complaint. Any such complaint may be amended by the judge conducting the hearing, upon the motion of the party filing the complaint, in the judge's discretion at any time prior to the issuance of an order based thereon. The person or entity so complained of shall have the right to file an answer to the original or amended complaint and to appear in person or otherwise and give testimony at the place and time fixed in the complaint.

(2) Judges hearing cases

Hearings on complaints under this subsection shall be considered before administrative law judges who are specially designated by the Attorney General as having special training respecting employment discrimination and, to the extent practicable, before such judges who only consider cases under this section.

(3) Complainant as party

Any person filing a charge with the Special Counsel respecting an unfair immigration-related employment practice shall be considered a party to any complaint before an administrative law judge respecting such practice and any subsequent appeal respecting that complaint. In the discretion of the judge conducting the hearing, any other person may be allowed to intervene in the proceeding and to present testimony.

(f) Testimony and authority of hearing officers

(1) Testimony

The testimony taken by the administrative law judge shall be reduced to writing. Thereafter, the judge, in his discretion, upon notice may provide for the taking of further testimony or hear argument.

(2) Authority of administrative law judges

In conducting investigations and hearings under this subsection and in accordance with regulations of the Attorney General, the Special Counsel and administrative law judges shall have reasonable access to examine evidence of any person or entity being investigated. The administrative law judges by subpoena may compel the attendance of witnesses and the production of evidence at any designated place or hearing. In case of contumacy or refusal to obey a subpoena lawfully issued under this paragraph and upon application of the administrative law judge, an appropriate district court of the United States may issue an order requiring compliance with such subpoena and any failure to obey such order may be punished by such court as a contempt thereof.

(g) Determinations

(1) Order

The administrative law judge shall issue and cause to be served on the parties to the proceeding an order, which shall be final unless appealed as provided under subsection (i) of this section.

(2) Orders finding violations

(A) In general

If, upon the preponderance of the evidence, an administrative law judge determines that any person or entity named in the complaint has engaged in or is engaging in any such unfair immigration-related employment practice, then the judge shall state his findings of fact and shall issue and cause to be served on such person or entity an order which requires such person or entity to cease and desist from such unfair immigration-related employment practice.

(B) Contents of order

Such an order also may require the person or entity—

(i) to comply with the requirements of section 1324a(b) of this title with respect to individuals hired (or recruited or referred for employment for a fee) during a period of up to three years;

(ii) to retain for the period referred to in clause (i) and only for purposes consistent with section 1324a(b)(5) of this title, the name and address of each individual who applies, in person or in writing, for hiring for an existing position, or for recruiting or referring for a fee, for employment in the United States;

(iii) to hire individuals directly and adversely affected, with or without back pay;

(iv)

(I) except as provided in subclauses (II) through (IV), to pay a civil penalty of not less than $250 and not more than $2,000 for each individual discriminated against,

(II) except as provided in subclauses (III) and (IV), in the case of a person or entity previously subject to a single order under this paragraph, to pay a civil penalty of not less than $2,000 and not more than $5,000 for each individual discriminated against,

(III) except as provided in subclause (IV), in the case of a person or entity previously subject to more than one order under this paragraph, to pay a civil penalty of not less than $3,000 and not more than $10,000 for each individual discriminated against, and

(IV) in the case of an unfair immigration-related employment practice described in subsection (a)(6) of this section, to pay a civil penalty of not less than $100 and not more than $1,000 for each individual discriminated against;

(v) to post notices to employees about their rights under this section and employers' obligations under section 1324a of this title;

(vi) to educate all personnel involved in hiring and complying with this section or section 1324a of this title about the requirements of this section or such section;

(vii) to remove (in an appropriate case) a false performance review or false warning from an employee's personnel file; and

(viii) to lift (in an appropriate case) any restrictions on an employee's assignments, work shifts, or movements.

(C) Limitation on back pay remedy

In providing a remedy under subparagraph (B)(iii), back pay liability shall not accrue from a date more than two years prior to the date of the filing of a charge with the Special Counsel. Interim earnings or amounts earnable with reasonable diligence by the individual or individuals discriminated against shall operate to reduce the back pay otherwise allowable under such subparagraph. No order shall require the hiring of an individual as an employee or the payment to an individual of any back pay, if the individual was refused employment for any reason other than discrimination on account of national origin or citizenship status.

(D) Treatment of distinct entities

In applying this subsection in the case of a person or entity composed of distinct, physically separate subdivisions each of which provides separately for the hiring, recruiting, or referring for employment, without reference to the practices of, and not under the control of or common control with, another subdivision, each such subdivision shall be considered a separate person or entity.

(3) Orders not finding violations

If upon the preponderance of the evidence an administrative law judge determines that the person or entity named in the complaint has not engaged and is not engaging in any such unfair immigration-related employment practice, then the judge shall state his findings of fact and shall issue an order dismissing the complaint.

(h) Awarding of attorney's fees

In any complaint respecting an unfair immigration-related employment practice, an administrative law judge, in the judge's discretion, may allow a prevailing party, other than the United States, a reasonable attorney's fee, if the losing party's argument is without reasonable foundation in law and fact.

(i) Review of final orders

(1) In general

Not later than 60 days after the entry of such final order, any person aggrieved by such final order may seek a review of such order in the United States court of appeals for the circuit in which the violation is alleged to have occurred or in which the employer resides or transacts business.

(2) Further review

Upon the filing of the record with the court, the jurisdiction of the court shall be exclusive and its judgment shall be final, except that the same shall be subject to review by the Supreme Court of the United States upon writ of certiorari or certification as provided in section 1254 of Title 28.

(j) Court enforcement of administrative orders

(1) In general

If an order of the agency is not appealed under subsection (i)(1) of this section, the Special Counsel (or, if the Special Counsel fails to act, the person filing the charge) may petition the United States district court for the district in which a violation of the order is alleged to have occurred, or in which the respondent resides or transacts business, for the enforcement of the order of the administrative law judge, by filing in such court a written petition praying that such order be enforced.

(2) Court enforcement order

Upon the filing of such petition, the court shall have jurisdiction to make and enter a decree enforcing the order of the administrative law judge. In such a proceeding, the order of the administrative law judge shall not be subject to review.

(3) Enforcement decree in original review

If, upon appeal of an order under subsection (i)(1) of this section, the United States court of appeals does not reverse such order, such court shall have the jurisdiction to make and enter a decree enforcing the order of the administrative law judge.

(4) Awarding of attorney's fees

In any judicial proceeding under subsection (i) of this section or this subsection, the court, in its discretion, may allow a prevailing party, other than the United States, a reasonable attorney's fee as part of costs but only if the losing party's argument is without reasonable foundation in law and fact.

(k) Termination dates

(1) This section shall not apply to discrimination in hiring, recruiting, referring, or discharging of individuals occurring after the date of any termination of the provisions of section 1324a of this title, under subsection (l) of that section.

(2) The provisions of this section shall terminate 30 calendar days after receipt of the last report required to be transmitted under section 1324a(j) of this title if—

(A) the Comptroller General determines, and so reports in such report that—

(i) no significant discrimination has resulted, against citizens or nationals of the United States or against any eligible workers seeking employment, from the implementation of section 1324a of this title, or

(ii) such section has created an unreasonable burden on employers hiring such workers; and

(B) there has been enacted, within such period of 30 calendar days, a joint resolution stating in substance that the Congress approves the findings of the Comptroller General contained in such report.

The provisions of subsections (m) and (n) of section 1324a of this title shall apply to any joint resolution under subparagraph (B) in the same manner as they apply to a joint resolution under subsection (l) of such section.

(l) Dissemination of information concerning anti-discrimination provisions

(1) Not later than 3 months after November 29, 1990, the Special Counsel, in cooperation with the chairman of the Equal Employment Opportunity Commission, the Secretary of Labor, and the Administrator of the Small Business Administration, shall conduct a campaign to disseminate information respecting the rights and remedies prescribed under this section and under title VII of the Civil Rights Act of 1964 *[42 U.S.C.A. § 2000e et seq.]* in connection with unfair immigration-related employment practices. Such campaign shall be aimed at increasing the knowledge of employers, employees, and the general public concerning employer and employee rights, responsibilities, and remedies under this section and such title.

(2) In order to carry out the campaign under this subsection, the Special Counsel—

(A) may, to the extent deemed appropriate and subject to the availability of appropriations, contract with public and private organizations for outreach activities under the campaign, and

(B) shall consult with the Secretary of Labor, the chairman of the Equal Employment Opportunity Commission, and the heads of such other agencies as may be appropriate.

(3) There are authorized to be appropriated to carry out this subsection $10,000,000 for each fiscal year (beginning with fiscal year 1991).

■

Chapter 12

National Labor Relations Act (NLRA)

Statute: 29 U.S.C. §§ 151-169
http://www4.law.cornell.edu/uscode/29/ch7schII.html

Regulations: 29 C.F.R. §§ 100-103; 1400–1471 (Federal Conciliation and Mediation Service)
http://lula.law.cornell.edu/cfr/cfr.php?title=29&type=chapter&value=1
http://lula.law.cornell.edu/cfr/cfr.php?title=29&type=chapter&value=12

Definition

Bargaining unit

A group of employees whom the union represents (or seeks to represent) in its dealings
with an employer. Workers in a bargaining
unit must have similar job duties, skills or
working conditions and have common
concerns about wages and hours. Usually,
professional and nonprofessional employees
will not be combined in a single bargaining
unit. A single workplace may contain more
than one bargaining unit (for example, the
butchers, checkers and janitors in a grocery
store might all be members of different bargaining units). A bargaining unit can include
workers from different facilities (for example,
all of the cashiers in a chain of retail stores).

Collective bargaining agreement

The contract between the union (on behalf of
the *bargaining unit* it represents) and the employer that governs the terms and conditions
of the workers' employment.

Federal Conciliation and Mediation Service

An agency of the federal government that
helps parties to a labor dispute reach a solu-
tion through negotiation and mediation.

Health care institution

Any hospital, convalescent hospital, health
maintenance organization, health clinic,

- retail enterpr total
  total annual
- those engage n total
  operation of
  ping centers t least
  annual rever e
  more comes ions
  meet any of es at
  standards ex
  purchase of 0,000
  nesses   urces
- public utiliti e for
  annual busir s
  direct sales
  or sales to grams:
- newspapers venue
  annual busi ices
- radio, teleg tribute
  phone com
  total annua
- hotels, mot 0 in
  buildings: a g
  annual bus ffect-
- privately op ave a
  at least $25 ense.
  volume for he
  ing homes er the
  and related the
- transportat ether
  in total an that
  interstate
  portation;
  for busine
  other juris
  the indire es of a
  for non-r wing:

- agricultural workers
- domestic servants
- anyone employed by a parent or spouse
- independent contractors
- *managers*
- *supervisors*
- government employees, and
- workers whose employer is subject to the Railway Labor Act.

B. Major Provisions of the NLRA

1. Organizing and Representation Elections

The NLRA establishes workers' basic right to organize—to form, join or assist a union; to choose their own representatives to negotiate with their employer over terms and conditions of employment; and to engage in other collective efforts to improve their work situations. The law also establishes procedures for determining whether a particular union should have the right to represent a group of workers.

Anatomy of an Election

In order to represent workers in negotiations with an employer, a union must have the support of a majority of workers in an appropriate *bargaining unit*. Unions generally demonstrate this support by asking workers to sign authorization cards, forms that each worker fills in and signs to indicate a desire to be represented by the union in dealings with the employer.

If the union gets the support of a majority of *bargaining unit* workers, it will often ask the employer to recognize the union voluntarily. If the employer agrees, the union will be the official bargaining representative of the unit, and employer and union can begin negotiating a *collective bargaining agreement*.

If the employer refuses to recognize the union—for example, if the employer believes the bargaining unit is improper or believes the union's support is not genuine—the workers or union can file a petition with the NLRB, asking it to hold an election. Their petition must be supported by authorization cards or other signed statements of union support of at least 30% of the workers in the *bargaining unit*. After it investigates and tries to resolve any disputes between the parties over the scope of the *bargaining unit* and the time and place of the election, the NLRB will hold a secret election. If the union receives a majority of the votes cast, it will be certified as the bargaining representative of the unit.

An employer may also petition the NLRB for an election, if more than one union claims the right to represent a particular *bargaining unit*.

Regulated Employers

All covered employers must comply with this provision.

Covered Workers

All protected workers are covered by this provision.

What's Prohibited: Employers

The NLRA prohibits employers from unfairly influencing their workers' decision to join or form a union, and from using threats or other coercive tactics to influence the outcome of an election. (However, employers still have free speech rights—see Section D4, below.)

Union Discussions in the Workplace

An employer may not prohibit all union discussions—including discussions that occur before workers are unionized, such as conversations about whether to form or join a union—in the workplace. Instead, employers must treat union-related communications like any other matter not related to work. The specific rules for union discussions depend on the employer's general rules on non-work communications:

- An employer may prohibit workers from talking about union matters in work areas during work hours, but only if the employer prohibits workers from talking about other non-work issues as well.
- An employer must allow workers to talk about union matters outside of work hours in non-work areas (like a lunchroom or locker room).
- An employer may prohibit union discussions outside of work hours in work areas only if such a rule is necessary to maintain productivity or discipline and the rule applies to all non-work topics.
- An employer may prohibit distribution of union literature (such as pamphlets or fact sheets) in work areas at all times, as long as the ban applies to all non-work literature.
- An employer may not prohibit workers from wearing clothing bearing a pro-union message or logo, unless that apparel creates a safety hazard.

Electronic mail systems have put a modern twist in these established rules—one that the legal system has not yet straightened out. Clearly, under the principles explained above, employers may not single out union-related email messages for prohibition: if an employer allows employees to use the company email system to send personal or non-business related messages, it must allow them to send messages relating to union matters. However, the law is unclear as to whether an employer can enforce a ban on all personal messages, union-related or not. The NLRB's General Counsel has argued that such a rule violates workers' rights to talk to each other about the union outside of work hours (assuming workers send these messages during breaks or after hours), and is therefore illegal as applied to union messages.

Election Conduct

Employers may not engage in conduct that tends to interfere with their workers' right to freely choose or reject a union, without fear of reprisal. If the NRLB finds that an employer has unfairly influenced the outcome of an election, it can set aside a vote rejecting the union—and even declare the union the victor by default. Here are some examples of prohibited employer conduct:

- **Punishing union supporters.** An employer may not retaliate or discriminate against workers who support the union.
- **Threats.** An employer cannot threaten to fire, demote or take any other negative job action against workers because they support a union, nor can it threaten to shut down or move the business if the union wins the election.
- **Inducements.** An employer cannot promise or give benefits to workers who oppose the union. Once an organizing campaign has begun, an employer may not increase workers' benefits to discourage them from forming or joining a union.
- **Infiltration.** An employer may not conduct surveillance or otherwise spy on union meetings or on employees who support the union.
- **Interrogation.** An employer may not question workers about their union membership, union meetings or their support for the union; nor may it ask employees to report on union activities or their co-workers' union views.

What's Prohibited: Unions

Like employers, unions are prohibited from unfairly influencing a worker's decision to support or reject the union or the outcome of an election. The list of prohibited actions for unions is similar to the list for employers. Here are some examples:

- **Threats.** A union may not threaten workers with job loss or other negative job actions for failing to support the union, nor may a union cause an employer to take negative job actions against such workers.
- **Takeovers.** A union may not enter into an agreement with an employer that recognizes the union as the exclusive bargaining representative of a bargaining unit if it does not have the support of a majority of unit employees.
- **Inducements.** A union may not promise or grant benefits to workers for supporting the union.
- **Violence.** A union may not use or threaten physical force against workers to influence their votes.

What's Required: Workers

Under some circumstances, workers must pay union dues (or an equivalent sum) even if they do not support the union. See "Exceptions," below.

Exceptions

Union Security Agreements

Although the NLRA protects a worker's right to freely choose whether to join or support a union, it also allows a union and employer to enter into a contract, called a union security agreement, requiring workers to make certain payments to the union as a condition of getting or keeping a job. If a union and employer have entered into a union security agreement, all workers must either join the union or make "agency fee" payments to the union as a condition of employment. If a worker refuses to pay up or join, the employer must fire the worker.

The NLRA allows states to prohibit union security agreements, and many have. In these states (called "right to work" states), workers who decide not to join the union cannot be required to pay any fees to the union—and can't be fired or otherwise penalized for failing to do so. See Section G for a list of "right to work" states.

Dues Objectors

Workers who object to paying union dues either on religious grounds or because they don't support the union's political or other activities can make alternative arrangements, even if they work in a state that allows union security agreements. A worker who has religious reasons for refusing to pay dues may be required to make a similar contribution to a non-labor, non-religious charity group.

In states that allow union security agreements, non-member workers who object to the union's use of their fees for political or other purposes are entitled to get that money back. However, they still have to pay their fair share of union money spent on representing the bargaining unit's workers. Some states require unions to get workers' permission before even collecting any fees for activities other than representing workers.

2. Unfair Labor Practices

In addition to the rules governing union organizing campaigns and elections, the NLRA prohibits a number of activities—called "unfair labor practices"—by employers and unions. Some of these rules apply to the interactions between employer and union; others protect individual workers from unfair treatment by an employer or a union.

Regulated Employers

All covered employers must comply with this provision.

Covered Workers

All protected workers are covered by this provision.

What's Prohibited: Employers

In addition to the prohibitions covered in Section B1 above, the NLRA prohibits employers from:

- interfering with an employee's right to organize, join or assist a union or engage in collective bargaining
- dominating or providing illegal assistance or support to a labor union (see "Company Unions," below)
- discriminating against employees for the purpose of encouraging or discouraging membership in a labor organization—this prohibition also covers replacing workers who strike to protest an unfair labor practice (see "Lawful Strikes," below)
- retaliating against an employee for filing a charge or giving testimony to the NLRB
- refusing to engage in good faith collective bargaining (see "Collective Bargaining," below), and
- making a *hot cargo agreement* with a union.

Company Unions

Employers may not establish, dominate or interfere with any labor organization. This rule exists to outlaw "sham unions"—company groups that appear to represent employees' interests, but are really controlled by the employer. To figure out whether an employer unfairly controls a particular workplace group, the NLRB looks at all the circumstances, including:

- whether the employer started the group
- whether the employer played a role in organizing the group and deciding how it will function
- whether management actually attends the group's meetings or otherwise tries to set the group's agenda
- the group's purpose, and
- how the group makes decisions.

The NLRB has held that workplace "committees"—informal groups in which workers and management meet to resolve workplace problems—violate this rule if they are effectively dominated by management and they deal with the employer on topics that must be collectively bargained (such as wages, hours or working conditions—see "Collective Bargaining," below).

Collective Bargaining

Collective bargaining is the negotiation process between the union (on behalf of the *bargaining unit* it represents) and the company to work out an agreement that will govern the terms and conditions of the workers' employment. Once a union has been elected, the NLRA requires employer and union to meet and negotiate over wages, hours and other significant terms of employment (called subjects of "mandatory bargaining"). The two sides don't have to reach an agreement, but they have to bargain in good faith.

Before an employer changes a workplace rule or policy that implicates a subject of mandatory bargaining, it must ask the union to negotiate the issue—even if the change will provide an overall benefit to workers. An employer who makes unilateral changes regarding mandatory bargaining issues commits an unfair labor practice.

Lawful Strikes

The NLRA protects the right to strike—but only if the strike has a lawful purpose. Generally, a strike has a lawful purpose if workers are striking for economic reasons (for example, to seek higher wages or better working conditions) or to protest an unfair labor practice by the employer (like discriminating against union members or refusing to bargain with the union). Strikes without a lawful purpose are illegal—see "What's Prohibited: Unions," below, for examples.

Even a strike with a lawful purpose might not be protected under the NLRA if the workers strike in violation of a "no strike" provision in the collective bargaining agreement or if the strikers engage in serious misconduct (like violence).

An employer may not fire or hire permanent replacements for workers who strike to protest an unfair labor practice. These workers are entitled to reinstatement once the strike is over.

However, workers who strike for economic reasons can be replaced permanently. Once the strike is over, they are entitled to their former jobs only if the employer did not hire permanent replacements. If the employer hired permanent replacements, the workers who went on strike are only entitled to be called back for job openings as those jobs become available—and only if they are unable to find regular and substantially similar work elsewhere.

What's Prohibited: Unions

In addition to the rules discussed in Section B1, above, the NLRA prohibits unions from:

- restraining or coercing employees in the free exercise of their right not to support a union (by, for example, threatening employees who don't want a union or expelling members for crossing an illegal picket line)
- restraining or coercing an employer in its choice of a bargaining representative (by insisting on meeting only with a particular management employee or refusing to bargain with the representative the employer chooses)
- causing or trying to cause an employer to discriminate against an employee for the purpose of encouraging or discouraging union membership (for example, convincing an employer to penalize employees who engage in anti-union activities)
- refusing to engage in good faith collective bargaining (refusing to come to the bargaining table or listen to any of the employer's proposals, for example)
- engaging in strikes, boycotts or other coercive action for an illegal purpose (see "Unlawful Strikes," below)
- charging excessive or discriminatory membership fees
- getting or trying to get an employer to agree to pay for work that is not performed ("featherbedding")
- for a union that is not certified to represent a group of workers, picketing or threatening to picket an employer in order to force the employer to recognize or bargain with the union or force the workers to accept the union as their representative if (1) another union already represents the workers, (2) a valid representation election was held in the past year, or (3) the union does not file a petition for an election with the NLRB within 30 days after the picketing starts
- making a *hot cargo agreement*
- striking, picketing or otherwise engaging in a collective work stoppage at any *health care institution* without giving at least ten days' written notice both to the institution and the *Federal Mediation and Conciliation Service.*

Unlawful Strikes

A union may not strike, boycott or use other means of persuasion or coercion for prohibited purposes. Such purposes include:

- forcing or requiring an employer to assign particular work to employees in a particular union, trade, craft or class
- forcing or requiring an employer to recognize or bargain with a particular union if another union has been duly certified as the representative of its employees
- forcing or requiring any person to stop doing business with any other business or to stop using, selling or transporting the products of any other business (such strikes or boycotts against a business other than the employer are called "secondary strikes")
- forcing or requiring an employer or self-employed person to join any labor or employer organization, or enter into a *hot cargo agreement* .

asking the NLRB to hold an election. The NLRB's procedures for handling charges and petitions are described below.

The NLRA cannot be enforced through private lawsuits—violations of the NLRA must be challenged through the NLRB.

C. How the NLRA Is Enforced

1. Individual Complaints

An employee, employer or union who believes that an unfair labor practice has been committed may file a charge with the NLRB. Unfair labor practice charges must be filed within six months of the incident alleged to be unfair.

If an employee, employer or union believes that a question of representation exists—that is, that there is some dispute over whether employees want a particular union to represent them—these parties may file a petition

2. Agency Enforcement

The NLRB handles two issues: representation questions (disputes over whether employees want a union) and unfair labor practices.

Representation Questions

Representation questions are brought to the NLRB when an employee, employer or union files a petition with the agency. If a union or employee files the petition, it must show that at least 30% of the affected workers want an election. An employer may petition the NLRB for an election only if more than one union claims the right to represent a particular *bargaining unit.*

Once a petition is filed, the NLRB will investigate. If it finds that the petition has merit, it will try to hammer out an agreement between the employees and employer regarding election issues—such as the scope of the *bargaining unit* and the time and place of the election. The NLRB will then order an election, by secret ballot, and certify a union if it receives a majority of votes cast. If a union is certified, it becomes the workers' representative and is entitled to bargain with the employer. If a union is not certified, it does not have the right to represent the workers.

Unfair Labor Practices

Unfair labor practices come to the NLRB when an employee, employer or union files a charge with the agency. The NLRB will investigate the charge and, if it finds reason to believe that the NLRA has been violated, will try to get the parties to settle their differences. If this fails, the NLRB will hold a hearing before an administrative law judge, who will issue a written decision. This decision may be appealed within the NLRB—if either party is dissatisfied with the NLRB's final decision, it may appeal the matter to the federal courts.

D. For Employers: Complying With the NLRA

1. Reporting Requirements

None. However, employers and unions have reporting requirements under the Labor Management Reporting & Disclosure Act or LMRDA (29 U.S.C. §§ 401-531).

2. Posting Requirements

Once the NLRB gets involved, it can require employers to post various notices relating to elections and the resolution of a particular charge of unfair labor practices. However, the NLRA doesn't require posting absent some NLRB action.

3. Recordkeeping Requirements

The NLRA does not impose recordkeeping requirements.

4. Practical Tips

Here are some practical tips for dealing with union issues:

- **If you want to keep a union out, make it superfluous.** The best way to keep your workplace union-free, if that's your goal, is to give your workers what the union would get for them. Unionization efforts take root when employees feel that they aren't being listened to or treated fairly. Make a union unnecessary by offering competitive pay, good benefits, safe working conditions, some form of job protection and a meaningful complaint process.
- **Review your employee handbook.** Your work rules must allow employees to exercise their rights under the NLRA, even if your workplace is not union-

ized. Make sure, for example, that your dress code doesn't prohibit workers from wearing pro-union messages and that your email policy doesn't single out messages about organizing or union issues. If you are already dealing with a union, make sure your policies accurately reflect what you've promised in the collective bargaining agreement.

- **You have free speech rights, too.** If you are facing an organizing campaign, you cannot threaten or punish employees to prevent them from supporting a union, or spy on employee meetings to find out about the union's support. But you are free to say your piece, as long as your statements are accurate and not coercive. For example, you can tell your workers why you don't want a union in the workplace, give employees true information about the union (such as how much it charges for dues and fees) and compare the benefits and wages you offer with what the union has been able to negotiate from other companies.

- **If things get down and dirty, talk to an expert.** Organizing campaigns can get downright ugly—the high stakes can lead people on both sides to go too far. Even after a union is elected, certain issues—like a bargaining impasse, layoffs or a threatened strike—can cause otherwise good relations to unravel. If you're faced with an escalating conflict, get some help from a management-side labor lawyer, who can let you know

what you should and shouldn't do before it's too late.

5. Penalties

If an employer, union or employee files a petition seeking an election, there are no penalties awarded. The NLRB simply holds an election and certifies the results.

If the NLRB finds that an employer has committed an unfair labor practice, during an organizing campaign or at any other time, the employer can be required to do any or all of the following:

- pay any compensation, benefits or other monetary losses the employee suffered ("back pay") as a result of the unfair practice—plus interest
- take action to remedy the problem, by reinstating an employee, changing workplace rules, stopping an illegal practice or recognizing a union
- pay attorney fees and costs (with some limitations)
- post a notice in the workplace regarding the unfair practice.

E. For Workers: Asserting Rights Under the NLRA

1. Where to Start

Your first steps depend on whether your complaint involves representation issues or unfair labor practices.

Representation Issues

Representation issues might come up in several different ways. If a particular union is trying to organize employees in your workplace and you would like to be represented by that union, talk to a union representative to make your feelings known—and sign an authorization card expressing your wishes. The union must be able to show the NLRB that it has the support of at least 30% of the workers in the *bargaining unit* before the NLRB will hold an election. Although either an individual employee or the union may file a petition seeking an election, it is generally easier to let the union do the work. If the union declines to file, you can file a petition on your own.

If several unions are fighting over (or claim to have) the right to represent you and your coworkers, tell your employer that you want the situation sorted out. Your employer can file a petition with the NLRB seeking an election in this type of situation—or you or the union can, if one union has the support of 30% of *bargaining unit* workers.

If you are currently represented by a union and you want the union out, you may file a petition with the NLRB. However, you must show that 30% of the employees currently represented by the union no longer want the union. This means that your first step should be to talk to your coworkers to find out what kind of support the union has.

Unfair Labor Practices

If you believe you have been a victim of an unfair labor practice, your first steps will depend on who committed the violation, whether you are represented by a union and, if so, whether the *collective bargaining agreement* calls for arbitration of the incident alleged to be unfair.

If a union that does not represent you committed the violation (for example, by intimidating workers during an organizing campaign), contact your local office of the NLRB to file a charge. If a union that represents you committed the violation (by charging excessive fees, for example), you may need to complain within the union before filing a charge with the NLRB. Contact your local office of the NLRB for assistance—you can find contact information in Section F.

If your employer committed the violation and you are not represented by a union. Contact the NLRB about filing a charge. If the violation occurred during an organizing campaign, you might also want to contact the union to let them know what happened. The union may be able to assist you with the charge.

If your employer committed the violation and you are represented by a union. You may have to "grieve the issue" (that is, file a union grievance that the union will arbitrate with your employer). If the *collective bargaining agreement* between the employer and the union calls for arbitration of grievances, the NLRB may tell you to take your charge to arbitration rather than to the NLRB hearing process. The NLRB will do this only if, among other things, your employer agrees to arbitrate the issue (even if you missed the deadline for submitting it to arbitration), the employer and union have a proven track record of working together, the subject of your complaint is one that must be arbitrated under the agreement and arbitration is likely to resolve the problem.

Luckily, the NLRB won't penalize you if you file a charge before filing a grievance—it will simply tell you to grieve the issue, if the conditions set forth above are met. In the meantime, the NLRB will retain its jurisdiction over your charge—if the grievance procedure doesn't work as it should, the NLRB can step back in and process the charge.

2. Required Forms

The NLRB has forms you can fill out to file a petition or an unfair labor practice charge. Contact your local NLRB office for information and assistance (see Section F for contact information).

3. Practical Tips

Here are some tips for asserting your rights under the NLRA:

- **For organizing help, go to an established union.** Some employees manage to form a union on their own. But the most common way for employees to organize their workplace is to bring in an existing union—one that already knows the ropes and has the financial and organizational wherewithal to weather an election campaign. Look in the phone book for unions that sound like they might represent workers in your industry or contact the AFL-CIO, a coalition of labor unions.

- **Comparison shop for the best deal.** If an existing union—or more than one union—is trying to organize your workplace, find out what the union has to offer. What will it charge in fees and dues? How successful has it been for workers at other companies? Is its management responsive to rank and file concerns? Some unions are strong advocates and savvy negotiators for the workers they represent; others are ineffective, bullying or crooked. Before you sign on the dotted line, make sure the union will meet the needs of your workplace.

- **Get the union's help.** Once you are represented by a union, part of the union's job is to represent your concerns to management. If you feel that your employer is committing an unfair labor practice, your first stop should be your shop steward or union representative. Even before a particular union gains the right to represent you, the union can help you deal with unfair labor practices during the organizing campaign—and perhaps file its own unfair labor practice charge with the NLRB.

- **Enlist your coworkers.** The theory behind unionization is strength in numbers—and it's a theory that applies equally to dealings with your employer and dealings with your union. You are more likely to get a problem resolved if a lot of people complain about it, whether the complaint is to your employer, your union or the NLRB.

F. Agency Charged With Enforcement & Compliance

National Labor Relations Board

1099 14th Street, NW

Washington, DC 20570

Phone: 202-273-1000

http://www.nlrb.gov

Agency Resources for Employers

(These can be obtained either at the Web addresses listed below or at the address and phone number listed above.)

- A description of how the NLRB processes charges of unfair labor practices
  Unfair Labor Practices Cases
  http://www.nlrb.gov/tri-ulp.html
- A description of how the NLRB processes election petitions
  Representation Cases
  http://www.nlrb.gov/tri-rcas.html
- A list of the NLRB's local offices
  National Labor Relations Board Field Offices
  http://www.nlrb.gov/fieldoff.html
- A comprehensive resource on the NLRA's provisions
  A Guide to Basic Law and Procedures under the National Labor Relations Act
  http://www.nlrb.gov/publications/nlrb2.pdf
- An explanation of the role of the NLRB
  The NLRB: What It Is, What It Does
  http://www.nlrb.gov/publications/whatitis.pdf

Agency Resources for Workers

(These can be obtained either at the Web addresses listed below or at the address and phone number listed above.)

- Description of representation election procedures
  Your Government Conducts an Election
  www.nlrb.gov/publications/election.pdf
- An explanation of election petitions
  The National Labor Relations Board and You: Representation Cases
  http://www.nlrb.gov/publications/engrep.pdf

- An explanation of unfair labor practice charges
  The National Labor Relations Board and You: Unfair Labor Practices
  http://www.nlrb.gov/publications/engulp.pdf
- A description of how the NLRB processes charges of unfair labor practices
  Unfair Labor Practices Cases
  http://www.nlrb.gov/tri-ulp.html
- A description of how the NLRB processes election petitions
  Representation Cases
  http://www.nlrb.gov/tri-rcas.html
- A list of the NLRB's local offices
  National Labor Relations Board Field Offices
  http://www.nlrb.gov/fieldoff.html
- A comprehensive resource on the NLRA's provisions
  A Guide to Basic Law and Procedures under the National Labor Relations Act
  http://www.nlrb.gov/publications/nlrb2.pdf
- An explanation of the role of the NLRB
  The NLRB: What It Is, What It Does
  http://www.nlrb.gov/publications/whatitis.pdf

G. State "Right to Work" Laws

The NLRA allows states to prohibit union security agreements. In the states listed below (called "right to work" states), workers who decide not to join the union cannot be required to pay any fees to the union—and can't be fired or otherwise penalized for failing to do so.

State	Right to Work Law
Alabama	Ala. Code § 25-7-32
Arizona	Ariz. Rev. Stat. § 23-1302
Arkansas	Ark. Code Ann. § 11-3-303
Florida	Fla. Stat. Ann. § 447.17
Georgia	Ga. Code Ann. § 34-6-21
Idaho	Idaho Code § 44-2003
Iowa	Iowa Code § 731.1
Kansas	Kan. Const. art. 15 § 12
Louisiana	La. Rev. Stat. Ann. §§ 23:983 (all workers) and 23:881 (agricultural workers)
Mississippi	Miss. Const. Art. 7, §198-A
Nebraska	Neb. Rev. Stat. § 48-217
Nevada	Nev. Rev. Stat. Ann. § 613.250
New Hampshire	N.H. Rev. Stat. Ann. § 275:1
New Mexico	N.M. Stat. Ann. § 50-2-4
North Carolina	N.C. Gen. Stat. § 95-80
North Dakota	N.D. Cent. Code § 34-01-14
Ohio	Ohio Rev. Code Ann. § 4113.02
Oklahoma	Okla. Const. Art. 23, § 1A
South Carolina	S.C. Code Ann. § 41-7-30
South Dakota	S.D. Const. art. VI, § 2
Tennessee	Tenn. Code Ann. § 50-1-201
Texas	Tex. Lab. Code Ann. § 101.052
Utah	Utah Code Ann. § 34-34-8
Virginia	Va. Code Ann. § 40.1-60
Wyoming	Wyo. Stat. § 27-7-109

H. Full Text of the NLRA

29 U.S.C. §§151-169
U.S. Code
Title 29: Labor
Chapter 7: Labor-Management Relations
Subchapter II: National Labor Relations

§ 151. Findings and declaration of policy
§ 152. Definitions
§ 153. National Labor Relations Board
§ 154. National Labor Relations Board; eligibility for reappointment; officers and employees; payment of expenses
§ 155. National Labor Relations Board; principal office, conducting inquiries throughout country; participation in decisions or inquiries conducted by member
§ 156. Rules and regulations
§ 157. Right of employees as to organization, collective bargaining, etc.
§ 158. Unfair labor practices
§ 158a. Providing facilities for operations of Federal Credit Unions
§ 159. Representatives and elections
§ 160. Prevention of unfair labor practices
§ 161. Investigatory powers of Board
§ 162. Offenses and penalties
§ 163. Right to strike preserved
§ 164. Construction of provisions
§ 165. Conflict of laws
§ 166. Separability
§ 167. Short title of subchapter
§ 168. Validation of certificates and other Board actions
§ 169. Employees with religious convictions; payment of dues and fees

§ 151. [§ 1] Findings and declaration of policy

The denial by some employers of the right of employees to organize and the refusal by some employers to accept the procedure of collective bargaining lead to strikes and other forms of industrial strife or unrest, which have the intent or the necessary effect of burdening or obstructing commerce by (a) impairing the efficiency, safety, or operation of the instrumentalities of commerce; (b) occurring in the current of commerce; (c) materially affecting, restraining, or controlling the flow of raw materials or manufactured or processed goods from or into the channels of commerce, or the prices of such materials or goods in commerce; or (d) causing diminution of employment and wages in such volume as substantially to impair or disrupt the market for goods flowing from or into the channels of commerce.

The inequality of bargaining power between employees who do not possess full freedom of association or actual liberty of contract and employers who are organized in the corporate or other forms of ownership association substantially burdens and affects the flow of commerce, and tends to aggravate recurrent business depressions, by depressing wage rates and the purchasing power of wage earners in industry and by preventing the stabilization of competitive wage rates and working conditions within and between industries.

Experience has proved that protection by law of the right of employees to organize and bargain collectively safeguards commerce from injury, impairment, or interruption, and promotes the flow of commerce by removing certain recognized sources of industrial strife and unrest, by encouraging practices fundamental to the friendly adjustment of industrial disputes arising out of differences as to wages, hours, or other working conditions, and by restoring equality of bargaining power between employers and employees.

Experience has further demonstrated that certain practices by some labor organizations, their officers, and members have the intent or the necessary effect of burdening or obstructing commerce by preventing the free flow of goods in such commerce through strikes and other forms of industrial unrest or through concerted activities which impair the interest of the public in the free flow of such commerce. The elimination of such practices is a necessary condition to the assurance of the rights herein guaranteed.

It is declared to be the policy of the United States to eliminate the causes of certain substantial obstructions to the free flow of commerce and to mitigate and eliminate these obstructions when they have occurred by encouraging the practice and procedure of collective bargaining and by protecting the exercise by workers of full freedom of association, self-organization, and designation of representatives of their own choosing, for the purpose of negotiating the terms and conditions of their employment or other mutual aid or protection.

§ 152. [§ 2] Definitions

When used in this Act *[subchapter]*—

(1) The term "person" includes one or more individuals, labor organizations, partnerships, associations,

corporations, legal representatives, trustees, trustees in cases under title 11 of the United States Code *[under title 11]*, or receivers.

(2) The term "employer" includes any person acting as an agent of an employer, directly or indirectly, but shall not include the United States or any wholly owned Government corporation, or any Federal Reserve Bank, or any State or political subdivision thereof, or any person subject to the Railway Labor Act *[45 U.S.C. Sec. 151 et seq.]*, as amended from time to time, or any labor organization (other than when acting as an employer), or anyone acting in the capacity of officer or agent of such labor organization. *[Pub. L. 93-360, Sec. 1(a), July 26, 1974, 88 Stat. 395, deleted the phrase "or any corporation or association operating a hospital, if no part of the net earnings inures to the benefit of any private shareholder or individual" from the definition of "employer."]*

(3) The term "employee" shall include any employee, and shall not be limited to the employees of a particular employer, unless the Act *[this subchapter]* explicitly states otherwise, and shall include any individual whose work has ceased as a consequence of, or in connection with, any current labor dispute or because of any unfair labor practice, and who has not obtained any other regular and substantially equivalent employment, but shall not include any individual employed as an agricultural laborer, or in the domestic service of any family or person at his home, or any individual employed by his parent or spouse, or any individual having the status of an independent contractor, or any individual employed as a supervisor, or any individual employed by an employer subject to the Railway Labor Act *[45 U.S.C. Sec. 151 et seq.]*, as amended from time to time, or by any other person who is not an employer as herein defined.

(4) The term "representatives" includes any individual or labor organization.

(5) The term "labor organization" means any organization of any kind, or any agency or employee representation committee or plan, in which employees participate and which exists for the purpose, in whole or in part, of dealing with employers concerning grievances, labor disputes, wages, rates of pay, hours of employment, or conditions of work.

(6) The term "commerce" means trade, traffic, commerce, transportation, or communication among the several States, or between the District of Columbia or any Territory of the United States and any State or other Territory, or between any foreign country and any State, Territory, or the District of Columbia, or

within the District of Columbia or any Territory, or between points in the same State but through any other State or any Territory or the District of Columbia or any foreign country.

(7) The term "affecting commerce" means in commerce, or burdening or obstructing commerce or the free flow of commerce, or having led or tending to lead to a labor dispute burdening or obstructing commerce or the free flow of commerce.

(8) The term "unfair labor practice" means any unfair labor practice listed in section 8 *[section 158 of this title]*.

(9) The term "labor dispute" includes any controversy concerning terms, tenure, or conditions of employment, or concerning the association or representation of persons in negotiating, fixing, maintaining, changing, or seeking to arrange terms or conditions of employment, regardless of whether the disputants stand in the proximate relation of employer and employee.

(10) The term "National Labor Relations Board" means the National Labor Relations Board provided for in section 3 of this Act *[section 153 of this title]*.

(11) The term "supervisor" means any individual having authority, in the interest of the employer, to hire, transfer, suspend, lay off, recall, promote, discharge, assign, reward, or discipline other employees, or responsibly to direct them, or to adjust their grievances, or effectively to recommend such action, if in connection with the foregoing the exercise of such authority is not of a merely routine or clerical nature, but requires the use of independent judgment.

(12) The term "professional employee" means—

   (a) any employee engaged in work (i) predominantly intellectual and varied in character as opposed to routine mental, manual, mechanical, or physical work; (ii) involving the consistent exercise of discretion and judgment in its performance; (iii) of such a character that the output produced or the result accomplished cannot be standardized in relation to a given period of time; (iv) requiring knowledge of an advanced type in a field of science or learning customarily acquired by a prolonged course of specialized intellectual instruction and study in an institution of higher learning or a hospital, as distinguished from a general academic education or from an apprenticeship or from training in the performance of routine mental, manual, or physical processes; or

   (b) any employee, who (i) has completed the courses of specialized intellectual instruction and study described in clause (iv) of paragraph (a), and

(ii) is performing related work under the supervision of a professional person to qualify himself to become a professional employee as defined in paragraph (a).

(13) In determining whether any person is acting as an "agent" of another person so as to make such other person responsible for his acts, the question of whether the specific acts performed were actually authorized or subsequently ratified shall not be controlling.

(14) The term "health care institution" shall include any hospital, convalescent hospital, health maintenance organization, health clinic, nursing home, extended care facility, or other institution devoted to the care of sick, infirm, or aged persons.

[Pub. L. 93-360, Sec. 1(b), July 26, 1974, 88 Stat. 395, added par. (14).]

§ 153. [§ 3] National Labor Relations Board

(a) *[Creation, composition, appointment, and tenure; Chairman; removal of members]* The National Labor Relations Board (hereinafter called the "Board") created by this Act *[subchapter]* prior to its amendment by the Labor Management Relations Act, 1947 *[29 U.S.C. Sec. 141 et seq.]*, is continued as an agency of the United States, except that the Board shall consist of five instead of three members, appointed by the President by and with the advice and consent of the Senate. Of the two additional members so provided for, one shall be appointed for a term of five years and the other for a term of two years. Their successors, and the successors of the other members, shall be appointed for terms of five years each, excepting that any individual chosen to fill a vacancy shall be appointed only for the unexpired term of the member whom he shall succeed. The President shall designate one member to serve as Chairman of the Board. Any member of the Board may be removed by the President, upon notice and hearing, for neglect of duty or malfeasance in office, but for no other cause.

(b) *[Delegation of powers to members and regional directors; review and stay of actions of regional directors; quorum; seal]* The Board is authorized to delegate to any group of three or more members any or all of the powers which it may itself exercise. The Board is also authorized to delegate to its regional directors its powers under section 9 *[section 159 of this title]* to determine the unit appropriate for the purpose of collective bargaining, to investigate and provide for hearings, and determine whether a question of representation exists, and to direct an election or take a secret ballot under subsection (c) or (e) of section 9 *[section 159 of this title]* and certify the results thereof, except that upon the filing of a request therefor with the Board by any interested person, the Board may review any action of a regional director delegated to him under this paragraph, but such a review shall not, unless specifically ordered by the Board, operate as a stay of any action taken by the regional director. A vacancy in the Board shall not impair the right of the remaining members to exercise all of the powers of the Board, and three members of the Board shall, at all times, constitute a quorum of the Board, except that two members shall constitute a quorum of any group designated pursuant to the first sentence hereof. The Board shall have an official seal which shall be judicially noticed.

(c) *[Annual reports to Congress and the President]* The Board shall at the close of each fiscal year make a report in writing to Congress and to the President summarizing significant case activities and operations for that fiscal year.

(d) *[General Counsel; appointment and tenure; powers and duties; vacancy]* There shall be a General Counsel of the Board who shall be appointed by the President, by and with the advice and consent of the Senate, for a term of four years. The General Counsel of the Board shall exercise general supervision over all attorneys employed by the Board (other than administrative law judges and legal assistants to Board members) and over the officers and employees in the regional offices. He shall have final authority, on behalf of the Board, in respect of the investigation of charges and issuance of complaints under section 10 *[section 160 of this title]*, and in respect of the prosecution of such complaints before the Board, and shall have such other duties as the Board may prescribe or as may be provided by law. In case of vacancy in the office of the General Counsel the President is authorized to designate the officer or employee who shall act as General Counsel during such vacancy, but no person or persons so designated shall so act (1) for more than forty days when the Congress is in session unless a nomination to fill such vacancy shall have been submitted to the Senate, or (2) after the adjournment sine die of the session of the Senate in which such nomination was submitted.

[The title "administrative law judge" was adopted in 5 U.S.C. Sec. 3105.]

§ 154. [§ 4] National Labor Relations Board; eligibility for reappointment; officers and employees; payment of expenses

(a) Each member of the Board and the General Counsel of the Board shall be eligible for reappointment, and shall not engage in any other business, vocation, or employment. The Board shall appoint an executive secretary, and such attorneys, examiners, and regional directors, and such other employees as it may from time to time find necessary for the proper performance of its duties. The Board may not employ any attorneys for the purpose of reviewing transcripts of hearings or preparing drafts of opinions except that any attorney employed for assignment as a legal assistant to any Board member may for such Board member review such transcripts and prepare such drafts. No administrative law judge's report shall be reviewed, either before or after its publication, by any person other than a member of the Board or his legal assistant, and no administrative law judge shall advise or consult with the Board with respect to exceptions taken to his findings, rulings, or recommendations. The Board may establish or utilize such regional, local, or other agencies, and utilize such voluntary and uncompensated services, as may from time to time be needed. Attorneys appointed under this section may, at the direction of the Board, appear for and represent the Board in any case in court. Nothing in this Act *[subchapter]* shall be construed to authorize the Board to appoint individuals for the purpose of conciliation or mediation, or for economic analysis.

[The title "administrative law judge" was adopted in 5 U.S.C. Sec. 3105.]

(b) All of the expenses of the Board, including all necessary traveling and subsistence expenses outside the District of Columbia incurred by the members or employees of the Board under its orders, shall be allowed and paid on the presentation of itemized vouchers therefor approved by the Board or by any individual it designates for that purpose.

§ 155. [§ 5] National Labor Relations Board; principal office, conducting inquiries throughout country; participation in decisions or inquiries conducted by member

The principal office of the Board shall be in the District of Columbia, but it may meet and exercise any or all of its powers at any other place. The Board may, by one or more of its members or by such agents or agencies as it may designate, prosecute any inquiry necessary to its functions in any part of the United States. A member who participates in such an inquiry shall not be disqualified from subsequently participating in a decision of the Board in the same case.

§ 156. [§ 6] Rules and regulations

The Board shall have authority from time to time to make, amend, and rescind, in the manner prescribed by the Administrative Procedure Act *[by subchapter II of chapter 5 of title 5]*, such rules and regulations as may be necessary to carry out the provisions of this Act *[subchapter]*.

Rights of Employees

§ 157. [§ 7] Right of employees as to organization, collective bargaining, etc.

Employees shall have the right to self-organization, to form, join, or assist labor organizations, to bargain collectively through representatives of their own choosing, and to engage in other concerted activities for the purpose of collective bargaining or other mutual aid or protection, and shall also have the right to refrain from any or all such activities except to the extent that such right may be affected by an agreement requiring membership in a labor organization as a condition of employment as authorized in section 8(a)(3) *[section 158(a)(3) of this title]*.

Unfair Labor Practices

§ 158. [§ 8] Unfair labor practices

(a) *[Unfair labor practices by employer]*

It shall be an unfair labor practice for an employer—

(1) to interfere with, restrain, or coerce employees in the exercise of the rights guaranteed in section 7 *[section 157 of this title]*;

(2) to dominate or interfere with the formation or administration of any labor organization or contribute financial or other support to it: Provided, That subject to rules and regulations made and published by the Board pursuant to section 6 *[section 156 of this title]*, an employer shall not be prohibited from permitting employees to confer with him during working hours without loss of time or pay;

(3) by discrimination in regard to hire or tenure of employment or any term or condition of employment to encourage or discourage membership in any labor organization: Provided, That nothing in this Act *[subchapter]*, or in any other statute of the United States, shall preclude an employer from making an agreement with a labor organization (not established, maintained, or assisted by any action defined in section 8(a) of this Act *[in this subsection]* as an unfair labor practice) to require as a condition of employment membership therein on or after the thirtieth day following the beginning of such employment or the effective date of such agreement,

whichever is the later, (i) if such labor organization is the representative of the employees as provided in section 9(a) *[section 159(a) of this title]*, in the appropriate collective-bargaining unit covered by such agreement when made, and (ii) unless following an election held as provided in section 9(e) *[section 159(e) of this title]* within one year preceding the effective date of such agreement, the Board shall have certified that at least a majority of the employees eligible to vote in such election have voted to rescind the authority of such labor organization to make such an agreement: Provided further, That no employer shall justify any discrimination against an employee for nonmembership in a labor organization (A) if he has reasonable grounds for believing that such membership was not available to the employee on the same terms and conditions generally applicable to other members, or (B) if he has reasonable grounds for believing that membership was denied or terminated for reasons other than the failure of the employee to tender the periodic dues and the initiation fees uniformly required as a condition of acquiring or retaining membership;

(4) to discharge or otherwise discriminate against an employee because he has filed charges or given testimony under this Act *[subchapter]*;

(5) to refuse to bargain collectively with the representatives of his employees, subject to the provisions of section 9(a) *[section 159(a) of this title]*.

(b) *[Unfair labor practices by labor organization]*

It shall be an unfair labor practice for a labor organization or its agents—

(1) to restrain or coerce (A) employees in the exercise of the rights guaranteed in section 7 *[section 157 of this title]*: Provided, That this paragraph shall not impair the right of a labor organization to prescribe its own rules with respect to the acquisition or retention of membership therein; or (B) an employer in the selection of his representatives for the purposes of collective bargaining or the adjustment of grievances;

(2) to cause or attempt to cause an employer to discriminate against an employee in violation of subsection (a)(3) *[of subsection (a)(3) of this section]* or to discriminate against an employee with respect to whom membership in such organization has been denied or terminated on some ground other than his failure to tender the periodic dues and the initiation fees uniformly required as a condition of acquiring or retaining membership;

(3) to refuse to bargain collectively with an employer, provided it is the representative of his employees

subject to the provisions of section 9(a) *[section 159(a) of this title]*;

(4)

(i) to engage in, or to induce or encourage any individual employed by any person engaged in commerce or in an industry affecting commerce to engage in, a strike or a refusal in the course of his employment to use, manufacture, process, transport, or otherwise handle or work on any goods, articles, materials, or commodities or to perform any services; or (ii) to threaten, coerce, or restrain any person engaged in commerce or in an industry affecting commerce, where in either case an object thereof is—

(A) forcing or requiring any employer or self-employed person to join any labor or employer organization or to enter into any agreement which is prohibited by section 8(e) *[subsection (e) of this section]*;

(B) forcing or requiring any person to cease using, selling, handling, transporting, or otherwise dealing in the products of any other producer, processor, or manufacturer, or to cease doing business with any other person, or forcing or requiring any other employer to recognize or bargain with a labor organization as the representative of his employees unless such labor organization has been certified as the representative of such employees under the provisions of section 9 *[section 159 of this title]*: Provided, That nothing contained in this clause (B) shall be construed to make unlawful, where not otherwise unlawful, any primary strike or primary picketing;

(C) forcing or requiring any employer to recognize or bargain with a particular labor organization as the representative of his employees if another labor organization has been certified as the representative of such employees under the provisions of section 9 *[section 159 of this title]*;

(D) forcing or requiring any employer to assign particular work to employees in a particular labor organization or in a particular trade, craft, or class rather than to employees in another labor organization or in another trade, craft, or class, unless such employer is failing to conform to an order or certification of the Board determining the bargaining representative for employees performing such work:

Provided, That nothing contained in this subsection (b) *[this subsection]* shall be construed to make

unlawful a refusal by any person to enter upon the premises of any employer (other than his own employer), if the employees of such employer are engaged in a strike ratified or approved by a representative of such employees whom such employer is required to recognize under this Act *[subchapter]*: Provided further, That for the purposes of this paragraph (4) only, nothing contained in such paragraph shall be construed to prohibit publicity, other than picketing, for the purpose of truthfully advising the public, including consumers and members of a labor organization, that a product or products are produced by an employer with whom the labor organization has a primary dispute and are distributed by another employer, as long as such publicity does not have an effect of inducing any individual employed by any person other than the primary employer in the course of his employment to refuse to pick up, deliver, or transport any goods, or not to perform any services, at the establishment of the employer engaged in such distribution;

(5) to require of employees covered by an agreement authorized under subsection (a)(3) *[of this section]* the payment, as a condition precedent to becoming a member of such organization, of a fee in an amount which the Board finds excessive or discriminatory under all the circumstances. In making such a finding, the Board shall consider, among other relevant factors, the practices and customs of labor organizations in the particular industry, and the wages currently paid to the employees affected;

(6) to cause or attempt to cause an employer to pay or deliver or agree to pay or deliver any money or other thing of value, in the nature of an exaction, for services which are not performed or not to be performed; and

(7) to picket or cause to be picketed, or threaten to picket or cause to be picketed, any employer where an object thereof is forcing or requiring an employer to recognize or bargain with a labor organization as the representative of his employees, or forcing or requiring the employees of an employer to accept or select such labor organization as their collective-bargaining representative, unless such labor organization is currently certified as the representative of such employees:

(A) where the employer has lawfully recognized in accordance with this Act *[subchapter]* any other labor organization and a question concerning representation may not appropriately be raised under section 9(c) of this Act *[section 159(c) of this title]*,

(B) where within the preceding twelve months a valid election under section 9(c) of this Act *[section 159(c) of this title]* has been conducted, or

(C) where such picketing has been conducted without a petition under section 9(c) *[section 159(c) of this title]* being filed within a reasonable period of time not to exceed thirty days from the commencement of such picketing: Provided, That when such a petition has been filed the Board shall forthwith, without regard to the provisions of section 9(c)(1) *[section 159(c)(1) of this title]* or the absence of a showing of a substantial interest on the part of the labor organization, direct an election in such unit as the Board finds to be appropriate and shall certify the results thereof: Provided further, That nothing in this subparagraph (C) shall be construed to prohibit any picketing or other publicity for the purpose of truthfully advising the public (including consumers) that an employer does not employ members of, or have a contract with, a labor organization, unless an effect of such picketing is to induce any individual employed by any other person in the course of his employment, not to pick up, deliver or transport any goods or not to perform any services.

Nothing in this paragraph (7) shall be construed to permit any act which would otherwise be an unfair labor practice under this section 8(b) *[this subsection]*.

(c) *[Expression of views without threat of reprisal or force or promise of benefit]* The expressing of any views, argument, or opinion, or the dissemination thereof, whether in written, printed, graphic, or visual form, shall not constitute or be evidence of an unfair labor practice under any of the provisions of this Act *[subchapter]*, if such expression contains no threat of reprisal or force or promise of benefit.

(d) *[Obligation to bargain collectively]* For the purposes of this section, to bargain collectively is the performance of the mutual obligation of the employer and the representative of the employees to meet at reasonable times and confer in good faith with respect to wages, hours, and other terms and conditions of employment, or the negotiation of an agreement or any question arising thereunder, and the execution of a written contract incorporating any agreement reached if requested by either party, but such obligation does not compel either party to agree to a proposal or require the making of a concession: Provided, That where there is in effect a collective-bargaining contract covering employees in an industry affecting commerce, the duty to bargain collectively shall also mean that no party to such contract shall terminate or modify such contract, unless the party desiring such termination or modification—

(1) serves a written notice upon the other party to the contract of the proposed termination or modification sixty days prior to the expiration date thereof, or in the event such contract contains no expiration date, sixty days prior to the time it is proposed to make such termination or modification;

(2) offers to meet and confer with the other party for the purpose of negotiating a new contract or a contract containing the proposed modifications;

(3) notifies the Federal Mediation and Conciliation Service within thirty days after such notice of the existence of a dispute, and simultaneously therewith notifies any State or Territorial agency established to mediate and conciliate disputes within the State or Territory where the dispute occurred, provided no agreement has been reached by that time; and

(4) continues in full force and effect, without resorting to strike or lockout, all the terms and conditions of the existing contract for a period of sixty days after such notice is given or until the expiration date of such contract, whichever occurs later:

The duties imposed upon employers, employees, and labor organizations by paragraphs (2), (3), and (4) *[paragraphs (2) to (4) of this subsection]* shall become inapplicable upon an intervening certification of the Board, under which the labor organization or individual, which is a party to the contract, has been superseded as or ceased to be the representative of the employees subject to the provisions of section 9(a) *[section 159(a) of this title]*, and the duties so imposed shall not be construed as requiring either party to discuss or agree to any modification of the terms and conditions contained in a contract for a fixed period, if such modification is to become effective before such terms and conditions can be reopened under the provisions of the contract. Any employee who engages in a strike within any notice period specified in this subsection, or who engages in any strike within the appropriate period specified in subsection (g) of this section, shall lose his status as an employee of the employer engaged in the particular labor dispute, for the purposes of sections 8, 9, and 10 of this Act *[sections 158, 159, and 160 of this title]*, but such loss of status for such employee shall terminate if and when he is reemployed by such employer. Whenever the collective bargaining involves employees of a health care institution, the provisions of this section 8(d) *[this subsection]* shall be modified as follows:

(A) The notice of section 8(d)(1) *[paragraph (1) of this subsection]* shall be ninety days; the notice of section 8(d)(3) *[paragraph (3) of this subsection]* shall be sixty days; and the contract period of section 8(d)(4) *[paragraph (4) of this subsection]* shall be ninety days.

(B) Where the bargaining is for an initial agreement following certification or recognition, at least thirty days' notice of the existence of a dispute shall be given by the labor organization to the agencies set forth in section 8(d)(3) *[in paragraph (3) of this subsection]*.

(C) After notice is given to the Federal Mediation and Conciliation Service under either clause (A) or (B) of this sentence, the Service shall promptly communicate with the parties and use its best efforts, by mediation and conciliation, to bring them to agreement. The parties shall participate fully and promptly in such meetings as may be undertaken by the Service for the purpose of aiding in a settlement of the dispute.

[Pub. L. 93-360, July 26, 1974, 88 Stat. 395, amended the last sentence of Sec. 8(d) by striking the words "the sixty-day" and inserting the words "any notice" and by inserting before the words "shall lose" the phrase, "or who engages in any strike within the appropriate period specified in subsection (g) of this section." It also amended the end of paragraph Sec. 8(d) by adding a new sentence "Whenever the collective bargaining ... aiding in a settlement of the dispute."]

(e) *[Enforceability of contract or agreement to boycott any other employer; exception]* It shall be an unfair labor practice for any labor organization and any employer to enter into any contract or agreement, express or implied, whereby such employer ceases or refrains or agrees to cease or refrain from handling, using, selling, transporting, or otherwise dealing in any of the products of any other employer, or cease doing business with any other person, and any contract or agreement entered into heretofore or hereafter containing such an agreement shall be to such extent unenforceable and void: Provided, That nothing in this subsection (e) *[this subsection]* shall apply to an agreement between a labor organization and an employer in the construction industry relating to the contracting or subcontracting of work to be done at the site of the construction, alteration, painting, or repair of a building, structure, or other work: Provided further,

That for the purposes of this subsection (e) and section 8(b)(4)(B) *[this subsection and subsection (b)(4)(B) of this section]* the terms "any employer," "any person engaged in commerce or an industry affecting commerce," and "any person" when used in relation to the terms "any other producer, processor, or manufacturer," "any other employer," or "any other person" shall not include persons in the relation of a jobber, manufacturer, contractor, or subcontractor working on the goods or premises of the jobber or manufacturer or performing parts of an integrated process of production in the apparel and clothing industry: Provided further, That nothing in this Act *[subchapter]* shall prohibit the enforcement of any agreement which is within the foregoing exception.

(f) *[Agreements covering employees in the building and construction industry]* It shall not be an unfair labor practice under subsections (a) and (b) of this Section for an employer engaged primarily in the building and construction industry to make an agreement covering employees engaged (or who, upon their employment, will be engaged) in the building and construction industry with a labor organization of which building and construction employees are members (not established, maintained, or assisted by any action defined in section 8(a) of this Act *[subsection (a) of this section]* as an unfair labor practice) because (1) the majority status of such labor organization has not been established under the provisions of section 9 of this Act *[section 159 of this title]* prior to the making of such agreement, or (2) such agreement requires as a condition of employment, membership in such labor organization after the seventh day following the beginning of such employment or the effective date of the agreement, whichever is later, or (3) such agreement requires the employer to notify such labor organization of opportunities for employment with such employer, or gives such labor organization an opportunity to refer qualified applicants for such employment, or (4) such agreement specifies minimum training or experience qualifications for employment or provides for priority in opportunities for employment based upon length of service with such employer, in the industry or in the particular geographical area: Provided, That nothing in this subsection shall set aside the final proviso to section 8(a)(3) of this Act *[subsection (a)(3) of this section]*: Provided further, That any agreement which would be invalid, but for clause (1) of this subsection, shall not be a bar to a petition filed pursuant to section 9(c) or 9(e) *[section 159(c) or 159(e) of this title]*.

(g) *[Notification of intention to strike or picket at any health care institution]* A labor organization before engaging in any strike, picketing, or other concerted refusal to work at any health care institution shall, not less than ten days prior to such action, notify the institution in writing and the Federal Mediation and Conciliation Service of that intention, except that in the case of bargaining for an initial agreement following certification or recognition the notice required by this subsection shall not be given until the expiration of the period specified in clause (B) of the last sentence of section 8(d) of this Act *[subsection (d) of this section]*. The notice shall state the date and time that such action will commence. The notice, once given, may be extended by the written agreement of both parties. *[Pub. L. 93-360, July 26, 1974, 88 Stat. 396, added subsec. (g).]*

§ 158a. Providing facilities for operations of Federal Credit Unions

[not printed here]

§ 159. [§ 9] Representatives and elections

(a) *[Exclusive representatives; employees' adjustment of grievances directly with employer]*
Representatives designated or selected for the purposes of collective bargaining by the majority of the employees in a unit appropriate for such purposes, shall be the exclusive representatives of all the employees in such unit for the purposes of collective bargaining in respect to rates of pay, wages, hours of employment, or other conditions of employment: Provided, That any individual employee or a group of employees shall have the right at any time to present grievances to their employer and to have such grievances adjusted, without the intervention of the bargaining representative, as long as the adjustment is not inconsistent with the terms of a collective-bargaining contract or agreement then in effect: Provided further, That the bargaining representative has been given opportunity to be present at such adjustment.

(b) *[Determination of bargaining unit by Board]* The Board shall decide in each case whether, in order to assure to employees the fullest freedom in exercising the rights guaranteed by this Act *[subchapter]*, the unit appropriate for the purposes of collective bargaining shall be the employer unit, craft unit, plant unit, or subdivision thereof: Provided, That the Board shall not (1) decide that any unit is appropriate for such purposes if such unit includes both professional employees and employees who are not professional employees unless a majority of such professional employees vote for inclusion in such unit; or (2) decide that any craft unit is inappropriate for such purposes on the ground that a

different unit has been established by a prior Board determination, unless a majority of the employees in the proposed craft unit votes against separate representation or (3) decide that any unit is appropriate for such purposes if it includes, together with other employees, any individual employed as a guard to enforce against employees and other persons rules to protect property of the employer or to protect the safety of persons on the employer's premises; but no labor organization shall be certified as the representative of employees in a bargaining unit of guards if such organization admits to membership, or is affiliated directly or indirectly with an organization which admits to membership, employees other than guards.

(c) *[Hearings on questions affecting commerce; rules and regulations]*

(1) Whenever a petition shall have been filed, in accordance with such regulations as may be prescribed by the Board—

(A) by an employee or group of employees or any individual or labor organization acting in their behalf alleging that a substantial number of employees (i) wish to be represented for collective bargaining and that their employer declines to recognize their representative as the representative defined in section 9(a) *[subsection (a) of this section]*, or (ii) assert that the individual or labor organization, which has been certified or is being currently recognized by their employer as the bargaining representative, is no longer a representative as defined in section 9(a) *[subsection (a) of this section]*; or

(B) by an employer, alleging that one or more individuals or labor organizations have presented to him a claim to be recognized as the representative defined in section 9(a) *[subsection (a) of this section]*; the Board shall investigate such petition and if it has reasonable cause to believe that a question of representation affecting commerce exists shall provide for an appropriate hearing upon due notice. Such hearing may be conducted by an officer or employee of the regional office, who shall not make any recommendations with respect thereto. If the Board finds upon the record of such hearing that such a question of representation exists, it shall direct an election by secret ballot and shall certify the results thereof.

(2) In determining whether or not a question of representation affecting commerce exists, the same regulations and rules of decision shall apply irrespective of the identity of the persons filing the petition or

the kind of relief sought and in no case shall the Board deny a labor organization a place on the ballot by reason of an order with respect to such labor organization or its predecessor not issued in conformity with section 10(c) *[section 160(c) of this title]*.

(3) No election shall be directed in any bargaining unit or any subdivision within which, in the preceding twelve-month period, a valid election shall have been held. Employees engaged in an economic strike who are not entitled to reinstatement shall be eligible to vote under such regulations as the Board shall find are consistent with the purposes and provisions of this Act *[subchapter]* in any election conducted within twelve months after the commencement of the strike. In any election where none of the choices on the ballot receives a majority, a runoff shall be conducted, the ballot providing for a selection between the two choices receiving the largest and second largest number of valid votes cast in the election.

(4) Nothing in this section shall be construed to prohibit the waiving of hearings by stipulation for the purpose of a consent election in conformity with regulations and rules of decision of the Board.

(5) In determining whether a unit is appropriate for the purposes specified in subsection (b) *[of this section]* the extent to which the employees have organized shall not be controlling.

(d) *[Petition for enforcement or review; transcript]*
Whenever an order of the Board made pursuant to section 10(c) *[section 160(c) of this title]* is based in whole or in part upon facts certified following an investigation pursuant to subsection (c) of this section and there is a petition for the enforcement or review of such order, such certification and the record of such investigation shall be included in the transcript of the entire record required to be filed under section 10(e) or 10(f) *[subsection (e) or (f) of section 160 of this title]*, and thereupon the decree of the court enforcing, modifying, or setting aside in whole or in part the order of the Board shall be made and entered upon the pleadings, testimony, and proceedings set forth in such transcript.

(e) *[Secret ballot; limitation of elections]*

(1) Upon the filing with the Board, by 30 per centum or more of the employees in a bargaining unit covered by an agreement between their employer and labor organization made pursuant to section 8(a)(3) *[section 158(a)(3) of this title]*, of a petition alleging they desire that such authorization be rescinded, the Board shall take a secret ballot of the employees in such unit and certify the results thereof to such labor organization and to the employer.

(2) No election shall be conducted pursuant to this subsection in any bargaining unit or any subdivision within which, in the preceding twelve-month period, a valid election shall have been held.

§ 160. [§ 10] Prevention of unfair labor practices

(a) *[Powers of Board generally]*
The Board is empowered, as hereinafter provided, to prevent any person from engaging in any unfair labor practice (listed in section 8 *[section 158 of this title]*) affecting commerce. This power shall not be affected by any other means of adjustment or prevention that has been or may be established by agreement, law, or otherwise: Provided, That the Board is empowered by agreement with any agency of any State or Territory to cede to such agency jurisdiction over any cases in any industry (other than mining, manufacturing, communications, and transportation except where predominately local in character) even though such cases may involve labor disputes affecting commerce, unless the provision of the State or Territorial statute applicable to the determination of such cases by such agency is inconsistent with the corresponding provision of this Act *[subchapter]* or has received a construction inconsistent therewith.

(b) *[Complaint and notice of hearing; six-month limitation; answer; court rules of evidence inapplicable]*
Whenever it is charged that any person has engaged in or is engaging in any such unfair labor practice, the Board, or any agent or agency designated by the Board for such purposes, shall have power to issue and cause to be served upon such person a complaint stating the charges in that respect, and containing a notice of hearing before the Board or a member thereof, or before a designated agent or agency, at a place therein fixed, not less than five days after the serving of said complaint: Provided, That no complaint shall issue based upon any unfair labor practice occurring more than six months prior to the filing of the charge with the Board and the service of a copy thereof upon the person against whom such charge is made, unless the person aggrieved thereby was prevented from filing such charge by reason of service in the armed forces, in which event the six-month period shall be computed from the day of his discharge. Any such complaint may be amended by the member, agent, or agency conducting the hearing or the Board in its discretion at any time prior to the issuance of an order based thereon. The person so complained of shall have the right to file an answer to the original or amended complaint and to appear in person or otherwise and give testimony at the place and time fixed in

the complaint. In the discretion of the member, agent, or agency conducting the hearing or the Board, any other person may be allowed to intervene in the said proceeding and to present testimony. Any such proceeding shall, so far as practicable, be conducted in accordance with the rules of evidence applicable in the district courts of the United States under the rules of civil procedure for the district courts of the United States, adopted by the Supreme Court of the United States pursuant to section 2072 of title 28, United States Code *[section 2072 of title 28]*.

(c) *[Reduction of testimony to writing; findings and orders of Board]*

The testimony taken by such member, agent, or agency, or the Board shall be reduced to writing and filed with the Board. Thereafter, in its discretion, the Board upon notice may take further testimony or hear argument. If upon the preponderance of the testimony taken the Board shall be of the opinion that any person named in the complaint has engaged in or is engaging in any such unfair labor practice, then the Board shall state its findings of fact and shall issue and cause to be served on such person an order requiring such person to cease and desist from such unfair labor practice, and to take such affirmative action including reinstatement of employees with or without backpay, as will effectuate the policies of this Act *[subchapter]*: Provided, That where an order directs reinstatement of an employee, backpay may be required of the employer or labor organization, as the case may be, responsible for the discrimination suffered by him: And provided further, That in determining whether a complaint shall issue alleging a violation of section 8(a)(1) or section 8(a)(2) *[subsection (a)(1) or (a)(2) of section 158 of this title]*, and in deciding such cases, the same regulations and rules of decision shall apply irrespective of whether or not the labor organization affected is affiliated with a labor organization national or international in scope. Such order may further require such person to make reports from time to time showing the extent to which it has complied with the order. If upon the preponderance of the testimony taken the Board shall not be of the opinion that the person named in the complaint has engaged in or is engaging in any such unfair labor practice, then the Board shall state its findings of fact and shall issue an order dismissing the said complaint. No order of the Board shall require the reinstatement of any individual as an employee who has been suspended or discharged, or the payment to him of any backpay, if such individual was suspended or discharged for cause. In case the evidence is presented before a member of the Board, or before an administrative law judge or

judges thereof, such member, or such judge or judges, as the case may be, shall issue and cause to be served on the parties to the proceeding a proposed report, together with a recommended order, which shall be filed with the Board, and if no exceptions are filed within twenty days after service thereof upon such parties, or within such further period as the Board may authorize, such recommended order shall become the order of the Board and become affective as therein prescribed. *[The title "administrative law judge" was adopted in 5 U.S.C. Sec. 3105.]*

(d) *[Modification of findings or orders prior to filing record in court]*

Until the record in a case shall have been filed in a court, as hereinafter provided, the Board may at any time, upon reasonable notice and in such manner as it shall deem proper, modify or set aside, in whole or in part, any finding or order made or issued by it.

(e) *[Petition to court for enforcement of order; proceedings; review of judgment]* The Board shall have power to petition any court of appeals of the United States, or if all the courts of appeals to which application may be made are in vacation, any district court of the United States, within any circuit or district, respectively, wherein the unfair labor practice in question occurred or wherein such person resides or transacts business, for the enforcement of such order and for appropriate temporary relief or restraining order, and shall file in the court the record in the proceeding, as provided in section 2112 of title 28, United States Code *[section 2112 of title 28]*. Upon the filing of such petition, the court shall cause notice thereof to be served upon such person, and thereupon shall have jurisdiction of the proceeding and of the question determined therein, and shall have power to grant such temporary relief or restraining order as it deems just and proper, and to make and enter a decree enforcing, modifying and enforcing as so modified, or setting aside in whole or in part the order of the Board. No objection that has not been urged before the Board, its member, agent, or agency, shall be considered by the court, unless the failure or neglect to urge such objection shall be excused because of extraordinary circumstances. The findings of the Board with respect to questions of fact if supported by substantial evidence on the record considered as a whole shall be conclusive. If either party shall apply to the court for leave to adduce additional evidence and shall show to the satisfaction of the court that such additional evidence is material and that there were reasonable grounds for the failure to adduce such evidence in the hearing before the Board, its member, agent, or agency, the court may order such additional evidence to be taken before the Board, its member, agent, or agency, and to be made a part of the record. The Board may modify its findings as to the facts, or make new findings, by reason of additional evidence so taken and filed, and it shall file such modified or new findings, which findings with respect to question of fact if supported by substantial evidence on the record considered as a whole shall be conclusive, and shall file its recommendations, if any, for the modification or setting aside of its original order. Upon the filing of the record with it the jurisdiction of the court shall be exclusive and its judgment and decree shall be final, except that the same shall be subject to review by the appropriate United States court of appeals if application was made to the district court as hereinabove provided, and by the Supreme Court of the United States upon writ of certiorari or certification as provided in section 1254 of title 28.

(f) *[Review of final order of Board on petition to court]*
Any person aggrieved by a final order of the Board granting or denying in whole or in part the relief sought may obtain a review of such order in any United States court of appeals in the circuit wherein the unfair labor practice in question was alleged to have been engaged in or wherein such person resides or transacts business, or in the United States Court of Appeals for the District of Columbia, by filing in such court a written petition praying that the order of the Board be modified or set aside. A copy of such petition shall be forthwith transmitted by the clerk of the court to the Board, and thereupon the aggrieved party shall file in the court the record in the proceeding, certified by the Board, as provided in section 2112 of title 28, United States Code *[section 2112 of title 28]*. Upon the filing of such petition, the court shall proceed in the same manner as in the case of an application by the Board under subsection (e) of this section, and shall have the same jurisdiction to grant to the Board such temporary relief or restraining order as it deems just and proper, and in like manner to make and enter a decree enforcing, modifying and enforcing as so modified, or setting aside in whole or in part the order of the Board; the findings of the Board with respect to questions of fact if supported by substantial evidence on the record considered as a whole shall in like manner be conclusive.

(g) *[Institution of court proceedings as stay of Board's order]*
The commencement of proceedings under subsection (e) or (f) of this section shall not, unless specifically ordered by the court, operate as a stay of the Board's order.

(h) *[Jurisdiction of courts unaffected by limitations prescribed in chapter 6 of this title]*

When granting appropriate temporary relief or a restraining order, or making and entering a decree enforcing, modifying and enforcing as so modified, or setting aside in whole or in part an order of the Board, as provided in this section, the jurisdiction of courts sitting in equity shall not be limited by sections 101 to 115 of title 29, United States Code *[chapter 6 of this title] [known as the "Norris-LaGuardia Act"]*.

(i) *Repealed.*

(j) *[Injunctions]*
The Board shall have power, upon issuance of a complaint as provided in subsection (b) *[of this section]* charging that any person has engaged in or is engaging in an unfair labor practice, to petition any United States district court, within any district wherein the unfair labor practice in question is alleged to have occurred or wherein such person resides or transacts business, for appropriate temporary relief or restraining order. Upon the filing of any such petition the court shall cause notice thereof to be served upon such person, and thereupon shall have jurisdiction to grant to the Board such temporary relief or restraining order as it deems just and proper.

(k) *[Hearings on jurisdictional strikes]*
Whenever it is charged that any person has engaged in an unfair labor practice within the meaning of paragraph (4)(D) of section 8(b) *[section 158(b) of this title]*, the Board is empowered and directed to hear and determine the dispute out of which such unfair labor practice shall have arisen, unless, within ten days after notice that such charge has been filed, the parties to such dispute submit to the Board satisfactory evidence that they have adjusted, or agreed upon methods for the voluntary adjustment of, the dispute. Upon compliance by the parties to the dispute with the decision of the Board or upon such voluntary adjustment of the dispute, such charge shall be dismissed.

(l) *[Boycotts and strikes to force recognition of uncertified labor organizations; injunctions; notice; service of process]*
Whenever it is charged that any person has engaged in an unfair labor practice within the meaning of paragraph (4)(A), (B), or (C) of section 8(b) *[section 158(b) of this title]*, or section 8(e) *[section 158(e) of this title]* or section 8(b)(7) *[section 158(b)(7) of this title]*, the preliminary investigation of such charge shall be made forthwith and given priority over all other cases except cases of like character in the office where it is filed or to which it is referred. If, after such investigation, the officer or regional attorney to whom the matter may be referred has reasonable cause to believe such charge is

true and that a complaint should issue, he shall, on behalf of the Board, petition any United States district court within any district where the unfair labor practice in question has occurred, is alleged to have occurred, or wherein such person resides or transacts business, for appropriate injunctive relief pending the final adjudication of the Board with respect to such matter. Upon the filing of any such petition the district court shall have jurisdiction to grant such injunctive relief or temporary restraining order as it deems just and proper, notwithstanding any other provision of law: Provided further, That no temporary restraining order shall be issued without notice unless a petition alleges that substantial and irreparable injury to the charging party will be unavoidable and such temporary restraining order shall be effective for no longer than five days and will become void at the expiration of such period: Provided further, That such officer or regional attorney shall not apply for any restraining order under section 8(b)(7) *[section 158(b)(7) of this title]* if a charge against the employer under section 8(a)(2) *[section 158(a)(2) of this title]* has been filed and after the preliminary investigation, he has reasonable cause to believe that such charge is true and that a complaint should issue. Upon filing of any such petition the courts shall cause notice thereof to be served upon any person involved in the charge and such person, including the charging party, shall be given an opportunity to appear by counsel and present any relevant testimony: Provided further, That for the purposes of this subsection district courts shall be deemed to have jurisdiction of a labor organization (1) in the district in which such organization maintains its principal office, or (2) in any district in which its duly authorized officers or agents are engaged in promoting or protecting the interests of employee members. The service of legal process upon such officer or agent shall constitute service upon the labor organization and make such organization a party to the suit. In situations where such relief is appropriate the procedure specified herein shall apply to charges with respect to section 8(b)(4)(D) *[section 158(b)(4)(D) of this title]*.

(m) *[Priority of cases]*

Whenever it is charged that any person has engaged in an unfair labor practice within the meaning of subsection (a)(3) or (b)(2) of section 8 *[section 158 of this title]*, such charge shall be given priority over all other cases except cases of like character in the office where it is filed or to which it is referred and cases given priority under subsection (l) *[of this section]*.

§ 161. [§ 11] Investigatory powers of Board

For the purpose of all hearings and investigations, which, in the opinion of the Board, are necessary and proper for the exercise of the powers vested in it by section 9 and section 10 *[sections 159 and 160 of this title]*—

(1) *[Documentary evidence; summoning witnesses and taking testimony]* The Board, or its duly authorized agents or agencies, shall at all reasonable times have access to, for the purpose of examination, and the right to copy any evidence of any person being investigated or proceeded against that relates to any matter under investigation or in question. The Board, or any member thereof, shall upon application of any party to such proceedings, forthwith issue to such party subpoenas requiring the attendance and testimony of witnesses or the production of any evidence in such proceeding or investigation requested in such application. Within five days after the service of a subpoena on any person requiring the production of any evidence in his possession or under his control, such person may petition the Board to revoke, and the Board shall revoke, such subpoena if in its opinion the evidence whose production is required does not relate to any matter under investigation, or any matter in question in such proceedings, or if in its opinion such subpoena does not describe with sufficient particularity the evidence whose production is required. Any member of the Board, or any agent or agency designated by the Board for such purposes, may administer oaths and affirmations, examine witnesses, and receive evidence. Such attendance of witnesses and the production of such evidence may be required from any place in the United States or any Territory or possession thereof, at any designated place of hearing.

(2) *[Court aid in compelling production of evidence and attendance of witnesses]* In case of contumacy or refusal to obey a subpoena issued to any person, any United States district court or the United States courts of any Territory or possession, within the jurisdiction of which the inquiry is carried on or within the jurisdiction of which said person guilty of contumacy or refusal to obey is found or resides or transacts business, upon application by the Board shall have jurisdiction to issue to such person an order requiring such person to appear before the Board, its member, agent, or agency, there to produce evidence if so ordered, or there to give testimony touching the matter under investigation or in question; and any failure to obey such order of the court may be punished by said court as a contempt thereof.

(3) *Repealed.*

[Immunity of witnesses. See 18 U.S.C. Sec. 6001 et seq.]

(4) *[Process, service, and return; fees of witnesses]* Complaints, orders and other process and papers of the Board, its member, agent, or agency, may be served either personally or by registered or certified mail or by telegraph or by leaving a copy thereof at the principal office or place of business of the person required to be served. The verified return by the individual so serving the same setting forth the manner of such service shall be proof of the same, and the return post office receipt or telegraph receipt therefor when registered or certified and mailed or when telegraphed as aforesaid shall be proof of service of the same. Witnesses summoned before the Board, its member, agent, or agency, shall be paid the same fees and mileage that are paid witnesses in the courts of the United States, and witnesses whose depositions are taken and the persons taking the same shall severally be entitled to the same fees as are paid for like services in the courts of the United States.

(5) *[Process, where served]* All process of any court to which application may be made under this Act *[subchapter]* may be served in the judicial district wherein the defendant or other person required to be served resides or may be found.

(6) *[Information and assistance from departments]* The several departments and agencies of the Government, when directed by the President, shall furnish the Board, upon its request, all records, papers, and information in their possession relating to any matter before the Board.

§ 162. [§ 12] Offenses and penalties

Any person who shall willfully resist, prevent, impede, or interfere with any member of the Board or any of its agents or agencies in the performance of duties pursuant to this Act *[subchapter]* shall be punished by a fine of not more than $5,000 or by imprisonment for not more than one year, or both.

§ 163. [§ 13] Right to strike preserved

Nothing in this Act *[subchapter]*, except as specifically provided for herein, shall be construed so as either to interfere with or impede or diminish in any way the right to strike or to affect the limitations or qualifications on that right.

§ 164. [§ 14] Construction of provisions

(a) *[Supervisors as union members]* Nothing herein shall prohibit any individual employed as a supervisor from becoming or remaining a member of a labor organization, but no employer subject to this Act *[subchapter]* shall be compelled to deem individuals defined herein as supervisors as employees for the purpose of any law, either national or local, relating to collective bargaining.

(b) *[Agreements requiring union membership in violation of State law]* Nothing in this Act *[subchapter]* shall be construed as authorizing the execution or application of agreements requiring membership in a labor organization as a condition of employment in any State or Territory in which such execution or application is prohibited by State or Territorial law.

(c) *[Power of Board to decline jurisdiction of labor disputes; assertion of jurisdiction by State and Territorial courts]*

(1) The Board, in its discretion, may, by rule of decision or by published rules adopted pursuant to the Administrative Procedure Act *[to subchapter II of chapter 5 of title 5]*, decline to assert jurisdiction over any labor dispute involving any class or category of employers, where, in the opinion of the Board, the effect of such labor dispute on commerce is not sufficiently substantial to warrant the exercise of its jurisdiction: Provided, That the Board shall not decline to assert jurisdiction over any labor dispute over which it would assert jurisdiction under the standards prevailing upon August 1, 1959.

(2) Nothing in this Act *[subchapter]* shall be deemed to prevent or bar any agency or the courts of any State or Territory (including the Commonwealth of Puerto Rico, Guam, and the Virgin Islands) from assuming and asserting jurisdiction over labor disputes over which the Board declines, pursuant to paragraph (1) of this subsection, to assert jurisdiction.

§ 165. [§ 15] Conflict of laws

[Reference to repealed provisions of bankruptcy statute.]

§ 166. [§ 16] Separability

If any provision of this Act *[subchapter]*, or the application of such provision to any person or circumstances, shall be held invalid, the remainder of this Act *[subchapter]*, or the application of such provision to persons or circumstances other than those as to which it is held invalid, shall not be affected thereby.

§ 167. [§ 17] Short title of subchapter

This Act *[subchapter]* may be cited as the "National Labor Relations Act."

§ 168. [§ 18] Validation of certificates and other Board actions

[Reference to former sec. 9(f), (g), and (h).]

§ 169. [§ 19] Employees with religious convictions; payment of dues and fees

Any employee who is a member of and adheres to established and traditional tenets or teachings of a bona fide religion, body, or sect which has historically held conscientious objections to joining or financially supporting labor organizations shall not be required to join or financially support any labor organization as a condition of employment; except that such employee may be required in a contract between such employee's employer and a labor organization in lieu of periodic dues and initiation fees, to pay sums equal to such dues and initiation fees to a nonreligious, nonlabor organization charitable fund exempt from taxation under section 501(c)(3) of title 26 of the Internal Revenue Code *[section 501(c)(3) of title 26]*, chosen by such employee from a list of at least three such funds, designated in such contract or if the contract fails to designate such funds, then to any such fund chosen by the employee. If such employee who holds conscientious objections pursuant to this section requests the labor organization to use the grievance-arbitration procedure on the employee's behalf, the labor organization is authorized to charge the employee for the reasonable cost of using such procedure.

[Sec. added, Pub. L. 93-360, July 26, 1974, 88 Stat. 397, and amended, Pub. L. 96-593, Dec. 24, 1980, 94 Stat. 3452.]

Chapter 13

The Occupational Safety and Health Act (the OSH Act)

Statute: 29 U.S.C. § 651 and following
http://www.osha-slc.gov/OshAct_toc/OshAct_toc_by_sect.html

Regulations: 29 C.F.R. § 1900 and following
http://cfr.law.cornell.edu/cfr/cfr.php?title=29&type=chapter&value=17

Definitions

Imminent danger

Any condition or practice that could reasonably be expected to cause death or serious physical harm immediately or before the danger can be eliminated through OSHA enforcement procedures.

Longshoring

The loading, unloading, moving or handling of ship's cargo, stores, gear or similar things into, onto, off of or out of a vessel.

Recognized hazard

A workplace hazard that an employer is, or should be, aware of. Under the general safety provisions of the OSH Act, employers must keep their workplace free of recognized hazards that are likely to cause death or serious physical harm. See Section B2, below.

Ship breaking

The breaking down of a vessel's structure for the purpose of scrapping the vessel, including removing gear, equipment or any part of the vessel.

Ship building

The construction of a vessel, including installing machinery and equipment on the vessel.

Ship repair

Any repair work done on a vessel, including alterations, conversions, installations, cleaning, painting and maintenance.

State plan state

Refers to a state that has submitted a workplace safety plan to the Secretary of Labor for approval. If the Secretary approves the plan, the state can retain control of work-related health and safety issues within its borders. For more on this, see Section G.

A. Overview of the OSH Act

1. Summary

Congress passed the Occupational Safety and Health Act in 1970 to ensure safe working conditions for all American workers. The Act requires employers to provide hazard-free working conditions, and it imposes stiff penalties on those who fail to do so.

The Act has three main provisions that employers must follow:

- **Compliance.** Employers must comply with standards issued by the Occupational Safety and Health Administration (OSHA) or, if they are in a *state plan state*, by the state agency. (See Section F, below, for more about OSHA. See Section G, below, for more about *state plan states*.)

- **Safety.** Employers must keep their workplace free of *recognized hazards* that are causing or likely to cause death or serious physical injury.
- **Inspection.** Employers must submit to inspections from OSHA inspectors or, if they are in a *state plan state*, from OSHA-approved state inspectors.

Compliance, safety and inspection provisions are covered in more detail in Sections B1, B2 and B3, respectively.

In addition, employers must maintain accurate records of all work-related accidents and diseases (see Section D3, below) and inform employees of their protections and duties under the Act (see Section D2, below).

The Act has literally thousands of regulations, covering everything from ladders to atomic substances. The type of business you engage in will determine which of these regulations you have to follow. This discussion addresses only general employer duties under the Act; it cannot begin to cover all of the regulations that employers may have to follow. To find out about specific regulations, refer to the agency resources in Section F.

The Act also has extensive provisions dealing with employee rights, which are discussed in more detail in Section B4.

Issues relating to multi-employer responsibility are quite complicated and are beyond the scope of this discussion.

2. Regulated Employers

The Act covers virtually all private businesses, regardless of size, so long as they employ at least one person and so long as they are located in one of the 50 states, the District of Columbia, the Virgin Islands, American Samoa, Puerto Rico, the Trust Territory of the Pacific Islands, the Canal Zone, the Outer Continental Shelf, the Wake Island or Johnson Island.

Even if an employer is covered by the federal law, the employer may or may not have to follow the federal law depending on the state in which the employer operates. This is because states may choose to take full responsibility for occupational health and safety administration and regulation within their borders. Private businesses that operate in one of the so-called *state plan states* must follow regulations issued by their state workplace heath and safety agency. (See Section G for more about this issue.)

The Act does not apply to state governments and their political subdivisions. However, if a state wants to take advantage of the state plan option, its plan must cover state employers. Thus, in all of the *state plan states*, state employers are subject to the state's equivalent of the OSH Act.

The Act does not apply to local governments and their political subdivisions.

The Act does not apply to the federal government and its political subdivisions. However, the Act does require each federal agency to devise health and safety standards that are consistent with the OSH Act. In addition, an executive order issued by President Carter also protects federal workers by requiring federal agencies to comply with OSH Act standards, to provide workplaces free of *recognized hazards* and to submit to inspections from the Department of Labor. The order also protects workers from retaliation for filing reports about unsafe working conditions.

3. Covered Workers

The Act applies to any employee of a covered employer (see Section A2, above), regardless of the individual's title, status or classification. Thus, the law applies to managers, supervisors, partners, stockholders, officers and employee family members as well as to rank-and-file employees.

The Act does not apply to independent contractors.

The Act does not apply to the immediate family members of a farm operator.

4. What's Prohibited: Employers

Employers may not retaliate or discriminate against employees who exercise their rights under the Act. (For information about employee rights, see Section B4.)

5. What's Required: Workers

All covered employees must comply with occupational safety and health standards and all of the rules, regulations and orders that apply to their actions and conduct.

6. Exceptions

The Act does not apply to businesses regulated under the Atomic Energy Act or under job safety rules of federal agencies other than the Department of Labor. For example, the Federal Aviation Administration has regulations on how to transport radioactive materials on airplanes. Those rules supercede OSHA regulations about radioactive hazards for airline workers.

There has been much dispute over which federal regulations fit within this exception and which do not, and the rules are court-made and quite complicated. Thus, the details of this exception are beyond the scope of this discussion.

B. Major Provisions of the OSH Act

1. Compliance

Since the OSH Act was passed in 1970, OSHA has been issuing standards designed to make workplaces as safe as possible. These standards fall into four broad categories: general industry, maritime and *longshoring*, construction and agricultural. Covered employers must follow the safety standards that apply to their business. This is referred to as "pre-inspection compliance," because employers must comply with the safety regulations before they are ever specifically told to do so by an OSHA inspector. If they don't, they face stiff fines and penalties.

Don't forget: If an employer operates its business in a *state plan state*, then it must follow its state plan standards, and not the OSH Act standards. See Section G, below, for information about *state plan states*.

Regulated Employers

See Section A2, above.

Covered Workers

See Section A3, above.

What's Required: Employers

Employers must follow the standards that apply to their industry:

- **General industry:** As a general rule, all covered employers must follow the general industry standards—unless the standard itself specifies the type of workplace to which it applies. (For example, there is a set of general industry standards that applies only to bakeries).
- **Construction:** As the name suggests, construction standards apply to covered employers who have employees who do construction work. This kind of work includes construction, alteration, repair, painting and decorating.
- **Maritime and longshoring:** These standards apply to covered employers who have employees involved in *ship repairing*, *ship building*, *ship breaking* and *longshoring*.
- **Agricultural:** These standards apply to any employer who has employees involved in the growing or harvesting of crops or the raising of livestock or poultry—or related activities—on sites such as farms, ranches, orchards or dairies.

Within each broad category are additional categories and levels of standards—and sometimes, two or more standards may apply

to the same thing. Thus, finding out which standards apply to any one business or to any one operation can be quite a daunting undertaking. OSHA and the *state plan states* provide resources to help employers understand which standards they must follow. To find out about these resources, see Sections G and H.

Employers must comply with the applicable standards in every detail. Even if the employer has developed its own safety standards or is following another public or private safety standard, the employer will violate the OSH Act if it fails to follow the OSHA standard. (Or, if the employer is in a *state plan state*, the employer will violate the state law if it fails to follow the state agency standard.)

The standards are meant to be taken literally. Whether or not an accident has occurred is irrelevant to determining whether a covered employer has violated the compliance provision. An employer can have no accidents for decades and still violate the OSH Act (or its state equivalent) if it doesn't follow the standard. Similarly, an employer can have a number of accidents and be in full compliance as long as it follows the standard (when this happens, the employer may have violated the OSH Act's safety provisions—or the safety provisions of its state equivalent—see Section B2, below).

The OSH Act requires employers to train employees adequately for their jobs. Some of the standards require employers to provide specific training to their employees.

In addition, covered employers must adequately supervise their employees.

Employers have a general duty to provide employees with tools and equipment that are in safe condition. Many of the standards require that employers provide their employees with specific types of safety equipment.

Some of the standards require employers to protect employees from health hazards, such as asbestos and lead.

There are a number of defenses that employers can raise if they are accused of failing to follow the standards. Those are beyond the scope of this discussion.

2. Safety

Covered employers have a general duty to provide their employees with employment and a place of employment free of *recognized hazards*. Congress enacted this provision to cover serious hazards that no OSHA standard applies to. If an OSHA standard does cover a hazard, then that hazard does not fall under this provision.

Don't forget: If an employer operates its business in a *state plan state*, then it must follow its state plan standards, and not the OSH Act standards. See Section G, below, for information about *state plan states*.

Regulated Employers
See Section A2.

Covered Workers
See Section A3.

What's Required: Employers
Covered employers must provide both employment and a place of employment free of hazards that they know about or should know about (so-called *recognized hazards*) and that are causing or likely to cause death or serious physical injury to employees. The fact that employers must provide both safe employment and a safe place of employment means that their duty to their employees extends beyond the four walls of their business. Anywhere that an employee is performing work for an employer is covered by the Act.

The question of what hazards are *recognized hazards* can be a difficult one, depending on the circumstances. Obviously, a hazard that an employer knows about is recognized, as is one that is common knowledge in the employer's industry. A hazard will also be recognized if the employer could easily detect it simply by walking through the workplace and using the five senses. Many courts have also held that hazards that the employer could detect through instruments are recognized.

Recognized hazards can encompass both conditions and practices.

3. Inspection

The chief way in which OSHA enforces the OSH Act is through on-site inspections. An OSHA inspection can take place in one of two circumstances:

- OSHA is conducting a random inspection, or
- OSHA is inspecting the worksite because it has received a complaint about unsafe conditions.

Employers who operate their businesses in *state plan states* face inspection from state inspectors, not OSHA inspectors. For more, see Section G, below.

Regulated Employers

See Section A2, above.

Covered Workers

See Section A3, above.

What's Required: Employers

If OSHA presents an employer with an inspection warrant, the employer must submit to the inspection. If OSHA appears without a warrant, however, the employer can consent to the inspection or refuse to consent and demand that OSHA get a warrant before entering the worksite.

4. Employee Rights

The Act gives employees numerous rights to take action to ensure that their workplace is safe. If an employee works for an employer that operates in a *state plan state*, the employee's rights may be slightly different from the ones described in this section. To learn more about *state plan states*, see Section G, below.

Although not all of the employee OSH Act rights are listed here, some of the major ones include:

- petitioning OSHA to adopt a standard
- filing a complaint with OSHA about unsafe working conditions or other OSH Act violations
- where imminent dangers exist, seeking a court order compelling the Secretary of Labor to conduct an inspection

- participating in conferences relating to the inspection
- participating in the inspection
- opposing settlements and withdrawals of contested cases
- inspecting their employer's log of occupational injuries and illnesses
- requesting a government determination as to whether there are any toxic substances in the workplace.

The Act also gives employees rights to information about workplace hazards. For example, when OSHA standards require employers to monitor employee exposure to toxic substances, the employers must:

- inform employees of the identity of certain toxic substances in the workplace
- allow employees to participate in the monitoring
- give employees all of the information obtained in the monitoring
- inform employees when they are being exposed to dangerous levels of toxins, and
- give employees access to exposure and their own medical records.

Although the OSH Act does not expressly allow employees to refuse to work in dangerous conditions, OSHA regulations do allow it when employees are faced with *imminent danger*. An employer may not discipline an employee for refusing to work if:

- the employee has a reasonable and good faith belief that performing the work presents a real danger of death or serious physical injury

- the employer will not correct the danger, and
- there isn't enough time to eliminate the danger through other channels, such as requesting an OSHA inspection.

In the case of a toxic substance or other health hazard, the worker must reasonably believe that the toxic substance or hazard is present and will shorten life or cause substantial reduction in physical or mental efficiency. The harm itself does not have to happen immediately.

State plan states—and unions—may have more lenient rules about when employees can refuse to work because of workplace hazards.

C. How the OSH Act Is Enforced

1. Individual Complaints

Individuals can complain to OSHA (or to the OSHA-approved agency in their state if they work in a *state plan state*) about safety hazards and violations.

Although individuals cannot privately sue to recover damages under the Act, they can sue in state court for injuries that they sustain in their workplaces—and use their employer's OSH Act violations as evidence of their employer's wrongdoing.

2. Agency Enforcement

Except in *state plan states*, the Act is enforced by the Occupational Safety and Health Administration (OSHA), which is a division of the U.S. Department of Labor. (See Section G, below, for a list of *state plan states*. See Section F, below, for more about OSHA.) In *state plan* jurisdictions, the law is enforced by an OSHA-approved state equivalent.

The principal method of enforcement is through on-site inspections by either federal OSHA inspectors or by OSHA-authorized state inspectors in *state plan* jurisdictions. If inspectors find violations, they will issue a citation to the employer along with a proposed penalty. Usually, the citation will also order that the employer cure the violation within a certain time period.

If the employer disagrees with the citation or wants to do something different from what the citation orders, the employer must say so within 15 days. If the employer doesn't act within 15 days, the citation becomes final. If the employer does act, it doesn't have to pay penalties or cure the alleged violation until an administrative law judge decides the matter.

D. For Employers: Complying With the OSH Act

1. Reporting Requirements

See Section D3, below.

2. Posting Requirements

All covered employers must post:

- an OSHA poster informing employees of their rights and obligations under the OSH Act
- a log and summary of occupational illnesses and injuries (see below for more about this)
- current citations that OSHA inspectors have issued to the employer (see Section C2 for more about citations), and
- any petitions that the employer has filed for modification or abatement.

Employers may have other posting requirements depending on the type of business that they run. Those additional posting requirements are beyond the scope of this discussion.

Employers that operate in a *state plan state* may have different posting responsibilities than the ones described above.

3. Recordkeeping Requirements

Although OSHA is the agency that issues recordkeeping regulations, the Department of Labor's Bureau of Labor Statistics compiles them.

There are numerous recordkeeping regulations. Generally speaking, however, covered employers must maintain the following:

- records of efforts to comply with the Act and to prevent occupational injuries and illnesses
- records of work-related deaths, injuries and illnesses, and
- records of employee exposure to potentially toxic substances or harmful physical agents.

There are a number of exemptions to various recordkeeping requirements, including ones for employers with fewer than 11 employees and for employers in low-hazard industries such as retail, service, finance, insurance and real estate. For more about these exemptions, contact the agencies listed in Section F.

Employers must use OSHA forms to keep their records. To obtain copies of the forms, contact OSHA (see Section F).

Employers must allow OSHA inspectors access to their logs and records.

Employers must also participate in any surveys that the Bureau of Labor Statistics sends to them.

OSHA has a "hazard communication standard" that requires chemical manufacturers and employers to provide information to their employees about hazardous chemicals.

For detailed information about OSHA's recordkeeping requirements, including training materials and forms, refer to the agency's recordkeeping website at http://www.osha-slc.gov/recordkeeping/index.html.

Remember: Employers who operate in *state plan states* may have to follow different recordkeeping rules. Those employers should contact their state agency (see Section G).

4. Practical Tips

If you keep your workplace as healthy and safe as possible, everyone wins. Employees will be more productive and perform better in a workplace that feels safe to them, and you will minimize the risk of fines and employee lawsuits. Even if it seems cheaper to cut corners in the short run, it won't be in the long run, especially if an employee is injured or killed.

Where your conduct violates an OSHA standard (or, if you operate in a *state plan state*, a state standard), you face fines and penalties for the violation. If you haven't violated a standard, you may not face fines, but you might face something even more costly: a lawsuit from an injured employee or, if the employee is dead, from the employee's family. Sometimes, employees will be limited to workers' compensation insurance. If your conduct is particularly grievous, however, employees will be allowed to sue you in state court—and damages in such lawsuits can extend into the millions of dollars, not to mention the cost of defending the suit.

5. Penalties

Employers face civil penalties and criminal prosecution for violating the Act.

In addition, some state prosecutors have charged employers with such things as manslaughter, murder and aggravated assault when employees have been severely injured or killed by poor working conditions. Sometimes, prosecutors will introduce OSH Act violations as evidence in these prosecutions.

In addition, workers and their families can sometimes sue employers outside of the workers' compensation system for injuries and deaths caused by unsafe workplaces.

E. For Workers: Asserting Rights Under OSHA

1. Where to Start

If You Are Not in Imminent Danger

If you see a hazard in your workplace and think that your employer might be amenable to hearing about the hazard, start by informing your employer. It is possible that your employer doesn't know about the hazard and will take care of the situation promptly. Be sure to document your request—either by making the request in writing or by writing a little note to yourself with the date that you made the request, the name of the person to whom you made it and a summary of what you and the person said. If you are afraid to complain to your employer, skip this step and start by complaining directly to OSHA (or, if you are in a *state plan state*, to your state agency).

If your employer doesn't address the hazard—or if your employer takes adverse action against you for complaining about the hazard—your next step is to complain to OSHA (or your state plan agency). You can make the complaint in writing or on the Internet. You can give your name or be anonymous.

The agency will decide what to do next. It might conduct an off-site investigation or an on-site inspection.

If You Are in Imminent Danger

Under the OSH act, if you think your life is in *imminent danger* because of a workplace hazard, you have the right to refuse to work.

(See Section B4, above, for more about *imminent danger.*) You should also call OSHA immediately at 800-321-OSHA. If you are in a *state plan state*, you may have a right to refuse to work even if the harm isn't life-threatening. Call your state plan office immediately for more information and to report the hazard. (See Section G, below, for more about *state plan states.*)

2. Required Forms

You can file a complaint with OSHA by using the agency's complaint form or by calling your OSHA regional office. If you live in a *state plan state*, your state office might have a different complaint process.

3. Practical Tips

OSHA empowers workers to be active participants in the effort to keep their workplace safe. Your OSHA (or *state plan*) rights can help you only if you use them, however. Read the agency resources list in Sections F and G, below, and use your rights to make sure that your workplace is as safe and healthy as possible. This includes requesting training from your employer and requesting information about toxic substances and hazards that you might be using.

You can also do a lot of research on OSHA's website about hazards in your industry and about your particular employer's inspection history.

If you complain to your employer or to OSHA or to your state plan agency about a workplace hazard, you do not have the right to walk off the job simply because you have filed a complaint. Under the federal OSH Act, you have this right only if you are faced with an *imminent danger* (see Section B4, above). If you are in a union or live in a *state plan state*, you may have additional rights in this regard.

Before you file a complaint with OSHA (or with your state agency if you live in a *state plan state*), be sure to find out what type of information the agency needs in order to take swift action. For example, OSHA lists 15 pieces of information that it finds useful when evaluating a complaint (see *How to File a Complaint* in the agency resources listed below). The more complete your complaint is, the more likely it is that you will get swift and effective action.

F. Agencies Charged With Enforcement & Compliance

Department of Labor
Occupational Safety and Health Administration
200 Constitution Avenue, NW
Washington, DC 20210
Phone: 202-693-2000
http://www.osha.gov

Agency Resources for Employers

(These can be obtained either at the Web addresses listed below or at the address and phone
number listed above.)

*   A concise summary of employer responsibilities under the OSH Act
    Employer Responsibilities
    http://www.osha.gov/as/opa/worker/employer-responsibility.html
*   Information about the agency's consulting service, including links to consulting offices in
    each state
    Consultation Service
    http://www.osha.gov/oshprogs/consult.html
*   A Web page with links organized by type of business (for example, auto body repair, dry
    cleaning, logging and so on). These links lead to information about the standards that an
    employer has to follow if it is engaged in that type of business.
    Industry Profiles
    http://www.osha-slc.gov/SLTC/industries.html
*   A Web page that contains links to numerous documents explaining OSHA's recordkeeping
    requirements
    Injury and Illness Recordkeeping
    http://www.osha-slc.gov/recordkeeping/index.html

Agency Resources for Workers

(These can be obtained either at the Web addresses listed below or at the address and phone
number listed above.)

*   Information on filing a complaint with OSHA, including links to a complaint form
    How to File a Complaint With OSHA
    http://www.osha.gov/as/opa/worker/complain.html
*   Information about how OSHA handles complaints from workers

Federal OSHA Complaint Handling Process

http://www.osha.gov/as/opa/worker/handling.html

- A good discussion on how workers can use their OSHA rights to be proactive in ensuring their workplaces are safe

Worker Rights Under the Occupational Safety and Health Act of 1970

http://www.osha.gov/as/opa/worker/rights.html

- A concise summary of employer responsibilities under the OSH Act

Employer Responsibilities

http://www.osha.gov/as/opa/worker/employer-responsibility.html

- A discussion of when a worker can refuse to work because of a workplace hazard

Refusing to Work Because Conditions Are Dangerous

http://www.osha.gov/as/opa/worker/refuse.html

Department of Health and Human Services

National Institute for Occupational Safety and Health (NIOSH)

Centers for Disease Control and Prevention

200 Independence Ave., SW

Washington, DC 20201

Phone: 800-356-4674

http://www.cdc.gov/niosh/homepage.html

NIOSH researches health and safety problems and develops criteria that OSHA can use when promulgating standards designed to cure those problems. As part of its research, NIOSH can inspect workplaces, issue subpoenas and interview employers and workers. NIOSH also conducts training and educational programs. The NIOSH website is rich in information about workplace hazards and safety strategies.

G. State Laws Relating to Occupational Safety and Health

When it was passed, the OSH Act pre-empted all state job safety and health laws. The states then had the option of submitting a plan to the Secretary of Labor for approval. If the secretary found the plan acceptable, then the state's law could stand. Below is a list of states that have exercised this *state plan* option.

If a state has an approved *state plan*, then that state can govern workplace health and safety with its own laws, regulations and standards.

If a state does not have an approved plan, then the federal law pre-empts state laws, regulations and standards relating to job health and safety—except in cases where the federal law doesn't cover an issue. For example, the federal law does not have standards relating to elevators. Therefore, states can have their own standards relating to elevators, even if they did not exercise the *state plan option*.

In addition, all states—even non-*state plan states*—can enforce laws, such as fire codes, that protect a wider class of people than just employees. All states can also train and educate and consult on job safety and health issues. And all states can have laws protecting state and local government employees.

State	State Plan Website
Alaska	http://www.labor.state.ak.us/lss/lss.htm?
Arizona	http://www.ica.state.az.us/ADOSH/oshatop.htm
California	http://www.dir.ca.gov/occupational_safety.html
Hawaii	http://www.state.hi.us/dlir/hiosh
Indiana	http://www.state.in.us/labor/iosha/iosha.html
Iowa	http://www.state.ia.us/iwd/labor/index.html
Kentucky	http://www.kylabor.net/kyosh/index.htm
Maryland	http://www.dllr.state.md.us/labor/mosh.html
Michigan	http://www.cis.state.mi.us/bsr
Minnesota	http://www.doli.state.mn.us/mnosha.html
Nevada	http://dirweb.state.nv.us
New Mexico	http://www.nmenv.state.nm.us/Ohsb/oshahome.htm
North Carolina	http://www.dol.state.nc.us/osha/osh.htm
Oregon	http://www.orosha.org
South Carolina	http://www.llr.state.sc.us/osha.asp
Tennessee	http://www.state.tn.us/labor-wfd
Utah	http://laborcommission.utah.gov/Utah_Occupational_Safety___Hea/ utah_occupational_safety___hea.html
Vermont	http://www.state.vt.us/labind/vosha.htm
Virginia	http://www.doli.state.va.us
Washington	http://www.lni.wa.gov/wisha
Wyoming	http://wydoe.state.wy.us/doe.asp?ID=7

H. Full Text of OSHA

U.S. Code
Title 29: Labor
Chapter 15: Occupational Safety and Health

§ 651. Congressional statement of findings and declaration of purpose and policy

§ 652. Definitions

§ 653. Geographic applicability; judicial enforcement; applicability to existing standards; report to Congress on duplication and coordination of Federal laws; workmen's compensation law or common law or statutory rights, duties, or liabilities of employers and employees unaffected

§ 654. Duties of employers and employees

§ 655. Standards

§ 656. Administration

§ 657. Inspections, investigations, and recordkeeping

§ 658. Citations

§ 659. Enforcement procedures

§ 660. Judicial review

§ 661. Occupational Safety and Health Review Commission

§ 662. Injunction proceedings

§ 663. Representation in civil litigation

§ 664. Disclosure of trade secrets; protective orders

§ 665. Variations, tolerances, and exemptions from required provisions; procedure; duration

§ 666. Civil and criminal penalties

§ 667. State jurisdiction and plans

§ 668. Programs of Federal agencies

§ 669. Research and related activities

§ 670. Training and employee education

§ 671. National Institute for Occupational Safety and Health

§ 671a. Workers' family protection

§ 672. Grants to States

§ 673. Statistics

§ 674. Audit of grant recipient; maintenance of records; contents of records; access to books, etc.

§ 675. Annual reports by Secretary of Labor and Secretary of Health and Human Services; contents

§ 676. National Commission on State Workmen's Compensation Laws

§ 677. Separability

§ 678. Authorization of appropriations

§ 651. Congressional Findings and Purpose

(a) The Congress finds that personal injuries and illnesses arising out of work situations impose a substantial burden upon, and are a hindrance to, interstate commerce in terms of lost production, wage loss, medical expenses, and disability compensation payments.

(b) The Congress declares it to be its purpose and policy, through the exercise of its powers to regulate commerce among the several States and with foreign nations and to provide for the general welfare, to assure so far as possible every working man and woman in the Nation safe and healthful working conditions and to preserve our human resources—

(1) by encouraging employers and employees in their efforts to reduce the number of occupational safety and health hazards at their places of employment, and to stimulate employers and employees to institute new and to perfect existing programs for providing safe and healthful working conditions;

(2) by providing that employers and employees have separate but dependent responsibilities and rights with respect to achieving safe and healthful working conditions;

(3) by authorizing the Secretary of Labor to set mandatory occupational safety and health standards applicable to businesses affecting interstate commerce, and by creating an Occupational Safety and Health Review Commission for carrying out adjudicatory functions under the Act;

(4) by building upon advances already made through employer and employee initiative for providing safe and healthful working conditions;

(5) by providing for research in the field of occupational safety and health, including the psychological factors involved, and by developing innovative methods, techniques, and approaches for dealing with occupational safety and health problems;

(6) by exploring ways to discover latent diseases, establishing causal connections between diseases and work in environmental conditions, and conducting other research relating to health problems, in recognition of the fact that occupational health standards present problems often different from those involved in occupational safety;

(7) by providing medical criteria which will assure insofar as practicable that no employee will suffer diminished health, functional capacity, or life expectancy as a result of his work experience;

(8) by providing for training programs to increase the number and competence of personnel engaged in the field of occupational safety and health;

(9) by providing for the development and promulgation of occupational safety and health standards;

(10) by providing an effective enforcement program which shall include a prohibition against giving advance notice of any inspection and sanctions for any individual violating this prohibition;

(11) by encouraging the States to assume the fullest responsibility for the administration and enforcement of their occupational safety and health laws by providing grants to the States to assist in identifying their needs and responsibilities in the area of occupational safety and health, to develop plans in accordance with the provisions of this Act, to improve the administration and enforcement of State occupational safety and health laws, and to conduct experimental and demonstration projects in connection therewith;

(12) by providing for appropriate reporting procedures with respect to occupational safety and health which procedures will help achieve the objectives of this Act and accurately describe the nature of the occupational safety and health problem;

(13) by encouraging joint labor-management efforts to reduce injuries and disease arising out of employment.

§ 652. Definitions

For the purposes of this Act—

(1) The term "Secretary" means the Secretary of Labor.

(2) The term "Commission" means the Occupational Safety and Health Review Commission established under this Act.

(3) The term "commerce" means trade, traffic, commerce, transportation, or communication among the several States, or between a State and any place outside thereof, or within the District of Columbia, or a possession of the United States (other than the Trust Territory of the Pacific Islands), or between points in the same State but through a point outside thereof.

(4) The term "person" means one or more individuals, partnerships, associations, corporations, business trusts, legal representatives, or any organized group of persons.

(5) The term "employer" means a person engaged in a business affecting commerce who has employees, but does not include the United States (not including the United States Postal Service) or any State or political subdivision of a State.

(6) The term "employee" means an employee of an employer who is employed in a business of his employer which affects commerce.

(7) The term "State" includes a State of the United States, the District of Columbia, Puerto Rico, the Virgin Islands, American Samoa, Guam, and the Trust Territory of the Pacific Islands.

(8) The term "occupational safety and health standard" means a standard which requires conditions, or the adoption or use of one or more practices, means, methods, operations, or processes, reasonably necessary or appropriate to provide safe or healthful employment and places of employment.

(9) The term "national consensus standard" means any occupational safety and health standard or modification thereof which (1), has been adopted and promulgated by a nationally recognized standards-producing organization under procedures whereby it can be determined by the Secretary that persons interested and affected by the scope or provisions of the standard have reached substantial agreement on its adoption, (2) was formulated in a manner which afforded an opportunity for diverse views to be considered and (3) has been designated as such a standard by the Secretary, after consultation with other appropriate Federal agencies.

(10) The term "established Federal standard" means any operative occupational safety and health standard established by any agency of the United States and presently in effect, or contained in any Act of Congress in force on the date of enactment of this Act.

(11) The term "Committee" means the National Advisory Committee on Occupational Safety and Health established under this Act.

(12) The term "Director" means the Director of the National Institute for Occupational Safety and Health.

(13) The term "Institute" means the National Institute for Occupational Safety and Health established under this Act.

(14) The term "Workmen's Compensation Commission" means the National Commission on State Workmen's Compensation Laws established under this Act.

§ 653. Applicability of This Act

(a) This Act shall apply with respect to employment performed in a workplace in a State, the District of Columbia, the Commonwealth of Puerto Rico, the Virgin Islands, American Samoa, Guam, the Trust Territory of the Pacific Islands, Wake Island, Outer Continental Shelf Lands defined in the Outer Continental Shelf Lands Act, Johnston Island, and the Canal Zone. The Secretary of the Interior shall, by regulation, provide for judicial enforcement of this Act by the courts established for areas in which there are no United States district courts having jurisdiction.

(b)

(1) Nothing in this Act shall apply to working conditions of employees with respect to which other Federal agencies, and State agencies acting under section 274 of the Atomic Energy Act of 1954, as amended (42 U.S.C. 2021), exercise statutory authority to prescribe or enforce standards or regulations affecting occupational safety or health.

(2) The safety and health standards promulgated under the Act of June 30, 1936, commonly known as the Walsh-Healey Act (41 U.S.C. 35 et seq.), the Service Contract Act of 1965 (41 U.S.C. 351 et seq.), Public Law 91-54, Act of August 9, 1969 (40 U.S.C. 333), Public Law 85-742, Act of August 23, 1958 (33 U.S.C. 941), and the National Foundation on Arts and Humanities Act (20 U.S.C. 951 et seq.) are superseded on the effective date of corresponding standards, promulgated under this Act, which are determined by the Secretary to be more effective. Standards issued under the laws listed in this paragraph and in effect on or after the effective date of this Act shall be deemed to be occupational safety and health standards issued under this Act, as well as under such other Acts.

(3) The Secretary shall, within three years after the effective date of this Act, report to the Congress his recommendations for legislation to avoid unnecessary duplication and to achieve coordination between this Act and other Federal laws.

(4) Nothing in this Act shall be construed to supersede or in any manner affect any workmen's compensation law or to enlarge or diminish or affect in any other manner the common law or statutory rights, duties, or liabilities of employers and employees under any law with respect to injuries, diseases, or death of employees arising out of, or in the course of, employment.

§ 654. Duties

(a) Each employer—

(1) shall furnish to each of his employees employment and a place of employment which are free from recognized hazards that are causing or are likely to cause death or serious physical harm to his employees;

(2) shall comply with occupational safety and health standards promulgated under this Act.

(b) Each employee shall comply with occupational safety and health standards and all rules, regulations, and orders issued pursuant to this Act which are applicable to his own actions and conduct.

§ 655. Occupational Safety and Health Standards

(a) Without regard to chapter 5 of title 5, United States Code, or to the other subsections of this section, the Secretary shall, as soon as practicable during the period beginning with the effective date of this Act and ending two years after such date, by rule promulgate as an occupational safety or health standard any national consensus standard, and any established Federal standard, unless he determines that the promulgation of such a standard would not result in improved safety or health for specifically designated employees. In the event of conflict among any such standards, the Secretary shall promulgate the standard which assures the greatest protection of the safety or health of the affected employees.

(b) The Secretary may by rule promulgate, modify, or revoke any occupational safety or health standard in the following manner:

(1) Whenever the Secretary, upon the basis of information submitted to him in writing by an interested person, a representative of any organization of employers or employees, a nationally recognized standards-producing organization, the Secretary of Health and Human Services, the National Institute for Occupational Safety and Health, or a State or political subdivision, or on the basis of information developed by the Secretary or otherwise available to him, determines that a rule should be promulgated in order to serve the objectives of this Act, the Secretary may request the recommendations of an advisory committee appointed under section 7 of this Act. The Secretary shall provide such an advisory committee with any proposals of his own or of the Secretary of Health and Human Services, together with all pertinent factual information developed by the Secretary or the Secretary of Health and Human Services, or otherwise available, including the results of research,

demonstrations, and experiments. An advisory committee shall submit to the Secretary its recommendations regarding the rule to be promulgated within ninety days from the date of its appointment or within such longer or shorter period as may be prescribed by the Secretary, but in no event for a period which is longer than two hundred and seventy days.

(2) The Secretary shall publish a proposed rule promulgating, modifying, or revoking an occupational safety or health standard in the Federal Register and shall afford interested persons a period of thirty days after publication to submit written data or comments. Where an advisory committee is appointed and the Secretary determines that a rule should be issued, he shall publish the proposed rule within sixty days after the submission of the advisory committee's recommendations or the expiration of the period prescribed by the Secretary for such submission.

(3) On or before the last day of the period provided for the submission of written data or comments under paragraph (2), any interested person may file with the Secretary written objections to the proposed rule, stating the grounds therefor and requesting a public hearing on such objections. Within thirty days after the last day for filing such objections, the Secretary shall publish in the Federal Register a notice specifying the occupational safety or health standard to which objections have been filed and a hearing requested, and specifying a time and place for such hearing.

(4) Within sixty days after the expiration of the period provided for the submission of written data or comments under paragraph (2), or within sixty days after the completion of any hearing held under paragraph (3), the Secretary shall issue a rule promulgating, modifying, or revoking an occupational safety or health standard or make a determination that a rule should not be issued. Such a rule may contain a provision delaying its effective date for such period (not in excess of ninety days) as the Secretary determines may be necessary to insure that affected employers and employees will be informed of the existence of the standard and of its terms and that employers affected are given an opportunity to familiarize themselves and their employees with the existence of the requirements of the standard.

(5) The Secretary, in promulgating standards dealing with toxic materials or harmful physical agents under this subsection, shall set the standard which most adequately assures, to the extent feasible, on the basis of the best available evidence, that no employee will suffer material impairment of health or functional capacity even if such employee has regular exposure to the hazard dealt with by such standard for the period of his working life. Development of standards under this subsection shall be based upon research, demonstrations, experiments, and such other information as may be appropriate. In addition to the attainment of the highest degree of health and safety protection for the employee, other considerations shall be the latest available scientific data in the field, the feasibility of the standards, and experience gained under this and other health and safety laws. Whenever practicable, the standard promulgated shall be expressed in terms of objective criteria and of the performance desired.

(6)

(A) Any employer may apply to the Secretary for a temporary order granting a variance from a standard or any provision thereof promulgated under this section. Such temporary order shall be granted only if the employer files an application which meets the requirements of clause (B) and establishes that (i) he is unable to comply with a standard by its effective date because of unavailability of professional or technical personnel or of materials and equipment needed to come into compliance with the standard or because necessary construction or alteration of facilities cannot be completed by the effective date, (ii) he is taking all available steps to safeguard his employees against the hazards covered by the standard, and (iii) he has an effective program for coming into compliance with the standard as quickly as practicable. Any temporary order issued under this paragraph shall prescribe the practices, means, methods, operations, and processes which the employer must adopt and use while the order is in effect and state in detail his program for coming into compliance with the standard. Such a temporary order may be granted only after notice to employees and an opportunity for a hearing: Provided, That the Secretary may issue one interim order to be effective until a decision is made on the basis of the hearing. No temporary order may be in effect for longer than the period needed by the employer to achieve compliance with the standard or one year, whichever is shorter, except that such an order may be renewed not more that twice (I) so long as the requirements of this paragraph are met and (II) if an application for renewal is filed at least 90 days prior to the expiration date of the order. No interim renewal of an order may remain in effect for longer than 180 days.

(B) An application for temporary order under this paragraph (6) shall contain:

(i) a specification of the standard or portion thereof from which the employer seeks a variance,

(ii) a representation by the employer, supported by representations from qualified persons having firsthand knowledge of the facts represented, that he is unable to comply with the standard or portion thereof and a detailed statement of the reasons therefor,

(iii) a statement of the steps he has taken and will take (with specific dates) to protect employees against the hazard covered by the standard,

(iv) a statement of when he expects to be able to comply with the standard and what steps he has taken and what steps he will take (with dates specified) to come into compliance with the standard, and

(v) a certification that he has informed his employees of the application by giving a copy thereof to their authorized representative, posting a statement giving a summary of the application and specifying where a copy may be examined at the place or places where notices to employees are normally posted, and by other appropriate means.

A description of how employees have been informed shall be contained in the certification. The information to employees shall also inform them of their right to petition the Secretary for a hearing.

(C) The Secretary is authorized to grant a variance from any standard or portion thereof whenever he determines, or the Secretary of Health and Human Services certifies, that such variance is necessary to permit an employer to participate in an experiment approved by him or the Secretary of Health and Human Services designed to demonstrate or validate new and improved techniques to safeguard the health or safety of workers.

(7) Any standard promulgated under this subsection shall prescribe the use of labels or other appropriate forms of warning as are necessary to insure that employees are apprised of all hazards to which they are exposed, relevant symptoms and appropriate emergency treatment, and proper conditions and precautions of safe use or exposure. Where appropriate, such standard shall also prescribe suitable protective equipment and control or technological procedures to be used in connection with such hazards and shall provide for monitoring or measuring employee exposure at such locations and intervals, and in such manner as may be necessary for the protection of employees. In addition, where appropriate, any such standard shall prescribe the type and frequency of medical examinations or other tests which shall be made available, by the employer or at his cost, to employees exposed to such hazards in order to most effectively determine whether the health of such employees is adversely affected by such exposure. In the event such medical examinations are in the nature of research, as determined by the Secretary of Health and Human Services, such examinations may be furnished at the expense of the Secretary of Health and Human Services. The results of such examinations or tests shall be furnished only to the Secretary or the Secretary of Health and Human Services, and, at the request of the employee, to his physician. The Secretary, in consultation with the Secretary of Health and Human Services, may by rule promulgated pursuant to section 553 of title 5, United States Code, make appropriate modifications in the foregoing requirements relating to the use of labels or other forms of warning, monitoring or measuring, and medical examinations, as may be warranted by experience, information, or medical or technological developments acquired subsequent to the promulgation of the relevant standard.

(8) Whenever a rule promulgated by the Secretary differs substantially from an existing national consensus standard, the Secretary shall, at the same time, publish in the Federal Register a statement of the reasons why the rule as adopted will better effectuate the purposes of this Act than the national consensus standard.

(c)

(1) The Secretary shall provide, without regard to the requirements of chapter 5, title 5, Unites States Code, for an emergency temporary standard to take immediate effect upon publication in the Federal Register if he determines (A) that employees are exposed to grave danger from exposure to substances or agents determined to be toxic or physically harmful or from new hazards, and (B) that such emergency standard is necessary to protect employees from such danger.

(2) Such standard shall be effective until superseded by a standard promulgated in accordance with the procedures prescribed in paragraph (3) of this subsection.

(3) Upon publication of such standard in the Federal Register the Secretary shall commence a proceeding

in accordance with section 6(b) of this Act, and the standard as published shall also serve as a proposed rule for the proceeding. The Secretary shall promulgate a standard under this paragraph no later than six months after publication of the emergency standard as provided in paragraph (2) of this subsection.

(d) Any affected employer may apply to the Secretary for a rule or order for a variance from a standard promulgated under this section. Affected employees shall be given notice of each such application and an opportunity to participate in a hearing. The Secretary shall issue such rule or order if he determines on the record, after opportunity for an inspection where appropriate and a hearing, that the proponent of the variance has demonstrated by a preponderance of the evidence that the conditions, practices, means, methods, operations, or processes used or proposed to be used by an employer will provide employment and places of employment to his employees which are as safe and healthful as those which would prevail if he complied with the standard. The rule or order so issued shall prescribe the conditions the employer must maintain, and the practices, means, methods, operations, and processes which he must adopt and utilize to the extent they differ from the standard in question. Such a rule or order may be modified or revoked upon application by an employer, employees, or by the Secretary on his own motion, in the manner prescribed for its issuance under this subsection at any time after six months from its issuance.

(e) Whenever the Secretary promulgates any standard, makes any rule, order, or decision, grants any exemption or extension of time, or compromises, mitigates, or settles any penalty assessed under this Act, he shall include a statement of the reasons for such action, which shall be published in the Federal Register.

(f) Any person who may be adversely affected by a standard issued under this section may at any time prior to the sixtieth day after such standard is promulgated file a petition challenging the validity of such standard with the United States court of appeals for the circuit wherein such person resides or has his principal place of business, for a judicial review of such standard. A copy of the petition shall be forthwith transmitted by the clerk of the court to the Secretary. The filing of such petition shall not, unless otherwise ordered by the court, operate as a stay of the standard. The determinations of the Secretary shall be conclusive if supported by substantial evidence in the record considered as a whole.

(g) In determining the priority for establishing standards under this section, the Secretary shall give due regard to the urgency of the need for mandatory safety and health standards for particular industries, trades, crafts, occupations, businesses, workplaces or work environments. The Secretary shall also give due regard to the recommendations of the Secretary of Health and Human Services regarding the need for mandatory standards in determining the priority for establishing such standards.

§ 656 Advisory Committees; Administration

(a)

(1) There is hereby established a National Advisory Committee on Occupational Safety and Health consisting of twelve members appointed by the Secretary, four of whom are to be designated by the Secretary of Health and Human Services, without regard to the provisions of title 5, United States Code, governing appointments in the competitive service, and composed of representatives of management, labor, occupational safety and occupational health professions, and of the public. The Secretary shall designate one of the public members as Chairman. The members shall be selected upon the basis of their experience and competence in the field of occupational safety and health.

(2) The Committee shall advise, consult with, and make recommendations to the Secretary and the Secretary of Health and Human Services on matters relating to the administration of the Act. The Committee shall hold no fewer than two meetings during each calendar year. All meetings of the Committee shall be open to the public and a transcript shall be kept and made available for public inspection.

(3) The members of the Committee shall be compensated in accordance with the provisions of section 3109 of title 5, United States Code.

(4) The Secretary shall furnish to the Committee an executive secretary and such secretarial, clerical, and other services as are deemed necessary to the conduct of its business.

(b) An advisory committee may be appointed by the Secretary to assist him in his standard-setting functions under section 6 of this Act. Each such committee shall consist of not more than fifteen members and shall include as a member one of more designees of the Secretary of Health and Human Services, and shall include among its members an equal number of persons qualified by experience and affiliation to present the viewpoint of the employers involved, and of persons similarly qualified to present the viewpoint of the workers involved, as well as one or more representatives of health and safety agencies of the States. An advisory committee may also include such other persons as the

Secretary may appoint who are qualified by knowledge and experience to make a useful contribution to the work of such committee, including one or more representatives of professional organizations of technicians or professionals specializing in occupational safety or health, and one or more representatives of nationally recognized standards-producing organizations, but the number of persons so appointed to any such advisory committee shall not exceed the number appointed to such committee as representatives of Federal and State agencies. Persons appointed to advisory committees from private life shall be compensated in the same manner as consultants or experts under section 3109 of title 5, United States Code. The Secretary shall pay to any State which is the employer of a member of such a committee who is a representative of the health or safety agency of that State, reimbursement sufficient to cover the actual cost to the State resulting from such representative's membership on such committee. Any meeting of such committee shall be open to the public and an accurate record shall be kept and made available to the public. No member of such committee (other than representatives of employers and employees) shall have an economic interest in any proposed rule.

(c) In carrying out his responsibilities under this Act, the Secretary is authorized to—

(1) use, with the consent of any Federal agency, the services, facilities, and personnel of such agency, with or without reimbursement, and with the consent of any State or political subdivision thereof, accept and use the services, facilities, and personnel of any agency of such State or subdivision with reimbursement; and

(2) employ experts and consultants or organizations thereof as authorized by section 3109 of title 5, United States Code, except that contracts for such employment may be renewed annually; compensate individuals so employed at rates not in excess of the rate specified at the time of service for grade GS-18 under section 5332 of title 5, United States Code, including travel time, and allow them while away from their homes or regular places of business, travel expenses (including per diem in lieu of subsistence) as authorized by section 5703 of title 5, United States Code, for persons in the Government service employed intermittently, while so employed.

§ 657. Inspections, Investigations, and Recordkeeping

(a) In order to carry out the purposes of this Act, the Secretary, upon presenting appropriate credentials to the owner, operator, or agent in charge, is authorized—

(1) to enter without delay and at reasonable times any factory, plant, establishment, construction site, or other area, workplace or environment where work is performed by an employee of an employer; and

(2) to inspect and investigate during regular working hours and at other reasonable times, and within reasonable limits and in a reasonable manner, any such place of employment and all pertinent conditions, structures, machines, apparatus, devices, equipment, and materials therein, and to question privately any such employer, owner, operator, agent or employee.

(b) In making his inspections and investigations under this Act the Secretary may require the attendance and testimony of witnesses and the production of evidence under oath. Witnesses shall be paid the same fees and mileage that are paid witnesses in the courts of the United States. In case of a contumacy, failure, or refusal of any person to obey such an order, any district court of the United States or the United States courts of any territory or possession, within the jurisdiction of which such person is found, or resides or transacts business, upon the application by the Secretary, shall have jurisdiction to issue to such person an order requiring such person to appear to produce evidence if, as, and when so ordered, and to give testimony relating to the matter under investigation or in question, and any failure to obey such order of the court may be punished by said court as a contempt thereof.

(c)

(1) Each employer shall make, keep and preserve, and make available to the Secretary or the Secretary of Health and Human Services, such records regarding his activities relating to this Act as the Secretary, in cooperation with the Secretary of Health and Human Services, may prescribe by regulation as necessary or appropriate for the enforcement of this Act or for developing information regarding the causes and prevention of occupational accidents and illnesses. In order to carry out the provisions of this paragraph such regulations may include provisions requiring employers to conduct periodic inspections. The Secretary shall also issue regulations requiring that employers, through posting of notices or other appropriate means, keep their employees informed of their protections and obligations under this Act, including the provisions of applicable standards.

(2) The Secretary, in cooperation with the Secretary of Health and Human Services, shall prescribe regulations requiring employers to maintain accurate records of, and to make periodic reports on, work-related deaths, injuries and illnesses other than minor injuries requiring only first aid treatment and which do not involve

medical treatment, loss of consciousness, restriction of work or motion, or transfer to another job.

(3) The Secretary, in cooperation with the Secretary of Health and Human Services, shall issue regulations requiring employers to maintain accurate records of employee exposures to potentially toxic materials or harmful physical agents which are required to be monitored or measured under section 6. Such regulations shall provide employees or their representatives with an opportunity to observe such monitoring or measuring, and to have access to the records thereof. Such regulations shall also make appropriate provision for each employee or former employee to have access to such records as will indicate his own exposure to toxic materials or harmful physical agents. Each employer shall promptly notify any employee who has been or is being exposed to toxic materials or harmful physical agents in concentrations or at levels which exceed those prescribed by an applicable occupational safety and health standard promulgated under section 6, and shall inform any employee who is being thus exposed of the corrective action being taken.

(d) Any information obtained by the Secretary, the Secretary of Health and Human Services, or a State agency under this Act shall be obtained with a minimum burden upon employers, especially those operating small businesses. Unnecessary duplication of efforts in obtaining information shall be reduced to the maximum extent feasible.

(e) Subject to regulations issued by the Secretary, a representative of the employer and a representative authorized by his employees shall be given an opportunity to accompany the Secretary or his authorized representative during the physical inspection of any workplace under subsection (a) for the purpose of aiding such inspection. Where there is no authorized employee representative, the Secretary or his authorized representative shall consult with a reasonable number of employees concerning matters of health and safety in the workplace.

(f)

(1) Any employees or representative of employees who believe that a violation of a safety or health standard exists that threatens physical harm, or that an imminent danger exists, may request an inspection by giving notice to the Secretary or his authorized representative of such violation or danger. Any such notice shall be reduced to writing, shall set forth with reasonable particularity the grounds for the notice, and shall be signed by the employees or representative of employees, and a copy shall be provided the employer or his agent no later than at the time of inspection, except that, upon the request of the person giving such notice, his name and the names of individual employees referred to therein shall not appear in such copy or on any record published, released, or made available pursuant to subsection (g) of this section. If upon receipt of such notification the Secretary determines there are reasonable grounds to believe that such violation or danger exists, he shall make a special inspection in accordance with the provisions of this section as soon as practicable, to determine if such violation or danger exists. If the Secretary determines there are no reasonable grounds to believe that a violation or danger exists he shall notify the employees or representative of the employees in writing of such determination.

(2) Prior to or during any inspection of a workplace, any employees or representative of employees employed in such workplace may notify the Secretary or any representative of the Secretary responsible for conducting the inspection, in writing, of any violation of this Act which they have reason to believe exists in such workplace. The Secretary shall, by regulation, establish procedures for informal review of any refusal by a representative of the Secretary to issue a citation with respect to any such alleged violation and shall furnish the employees or representative of employees requesting such review a written statement of the reasons for the Secretary's final disposition of the case.

(g)

(1) The Secretary and Secretary of Health and Human Services are authorized to compile, analyze, and publish, either in summary or detailed form, all reports or information obtained under this section.

(2) The Secretary and the Secretary of Health and Human Services shall each prescribe such rules and regulations as he may deem necessary to carry out their responsibilities under this Act, including rules and regulations dealing with the inspection of an employer's establishment.

(h) The Secretary shall not use the results of enforcement activities, such as the number of citations issued or penalties assessed, to evaluate employees directly involved in enforcement activities under this Act or to impose quotas or goals with regard to the results of such activities.

§ 658. Citations

(a) If, upon inspection or investigation, the Secretary or his authorized representative believes that an employer has violated a requirement of section 5 of this Act, of any standard, rule or order promulgated pursuant to section 6 of this Act, or of any regulations prescribed pursuant to this Act, he shall with reasonable promptness issue a citation to the employer. Each citation shall be in writing and shall describe with particularity the nature of the violation, including a reference to the provision of the Act, standard, rule, regulation, or order alleged to have been violated. In addition, the citation shall fix a reasonable time for the abatement of the violation. The Secretary may prescribe procedures for the issuance of a notice in lieu of a citation with respect to de minimis violations which have no direct or immediate relationship to safety or health.

(b) Each citation issued under this section, or a copy or copies thereof, shall be prominently posted, as prescribed in regulations issued by the Secretary, at or near each place a violation referred to in the citation occurred.

(c) No citation may be issued under this section after the expiration of six months following the occurrence of any violation.

§ 659. Procedure for Enforcement

(a) If, after an inspection or investigation, the Secretary issues a citation under section 9(a), he shall, within a reasonable time after the termination of such inspection or investigation, notify the employer by certified mail of the penalty, if any, proposed to be assessed under section 17 and that the employer has fifteen working days within which to notify the Secretary that he wishes to contest the citation or proposed assessment of penalty. If, within fifteen working days from the receipt of the notice issued by the Secretary the employer fails to notify the Secretary that he intends to contest the citation or proposed assessment of penalty, and no notice is filed by any employees or representative of employees under subsection (c) within such time, the citation and the assessment, as proposed, shall be deemed a final order of the Commission and not subject to review by any court or agency.

(b) If the Secretary has reason to believe that an employer has failed to correct a violation for which a citation has been issued within the period permitted for its correction (which period shall not begin to run until the entry of a final order by the Commission in the case of any review proceedings under this Section initiated by the employer in good faith and not solely for delay or avoidance of penalties), the Secretary shall notify the employer by certified mail of such failure and of the penalty proposed to be assessed under section 17 by reason of such failure, and that the employer has fifteen working days

within which to notify the Secretary that he wishes to contest the Secretary's notification or the proposed assessment of penalty. If, within fifteen working days from the receipt of notification issued by the Secretary, the employer fails to notify the Secretary that he intends to contest the notification or proposed assessment of penalty, the notification and assessment, as proposed, shall be deemed a final order of the Commission and not subject to review by any court or agency.

(c) If an employer notifies the Secretary that he intends to contest a citation issued under section 9(a) or notification issued under subsection (a) or (b) of this section, or if, within fifteen working days of the issuance of a citation under section 9(a), any employee or representative of employees files a notice with the Secretary alleging that the period of time fixed in the citation for the abatement of the violation is unreasonable, the Secretary shall immediately advise the Commission of such notification, and the Commission shall afford an opportunity for a hearing (in accordance with section 554 of title 5, United States Code, but without regard to subsection (a)(3) of such section). The Commission shall thereafter issue an order, based on findings of fact, affirming, modifying, or vacating the Secretary's citation or proposed penalty, or directing other appropriate relief, and such order shall become final thirty days after its issuance. Upon a showing by an employer of a good faith effort to comply with the abatement requirements of a citation, and that abatement has not been completed because of factors beyond his reasonable control, the Secretary, after an opportunity for a hearing as provided in this subsection, shall issue an order affirming or modifying the abatement requirements in such citation. The rules of procedure prescribed by the Commission shall provide affected employees or representatives of affected employees an opportunity to participate as parties to hearings under this subsection.

§ 660. Judicial Review

(a) Any person adversely affected or aggrieved by an order of the Commission issued under subsection (c) of section 10 may obtain a review of such order in any United States court of appeals for the circuit in which the violation is alleged to have occurred or where the employer has its principal office, or in the Court of Appeals for the District of Columbia Circuit, by filing in such court within sixty days following the issuance of such order a written petition praying that the order be modified or set aside. A copy of such petition shall be forthwith transmitted by the clerk of the court to the Commission and to the other parties, and thereupon the

Commission shall file in the court the record in the proceeding as provided in section 2112 of title 28, United States Code. Upon such filing, the court shall have jurisdiction of the proceeding and of the question determined therein, and shall have power to grant such temporary relief or restraining order as it deems just and proper, and to make and enter upon the pleadings, testimony, and proceedings set forth in such record a decree affirming, modifying, or setting aside in whole or in part, the order of the Commission and enforcing the same to the extent that such order is affirmed or modified. The commencement of proceedings under this subsection shall not, unless ordered by the court, operate as a stay of the order of the Commission. No objection that has not been urged before the Commission shall be considered by the court, unless the failure or neglect to urge such objection shall be excused because of extraordinary circumstances. The findings of the Commission with respect to questions of fact, if supported by substantial evidence on the record considered as a whole, shall be conclusive. If any party shall apply to the court for leave to adduce additional evidence and shall show to the satisfaction of the court that such additional evidence is material and that there were reasonable grounds for the failure to adduce such evidence in the hearing before the Commission, the court may order such additional evidence to be taken before the Commission and to be made a part of the record. The Commission may modify its findings as to the facts, or make new findings, by reason of additional evidence so taken and filed, and it shall file such modified or new findings, which findings with respect to questions of fact, if supported by sub-stantial evidence on the record considered as a whole, shall be conclusive, and its recommendations, if any, for the modification or setting aside of its original order. Upon the filing of the record with it, the jurisdiction of the court shall be exclusive and its judgment and decree shall be final, except that the same shall be subject to review by the Supreme Court of the United States, as provided in section 1254 of title 28, United States Code.

(b) The Secretary may also obtain review or enforcement of any final order of the Commission by filing a petition for such relief in the United States court of appeals for the circuit in which the alleged violation occurred or in which the employer has its principal office, and the provisions of subsection (a) shall govern such proceedings to the extent applicable. If no petition for review, as provided in subsection (a), is filed within sixty days after service of the Commission's order, the Commission's findings of fact and order shall be conclusive in connection with any petition for enforcement which is filed by the Secretary after the expiration of such sixty-day period. In

any such case, as well as in the case of a noncontested citation or notification by the Secretary which has become a final order of the Commission under subsection (a) or (b) of section 10, the clerk of the court, unless otherwise ordered by the court, shall forthwith enter a decree enforcing the order and shall transmit a copy of such decree to the Secretary and the employer named in the petition. In any contempt proceeding brought to enforce a decree of a court of appeals entered pursuant to this subsection or subsection (a), the court of appeals may assess the penalties provided in section 17, in addition to invoking any other available remedies.

(c)

(1) No person shall discharge or in any manner discriminate against any employee because such employee has filed any complaint or instituted or caused to be instituted any proceeding under or related to this Act or has testified or is about to testify in any such proceeding or because of the exercise by such employee on behalf of himself or others of any right afforded by this Act.

(2) Any employee who believes that he has been discharged or otherwise discriminated against by any person in violation of this subsection may, within thirty days after such violation occurs, file a complaint with the Secretary alleging such discrimination. Upon receipt of such complaint, the Secretary shall cause such investigation to be made as he deems appropriate. If upon such investigation, the Secretary determines that the provisions of this subsection have been violated, he shall bring an action in any appropriate United States district court against such person. In any such action the United States district courts shall have jurisdiction, for cause shown to restrain violations of paragraph (1) of this subsection and order all appropriate relief including rehiring or reinstatement of the employee to his former position with back pay.

(3) Within 90 days of the receipt of a complaint filed under this subsection the Secretary shall notify the complainant of his determination under paragraph 2 of this subsection.

§ 661. The Occupational Safety and Health Review Commission

(a) The Occupational Safety and Health Review Commis-sion is hereby established. The Commission shall be composed of three members who shall be appointed by the President, by and with the advice and consent of the Senate, from among persons who by reason of training, education, or experience are qualified to carry out the functions of the Commission under this Act. The President shall designate one of the members of the Commission to serve as Chairman.

(b) The terms of members of the Commission shall be six years except that (1) the members of the Commission first taking office shall serve, as designated by the President at the time of appointment, one for a term of two years, one for a term of four years, and one for a term of six years, and (2) a vacancy caused by the death, resignation, or removal of a member prior to the expiration of the term for which he was appointed shall be filled only for the remainder of such unexpired term. A member of the Commission may be removed by the President for inefficiency, neglect of duty, or malfeasance in office.

(c)

(1) Section 5314 of title 5, United States Code, is amended by adding at the end thereof the following new paragraph:

"(57) Chairman, Occupational Safety and Health Review Commission."

(2) Section 5315 of title 5, United States Code, is amended by adding at the end thereof the following new paragraph:

"(94) Members, Occupational Safety and Health Review Commission."

(d) The principal office of the Commission shall be in the District of Columbia. Whenever the Commission deems that the convenience of the public or of the parties may be promoted, or delay or expense may be minimized, it may hold hearings or conduct other proceedings at any other place.

(e) The Chairman shall be responsible on behalf of the Commission for the administrative operations of the Commission and shall appoint such administrative law judges and other employees as he deems necessary to assist in the performance of the Commission's functions and to fix their compensation in accordance with the provisions of chapter 51 and subchapter III of chapter 53 of title 5, United States Code, relating to classification and General Schedule pay rates: Provided, That assignment, removal and compensation of administrative law judges shall be in accordance with sections 3105, 3344, 5372, and 7521 of title 5, United States Code.

(f) For the purpose of carrying out its functions under this Act, two members of the Commission shall constitute a quorum and official action can be taken only on the affirmative vote of at least two members.

(g) Every official act of the Commission shall be entered of record, and its hearings and records shall be open to the public. The Commission is authorized to make such rules as are necessary for the orderly transaction of its proceedings. Unless the Commission has adopted a different rule, its proceedings shall be in accordance with the Federal Rules of Civil Procedure.

(h) The Commission may order testimony to be taken by deposition in any proceedings pending before it at any state of such proceeding. Any person may be compelled to appear and depose, and to produce books, papers, or documents, in the same manner as witnesses may be compelled to appear and testify and produce like documentary evidence before the Commission. Witnesses whose depositions are taken under this subsection, and the persons taking such depositions, shall be entitled to the same fees as are paid for like services in the courts of the United States.

(i) For the purpose of any proceeding before the Commission, the provisions of section 11 of the National Labor Relations Act (29 U.S.C. 161) are hereby made applicable to the jurisdiction and powers of the Commission.

(j) A administrative law judge appointed by the Commission shall hear, and make a determination upon, any proceeding instituted before the Commission and any motion in connection therewith, assigned to such administrative law judge by the Chairman of the Commission, and shall make a report of any such determination which constitutes his final disposition of the proceedings. The report of the administrative law judge shall become the final order of the Commission within thirty days after such report by the administrative law judge, unless within such period any Commission member has directed that such report shall be reviewed by the Commission.

(k) Except as otherwise provided in this Act, the administrative law judges shall be subject to the laws governing employees in the classified civil service, except that appointments shall be made without regard to section 5108 of title 5, United States Code. Each administrative law judge shall receive compensation at a rate not less than that prescribed for GS-16 under section 5332 of title 5, United States Code.

§ 662. Procedures to Counteract Imminent Dangers

(a) The United States district courts shall have jurisdiction, upon petition of the Secretary, to restrain any conditions or practices in any place of employment which are such that a danger exists which could reasonably be expected to cause death or serious physical harm immediately or before the imminence of such danger can be eliminated through the enforcement procedures otherwise provided by this Act. Any order issued under this section may require such steps to be taken as may be necessary to avoid, correct, or remove such imminent danger and prohibit the employment or presence of any individual in locations or under conditions where such imminent danger exists, except individuals whose presence is necessary to avoid, correct, or remove such imminent danger or to maintain the capacity of a continuous process operation to resume normal operations without a complete cessation of operations, or where a cessation of operations is necessary, to permit such to be accomplished in a safe and orderly manner.

(b) Upon the filing of any such petition the district court shall have jurisdiction to grant such injunctive relief or temporary restraining order pending the outcome of an enforcement proceeding pursuant to this Act. The proceeding shall be as provided by Rule 65 of the Federal Rules, Civil Procedure, except that no temporary restraining order issued without notice shall be effective for a period longer than five days.

(c) Whenever and as soon as an inspector concludes that conditions or practices described in subsection (a) exist in any place of employment, he shall inform the affected employees and employers of the danger and that he is recommending to the Secretary that relief be sought.

(d) If the Secretary arbitrarily or capriciously fails to seek relief under this section, any employee who may be injured by reason of such failure, or the representative of such employees, might bring an action against the Secretary in the United States district court for the district in which the imminent danger is alleged to exist or the employer has its principal office, or for the District of Columbia, for a writ of mandamus to compel the Secretary to seek such an order and for such further relief as may be appropriate.

§ 663. Representation in Civil Litigation

Except as provided in section 518(a) of title 28, United States Code, relating to litigation before the Supreme Court, the Solicitor of Labor may appear for and represent the Secretary in any civil litigation brought under this Act but all such litigation shall be subject to the direction and control of the Attorney General.

§ 664. Confidentiality of Trade Secrets

All information reported to or otherwise obtained by the Secretary or his representative in connection with any inspection or proceeding under this Act which contains or which might reveal a trade secret referred to in section 1905 of title 18 of the United States Code shall be considered confidential for the purpose of that section, except that such information may be disclosed to other officers or employees concerned with carrying out this Act or when relevant in any proceeding under this Act. In any such proceeding the Secretary, the Commission, or the court shall issue such orders as may be appropriate to protect the confidentiality of trade secrets.

§ 665. Variations, Tolerances, and Exemptions

The Secretary, on the record, after notice and opportunity for a hearing may provide such reasonable limitations and may make such rules and regulations allowing reasonable variations, tolerances, and exemptions to and from any or all provisions of this Act as he may find necessary and proper to avoid serious impairment of the national defense. Such action shall not be in effect for more than six months without notification to affected employees and an opportunity being afforded for a hearing.

§ 666. Penalties

(a) Any employer who willfully or repeatedly violates the requirements of section 5 of this Act, any standard, rule, or order promulgated pursuant to section 6 of this Act, or regulations prescribed pursuant to this Act, may be assessed a civil penalty of not more than $70,000 for each violation, but not less than $5,000 for each willful violation.

[Maximum allowed criminal fines under this subsection have been increased by the Sentencing Reform Act of 1984, 18 USC § 3551 et seq.]

(b) Any employer who has received a citation for a serious violation of the requirements of section 5 of this Act, of any standard, rule, or order promulgated pursuant to section 6 of this Act, or of any regulations prescribed pursuant to this Act, shall be assessed a civil penalty of up to $7,000 for each such violation.

(c) Any employer who has received a citation for a violation of the requirements of section 5 of this Act, of any standard, rule, or order promulgated pursuant to section 6 of this Act, or of regulations prescribed pursuant to this Act, and such violation is specifically determined not to be of a serious nature, may be assessed a civil penalty of up to $7,000 for each violation.

(d) Any employer who fails to correct a violation for which a citation has been issued under section 9(a) within the period permitted for its correction (which period shall not begin to run until the date of the final order of the Commission in the case of any review proceeding under section 10 initiated by the employer in good faith and not solely for delay or avoidance of penalties), may be assessed a civil penalty of not more than $7,000 for each day during which such failure or violation continues.

(e) Any employer who willfully violates any standard, rule, or order promulgated pursuant to section 6 of this Act, or of any regulations prescribed pursuant to this Act, and that violation caused death to any employee, shall, upon conviction, be punished by a fine of not more than $10,000 or by imprisonment for not more than six months, or by both; except that if the conviction is for a violation committed after a first conviction of such person, punishment shall be by a fine of not more than $20,000 or by imprisonment for not more than one year, or by both.

(f) Any person who gives advance notice of any inspection to be conducted under this Act, without authority from the Secretary or his designees, shall, upon conviction, be punished by a fine of not more than $1,000 or by imprisonment for not more than six months, or by both.

(g) Whoever knowingly makes any false statement, representation, or certification in any application, record, report, plan, or other document filed or required to be maintained pursuant to this Act shall, upon conviction, be punished by a fine of not more than $10,000, or by imprisonment for not more than six months, or by both.

(h)

(1) Section 1114 of title 18, United States Code, is hereby amended by striking out "designated by the Secretary of Health and Human Services to conduct investigations, or inspections under the Federal Food, Drug, and Cosmetic Act" and inserting in lieu thereof "or of the Department of Labor assigned to perform investigative, inspection, or law enforcement functions".

(2) Notwithstanding the provisions of sections 1111 and 1114 of title 18, United States Code, whoever, in violation of the provisions of section 1114 of such title, kills a person while engaged in or on account of the performance of investigative, inspection, or law enforcement functions added to such section 1114 by paragraph (1) of this subsection, and who would otherwise be subject to the penalty provisions of such section 1111, shall be punished by imprisonment for any term of years or for life.

(i) Any employer who violates any of the posting requirements, as prescribed under the provisions of this Act, shall be assessed a civil penalty of up to $7,000 for each violation.

(j) The Commission shall have authority to assess all civil penalties provided in this section, giving due consideration to the appropriateness of the penalty with respect to the size of the business of the employer being charged, the gravity of the violation, the good faith of the employer, and the history of previous violations.

(k) For purposes of this section, a serious violation shall be deemed to exist in a place of employment if there is a substantial probability that death or serious physical harm could result from a condition which exists, or from one or more practices, means, methods, operations, or processes which have been adopted or are in use, in such place of employment unless the employer did not, and could not with the exercise of reasonable diligence, know of the presence of the violation.

(l) Civil penalties owed under this Act shall be paid to the Secretary for deposit into the Treasury of the United States and shall accrue to the United States and may be recovered in a civil action in the name of the United States brought in the United States district court for the district where the violation is alleged to have occurred or where the employer has its principal office.

§ 667. State Jurisdiction and State Plans

(a) Nothing in this Act shall prevent any State agency or court from asserting jurisdiction under State law over any occupational safety or health issue with respect to which no standard is in effect under section 6.

(b) Any State which, at any time, desires to assume responsibility for development and enforcement therein of occupational safety and health standards relating to any occupational safety or health issue with respect to which a Federal standard has been promulgated under section 6 shall submit a State plan for the development of such standards and their enforcement.

(c) The Secretary shall approve the plan submitted by a State under subsection (b), or any modification thereof, if such plan in his judgement—

(1) designates a State agency or agencies as the agency or agencies responsible for administering the plan throughout the State,

(2) provides for the development and enforcement of safety and health standards relating to one or more safety or health issues, which standards (and the enforcement of which standards) are or will be at least as effective in providing safe and healthful employment and places of employment as the standards promulgated under section 6 which relate to the same issues, and which standards, when applicable to products which are distributed or used in interstate commerce, are required by compelling local conditions and do not unduly burden interstate commerce,

(3) provides for a right of entry and inspection of all workplaces subject to the Act which is at least as effective as that provided in section 8, and includes a prohibition on advance notice of inspections,

(4) contains satisfactory assurances that such agency or agencies have or will have the legal authority and qualified personnel necessary for the enforcement of such standards,

(5) gives satisfactory assurances that such State will devote adequate funds to the administration and enforcement of such standards,

(6) contains satisfactory assurances that such State will, to the extent permitted by its law, establish and maintain an effective and comprehensive occupational safety and health program applicable to all employees of public agencies of the State and its political subdivisions, which program is as effective as the standards contained in an approved plan,

(7) requires employers in the State to make reports to the Secretary in the same manner and to the same extent as if the plan were not in effect, and

(8) provides that the State agency will make such reports to the Secretary in such form and containing such information, as the Secretary shall from time to time require.

(d) If the Secretary rejects a plan submitted under subsection (b), he shall afford the State submitting the plan due notice and opportunity for a hearing before so doing.

(e) After the Secretary approves a State plan submitted under subsection (b), he may, but shall not be required to, exercise his authority under sections 8, 9, 10, 13, and 17 with respect to comparable standards promulgated under section 6, for the period specified in the next sentence. The Secretary may exercise the authority referred to above until he determines, on the basis of actual operations under the State plan, that the criteria set forth in subsection (c) are being applied, but he shall not make such determination for at least three years after the plan's approval under subsection (c). Upon making the determination referred to in the preceding sentence, the provisions of sections 5(a)(2), 8 (except for the purpose of carrying out subsection (f) of this section), 9, 10, 13, and 17, and standards promulgated under section 6 of this Act, shall not apply with respect to any occupational safety or health issues covered under the plan, but the Secretary may retain jurisdiction under the above provisions in any proceeding commenced under section 9 or 10 before the date of determination.

(f) The Secretary shall, on the basis of reports submitted by the State agency and his own inspections make a continuing evaluation of the manner in which each State having a plan approved under this Section is carrying out such plan. Whenever the Secretary finds, after affording due notice and opportunity for a hearing, that in the administration of the State plan there is a failure to comply substantially with any provision of the State plan (or any assurance contained therein), he shall notify the State agency of his withdrawal of approval of such plan and upon receipt of such notice such plan shall cease to be in effect, but the State may retain jurisdiction in any case commenced before the withdrawal of the plan in order to enforce standards under the plan whenever the issues involved do not relate to the reasons for the withdrawal of the plan.

(g) The State may obtain a review of a decision of the Secretary withdrawing approval of or rejecting its plan by the United States court of appeals for the circuit in which the State is located by filing in such court within thirty days following receipt of notice of such decision a petition to modify or set aside in whole or in part the action of the Secretary. A copy of such petition shall forthwith be served upon the Secretary, and thereupon the Secretary shall certify and file in the court the record upon which the decision complained of was issued as provided in section 2112 of title 28, United States Code. Unless the court finds that the Secretary's decision in rejecting a proposed State plan or withdrawing his approval of such a plan is not supported by substantial evidence the court shall affirm the Secretary's decision. The judgment of the court shall be subject to review by the Supreme Court of the United States upon certiorari or certification as provided in section 1254 of title 28, United States Code.

(h) The Secretary may enter into an agreement with a State under which the State will be permitted to continue to enforce one or more occupational health and safety standards in effect in such State until final action is taken by the Secretary with respect to a plan submitted by a State under subsection (b) of this section, or two years from the date of enactment of this Act, whichever is earlier.

§ 668. Federal Agency Safety Programs and Responsibilities

(a) It shall be the responsibility of the head of each Federal agency (not including the United States Postal Service) to establish and maintain an effective and comprehensive occupational safety and health program which is consistent with the standards promulgated under section 6. The head of each agency shall (after consultation with representatives of the employees thereof)—

(1) provide safe and healthful places and conditions of employment, consistent with the standards set under section 6;

(2) acquire, maintain, and require the use of safety equipment, personal protective equipment, and devices reasonably necessary to protect employees;

(3) keep adequate records of all occupational accidents and illnesses for proper evaluation and necessary corrective action;

(4) consult with the Secretary with regard to the adequacy as to form and content of records kept pursuant to subsection (a)(3) of this section; and

(5) make an annual report to the Secretary with respect to occupational accidents and injuries and the agency's program under this section. Such report shall include any report submitted under section 7902(e)(2) of title 5, United States Code.

(b) The Secretary shall report to the President a summary or digest of reports submitted to him under subsection (a)(5) of this section, together with his evaluations of and recommendations derived from such reports.

(c) Section 7902(c)(1) of title 5, United States Code, is amended by inserting after "agencies" the following: "and of labor organizations representing employees".

(d) The Secretary shall have access to records and reports kept and filed by Federal agencies pursuant to subsections (a)(3) and (5) of this section unless those records and reports are specifically required by Executive order to be kept secret in the interest of the national defense or foreign policy, in which case the Secretary shall have access to such information as will not jeopardize national defense or foreign policy.

§ 669. Research and Related Activities

(a)

(1) The Secretary of Health and Human Services, after consultation with the Secretary and with other appropriate Federal departments or agencies, shall conduct (directly or by grants or contracts) research, experiments, and demonstrations relating to occupational safety and health, including studies of psychological factors involved, and relating to innovative methods, techniques, and approaches for dealing with occupational safety and health problems.

(2) The Secretary of Health and Human Services shall from time to time consult with the Secretary in order to develop specific plans for such research, demonstrations, and experiments as are necessary to produce criteria, including criteria identifying toxic substances,

enabling the Secretary to meet his responsibility for the formulation of safety and health standards under this Act; and the Secretary of Health and Human Services, on the basis of such research, demonstrations, and experiments and any other information available to him, shall develop and publish at least annually such criteria as will effectuate the purposes of this Act.

(3) The Secretary of Health and Human Services, on the basis of such research, demonstrations, and experiments, and any other information available to him, shall develop criteria dealing with toxic materials and harmful physical agents and substances which will describe exposure levels that are safe for various periods of employment, including but not limited to the exposure levels at which no employee will suffer impaired health or functional capacities or diminished life expectancy as a result of his work experience.

(4) The Secretary of Health and Human Services shall also conduct special research, experiments, and demonstrations relating to occupational safety and health as are necessary to explore new problems, including those created by new technology in occupational safety and health, which may require ameliorative action beyond that which is otherwise provided for in the operating provisions of this Act. The Secretary of Health and Human Services shall also conduct research into the motivational and behavioral factors relating to the field of occupational safety and health.

(5) The Secretary of Health and Human Services, in order to comply with his responsibilities under paragraph (2), and in order to develop needed information regarding potentially toxic substances or harmful physical agents, may prescribe regulations requiring employers to measure, record, and make reports on the exposure of employees to substances or physical agents which the Secretary of Health and Human Services reasonably believes may endanger the health or safety of employees. The Secretary of Health and Human Services also is authorized to establish such programs of medical examinations and tests as may be necessary for determining the incidence of occupational illnesses and the susceptibility of employees to such illnesses. Nothing in this or any other provision of this Act shall be deemed to authorize or require medical examination, immunization, or treatment for those who object thereto on religious grounds, except where such is necessary for the protection of the health or safety of others. Upon the request of any employer who is required to measure

and record exposure of employees to substances or physical agents as provided under this subsection, the Secretary of Health and Human Services shall furnish full financial or other assistance to such employer for the purpose of defraying any additional expense incurred by him in carrying out the measuring and recording as provided in this subsection.

(6) The Secretary of Health and Human Services shall publish within six months of enactment of this Act and thereafter as needed but at least annually a list of all known toxic substances by generic family or other useful grouping, and the concentrations at which such toxicity is known to occur. He shall determine following a written request by any employer or authorized representative of employees, specifying with reasonable particularity the grounds on which the request is made, whether any substance normally found in the place of employment has potentially toxic effects in such concentrations as used or found; and shall submit such determination both to employers and affected employees as soon as possible. If the Secretary of Health and Human Services determines that any substance is potentially toxic at the concentrations in which it is used or found in a place of employment, and such substance is not covered by an occupational safety or health standard promulgated under section 6, the Secretary of Health and Human Services shall immediately submit such determination to the Secretary, together with all pertinent criteria.

(7) Within two years of enactment of the Act, and annually thereafter the Secretary of Health and Human Services shall conduct and publish industry wide studies of the effect of chronic or low-level exposure to industrial materials, processes, and stresses on the potential for illness, disease, or loss of functional capacity in aging adults.

(b) The Secretary of Health and Human Services is authorized to make inspections and question employers and employees as provided in section 8 of this Act in order to carry out his functions and responsibilities under this section.

(c) The Secretary is authorized to enter into contracts, agreements, or other arrangements with appropriate public agencies or private organizations for the purpose of conducting studies relating to his responsibilities under this Act. In carrying out his responsibilities under this subsection, the Secretary shall cooperate with the Secretary of Health and Human Services in order to avoid any duplication of efforts under this section.

(d) Information obtained by the Secretary and the Secretary of Health and Human Services under this section shall be disseminated by the Secretary to employers and employees and organizations thereof.

(e) The functions of the Secretary of Health and Human Services under this Act shall, to the extent feasible, be delegated to the Director of the National Institute for Occupational Safety and Health established by section 22 of this Act.

§ 670. Training and Employee Education

(a) The Secretary of Health and Human Services, after consultation with the Secretary and with other appropriate Federal departments and agencies, shall conduct, directly or by grants or contracts (1) education programs to provide an adequate supply of qualified personnel to carry out the purposes of this Act, and (2) informational programs on the importance of and proper use of adequate safety and health equipment.

(b) The Secretary is also authorized to conduct, directly or by grants or contracts, short-term training of personnel engaged in work related to his responsibilities under this Act.

(c) The Secretary, in consultation with the Secretary of Health and Human Services, shall (1) provide for the establishment and supervision of programs for the education and training of employers and employees in the recognition, avoidance, and prevention of unsafe or unhealthful working conditions in employments covered by this Act, and (2) consult with and advise employers and employees, and organizations representing employers and employees as to effective means of preventing occupational injuries and illnesses.

(d)

(1) The Secretary shall establish and support cooperative agreements with the States under which employers subject to this Act may consult with State personnel with respect to—

(A) the application of occupational safety and health requirements under this Act or under State plans approved under section 18; and

(B) voluntary efforts that employers may undertake to establish and maintain safe and healthful employment and places of employment. Such agreements may provide, as a condition of receiving funds under such agreements, for contributions by States towards meeting the costs of such agreements.

(2) Pursuant to such agreements the State shall provide on-site consultation at the employer's worksite to employers who request such assistance. The State may also provide other education and training programs for employers and employees in

the State. The State shall ensure that on-site consultations conducted pursuant to such agreements include provision for the participation by employees.

(3) Activities under this subsection shall be conducted independently of any enforcement activity. If an employer fails to take immediate action to eliminate employee exposure to an imminent danger identified in a consultation or fails to correct a serious hazard so identified within a reasonable time, a report shall be made to the appropriate enforcement authority for such action as is appropriate.

(4) The Secretary shall, by regulation after notice and opportunity for comment, establish rules under which an employer—

(A) which requests and undergoes an on-site consultative visit provided under this subsection;

(B) which corrects the hazards that have been identified during the visit within the time frames established by the State and agrees to request a subsequent consultative visit if major changes in working conditions or work processes occur which introduce new hazards in the workplace; and

(C) which is implementing procedures for regularly identifying and preventing hazards regulated under this Act and maintains appropriate involvement of, and training for, management and non-management employees in achieving safe and healthful working conditions, may be exempt from an inspection (except an inspection requested under section 8(f) or an inspection to determine the cause of a workplace accident which resulted in the death of one or more employees or hospitalization for three or more employees) for a period of 1 year from the closing of the consultative visit.

(5) A State shall provide worksite consultations under paragraph (2) at the request of an employer. Priority in scheduling such consultations shall be assigned to requests from small businesses which are in higher hazard industries or have the most hazardous conditions at issue in the request.

§ 671. National Institute for Occupational Safety and Health

(a) It is the purpose of this section to establish a National Institute for Occupational Safety and Health in the Department of Health and Human Services in order to carry out the policy set forth in section 2 of this Act and to perform the functions of the Secretary of Health and Human Services under sections 20 and 21 of this Act.

(b) There is hereby established in the Department of Health and Human Services a National Institute for Occupational Safety and Health. The Institute shall be headed by a Director who shall be appointed by the Secretary of Health and Human Services, and who shall serve for a term of six years unless previously removed by the Secretary of Health and Human Services.

(c) The Institute is authorized to—

(1) develop and establish recommended occupational safety and health standards; and

(2) perform all functions of the Secretary of Health and Human Services under sections 20 and 21 of this Act.

(d) Upon his own initiative, or upon the request of the Secretary of Health and Human Services, the Director is authorized (1) to conduct such research and experimental programs as he determines are necessary for the development of criteria for new and improved occupational safety and health standards, and (2) after consideration of the results of such research and experimental programs make recommendations concerning new or improved occupational safety and health standards. Any occupational safety and health standard recommended pursuant to this section shall immediately be forwarded to the Secretary of Labor, and to the Secretary of Health and Human Services.

(e) In addition to any authority vested in the Institute by other provisions of this section, the Director, in carrying out the functions of the Institute, is authorized to—

(1) prescribe such regulations as he deems necessary governing the manner in which its functions shall be carried out;

(2) receive money and other property donated, bequeathed, or devised, without condition or restriction other than that it be used for the purposes of the Institute and to use, sell, or otherwise dispose of such property for the purpose of carrying out its functions;

(3) receive (and use, sell, or otherwise dispose of, in accordance with paragraph (2)), money and other property donated, bequeathed, or devised to the Institute with a condition or restriction, including a condition that the Institute use other funds of the Institute for the purposes of the gift;

(4) in accordance with the civil service laws, appoint and fix the compensation of such personnel as may be necessary to carry out the provisions of this section;

(5) obtain the services of experts and consultants in accordance with the provisions of section 3109 of title 5, United States Code;

(6) accept and utilize the services of voluntary and noncompensated personnel and reimburse them for travel expenses, including per diem, as authorized by section 5703 of title 5, United States Code;

(7) enter into contracts, grants or other arrangements, or modifications thereof to carry out the provisions of this section, and such contracts or modifications thereof may be entered into without performance or other bonds, and without regard to section 3709 of the Revised Statutes, as amended (41 U.S.C. 5), or any other provision of law relating to competitive bidding;

(8) make advance, progress, and other payments which the Director deems necessary under this title without regard to the provisions of section 3324 (a) and (b) of Title 31; and

(9) make other necessary expenditures.

(f) The Director shall submit to the Secretary of Health and Human Services, to the President, and to the Congress an annual report of the operations of the Institute under this Act, which shall include a detailed statement of all private and public funds received and expended by it, and such recommendations as he deems appropriate.

(g) LEAD-BASED PAINT ACTIVITIES.

(1) Training Grant Program.—

(A) The Institute, in conjunction with the Administrator of the Environmental Protection Agency, may make grants for the training and education of workers and supervisors who are or may be directly engaged in lead-based paint activities.

(B) Grants referred to in subparagraph (A) shall be awarded to nonprofit organizations (including colleges and universities, joint labor-management trust funds, States, and nonprofit government employee organizations)—

(i) which are engaged in the training and education of workers and supervisors who are or who may be directly engaged in lead-based paint activities (as defined in Title IV of the Toxic Substances Control Act), [15 USC 2681 et. seq.]

(ii) which have demonstrated experience in implementing and operating health and safety training and education programs, and

(iii) with a demonstrated ability to reach, and involve in lead-based paint training programs, target populations of individuals who are or will be engaged in lead-based paint activities.

Grants under this subsection shall be awarded only to those organizations that fund at least 30

percent of their lead-based paint activities training programs from non-Federal sources, excluding in-kind contributions. Grants may also be made to local governments to carry out such training and education for their employees.

(C) There are authorized to be appropriated, a minimum, $10,000,000 to the Institute for each of the fiscal years 1994 through 1997 to make grants under this paragraph.

(2) Evaluation of Programs.— The Institute shall conduct periodic and comprehensive assessments of the efficacy of the worker and supervisor training programs developed and offered by those receiving grants under this section. The Director shall prepare reports on the results of these assessments addressed to the Administrator of the Environmental Protection Agency to include recommendations as may be appropriate for the revision of these programs. The sum of $500,000 is authorized to be appropriated to the Institute for each of the fiscal years 1994 through 1997 to carry out this paragraph.

§ 672. Grants to the States

(a) The Secretary is authorized, during the fiscal year ending June 30, 1971, and the two succeeding fiscal years, to make grants to the States which have designated a State agency under section 18 to assist them—

(1) in identifying their needs and responsibilities in the area of occupational safety and health,

(2) in developing State plans under section 18, or

(3) in developing plans for—

(A) establishing systems for the collection of information concerning the nature and frequency of occupational injuries and diseases;

(B) increasing the expertise and enforcement capabilities of their personnel engaged in occupational safety and health programs; or

(C) otherwise improving the administration and enforcement of State occupational safety and health laws, including standards thereunder, consistent with the objectives of this Act.

(b) The Secretary is authorized, during the fiscal year ending June 30, 1971, and the two succeeding fiscal years, to make grants to the States for experimental and demonstration projects consistent with the objectives set forth in subsection (a) of this section.

(c) The Governor of the State shall designate the appropriate State agency for receipt of any grant made by the Secretary under this section.

(d) Any State agency designated by the Governor of the State desiring a grant under this section shall submit an application therefor to the Secretary.

(e) The Secretary shall review the application, and shall, after consultation with the Secretary of Health and Human Services, approve or reject such application.

(f) The Federal share for each State grant under subsection (a) or (b) of this section may not exceed 90 per centum of the total cost of the application. In the event the Federal share for all States under either such subsection is not the same, the differences among the States shall be established on the basis of objective criteria.

(g) The Secretary is authorized to make grants to the States to assist them in administering and enforcing programs for occupational safety and health contained in State plans approved by the Secretary pursuant to section 18 of this Act. The Federal share for each State grant under this subsection may not exceed 50 per centum of the total cost to the State of such a program. The last sentence of subsection (f) shall be applicable in determining the Federal share under this subsection.

(h) Prior to June 30, 1973, the Secretary shall, after consultation with the Secretary of Health and Human Services, transmit a report to the President and to the Congress, describing the experience under the grant programs authorized by this section and making any recommendations he may deem appropriate.

§ 673. Statistics

(a) In order to further the purposes of this Act, the Secretary, in consultation with the Secretary of Health and Human Services, shall develop and maintain an effective program of collection, compilation, and analysis of occupational safety and health statistics. Such program may cover all employments whether or not subject to any other provisions of this Act but shall not cover employments excluded by section 4 of the Act. The Secretary shall compile accurate statistics on work injuries and illnesses which shall include all disabling, serious, or significant injuries and illnesses, whether or not involving loss of time from work, other than minor injuries requiring only first aid treatment and which do not involve medical treatment, loss of consciousness, restriction of work or motion, or transfer to another job.

(b) To carry out his duties under subsection (a) of this section, the Secretary may—

(1) promote, encourage, or directly engage in programs of studies, information and communication concerning occupational safety and health statistics;

(2) make grants to States or political subdivisions thereof in order to assist them in developing and administering programs dealing with occupational safety and health statistics; and

(3) arrange, through grants or contracts, for the conduct of such research and investigations as give promise of furthering the objectives of this section.

(c) The Federal share for each grant under subsection (b) of this section may be up to 50 per centum of the State's total cost.

(d) The Secretary may, with the consent of any State or political subdivision thereof, accept and use the services, facilities, and employees of the agencies of such State or political subdivision, with or without reimbursement, in order to assist him in carrying out his functions under this section.

(e) On the basis of the records made and kept pursuant to section 8(c) of this Act, employers shall file such reports with the Secretary as he shall prescribe by regulation, as necessary to carry out his functions under this Act.

(f) Agreements between the Department of Labor and States pertaining to the collection of occupational safety and health statistics already in effect on the effective date of this Act shall remain in effect until superseded by grants or contracts made under this Act.

§ 674. Audits

(a) Each recipient of a grant under this Act shall keep such records as the Secretary or the Secretary of Health and Human Services shall prescribe, including records which fully disclose the amount and disposition by such recipient of the proceeds of such grant, the total cost of the project or undertaking in connection with which such grant is made or used, and the amount of that portion of the cost of the project or undertaking supplied by other sources, and such other records as will facilitate an effective audit.

(b) The Secretary or the Secretary of Health and Human Services, and the Comptroller General of the United States, or any of their duly authorized representatives, shall have access for the purpose of audit and examination to any books, documents, papers, and records of the recipients of any grant under this Act that are pertinent to any such grant.

§ 675. Annual Report

Within one hundred and twenty days following the convening of each regular session of each Congress, the Secretary and the Secretary of Health and Human Services shall each prepare and submit to the President for transmittal to the Congress a report upon the subject matter of this Act, the progress toward achievement of the purpose of this Act, the needs and requirements in the field of occupational safety and health, and any other relevant information. Such reports shall include information regarding occupational safety and health standards, and criteria for such standards, developed during the preceding year; evaluation of standards and criteria previously developed under this Act, defining areas of emphasis for new criteria and standards; an evaluation of the degree of observance of applicable occupational safety and health standards, and a summary of inspection and enforcement activity undertaken; analysis and evaluation of research activities for which results have been obtained under governmental and nongovernmental sponsorship; an analysis of major occupational diseases; evaluation of available control and measurement technology for hazards for which standards or criteria have been developed during the preceding year; description of cooperative efforts under-taken between Government agencies and other interested parties in the implementation of this Act during the preceding year; a progress report on the development of an adequate supply of trained manpower in the field of occupational safety and health, including estimates of future needs and the efforts being made by Government and others to meet those needs; listing of all toxic sub-stances in industrial usage for which labeling requirements, criteria, or standards have not yet been established; and such recommendations for additional legislation as are deemed necessary to protect the safety and health of the worker and improve the administration of this Act.

§ 676. National Commission on State Workmen's Compensation Laws

(a)

    (1) The Congress hereby finds and declares that—

      (A) the vast majority of American workers, and their families, are dependent on workmen's compensation for their basic economic security in the event such workers suffer disabling injury or death in the course of their employment; and that the full protection of American workers from job-related injury or death requires an adequate, prompt, and equitable system of workmen's compensation as well as an effective program of occupational health and safety regulation; and

      (B) in recent years serious questions have been raised concerning the fairness and adequacy of present workmen's compensation laws in the light of the growth of the economy, the changing nature of the labor force, increases in medical knowledge, changes in the hazards associated with various types of employment, new technology creating new risks to health and safety, and increases in the general level of wages and the cost of living.

(2) The purpose of this Section is to authorize an effective study and objective evaluation of State workmen's compensation laws in order to determine if such laws provide an adequate, prompt, and equitable system of compensation for injury or death arising out of or in the course of employment.

§ 677. Separability

If any provision of this Act, or the application of such provision to any person or circumstance, shall be held invalid, the remainder of this Act, or the application of such provision to persons or circumstances other than those as to which it is held invalid, shall not be affected thereby.

§ 678. Appropriations

There are authorized to be appropriated to carry out this Act for each fiscal year such sums as the Congress shall deem necessary.

■

Chapter 14

Older Workers Benefit Protection Act (OWBPA)

Statute: 29 U.S.C. §§ 623 & 626
http://www4.law.cornell.edu/uscode/29/ch14.html

Regulations: 29 C.F.R. §§ 1625.10, 1625.22 & 1625.23
http://cfr.law.cornell.edu/cfr/cfr.php?title=29&type=part&value=1625

Definitions

Bona fide employee benefit plan
A benefit plan that has been accurately described, in writing, to all employees and that actually provides the benefits promised.

Early retirement incentive plan
A voluntary program in which employers offer employees the opportunity to retire early—before they reach normal retirement age under the employer's pension or other retirement plan—in exchange for additional benefits to which they would not otherwise have been entitled. Many employers credit employees who agree to retire early with additional years of service for purposes of pension accrual, so the employee will be eligible to receive an immediate *unreduced pension*.

Exit incentive program
A voluntary program offered to a group or class of at least two employees, whereby the employees are offered something of value (such as enhanced benefits or compensation) in exchange for their decision to resign and sign a *waiver*.

Other employment termination program
A program by which a group or class of at least two employees are terminated involuntarily (through a layoff or reduction in force, for example) and are offered something of value in exchange for their decision to sign a *waiver*.

Unreduced pension
The full pension an employee will receive under an employer's pension plan as long as the employee works until normal retirement age.

Waiver
A legal agreement or contract between an employer and an employee in which the employee gives up ("waives") the right to sue the employer for specified claims. Generally, a waiver may cover every potential legal claim an employee might have against an employer or may be limited to only certain claims. The requirements of the OWBPA apply only to waivers of claims for age discrimination under the Age Discrimination in Employment Act (ADEA). A waiver is sometimes also referred to as a "release" or "release of claims."

A. Overview of OWBPA

1. Summary

Passed in 1989, the Older Workers Benefit Protection Act (OWBPA) explains how courts will decide whether the benefits employers offer to older workers are equal to the benefits offered to younger workers—a requirement under the Age Discrimination in Employment Act (ADEA). OWBPA also regulates *waivers*, and requires employers to take certain steps to make sure that these agreements are knowing and voluntary.

The OWBPA includes provisions on:

- **Benefits:** Employers must offer older workers benefits that are equal to or, in some cases, cost the employer as much as, the benefits offered to younger workers. The rules for determining whether benefits are equal depend on the type of benefits offered.
- **Waivers:** A *waiver* of the right to sue for age discrimination is valid only if it meets certain standards, designed to ensure that the waiver is knowing and voluntary.

Although technically an amendment to the Age Discrimination in Employment Act (ADEA), OWBPA addresses issues that were not covered in the original ADEA. For this reason, human resources professionals and lawyers generally refer to it by its own name as a separate law—as do we.

2. Regulated Employers

OWBPA applies to all employers covered by the ADEA (see the chapter on the ADEA).

3. Covered Workers

OWBPA protects all workers covered by the ADEA (see the chapter on the ADEA).

B. Major Provisions of OWBPA

1. Benefits

Congress passed OWBPA to prohibit age discrimination in the provision of fringe benefits (such as life insurance, health insurance, disability benefits, pensions and retirement benefits), while at the same time allowing employers to reduce benefits to older workers when justified by significant cost considerations. In most situations, employers must provide equal benefits to older and younger workers. For some types of benefits, however, employers can meet this requirement by spending the same amount on the benefit provided to each group, even if older workers receive lesser benefits. Employers are also allowed, in some circumstances, to provide lesser benefits to older workers if the older workers receive (from the employer or the government) additional benefits to make up the difference.

Regulated Employers

All regulated employers must comply with these provisions. See Section A2.

Covered Workers

These provisions protect all covered workers. See Section A3.

What's Prohibited: Employers

Employers may not rely on the provisions of a benefit plan to

- refuse to hire anyone based on the person's age, or
- require anyone to retire involuntarily because of that person's age.

What's Required: Employers

Employers are not always required to provide precisely the same benefit to older workers as they provide to younger workers. In some cases, employers may comply with OWBPA by showing that although the benefits to each group aren't identical, they paid the same amount for benefits to older and younger workers (the "equal cost" defense), or that any shortfall in benefits to older workers was made up ("offset") by additional benefits provided by the employer or by the government.

Below, we explain how these defenses work, then explain a few special rules that apply to certain types of benefits.

The Equal Cost Defense

An employer may offer a lesser benefit to older workers if it costs the same as the benefit offered to younger workers. However, this rule applies only to certain types of

benefits and is subject to several conditions. An employer may use the equal cost defense only if *all* of the following are true:

- The benefit is one that becomes more costly to provide as workers grow older. This is true of life insurance, health insurance and disability insurance, for example—as workers age, it becomes more likely that they will use these benefits, and insurers often charge more for coverage to guard against this possibility. Because benefits such as severance pay or paid vacations do not cost more to provide to older workers, the equal cost defense does not apply to these benefits.
- The benefit is not a retirement benefit (to which the equal cost defense does not apply).
- The benefit is provided as part of a *bona fide employee benefit plan.*
- The benefit plan explicitly requires lower benefits for older workers. An employer cannot use the equal cost defense if the benefit plan gives the employer discretion to pay lower benefits to older workers if it chooses—the plan must require benefits to diminish for older workers.
- The employer must pay the same amount (as a premium, for example) for coverage for older and younger workers—this is the equal cost requirement.
- Benefit levels for older workers have not been reduced more than is necessary to achieve equal cost for coverage of older and younger workers.

- When comparing coverage costs, the employer has not used age brackets of more than five years. That is, an employer who wishes to reduce a benefit for workers ages 61 through 65 must compare the cost of covering those workers with the cost of covering workers ages 56 through 60—not the cost of covering workers in their 20s or 30s.

Offsets

In some cases, employers may offer older employees lesser benefits if those employees receive additional benefits from the employer or the government that make up the difference. The employer may use these additional benefits to "offset" the shortfall and bring the older workers' benefits up to the same level offered to younger employees.

Offsets may be used only in the following circumstances:

- Employers can use government-provided disability benefits to offset disability benefits or disability retirement benefits provided by the employer. For example, if a disabled employee collects workers' compensation or Social Security disability payments, the employer can count that money towards the total disability benefit it offers older workers for purposes of the equal benefit rule.
- Employers can use the portion of an older worker's pension benefit that is attributable to employer contributions to offset long-term disability benefits if (1) the worker voluntarily elects to

receive the pension (at any age) or (2) the worker has reached the later of age 62 or the pension plan's normal retirement age and is eligible for an *unreduced pension.*

- Employers can use retiree health benefits provided to an employee to offset severance benefits if (1) the retiree actually receives the health benefit coverage (if an employer offers the benefit but the retiree turns it down, this requirement has not been met); (2) the retiree health benefits are at least comparable to Medicare benefits in type and value, or to ¼ the value of Medicare benefits, if the retiree is over the age of 64; and (3) the retiree is eligible for an immediate pension. If these requirements are met, the employer may take the following offsets: for health benefits provided for an unlimited time period (for example, for the rest of the employee's lifetime), the employer may offset $48,000 if the employee is younger than 65, and $24,000 if the employee is 65 or older at the time of retirement. For benefits of limited duration, the employer may deduct $3,000 per year of benefits paid before the employee reaches the age of 65, and $750 per year once the employee reaches 65.
- Employers can use additional pension benefits to offset severance benefits if (1) the additional pension benefits are made available solely because of the employee's separation from employment,

and (2) counting the additional pension benefit, the employee is eligible for an immediate and *unreduced pension.*

- Employers who increase the value of a pension benefit for employees who work beyond normal retirement age may use that increased value to offset the employee's pension accrual. For example, if a pension accrues a benefit of $50 per year of service, but pays employees $75 for each year of work beyond normal retirement age, the employer is not required to pay both amounts—the $75 increased value offsets the $50 benefit.

- Employers who begin pension payments while an employee is still working may use the actuarial value of those payments to offset the employee's pension accrual. For example, if an employee works for one year beyond normal retirement age and receives $10,000 in pension payments during that time, the employer may use the actuarial value of those payments (what that amount would be worth to the employee per month over the course of the employee's lifetime) to offset pension accrual (how much the employee is entitled to earn per year of service).

- Employers may use Social Security Old Age benefits to offset pension benefits, in some cases.

Special Rules for Certain Benefits

OWBPA places special requirements on certain types of benefits.

Employee Contribution Plans

If an employee contributes a portion of the costs of a required benefit (for example, an employee pays part of a health insurance or life insurance premium for a benefit that all employees are required to have), the employer may not require an older employee, as a condition of employment, to pay a higher contribution than younger employees. However, the employer may require an older employee to contribute more to participate in a voluntary benefit plan, as long as that higher contribution is justified by the equal cost defense. The employer may also allow older workers to pay more to maintain their benefit at the same level provided to younger employees.

Benefit Packages

The equal cost approach applies to benefit packages as well as individual benefits—that is, an employer may offer a different total benefit package to older employees than to younger employees, as long as the difference is justified by the equal cost defense. However, the following requirements apply:

- Only those benefits that become more costly to provide with increasing age may be included in the benefit package. Retirement or pension plans may not be included.

- Employers may not use the benefit package approach to reduce health benefits beyond what would be allowed under an individual benefit comparison. Any reductions in health insurance must be justified by the increased cost to the employer of providing that benefit alone.

- If an older worker is deprived of a particular benefit because of the increased cost of providing that benefit as workers age, the worker must receive additional benefits in exchange. Considered as a whole, the entire benefit package for older workers must be no worse than they would have received had the employer compared benefits individually under the equal cost defense.

Long-Term Disability Benefits

OWBPA provides a safe harbor for employers who offer long-term disability benefits. Under this rule, an employer may stop disability benefits at age 65 for an employee who is disabled at the age of 60 or younger, and may stop disability benefits five years after the disability is incurred for workers who become disabled past the age of 60.

Pension Benefits

An employer who offers pension benefits is legally allowed to set a normal or early retirement age for receipt of benefits, require a specified number of years of service before an employee will be eligible to retire and receive benefits and limit the total amount of benefits provided or the total number of years of service that will be credited in calculating pension benefits. However, employers may not:

- prevent an employee from participating in a pension plan solely because that employee is near the plan's normal retirement age when hired

- discontinue benefit accrual based on an employee's age, or
- stop contributing to an employee's pension account because of the employee's age.

Early Retirement Incentive Plans

Early retirement incentive plans sometimes provide a greater benefit to younger employees —if the plan offers an unreduced pension benefit to employees who have not yet reached normal retirement age, the youngest employees benefit the most from such a plan. Nevertheless, an *early retirement incentive* that doesn't provide equal benefits to older and younger employees is legal if it is voluntary (that is, it does not require any employee to retire) and it meets one of these additional requirements:

- The plan subsidizes a retirement plan, by paying employees who agree to retire additional pension benefits. An employer may pay retiring employees an additional subsidy to bring that employee's retirement benefits up to the level of an *unreduced pension.*
- The plan provides Social Security supplements to retiring employees who are not yet eligible for Social Security, as long as the payments do not exceed the amount that would be paid if the employee received Social Security. Such payments must stop when the employee becomes eligible for Social Security.
- The plan is offered by an institution of higher education to tenured faculty, as long as the plan does not reduce or

eliminate other benefits or repackage benefits that were already offered to the retiring employees during the year prior to the incentive.

- The plan otherwise treats employees equally without regard to age. For example, an employer may offer employees additional compensation to retire (a set dollar amount, additional money based on years of service, a percentage or set dollar increase in pension benefits or credit for additional years of service) as long as the same benefits are offered to all employees eligible for the retirement incentive.

2. Waivers

Under OWBPA, a *waiver* of the right to sue for age discrimination is valid only if it is knowing and voluntary. A court will not find that a *waiver* is knowing and voluntary unless it meets certain minimum requirements.

Regulated Employers
All regulated employers must comply with these provisions when seeking *waivers* of ADEA (Age Discrimination in Employment Act) claims from their employees. See Section A2.

Covered Workers
These provisions protect all covered workers whose employers ask them to waive ADEA (Age Discrimination in Employment Act) claims. See Section A3.

What's Required: Employers
A *waiver* is valid only if it is knowing and voluntary. Because these terms are open to interpretation, Congress decided that an agreement will not be considered knowing and voluntary unless it meets certain minimum requirements.

Waivers that do not meet these requirements are invalid. This means that a court will not enforce the *waiver*—the worker will be able to sue for age discrimination despite the agreement.

Even if a *waiver* meets these minimum standards, a court still might find it invalid if other evidence demonstrates that the worker did not knowingly and voluntarily agree to the *waiver*. For example, if the *waiver* is misleading or omits important information, a court might throw the *waiver* out—even if it meets the specifications listed below.

Requirements for a Knowing and Voluntary Agreement
A *waiver* will be considered knowing and voluntary only if it:

- is part of an agreement between the employer and the employee that is written in a manner calculated to be understood by the employee, or in the case of an offer made to a group (such as an *exit incentive program*), by the average employee eligible to participate
- specifically refers to the worker's rights or claims under the ADEA
- does not require the employee to waive any rights or claims that may arise after the agreement is signed, and

- gives the employee something of value (such as cash or continued benefits) in exchange for the *waiver*, over and above anything to which the employee is already entitled (for example, if all employees receive a set amount of severance pay, the employer must give an employee who signs an ADEA *waiver* something in addition to that pay).

In addition, employers must:

- advise the employee, in writing, to consult with an attorney before signing the agreement
- give the employee at least 21 days to consider the agreement, or 45 days if the *waiver* is requested in connection with an exit incentive or other employment termination program offered to a group of employees (the employee can accept the agreement after a shorter period of deliberation, as long as the employee had the opportunity to take as long as the statute allows)
- give the employee at least seven days after signing to revoke the agreement.

Additional Rules for Exit Incentive or Other Employment Termination Programs

If the *waiver* is requested in connection with an *exit incentive program* or other *employment termination program* offered to a group of employees, the employer must also inform the employee, in writing, of:

- any class, unit or group of individuals covered by the program, any eligibility rules for the program and any time limits applicable to the program, and

- the job titles and ages of all individuals eligible or selected for the program, and the ages of all individuals in the same job classification or organizational unit who are not eligible or selected for the program.

Rules for Waivers to Settle an EEOC Charge or Lawsuit

If the employee has already filed a charge of age discrimination with the EEOC or filed a lawsuit against the employer for age discrimination (see Section E, below), the rules for *waivers* are less strict. In these situations, the employer does not have to allow a revocation period of seven days, provide 21 or 45 days for the employee to consider the agreement or give the additional information (on eligible employees and their ages, etc.) required for a group exit program.

However, the *waiver* must meet the other requirements listed above. In addition, the employee must be given a reasonable period of time to consider the settlement.

Lawsuits Filed after a Waiver— the Tender Back Rule

If a worker tries to sue an employer after signing a *waiver*, traditional legal principles require that worker first give back whatever he received (for example, severance pay or continued benefits) in exchange for giving up the right to sue. This requirement, referred to as the "tender back" rule, requires a worker to put his money where his mouth is—in order to argue that the *waiver* should not be enforced to prevent a lawsuit, the worker must give up his rights under the *waiver*.

However, the tender back rule does not apply to workers who file age discrimination lawsuits—older workers may keep their release money AND file an ADEA claim. If the worker wins the lawsuit, the employer is entitled to reimbursement of the money paid for the release. The employer can recover either the full amount paid for the release or the full amount the worker wins in the lawsuit, whichever is less.

Employers may not include in the *waiver* any penalty for filing a lawsuit. For example, some *waivers* require an employee to pay the employer's attorney fees if the employee files a lawsuit—such a requirement is illegal. Employers also may not stop fulfilling their obligations under a *waiver* if a lawsuit is filed. For example, many *waivers* provide that an employee will be paid a monthly severance check or will receive certain retirement benefits for a period of time. The employer cannot stop honoring these agreements simply because the employee files a lawsuit claiming the *waiver* is invalid.

C. How OWBPA Is Enforced

1. Individual Complaints

Employees may file a charge (complaint) of age discrimination with the Equal Employment Opportunity Commission (EEOC). The deadlines for filing a charge depend on whether the state where the discrimination charge will be filed also has an anti-discrimination law. In states without anti-discrimination laws, an employee has 180 days from the date of the discriminatory act to complain. In states with an anti-discrimination law, this deadline is extended to 300 days. (See Section G for a list of states with anti-discrimination laws.)

An employee may also file a lawsuit for age discrimination. However, the employee must file a charge of discrimination with the EEOC and get a "right to sue" letter first (see Section C2, below). An employee must file the lawsuit within 90 days of receiving a right to sue letter from the EEOC.

2. Agency Enforcement

The federal agency responsible for investigating OWBPA complaints is the EEOC. An employee usually initiates the process by filing a charge (complaint) with the EEOC, although the agency can also act on its own initiative. The EEOC has the power to investigate, negotiate with employers and bring lawsuits against employers to stop discriminatory practices.

Once an employee files a charge with the EEOC, the employee cannot file a lawsuit until the EEOC gives the employee a "right to sue" letter. The EEOC generally issues such a letter when it finishes processing the charge —and it must issue a right to sue letter if it has not filed its own lawsuit against the employer within 180 days after the charge is filed. However, an employee who wants to file a lawsuit before the EEOC has completed its investigation or before 180 days have passed can request a right to sue letter from the agency—the EEOC will generally comply with these requests.

D. For Employers: Complying With OWBPA

1. Reporting Requirements

OWBPA imposes no reporting requirements.

2. Posting Requirements

OWBPA has no separate posting requirements; it is covered in the posting requirements for the ADEA (see Section C of the chapter on the ADEA).

3. Recordkeeping Requirements

OWBPA has no separate recordkeeping requirements; it is covered in the record-keeping requirements for the ADEA (see Section C of the chapter on the ADEA).

4. Practical Tips

OWBPA is not the most user-friendly law. Its requirements can be difficult to understand and implement. Here are some tips that can help you comply:

- **Follow OWBPA's waiver requirements for all employees over the age of 39.** Whenever you ask an employee who is

protected by the ADEA to sign a *waiver,* make sure the *waiver* complies with OWBPA—even if you don't think the worker has any potential claims of age discrimination. The sad truth is that you cannot predict what you might later be sued for. And if you don't follow OWBPA, the worker will be allowed to sue you for age discrimination despite having signed a *waiver.*

- **Offer equal benefits to older and younger workers, if possible.** In a few cases, it will be easy to apply the equal cost defense or use offsets to justify giving lesser benefits to older workers. In some cases, however, it will be more complicated—and may require expensive actuarial analyses. You can avoid the whole issue by simply offering equal benefits to all of your workers.

- **Get some help with the technicalities.** Before you offer a *waiver* to a worker, consider asking a lawyer to look over the agreement. Once you are sure you've met all of OWBPA's requirements, you can keep using that language in any future *waivers* you execute. And you might want to ask a lawyer or insurance expert to review any planned reductions in older workers' benefits.

5. Penalties

The penalties for violating OWBPA are the same as those for violating the ADEA. See Section C of the chapter on the ADEA.

E. For Workers: Asserting Rights Under OWBPA

1. Where to Start

If you believe your employer has violated OWBPA, your first course of action should be to make an internal complaint. Follow your company's complaint policy or, if there is no policy, complain to a human resources representative or a member of management. If you are a union member, talk to your shop steward or union representative.

If you no longer work for the employer whom you believe violated your rights (for example, if your employment was terminated and you signed a *waiver* that you think is invalid under OWBPA), you may want to contact your former employer to see if you can resolve the problem informally. However, many former employees choose to go straight to the EEOC instead.

If internal and union complaints don't work, your next step is to file a charge of discrimination with the EEOC (see Section C2, above). You can file a charge by mail or in person at your nearest EEOC office. To find the office closest to you, call 800-669-4000 or refer to the agency's website at http://www.eeoc.gov/teledir.html.

Once the EEOC has issued you a "right to sue" letter, you can also file a lawsuit in state or federal court against your employer.

2. Required Forms

If you decide to file a charge with the EEOC, you will have to use their charge form. This form is available at EEOC offices and through the EEOC's website (see Section 1, above).

3. Practical Tips

Here are a few tips for asserting your rights under OWBPA:

- **Act fast.** If you believe that your employer (or former employer) has violated your rights, take action quickly. If you wait too long, you might miss the deadline for filing an EEOC charge.
- **Make sure it's worth your while to challenge a waiver.** If you convince a court that your *waiver* is invalid under OWBPA, you win the right to sue your employer for age discrimination. However, if you win your discrimination claim, you will have to give back whatever your employer paid you to sign the *waiver*, up to the total amount of money you win in court. Before you spend a lot of time and money bringing a lawsuit, make sure that your claims are worth a lot more than you got for your *waiver*.
- **Take your time when considering a waiver.** OWBPA gives you plenty of time to consider (and reconsider) whether to sign a *waiver*. Use as much of that time as you need to decide whether it's a good deal. Remember, you are giving up your right to sue for age discrimination—a right that might be worth quite a bit, depending on your circumstances. Consider consulting with a lawyer before you sign away your rights—and don't make any rash decisions.

- **Scrutinize benefits documents carefully.** In order to take advantage of the equal cost defense, your employer must give you written details about your benefits. Read these documents carefully to make sure the benefits comply with OWBPA. If you feel strongly that your employer is violating the law, you might want to ask an insurance expert or attorney to review the documents as well.

- **Get free help.** Because the requirements of OWBPA are quite technical, it can be tough to figure out whether you have a legitimate gripe with your employer. Consider getting free assistance—from the EEOC or from a local or national group that advocates for seniors—to help you figure out whether you have a sound legal claim.

F. Agency Charged With Enforcement & Compliance

Equal Employment Opportunity Commission

1801 L Street, NW
Washington, DC 20507
Phone: 202-663-4900
TTY: 202-663-4494
http://www.eeoc.gov

Agency Resources for Employers and Workers

(These can be obtained either at the Web addresses listed below or at the address and phone numbers listed above.)

- Information on the "tender back" rule

  Questions and Answers: Final Regulation on 'Tender Back' and Related Issues Concerning ADEA Waivers

  http://www.eeoc.gov/regs/tenderback-qanda.html

- Detailed explanations and examples of OWBPA's benefits rules

  EEOC Compliance Manual: Employee Benefits

  http://www.eeoc.gov/docs/benefits.html

- Basic information on OWBPA's benefits rules

  Questions and Answers: Compliance Manual Section on Employee Benefits

  http://www.eeoc.gov/docs/qanda-benefits.html

G. State Laws Relating to Age Discrimination

See Section F of the chapter on Title VII for a chart of state laws relating to fair employment —this chart includes laws prohibiting age discrimination.

H. Full Text of OWBPA

U.S. Code
Title 29: Labor
Chapter 14: Age Discrimination in Employment

...

§ 623. Prohibition of age discrimination

...

§ 626 Recordkeeping, Investigation, and Enforcement

...

§ 623. Prohibition of Age Discrimination

(a) It shall be unlawful for an employer—

(1) to fail or refuse to hire or to discharge any individual or otherwise discriminate against any individual with respect to his compensation, terms, conditions, or privileges of employment, because of such individual's age;

(2) to limit, segregate, or classify his employees in any way which would deprive or tend to deprive any individual of employment opportunities or otherwise adversely affect his status as an employee, because of such individual's age; or

(3) to reduce the wage rate of any employee in order to comply with this chapter.

(b) It shall be unlawful for an employment agency to fail or refuse to refer for employment, or otherwise to discriminate against, any individual because of such individual's age, or to classify or refer for employment any individual on the basis of such individual's age.

(c) It shall be unlawful for a labor organization—

(1) to exclude or to expel from its membership, or otherwise to discriminate against, any individual because of his age;

(2) to limit, segregate, or classify its membership, or to classify or fail or refuse to refer for employment any individual, in any way which would deprive or tend to deprive any individual of employment opportunities, or would limit such employment opportunities or otherwise adversely affect his status as an employee or as an applicant for employment, because of such individual's age;

(3) to cause or attempt to cause an employer to discriminate against an individual in violation of this section.

(d) It shall be unlawful for an employer to discriminate against any of his employees or applicants for employment, for an employment agency to discriminate against any individual, or for a labor organization to discriminate against any member thereof or applicant for membership, because such individual, member or applicant for membership has opposed any practice made unlawful by this section, or because such individual, member or applicant for membership has made a charge, testified, assisted, or participated in any manner in an investigation, proceeding, or litigation under this chapter.

(e) It shall be unlawful for an employer, labor organization, or employment agency to print or publish, or cause to be printed or published, any notice or advertisement relating to employment by such an employer or membership in or any classification or referral for employment by such a labor organization, or relating to any classification or referral for employment by such an employment agency, indicating any preference, limitation, specification, or discrimination, based on age.

(f) It shall not be unlawful for an employer, employment agency, or labor organization—

(1) to take any action otherwise prohibited under subsections (a), (b), (c), or (e) of this section where age is a bona fide occupational qualification reasonably necessary to the normal operation of the particular business, or where the differentiation is based on reasonable factors other than age, or where such practices involve an employee in a workplace in a foreign country, and compliance with such subsections would cause such employer, or a corporation controlled by such employer, to violate the laws of the country in which such workplace is located;

(2) to take any action otherwise prohibited under subsection (a), (b), (c), or (e) of this section—

(A) to observe the terms of a bona fide seniority system that is not intended to evade the purposes of this chapter, except that no such seniority system shall require or permit the involuntary retirement of any individual specified by section

631(a) of this title because of the age of such individual; or

(B) to observe the terms of a bona fide employee benefit plan—

(i) where, for each benefit or benefit package, the actual amount of payment made or cost incurred on behalf of an older worker is no less than that made or incurred on behalf of a younger worker, as permissible under section 1625.10, title 29, Code of Federal Regulations (as in effect on June 22, 1989); or

(ii) that is a voluntary early retirement incentive plan consistent with the relevant purpose or purposes of this chapter. Notwithstanding clause (i) or (ii) of subparagraph (B), no such employee benefit plan or voluntary early retirement incentive plan shall excuse the failure to hire any individual, and no such employee benefit plan shall require or permit the involuntary retirement of any individual specified by section 631(a) of this title, because of the age of such individual. An employer, employment agency, or labor organization acting under subparagraph (A), or under clause (i) or (ii) of subparagraph (B), shall have the burden of proving that such actions are lawful in any civil enforcement proceeding brought under this chapter; or

(3) to discharge or otherwise discipline an individual for good cause.

(g) *[Repealed]*

(h)

(1) If an employer controls a corporation whose place of incorporation is in a foreign country, any practice by such corporation prohibited under this section shall be presumed to be such practice by such employer.

(2) The prohibitions of this section shall not apply where the employer is a foreign person not controlled by an American employer.

(3) For the purpose of this subsection the determination of whether an employer controls a corporation shall be based upon the—

(A) interrelation of operations,

(B) common management,

(C) centralized control of labor relations, and

(D) common ownership or financial control, of the employer and the corporation.

(i) It shall not be unlawful for an employer which is a State, a political subdivision of a State, an agency or instrumentality of a State or a political subdivision of a State, or an interstate agency to fail or refuse to hire or to discharge any individual because of such individual's age if such action is taken—

(1) with respect to the employment of an individual as a firefighter or as a law enforcement officer and the individual has attained the age of hiring or retirement in effect under applicable State or local law on March 3, 1983, and

(2) pursuant to a bona fide hiring or retirement plan that is not a subterfuge to evade the purposes of this chapter.

(j)

(1) Except as otherwise provided in this subsection, it shall be unlawful for an employer, an employment agency, a labor organization, or any combination thereof to establish or maintain an employee pension benefit plan which requires or permits—

(A) in the case of a defined benefit plan, the cessation of an employee's benefit accrual, or the reduction of the rate of an employee's benefit accrual, because of age, or

(B) in the case of a defined contribution plan, the cessation of allocations to an employee's account, or the reduction of the rate at which amounts are allocated to an employee's account, because of age.

(2) Nothing in this section shall be construed to prohibit an employer, employment agency, or labor organization from observing any provision of an employee pension benefit plan to the extent that such provision imposes (without regard to age) a limitation on the amount of benefits that the plan provides or a limitation on the number of years of service or years of participation which are taken into account for purposes of determining benefit accrual under the plan.

(3) In the case of any employee who, as of the end of any plan year under a defined benefit plan, has attained normal retirement age under such plan—

(A) if distribution of benefits under such plan with respect to such employee has commenced as of the end of such plan year, then any requirement of this subsection for continued accrual of benefits under such plan with respect to such employee during such plan year shall be treated as satisfied to the extent of the actuarial equivalent of inservice distribution of benefits, and

(B) if distribution of benefits under such plan with respect to such employee has not commenced as of the end of such year in accordance with section 1056(a)(3) of this title *[section 206(a)(3) of the*

Employee Retirement Income Security Act of 1974] and section 401(a)(14)(C) of title 26 *[the Internal Revenue Code of 1986]*, and the payment of benefits under such plan with respect to such employee is not suspended during such plan year pursuant to section 1053(a)(3)(B) of this title *[section 203(a)(3)(B) of the Employee Retirement Income Security Act of 1974]* or section 411(a)(3)(B) of title 26 *[the Internal Revenue Code of 1986]*, then any requirement of this subsection for continued accrual of benefits under such plan with respect to such employee during such plan year shall be treated as satisfied to the extent of any adjustment in the benefit payable under the plan during such plan year attributable to the delay in the distribution of benefits after the attainment of normal retirement age. The provisions of this paragraph shall apply in accordance with regulations of the Secretary of the Treasury. Such regulations shall provide for the application of the preceding provisions of this paragraph to all employee pension benefit plans subject to this subsection and may provide for the application of such provisions, in the case of any such employee, with respect to any period of time within a plan year.

(4) Compliance with the requirements of this subsection with respect to an employee pension benefit plan shall constitute compliance with the requirements of this section relating to benefit accrual under such plan.

(5) Paragraph (1) shall not apply with respect to any employee who is a highly compensated employee (within the meaning of section 414(q) of title 26 *[the Internal Revenue Code of 1986]*) to the extent provided in regulations prescribed by the Secretary of the Treasury for purposes of precluding discrimination in favor of highly compensated employees within the meaning of subchapter D of chapter 1 of title 26 *[the Internal Revenue Code of 1986]*.

(6) A plan shall not be treated as failing to meet the requirements of paragraph (1) solely because the subsidized portion of any early retirement benefit is disregarded in determining benefit accruals.

(7) Any regulations prescribed by the Secretary of the Treasury pursuant to clause (v) of section 411(b)(1)(H) of title 26 *[the Internal Revenue Code of 1986]* and subparagraphs c and (D) of section 411(b)(2) of title 26 *[the Internal Revenue Code of 1986]* shall apply with respect to the requirements of this subsection in the same manner and to the same extent as such

regulations apply with respect to the requirements of such sections 411(b)(1)(H) and 411(b)(2).

(8) A plan shall not be treated as failing to meet the requirements of this section solely because such plan provides a normal retirement age described in section 1002(24)(B) of this title *[section 3(24)(B) of the Employee Retirement Income Security Act of 1974]* and section 411(a)(8)(B) of title 26 *[the Internal Revenue Code of 1986]*.

(9) For purposes of this subsection—

(A) The terms "employee pension benefit plan", "defined benefit plan", "defined contribution plan", and "normal retirement age" have the meanings provided such terms in section 1002 of this title *[section 3 of the Employee Retirement Income Security Act of 1974]*.

(B) The term "compensation" has the meaning provided by section 414(s) of title 26 *[the Internal Revenue Code of 1986]*.

(k) A seniority system or employee benefit plan shall comply with this chapter regardless of the date of adoption of such system or plan.

(l) Notwithstanding clause (i) or (ii) of subsection (f)(2)(B) of this section—

(1) It shall not be a violation of subsection (a), (b), (c), or (e) of this section solely because—

(A) an employee pension benefit plan (as defined in section 1002(2) of this title *[section 3(2) of the Employee Retirement Income Security Act of 1974]*) provides for the attainment of a minimum age as a condition of eligibility for normal or early retirement benefits; or

(B) a defined benefit plan (as defined in section 1002(35) of this title *[section 3(35) of such Act]*) provides for—

(i) payments that constitute the subsidized portion of an early retirement benefit; or

(ii) social security supplements for plan participants that commence before the age and terminate at the age (specified by the plan) when participants are eligible to receive reduced or unreduced old-age insurance benefits under title II of the Social Security Act (42 U.S.C. 401 et seq.), and that do not exceed such old-age insurance benefits.

(2)

(A) It shall not be a violation of subsection (a), (b), (c), or (e) of this section solely because following a contingent event unrelated to age

(i) the value of any retiree health benefits received by an individual eligible for an immediate pension;

(ii) the value of any additional pension benefits that are made available solely as a result of the contingent event unrelated to age and following which the individual is eligible for not less than an immediate and unreduced pension; or

(iii) the values described in both clauses (i) and (ii); are deducted from severance pay made available as a result of the contingent event unrelated to age.

(B) For an individual who receives immediate pension benefits that are actuarially reduced under subparagraph (A)(i), the amount of the deduction available pursuant to subparagraph (A)(i) shall be reduced by the same percentage as the reduction in the pension benefits.

(C) For purposes of this paragraph, severance pay shall include that portion of supplemental unemployment compensation benefits (as described in section 501c(17) of title 26 *[the Internal Revenue Code of 1986]*) that—

(i) constitutes additional benefits of up to 52 weeks;

(ii) has the primary purpose and effect of continuing benefits until an individual becomes eligible for an immediate and unreduced pension; and

(iii) is discontinued once the individual becomes eligible for an immediate and unreduced pension.

(D) For purposes of this paragraph and solely in order to make the deduction authorized under this paragraph, the term "retiree health benefits" means benefits provided pursuant to a group health plan covering retirees, for which (determined as of the contingent event unrelated to age)—

(i) the package of benefits provided by the employer for the retirees who are below age 65 is at least comparable to benefits provided under title XVIII of the Social Security Act (42 U.S.C. 1395 et seq.);

(ii) the package of benefits provided by the employer for the retirees who are age 65 and above is at least comparable to that offered under a plan that provides a benefit package with one fourth the value of benefits provided under title XVIII of such Act; or

(iii) the package of benefits provided by the employer is as described in clauses (i) and (ii).

(E)

(i) If the obligation of the employer to provide retiree health benefits is of limited duration, the value for each individual shall be calculated at a rate of $3,000 per year for benefit years before age 65, and $750 per year for benefit years beginning at age 65 and above.

(ii) If the obligation of the employer to provide retiree health benefits is of unlimited duration, the value for each individual shall be calculated at a rate of $48,000 for individuals below age 65, and $24,000 for individuals age 65 and above.

(iii) The values described in clauses (i) and (ii) shall be calculated based on the age of the individual as of the date of the contingent event unrelated to age. The values are effective on October 16, 1990, and shall be adjusted on an annual basis, with respect to a contingent event that occurs subsequent to the first year after October 16, 1990, based on the medical component of the Consumer Price Index for all urban consumers published by the Department of Labor.

(iv) If an individual is required to pay a premium for retiree health benefits, the value calculated pursuant to this subparagraph shall be reduced by whatever percentage of the overall premium the individual is required to pay.

(F) If an employer that has implemented a deduction pursuant to subparagraph (A) fails to fulfill the obligation described in subparagraph (E), any aggrieved individual may bring an action for specific performance of the obligation described in subparagraph (E). The relief shall be in addition to any other remedies provided under Federal or State law.

(3) It shall not be a violation of subsection (a), (b), (c), or (e) of this section solely because an employer provides a bona fide employee benefit plan or plans under which long-term disability benefits received by an individual are reduced by any pension benefits (other than those attributable to employee contributions)—

(A) paid to the individual that the individual voluntarily elects to receive; or

(B) for which an individual who has attained the later of age 62 or normal retirement age is eligible.

§ 626. Recordkeeping, Investigation, and Enforcement

(a) The Equal Employment Opportunity Commission shall have the power to make investigations and require the keeping of records necessary or appropriate for the administration of this chapter in accordance with the powers and procedures provided in sections 209 and 211 of this title *[sections 9 and 11 of the Fair Labor Standards Act of 1938, as amended]*.

(b) The provisions of this chapter shall be enforced in accordance with the powers, remedies, and procedures provided in sections 211(b), 216 (except for subsection (a) thereof), and 217 of this title *[sections 11(b), 16 (except for subsection (a) thereof), and 17 of the Fair Labor Standards Act of 1938, as amended]*, and subsection c of this section. Any act prohibited under section 623 of this title *[section 4]* shall be deemed to be a prohibited act under section 215 of this title *[section 15 of the Fair Labor Standards Act of 1938, as amended]*. Amounts owing to a person as a result of a violation of this chapter shall be deemed to be unpaid minimum wages or unpaid overtime compensation for purposes of sections 216 and 217 of this title *[sections 16 and 17 of the Fair Labor Standards Act of 1938, as amended]*: Provided, That liquidated damages shall be payable only in cases of willful violations of this chapter. In any action brought to enforce this chapter the court shall have jurisdiction to grant such legal or equitable relief as may be appropriate to effectuate the purposes of this chapter, including without limitation judgments compelling employment, reinstatement or promotion, or enforcing the liability for amounts deemed to be unpaid minimum wages or unpaid overtime compensation under this section. Before instituting any action under this section, the Equal Employment Opportunity Commission shall attempt to eliminate the discriminatory practice or practices alleged, and to effect voluntary compliance with the requirements of this chapter through informal methods of conciliation, conference, and persuasion.

(c)

(1) Any person aggrieved may bring a civil action in any court of competent jurisdiction for such legal or equitable relief as will effectuate the purposes of this chapter: Provided, That the right of any person to bring such action shall terminate upon the commencement of an action by the Equal Employment Opportunity Commission to enforce the right of such employee under this chapter.

(2) In an action brought under paragraph (1), a person shall be entitled to a trial by jury of any issue of fact in any such action for recovery of amounts owing as a result of a violation of this chapter, regardless of whether equitable relief is sought by any party in such action.

(d) No civil action may be commenced by an individual under this section until 60 days after a charge alleging unlawful discrimination has been filed with the Equal Employment Opportunity Commission. Such a charge shall be filed—

(1) within 180 days after the alleged unlawful practice occurred; or

(2) in a case to which section 633(b) of this title applies, within 300 days after the alleged unlawful practice occurred, or within 30 days after receipt by the individual of notice of termination of proceedings under State law, whichever is earlier. Upon receiving such a charge, the Commission shall promptly notify all persons named in such charge as prospective defendants in the action and shall promptly seek to eliminate any alleged unlawful practice by informal methods of conciliation, conference, and persuasion.

(e) Section 259 of this title *[section 10 of the Portal-to-Portal Act of 1947]* shall apply to actions under this chapter. If a charge filed with the Commission under this chapter is dismissed or the proceedings of the Commission are otherwise terminated by the Commission, the Commission shall notify the person aggrieved. A civil action may be brought under this section by a person defined in section 630(a) of this title *[section 11(a)]* against the respondent named in the charge within 90 days after the date of the receipt of such notice.

(f)

(1) An individual may not waive any right or claim under this chapter unless the waiver is knowing and voluntary. Except as provided in paragraph (2), a waiver may not be considered knowing and voluntary unless at a minimum—

(A) the waiver is part of an agreement between the individual and the employer that is written in a manner calculated to be understood by such individual, or by the average individual eligible to participate;

(B) the waiver specifically refers to rights or claims arising under this chapter;

(C) the individual does not waive rights or claims that may arise after the date the waiver is executed;

(D) the individual waives rights or claims only in exchange for consideration in addition to anything of value to which the individual already is entitled;

(E) the individual is advised in writing to consult with an attorney prior to executing the agreement;

(F)

(i) the individual is given a period of at least 21 days within which to consider the agreement; or

(ii) if a waiver is requested in connection with an exit incentive or other employment termination program offered to a group or class of employees, the individual is given a period of at least 45 days within which to consider the agreement;

(G) the agreement provides that for a period of at least 7 days following the execution of such agreement, the individual may revoke the agreement, and the agreement shall not become effective or enforceable until the revocation period has expired;

(H) if a waiver is requested in connection with an exit incentive or other employment termination program offered to a group or class of employees, the employer (at the commencement of the period specified in subparagraph (F)) informs the individual in writing in a manner calculated to be understood by the average individual eligible to participate, as to—

(i) any class, unit, or group of individuals covered by such program, any eligibility factors for such program, and any time limits applicable to such program; and

(ii) the job titles and ages of all individuals eligible or selected for the program, and the ages of all individuals in the same job classification or organizational unit who are not eligible or selected for the program.

(2) A waiver in settlement of a charge filed with the Equal Employment Opportunity Commission, or an action filed in court by the individual or the individual's representative, alleging age discrimination of a kind prohibited under section 623 or 633a of this title *[section 4 or 15]* may not be considered knowing and voluntary unless at a minimum—

(A) subparagraphs (A) through (E) of paragraph (1) have been met; and

(B) the individual is given a reasonable period of time within which to consider the settlement agreement.

(3) In any dispute that may arise over whether any of the requirements, conditions, and circumstances set forth in subparagraph (A), (B), (C), (D), (E), (F), (G), or (H) of paragraph (1), or subparagraph (A) or (B) of paragraph (2), have been met, the party asserting the validity of a waiver shall have the burden of proving in a court of competent jurisdiction that a waiver was knowing and voluntary pursuant to paragraph (1) or (2).

Chapter 15

Pregnancy Discrimination Act (PDA)

Statute: 42 U.S.C. § 2000e(k)

http://www.eeoc.gov/35th/thelaw/pregnancy_discrimination-1978.html

Regulations: 29 C.F.R. § 1604, appendix

http://cfr.law.cornell.edu/cfr/cfr.php?title=29&type=part&value=1604

Definitions

The Definitions for the Pregnancy Discrimination Act are the same as those for Title VII.

A. Overview of the Pregnancy Discrimination Act

1. Summary

The Pregnancy Discrimination Act amended Title VII to prohibit discrimination on the basis of pregnancy, childbirth and related medical conditions in employment opportunities, health insurance plans, disability insurance plans and sick leave plans. (See the chapter on Title VII for more information.) Under the Act, pregnancy discrimination is considered a type of unlawful sex discrimination.

2. Regulated Employers

The Pregnancy Discrimination Act covers the same employers as does Title VII. Those are:

- private employers with 15 or more employees
- the federal government, its agencies and political subdivisions
- state governments, their agencies and political subdivisions
- local governments, their agencies and political subdivisions
- private and public employment agencies
- labor organizations, and
- joint labor/management committees.

3. Covered Workers

The Act protects all prospective and current employees of a covered employer.

4. What's Prohibited: Employers

The Act prohibits employers from discriminating against prospective and current employees on the basis of pregnancy, childbirth or related medical conditions. For general information about employment discrimination, see "What Is Discrimination" in Section A4 of the chapter on Title VII. For more information about related medical conditions, see "What Is a Related Medical Condition," below.

The Act applies to all terms and benefits of employment, including:

- hiring
- firing
- compensation and benefits
- job assignment
- employee classification
- transfer
- promotion
- layoff or recall
- training and apprenticeship programs
- use of company facilities
- retirement plans, and
- leave.

For example, if an individual is able to perform the major functions of a job, an employer cannot refuse to hire an individual simply because she is pregnant.

The Act also prohibits employers from retaliating against people who complain or who otherwise assert their rights under the law. For example, an employer cannot fire someone for complaining about pregnancy discrimination. For more, see "What Is Retaliation," in Section A4 in the chapter on Title VII.

What Is a Related Medical Condition

Unfortunately, the Act does not define the term "related medical condition," so the task of giving this term meaning has been left to the courts. They haven't done a very good job of it, and there is more disagreement than agreement among them.

Nonetheless, a few things seem clear. If a woman suffers from a medical complication or disability as a direct result of pregnancy or childbirth that requires medical treatment, her condition is a related medical condition. For example, recovery from childbirth (even if the birth was uneventful), miscarriage or abortion fall within this interpretation.

In addition, women are protected from discrimination based on their potential to become pregnant.

On the other side of the spectrum, breastfeeding and child care are not related medical conditions and are therefore not protected by the Act.

Courts are divided as to whether infertility is a related medical condition.

5. What's Required: Employers

If an employee is temporarily disabled by pregnancy, childbirth or a related medical condition, the employer must treat the employee the same way the employer would treat any other temporarily disabled employee —for example, by temporarily modifying the job, providing disability leave or providing unpaid leave.

Similarly, rules pertaining to things such as benefit accrual, seniority, vacation calculation, pay increases and other benefits should apply the same way to employees on pregnancy disability leave as to employees on any other disability leave.

If an employee is absent because of pregnancy, childbirth or a related medical condition, the employer must hold the employee's job open for the same amount of time that the employer would hold open the job of an employee who is on leave for illness or disability.

Employers must allow pregnant employees to work for as long as they are able to do their jobs. For example, an employer cannot require a pregnant employee to go on leave until the baby's birth—paid or unpaid—if the employee does not want to.

If the employer provides health insurance as a benefit to employees, the policy must cover expenses for pregnancy, childbirth and related medical conditions to the same extent that it covers expenses for other medical conditions.

However, employers do not have to provide benefits to pay for an abortion unless the life of the mother would be endangered if she carried the fetus to term. If a woman does have an abortion, the employer's health benefits must cover any medical complications arising from that abortion, whether or not the benefits paid for the abortion in the first place.

If the husbands of female employees get comprehensive medical benefits, then the wives of male employees must also get comprehensive medical benefits—including those for pregnancy and so on.

6. Exceptions

The exceptions to the Pregnancy Discrimination Act are the same as those for Title VII.

B. How the Pregnancy Discrimination Act Is Enforced

1. Individual Complaints

The enforcement provisions of Title VII apply to the Pregnancy Discrimination Act. See Section B1 of the chapter on Title VII.

2. Agency Enforcement

The enforcement provisions of Title VII apply to the Pregnancy Discrimination Act. See Section B2 of the chapter on Title VII.

C. For Employers: Complying With the Pregnancy Discrimination Act

1. Reporting Requirements

The reporting requirements for the Pregnancy Discrimination Act are the same as those for Title VII. See Section C1 of the chapter on Title VII.

2. Recordkeeping Requirements

The recordkeeping requirements for the Pregnancy Discrimination Act are the same as those for Title VII. See Section C2 of the chapter on Title VII.

3. Practical Tips

The practical tips for the Pregnancy Discrimination Act are the same as those for Title VII. See Section C3 of the chapter on Title VII.

D. For Workers: Asserting Rights Under the Pregnancy Discrimination Act

1. Where to Start

Follow the same procedures that you would follow for any employment discrimination problem. See Section D1 of the chapter on Title VII.

2. Required Forms

Contact your local EEOC office to see if it has a standard charge form that you must file.

3. Practical Tips

For practical tips on employment discrimination, including pregnancy discrimination, see Section D3 of the chapter on Title VII.

If you are pregnant or have recently had a child, you may also have rights under the Family and Medical Leave Act (see the chapter on the FMLA).

As we explained above, breastfeeding isn't covered by the Act. However, an increasing number of states are requiring employers to accommodate their employees' desire to breastfeed their children. To find out if your state has such a law, contact your state labor department. (See Appendix for contact details.)

E. Agency Charged With Enforcement & Compliance

Equal Employment Opportunity Commission (EEOC)
1801 L Street, NW
Washington, DC 20507
Phone: 202-663-4900
http://www.eeoc.gov
To find your local EEOC office, refer to http://www.eeoc.gov/teledir.html

F. Full Text of the Pregnancy Discrimination Act

Note: The Pregnancy Discrimination Act is part of Title VII. To see the full text of the statute, see the chapter on Title VII.

U.S. Code
Title 42: Labor
Chapter 21: Civil Rights
Subchapter VI: Equal Employment Opportunity

§ 2000e. Definitions

....

(k) The terms "because of sex" or "on the basis of sex" include, but are not limited to, because of or on the basis of pregnancy, childbirth, or related medical conditions; and women affected by pregnancy, childbirth, or related medical conditions shall be treated the same for all employment-related purposes, including receipt of benefits under fringe benefit programs, as other persons not so affected but similar in their ability or inability to work, and nothing in section 2000e-2(h) of this title shall be interpreted to permit otherwise. This subsection shall not require an employer to pay for health insurance benefits for abortion, except where the life of the mother would be endangered if the fetus were carried to term, or except where medical complications have arisen from an abortion: Provided, That nothing herein shall preclude an employer from providing abortion benefits or otherwise affect bargaining agreements in regard to abortion.

...

■

Chapter 16

Personal Responsibility and Work Opportunity Reconciliation Act (PRWORA)

Statute: 42 U.S.C. § 653a

http://www4.law.cornell.edu/uscode/42/653a.html

Regulations: None

Definitions

Date of hire

The first day on which an employee performs services for wages—in other words, an employee's first actual workday. The date of hire is not the same as the day on which a job offer is made or accepted—but it can be if the employee begins work on the day the offer is accepted.

Independent contractor

PRWORA uses the Internal Revenue Service's definitions of employee and independent

contractor. Under the IRS rule, a worker will usually be classified as an independent contractor if the person paying the worker has the right to control or direct only the result of the work, not the means or methods by which that result is to be accomplished. For more information on the IRS definitions, see http://www.irs.gov/prod/tax_edu/teletax/tc762.html.

Multistate employer

An employer that has employees working in more than one state.

A. Overview of PRWORA

1. Summary

This law enlists employers in the effort to help parents collect child support. Passed in 1996 as part of President Clinton's welfare reform effort, the PRWORA requires employers to report all new hires to a state registry, which uses this information to try to track down parents who aren't meeting their child support obligations.

The PRWORA is a broad welfare law, with provisions on nutrition programs, teen pregnancy prevention, welfare-to-work requirements and more. This book discusses only the law's provision for collecting child support in the employment context.

2. Regulated Employers

The law covers:

- state and local governments
- the federal government
- all private employers
- union hiring halls, if they retain an employment relationship with the workers whom they refer for jobs (for example, if the union rather than the company to which the worker is referred pays the worker's wages)
- unions that employ workers for wages (as paid organizers or administrative workers, for example)
- temporary or placement agencies that retain an employment relationship with the workers whom they place (for

example, agencies that collect an hourly rate from the companies in which workers are placed, then pay a portion of that rate to the workers as wages).

Employers on Native American reservations and lands are not required to comply with the law.

3. Covered Workers

PRWORA applies to all newly hired employees. This definition includes:

- former employees who are rehired
- agricultural and domestic workers (housekeepers and child care workers, for example)
- short-term employees (workers who quit or are fired before the 20-day deadline for reporting new hires has passed—see "What's Required: Employers" for more on this deadline).

However, the law does not cover:

- employees acquired through a merger or reorganization (for example, if one company buys another company and acquires the purchased company's workers, the purchasing company need not report those employees as new hires)
- *independent contractors*
- employees working outside of the United States, even if they work for an American employer
- employees of a federal or state agency who perform intelligence or counterintelligence functions, if the head of the agency determines that reporting such employees could endanger the employee's

safety or compromise an ongoing investigation or intelligence mission.

4. What's Required: Employers

Employers must report all new hires to a state agency, the State Directory of New Hires (PRWORA requires each state to establish such an agency). Employers must make this report to the state agency in the state where the employee works (although *multistate employers* may designate one state as the recipient of all new hire reports—see "Exceptions," below).

Required Information

The employer must submit the following information every time it makes a new hire:

- employee's name
- employee's address
- employee's Social Security number
- employer's name
- employer's address, and
- employer's federal employer identification number.

The employer may comply with this requirement by submitting the employee's W-4 form or by supplying the information in a different format.

PRWORA allows states to require employers to submit additional information on new hires, such as the *date of hire* and the employee's birth date.

Deadlines for Submitting Information

Employers must submit the required information within 20 days after a new employee's *date of hire*. Employers who choose to report new hire information electronically or by magnetic media (on a magnetic tape, for example) must report at least twice a month (if necessary). These reports must be no less than 12, and no more than 16, days apart.

5. What's Required: Workers

The law places no obligations on workers.

6. Exceptions

Multistate Employers

The law does not require *multistate employers* to report each new hire to the state agency where the employee works. Instead, a *multistate employer* can designate one state agency as the recipient of all new hire reports, regardless of where these employees actually work. To use this exception, the *multistate employer* must:

- choose a state in which it has employees
- submit its new hire information electronically or by magnetic media (on tape), and
- tell the office of the Secretary of Health and Human Services, in writing, which state it has designated to receive new hire reports.

B. How PRWORA Is Enforced

Under PRWORA, state agencies are responsible for policing an employer's compliance with the law's reporting requirement. Although a federal agency (the Office of Child Support Enforcement, a division of the Department of Health and Human Services—see "Agency Charged With Enforcement & Compliance," below) oversees the entire program, each state is responsible for making sure that employers within its borders comply with the law.

C. For Employers: Complying With PRWORA

1. Reporting Requirements

The law is essentially a reporting requirement. For details, see "What's Required: Employers," above.

2. Recordkeeping Requirements

PRWORA imposes no special recordkeeping requirements on employers—there is no requirement that employers keep a copy of the information they send to the state directory of new hires for any length of time, for example.

3. Practical Tips

Here are some tips for complying with PRWORA:

- **Check your state's laws.** PRWORA gives each state the right to impose additional requirements on employers—to request more information or shorten the report-

ing deadline, for example. And some states provide their own form that you can use for reporting. To check your state's rules, go to the website listed in Section F, below.

- **Make the new hire form part of your first-day paperwork.** When you ask your new employees to fill out W-4s, insurance forms and the like, also get the information you need to send to the new hire directory. If your state allows you to use a particular form, fill that form out on the first day.
- **Take advantage of *multistate employer* procedures.** If you have employees in more than one state, designate one state's directory as the agency to which you will send information on all new hires. This will simplify your paperwork —and relieve you of the need to learn the reporting requirements of several different states.

- **Respond quickly to withholding orders.** Once you send your new hire information to the state directory, the state will check that information against its list of parents who owe child support. If the government finds a match, you will receive a withholding order directing you to withhold money from that employee's income to pay the employee's monthly child support obligation. If you get such an order, obey it—and fast. Otherwise, you might have to pay the full amount that you should have withheld to the custodial parent.

4. Penalties

PRWORA authorizes states to impose penalties on employers who fail to report new hires as required by the law. If a state chooses to impose such a penalty, it may not exceed:

- $25 for each new hire whom the employer fails to report, or
- if the employer and employee conspire in the failure to report (for example, if an employer agrees to an employee's request that it not file the report so that the employee can evade child support obligations), $500 for each new hire.

D. For Workers: Asserting Rights Under PRWORA

PRWORA does not give workers any independent rights, nor does it impose any obligations on workers.

E. Agency Charged With Enforcement & Compliance

Department of Health and Human Services
Administration for Children & Families
Office of Child Support Enforcement
370 L'Enfant Promenade SW
Washington, DC 20447
http://www.acf.dhhs.gov/programs/cse

Agency Resources for Employers
(These can be obtained either at the Web addresses listed below or at the address listed above.)

- An employer's guide to complying with PRWORA's reporting requirements
  New Hire Reporting Program
  http://www.acf.dhhs.gov/programs/cse/newhire/nh/abc/new_hire.htm
- An explanation of employers' responsibilities under PRWORA; includes a 50-state list of child support enforcement agencies
  The Child Support Program and Employers
  http://www.acf.dhhs.gov/programs/cse/newhire/nh/csprog/ecsprog.doc
- A form multistate employers can use to designate the state to which they will submit new hire information
  Multistate Employer Notification Form for New Hire Reporting
  http://www.acf.dhhs.gov/programs/cse/newhire/docs/mseform6.pdf

F. State Laws Relating to PRWORA

PRWORA gives states the leeway to impose stricter requirements on employers. For example, although the federal law doesn't require it, states may choose to enact laws requiring employers to:

- report *independent contractors* as well as employees

- submit new hire information within a shorter time limit (that is, shorter than the 20 days allowed under PRWORA)
- provide more information about new hires than the federal law requires
- impose penalties on employers who don't comply with the law.

You can find information on each state's requirements, as well as citations to your state's law and the address of your state's enforcement agency, on the website of the Office of Child Support Enforcement: http://www.acf.dhhs.gov/programs/cse/newhire/docs/nhstmtrx.htm.

G. Full Text of PRWORA

U.S Code
Title 42: The Public Health and Welfare
Chapter 7: Social Security
Subchapter IV: Grants to States for Aid and Services to Needy Families With Children and for Child-Welfare Services
Part D: Child Support and Establishment of Paternity

§ 635a. State Directory of New Hires

(a) Establishment

(1) In general

(A) Requirement for States that have no directory

Except as provided in subparagraph (B), not later than October 1, 1997, each State shall establish an automated directory (to be known as the "State Directory of New Hires") which shall contain information supplied in accordance with subsection (b) of this section by employers on each newly hired employee.

(B) States with new hire reporting law in existence

A State which has a new hire reporting law in existence on August 22, 1996, may continue to operate under the State law, but the State must meet the requirements of subsection (g)(2) of this section not later than October 1, 1997, and the requirements of this section (other than subsection (g)(2) of this section) not later than October 1, 1998.

(2) Definitions

As used in this section:

(A) Employee

The term "employee"—

(i)

means an individual who is an employee within the meaning of chapter 24 of the Internal Revenue Code of 1986; and

(ii)

does not include an employee of a Federal or State agency performing intelligence or counter-intelligence functions, if the head of such agency has determined that reporting pursuant to paragraph (1) with respect to the employee could endanger the safety of the employee or compromise an ongoing investigation or intelligence mission.

(B) Employer

(i) In general

The term "employer" has the meaning given such term in section 3401(d) of the Internal Revenue Code of 1986 and includes any governmental entity and any labor organization.

(ii) Labor organization

The term "labor organization" shall have the meaning given such term in section 152(5) of title 29, and includes any entity (also known as a "hiring hall") which is used by the organization and an employer to carry out requirements described in section 158(f)(3) of title 29 of an agreement between the organization and the employer.

(b) Employer information

(1) Reporting requirement

(A) In general

Except as provided in subparagraphs (B) and (C), each employer shall furnish to the Directory of New Hires of the State in which a newly hired employee works, a report that contains the name, address, and social security number of the employee, and the name and address of, and identifying number assigned under section 6109 of the Internal Revenue Code of 1986 to, the employer.

(B) Multistate employers

An employer that has employees who are employed in 2 or more States and that transmits reports magnetically or electronically may comply with subparagraph (A) by designating 1 State in which such employer has employees to which the employer will transmit the report described in subparagraph (A), and transmitting such report to such State. Any employer that transmits reports pursuant to this subparagraph shall notify the

Secretary in writing as to which State such employer designates for the purpose of sending reports.

(C) Federal Government employers

Any department, agency, or instrumentality of the United States shall comply with subparagraph (A) by transmitting the report described in subparagraph (A) to the National Directory of New Hires established pursuant to section 653 of this title.

(2) Timing of report

Each State may provide the time within which the report required by paragraph (1) shall be made with respect to an employee, but such report shall be made—

(A) not later than 20 days after the date the employer hires the employee; or

(B) in the case of an employer transmitting reports magnetically or electronically, by 2 monthly transmissions (if necessary) not less than 12 days nor more than 16 days apart.

(c) Reporting format and method

Each report required by subsection (b) of this section shall be made on a W-4 form or, at the option of the employer, an equivalent form, and may be transmitted by 1st class mail, magnetically, or electronically.

(d) Civil money penalties on noncomplying employers

The State shall have the option to set a State civil money penalty which shall not exceed—

(1) $25 per failure to meet the requirements of this section with respect to a newly hired employee; or

(2) $500 if, under State law, the failure is the result of a conspiracy between the employer and the employee to not supply the required report or to supply a false or incomplete report.

(e) Entry of employer information

Information shall be entered into the data base maintained by the State Directory of New Hires within 5 business days of receipt from an employer pursuant to subsection (b) of this section.

(f) Information comparisons

(1) In general

Not later than May 1, 1998, an agency designated by the State shall, directly or by contract, conduct automated comparisons of the social security numbers reported by employers pursuant to subsection (b) of this section and the social security numbers appearing in the records of the State case registry for cases being enforced under the State plan.

(2) Notice of match

When an information comparison conducted under paragraph (1) reveals a match with respect to the social security number of an individual required to provide support under a support order, the State Directory of New Hires shall provide the agency administering the State plan approved under this part of the appropriate State with the name, address, and social security number of the employee to whom the social security number is assigned, and the name and address of, and identifying number assigned under section 6109 of the Internal Revenue Code of 1986 to, the employer.

(g) Transmission of information

(1) Transmission of wage withholding notices to employers

Within 2 business days after the date information regarding a newly hired employee is entered into the State Directory of New Hires, the State agency enforcing the employee's child support obligation shall transmit a notice to the employer of the employee directing the employer to withhold from the income of the employee an amount equal to the monthly (or other periodic) child support obligation (including any past due support obligation) of the employee, unless the employee's income is not subject to withholding pursuant to section 666(b)(3) of this title.

(2) Transmissions to the National Directory of New Hires

(A) New hire information

Within 3 business days after the date information regarding a newly hired employee is entered into the State Directory of New Hires, the State Directory of New Hires shall furnish the information to the National Directory of New Hires.

(B) Wage and unemployment compensation information

The State Directory of New Hires shall, on a quarterly basis, furnish to the National Directory of New Hires information concerning the wages and unemployment compensation paid to individuals, by such dates, in such format, and containing such information as the Secretary of Health and Human Services shall specify in regulations.

(3) "Business day" defined

As used in this subsection, the term "business day" means a day on which State offices are open for regular business.

(h) Other uses of new hire information

(1) Location of child support obligors

The agency administering the State plan approved under this part shall use information received pursuant to subsection (f)(2) of this section to locate individuals for purposes of establishing paternity and establishing, modifying, and enforcing child support obligations, and may disclose such information to any agent of the agency that is under contract with the agency to carry out such purposes.

(2) Verification of eligibility for certain programs

A State agency responsible for administering a program specified in section 1320b-7(b) of this title shall have access to information reported by employers pursuant to subsection (b) of this section for purposes of verifying eligibility for the program.

(3) Administration of employment security and workers' compensation

State agencies operating employment security and workers' compensation programs shall have access to information reported by employers pursuant to subsection (b) of this section for the purposes of administering such programs.

∎

Chapter 17

Civil Rights Act of 1866 (Section 1981)

Statute: 42 U.S.C. § 1981

http://www4.law.cornell.edu/uscode/42/1981.html

Regulations: None

Definitions

At-will employee
An employee who can quit or be fired at any time, for any reason that is not illegal. In this country, a worker is employed at will unless he has an employment contract that limits the employer's right to fire him. Such an employment contract may be written, oral or implied from the conduct of the employer and employee.

A. Overview of Section 1981

1. Summary

Passed despite President Andrew Johnson's veto during the Reconstruction Era immediately following the Civil War, the Civil Rights Act of 1866 declared African-Americans to be citizens, entitled to a series of rights previously reserved to white men. This law is known as Section 1981 because of its location in the United States Code.

Section 1981 confers a number of rights, including the right to sue or be sued in court, to give evidence and to purchase property. This book discusses only one of the law's protections: the right to make and enforce contracts, which courts have found prohibits racial discrimination in the employment relationship.

Although the law's original purpose was to protect African-Americans, courts have interpreted it to protect people of all races from discrimination and harassment.

2. Regulated Employers

Section 1981 applies to all employers:
- state governments
- the federal government
- private employers of any size.

Section 1981 also applies to some entities that are not employers in the legal sense, but have a contractual relationship with persons performing work for them. For example, partners in a partnership are covered by Section 1981 (but not by other federal anti-discrimination statutes, such as Title VII, the Age Discrimination in Employment Act or the Americans With Disabilities Act). Most courts have also found that firms hiring independent contractors are covered by Section 1981 (see Section A3, below).

3. Covered Workers

All private and government employees are covered by Section 1981. In addition, the law covers partners in a partnership.

At-Will Employees

Section 1981 protects the right to make and enforce contracts, including employment contracts. Historically, this provision of the law was intended to help African-Americans achieve some measure of economic independence by supplanting slavery and the coercive labor arrangements that took its place with freely negotiated contractual agreements.

However, courts have not yet reached a consensus on whether all employees are protected by this provision, or whether it applies only to employees with a traditional employment contract. Courts agree that, in order to sue under this law, an employee must either have a contract or have been denied a contract. However, courts disagree as to whether *at-will employees* have a contract of employment and, therefore, can sue under Section 1981.

Most federal courts that have considered this issue—including several federal courts of appeal—have decided that *at-will employees* may sue an employer for violating Section 1981, even though they do not have employment contracts limiting the employer's right to fire them. These courts reasoned that *at-will employees* have very basic employment contracts (covering, for example, wages and work to be performed), although those contracts offer no job protection.

However, several federal district courts have refused to allow *at-will employees* to bring a lawsuit under Section 1981.

The United States Supreme Court has not yet considered this issue.

Independent Contractors

Section 1981 protects independent contractors from race discrimination by their hiring firm. However, at least one court (a federal court in Alabama) has decided that this protection does not extend to claims of harassment. The United States Supreme Court has not yet considered this issue.

4. What's Prohibited: Employers

Section 1981 prohibits discrimination on the basis of race in the making or enforcement of employment contracts. This language has been interpreted broadly to prohibit any intentional workplace discrimination—including harassment—on the basis of race. Some courts have also found that Section 1981 prohibits discrimination and harassment on the basis of ethnicity, at least where that ethnicity has a racial component (see "Race and Ethnicity," below).

Covered Employment Practices

Employers may not discriminate on the basis of race in any aspect of employment, including:

- hiring
- promotions
- employment benefits
- pay
- firing.

Racial Harassment

Today, it is undisputed that Section 1981 prohibits racial harassment. However, this issue was fiercely contested in the last decade, in a battle between Congress and the Supreme Court.

In 1989, the United States Supreme Court decided that Section 1981 covered only the right to enter into a contract in the first place, and did not extend to any problems or issues that might later arise in the employment relationship—such as harassment. (*Patterson v. McClean Credit Union,* 491 U.S. 164). In response to this and several other decisions in the same term that narrowed employees' rights, Congress passed the Civil Rights Act of 1991. Among other things, this law overruled *Patterson* and amended Section 1981 so that it now clearly prohibits racial harassment.

An employee claiming racial harassment in violation of Section 1981 must show that he was subjected to unwelcome racial comments or offensive conduct that was severe or pervasive enough to alter the conditions of his employment. This test is the same as that used under Title VII (see the chapter on Title VII for more about harassment).

Race and Ethnicity

Although Section 1981 was originally intended to protect the newly freed slaves, courts have consistently interpreted the law to protect people of any race (including white people) from intentional race discrimination.

Some courts have also found that Section 1981 prohibits discrimination on the basis of ethnicity—but only if that discrimination is racial in character. For example, courts have held that discrimination against Hispanic-Americans, Arab-Americans and Asian-Americans violates Section 1981—but discrimination against persons of Slavic or Italian origin does not.

In deciding whether ethnic discrimination constitutes race discrimination under Section 1981, courts have looked at several factors, including:

- whether the discriminator perceived or characterized the victim as belonging to a separate race because of his ethnicity
- whether the victim belongs to an ethnicity that is perceived as "nonwhite"
- whether the victim belongs to an ethnicity that has traditionally been subject to discrimination
- whether the victim is claiming discrimination based on characteristics commonly associated with national origin (country of birth, language skills and surname, for example), which is not a violation of Section 1981; or on characteristics commonly associated with race (physical characteristics or skin color, for example), which is.

5. What's Required: Workers

Section 1981 imposes no obligations on workers.

6. Exceptions

Other Types of Discrimination

Section 1981 prohibits only discrimination based on race or ethnicity. It does not prohibit discrimination based on sex, religion, disability or age.

Disparate Impact Claims

Only intentional race discrimination violates Section 1981. Unintentional discrimination—such as the use of seemingly neutral hiring criteria that disproportionately weed out applicants of a particular race—does not violate the law. Lawsuits for unintentional discrimination (called "disparate impact" lawsuits) are allowed under other anti-discrimination laws, such as Title VII.

B. How Section 1981 Is Enforced

1. Individual Complaints

Employees or applicants who believe that their rights under Section 1981 have been violated may file a lawsuit in state court or in a federal district court.

No government agency takes complaints about violations of Section 1981 or enforces the law against private employers. Therefore, an employee's only official avenue of redress is through the courts.

If your employer is covered by Title VII (see Chapter 18, Section A), you can also file a charge of race discrimination with the Equal Employment Opportunity Commission (EEOC). However, the EEOC will only enforce your rights under Title VII, not your Section 1981 rights. For more information—including how to file a charge (complaint) of discrimination with the EEOC—see the chapter on Title VII.

2. Agency Enforcement

No agency enforces Section 1981 against private employers.

C. For Employers: Complying With Section 1981

1. Reporting Requirements

Section 1981 imposes no reporting requirements.

2. Posting Requirements

Posting is not required under Section 1981.

3. Recordkeeping Requirements

Section 1981 does not require employers to keep any particular records.

4. Practical Tips

Here are a few practical tips for complying with Section 1981:

- **Smaller employers beware.** Unlike most federal anti-discrimination laws, Section 1981 applies to every employer, regardless of size. Even if you have fewer than 15 employees (and therefore are not covered by Title VII), you should familiarize yourself with the basics of anti-discrimination law by reading the Title VII chapter. Courts will apply these rules in deciding race discrimination cases under Section 1981 (except the rules regarding disparate impact cases, which do not apply to Section 1981—see Section C6, above).

- **Keep a written record.** To succeed in a lawsuit under Section 1981, an employee must show that you intentionally discriminated. This means that your grounds for taking any employment action are very important—you should be ready to prove that you had legitimate business reasons for the decision you made. And the best way to prove anything in court is with documents, particularly documents that were made at the time of the disputed incident, rather than created after the fact. Keep track, in writing, of your reasons for refusing to hire, failing to promote or firing any employee. And keep copies of any documents that support your decision (like customer complaints, poor performance evaluations or poor productivity numbers).

- **Take quick action if you receive a complaint.** If an employee complains of racial discrimination or racial harassment, investigate the complaint immediately. If you find that the complaint is warranted —for example, if one of your supervisors made offensive racial comments or can't seem to get along with workers of another race—take action right away to remedy the situation.

5. Penalties

If an employee wins a lawsuit for violation of Section 1981, the employer may be required to:

- pay the employee back pay and benefits lost as a result of the discrimination or harassment
- pay the employee compensatory damages for emotional distress, such as pain and suffering
- pay punitive damages, a sum of money intended to punish the employer for violating the law
- take action to remedy its discrimination, such as promoting, hiring or reinstating a worker who was discriminated against
- pay the employee's attorney fees and court costs.

D. For Workers: Asserting Rights Under Section 1981

1. Where to Start

If you believe that your employer or a prospective employer has violated Section 1981, you should start by complaining internally to the company. If the company has a complaint policy, follow the designated procedures to file a complaint. If the company has no complaint policy, talk to a human resources representative or a member of management.

If you are a union member, talk to your shop steward or union representative.

If internal complaints and/or union complaints don't work, your only official resort is to file a lawsuit in federal district court or state court. Remember, however, that you may also have rights under Title VII—and you can complain to the EEOC if you believe those rights have been violated. (See the chapter on Title VII for more information.)

2. Required Forms

None.

3. Practical Tips

Here are some tips for asserting your rights under Section 1981:

- **Gather your evidence while ye may.** In any discrimination lawsuit, it is very important for employees to collect evidence—documents and witness statements, in particular—right away. Memories fade, co-workers grow fearful or take new jobs and documents and other tangible evidence of discrimination (like an offensive cartoon or email) disappear. Because Section 1981 claims can be brought up to several years after a discriminatory or harassing incident, preserving evidence is especially important in these cases.
- **Damages are unlimited under Section 1981.** If you have been discriminated against on the basis of race, you can file a charge (complaint) with the EEOC, claiming that your Title VII rights have been violated. And many employees choose to do just that, to take advantage of the EEOC's investigative and settlement procedures. However, if you end up filing a lawsuit, be sure to include a claim that your employer violated Section

1981. The reason is simple: while Title VII limits the damages you can collect from your employer, Section 1981 does not.

- **Longer time limits generally apply to Section 1981 claims.** Under Title VII, you must complain to the Equal Employment Opportunity Commission (EEOC) before you can file a lawsuit—and you must get to the EEOC within 180 to 300 days after the discriminatory incident. Section 1981 doesn't impose these requirements. Because no agency enforces the law, you don't have to complain to an agency before you can go to court. The time limit for filing a Section 1981 case is based on state law, but will generally be longer than the EEOC's requirement. So even if you missed your chance to file a Title VII race discrimination claim, you may still be able to sue under Section 1981.

E. Agency Charged With Enforcement & Compliance

No agency enforces Section 1981 against private employers.

F. State Laws Relating to Race Discrimination

See the chapter on Title VII, which lists state anti-discrimination laws.

G. Full Text of Section 1981

U.S. Code
Title 42: The Public Health and Welfare
Chapter 21: Civil Rights
Subchapter 1: Generally

§ 1981. Equal Rights Under the Law

(a) Statement of equal rights

All persons within the jurisdiction of the United States shall have the same right in every State and Territory to make and enforce contracts, to sue, be parties, give evidence, and to the full and equal benefit of all laws and proceedings for the security of persons and property as is enjoyed by white citizens, and shall be subject to like punishment, pains, penalties, taxes, licenses, and exactions of every kind, and to no other.

(b) "Make and enforce contracts" defined

For purposes of this section, the term "make and enforce contracts" includes the making, performance, modification, and termination of contracts, and the enjoyment of all benefits, privileges, terms, and conditions of the contractual relationship.

(c) Protection against impairment

The rights protected by this section are protected against impairment by nongovernmental discrimination and impairment under color of State law.

■

Chapter 18

Title VII of the Civil Rights Act of 1964 (Title VII)

Statute: 42 U.S.C. § 2000e

http://www.eeoc.gov/laws/vii.html

Regulations: 29 C.F.R. §§ 1600 through 1609

http://lula.law.cornell.edu/cfr/cfr.php?title=29&type=chapter&value=14

Definitions

Bona fide occupational qualification (BFOQ)
An exception to Title VII's general prohibition to discrimination that allows employers to discriminate when the very nature of the job requires them to do so. For more about BFOQs, see Section A6.

Disparate impact
A type of unlawful discrimination that occurs when a seemingly neutral policy disproportionately affects people of a *protected class*. For more about disparate impact discrimination, see "What Is Discrimination" in Section A4.

Harassment
Work conditions or behavior by coworkers, superiors, managers or others that subjects employees who are members of a protected class to a work environment that is hostile, intimidating or offensive. For more about harassment, see "What Is Harassment" in Section A4.

Protected class
A group specifically protected by Title VII. For example, because Title VII prohibits discrimination based on sex, both men and women are protected classes. People with red hair, however, are not members of a protected class because there is no ban against discrimination based on hair color. For more, see Section A4.

Retaliation
Any adverse action that an employer or someone who works for the employer takes against an employee for complaining about *harassment* or discrimination. For more about this, see "What Is Retaliation" in Section A4.

Sexual harassment
Any unwelcome sexual advance or conduct on the job that creates an intimidating, hostile or offensive working environment. For more about this, see "What Is Sexual Harassment" in Section A4.

A. Overview of Title VII

1. Summary

Title VII prohibits employment discrimination based on race, religion, color, sex and national origin.

2. Regulated Employers

Title VII covers the following employers:
- private employers with 15 or more employees
- the federal government, its agencies and political subdivisions

- the state governments, their agencies and political subdivisions
- local governments, their agencies and political subdivisions
- private and public employment agencies
- labor organizations, and
- joint labor/management committees.

3. Covered Workers

Title VII protects all prospective and current employees of a covered employer.

4. What's Prohibited: Employers

Title VII prohibits employers from discriminating against prospective and current employees on the basis of the following characteristics: race, color, religion, sex and national origin. (For detailed information about each characteristic, see "Protected Classes," below.)

Title VII was amended in 1978 to add pregnancy as a *protected class*. To learn more about pregnancy discrimination, see the chapter on the Pregnancy Discrimination Act (PDA).

Title VII applies to all terms and benefits of employment, including:

- hiring
- firing
- compensation and benefits
- job assignment
- employee classification
- transfer
- promotion
- layoff or recall

- training and apprenticeship programs
- use of company facilities
- retirement plans, and
- leave.

Title VII also prohibits employers from *retaliating* against people who complain or who otherwise assert their rights under the law. For example, an employer cannot fire someone for complaining about race discrimination. For more, see "What Is Retaliation," below.

What Is Discrimination

Unlawful discrimination includes the following practices:

- giving some people preferential treatment over others based on their membership in a *protected class*
- treating some people worse than others based on their membership in a *protected class*
- *harassing* people because of their membership in a *protected class* (for more about this issue, see "What Is Harassment," below)
- making decisions based on stereotypes about people of a *protected class* (for example, refusing to hire a woman as a police officer because of a belief that women are too emotional and not mentally tough enough)
- treating people differently because of their marriage to or association with members of a *protected class* (for example, refusing to hire a white man because he is married to an Asian woman).

Title VII outlaws both intentional discrimination and any practices that have a discriminatory effect, whether or not the employer intended for those practices to discriminate. This discriminatory effect is called *"disparate impact,"* and it happens when a practice that seems fair and neutral actually affects a *protected class* in a disproportionate and unfair way. Unless the employer has a legitimate and nondiscriminatory business reason for using that practice, the law will view that practice as unlawful. For example, if an employer refuses to hire people who don't meet minimum height and weight criteria, the employer may be discriminating against people of Asian descent, who will be disproportionately affected by this rule. The rule will pass legal muster only if the employer can show it is clearly related to the physical demands of the particular job—heavy lifting in a warehouse, for example.

What Is Harassment

Harassment occurs any time people are forced to endure a work environment that is hostile or intimidating or offensive to them because of their membership in a *protected class. Harassing* acts can include:

- slurs
- offensive "jokes"
- offensive remarks based on a protected characteristic
- drawings or pictures that depict people with a protected characteristic in an unfavorable light
- threats

- intimidation
- hostile demeanor
- physical violence.

What Is Sexual Harassment

Sexual harassment is a type of gender discrimination. It is any unwelcome sexual advance or conduct on the job that creates an intimidating, hostile or offensive working environment. Any conduct of a sexual nature that makes an employee uncomfortable has the potential to be sexual harassment.

Given such a broad definition, it is not surprising that sexual harassment comes in many forms. The following are all examples of sexual harassment:

- A supervisor implies to an employee that the employee must sleep with him to keep a job. (In legal lingo, this is sometimes called "quid pro quo" harassment.)
- A sales clerk makes demeaning comments about female customers to his co-workers.
- Lawyers regularly tell sexually explicit jokes in earshot of the office manager, who finds the jokes offensive.
- A cashier at a store pinches and fondles a co-worker against the co-worker's will.
- A secretary's co-workers belittle her and refer to her by sexist or demeaning terms.
- Several employees post sexually explicit jokes on an office intranet bulletin board.

- An employee sends emails to co-workers that contain sexually explicit language and jokes.

The harasser can be the victim's supervisor, manager or co-worker. The harasser can even be a non-employee, if the person is on the premises with permission (for example, a customer or a vendor).

Sexual harassment knows no gender: Men can sexually harass women, and women can sexually harass men.

What Is Retaliation

Retaliation means any adverse action that an employer or someone who works for the employer takes against an employee for complaining about *harassment* or discrimination. Adverse action includes demotion, discipline, firing, salary reduction, negative evaluation, change in job assignment or change in shift assignment.

Retaliation can also include hostile behavior or attitudes toward an employee who complains.

Although *retaliation* obviously includes any action taken with malice or bad intent, it can also include actions taken with the best of intentions—if those actions have a negative impact on the employee. For example:

- A female employee complains that her supervisor is sexually harassing her. In response, the employer changes the employee from the day shift to the night shift so that she doesn't have to work with the supervisor any more. Even though the employer didn't intend to hurt the employee, this action could

be *retaliatory* if the employee preferred the day shift.

- An African-American employee complains to his employer that the store in which he works is racially hostile toward him because his co-workers tell racial jokes and refer to him with racially derogatory names. In response, the employer transfers him to another store. This action could be retaliatory if the new store is farther from the employee's home or is less desirable in some other way.

Protected Classes
Race

Title VII includes more than a prohibition against discrimination against specific races. It also forbids discriminating against people because they have immutable characteristics carried by people of a certain race, such as skin color, hair texture or other physical features.

Title VII's prohibition against race discrimination also includes physically isolating individuals based on their race.

Coding applications or resumes to indicate an applicant's race can be evidence of discrimination, as can questions that elicit information about an applicant's race.

Religion

Title VII both *prohibits* employers from making decisions based on a person's religion and *requires* employers to make decisions based on a person's religion.

This seeming contradiction comes from the fact that religion is more than just a characteristic. Religion is also a set of practices and beliefs. The law prohibits employers from discriminating based on the fact of someone's religion (for example, that an employee is Jewish or Catholic or Baptist), and it requires employers to make allowances for a person's religious practices and beliefs (for example, that an employee needs time after lunch to pray or that an employee needs Saturdays off to observe her Sabbath).

The first part is fairly simple. Employers can't refuse to hire someone because he or she is Jewish; they can't promote someone because he or she is Muslim. Employers must make those decisions for non-discriminatory reasons.

The second part is more complicated. Employers must work with their employees to make it possible for the employees to practice their religious beliefs—within reason. This might mean not scheduling an employee to work on her Sabbath day or relaxing a dress code so that an employee can wear religious garments. In legal parlance, these allowances are called "accommodations." The only time employers do not have to accommodate an employee is if it would cause the business too much hardship. For instance, if changing an employee's schedule to accommodate a religious belief would wreak havoc with a seniority system and cause severe morale problems among other employees, the employer might not have to accommodate the worker.

National Origin

The prohibition against national origin discrimination generally means that employers cannot make employment decisions based on an individual's:

- birthplace
- ancestry
- culture
- native language
- accent (unless the accent affects the individual's ability to perform the job)
- marriage or association with people of a national ethnic group
- membership or association with a ethnic cultural organization
- attendance or participation in schools, churches, temples or mosques that are generally associated with a specific ethnic group, or
- name that is associated with a specific ethnic group.

A rule requiring employees to speak only English at work may violate Title VII unless the employer can show that the rule is critical for business purposes.

National origin discrimination is also prohibited by the federal Immigration Reform and Control Act (see the chapter on IRCA).

Sex

Title VII's prohibition against sex discrimination protects both men and women from discrimination and *harassment* based on gender.

Sex discrimination includes making decisions based on the fact that a person doesn't fit the employer's concept of what people of a certain gender should be like. For example, a restaurant couldn't refuse to hire a woman because she isn't feminine enough.

Currently, it is an open question as to whether Title VII prohibits discrimination based on sexual orientation. However, many states have explicitly added this protection to their own fair employment laws (see Section F).

5. What's Required: Employers

Employers must provide their employees with a workplace free of unlawful discrimination and *harassment*. This means that employers must act when they learn that an employee, manager or supervisor is discriminating against or *harassing* another employee or group of employees. Employers must take effective and immediate action to stop such conduct. This action might include investigating the situation and disciplining (up to and including terminating) the offender.

6. Exceptions

In a very rare and narrow exception to Title VII, employers can discriminate against people on the basis of gender, religion and national origin (but never race or color) if the very nature of the job requires them to do so.

This exception is called the *bona fide occupational qualification* exception *(BFOQ)*. It reflects Congress's recognition that some jobs must be filled by people who have certain characteristics—even though normally the law would protect those who don't fit the bill.

For example, a movie director searching for someone to play the role of Hamlet's mother may consider only women for the job—and thus discriminate against men in filling the part. Or, an official in the Catholic Church can insist on hiring only Catholics—and discriminate against non-Catholics—when hiring Sunday school teachers.

In order to use this exception, the employer must prove that no member of the group that's being discriminated against can perform the job. This is a very tough thing to prove, and courts often reject arguments that most employers find perfectly legitimate. For example, the airlines can't discriminate against older applicants when hiring flight attendants simply because they think that passengers prefer young pretty faces. Many years ago, the courts held that a 45-year-old individual is just as able to perform the actual duties of the job—maintaining order in the plane's cabin, serving meals and beverages—as a 25-year-old.

There are times, however, when an employer has no choice but to use the *BFOQ* exception. For example, the law has allowed *BFOQs* in the following instances:

- An employer was allowed to hire only male attendants for its company bathroom.
- An airline was allowed to discriminate on the basis of religion and hire only Moslem pilots to fly certain routes in Saudi Arabia where Saudi Arabian law prohibited, under punishment of death, any non-Moslems to enter the area.

B. How Title VII Is Enforced

1. Individual Complaints

Individuals may file a complaint (also called a charge) with the federal Equal Employment Opportunity Commission (EEOC) (see Section E, below).

Individuals may also file a lawsuit. However, they must first file a complaint with the EEOC or their state fair employment office (if their state has one—see Section F, below) and then receive what is called a "right to sue" letter. Once they receive that letter, they have 90 days to file suit.

2. Agency Enforcement

The EEOC may act in its own initiative or after receiving a charge. It has the authority to investigate a charge, negotiate a settlement, mediate the charge and bring a suit in federal court. The EEOC also issues regulatory and other forms of guidance interpreting Title VII. In the event that the employee has signed an arbitration agreement limiting her rights to sue, the EEOC may sue on her behalf.

C. For Employers: Complying With Title VII

1. Reporting Requirements

Only large employers (100 or more employees) with federal contracts must file annual reports with the EEOC.

2. Recordkeeping Requirements

EEOC regulations require employers to keep personnel and employment records for at least one year. If an employer terminates an employee, the employer must keep that employee's records for a year after the termination.

3. Practical Tips

Discrimination and harassment are evils that you must not tolerate in your workplace—both for your good and that of your employees. The following practices can help:

- Train your employees, managers and supervisors about anti-discrimination laws, including Title VII.
- Take swift and immediate action if you suspect discrimination and harassment —or if someone complains. This action includes investigating complaints and disciplining wrongdoers.
- Have legitimate nondiscriminatory reasons for all of the business decisions you make. That way an employee can't claim that the decisions were really based on bias or prejudice.
- Know your workplace. Get out among your workers and find out what is going on. Chat with them to see if they have any concerns or gripes. Look around the office to see if there are any posters or pictures that are offensive or harassing.
- Have written documentation to support all of the decisions you make.

- Keep records of all complaints of discrimination and the actions that you took in response to them.
- Don't retaliate against people who complain—even if you think the complaint lacks merit.
- Have a written policy prohibiting discrimination and harassment in your workplace.
- Write and distribute to your employees a procedure that they can follow to complain about discrimination and harassment.

4. Penalties

If an employer is found guilty of discrimination or harassment, the penalties might include the following:

- lost wages
- hiring the aggrieved employee(s)
- promoting the aggrieved employee(s)
- reinstating the aggrieved employee(s)
- paying for mental anguish and inconvenience
- paying punitive damages
- providing a reasonable accommodation
- taking corrective and preventative measures to cure discrimination in the workplace
- paying attorney's fees, expert witness fees and court costs.

D. For Workers: Asserting Rights Under Title VII

1. Where to Start

If you feel that you are a victim of discrimination or harassment, the very first place to go for help is, believe it or not, your employer. After all, an employer can't fix a situation that it doesn't know about, and the law will not hold an employer responsible in cases where employees did not use employer complaint procedures. If your employer has written complaint procedures, follow them. If there are no written complaint procedures, complain to the human resources department and any manager or supervisor.

If your employer does not act to stop the discrimination or harassment, your next step is to file a complaint (also called a charge) with the EEOC (see Section E) or with your state fair employment office if your state has one (see Section F). You can file a charge by mail or in person at your nearest EEOC office. To find the office closest to you, call 800-669-4000 or refer to the agency's website at http://www.eeoc.gov/teledir.html.

Whatever you do, don't let too much time pass before filing your charge. Strict time limits apply, and if you miss the deadline, you will not be allowed to sue your employer. The deadlines depend on whether your state also has an anti-discrimination law. In states without anti-discrimination laws, you have 180 days from the date of the discriminatory act to complain. In states with an anti-discrimination law, you have 300 days to complain. (See Section F for a list of states with anti-discrimination laws.)

The agency will investigate your complaint. It will either try to resolve the situation or inform you that it didn't find any evidence of discrimination.

Regardless of what the agency does, you may also contact an attorney about negotiating a settlement or filing a lawsuit on your behalf. The attorney will have to obtain a "right to sue" letter from the agency before filing a lawsuit. The attorney will then have 90 days to file suit.

2. Required Forms

Contact your local EEOC office or state fair employment office to see if they have a standard charge form that you must file.

3. Practical Tips

If you suspect that you are a victim of discrimination and harassment, act—and act fast.

Even though it is extremely difficult to assert your rights in this sort of situation, the law does not protect those who keep quiet and passively endure unlawful treatment.

The first place you must go is to your employer, but don't let yourself get delayed too long at this step. If you wait more than 180 days before filing a charge with the EEOC or your state fair employment office, you may be out of luck. (If 180 days have already passed, don't give up. Go ahead and file a charge. The deadline has numerous exceptions, and you may fit into one of them without knowing it.)

Keep a written record of everything related to the discrimination and harassment. Be sure to include dates and the names of any people who might have seen or heard something. When you complain to your employer, do it in writing. Keep a copy of the complaint and any response you receive from your employer. Remember: You will win your case only if you can prove it, and written documentation is a powerful form of proof.

E. Agency Charged With Enforcement & Compliance

Equal Employment Opportunity Commission (EEOC)
1801 L Street, NW
Washington, DC 20507
Phone: 202-663-4900
http://www.eeoc.gov
To find your local EEOC office, refer to **http://www.eeoc.gov/teledir.html.**

Agency Resources for Employers

(These can be obtained either at the Web addresses listed below or at the address and phone number listed above.)

- Information about different types of discrimination, including national origin discrimination and race discrimination
  Fact Sheets
  http://www.eeoc.gov/eeoinfo.html
- Information on complying with federal anti-discrimination laws
  Information for Small Employers
  http://www.eeoc.gov/small/index.html
- A description of the EEOC and how it works
  The U.S. Equal Employment Opportunity Commission: An Overview
  http://www.eeoc.gov/facts/overview.html
- Information about anti-discrimination laws
  Federal Laws Prohibiting Job Discrimination: Questions and Answers
  http://www.eeoc.gov/facts/qanda.html

Agency Resources for Workers

(These can be obtained either at the Web addresses listed below or at the address and phone number listed above.)

- Information about different types of discrimination, including national origin discrimination and race discrimination
  Fact Sheets
  http://www.eeoc.gov/eeoinfo.html
- A description of the EEOC and how it works
  The U.S. Equal Employment Opportunity Commission: An Overview
  http://www.eeoc.gov/facts/overview.html
- Information about anti-discrimination laws
  Federal Laws Prohibiting Job Discrimination: Questions and Answers
  http://www.eeoc.gov/facts/qanda.html
- Instructions on how to file a charge of discrimination with the EEOC
  Filing a Charge
  http://www.eeoc.gov/facts/howtofil.html

F. State Laws Relating to Fair Employment

Many states and localities have anti-discrimination laws and fair employment agencies responsible for enforcing those laws. If an employee lives in such a state or locality, a charge that an employee files with the EEOC is cross-filed with the state fair employment agency and vice versa. That way, one charge protects the employee under both state and federal law.

State fair employment laws are often broader than Title VII, covering more employers and protecting more classes of employees.

Laws Prohibiting Discrimination in Employment

"Employer" refers to:

- private employers
- labor unions
- employment agencies.

Certain religious and educational organizations may be exempt.

State	Law applies to employers with	Age	Ancestry or national origin	Disability	AIDS/HIV	Gender	Marital status	Pregnancy, childbirth and related medical conditions	Race or color	Religion or creed	Sexual orientation	Genetic testing information	Additional protected categories
Alabama Ala. Code §§ 21-7-1; 25-1-20	20 or more employees	40 and older											
Alaska Alaska Stat. §§ 18.80.220; 47.30.865	One or more employees	40 and older	✓	Physical and mental	✓	✓	✓ (Includes changes in status)	✓ (Includes parenthood)	✓	✓			Mental illness
Arizona Ariz. Rev. Stat. § 41-1461	15 or more employees	40 and older	✓	Physical	✓	✓			✓	✓		✓	
Arkansas Ark. Code Ann. §§ 16-123-101; 11-4-601; 11-5-403	9 or more employees		✓	Physical and mental		✓		✓	✓	✓		✓[1]	
California Cal. Gov't. Code §§ 12920,12941; Cal. Lab. Code § 1101	5 or more employees	40 and older	✓	Physical and mental	✓	✓	✓	✓		✓	✓	✓	• Medical condition • Political activities or affiliations

"Private employers may not make employment decisions based on"

[1] Employers covered by FLSA

State	Law applies to employers with	Age	Ancestry or national origin	Disability	AIDS/HIV	Gender	Marital status	Pregnancy, childbirth and related medical conditions	Race or color	Religion or creed	Sexual orientation	Genetic testing information	Additional protected categories
			Private employers may not make employment decisions based on										
Colorado Colo. Rev. Stat. §§ 24-34-301, 24-34-401; 27-10-115	Law applies to all employers.	40 to 70	✓	Physical, mental and learning	✓	✓		✓	✓	✓			• Lawful conduct outside of work • Mental illness
Connecticut Conn. Gen. Stat. Ann. §§ 46a-51, 46a-60	3 or more employees	40 and older	✓	Present or past physical, mental or learning	✓	✓	✓	✓	✓	✓		✓	Mental retardation
Delaware Del. Code Ann. tit. 19, § 710	4 or more employees	40 to 70	✓	Physical or mental	✓	✓	✓	✓	✓	✓		✓	
District of Columbia D.C. Code Ann. §§ 2-1401.01; 7-1703.03	Law applies to all employers.	18 and older	✓	Physical or mental	✓	✓	✓	✓ (Includes parenthood)	✓	✓	✓		• Enrollment in vocational or professional or college education • Family duties • Personal appearance • Political affiliation • Smoker
Florida Fla. Stat. Ann. §§ 760.01, 760.50; 448.075	15 or more employees	No age limit	✓	"Handicap"	✓	✓	✓		✓	✓			Sickle cell trait
Georgia Ga. Code Ann. §§ 34-6A-1; 34-1-23; 34-5-1	15 or more employees (disability) 10 or more employees (gender)	40 to 70		Physical or mental		✓[2]							
Hawaii Haw. Rev. Stat. § 378-1	One or more employees	No age limit	✓	Physical or mental	✓	✓	✓	✓ (Includes breastfeeding)	✓	✓	✓		Arrest and court record (unless there is a conviction directly related to job)

[2] Wage discrimination only

State	Law applies to employers with	Age	Ancestry or national origin	Disability	AIDS/HIV	Gender	Marital status	Pregnancy, childbirth and related medical conditions	Race or color	Religion or creed	Sexual orientation	Genetic testing information	Additional protected categories
Idaho Idaho Code § 67-5909	5 or more employees	40 and older	✓	Physical or mental		✓		✓	✓	✓			
Illinois 775 Ill. Comp. Stat. §§ 5/1-101, 5/2-101; Ill. Admin. Code tit. 56, § 5210.110	15 or more employees	40 and older	✓	Physical or mental	✓	✓	✓	✓	✓	✓			• Arrest record • Citizen status • Military status • Unfavorable military discharge
Indiana Ind. Code Ann. §§ 22-9-1-1, 22-9-2-1	6 or more employees	40 to 70	✓	Physical or mental		✓			✓	✓			
Iowa Iowa Code § 216.1	4 or more employees	18 or older	✓	Physical or mental	✓	✓		✓	✓	✓			
Kansas Kan. Stat. Ann. §§ 44-1001, 44-1111, 44-1125; 65-6002(e)	4 or more employees	18 or older	✓	Physical or mental	✓	✓			✓	✓		✓	Military status
Kentucky Ky. Rev. Stat. Ann. § 344.040; 207.130; 342.197	8 or more employees	40 or older	✓	Physical (Includes black lung disease)	✓	✓			✓	✓			Smoker or nonsmoker
Louisiana La. Rev. Stat. Ann. §§ 23:301 to 23:352	20 or more employees		✓	Physical or mental		✓		✓ (Applies to employers with 25 or more employees)	✓	✓		✓	Sickle cell trait
Maine Me. Rev. Stat. Ann. tit. 5, §§ 4551, 4571	Law applies to all employers.	No age limit	✓	Physical or mental		✓		✓	✓	✓	✓	✓	
Maryland Md. Code 1957 Art. 49B, § 15	15 or more employees	No age limit	✓	Physical or mental	✓	✓	✓	✓	✓	✓	✓	✓	
Massachusetts Mass. Gen. Laws ch. 151B, § 1	6 or more employees	40 or older	✓	Physical or mental	✓	✓			✓	✓	✓	✓	

Private employers may not make employment decisions based on

State	Law applies to employers with	Age	Ancestry or national origin	Disability	AIDS/HIV	Gender	Marital status	Pregnancy, childbirth and related medical conditions	Race or color	Religion or creed	Sexual orientation	Genetic testing information	Additional protected categories
Private employers may not make employment decisions based on													
Michigan Mich. Comp. Laws §§ 37.1201, 37.2201, 37.1103	One or more employees	No age limit	✓	Physical or mental	✓	✓	✓	✓	✓	✓		✓	• Height or weight • Arrest record
Minnesota Minn. Stat. Ann. §§ 363.01; 181.974	One or more employees	18 or older	✓	Physical or mental	✓	✓	✓		✓	✓	✓	✓	• Member of local commission • Receiving public assistance
Missouri Mo. Rev. Stat. §§ 213.010; 191.665; 375.1306	6 or more employees	40 to 70	✓	Physical or mental	✓	✓			✓	✓	✓		
Montana Mont. Code Ann. §§ 49-2-101, 49-2-303	One or more employees	No age limit	✓	Physical or mental		✓			✓	✓	✓		
Nebraska Neb. Rev. Stat. §§ 48-1101; 48-1001; 20-168	15 or more employees	40 to 70[3]	✓	Physical or mental	✓	✓	✓		✓	✓	✓		
Nevada Nev. Rev. Stat. Ann. § 613.310 and foll.	15 or more employees	40 or older	✓	Physical or mental		✓			✓	✓	✓	✓	✓	Lawful use of any product when not at work
New Hampshire N.H. Rev. Stat. Ann. §§ 354-A: 2 and foll.; 141-H:3	6 or more employees	No age limit	✓	Physical or mental		✓	✓		✓	✓	✓	✓	✓	
New Jersey N.J. Stat. Ann. §§ 10:5-1; 34: 6B-1	Law applies to all employers.	18 to 70	✓	Past or present physical or mental	✓	✓	✓		✓	✓	✓	✓	✓	• Hereditary cellular or blood trait • Military service or status • Smoker or nonsmoker

[3] Employers with 25 or more employees

			Private employers may not make employment decisions based on											
State	Law applies to employers with	Age	Ancestry or national origin	Disability	AIDS/HIV	Gender	Marital status	Pregnancy, childbirth and related medical conditions	Race or color	Religion or creed	Sexual orientation	Genetic testing information	Additional protected categories
New Mexico N.M. Stat. Ann. § 28-1-1	4 or more employees	40 or older	✓	Physical or mental		✓	✓ (Applies to employers with 50 or more employees)	✓	✓	✓			Serious medical condition
New York N.Y. Exec. Law § 292; N.Y. Lab. Law § 201-d	4 or more employees	18 and over	✓	Physical or mental	✓	✓	✓	✓	✓	✓		✓	• Lawful use of any product when not at work • Political activities
North Carolina N.C. Gen. Stat. §§ 143-422.2; 168A-1; 95-28.1; 130A-148	15 or more employees	No age limit	✓	Physical or mental	✓	✓			✓	✓		✓	• Lawful use of any product when not at work • Sickle cell trait
North Dakota N.D. Cent. Code §§ 14-02.4-01; 34-01-17	One or more employees	40 or older	✓	Physical or mental		✓	✓	✓	✓	✓			• Lawful conduct outside of work • Receiving public assistance
Ohio Ohio Rev. Code Ann. §§ 4111.17; 4112.01	4 or more employees	40 or older	✓	Physical, mental or learning		✓		✓	✓	✓			
Oklahoma Okla. Stat. Ann. tit. 25, § 1301; tit. 36, § 3614.2; tit. 40, § 500; tit. 44, § 208	15 or more employees	40 or older	✓	Physical or mental		✓			✓	✓		✓	• Military service • Smoker or nonsmoker
Oregon Or. Rev. Stat. §§ 659A.100 and foll.; 659A.303	One or more employees	18 or older	✓	Physical or mental[4]		✓		✓	✓	✓	✓		

[4] Employers with 6 or more employees

State	Law applies to employers with	Age	Ancestry or national origin	Disability	AIDS/HIV	Gender	Marital status	Pregnancy, childbirth and related medical conditions	Race or color	Religion or creed	Sexual orientation	Genetic testing information	Additional protected categories
Pennsylvania 43 Pa. Cons. Stat. Ann. § 953, 336.3	4 or more employees	40 to 70	✓	Physical or mental		✓		✓ (Pregnancy not treated as a disability in terms of benefits)	✓	✓			• Familial status • GED rather than high school diploma
Rhode Island R.I. Gen. Laws §§ 28-6-17; 28-5-11; 2-28-10; 23-6-22; 23-20.7.1-1	4 or more employees	40 or older	✓	Physical or mental	✓	✓		✓	✓	✓	✓	✓	• Domestic abuse victim • Gender identity or expression • Smoker or nonsmoker
South Carolina S.C. Code Ann. § 1-13-20 and foll.	15 or more employees	40 or older	✓	Physical or mental		✓		✓	✓	✓			
South Dakota S.D. Codified Laws Ann. §§ 20-13-1; 60-12-15; 60-2-20; 62-1-17	Law applies to all employers.		✓	Physical, mental and learning		✓			✓	✓		✓	Preexisting injury
Tennessee Tenn. Code Ann. §§ 4-21-102; 4-21-401 and foll.; 8-50-103; 50-2-202	8 or more employees	40 or older	✓	Physical or mental		✓		✓ (Full-time employee who worked the previous 12 months is entitled to 4 months maternity leave. Pay at discretion of employer.)[5]	✓	✓			
Texas Tex. Lab. Code Ann. §§ 21.002, 21.101, 21.401	15 or more employees	40 or older	✓	Physical or mental		✓		✓	✓	✓		✓	
Utah Utah Code Ann. § 34A-5-102	15 or more employees	40 or older	✓	Follows federal law	✓[6]	✓		✓	✓	✓			

[5] Employers with 100 or more employees

[6] Follows federal ADA statutes

					Private employers may not make employment decisions based on								
State	Law applies to employers with	Age	Ancestry or national origin	Disability	AIDS/HIV	Gender	Marital status	Pregnancy, childbirth and related medical conditions	Race or color	Religion or creed	Sexual orientation	Genetic testing information	Additional protected categories
Vermont Vt. Stat. Ann. tit. 21, § 495; tit. 18, § 9333	One or more employees	18 or older	✓	Physical, mental or learning	✓	✓			✓	✓	✓	✓	Place of birth
Virginia Va. Code Ann. §§ 2.2-3900; 40.1-28.6; 51.5-3	Law applies to all employers.	No age limit	✓	Physical or mental		✓	✓	✓	✓	✓			
Washington Wash. Rev. Code Ann. §§ 49.60.040, 49.60.172 and foll.; 49.12.175; 49.44.090; Wash. Admin. Code § 162-30-020	8 or more employees	40 or older	✓	Physical, mental or sensory	✓	✓	✓	✓	✓	✓			Member of state militia
West Virginia W. Va. Code §§ 5-11-3, 5-11-9; 21-5B-1	12 or more employees	40 or older	✓	Physical or mental	✓	✓[7]			✓	✓			Smoker or nonsmoker
Wisconsin Wis. Stat. Ann. § 111.32	One or more employees	40 or older	✓	Physical or mental	✓	✓	✓	✓	✓	✓	✓	✓	• Arrest or conviction • Lawful use of any product when not at work • Military service or status
Wyoming Wyo. Stat. §§ 27-9-105; 19-11-104	2 or more employees	40 to 69	✓			✓			✓	✓			• Military service or status • Smoker or nonsmoker

[7] Employers with one or more employees

G. Full Text of Title VII

U.S. Code
Title 42: The Public Health and Welfare
Chapter 21: Civil Rights
Subchapter VI: Equal Employment Opportunities

An Act

To enforce the constitutional right to vote, to confer jurisdiction upon the district courts of the United States to provide injunctive relief against discrimination in public accommodations, to authorize the Attorney General to institute suits to protect constitutional rights in public facilities and public education, to extend the Commission on Civil Rights, to prevent discrimination in federally assisted programs, to establish a Commission on Equal Employment Opportunity, and for other purposes.

Be it enacted by the Senate and House of Representatives of the United States of America in Congress assembled, That this Act may be cited as the "Civil Rights Act of 1964".

    * * *

§ 2000e. [Sec. 701] Definitions

For the purposes of this subchapter—

(a) The term "person" includes one or more individuals, governments, governmental agencies, political sub-divisions, labor unions, partnerships, associations, corporations, legal representatives, mutual companies, joint-stock companies, trusts, unincorporated organizations, trustees, trustees in cases under title 11 [bankruptcy], or receivers.

(b) The term "employer" means a person engaged in an industry affecting commerce who has fifteen or more employees for each working day in each of twenty or more calendar weeks in the current or preceding calendar year, and any agent of such a person, but such term does not include (1) the United States, a corporation wholly owned by the Government of the United States, an Indian tribe, or any department or agency of the District of Columbia subject by statute to procedures of the competitive service (as defined in section 2102 of title 5 [of the United States Code]), or (2) a bona fide private membership club (other than a labor organization) which is exempt from taxation under section 501(c) of title 26 [the Internal Revenue Code of 1954], except that

during the first year after March 24, 1972 [the date of enactment of the Equal Employment Opportunity Act of 1972], persons having fewer than twenty-five employees (and their agents) shall not be considered employers.

(c) The term "employment agency" means any person regularly undertaking with or without compensation to procure employees for an employer or to procure for employees opportunities to work for an employer and includes an agent of such a person.

(d) The term "labor organization" means a labor organization engaged in an industry affecting commerce, and any agent of such an organization, and includes any organization of any kind, any agency, or employee representation committee, group, association, or plan so engaged in which employees participate and which exists for the purpose, in whole or in part, of dealing with employers concerning grievances, labor disputes, wages, rates of pay, hours, or other terms or conditions of employment, and any conference, general committee, joint or system board, or joint council so engaged which is subordinate to a national or international labor organization.

(e) A labor organization shall be deemed to be engaged in an industry affecting commerce if

(1) it maintains or operates a hiring hall or hiring office which procures employees for an employer or procures for employees opportunities to work for an employer, or

(2) the number of its members (or, where it is a labor organization composed of other labor organizations or their representatives, if the aggregate number of the members of such other labor organization) is

(A) twenty-five or more during the first year after March 24, 1972 [the date of enactment of the Equal Employment Opportunity Act of 1972], or

(B) fifteen or more thereafter, and such labor organization—

(1) is the certified representative of employees under the provisions of the National Labor Relations Act, as amended [29 U.S.C. 151 et seq.], or the Railway Labor Act, as amended [45 U.S.C. 151 et seq.];

(2) although not certified, is a national or inter-national labor organization or a local labor organization recognized or acting as the repre-sentative of employees of an employer or employers engaged in an industry affecting commerce; or

(3) has chartered a local labor organization or subsidiary body which is representing or actively

seeking to represent employees of employers within the meaning of paragraph (1) or (2); or

(4) has been chartered by a labor organization representing or actively seeking to represent employees within the meaning of paragraph (1) or (2) as the local or subordinate body through which such employees may enjoy membership or become affiliated with such labor organization; or

(5) is a conference, general committee, joint or system board, or joint council subordinate to a national or international labor organization, which includes a labor organization engaged in an industry affecting commerce within the meaning of any of the preceding paragraphs of this subsection.

(f) The term "employee" means an individual employed by an employer, except that the term "employee" shall not include any person elected to public office in any State or political subdivision of any State by the qualified voters thereof, or any person chosen by such officer to be on such officer's personal staff, or an appointee on the policy making level or an immediate adviser with respect to the exercise of the constitutional or legal powers of the office. The exemption set forth in the preceding sentence shall not include employees subject to the civil service laws of a State government, governmental agency or political subdivision. With respect to employment in a foreign country, such term includes an individual who is a citizen of the United States.

(g) The term "commerce" means trade, traffic, commerce, transportation, transmission, or communication among the several States; or between a State and any place outside thereof; or within the District of Columbia, or a possession of the United States; or between points in the same State but through a point outside thereof.

(h) The term "industry affecting commerce" means any activity, business, or industry in commerce or in which a labor dispute would hinder or obstruct commerce or the free flow of commerce and includes any activity or industry "affecting commerce" within the meaning of the Labor-Management Reporting and Disclosure Act of 1959 [29 U.S.C. 401 et seq.], and further includes any governmental industry, business, or activity.

(i) The term "State" includes a State of the United States, the District of Columbia, Puerto Rico, the Virgin Islands, American Samoa, Guam, Wake Island, the Canal Zone, and Outer Continental Shelf lands defined in the Outer Continental Shelf Lands Act [43 U.S.C. 1331 et seq.].

(j) The term "religion" includes all aspects of religious observance and practice, as well as belief, unless an

employer demonstrates that he is unable to reasonably accommodate to an employee's or prospective employee's religious observance or practice without undue hardship on the conduct of the employer's business.

(k) The terms "because of sex" or "on the basis of sex" include, but are not limited to, because of or on the basis of pregnancy, childbirth, or related medical conditions; and women affected by pregnancy, childbirth, or related medical conditions shall be treated the same for all employment-related purposes, including receipt of benefits under fringe benefit programs, as other persons not so affected but similar in their ability or inability to work, and nothing in section 2000e-2(h) of this title [section 703(h)] shall be interpreted to permit otherwise. This subsection shall not require an employer to pay for health insurance benefits for abortion, except where the life of the mother would be endangered if the fetus were carried to term, or except where medical complications have arisen from an abortion: Provided, That nothing herein shall preclude an employer from providing abortion benefits or otherwise affect bargaining agreements in regard to abortion.

(l) The term "complaining party" means the Commission, the Attorney General, or a person who may bring an action or proceeding under this subchapter.

(m) The term "demonstrates" means meets the burdens of production and persuasion.

(n) The term "respondent" means an employer, employment agency, labor organization, joint labor-management committee controlling apprenticeship or other training or retraining program, including an on-the-job training program, or Federal entity subject to section 2000e-16 of this title.

§ 2000e-1. [Sec. 702] Exemption

(a) This subchapter shall not apply to an employer with respect to the employment of aliens outside any State, or to a religious corporation, association, educational institution, or society with respect to the employment of individuals of a particular religion to perform work connected with the carrying on by such corporation, association, educational institution, or society of its activities.

(b) It shall not be unlawful under section 2000e-2 or 2000e-3 of this title [section 703 or 704] for an employer (or a corporation controlled by an employer), labor organization, employment agency, or joint labor-management committee controlling apprenticeship or other training or retraining (including on-the-job training programs) to take any action otherwise prohibited by such section, with respect to an employee in a workplace in a foreign country if compliance with such section would cause such employer (or such corporation), such organization, such agency, or such committee to violate the law of the foreign country in which such workplace is located.

(c)

(1) If an employer controls a corporation whose place of incorporation is a foreign country, any practice prohibited by section 2000e-2 or 2000e-3 of this title *[section 703 or 704]* engaged in by such corporation shall be presumed to be engaged in by such employer.

(2) Sections 2000e-2 and 2000e-3 of this title *[sections 703 and 704]* shall not apply with respect to the foreign operations of an employer that is a foreign person not controlled by an American employer.

(3) For purposes of this subsection, the determination of whether an employer controls a corporation shall be based on—

(A) the interrelation of operations;

(B) the common management;

(C) the centralized control of labor relations; and

(D) the common ownership or financial control, of the employer and the corporation.

§ 2000e-2. [Sec. 703] Unlawful Employment Practices

(a) It shall be an unlawful employment practice for an employer —

(1) to fail or refuse to hire or to discharge any individual, or otherwise to discriminate against any individual with respect to his compensation, terms, conditions, or privileges of employment, because of such individual's race, color, religion, sex, or national origin; or

(2) to limit, segregate, or classify his employees or applicants for employment in any way which would deprive or tend to deprive any individual of employment opportunities or otherwise adversely affect his status as an employee, because of such individual's race, color, religion, sex, or national origin.

(b) It shall be an unlawful employment practice for an employment agency to fail or refuse to refer for employment, or otherwise to discriminate against, any individual because of his race, color, religion, sex, or national origin, or to classify or refer for employment any individual on the basis of his race, color, religion, sex, or national origin.

(c) It shall be an unlawful employment practice for a labor organization—

(1) to exclude or to expel from its membership, or otherwise to discriminate against, any individual because of his race, color, religion, sex, or national origin;

(2) to limit, segregate, or classify its membership or applicants for membership, or to classify or fail or refuse to refer for employment any individual, in any way which would deprive or tend to deprive any individual of employment opportunities, or would limit such employment opportunities or otherwise adversely affect his status as an employee or as an applicant for employment, because of such individual's race, color, religion, sex, or national origin; or

(3) to cause or attempt to cause an employer to discriminate against an individual in violation of this section.

(d) It shall be an unlawful employment practice for any employer, labor organization, or joint labor-management committee controlling apprenticeship or other training or retraining, including on-the-job training programs to discriminate against any individual because of his race, color, religion, sex, or national origin in admission to, or employment in, any program established to provide apprenticeship or other training.

(e) Notwithstanding any other provision of this subchapter,

(1) it shall not be an unlawful employment practice for an employer to hire and employ employees, for an employment agency to classify, or refer for employment any individual, for a labor organization to classify its membership or to classify or refer for employment any individual, or for an employer, labor organization, or joint labor-management committee controlling apprenticeship or other training or retraining programs to admit or employ any individual in any such program, on the basis of his religion, sex, or national origin in those certain instances where religion, sex, or national origin is a bona fide occupational qualification reasonably necessary to the normal operation of that particular business or enterprise, and

(2) it shall not be an unlawful employment practice for a school, college, university, or other educational institution or institution of learning to hire and employ employees of a particular religion if such school, college, university, or other educational institution or institution of learning is, in whole or in substantial part, owned, supported, controlled, or managed by a particular religion or by a particular religious corporation, association, or society, or if the curriculum of such school, college, university, or other educational

institution or institution of learning is directed toward the propagation of a particular religion.

(f) As used in this subchapter, the phrase "unlawful employment practice" shall not be deemed to include any action or measure taken by an employer, labor organization, joint labor-management committee, or employment agency with respect to an individual who is a member of the Communist Party of the United States or of any other organization required to register as a Communist-action or Communist-front organization by final order of the Subversive Activities Control Board pursuant to the Subversive Activities Control Act of 1950 [50 U.S.C. 781 et seq.].

(g) Notwithstanding any other provision of this subchapter, it shall not be an unlawful employment practice for an employer to fail or refuse to hire and employ any individual for any position, for an employer to discharge any individual from any position, or for an employment agency to fail or refuse to refer any individual for employment in any position, or for a labor organization to fail or refuse to refer any individual for employment in any position, if—

(1) the occupancy of such position, or access to the premises in or upon which any part of the duties of such position is performed or is to be performed, is subject to any requirement imposed in the interest of the national security of the United States under any security program in effect pursuant to or administered under any statute of the United States or any Executive order of the President; and

(2) such individual has not fulfilled or has ceased to fulfill that requirement.

(h) Notwithstanding any other provision of this subchapter, it shall not be an unlawful employment practice for an employer to apply different standards of compensation, or different terms, conditions, or privileges of employment pursuant to a bona fide seniority or merit system, or a system which measures earnings by quantity or quality of production or to employees who work in different locations, provided that such differences are not the result of an intention to discriminate because of race, color, religion, sex, or national origin, nor shall it be an unlawful employment practice for an employer to give and to act upon the results of any professionally developed ability test provided that such test, its administration or action upon the results is not designed, intended or used to discriminate because of race, color, religion, sex or national origin. It shall not be an unlawful employment practice under this subchapter for any employer to differentiate upon the basis of sex in determining the amount of the wages or compensation paid or to be paid to employees of such employer if such differentiation is authorized by the provisions of section 206(d) of title 29 [section 6(d) of the Fair Labor Standards Act of 1938, as amended].

(i) Nothing contained in this subchapter shall apply to any business or enterprise on or near an Indian reservation with respect to any publicly announced employment practice of such business or enterprise under which a preferential treatment is given to any individual because he is an Indian living on or near a reservation.

(j) Nothing contained in this subchapter shall be interpreted to require any employer, employment agency, labor organization, or joint labor-management committee subject to this subchapter to grant preferential treatment to any individual or to any group because of the race, color, religion, sex, or national origin of such individual or group on account of an imbalance which may exist with respect to the total number or percentage of persons of any race, color, religion, sex, or national origin employed by any employer, referred or classified for employment by any employment agency or labor organization, admitted to membership or classified by any labor organization, or admitted to, or employed in, any apprenticeship or other training program, in comparison with the total number or percentage of persons of such race, color, religion, sex, or national origin in any community, State, section, or other area, or in the available work force in any community, State, section, or other area.

(k)

(1)

(A) An unlawful employment practice based on disparate impact is established under this title only if—

(i) a complaining party demonstrates that a respondent uses a particular employment practice that causes a disparate impact on the basis of race, color, religion, sex, or national origin and the respondent fails to demonstrate that the challenged practice is job related for the position in question and consistent with business necessity; or

(ii) the complaining party makes the demonstration described in subparagraph (C) with respect to an alternative employment practice and the respondent refuses to adopt such alternative employment practice.

(B)

(i) With respect to demonstrating that a particular employment practice causes a disparate impact as described in subparagraph (A)(i), the complaining party shall demonstrate that each particular challenged employment practice causes a disparate impact, except that if the complaining party can demonstrate to the court that the elements of a respondent's decision-making process are not capable of separation for analysis, the decision-making process may be analyzed as one employment practice.

(ii) If the respondent demonstrates that a specific employment practice does not cause the disparate impact, the respondent shall not be required to demonstrate that such practice is required by business necessity.

(C) The demonstration referred to by subparagraph (A)(ii) shall be in accordance with the law as it existed on June 4, 1989, with respect to the concept of "alternative employment practice".

(2) A demonstration that an employment practice is required by business necessity may not be used as a defense against a claim of intentional discrimination under this title.

(3) Notwithstanding any other provision of this title, a rule barring the employment of an individual who currently and knowingly uses or possesses a controlled substance, as defined in schedules I and II of section 102(6) of the Controlled Substances Act (21 U.S.C. 802(6)), other than the use or possession of a drug taken under the supervision of a licensed health care professional, or any other use or possession authorized by the Controlled Substances Act *[21 U.S.C. 801 et seq.]* or any other provision of Federal law, shall be considered an unlawful employment practice under this title only if such rule is adopted or applied with an intent to discriminate because of race, color, religion, sex, or national origin.

(l) It shall be an unlawful employment practice for a respondent, in connection with the selection or referral of applicants or candidates for employment or promotion, to adjust the scores of, use different cutoff scores for, or otherwise alter the results of, employment related tests on the basis of race, color, religion, sex, or national origin.

(m) Except as otherwise provided in this title, an unlawful employment practice is established when the complaining party demonstrates that race, color, religion, sex, or national origin was a motivating factor for any employment practice, even though other factors also motivated the practice.

(n)

(1)

(A) Notwithstanding any other provision of law, and except as provided in paragraph (2), an employment practice that implements and is within the scope of a litigated or consent judgment or order that resolves a claim of employment discrimination under the Constitution or Federal civil rights laws may not be challenged under the circumstances described in subparagraph (B).

(B) A practice described in subparagraph (A) may not be challenged in a claim under the Constitution or Federal civil rights laws—

(i) by a person who, prior to the entry of the judgment or order described in subparagraph (A), had—

(I) actual notice of the proposed judgment or order sufficient to apprise such person that such judgment or order might adversely affect the interests and legal rights of such person and that an opportunity was available to present objections to such judgment or order by a future date certain; and

(II) a reasonable opportunity to present objections to such judgment or order; or

(ii) by a person whose interests were adequately represented by another person who had previously challenged the judgment or order on the same legal grounds and with a similar factual situation, unless there has been an intervening change in law or fact.

(2) Nothing in this subsection shall be construed to—

(A) alter the standards for intervention under rule 24 of the Federal Rules of Civil Procedure or apply to the rights of parties who have successfully intervened pursuant to such rule in the proceeding in which the parties intervened;

(B) apply to the rights of parties to the action in which a litigated or consent judgment or order was entered, or of members of a class represented or sought to be represented in such action, or of members of a group on whose behalf relief was sought in such action by the Federal Government;

(C) prevent challenges to a litigated or consent judgment or order on the ground that such judgment or order was obtained through collusion or fraud, or is transparently invalid or was entered by a court lacking subject matter jurisdiction; or

(D) authorize or permit the denial to any person of the due process of law required by the Constitution.

(3) Any action not precluded under this subsection that challenges an employment consent judgment or order described in paragraph (1) shall be brought in the court, and if possible before the judge, that entered

such judgment or order. Nothing in this subsection shall preclude a transfer of such action pursuant to section 1404 of title 28, United States Code.

§ 2000e-3. [Sec. 704] Other Unlawful Employment Practices

(a) It shall be an unlawful employment practice for an employer to discriminate against any of his employees or applicants for employment, for an employment agency, or joint labor-management committee controlling apprenticeship or other training or retraining, including on-the-job training programs, to discriminate against any individual, or for a labor organization to discriminate against any member thereof or applicant for membership, because he has opposed any practice made an unlawful employment practice by this subchapter, or because he has made a charge, testified, assisted, or participated in any manner in an investigation, proceeding, or hearing under this subchapter.

(b) It shall be an unlawful employment practice for an employer, labor organization, employment agency, or joint labor-management committee controlling apprenticeship or other training or retraining, including on-the-job training programs, to print or publish or cause to be printed or published any notice or advertisement relating to employment by such an employer or membership in or any classification or referral for employment by such a labor organization, or relating to any classification or referral for employment by such an employment agency, or relating to admission to, or employment in, any program established to provide apprenticeship or other training by such a joint labor-management committee, indicating any preference, limitation, specification, or discrimination, based on race, color, religion, sex, or national origin, except that such a notice or advertisement may indicate a preference, limitation, specification, or discrimination based on religion, sex, or national origin when religion, sex, or national origin is a bona fide occupational qualification for employment.

§ 2000e-4. [Sec. 705] Equal Employment Opportunity Commission

(a) There is hereby created a Commission to be known as the Equal Employment Opportunity Commission, which shall be composed of five members, not more than three of whom shall be members of the same political party. Members of the Commission shall be appointed by the President by and with the advice and consent of the Senate for a term of five years. Any individual chosen to fill a vacancy shall be appointed only for the unexpired term of the member whom he

shall succeed, and all members of the Commission shall continue to serve until their successors are appointed and qualified, except that no such member of the Commission shall continue to serve

(1) for more than sixty days when the Congress is in session unless a nomination to fill such vacancy shall have been submitted to the Senate, or

(2) after the adjournment sine die of the session of the Senate in which such nomination was submitted. The President shall designate one member to serve as Chairman of the Commission, and one member to serve as Vice Chairman. The Chairman shall be responsible on behalf of the Commission for the administrative operations of the Commission, and, except as provided in subsection (b) of this section, shall appoint, in accordance with the provisions of title 5 *[United States Code]* governing appointments in the competitive service, such officers, agents, attorneys, administrative law judges *[hearing examiners]*, and employees as he deems necessary to assist it in the performance of its functions and to fix their compensation in accordance with the provisions of chapter 51 and subchapter III of chapter 53 of title 5 *[United States Code]*, relating to classification and General Schedule pay rates: Provided, That assignment, removal, and compensation of administrative law judges *[hearing examiners]* shall be in accordance with sections 3105, 3344, 5372, and 7521 of title 5 *[United States Code]*.

(b)

(1) There shall be a General Counsel of the Commission appointed by the President, by and with the advice and consent of the Senate, for a term of four years. The General Counsel shall have responsibility for the conduct of litigation as provided in sections 2000e-5 and 2000e-6 of this title *[sections 706 and 707]*. The General Counsel shall have such other duties as the Commission may prescribe or as may be provided by law and shall concur with the Chairman of the Commission on the appointment and supervision of regional attorneys. The General Counsel of the Commission on the effective date of this Act shall continue in such position and perform the functions specified in this subsection until a successor is appointed and qualified.

(2) Attorneys appointed under this section may, at the direction of the Commission, appear for and represent the Commission in any case in court, provided that the Attorney General shall conduct all litigation to which the Commission is a party in the Supreme Court pursuant to this subchapter.

(c) A vacancy in the Commission shall not impair the right of the remaining members to exercise all the powers of the Commission and three members thereof shall constitute a quorum.

(d) The Commission shall have an official seal which shall be judicially noticed.

(e) The Commission shall at the close of each fiscal year report to the Congress and to the President concerning the action it has taken *[the names, salaries, and duties of all individuals in its employ]* and the moneys it has disbursed. It shall make such further reports on the cause of and means of eliminating discrimination and such recommendations for further legislation as may appear desirable.

(f) The principal office of the Commission shall be in or near the District of Columbia, but it may meet or exercise any or all its powers at any other place. The Commission may establish such regional or State offices as it deems necessary to accomplish the purpose of this subchapter.

(g) The Commission shall have power—

(1) to cooperate with and, with their consent, utilize regional, State, local, and other agencies, both public and private, and individuals;

(2) to pay to witnesses whose depositions are taken or who are summoned before the Commission or any of its agents the same witness and mileage fees as are paid to witnesses in the courts of the United States;

(3) to furnish to persons subject to this subchapter such technical assistance as they may request to further their compliance with this subchapter or an order issued thereunder;

(4) upon the request of (i) any employer, whose employees or some of them, or (ii) any labor organization, whose members or some of them, refuse or threaten to refuse to cooperate in effectuating the provisions of this subchapter, to assist in such effectuation by conciliation or such other remedial action as is provided by this subchapter;

(5) to make such technical studies as are appropriate to effectuate the purposes and policies of this sub-chapter and to make the results of such studies available to the public;

(6) to intervene in a civil action brought under section 2000e-5 of this title *[section 706]* by an aggrieved party against a respondent other than a government, governmental agency or political subdivision.

(h)

(1) The Commission shall, in any of its educational or promotional activities, cooperate with other departments and agencies in the performance of such educational and promotional activities.

(2) In exercising its powers under this title, the Commission shall carry out educational and outreach activities (including dissemination of information in languages other than English) targeted to—

(A) individuals who historically have been victims of employment discrimination and have not been equitably served by the Commission; and

(B) individuals on whose behalf the Commission has authority to enforce any other law prohibiting employment discrimination, concerning rights and obligations under this title or such law, as the case may be.

(i) All officers, agents, attorneys, and employees of the Commission shall be subject to the provisions of section 7324 of title 5 *[section 9 of the Act of August 2, 1939, as amended (the Hatch Act)]*, notwithstanding any exemption contained in such section.

(j)

(1) The Commission shall establish a Technical Assistance Training Institute, through which the Commission shall provide technical assistance and training regarding the laws and regulations enforced by the Commission.

(2) An employer or other entity covered under this title shall not be excused from compliance with the requirements of this title because of any failure to receive technical assistance under this subsection.

(3) There are authorized to be appropriated to carry out this subsection such sums as may be necessary for fiscal year 1992.

§ 2000e-5. [Sec. 706] Enforcement Provisions

(a) The Commission is empowered, as hereinafter provided, to prevent any person from engaging in any unlawful employment practice as set forth in section 2000e-2 or 2000e-3 of this title *[section 703 or 704]*.

(b) Whenever a charge is filed by or on behalf of a person claiming to be aggrieved, or by a member of the Commission, alleging that an employer, employment agency, labor organization, or joint labor-management committee controlling apprenticeship or other training or retraining, including on-the-job training programs, has engaged in an unlawful employment practice, the Commission shall serve a notice of the charge (including the date, place and circumstances of the alleged unlaw-ful employment practice) on such employer, employment agency, labor organization, or joint labor-management committee (hereinafter referred to as the "respondent") within ten days, and shall make an investigation thereof. Charges shall be in writing under oath or affirmation and shall contain such information and be in such form as the Commission requires. Charges shall not be made public by the Commission. If the Commission determines after such investigation that there is not reasonable cause to believe that the charge is true, it shall dismiss the charge and promptly notify the person claiming to be aggrieved and the respondent of its action. In determining whether reasonable cause exists, the Commission shall accord substantial weight to final findings and orders made by State or local authorities in proceedings commenced under State or local law pursuant to the requirements of subsections (c) and (d) of this section. If the Commission determines after such investigation that there is reasonable cause to believe that the charge is true, the Commission shall endeavor to eliminate any such alleged unlawful employment practice by informal methods of conference, conciliation, and persuasion. Nothing said or done during and as a part of such informal endeavors may be made public by the Commission, its officers or employees, or used as evidence in a subsequent proceeding without the written consent of the persons concerned. Any person who makes public information in violation of this subsection shall be fined not more than $1,000 or imprisoned for not more than one year, or both. The Commission shall make its determination on reasonable cause as promptly as possible and, so far as practicable, not later than one hundred and twenty days from the filing of the charge or, where applicable under subsection (c) or (d) of this section, from the date upon which the Commission is authorized to take action with respect to the charge.

(c) In the case of an alleged unlawful employment practice occurring in a State, or political subdivision of a State, which has a State or local law prohibiting the unlawful employment practice alleged and establishing or authorizing a State or local authority to grant or seek relief from such practice or to institute criminal proceedings with respect thereto upon receiving notice thereof, no charge may be filed under subsection (a) of this section by the person aggrieved before the expiration of sixty days after proceedings have been commenced under the State or local law, unless such proceedings have been earlier terminated, provided that such sixty-day period shall be extended to one hundred and twenty days during the first year after the effective date of such State or local law. If any requirement for the commencement of such proceedings is imposed by a State or local authority other than a requirement of the filing of a written and signed statement of the facts upon which the proceeding is based, the proceeding shall be deemed to have been commenced for the purposes of this subsection at the time such statement is sent by registered mail to the appropriate State or local authority.

(d) In the case of any charge filed by a member of the Commission alleging an unlawful employment practice occurring in a State or political subdivision of a State which has a State or local law prohibiting the practice alleged and establishing or authorizing a State or local authority to grant or seek relief from such practice or to institute criminal proceedings with respect thereto upon receiving notice thereof, the Commission shall, before taking any action with respect to such charge, notify the appropriate State or local officials and, upon request, afford them a reasonable time, but not less than sixty days (provided that such sixty-day period shall be extended to one hundred and twenty days during the first year after the effective day of such State or local law), unless a shorter period is requested, to act under such State or local law to remedy the practice alleged.

(e)

(1) A charge under this section shall be filed within one hundred and eighty days after the alleged unlawful employment practice occurred and notice of the charge (including the date, place and circumstances of the alleged unlawful employment practice) shall be served upon the person against whom such charge is made within ten days thereafter, except that in a case of an unlawful employment practice with respect to which the person aggrieved has initially instituted proceedings with a State or local agency with authority to grant or seek relief from such practice or to institute criminal proceedings with respect thereto upon receiving notice thereof, such charge shall be filed by or on behalf of the person aggrieved within three hundred days after the alleged unlawful employment practice occurred, or within thirty days after receiving notice that the State or local agency has terminated the proceedings under the State or local law, whichever is earlier, and a copy of such charge shall be filed by the Commission with the State or local agency.

(2) For purposes of this section, an unlawful employment practice occurs, with respect to a seniority system that has been adopted for an intentionally discriminatory purpose in violation of this title (whether or not that discriminatory purpose is apparent on the face of the seniority provision), when the seniority system is adopted, when an individual becomes subject to the seniority system, or when a person aggrieved is injured by the application of the seniority system or provision of the system.

(f)

(1) If within thirty days after a charge is filed with the Commission or within thirty days after expiration of

any period of reference under subsection (c) or (d) of this section, the Commission has been unable to secure from the respondent a conciliation agreement acceptable to the Commission, the Commission may bring a civil action against any respondent not a government, governmental agency, or political sub-division named in the charge. In the case of a respondent which is a government, governmental agency, or political subdivision, if the Commission has been unable to secure from the respondent a conciliation agreement acceptable to the Commission, the Commission shall take no further action and shall refer the case to the Attorney General who may bring a civil action against such respondent in the appropriate United States district court. The person or persons aggrieved shall have the right to intervene in a civil action brought by the Commission or the Attorney General in a case involving a government, govern-mental agency, or political subdivision. If a charge filed with the Commission pursuant to subsection (b) of this section, is dismissed by the Commission, or if within one hundred and eighty days from the filing of such charge or the expiration of any period of reference under subsection (c) or (d) of this section, whichever is later, the Commission has not filed a civil action under this section or the Attorney General has not filed a civil action in a case involving a government, governmental agency, or political subdivision, or the Commission has not entered into a conciliation agreement to which the person aggrieved is a party, the Commission, or the Attorney General in a case involving a government, governmental agency, or political subdivision, shall so notify the person aggrieved and within ninety days after the giving of such notice a civil action may be brought against the respondent named in the charge (A) by the person claiming to be aggrieved or (B) if such charge was filed by a member of the Commission, by any person whom the charge alleges was aggrieved by the alleged unlawful employment practice. Upon application by the complainant and in such circumstances as the court may deem just, the court may appoint an attorney for such complainant and may authorize the commencement of the action without the payment of fees, costs, or security. Upon timely application, the court may, in its discretion, permit the Commission, or the Attorney General in a case involving a govern-ment, governmental agency, or political subdivision, to intervene in such civil action upon certification that the case is of general public importance. Upon request, the court may, in its discretion, stay further proceedings for not more than sixty days pending the termination of State or local proceedings described in subsection (c) or (d) of this section or further efforts of the Commission to obtain voluntary compliance.

(2) Whenever a charge is filed with the Commission and the Commission concludes on the basis of a preliminary investigation that prompt judicial action is necessary to carry out the purposes of this Act, the Commission, or the Attorney General in a case involving a government, governmental agency, or political subdivision, may bring an action for appropriate temporary or preliminary relief pending final dis-position of such charge. Any temporary restraining order or other order granting preliminary or temporary relief shall be issued in accordance with rule 65 of the Federal Rules of Civil Procedure. It shall be the duty of a court having jurisdiction over proceedings under this section to assign cases for hearing at the earliest practicable date and to cause such cases to be in every way expedited.

(3) Each United States district court and each United States court of a place subject to the jurisdiction of the United States shall have jurisdiction of actions brought under this subchapter. Such an action may be brought in any judicial district in the State in which the unlawful employment practice is alleged to have been committed, in the judicial district in which the employment records relevant to such practice are maintained and administered, or in the judicial district in which the aggrieved person would have worked but for the alleged unlawful employment practice, but if the respondent is not found within any such district, such an action may be brought within the judicial district in which the respondent has his principal office. For purposes of sections 1404 and 1406 of title 28 *[of the United States Code]*, the judicial district in which the respondent has his principal office shall in all cases be considered a district in which the action might have been brought.

(4) It shall be the duty of the chief judge of the district (or in his absence, the acting chief judge) in which the case is pending immediately to designate a judge in such district to hear and determine the case. In the event that no judge in the district is available to hear and determine the case, the chief judge of the district, or the acting chief judge, as the case may be, shall certify this fact to the chief judge of the circuit (or in his absence, the acting chief judge) who shall then designate a district or circuit judge of the circuit to hear and determine the case.

(5) It shall be the duty of the judge designated pursuant to this subsection to assign the case for hearing at the

earliest practicable date and to cause the case to be in every way expedited. If such judge has not scheduled the case for trial within one hundred and twenty days after issue has been joined, that judge may appoint a master pursuant to rule 53 of the Federal Rules of Civil Procedure.

(g)

(1) If the court finds that the respondent has intentionally engaged in or is intentionally engaging in an unlawful employment practice charged in the complaint, the court may enjoin the respondent from engaging in such unlawful employment practice, and order such affirmative action as may be appropriate, which may include, but is not limited to, reinstatement or hiring of employees, with or without back pay (payable by the employer, employment agency, or labor organization, as the case may be, responsible for the unlawful employment practice), or any other equitable relief as the court deems appropriate. Back pay liability shall not accrue from a date more than two years prior to the filing of a charge with the Commission. Interim earnings or amounts earnable with reasonable diligence by the person or persons discriminated against shall operate to reduce the back pay otherwise allowable.

(2)

(A) No order of the court shall require the admission or reinstatement of an individual as a member of a union, or the hiring, reinstatement, or promotion of an individual as an employee, or the payment to him of any back pay, if such individual was refused admission, suspended, or expelled, or was refused employment or advancement or was suspended or discharged for any reason other than discrimination on account of race, color, religion, sex, or national origin or in violation of section 2000e-3(a) of this title *[section 704(a)]*.

(B) On a claim in which an individual proves a violation under section 2000e-2(m) of this title *[section 703(m)]* and a respondent demonstrates that the respondent would have taken the same action in the absence of the impermissible motivating factor, the court—

(i) may grant declaratory relief, injunctive relief (except as provided in clause (ii)), and attorney's fees and costs demonstrated to be directly attributable only to the pursuit of a claim under section 2000e-2(m) of this title *[section 703(m)]*; and

(ii) shall not award damages or issue an order requiring any admission, reinstatement, hiring, promotion, or payment, described in subparagraph (A).

(h) The provisions of chapter 6 of title 29 *[the Act entitled "An Act to amend the Judicial Code and to define and limit the jurisdiction of courts sitting in equity, and for other purposes," approved March 23, 1932 (29 U.S.C. 105-115)]* shall not apply with respect to civil actions brought under this section.

(i) In any case in which an employer, employment agency, or labor organization fails to comply with an order of a court issued in a civil action brought under this section, the Commission may commence proceedings to compel compliance with such order.

(j) Any civil action brought under this section and any proceedings brought under subsection (i) of this section shall be subject to appeal as provided in sections 1291 and 1292, title 28 *[United States Code]*.

(k) In any action or proceeding under this subchapter the court, in its discretion, may allow the prevailing party, other than the Commission or the United States, a reasonable attorney's fee (including expert fees) as part of the costs, and the Commission and the United States shall be liable for costs the same as a private person.

§ 2000e-6. [Sec. 707] Civil Actions by the Attorney General

(a) Whenever the Attorney General has reasonable cause to believe that any person or group of persons is engaged in a pattern or practice of resistance to the full enjoyment of any of the rights secured by this subchapter, and that the pattern or practice is of such a nature and is intended to deny the full exercise of the rights herein described, the Attorney General may bring a civil action in the appropriate district court of the United States by filing with it a complaint (1) signed by him (or in his absence the Acting Attorney General), (2) setting forth facts pertaining to such pattern or practice, and (3) requesting such relief, including an application for a permanent or temporary injunction, restraining order or other order against the person or persons responsible for such pattern or practice, as he deems necessary to insure the full enjoyment of the rights herein described.

(b) The district courts of the United States shall have and shall exercise jurisdiction of proceedings instituted pursuant to this section, and in any such proceeding the Attorney General may file with the clerk of such court a request that a court of three judges be convened to hear and determine the case. Such request by the Attorney General shall be accompanied by a certificate that, in his opinion, the case is of general public importance. A copy of the certificate and request for a three-judge court shall be immediately furnished by such clerk to the chief judge of the circuit (or in his absence, the presiding circuit judge of the circuit) in which the case is pending. Upon receipt of such request it shall be the duty of the chief judge of the circuit or the presiding circuit judge, as the case may be, to designate immediately three judges in such circuit, of whom at least one shall be a circuit judge and another of whom shall be a district judge of the court in which the proceeding was instituted, to hear and determine such case, and it shall be the duty of the judges so designated to assign the case for hearing at the earliest practicable date, to participate in the hearing and determination thereof, and to cause the case to be in every way expedited. An appeal from the final judgment of such court will lie to the Supreme Court.

In the event the Attorney General fails to file such a request in any such proceeding, it shall be the duty of the chief judge of the district (or in his absence, the acting chief judge) in which the case is pending immediately to designate a judge in such district to hear and determine the case. In the event that no judge in the district is available to hear and determine the case, the chief judge of the district, or the acting chief judge, as the case may be, shall certify this fact to the chief judge of the circuit (or in his absence, the acting chief judge) who shall then designate a district or circuit judge of the circuit to hear and determine the case.

It shall be the duty of the judge designated pursuant to this section to assign the case for hearing at the earliest practicable date and to cause the case to be in every way expedited.

(c) Effective two years after March 24, 1972 [the date of enactment of the Equal Employment Opportunity Act of 1972], the functions of the Attorney General under this section shall be transferred to the Commission, together with such personnel, property, records, and unexpended balances of appropriations, allocations, and other funds employed, used, held, available, or to be made available in connection with such functions unless the President submits, and neither House of Congress vetoes, a reorganization plan pursuant to chapter 9 of title 5 [United States Code], inconsistent with the provisions of this subsection. The Commission shall carry out such functions in accordance with subsections (d) and (e) of this section.

(d) Upon the transfer of functions provided for in subsection (c) of this section, in all suits commenced pursuant to this section prior to the date of such transfer, proceedings shall continue without abatement, all court orders and decrees shall remain in effect, and the Commission shall be substituted as a party for the United States of America, the Attorney General, or the Acting Attorney General, as appropriate.

(e) Subsequent to March 24, 1972 [the date of enactment of the Equal Employment Opportunity Act of 1972], the Commission shall have authority to investigate and act on a charge of a pattern or practice of discrimination, whether filed by or on behalf of a person claiming to be aggrieved or by a member of the Commission. All such actions shall be conducted in accordance with the procedures set forth in section 2000e-5 of this title [section 706].

§ 2000e-7. [Sec. 708] Effect on State Laws

Nothing in this subchapter shall be deemed to exempt or relieve any person from any liability, duty, penalty, or punishment provided by any present or future law of any State or political subdivision of a State, other than any such law which purports to require or permit the doing of any act which would be an unlawful employment practice under this subchapter.

§ 2000e-8. [Sec. 709] Investigations, Inspections, Records, State Agencies

(a) In connection with any investigation of a charge filed under section 2000e-5 of this title [section 706], the Commission or its designated representative shall at all reasonable times have access to, for the purposes of examination, and the right to copy any evidence of any person being investigated or proceeded against that relates to unlawful employment practices covered by this subchapter and is relevant to the charge under investigation.

(b) The Commission may cooperate with State and local agencies charged with the administration of State fair employment practices laws and, with the consent of such agencies, may, for the purpose of carrying out its functions and duties under this subchapter and within the limitation of funds appropriated specifically for such purpose, engage in and contribute to the cost of research and other projects of mutual interest undertaken by such agencies, and utilize the services of such agencies and their employees, and, notwithstanding any other provision of law, pay by advance or reimbursement such agencies and their employees for services rendered to assist the Commission in carrying out this subchapter. In furtherance of such cooperative efforts, the Commission may enter into written agreements with such State or local agencies and such agreements may include provisions under which the Commission shall refrain from processing a charge in any cases or class of cases specified in such agreements or under which the Commission shall relieve any person or class of persons in such State or locality from requirements imposed under this section. The Commission shall rescind any such agreement whenever it determines that the agreement no longer serves the interest of effective enforcement of this subchapter.

(c) Every employer, employment agency, and labor organization subject to this subchapter shall

(1) make and keep such records relevant to the determinations of whether unlawful employment practices have been or are being committed,

(2) preserve such records for such periods, and

(3) make such reports therefrom as the Commission shall prescribe by regulation or order, after public hearing, as reasonable, necessary, or appropriate for the enforcement of this subchapter or the regulations or orders thereunder.

The Commission shall, by regulation, require each employer, labor organization, and joint labor-management committee subject to this subchapter which controls an apprenticeship or other training program to maintain such records as are reasonably necessary to carry out the purposes of this subchapter, including, but not limited to, a list of applicants who wish to participate in such program, including the chronological order in which applications were received, and to furnish to the Commission upon request, a detailed description of the manner in which persons are selected to participate in the apprenticeship or other training program. Any employer, employment agency, labor organization, or joint labor-management committee which believes that the application to it of any regulation or order issued under this section would result in undue hardship may apply to the Commission for an exemption from the application of such regulation or order, and, if such application for an exemption is denied, bring a civil action in the United States district court for the district where such records are kept. If the Commission or the court, as the case may be, finds that the application of the regulation or order to the employer, employment agency, or labor organization in question would impose an undue hardship, the Commission or the court, as the case may be, may grant appropriate relief. If any person required to comply with the provisions of this subsection fails or refuses to do so, the United States district court for the district in which such person is found, resides, or transacts business, shall, upon application of the Commission, or the Attorney General in a case involving a government, governmental agency or political subdivision, have jurisdiction to issue to such person an order requiring him to comply.

(d) In prescribing requirements pursuant to subsection (c) of this section, the Commission shall consult with other interested State and Federal agencies and shall endeavor to coordinate its requirements with those adopted by such agencies. The Commission shall furnish upon request and without cost to any State or local agency charged with the administration of a fair employment practice law information obtained pursuant to subsection (c) of this section from any employer, employment agency, labor organization, or joint labor-management committee subject to the jurisdiction of such agency. Such information shall be furnished on condition that it not be made public by the recipient agency prior to the institution of a proceeding under State or local law involving such information. If this condition is violated by a recipient agency, the Commission may decline to honor subsequent requests pursuant to this subsection.

(e) It shall be unlawful for any officer or employee of the Commission to make public in any manner whatever any information obtained by the Commission pursuant to its authority under this section prior to the institution of any proceeding under this subchapter involving such information. Any officer or employee of the Commission who shall make public in any manner whatever any information in violation of this subsection shall be guilty of a misdemeanor and upon conviction thereof, shall be fined not more than $1,000, or imprisoned not more than one year.

§ 2000e-9. [Sec. 710] Investigatory Powers

For the purpose of all hearings and investigations conducted by the Commission or its duly authorized agents or agencies, section 161 of title 29 *[section 11 of the National Labor Relations Act]* shall apply.

§ 2000e-10. [Sec. 711] Posting of Notices; Penalties

(a) Every employer, employment agency, and labor organization, as the case may be, shall post and keep posted in conspicuous places upon its premises where notices to employees, applicants for employment, and members are customarily posted a notice to be prepared or approved by the Commission setting forth excerpts, from or, summaries of, the pertinent provisions of this subchapter and information pertinent to the filing of a complaint.

(b) A willful violation of this section shall be punishable by a fine of not more than $100 for each separate offense.

§ 2000e-11. [Sec. 712] Veterans' Special Rights or Preference

Nothing contained in this subchapter shall be construed to repeal or modify any Federal, State, territorial, or local law creating special rights or preference for veterans.

§ 2000e-12. [Sect. 713] Rules and Regulations

(a) The Commission shall have authority from time to time to issue, amend, or rescind suitable procedural regulations to carry out the provisions of this subchapter. Regulations issued under this section shall be in conformity with the standards and limitations of subchapter II of chapter 5 of title 5 *[the Administrative Procedure Act]*.

(b) In any action or proceeding based on any alleged unlawful employment practice, no person shall be subject to any liability or punishment for or on account of

(1) the commission by such person of an unlawful employment practice if he pleads and proves that the act or omission complained of was in good faith, in conformity with, and in reliance on any written interpretation or opinion of the Commission, or

(2) the failure of such person to publish and file any information required by any provision of this subchapter if he pleads and proves that he failed to publish and file such information in good faith, in conformity with the instructions of the Commission issued under this subchapter regarding the filing of such information. Such a defense, if established, shall be a bar to the action or proceeding, notwithstanding that

(A) after such act or omission, such interpretation or opinion is modified or rescinded or is determined by judicial authority to be invalid or of no legal effect, or

(B) after publishing or filing the description and annual reports, such publication or filing is determined by judicial authority not to be in conformity with the requirements of this subchapter.

§ 2000e-13. [Sec. 714] Forcibly Resisting the Commission or Its Representatives

The provisions of sections 111 and 1114, title 18 *[United States Code]*, shall apply to officers, agents, and employees of the Commission in the performance of their official duties. Notwithstanding the provisions of sections 111 and 1114 of title 18 *[United States Code]*, whoever in violation of the provisions of section 1114 of such title kills a person while engaged in or on account of the performance of his official functions under this Act shall be punished by imprisonment for any term of years or for life.

TRANSFER OF AUTHORITY

[Administration of the duties of the Equal Employment Opportunity Coordinating Council was transferred to the Equal Employment Opportunity Commission effective July 1, 1978, under the President's Reorganization Plan of 1978.]

§ 2000e-14. [Sec. 715] Equal Employment Opportunity Coordinating Council

The Equal Employment Opportunity Commission shall have the responsibility for developing and implementing agreements, policies and practices designed to maximize effort, promote efficiency, and eliminate conflict, competition, duplication and inconsistency among the operations, functions and jurisdictions of the various departments, agencies and branches of the Federal Government responsible for the implementation and enforcement of equal employment opportunity legislation, orders, and policies. On or before October 1 of each year, the Equal Employment Opportunity Commission shall transmit to the President and to the Congress a report of its activities, together with such recommendations for legislative or administrative changes as it concludes are desirable to further promote the purposes of this section.

§ 2000e-15. [Sec. 716] Effective Date

The President shall, as soon as feasible after July 2, 1964 *[the enactment of this title]*, convene one or more conferences for the purpose of enabling the leaders of groups whose members will be affected by this subchapter to become familiar with the rights afforded and obligations imposed by its provisions, and for the purpose of making plans which will result in the fair and effective administration of this subchapter when all of its provisions become effective. The President shall invite the participation in such conference or conferences of (1) the members of the President's Committee on Equal Employment Opportunity, (2) the members of the Commission on Civil Rights, (3) representatives of State and local agencies engaged in furthering equal employment opportunity, (4) representatives of private agencies engaged in furthering equal employment opportunity, and (5) representatives of employers, labor organizations, and employment agencies who will be subject to this subchapter.

TRANSFER OF AUTHORITY

[Enforcement of Section 717 was transferred to the Equal Employment Opportunity Commission from the Civil Service Commission (Office of Personnel Management) effective January 1, 1979, under the President's Reorganization Plan No. 1 of 1978.]

§ 2000e-16. [Sec. 717] Employment by Federal Government

(a) All personnel actions affecting employees or applicants for employment (except with regard to aliens employed outside the limits of the United States) in military departments as defined in section 102 of title 5 *[United States Code]*, in executive agencies *[other than the General Accounting Office]* as defined in section 105 of title 5 *[United States Code]* (including employees and applicants for employment who are paid from non-appropriated funds), in the United States Postal Service and the Postal Rate Commission, in those units of the Government of the District of Columbia having positions in the competitive service, and in those units of the legislative and judicial branches of the Federal Government having positions in the competitive service, in the Smithsonian Institution, and in the Government Printing Office, the General Accounting Office, and the Library of Congress shall be made free from any discrimination based on race, color, religion, sex, or national origin.

(b) Except as otherwise provided in this subsection, the Equal Employment Opportunity Commission *[Civil Service Commission]* shall have authority to enforce the provisions of subsection (a) of this section through appropriate remedies, including reinstatement or hiring of employees with or without back pay, as will effectuate the policies of this section, and shall issue such rules, regulations, orders and instructions as it deems necessary and appropriate to carry out its responsibilities under this section. The Equal Employment Opportunity Commission *[Civil Service Commission]* shall—

(1) be responsible for the annual review and approval of a national and regional equal employment opportunity plan which each department and agency and each appropriate unit referred to in subsection (a) of this section shall submit in order to maintain an affirmative program of equal employment opportunity for all such employees and applicants for employment;

(2) be responsible for the review and evaluation of the operation of all agency equal employment opportunity programs, periodically obtaining and publishing (on at least a semiannual basis) progress reports from each such department, agency, or unit; and

(3) consult with and solicit the recommendations of interested individuals, groups, and organizations relating to equal employment opportunity.

The head of each such department, agency, or unit shall comply with such rules, regulations, orders, and instructions which shall include a provision that an employee or applicant for employment shall be notified of any final action taken on any complaint of discrimination filed by him thereunder. The plan submitted by each department, agency, and unit shall include, but not be limited to—

(1) provision for the establishment of training and education programs designed to provide a maximum opportunity for employees to advance so as to perform at their highest potential; and

(2) a description of the qualifications in terms of training and experience relating to equal employment opportunity for the principal and operating officials of each such department, agency, or unit responsible for carrying out the equal employment opportunity program and of the allocation of personnel and resources proposed by such department, agency, or unit to carry out its equal employment opportunity program.

With respect to employment in the Library of Congress, authorities granted in this subsection to the Equal Employment Opportunity Commission *[Civil Service Commission]* shall be exercised by the Librarian of Congress.

(c) Within 90 days of receipt of notice of final action taken by a department, agency, or unit referred to in subsection (a) of this section, or by the Equal Employment Opportunity Commission *[Civil Service Commission]* upon an appeal from a decision or order of such department, agency, or unit on a complaint of discrimination based on race, color, religion, sex or national origin, brought pursuant to subsection (a) of this section, Executive Order 11478 or any succeeding Executive orders, or after one hundred and eighty days from the filing of the initial charge with the department, agency, or unit or with the Equal Employment Opportunity Commission *[Civil Service Commission]* on appeal from a decision or order of such department, agency, or unit until such time as final action may be taken by a department, agency, or unit, an employee or applicant for employment, if aggrieved by the final disposition of his complaint, or by the failure to take final action on his complaint, may file a civil action as provided in section 2000e-5 of this title *[section 706]*, in which civil action the head of the department, agency, or unit, as appropriate, shall be the defendant.

(d) The provisions of section 2000e-5(f) through (k) of this title *[section 706(f) through (k)]*, as applicable, shall govern civil actions brought hereunder, and the same interest to compensate for delay in payment shall be available as in cases involving nonpublic parties.

(e) Nothing contained in this Act shall relieve any Government agency or official of its or his primary responsibility to assure nondiscrimination in employment as required by the Constitution and statutes or of its or his responsibilities under Executive Order 11478 relating to equal employment opportunity in the Federal Government.

§ 2000e-17. [Sec. 718] Special Provisions with Respect to Denial, Termination, and Suspension of Government Contracts

No Government contract, or portion thereof, with any employer, shall be denied, withheld, terminated, or suspended, by any agency or officer of the United States under any equal employment opportunity law or order, where such employer has an affirmative action plan which has previously been accepted by the Government for the same facility within the past twelve months without first according such employer full hearing and adjudication under the provisions of section 554 of title 5 *[United States Code]*, and the following pertinent sections: Provided, That if such employer has deviated substantially from such previously agreed to affirmative action plan, this section shall not apply: Provided further, That for the purposes of this section an affirmative action plan shall be deemed to have been accepted by the Government at the time the appropriate compliance agency has accepted such plan unless within forty-five days thereafter the Office of Federal Contract Compliance has disapproved such plan.

Chapter 19

Uniformed Services Employment and Reemployment Rights Act (USERRA)

Statute: 38 U.S.C. §§ 4301-4333

http://www.dol.gov/dol/vets/public/usc/vpl/usc38.htmphttp://www4.law.cornell.edu/uscode/38/4301.html

Regulations: none

Definitions

Uniformed services

The following branches of the United States military:

- Army
- Navy
- Marine Corps
- Air Force
- Coast Guard
- Reserves
- Army or Air National Guard, and
- Commissioned Corps of the Public Health Service.

Service in the uniformed services

Voluntary or involuntary performance of duties in a *uniformed service*, including:

- active duty
- active duty for training
- initial active duty for training
- inactive duty training
- full-time National Guard duty
- absence for an examination to determine a worker's fitness for any of the above types of duty, or

- funeral honors duty performed by National Guard or reserve members.

Undue hardship

The actions an employer would have to take to accommodate an employee returning from military leave constitute an undue hardship if they would involve significant difficulty or expense for the employer, in light of:

- the nature and cost of the action
- the overall financial resources of the particular facility where the action would be taken
- the number of persons employed at the facility
- the impact the action would have on the facility's operation, including expenses and resources
- the overall financial resources and size of the employer, including the size, number and nature of its facilities, and
- the type of operations in which the employer engages.

A. Overview of USERRA

1. Summary

Since 1940, federal law has guaranteed certain employment rights to workers who are in the *uniformed services*. In 1994, following the Persian Gulf War, Congress passed its most recent revision of this law, now called the

Uniformed Services Employment and Reemployment Rights Act. The law includes provisions on:

- **Discrimination:** Employers may not discriminate against members of the *uniformed services.*
- **Reinstatement:** Employers must reinstate employees upon their return from up to

five years of leave for *service in the uniformed services.*

- **Benefits:** Employers must restore all benefits to returning service members. For purposes of benefit eligibility, accrual of seniority-based benefits and vesting (that is, rules providing that employees are not entitled to collect or use benefits until they have worked for a certain period of time), time spent on leave must be treated as time worked.

- **Job Security:** Employers may not fire returning service members without good cause for up to one year after they return from military duty.

2. Regulated Employers

This law covers all employers of all sizes, including

- all private employers
- businesses that are incorporated or otherwise organized in a foreign country, if that business is controlled by an employer in the United States
- the federal government, and
- state and local governments.

3. Covered Workers

An employee is not entitled to any of the benefits of this law if the employee is:

- separated from a *uniformed service* under other than honorable conditions (such as a dishonorable discharge, bad conduct discharge or a discharge under "other than honorable" conditions)

- dropped from the rolls based on an absence without authority of more than three months or imprisonment by a civilian court, or
- in the case of a commissioned officer, dismissed from the *uniformed service* in a court martial or by order of the President in time of war.

B. Major Provisions of USERRA

1. Discrimination

Employers may not discriminate against members of the *uniformed services* or retaliate against workers who exercise their rights under USERRA.

Regulated Employers
All employers must comply with this provision.

Covered Workers
All members of, and applicants for membership in, the *uniformed services* are covered by this provision. In addition, any person who participates in a proceeding to enforce USERRA rights (a witness in an investigation, hearing or lawsuit, for example) is protected from retaliation, whether or not the person is a member of the *uniformed services.*

What's Prohibited: Employers

Discrimination
Employers may not take any negative job action against an employee or applicant based on

that person's membership in the *uniformed services*. Negative job actions include:

- firing
- demoting
- reducing pay or benefits
- transferring, and
- refusing to hire.

Retaliation

Employers also may not retaliate (by taking any negative job action, as described above) against any person who

- takes action to enforce USERRA rights
- testifies or makes a statement in connection with any USERRA enforcement proceeding
- participates in an investigation of a USERRA violation, or
- exercises his rights under USERRA.

2. Reinstatement

Employers must reinstate employees upon their return from up to five years of leave for *service in the uniformed services*.

Regulated Employers

All employers must comply with this provision.

Covered Workers

Reinstatement rights are available only to employees who have been absent from employment due to *service in the uniformed services*. In addition, employees are eligible for reinstatement only if:

- the employee gave the employer notice, before taking leave, that the leave was

for military service—this notice may be oral or written
- the employee spent no more than five years, cumulatively, on leave for military service (with certain exceptions—see "Exceptions," below)
- the employee was released from military service under honorable conditions, and
- the employee reports back or applies for reinstatement within specified time limits (these limits vary depending on the length of the employee's leave and whether the employee suffered or aggravated a disability while serving— see "What's Required: Workers," below)

What's Prohibited: Employers

Employers cannot require service members to use accrued vacation time for military service. However, if a service member asks to use vacation time for this purpose, the employer must allow it.

What's Required: Employers

Employers must reinstate workers who have taken up to a total of five years of leave to serve in the *uniformed services* to the position they would have held had they been continuously employed. Returning employees are entitled to any promotions, raises and other seniority-based benefits that they would have received had they not taken leave (see "Benefits," below).

If the worker is not qualified for the position, the employer must make reasonable efforts to help the employee qualify (by offering training, for example).

What's Required: Workers

Otherwise eligible employees must do two things to qualify for reinstatement:

- give the employer oral or written notice, before going on leave, that the leave is for military service, and
- report back or apply for reinstatement within specified time limits (see below).

Time Limits for Reporting for Work or Reinstatement

The time limits for reporting back depend on how long the worker was out on leave:

- workers who were on leave for 30 or fewer days must report back on the first regularly scheduled work day following the completion of their service, taking into consideration the time it takes for their safe transportation home from service and an additional eight-hour period.
- workers who were on leave for more than 30 but fewer than 181 days must submit an application for reemployment within 14 days after their period of service is complete. Many employers do not require workers to actually submit an application, but instead allow them to return to work on an agreed-upon date—but employers have the right to request an application, if they wish.
- workers who were on leave for more than 181 days must submit an application for reemployment within 90 days after their period of service is complete. Again, some employers do not require workers to actually submit an applica-

tion, but simply arrange for a return-to-work date.

- workers who are injured or become ill while performing service must report to the employer or submit an application for reemployment once they have recovered. This recovery period may not exceed two years.

Exceptions

Exceptions to the reinstatement right:

An employer does not have to reinstate an employee if:

- the employer's circumstances have changed so much as to make reemployment impossible or unreasonable
- the job was for a brief, non-recurrent period, and the worker had no reasonable expectation that the job would continue indefinitely or for a significant period, or
- in the case of an employee disabled during military service or otherwise unqualified for the position to which he is entitled to be reinstated, if reinstatement would impose an *undue hardship* on the employer.

Exceptions to the five-year limit:

An employee who takes more than a total of five years of leave is still entitled to reinstatement if:

- the employee's initial service obligation exceeds five years (for example, some military specialties require members to serve an initial term of more than five years)

- the employee is unable to obtain a release from duty within five years (this exception applies to service members who are involuntarily retained on active duty after their initial service obligation ends)
- the employee takes time off for reserve or National Guard training—this training does not count towards the five-year limit
- the employee is ordered to remain or go on active duty during a domestic emergency, a national security situation, a war or national emergency declared by the President or Congress
- the employee volunteers for active duty in support of an operational mission for which members of the Selected Reserve have been involuntarily ordered to active duty (this exception applies to workers who volunteered to support operational missions in Haiti and Bosnia, for example)
- the employee volunteers for active duty in support of a critical mission or requirement (as certified by the Secretary of the *uniformed service* involved), when no war or national emergency has been declared and no involuntary call-up is in effect, or
- the employee is a member of the National Guard called into federal service by the President to suppress an insurrection, repel an invasion or execute the laws of the U.S.

3. Benefits

Employers must make certain employment benefits available to workers who take leave for *service in the uniformed services*. In addition, returning workers are entitled to have their benefits restored.

Regulated Employers

All employers must comply with this provision.

Covered Workers

Workers who take leave from work for *service in the uniformed services* are eligible for benefits continuation while on leave. Only workers who are entitled to reinstatement following *service in the uniformed services* are eligible for benefits reinstatement. See "Covered Workers" under Reinstatement, above.

What's Required: Employers

Benefits During Leave

While a worker is on leave, the employer has the following obligations, depending on the type of benefits:

- **Health insurance.** Employers must continue to provide health insurance for up to 18 months after a worker goes on leave for *service in the uniformed services*. If the worker is absent for 30 or fewer days, the worker may not be required to pay more than the employee share, if any, for such coverage. If the worker is absent for more than 30 days, the worker may be required to pay up to 102% of the full premium for such coverage.
- **Other benefits.** The employer must give the worker the same benefits that are generally provided to workers in similar

positions who take a leave of absence. If such workers are generally required to pay the employee cost of a funded benefit, workers on leave for military service may also be required to pay.

Benefits After Reinstatement

Once a worker is reinstated following leave for *service in the uniformed services*, an employer has the following obligations:

- **Health insurance.** If the worker's health insurance coverage was terminated during the leave, this coverage must be reinstated without an exclusion or waiting period for the worker and any others (spouse and dependents, for example) covered under the worker's insurance.
- **Seniority-based benefits.** A reinstated worker is entitled to the seniority, and any rights and benefits based on seniority, that he would have attained had he been continuously employed.
- **Benefits not based on seniority.** A reinstated worker is entitled to the same benefits not based on seniority that are generally provided to employees who take a furlough or leave of absence for non-military reasons.
- **Pensions.** A reinstated worker's time on leave must not be treated as a break in service for purposes of an employer-maintained pension plan. For purposes of vesting and benefit accrual, the worker's military service must be considered service with the employer. The employee must be allowed to make up any employee contributions he missed

because of *service in the uniformed services*—and the employer must match these contributions to the same extent it matches contributions by other employees. The worker can take up to three times the length of his military service or five years, whichever is shorter, to make these contributions.

4. Job Security

Employers may not fire an employee, except for good cause, for up to one year after the employee returns to work after *service in the uniformed services*. Good cause means a good-faith, legitimate, business-related reason for firing. Examples of good cause include stealing from the employer, poor performance or serious misconduct.

Regulated Employers

All employers must comply with this provision.

Covered Workers

Only employees who served for at least 31 days in the *uniformed services* are entitled to this limited job protection.

What's Prohibited: Employers

Employers are prohibited from firing an employee who returns to work after *service in the uniformed services*, except for good cause, for:

- 180 days after the worker is reinstated, if the worker served in the *uniformed services* for 31 to 180 days, or

- one year after the worker is reinstated, if the worker served in the *uniformed services* for more than 180 days.

C. How USERRA Is Enforced

1. Individual Complaints

An employee whose USERRA rights have been violated has two choices. The employee may file a complaint with the Veterans Employment and Training Service ("VETS"), an agency within the Department of Labor, which will investigate and attempt to resolve the complaint. (See "Agency Enforcement," below.)

An employee does not have to complain to the VETS, however. The employee can go directly to federal district court and file a lawsuit against the employer. USERRA has no statute of limitations—this means that employees may file a lawsuit at any time, no matter how much time has passed since their employer violated USERRA.

2. Agency Enforcement

VETS has the authority to investigate complaints of USERRA violations. Once it has investigated, it will attempt to resolve the complaint. However, VETS cannot force an employer to comply with the law, nor can it impose penalties or fines on an employer that refuses to comply. If VETS's efforts at resolution are unsuccessful, it will inform the complaining employee, in writing, of the results of the investigation and the employee's right to continue to press the complaint.

Once VETS has investigated and attempted, unsuccessfully, to resolve a USERRA complaint, an employee can either file a lawsuit or ask VETS to refer the complaint to the Attorney General's office.

If the Attorney General's office decides that the complaint has merit, a lawyer from that office may bring a lawsuit against the employer to enforce the complaining employee's USERRA rights. If the Attorney General's office decides not to take the case, the employee can still file a private lawsuit.

D. For Employers: Complying With USERRA

1. Reporting Requirements

USERRA imposes no reporting requirements.

2. Posting Requirements

Employers are not required to post any notice under USERRA.

3. Recordkeeping Requirements

USERRA does not require employers to keep any particular records.

4. Practical Tips

Here are some tips for complying with USERRA:

- **Talk to your employees about their military responsibilities.** If you have workers who serve in the *uniformed services*, find out what that commitment entails, including how often they will have to attend training, when they expect to be out on leave and what the military expects of them. Of course, your workers won't always know ahead of time when they will be pressed into service, but getting as much information as you can will help you plan ahead for foreseeable absences.
- **Review your personnel policies.** Some employers have gotten into trouble because their policies don't allow employees to take the leave allowed under USERRA. For example, if your policies allow workers to take only a certain amount of leave each year or state that workers will be terminated if they are out of work for a certain period of time, these policies should be rewritten to state that they do not apply to employees taking leave that is protected by USERRA. And make sure your policies offer the same benefits to workers on military leaves of absence that you offer to workers on other types of leave.
- **Choose a USERRA point person.** Designate one manager to be the designated contact for workers on leave for military service. Let employees know that they can get in touch with this person to give notice of service, to find out about benefits while they are on leave and to notify the company when they will be returning to the workforce.

- **Document everything.** USERRA is very protective of employees' rights—and courts have generally interpreted it against employers. This means you must be prepared to offer evidence that you complied with the law. Make a practice of documenting your decisions and actions towards returning service members. For example, if you decide to fire a reinstated employee for good cause, find that reinstating a particular employee would pose an *undue hardship* or decide not to reinstate a worker who has taken more than five years of leave, you must carefully document the reasons for your decision.

5. Penalties

Employers who violate USERRA may be required to:

- comply with the law (for example, by reinstating a worker or restoring a worker's benefits)
- pay the worker for any benefits or wages lost because of the employer's violation, and
- pay the worker's attorney fees and court costs.

If a court finds that the employer's violation was willful (for example, that the employer knew or should have know that its acts were against the law), the employer can be ordered to pay *twice* the amount of the worker's lost benefits and wages, in addition to an order to comply with the law and pay attorney's fees and costs.

E. For Workers: Asserting Rights Under USERRA

1. Where to Start

A worker who believes that his rights under USERRA have been violated should start by complaining internally at his company. If the company has a complaint policy, the worker should follow the designated procedures. If the company has no complaint policy, the worker should complain to a human resources representative or a member of management.

A worker who is a union member should talk to a shop steward or union representative.

If internal complaints and/or union complaints don't work, a worker can either file a lawsuit in federal district court or file a complaint with VETS. For more on agency enforcement, see "How USERRA Is Enforced," above.

2. Required Forms

Workers should contact their local office of the VETS to find out whether they have to use a particular form to file their complaint.

3. Practical Tips

If you feel that your employer has discriminated against you because of your military service, or you haven't received the reinstatement rights to which you are entitled under USERRA, consider these tips:

- **Complain to your employer as soon as you believe that your rights have been violated.** Talk to your employer immediately if you think your rights were violated. The sooner you assert your rights, the sooner you will know whether your employer will work with you to resolve the problem—or whether you will have to get some outside help.
- **Don't delay in filing a lawsuit or administrative complaint.** Even though USERRA has no statute of limitations, you should still file a complaint with VETS or a lawsuit fairly quickly. After all, you will have to prove that you met all of USERRA's requirements (that is, that you were discharged honorably, that your service did not exceed five years and so on) and that your employer violated your rights. And it's much harder to prove something years after the fact.
- **Put everything in writing.** Handle important communications relating to your USERRA rights (such as your notice of leave and application for reinstatement) in writing. Take notes of every action, statement or other incident that relates to your complaint. If you file a written complaint with your company, keep a copy. Keep copies of every document relating to your complaint (such as a termination letter or a denial of insurance benefits). If you later have to take your employer to court, these documents will help you prove your case.
- **Make your rights known.** Many employers are not aware of their obligations under USERRA—or even of the law's existence. Although it isn't your responsibility to

explain the law to your employer, doing so can save you a lot of time and trouble in the long run. Point your employer to some of the internet resources listed under "Agency Resources for Employers," below.

- **Get the government's help.** You don't have to file a complaint with VETS—you can go straight to court and file a lawsuit, if you wish. But if you file a

complaint with VETS, it will investigate your complaint and try to get your employer to comply with the law—at no cost to you. If VETS is successful, you won't have to take further action to enforce your rights. But even if VETS can't convince your employer to do the right thing, you can use the information VETS gathers in its investigation to prepare your lawsuit.

F. Agency Charged With Enforcement & Compliance

Veterans Employment and Training Service, Department of Labor

200 Constitution Avenue, NW, Room S-1316
Washington, DC 20210
Phone: 202-693-4700
http://www.dol.gov/dol/vets

Agency Resources for Employers and Workers

(These can be obtained either at the Web addresses listed below or at the address and phone number listed above.)

- Detailed explanations of the law's requirements
  A Non-Technical Resource Guide to USERRA
  http://www.dol.gov/dol/vets/public/whatsnew/uguide.pdfp
  http://www.dol.gov/elaws/userra0.htm
- A directory of VETS offices nationwide
  Index to Regional and 50-State VETS Offices
  http://www.dol.gov/dol/vets/public/aboutvets/contacts/main.htm
- A factsheet about USERRA's basic provisions
  USERRA Small Business Handbook
  http://www.dol.gov/asp/programs/handbook/userra.htm
- An interactive guide to USERRA for employers and employees
  Uniformed Services Employment & Reemployment Rights Act (USERRA) Advisor
  http://www.dol.gov/elaws/userra0.htm

G. State Laws Relating to Military Service

Alaska	Alaska Stat. § 26.05.075
Employees covered	Employees called to active service in the state militia.
Amount of leave	Unlimited unpaid leave.
Reinstatement	To former or comparable position at same pay, seniority and benefits as before military service.
Return to work	Next workday after time required to travel from service site.
Disability due to service	If disability leaves employee unable to perform job duties, must be offered another position with similar pay and benefits. Employee must request reemployment within 30 days of being released to return to work.
Arizona	Ariz. Rev. Stat. §§ 26-167, 26-168
Employees covered	Members of state military forces or National Guard members called up by state.
Amount of leave	Unlimited unpaid leave. Does not affect vacation rights that already exist, but is not considered work for purpose of accruing vacation benefits and pay.
Reinstatement	To former or comparable position at same pay, seniority and benefits as before military service.
Benefits and rights	Employer may not dissuade employees from enlisting in state or national military forces by threatening economic reprisal.
Employer penalties	Discrimination or opposing service is a class 2 misdemeanor, which carries a fine of up to $750 or imprisonment of up to 4 months, or both. Violating leave provisions is a class 3 misdemeanor, which carries a fine of up to $500 or imprisonment of up to 30 days, or both.
Arkansas	Ark. Code Ann. § 12-62-413
Employees covered	Employees called by the governor to active duty in the Arkansas National Guard or the state militia have the same leave and reinstatement rights and benefits as members of the U.S. uniformed services.
California	Cal. Mil. & Vet. Code §§ 394 to 394.5
Employees covered	Employees who are called into service or training in the state military or naval forces have same leave and reinstatement rights and benefits as members of the U.S. uniformed services.

Amount of leave	Employees who are in the U.S. armed forces, National Guard or Naval Militia reserves entitled to 17 days unpaid leave per year for training or special exercises.
Benefits and rights	Employer may not discriminate in hiring or dissuade employee from enlisting. May not terminate or limit any benefits or seniority because of temporary disability (52 weeks or less).
Colorado	Colo. Rev. Stat. § 28-3-609
Employees covered	Permanent employees who are members of Colorado National Guard or U.S. armed forces reserves.
Amount of leave	15 days unpaid leave per year for training.
Reinstatement	Same or similar position with same status, pay and seniority.
Florida	Fla. Stat. Ann. §§ 250.482; 627.6692(h) to (j)
Employees covered	Employees who are members of the Florida National Guard and are called into active duty by the governor have the same leave and reinstatement rights as members of the U.S. uniformed services.
Benefits and rights	Employees not covered by COBRA whose employment is terminated while on active duty are entitled to a new 18-month benefit period beginning when active duty or job ends, whichever is later.
Employer penalties	Employee who has worked at least 1 year may sue employer who violates law for actual damages or $500, whichever is greater.
Georgia	Ga. Code Ann. § 38-2-280
Employees covered	Members of U.S. armed forces or Georgia National Guard called into active federal or state service.
Amount of leave	Unlimited unpaid leave for active service. Up to 6 months leave for service school or annual training, but no more than 6 months total during any 4-year period.
Reinstatement	Reinstatement with full benefits unless employer's circumstances have changed and reemployment is impossible or unreasonable. Employee must apply within 90 days of discharge from active duty or within 10 days of completing school or training.
Employer penalties	Employer who does not reinstate employee with full benefits is liable to employee for lost wages and benefits; upon request, employee may be represented by the state Attorney General.

Hawaii	Haw. Rev. Stat. § 121-43
Employees covered	Employees serving in the state National Guard are entitled to the same protections as those called into active duty in U.S. uniformed services.
Idaho	Idaho Code §§ 46-224 to 46-225
Employees covered	Members of National Guard and armed forces reserves.
Amount of leave	15 days unpaid (or paid at employer's discretion) leave per year for training. Leave does not affect vacation, sick leave, bonus or promotion rights. Employee must give 90 days' notice of training dates.
Reinstatement	Entitled to same position with no loss of seniority or benefits.
Illinois	20 Ill. Comp. Stat. §§ 1805/100, 1815/79; 225 Ill. Comp. Stat. §§ 60/21, 80/16, 115/15, 415/17, 441/5-16, 450/17.1, 458/5-25
Employees covered	Members of Illinois State Guard and members of U.S. uniformed services.
Benefits and rights	Employer may not in any way discriminate against employees who are members of the military, obstruct their employment or dissuade them from enlisting. Many occupations including veterinary technician, court reporter, real estate appraiser, home inspector, optometrist and accountant may renew licenses that expired during military service or training without paying late fees or fulfilling continuing education requirements.
Employer penalties	Discrimination is a petty offense, punishable by a fine of up to $1,000.
Indiana	Ind. Code Ann. §§ 10-5-9-1 to 10-5-9-2
Employees covered	Members of U.S. armed services reserves.
Amount of leave	15 days unpaid (or paid at employer's discretion) leave per year for training. Leave does not affect vacation, sick leave, bonus or promotion rights.
Reinstatement	Entitled to same or similar position with no loss of seniority or benefits.
Iowa	Iowa Code § 29A.43
Employees covered	Members of state military forces called into temporary duty have same protections as members of U.S. uniformed services called into active duty.
Kansas	Kan. Stat. Ann. § 48-222
Employees covered	Members of state military forces called into active duty by the state entitled to same protections as members of U.S. uniformed services.
Amount of leave	In addition to unlimited leave for active duty, 5 to 10 days leave each year to attend state National Guard training camp.

| Return to work | Must report to work within 72 hours of release from duty or recovery from service-related injury or illness. |
| Employer penalties | Failure to excuse employee for training or duty: $5 to $50 fine for each offense. Failure to fully reinstate employee: liable for lost wages or benefits or double that amount if failure is willful. |

Kentucky	Ky. Rev. Stat. Ann. §§ 38.238, 38.460
Employees covered	Members of Kentucky National Guard or Kentucky active militia.
Amount of leave	Unlimited unpaid leave for training.
Reinstatement	To former position with no loss of seniority, pay or benefits.
Benefits and rights	Employer may not in any way discriminate against employee or threaten to prevent employee from enlisting in the Kentucky National Guard or active militia.

Louisiana	La. Rev. Stat. Ann. §§ 29:38 to 29:38.1, 29:410
Employees covered	Employees called into active duty in any branch of the state military forces have the same leave and reinstatement rights and benefits as members of the U.S. uniformed services.
Return to work	Must report to work within 72 hours of release from state military duty or recovery from state service-related injury or illness.
Employer penalties	Employer who fails to comply liable for lost wages and benefits; upon request employee may be represented by the parish district attorney.

Maine	Me. Rev. Stat. Ann. tit. 37-B, § 342(5)
Employees covered	Members of state military forces.
Benefits and rights	Employer may not discriminate against employee for membership or service in state military forces.
Employer penalties	Employer who discriminates is guilty of a Class E crime, punishable by up to 6 months in the county jail or a fine of up to $1,000.

Maryland	Md. Code 1957 Art. 65, § 32A
Employees covered	Members of the organized militia called to active duty or training by the governor are entitled to the same leave and reinstatement rights and benefits as members of the U.S. uniformed services.
Reinstatement	Must apply for reemployment within 30 days of release from duty or training.
Employer penalties	Liable for lost wages and benefits.

Massachusetts	Mass. Gen. Laws ch. 33, § 13; ch. 149, § 52A
Employees covered	Employees who are members of U.S. armed forces reserves or who are members or connected with the state armed forces.
Amount of leave	17 days per year for training in the U.S. armed forces reserves. Leave does not affect vacation, sick leave, bonus or promotion rights.
Reinstatement	Employee who is still qualified must be reinstated in former or similar position with no loss of status, pay or seniority.
Benefits and rights	Employer may not in any way discriminate against employee or threaten to prevent employee from enlisting in the state armed forces.
Employer penalties	Employers who violate law protecting members of state armed forces are subject to a fine of up to $500, or up to 6 months imprisonment, or both.
Michigan	Mich. Comp. Laws §§ 32.271 to 32.274
Employees covered	Members of state or U.S. uniformed services.
Amount of leave	Unpaid leave authorized for taking a physical, enlisting, being inducted, attending encampment or drill or instruction.
Reinstatement	Employee must be reinstated to former position with no loss of seniority, benefits or pay; must apply within 15 days of release or rejection from service.
Benefits and rights	Employer may not in any way discriminate against employee or threaten to prevent employee from enlisting in the state armed forces.
Employer penalties	Violations of the law are a misdemeanor.
Minnesota	Minn. Stat. Ann. § 192.34
Employees covered	Employees who are members of the U.S., Minnesota or any other state military or naval forces.
Benefits and rights	Employer may not discharge employee or interfere with military service or dissuade employee from enlisting by threatening employee's job.
Employer penalties	Employer who violates law is guilty of a gross misdemeanor and is subject to a fine of up to $3,000, or up to one year imprisonment, or both.
Mississippi	Miss. Code Ann. § 33-1-19
Employees covered	Members of U.S. uniformed services and Mississippi armed forces.
Amount of leave	Unpaid leave for active state duty or state training duty.
Reinstatement	If still qualified to perform job duties, employee entitled to previous or similar position with no loss of seniority, status or pay.

Missouri	Mo. Rev. Stat. § 41.730
Employees covered	Members of state organized militia.
Benefits and rights	Employer may not discharge employee or interfere with employee's military service or threaten to dissuade employee from enlisting.
Employer penalties	Violations of the law are a class A misdemeanor punishable by a fine of up to $1,000 or by up to one year imprisonment.
Montana	Mont. Code Ann. § 10-1-603
Employees covered	Members of the state organized militia called to active service during a state-declared disaster or emergency.
Amount of leave	Unpaid leave for duration of service. Leave may not be deducted from sick leave or vacation or other leave, although employee may voluntarily use that leave.
Reinstatement	To same or similar position.
Benefits and rights	Employer may not in any way discriminate against employee or dissuade employee from enlisting by threatening employee's job.
Nevada	Nev. Rev. Stat. Ann. §§ 412.139, 412.606; 683A.261
Employees covered	Members of Nevada National Guard called into active service by the governor.
Benefits and rights	Employers may not discriminate against members of the Nevada National Guard and may not discharge any employee who is called into active service. Insurance brokers given extended time to renew license and fines and examinations waived.
Employer penalties	Employer who violates the law is guilty of a misdemeanor punishable by a fine of up to $1,000, or up to 6 months in the county jail, or both.
New Hampshire	N.H. Rev. Stat. Ann. § 110-B:65(II)
Employees covered	Members of state National Guard.
Benefits and rights	Employer may not discriminate against employee because of connection or service with National Guard; may not dissuade employee from enlisting by threatening job.
Employer penalties	Violation of the law is a misdemeanor which carries a fine of up to $1,000 and up to 1 year in prison.
New Jersey	N.J. Stat. Ann. § 38A:14-4
Employees covered	Members of state organized militia.
Benefits and rights	Employer may not discharge employee or interfere with military service or dissuade employee from enlisting by threatening employee's job.

Employer penalties	Violation of the law is a misdemeanor.
New Mexico	N.M. Stat. Ann. §§ 20-4-6; 28-15-1 to 28-15-3
Employees covered	Members of the state National Guard.
Benefits and rights	Employer may not discriminate against or discharge employee because of membership in the National Guard; may not prevent employee from performing military service.
Employer penalties	Employer who willfully violates law is guilty of a misdemeanor and subject to a fine of up to $1,000, imprisonment of up to 1 year, or both.
New York	N.Y. Mil. Law §§ 317 to 318
Employees covered	Members of state military forces called up by governor and members of U.S. uniformed services.
Amount of leave	Unpaid leave available for: active service; reserve drills or annual training; service school; initial full-time or active duty training.
Reinstatement	Employee entitled to previous position, or to one with the same seniority, status and pay, unless the employer's circumstances have changed and reemployment is impossible or unreasonable. Employee must apply within: 90 days of discharge from active service; 10 days of completion of annual training or school; 60 days of completion of initial training.
Benefits and rights	It is state policy not to discriminate against employees who are subject to state or federal military service. Employee who is discharged or suspended and who applies for reemployment within 10 days of termination must be fully reinstated (does not apply to routine R.O.T.C. training).
Employer penalties	Employer may be liable to employee for lost wages and benefits; upon request state attorney general may appear and act on employee's behalf.
North Carolina	N.C. Gen. Stat. §§ 127A-201 and following; 127B-14
Employees covered	Members of the North Carolina National Guard called to active duty by the governor.
Reinstatement	Must make written application for reemployment within 5 days of release from state duty or recovery from service-related injury or illness.
Benefits and rights	It is state policy to protect an individual's right to serve in the state National Guard without fear of employment discrimination or reprisal. Employer may not deny employment, promotion or any benefit because employee is a member, enlists or serves in the state National Guard; employer may not discharge employee called up for emergency military service.

Oklahoma	Okla. Stat. Ann. tit. 44, §§ 71, 208
Employees covered	Members of state military forces. Employees called to state active duty in the Oklahoma National Guard have the same leave and reinstatement rights and benefits guaranteed under USERRA.
Benefits and rights	Employer may not discharge employee or hinder or prevent employee from performing military service.
Employer penalties	For discharge or obstructing service: fine of up to $100, or up to 30 days in the county jail, or both.
Oregon	Or. Rev. Stat. § 399.230
Employees covered	Members of state organized militia called into active duty by the governor.
Amount of leave	Unpaid leave for term of service.
Reinstatement	Full reinstatement with no loss of seniority or benefits including sick leave, vacation or service credits under a pension plan.
Pennsylvania	51 Pa. Cons. Stat. Ann. §§ 7302, 7309
Employees covered	Members of National Guard or U.S. armed forces reserves called into active or emergency state duty by the governor.
Amount of leave	Employee who enlists or is drafted during a time of war or emergency called by the president or governor entitled to unpaid military leave along with reservists called into active duty.
Reinstatement	Employee must be restored to same or similar position with same status, seniority and pay.
Benefits and rights	Employers may not discharge or discriminate against any employee because of membership or service in the military. Employees called to active duty are entitled to 30 days health insurance continuation benefits at no cost.
Disability due to service	If disability leaves employee unable to perform job duties, must be restored to another position with similar pay and benefits.
Rhode Island	R.I. Gen. Laws §§ 30-11-2 to 30-11-6; 30-21-1
Employees covered	Members of state military forces. National Guard members on state active duty entitled to same rights and protections as those granted under USERRA.
Amount of leave	Unpaid leave of absence for state active duty.

Reinstatement	If still qualified to perform duties, employee must be restored to same or similar position with no loss of status, seniority or pay. Employee who enlists in U.S. Army, Navy or Air Force entitled to reinstatement in former or similar position if: employee makes request within 40 days of discharge; employee is still qualified to do job; employer's circumstances have not changed so that reemployment is impossible or unreasonable.
Benefits and rights	Employer may not discharge employee because of membership, or interfere with military service or dissuade employee from enlisting by threatening employee's job.
Employer penalties	Employer who discriminates is guilty of a misdemeanor which carries a fine of up to $1,000, up to 1 year imprisonment, or both; employer who does not reinstate an enlisted veteran subject to a fine of $50 to $500.
South Carolina	S.C. Code Ann. §§ 25-1-2310 to 25-1-2340
Employees covered	Members of South Carolina National Guard and State Guard called to state duty by the governor.
Reinstatement	If still qualified employee must be restored to previous position or one with same seniority, status and salary; if no longer qualified must be given another position, unless employer's circumstances make reinstatement unreasonable. Employee must apply in writing within 5 days of discharge from service or from related hospitalization.
South Dakota	S.D. Codified Laws Ann. § 33-17-15
Employees covered	Members of the South Dakota National Guard ordered to active duty by the governor or president entitled to same protections as members of U.S. uniformed services on active federal duty.
Tennessee	Tenn. Code Ann. § 58-1-604
Employees covered	Members of Tennessee National Guard.
Benefits and rights	Employer may not refuse to hire or discharge employee because of National Guard membership or because employee is absent for a required drill or annual training.
Employer penalties	Violation of law is a class E felony which is subject to a prison term of 1 to 2 years and a possible fine of up to $3,000.
Texas	Tex. Gov't. Code Ann. § 431.006
Employees covered	Members of state military forces called to active duty or training.

Reinstatement	Employee entitled to return to same position with no loss of time, efficiency rating, vacation or benefits unless employer's circumstances have changed so that reemployment is impossible or unreasonable.
Benefits and rights	Employer may not terminate employee in service.
Employer penalties	Employer may be liable for up to 6 months' compensation and attorney fees.
Utah	Utah Code Ann. § 39-1-36
Employees covered	Members of U.S. armed forces reserves who are called to active duty, active duty for training, inactive duty training or state active duty.
Amount of leave	Up to 5 years leave.
Reinstatement	Upon release from duty, training or related hospitalization employee entitled to return to previous employment with same seniority, status, pay and vacation rights.
Benefits and rights	Employer may not discriminate against employee based on membership in armed forces reserves.
Employer penalties	Employer who willfully discriminates, discharges or refuses to rehire is guilty of a class B misdemeanor which carries a fine of up to $1,000 or up to 6 months imprisonment.
Vermont	Vt. Stat. Ann. tit. 21, § 491
Employees covered	Permanent employees who are members of an organized unit of the National Guard or the ready reserves and are called to active state duty or training with the U.S. military.
Amount of leave	Leave of absence with or without pay. Employee must give 30 days' notice for U.S. training and as much notice as possible for state duty.
Reinstatement	If still qualified, to former position with the same status, pay and seniority, including seniority that accrued during the leave of absence.
Benefits and rights	Employer may not discriminate against employee who is a member or an applicant for membership in the state or federal National Guard.
Virginia	Va. Code Ann. §§ 44-93.2 to 44-93.5; 44-98
Employees covered	Member or the Virginia National Guard, Virginia State Defense Force or naval militia called to active state duty by the governor.
Amount of leave	Leave of absence with or without pay. May not be required to use vacation or any other accrued leave unless employee wants to.

Reinstatement	To previous position or one with same seniority, status and pay; if no such position exists, to a comparable position, unless reemployment would be unreasonable. Must apply in writing within 5 days of release from duty or from related hospitalization.
Benefits and rights	Employees may not be discriminated against in hiring, retention, promotion or benefits.
Employer penalties	Employer who discriminates or who violates leave provisions may be liable for any loss of wages or benefits. In addition any employer who tries to hinder or dissuade an employee from serving in the state military is liable for a fine of up to $500 or up to $30 days in jail or both.
Washington	Wash. Rev. Code Ann. §§ 73.16.032 to 73.16.035
Employees covered	Permanent employees who are Washington residents or employed within the state and who volunteer or are called to serve in the uniformed services have all the rights and protections guaranteed under USERRA.
West Virginia	W.Va. Code § 15-1F-8
Employees covered	Employees who are members of the organized militia in active state service have the same reemployment rights as members of the U.S. uniformed services under USERRA.
Wisconsin	Wis. Stat. Ann. §§ 45.50; 21.72
Employees covered	Permanent employees who enlist, are inducted or called to serve in the uniformed services; civilians requested to perform national defense work during an officially proclaimed emergency.
Amount of leave	Up to 4 years for service and or training unless period extended by law.
Reinstatement	To same or equivalent position with no loss of seniority, pay or benefits.
Return to work	Within 90 days of release from service or within 6 months of release from service-related hospitalization.
Benefits and rights	A member of the uniformed services on active federal or state duty after 9/11/2001 may renew any license that expired during that period within 90 days after discharge.
Employer penalties	May be liable for lost wages and benefits.
Wyoming	Wyo. Stat. § 19-11-104
Employees covered	Members of the uniformed services.
Benefits and rights	May not be discriminated against in hiring, reemployment, retention, promotion or any benefit because of membership, service or enlisting in uniformed services.

H. Full Text of USERRA

U.S Code
Title 38: Veterans' Benefits
Part III: Readjustment and Related Benefits
Chapter 43—Employment and Reemployment Rights of Members of the Uniformed Services

SUBCHAPTER I—GENERAL

§ 4301. Purposes; sense of Congress

(a) The purposes of this chapter are—

(1) to encourage noncareer service in the uniformed services by eliminating or minimizing the disadvantages to civilian careers and employment which can result from such service;

(2) to minimize the disruption to the lives of persons performing service in the uniformed services as well as to their employers, their fellow employees, and their communities, by providing for the prompt reemployment of such persons upon their completion of such service; and

(3) to prohibit discrimination against persons because of their service in the uniformed services.

(b) It is the sense of Congress that the Federal Government should be a model employer in carrying out the provisions of this chapter.

§ 4302. Relation to other law and plans or agreements

(a) Nothing in this chapter shall supersede, nullify or diminish any Federal or State law (including any local law or ordinance), contract, agreement, policy, plan, practice, or other matter that establishes a right or benefit that is more beneficial to, or is in addition to, a right or benefit provided for such person in this chapter.

(b) This chapter supersedes any State law (including any local law or ordinance), contract, agreement, policy, plan, practice, or other matter that reduces, limits, or eliminates in any manner any right or benefit provided by this chapter, including the establishment of additional prerequisites to the exercise of any such right or the receipt of any such benefit.

§ 4303. Definitions

For the purposes of this chapter—

(1) The term "Attorney General" means the Attorney General of the United States or any person designated by the Attorney General to carry out a responsibility of the Attorney General under this chapter.

(2) The term "benefit", "benefit of employment", or "rights and benefits" means any advantage, profit, privilege, gain, status, account, or interest (other than wages or salary for work performed) that accrues by reason of an employment contract or agreement or an employer policy, plan, or practice and includes rights and benefits under a pension plan, a health plan, an employee stock ownership plan, insurance coverage and awards, bonuses, severance pay, supplemental unemployment benefits, vacations, and the opportunity to select work hours or location of employment.

(3) The term "employee" means any person employed by an employer. Such term includes any person who is a citizen, national or permanent resident alien of the United States employed in a workplace in a foreign country by an employer that is an entity incorporated or otherwise organized in the United States or that is controlled by an entity organized in the United States, within the meaning of Section 4319(c) of this title.

(4)

(A) Except as provided in subparagraphs (B) and (C), the term "employer" means any person, institution, organization, or other entity that pays salary or wages for work performed or that has control over employment opportunities, including—

(i) a person, institution, organization, or other entity to whom the employer has delegated the performance of employment-related responsibilities;

(ii) the Federal Government;

(iii) a State;

(iv) any successor in interest to a person, institution, organization, or other entity referred to in this subparagraph; and

(v) a person, institution, organization, or other entity that has denied initial employment in violation of section 4311.

(B) In the case of a National Guard technician employed under section 709 of title 32, the term "employer" means the adjutant general of the State in which the technician is employed.

(C) Except as an actual employer of employees, an employee pension benefit plan described in section 3(2) of the Employee Retirement Income Security Act of 1974 (29 U.S.C. 1002(2)) shall be deemed to be an employer only with respect to the obligation to provide benefits described in section 4318.

(5) The term "Federal executive agency" includes the United States Postal Service, the Postal Rate Commission, any nonappropriated fund instrumentality of the United States, any Executive agency (as that term is defined in section 105 of title 5) other than an agency referred to in section 2302(a)(2)(C)(ii) of title 5, and any military department (as that term is defined in section 102 of title 5) with respect to the civilian employees of that department.

(6) The term "Federal Government" includes any Federal executive agency, the legislative branch of the United States, and the judicial branch of the United States.

(7) The term "health plan" means an insurance policy or contract, medical or hospital service agreement, membership or subscription contract, or other arrangement under which health services for individuals are provided or the expenses of such services are paid.

(8) The term "notice" means (with respect to subchapter II) any written or verbal notification of an obligation or intention to perform service in the uniformed services provided to an employer by the employee who will perform such service or by the uniformed service in which such service is to be performed.

(9) The term "qualified", with respect to an employment position, means having the ability to perform the essential tasks of the position.

(10) The term "reasonable efforts", in the case of actions required of an employer under this chapter, means actions, including training provided by an employer, that do not place an undue hardship on the employer.

(11) Notwithstanding section 101, the term "Secretary" means the Secretary of Labor or any person designated by such Secretary to carry out an activity under this chapter.

(12) The term "seniority" means longevity in employment together with any benefits of employment which accrue with, or are determined by, longevity in employment.

(13) The term "service in the uniformed services" means the performance of duty on a voluntary or involuntary basis in a uniformed service under competent authority and includes: full-time National Guard, a period for which a person is absent from a position of employment for the purpose of

performing funeral honors duty as authorized by section 12503 of title 10 of section 115 of title 32.

(14) The term "State" means each of the several States of the United States, the District of Columbia, the Commonwealth of Puerto Rico, Guam, the Virgin Islands, and other territories of the United States (including the agencies and political subdivisions thereof).

(15) The term "undue hardship", in the case of actions taken by an employer, means actions requiring significant difficulty or expense, when considered in light of—

(A) the nature and cost of the action needed under this chapter;

(B) the overall financial resources of the facility or facilities involved in the provision of the action; the number of persons employed at such facility; the effect on expenses and resources, or the impact otherwise of such action upon the operation of the facility;

(C) the overall financial resources of the employer; the overall size of the business of an employer with respect to the number of its employees; the number, type, and location of its facilities; and

(D) the type of operation or operations of the employer, including the composition, structure, and functions of the work force of such employer; the geographic separateness, administrative, or fiscal relationship of the facility or facilities in question to the employer.

(16) The term "uniformed services" means the Armed Forces, the Army National Guard and the Air National Guard when engaged in active duty for training, inactive duty training, or full-time National Guard duty, the commissioned corps of the Public Health Service, and any other category of persons designated by the President in time of war or national emergency.

§ 4304. Character of service

A person's entitlement to the benefits of this chapter by reason of the service of such person in one of the uniformed services terminates upon the occurrence of any of the following events:

(1) A separation of such person from such uniformed service with a dishonorable or bad conduct discharge.

(2) A separation of such person from such uniformed service under other than honorable conditions, as characterized pursuant to regulations prescribed by the Secretary concerned.

(3) A dismissal of such person permitted under section 1161(a) of title 10.

(4) A dropping of such person from the rolls pursuant to section 1161(b) of title 10.

SUBCHAPTER II—EMPLOYMENT AND REEMPLOYMENT RIGHTS AND LIMITATIONS; PROHIBITIONS

§ 4311. Discrimination against persons who serve in the uniformed services and acts of reprisal prohibited

(a) A person who is a member of, applies to be a member of, performs, has performed, applies to perform, or has an obligation to perform service in a uniformed service shall not be denied initial employment, reemployment, retention in employment, promotion, or any benefit of employment by an employer on the basis of that membership, application for membership, performance of service, application for service, or obligation.

(b) An employer may not discriminate in employment against or take any adverse employment action against any person because such person (1) has taken an action to enforce a protection afforded any person under this chapter, (2) has testified or otherwise made a statement in or in connection with any proceeding under this chapter, (3) has assisted or otherwise participated in an investigation under this chapter, or (4) has exercised a right provided for in this chapter. The prohibition in this subsection shall apply with respect to a person regardless of whether that person has performed service in the uniformed services.

(c) An employer shall be considered to have engaged in actions prohibited—

(1) under subsection (a), if the person's membership, application for membership, service, application for service, or obligation for service in the uniformed services is a motivating factor in the employer's action, unless the employer can prove that the action would have been taken in the absence of such membership, application for membership, service, application for service, or obligation for service; or

(2) under subsection (b), if the person's (A) action to enforce a protection afforded any person under this chapter, (B) testimony or making of a statement in or in connection with any proceeding under this chapter, (C) assistance or other participation in an investigation under this chapter, or (D) exercise of a right provided for in this chapter, is a motivating factor in the employer's action, unless the employer can prove that the action would have been taken in the absence

of such person's enforcement action, testimony, statement, assistance, participation, or exercise of a right.

(d) The prohibitions in subsections (a) and (b) shall apply to any position of employment, including a position that is described in section 4312(d)(1)(C) of this title.

§ 4312. Reemployment rights of persons who serve in the uniformed services

(a) Subject to subsections (b), (c), and (d) and to section 4304, any person whose absence from a position of employment is necessitated by reason of service in the uniformed services shall be entitled to the reemployment rights and benefits and other employment benefits of this chapter if—

(1) the person (or an appropriate officer of the uniformed service in which such service is performed) has given advance written or verbal notice of such service to such person's employer;

(2) the cumulative length of the absence and of all previous absences from a position of employment with that employer by reason of service in the uniformed services does not exceed five years; and

(3) except as provided in subsection (f), the person reports to, or submits an application for reemployment to, such employer in accordance with the provisions of subsection (e).

(b) No notice is required under subsection (a)(1) if the giving of such notice is precluded by military necessity or, under all of the relevant circumstances, the giving of such notice is otherwise impossible or unreasonable. A determination of military necessity for the purposes of this subsection shall be made pursuant to regulations prescribed by the Secretary of Defense and shall not be subject to judicial review.

(c) Subsection (a) shall apply to a person who is absent from a position of employment by reason of service in the uniformed services if such person's cumulative period of service in the uniformed services, with respect to the employer relationship for which a person seeks reemployment, does not exceed five years, except that any such period of service shall not include any service—

(1) that is required, beyond five years, to complete an initial period of obligated service;

(2) during which such person was unable to obtain orders releasing such person from a period of service in the uniformed services before the expiration of such five-year period and such inability was through no fault of such person;

(3) performed as required pursuant to section 10147 of title 10, under section 502(a) or 503 of title 32, or to fulfill additional training requirements determined and certified in writing by the Secretary concerned, to be necessary for professional development, or for completion of skill training or retraining; or

(4) performed by a member of a uniformed service who is—

(A) ordered to or retained on active duty under section 688, 12301(a), 12301(g), 12302, 12304, or 12305 of title 10 or under section 331, 332, 359, 360, 367, or 712 of title 14;

(B) ordered to or retained on active duty (other than for training) under any provision of law because of a war or national emergency declared by the President or the Congress, as determined by the Secretary concerned;

(C) ordered to active duty (other than for training) in support, as determined by the Secretary concerned, of an operational mission for which personnel have been ordered to active duty under section 12304 of title 10;

(D) ordered to active duty in support, as determined by the Secretary concerned, of a critical mission or requirement of the uniformed services; or

(E) called into Federal service as a member of the National Guard under chapter 15 of title 10 or under section 12406 of title 10.

(d)

(1) An employer is not required to reemploy a person under this chapter if—

(A) the employer's circumstances have so changed as to make such reemployment impossible or unreasonable;

(B) in the case of a person entitled to reemployment under subsection (a)(3), (a)(4), or (b)(2)(B) of section 4313, such employment would impose an undue hardship on the employer; or

(C) the employment from which the person leaves to serve in the uniformed services is for a brief, nonrecurrent period and there is no reasonable expectation that such employment will continue indefinitely or for a significant period.

(2) In any proceeding involving an issue of whether—

(A) any reemployment referred to in paragraph (1) is impossible or unreasonable because of a change in an employer's circumstances,

(B) any accommodation, training, or effort referred to in subsection (a)(3), (a)(4), or (b)(2)(B) of section 4313 would impose an undue hardship on the employer, or

(C) the employment referred to in paragraph (1)(C) is for a brief, nonrecurrent period and there is no reasonable expectation that such employment will continue indefinitely or for a significant period, the employer shall have the burden of proving the impossibility or unreasonableness, undue hardship, or the brief or nonrecurrent nature of the employment without a reasonable expectation of continuing indefinitely or for a significant period.

(e)

(1) Subject to paragraph (2), a person referred to in subsection (a) shall, upon the completion of a period of service in the uniformed services, notify the employer referred to in such subsection of the person's intent to return to a position of employment with such employer as follows:

(A) In the case of a person whose period of service in the uniformed services was less than 31 days, by reporting to the employer—

(i) not later than the beginning of the first full regularly scheduled work period on the first full calendar day following the completion of the period of service and the expiration of eight hours after a period allowing for the safe transportation of the person from the place of that service to the person's residence; or

(ii) as soon as possible after the expiration of the eight-hour period referred to in clause (i), if reporting within the period referred to in such clause is impossible or unreasonable through no fault of the person.

(B) In the case of a person who is absent from a position of employment for a period of any length for the purposes of an examination to determine the person's fitness to perform service in the uniformed services, by reporting in the manner and time referred to in subparagraph (A).

(C) In the case of a person whose period of service in the uniformed services was for more than 30 days but less than 181 days, by submitting an application for reemployment with the employer not later than 14 days after the completion of the period of service or if submitting such application within such period is impossible or unreasonable through no fault of the person, the next first full calendar day when submission of such application becomes possible.

(D) In the case of a person whose period of service in the uniformed services was for more than 180

days, by submitting an application for reemployment with the employer not later than 90 days after the completion of the period of service.

(2)

(A) A person who is hospitalized for, or convalescing from, an illness or injury incurred in, or aggravated during, the performance of service in the uniformed services shall, at the end of the period that is necessary for the person to recover from such illness or injury, report to the person's employer (in the case of a person described in subparagraph (A) or (B) of paragraph (1)) or submit an application for reemployment with such employer (in the case of a person described in subparagraph (C) or (D) of such paragraph). Except as provided in subparagraph (B), such period of recovery may not exceed two years.

(B) Such two-year period shall be extended by the minimum time required to accommodate the circumstances beyond such person's control which make reporting within the period specified in subparagraph (A) impossible or unreasonable.

(3) A person who fails to report or apply for employment or reemployment within the appropriate period specified in this subsection shall not automatically forfeit such person's entitlement to the rights and benefits referred to in subsection (a) but shall be subject to the conduct rules, established policy, and general practices of the employer pertaining to explanations and discipline with respect to absence from scheduled work.

(f)

(1) A person who submits an application for reemployment in accordance with subparagraph (C) or (D) of subsection (e)(1) or subsection (e)(2) shall provide to the person's employer (upon the request of such employer) documentation to establish that—

(A) the person's application is timely;

(B) the person has not exceeded the service limitations set forth in subsection (a)(2) (except as permitted under subsection (c)); and

(C) the person's entitlement to the benefits under this chapter has not been terminated pursuant to section 4304.

(2) Documentation of any matter referred to in paragraph (1) that satisfies regulations prescribed by the Secretary shall satisfy the documentation requirements in such paragraph.

(3)

(A) Except as provided in subparagraph (B), the failure of a person to provide documentation that satisfies regulations prescribed pursuant to paragraph (2) shall not be a basis for denying reemployment in accordance with the provisions of this chapter if the failure occurs because such documentation does not exist or is not readily available at the time of the request of the employer. If, after such reemployment, documentation becomes available that establishes that such person does not meet one or more of the requirements referred to in subparagraphs (A), (B), and (C) of paragraph (1), the employer of such person may terminate the employment of the person and the provision of any rights or benefits afforded the person under this chapter.

(B) An employer who reemploys a person absent from a position of employment for more than 90 days may require that the person provide the employer with the documentation referred to in subparagraph (A) before beginning to treat the person as not having incurred a break in service for pension purposes under section 4318(a)(2)(A).

(4) An employer may not delay or attempt to defeat a reemployment obligation by demanding documentation that does not then exist or is not then readily available.

(g) The right of a person to reemployment under this section shall not entitle such person to retention, preference, or displacement rights over any person with a superior claim under the provisions of title 5, United States Code, relating to veterans and other preference eligibles.

(h) In any determination of a person's entitlement to protection under this chapter, the timing, frequency, and duration of the person's training or service, or the nature of such training or service (including voluntary service) in the uniformed services, shall not be a basis for denying protection of this chapter if the service does not exceed the limitations set forth in subsection (c) and the notice requirements established in subsection (a)(1) and the notification requirements established in subsection (e) are met.

§ 4313. Reemployment positions

(a) Subject to subsection (b) (in the case of any employee) and sections 4314 and 4315 (in the case of an employee of the Federal Government), a person entitled to reemployment under section 4312, upon completion of a period of service in the uniformed services, shall be promptly reemployed in a position of employment in accordance with the following order of priority:

(1) Except as provided in paragraphs (3) and (4), in the case of a person whose period of service in the uniformed services was for less than 91 days—

(A) in the position of employment in which the person would have been employed if the continuous employment of such person with the employer had not been interrupted by such service, the duties of which the person is qualified to perform; or

(B) in the position of employment in which the person was employed on the date of the commencement of the service in the uniformed services, only if the person is not qualified to perform the duties of the position referred to in subparagraph (A) after reasonable efforts by the employer to qualify the person.

(2) Except as provided in paragraphs (3) and (4), in the case of a person whose period of service in the uniformed services was for more than 90 days—

(A) in the position of employment in which the person would have been employed if the continuous employment of such person with the employer had not been interrupted by such service, or a position of like seniority, status and pay, the duties of which the person is qualified to perform; or

(B) in the position of employment in which the person was employed on the date of the commencement of the service in the uniformed services, or a position of like seniority, status and pay, the duties of which the person is qualified to perform, only if the person is not qualified to perform the duties of a position referred to in subparagraph (A) after reasonable efforts by the employer to qualify the person.

(3) In the case of a person who has a disability incurred in, or aggravated during, such service, and who (after reasonable efforts by the employer to accommodate the disability) is not qualified due to such disability to be employed in the position of employment in which the person would have been employed if the continuous employment of such person with the employer had not been interrupted by such service—

(A) in any other position which is equivalent in seniority, status, and pay, the duties of which the person is qualified to perform or would become qualified to perform with reasonable efforts by the employer; or

(B) if not employed under subparagraph (A), in a position which is the nearest approximation to a position referred to in subparagraph (A) in terms of seniority, status, and pay consistent with circumstances of such person's case.

(4) In the case of a person who (A) is not qualified to be employed in (i) the position of employment in which the person would have been employed if the

continuous employment of such person with the employer had not been interrupted by such service, or (ii) in the position of employment in which such person was employed on the date of the commencement of the service in the uniform services for any reason (other than disability incurred in, or aggravated during, service in the uniformed services), and (B) cannot become qualified with reasonable efforts by the employer, in any other position which is the nearest approximation to a position referred to first in clause (A)(i) and then in clause (A)(ii) which such person is qualified to perform, with full seniority.

(b)

(1) If two or more persons are entitled to reemployment under section 4312 in the same position of employment and more than one of them has reported for such reemployment, the person who left the position first shall have the prior right to reemployment in that position.

(2) Any person entitled to reemployment under section 4312 who is not reemployed in a position of employment by reason of paragraph (1) shall be entitled to be reemployed as follows:

(A) Except as provided in subparagraph (B), in any other position of employment referred to in subsection (a)(1) or (a)(2), as the case may be (in the order of priority set out in the applicable subsection), that provides a similar status and pay to a position of employment referred to in paragraph (1) of this subsection, consistent with the circumstances of such person's case, with full seniority.

(B) In the case of a person who has a disability incurred in, or aggravated during, a period of service in the uniformed services that requires reasonable efforts by the employer for the person to be able to perform the duties of the position of employment, in any other position referred to in subsection (a)(3) (in the order of priority set out in that subsection) that provides a similar status and pay to a position referred to in paragraph (1) of this subsection, consistent with circumstances of such person's case, with full seniority.

§ 4314. Reemployment by the Federal Government

(a) Except as provided in subsections (b), (c), and (d), if a person is entitled to reemployment by the Federal Government under section 4312, such person shall be reemployed in a position of employment as described in section 4313.

(b)

(1) If the Director of the Office of Personnel Management makes a determination described in paragraph (2) with respect to a person who was employed by a Federal executive agency at the time the person entered the service from which the person seeks reemployment under this section, the Director shall—

(A) identify a position of like seniority, status, and pay at another Federal executive agency that satisfies the requirements of section 4313 and for which the person is qualified; and

(B) ensure that the person is offered such position.

(2) The Director shall carry out the duties referred to in subparagraphs (A) and (B) of paragraph (1) if the Director determines that—

(A) the Federal executive agency that employed the person referred to in such paragraph no longer exists and the functions of such agency have not been transferred to another Federal executive agency; or

(B) it is impossible or unreasonable for the agency to reemploy the person.

(c) If the employer of a person described in subsection (a) was, at the time such person entered the service from which such person seeks reemployment under this section, a part of the judicial branch or the legislative branch of the Federal Government, and such employer determines that it is impossible or unreasonable for such employer to reemploy such person, such person shall, upon application to the Director of the Office of Personnel Management, be ensured an offer of employment in an alternative position in a Federal executive agency on the basis described in subsection (b).

(d) If the adjutant general of a State determines that it is impossible or unreasonable to reemploy a person who was a National Guard technician employed under section 709 of title 32, such person shall, upon application to the Director of the Office of Personnel Management, be ensured an offer of employment in an alternative position in a Federal executive agency on the basis described in subsection (b).

§ 4315. Reemployment by certain Federal agencies

(a) The head of each agency referred to in section 2302(a)(2)(C)(ii) of title 5 shall prescribe procedures for ensuring that the rights under this chapter apply to the employees of such agency.

(b) In prescribing procedures under subsection (a), the head of an agency referred to in that subsection shall ensure, to the maximum extent practicable, that the procedures of the agency for reemploying persons who serve in the uniformed services provide for the reemployment of such persons in the agency in a manner similar to the manner of reemployment described in section 4313.

(c)

(1) The procedures prescribed under subsection (a) shall designate an official at the agency who shall determine whether or not the reemployment of a person referred to in subsection (b) by the agency is impossible or unreasonable.

(2) Upon making a determination that the reemployment by the agency of a person referred to in subsection (b) is impossible or unreasonable, the official referred to in paragraph (1) shall notify the person and the Director of the Office of Personnel Management of such determination.

(3) A determination pursuant to this subsection shall not be subject to judicial review.

(4) The head of each agency referred to in subsection (a) shall submit to the Select Committee on Intelligence and the Committee on Veterans' Affairs of the Senate and the Permanent Select Committee on Intelligence and the Committee on Veterans' Affairs of the House of Representatives on an annual basis a report on the number of persons whose reemployment with the agency was determined under this subsection to be impossible or unreasonable during the year preceding the report, including the reason for each such determination.

(d)

(1) Except as provided in this section, nothing in this section, section 4313, or section 4325 shall be construed to exempt any agency referred to in subsection (a) from compliance with any other substantive provision of this chapter.

(2) This section may not be construed—

(A) as prohibiting an employee of an agency referred to in subsection (a) from seeking information from the Secretary regarding assistance in seeking reemployment from the agency under this chapter, alternative employment in the Federal Government under this chapter, or information relating to the rights and obligations of employee and Federal agencies under this chapter; or

(B) as prohibiting such an agency from voluntarily cooperating with or seeking assistance in or of clarification from the Secretary or the Director of the Office of Personnel Management of any matter arising under this chapter.

(e) The Director of the Office of Personnel Management shall ensure the offer of employment to a person in a position in a Federal executive agency on the basis described in subsection (b) if—

(1) the person was an employee of an agency referred to in section 2302(a)(2)(C)(ii) of title 5 at the time the person entered the service from which the person seeks reemployment under this section;

(2) the appropriate officer of the agency determines under subsection (c) that reemployment of the person by the agency is impossible or unreasonable; and

(3) the person submits an application to the Director for an offer of employment under this subsection.

§ 4316. Rights, benefits, and obligations of persons absent from employment for service in a uniformed service

(a) A person who is reemployed under this chapter is entitled to the seniority and other rights and benefits determined by seniority that the person had on the date of the commencement of service in the uniformed services plus the additional seniority and rights and benefits that such person would have attained if the person had remained continuously employed.

(b)

(1) Subject to paragraphs (2) through (6), a person who is absent from a position of employment by reason of service in the uniformed services shall be—

(A) deemed to be on furlough or leave of absence while performing such service; and

(B) entitled to such other rights and benefits not determined by seniority as are generally provided by the employer of the person to employees having similar seniority, status, and pay who are on furlough or leave of absence under a contract, agreement, policy, practice, or plan in effect at the commencement of such service or established while such person performs such service.

(2)

(A) Subject to subparagraph (B), a person who—

(i) is absent from a position of employment by reason of service in the uniformed services, and

(ii) knowingly provides written notice of intent not to return to a position of employment after service in the uniformed service, is not entitled to rights and benefits under paragraph (1)(B).

(B) For the purposes of subparagraph (A), the employer shall have the burden of proving that a person knowingly provided clear written notice of intent not to return to a position of employment after service in the uniformed service and, in doing so, was aware of the specific rights and benefits to be lost under subparagraph (A).

(3) A person deemed to be on furlough or leave of absence under this subsection while serving in the uniformed services shall not be entitled under this subsection to any benefits to which the person would not otherwise be entitled if the person had remained continuously employed.

(4) Such person may be required to pay the employee cost, if any, of any funded benefit continued pursuant to paragraph (1) to the extent other employees on furlough or leave of absence are so required.

(5) The entitlement of a person to coverage under a health plan is provided for under section 4317.

(6) The entitlement of a person to a right or benefit under an employee pension benefit plan is provided for under section 4318.

(c) A person who is reemployed by an employer under this chapter shall not be discharged from such employment, except for cause—

(1) within one year after the date of such reemployment, if the person's period of service before the reemployment was more than 180 days; or

(2) within 180 days after the date of such reemployment, if the person's period of service before the reemployment was more than 30 days but less than 181 days.

(d) Any person whose employment with an employer is interrupted by a period of service in the uniformed services shall be permitted, upon request of that person, to use during such period of service any vacation, annual, or similar leave with pay accrued by the person before the commencement of such service. No employer may require any such person to use vacation, annual, or similar leave during such period of service.

(e)

(1) An employer shall grant an employee who is a member of a reserve component an authorized leave of absence from a position of employment to allow that employee to perform funeral honors duty as authorized by section 12503 of title 10 or section 115.

(2) For purposes of section 4312 (e)(1) of this title, an employee who takes an authorized leave of absence under paragraph (1) is deemed to have notified the employer of the employee's intent to return of such position of employment.

§ 4317. Health plans

(a)

(1) In any case in which a person (or the person's dependents) has coverage under a health plan in connection with the person's position of employment, including a group health plan (as defined in section 607(1) of the Employee Retirement Income Security Act of 1974), and such person is absent from such position of employment by reason of service in the uniformed services, the plan shall provide that the person may elect to continue such coverage as provided in this subsection. The maximum period of coverage of a person and the person's dependents under such an election shall be the lesser of—

(A) the 18-month period beginning on the date on which the person's absence begins; or

(B) the day after the date on which the person fails to apply for or return to a position of employment, as determined under section 4312(e).

(2) A person who elects to continue health-plan coverage under this paragraph may be required to pay not more than 102 percent of the full premium under the plan (determined in the same manner as the applicable premium under section 4980B(f)(4) of the Internal Revenue Code of 1986) associated with such coverage for the employer's other employees, except that in the case of a person who performs service in the uniformed services for less than 31 days, such person may not be required to pay more than the employee share, if any, for such coverage.

(3) In the case of a health plan that is a multiemployer plan, as defined in section 3(37) of the Employee Retirement Income Security Act of 1974, any liability under the plan for employer contributions and benefits arising under this paragraph shall be allocated—

(A) by the plan in such manner as the plan sponsor shall provide; or

(B) if the sponsor does not provide—

(i) to the last employer employing the person before the period served by the person in the uniformed services, or

(ii) if such last employer is no longer functional, to the plan.

(b)

(1) Except as provided in paragraph (2), in the case of a person whose coverage under a health plan was terminated by reason of service in the uniformed services, an exclusion or waiting period may not be imposed in connection with the reinstatement of such coverage upon reemployment under this chapter if an

exclusion or waiting period would not have been imposed under a health plan had coverage of such person by such plan not been terminated as a result of such service. This paragraph applies to the person who is reemployed and to any individual who is covered by such plan by reason of the reinstatement of the coverage of such person.

(2) Paragraph (1) shall not apply to the coverage of any illness or injury determined by the Secretary of Veterans Affairs to have been incurred in, or aggravated during, performance of service in the uniformed services.

§ 4318. Employee pension benefit plans

(a)

(1)

(A) Except as provided in subparagraph (B), in the case of a right provided pursuant to an employee pension benefit plan (including those described in sections 3(2) and 3(33) of the Employee Retirement Income Security Act of 1974) or a right provided under any Federal or State law governing pension benefits for governmental employees, the right to pension benefits of a person reemployed under this chapter shall be determined under this section.

(B) In the case of benefits under the Thrift Savings Plan, the rights of a person reemployed under this chapter shall be those rights provided in section 8432b of title 5. The first sentence of this subparagraph shall not be construed to affect any other right or benefit under this chapter.

(2)

(A) A person reemployed under this chapter shall be treated as not having incurred a break in service with the employer or employers maintaining the plan by reason of such person's period or periods of service in the uniformed services.

(B) Each period served by a person in the uniformed services shall, upon reemployment under this chapter, be deemed to constitute service with the employer or employers maintaining the plan for the purpose of determining the nonforfeitability of the person's accrued benefits and for the purpose of determining the accrual of benefits under the plan.

(b)

(1) An employer reemploying a person under this chapter shall, with respect to a period of service described in subsection (a)(2)(B), be liable to an employee pension benefit plan for funding any obligation of the plan to provide the benefits

described in subsection (a)(2) and shall allocate the amount of any employer contribution for the person in the same manner and to the same extent the allocation occurs for other employees during the period of service. For purposes of determining the amount of such liability and any obligation of the plan, earnings and forfeitures shall not be included. For purposes of determining the amount of such liability and for purposes of section 515 of the Employee Retirement Income Security Act of 1974 or any similar Federal or State law governing pension benefits for governmental employees, service in the uniformed services that is deemed under subsection (a) to be service with the employer shall be deemed to be service with the employer under the terms of the plan or any applicable collective bargaining agreement. In the case of a multiemployer plan, as defined in section 3(37) of the Employee Retirement Income Security Act of 1974, any liability of the plan described in this paragraph shall be allocated—

(A) by the plan in such manner as the sponsor maintaining the plan shall provide; or

(B) if the sponsor does not provide—

(i) to the last employer employing the person before the period served by the person in the uniformed services, or

(ii) if such last employer is no longer functional, to the plan.

(2) A person reemployed under this chapter shall be entitled to accrued benefits pursuant to subsection (a) that are contingent on the making of, or derived from, employee contributions or elective deferrals (as defined in section 402(g)(3) of the Internal Revenue Code of 1986) only to the extent the person makes payment to the plan with respect to such contributions or deferrals. No such payment may exceed the amount the person would have been permitted or required to contribute had the person remained continuously employed by the employer throughout the period of service described in subsection (a)(2)(B). Any payment to the plan described in this paragraph shall be made during the period beginning with the date of reemployment and whose duration is three times the period of the person's services in the uniformed services, such payment period not to exceed five years.

(3) For purposes of computing an employer's liability under paragraph (1) or the employee's contributions under paragraph (2), the employee's compensation during the period of service described in subsection (a)(2)(B) shall be computed—

(A) at the rate the employee would have received but for the period of service described in subsection (a)(2)(B), or

(B) in the case that the determination of such rate is not reasonably certain, on the basis of the employee's average rate of compensation during the 12-month period immediately preceding such period (or, if shorter, the period of employment immediately preceding such period).

(c) Any employer who reemploys a person under this chapter and who is an employer contributing to a multi-employer plan, as defined in section 3(37) of the Employee Retirement Income Security Act of 1974, under which benefits are or may be payable to such person by reason of the obligations set forth in this chapter, shall, within 30 days after the date of such reemployment, provide information, in writing, of such reemployment to the administrator of such plan.

§ 4319. Employment and reemployment rights in foreign countries

(a) LIABILITY OF CONTROLLING UNITED STATES EMPLOYER OF FOREIGN ENTITY—If an employer controls an entity that is incorporated or otherwise organized in a foreign country, any denial of employment, reemployment, or benefit by such entity shall be presumed to be by such employer.

(b) INAPPLICABILITY TO FOREIGN EMPLOYER—This subchapter does not apply to foreign operations of an employer that is a foreign person not controlled by or United States employer.

(c) DETERMINATION OF CONTROLLING EMPLOYER—For the purpose of this section, the determination of whether an employer controls an entity shall be based upon the interrelations of operations, common management, centralized control of labor relations, and common ownership or financial control of the employer and the entity.

(d) EXEMPTION—Notwithstanding any other provision of this subchapter, an employer, or an entity controlled by an employer, shall be exempt from compliance with any of section 4311 through 4318 of this title with respect to an employee in a workplace in a foreign country, if compliance with that section would cause such employer, or such entity controlled by an employer, to violate the law of the foreign country in which the workplace is located.

SUBCHAPTER III—PROCEDURES FOR ASSISTANCE, ENFORCEMENT, AND INVESTIGATION

§ 4321. Assistance in obtaining reemployment or other employment rights or benefits

The Secretary (through the Veterans' Employment and Training Service) shall provide assistance to any person with respect to the employment and reemployment rights and benefits to which such person is entitled under this chapter. In providing such assistance, the Secretary may request the assistance of existing Federal and State agencies engaged in similar or related activities and utilize the assistance of volunteers.

§ 4322. Enforcement of employment or reemployment rights

(a) A person who claims that—

(1) such person is entitled under this chapter to employment or reemployment rights or benefits with respect to employment by an employer; and

(2)

(A) such employer has failed or refused, or is about to fail or refuse, to comply with the provisions of this chapter; or

(B) in the case that the employer is a Federal executive agency, such employer or the Office of Personnel Management has failed or refused, or is about to fail or refuse, to comply with the provisions of this chapter, may file a complaint with the Secretary in accordance with subsection (b), and the Secretary shall investigate such complaint.

(b) Such complaint shall be in writing, be in such form as the Secretary may prescribe, include the name and address of the employer against whom the complaint is filed, and contain a summary of the allegations that form the basis for the complaint.

(c) The Secretary shall, upon request, provide technical assistance to a potential claimant with respect to a complaint under this subsection, and when appropriate, to such claimant's employer.

(d) The Secretary shall investigate each complaint submitted pursuant to subsection (a). If the Secretary determines as a result of the investigation that the action alleged in such complaint occurred, the Secretary shall attempt to resolve the complaint by making reasonable efforts to ensure that the person or entity named in the complaint complies with the provisions of this chapter.

(e) If the efforts of the Secretary with respect to any complaint filed under subsection (a) do not resolve the complaint, the Secretary shall notify the person who submitted the complaint of—

(1) the results of the Secretary's investigation; and

(2) the complainant's entitlement to proceed under the enforcement of rights provisions provided under section 4323 (in the case of a person submitting a complaint against a State or private employer) or section 4324 (in the case of a person submitting a complaint against a Federal executive agency or the Office of Personnel Management).

(f) This subchapter does not apply to any action relating to benefits to be provided under the Thrift Savings Plan under title 5.

§ 4323. Enforcement of rights with respect to a State or private employer

(a) ACTION FOR RELIEF—

(1) A person who receives from the Secretary a notification pursuant to section 4322(e) of this title of an unsuccessful effort to resolve a complaint relating to a State (as an employer) or a private employer may request that the Secretary refer the complaint to the Attorney General. If the Attorney General is responsibly satisfied that the person on whose behalf the complaint is referred is entitled to the rights or benefits sought, the Attorney General may appear on behalf of, and act as attorney for, the person on whose behalf the complaint is submitted and commence an action for relief under this chapter for such person. In the case of such an action against a State (as an employer), the action shall be brought in the name of the United States as the plaintiff in the action.

(2) A person may commence an action for relief with respect to a complaint against a State (as an employer) or a private employer if the person—

(A) has chosen not to apply to the Secretary for assistance under section 4322(a) of this title;

(B) has chosen not to request that the Secretary refer the complaint to the Attorney General under paragraph (1); or

(C) has been refused representation by the Attorney General with respect to the complaint under such paragraph .

(b) JURISDICTION—

(1) In the case of an action against a State (as an employer) or a private employer commenced by the United States, the district courts of the United States shall have jurisdiction over the action.

(2) In the case of action against a State (as an employer) by a person, the action may be brought in a State court of competent jurisdiction in accordance with the laws of the State.

(3) In the case of an action against a private employer by a person, the district courts of the United States shall have jurisdiction of the action.

(c) VENUE—

(1) In the case of an action by the United States against a State (as an employer), the action may proceed in the United States district court for any district in which the State exercises any authority or carries out any function.

(2) In the case of an action against a private employer, the action may proceed in the United States district court for any district in which the private employer of the person maintains a place of business.

(d) REMEDIES—

(1) In any action under this section, the court may award relief as follows:

(A) The court may require the employer to comply with the provisions of this chapter.

(B) The court may require the employer to compensate the person for any loss of wages or benefits suffered by reason of such employer's failure to comply with the provisions of this chapter.

(C) The court may require the employer to play the person an amount equal to the amount referred to in subparagraph (B) as liquidated damages, if the court determines that the employer's failure to comply with the provisions of this chapter was willful.

(2)

(A) Any compensation awarded under subparagraph (B) or (C) of paragraph (1) shall be in addition to, and shall not diminish, any of the other rights and benefits provided for under this chapter.

(B) In the case of an action commenced in the name of the United States for which the relief includes compensation awarded under subparagraph (B) or (C) of paragraph (1), such compensation shall be held in a special deposit account and shall be paid, on order of the Attorney General, directly to the person. If the compensation is not paid to the person because of inability to do so within a period of 3 years, the compensation shall be converted into the Treasury of the United States as miscellaneous receipts.

(3) A State shall be subject to the same remedies, including prejudgment interest, as may be imposed upon any private employer under this section.

(e) EQUITY POWERS—The court may use its full equity powers, including temporary or permanent injunctions, temporary restraining orders, and contempt orders, to vindicate fully the rights of benefits of persons under this chapter.

(f) STANDING—An action under this chapter may be initiated only by a person claiming rights or benefits under this chapter under subsection (a) or by the United States under subsection (a)(1).

(g) RESPONDENT—In any action under this chapter, only an employer or a potential employer, as the case may be, shall be a necessary party respondent.

(h) FEES, COURT COSTS—

(1) No fees or court costs may be charged or taxed against any person claiming rights under this chapter.

(2) In any action or proceeding to enforce a provision of this chapter by a person under subsection (a)(2) who obtained private counsel for such action or proceeding, the court may award any such person who prevails in such action or proceeding reasonable attorney fees, expert witness fees, and other litigation expenses.

(i) INAPPLICABILITY OF STATE STATUTE OF LIMITATIONS—No State statute of limitations shall apply to any proceeding under this chapter.

(j) DEFINITION—In this section, the term "private employer" includes a political subdivision of a State.

§ 4324. Enforcement of rights with respect to Federal executive agencies

(a)

(1) A person who receives from the Secretary a notification pursuant to section 4322(e) may request that the Secretary refer the complaint for litigation before the Merit Systems Protection Board. The Secretary shall refer the complaint to the Office of Special Counsel established by section 1211 of title 5.

(2)

(A) If the Special Counsel is reasonably satisfied that the person on whose behalf a complaint is referred under paragraph (1) is entitled to the rights or benefits sought, the Special Counsel (upon the request of the person submitting the complaint) may appear on behalf of, and act as attorney for, the person and initiate an action regarding such complaint before the Merit Systems Protection Board.

(B) If the Special Counsel declines to initiate an action and represent a person before the Merit Systems Protection Board under subparagraph (A), the Special Counsel shall notify such person of that decision.

(b) A person may submit a complaint against a Federal executive agency or the Office of Personnel Management under this subchapter directly to the Merit Systems Protection Board if that person—

(1) has chosen not to apply to the Secretary for assistance under section 4322(a);

(2) has received a notification from the Secretary under section 4322(e);

(3) has chosen not to be represented before the Board by the Special Counsel pursuant to subsection (a)(2)(A); or

(4) has received a notification of a decision from the Special Counsel under subsection (a)(2)(B).

(c)

(1) The Merit Systems Protection Board shall adjudicate any complaint brought before the Board pursuant to subsection (a)(2)(A) or (b), without, regard as to whether the complaint accured before, on, or after October 13, 1994. A person who seeks a hearing or adjudication by submitting such a complaint under this paragraph may be represented at such hearing or adjudication in accordance with the rules of the Board.

(2) If the Board determines that a Federal executive agency or the Office of Personnel Management has not complied with the provisions of this chapter relating to the employment or reemployment of a person by the agency, the Board shall enter an order requiring the agency or Office to comply with such provisions and to compensate such person for any loss of wages or benefits suffered by such person by reason of such lack of compliance.

(3) Any compensation received by a person pursuant to an order under paragraph (2) shall be in addition to any other right or benefit provided for by this chapter and shall not diminish any such right or benefit.

(4) If the Board determines as a result of a hearing or adjudication conducted pursuant to a complaint submitted by a person directly to the Board pursuant to subsection (b) that such person is entitled to an order referred to in paragraph (2), the Board may, in its discretion, award such person reasonable attorney fees, expert witness fees, and other litigation expenses.

(d)

(1) A person adversely affected or aggrieved by a final order or decision of the Merit Systems Protection Board under subsection (c) may petition the United States Court of Appeals for the Federal Circuit to review the final order or decision. Such petition and review shall be in accordance with the procedures set forth in section 7703 of title 5.

(2) Such person may be represented in the Federal Circuit proceeding by the Special Counsel unless the person was not represented by the Special Counsel before the Merit Systems Protection Board regarding such order or decision.

§ 4325. Enforcement of rights with respect to certain Federal agencies

(a) This section applies to any person who alleges that—

(1) the reemployment of such person by an agency referred to in subsection (a) of section 4315 was not in accordance with procedures for the reemployment of such person under subsection (b) of such section; or

(2) the failure of such agency to reemploy the person under such section was otherwise wrongful.

(b) Any person referred to in subsection (a) may submit a claim relating to an allegation referred to in that subsection to the inspector general of the agency which is the subject of the allegation. The inspector general shall investigate and resolve the allegation pursuant to procedures prescribed by the head of the agency.

(c) In prescribing procedures for the investigation and resolution of allegations under subsection (b), the head of an agency shall ensure, to the maximum extent practicable, that the procedures are similar to the procedures for investigating and resolving complaints utilized by the Secretary under section 4322(d).

(d) This section may not be construed—

(1) as prohibiting an employee of an agency referred to in subsection (a) from seeking information from the Secretary regarding assistance in seeking reemployment from the agency under this chapter, or information relating to the rights and obligations of employees and Federal agencies under this chapter; or

(2) as prohibiting such an agency from voluntarily cooperating with or seeking assistance in or of clarification from the Secretary or the Director of the Office of Personnel Management of any matter arising under this chapter.

§ 4326. Conduct of investigation; subpoenas

(a) In carrying out any investigation under this chapter, the Secretary's duly authorized representatives shall, at all reasonable times, have reasonable access to and the right to interview persons with information relevant to the investigation and shall have reasonable access to, for purposes of examination, and the right to copy and receive, any documents of any person or employer that the Secretary considers relevant to the investigation.

(b) In carrying out any investigation under this chapter, the Secretary may require by subpoena the attendance and testimony of witnesses and the production of documents relating to any matter under investigation. In case of disobedience of the subpoena or contumacy and on request of the Secretary, the Attorney General may apply to any district court of the United States in whose jurisdiction such disobedience or contumacy occurs for an order enforcing the subpoena.

(c) Upon application, the district courts of the United States shall have jurisdiction to issue writs commanding any person or employer to comply with the subpoena of the Secretary or to comply with any order of the Secretary made pursuant to a lawful investigation under this chapter and the district courts shall have jurisdiction to punish failure to obey a subpoena or other lawful order of the Secretary as a contempt of court.

(d) Subsections (b) and (c) shall not apply to the legislative branch or the judicial branch of the United States.

SUBCHAPTER IV—MISCELLANEOUS PROVISIONS

§ 4331. Regulations

(a) The Secretary (in consultation with the Secretary of Defense) may prescribe regulations implementing the provisions of this chapter with regard to the application of this chapter to States, local governments, and private employers.

(b)

(1) The Director of the Office of Personnel Management (in consultation with the Secretary and the Secretary of Defense) may prescribe regulations implementing the provisions of this chapter with regard to the application of this chapter to Federal executive agencies (other than the agencies referred to in paragraph (2)) as employers. Such regulations shall be consistent with the regulations pertaining to the States as employers and private employers, except that employees of the

Federal Government may be given greater or additional rights.

(2) The following entities may prescribe regulations to carry out the activities of such entities under this chapter:

(A) The Merit Systems Protection Board.

(B) The Office of Special Counsel.

(C) The agencies referred to in section 2303(a)(2)(C)(ii) of title 5.

§ 4332. Reports

The Secretary shall, after consultation with the Attorney General and the Special Counsel referred to in section 4324(a)(1) and no later than February 1, 1996, and annually thereafter through 2000, transmit to the Congress, a report containing the following matters for the fiscal year ending before such February 1:

(1) The number of cases reviewed by the Department of Labor under this chapter during the fiscal year for which the report is made.

(2) The number of cases referred to the Attorney General or the Special Counsel pursuant to section 4323 or 4324, respectively, during such fiscal year.

(3) The number of complaints filed by the Attorney General pursuant to section 4323 during such fiscal year.

(4) The nature and status of each case reported on pursuant to paragraph (1), (2), or (3).

(5) An indication of whether there are any apparent patterns of violation of the provisions of this chapter, together with an explanation thereof.

(6) Recommendations for administrative or legislative action that the Secretary, the Attorney General, or the Special Counsel considers necessary for the effective implementation of this chapter, including any action that could be taken to encourage mediation, before claims are filed under this chapter, between employers and persons seeking employment or reemployment.

§ 4333. Outreach

The Secretary, the Secretary of Defense, and the Secretary of Veterans Affairs shall take such actions as such Secretaries determine are appropriate to inform persons entitled to rights and benefits under this chapter and employers of the rights, benefits, and obligations of such persons and such employers under this chapter. ■

Chapter 20

Worker Adjustment and Retraining Notification Act (WARN)

Statute: 29 U.S.C. §§ 2101-2109
http://www4.law.cornell.edu/uscode/29/ch23.html

Regulations: 20 C.F.R. § 639
http://cfr.law.cornell.edu/cfr/cfr.php?title=20&type=part&value=639

Definitions

Affected employees

Employees who may reasonably be expected to suffer an *employment loss* as a result of a proposed *plant closing* or *mass layoff* by their employer.

Employment loss

An employment loss is

- an employment termination for reasons other than cause, voluntary departure or retirement
- a layoff of longer than six months, or
- a reduction of more than 50% in an employee's work hours for six consecutive months.

An employee has not suffered an employment loss if the employer conducted a *plant closing* or *mass layoff* as part of a relocation or consolidation of its business and either:

- prior to the *closing* or *layoff*, the employer offered to transfer the employee to a different employment site within a reasonable commuting distance with no more than a six-month break in employment, or
- the employer offered to transfer the employee to any other employment site (regardless of commuting distance) with no more than a six-month break in employment, and the employee accepted this offer within 30 days of the offer or 30 days of the *closing* or *layoff*, whichever is later.

Facility

A building or buildings in which an employer operates.

Mass layoff

A reduction in force which is not the result of a *plant closing* and results in an *employment loss* at a *single site of employment* during any 30-day period for:

- 500 or more employees (excluding *part-time employees*), or
- 50 to 499 employees (excluding *part-time employees*), if the number of employees laid off make up at least 33% of the employer's active workforce.

Operating unit

An organizationally or operationally distinct product, operation or specific work function within or across facilities at a *single site of employment* (for example, a sales force or production line).

Part-time employee

An employee who

- works, on average, fewer than 20 hours per week, or
- has been employed for fewer than six of the 12 months preceding the date on which notice would be required under WARN.

Plant closing

The permanent or temporary shutdown of a *single site of employment*, or one or more *facilities* or *operating units* within a *single site of employment*, which results in an *employ-*

ment loss for 50 or more employees (excluding *part-time employees*), during any 30-day period.

Single site of employment

One geographical location of an employer's operations. A single site may consist of one building, an office or a suite of offices in a building; or a group of buildings that form a campus or industrial park, for example.

Separate buildings or areas that are not in immediate proximity may nonetheless constitute a single site of employment if they
- are reasonably close together
- are used for the same purpose, and
- share the same staff and equipment (for example, two warehouses might be a single site if the employer rotates employees from one to the other).

A. Overview of WARN

1. Summary

The Worker Adjustment and Retraining Notification Act (WARN) requires certain larger employers to give some advance notice of an impending *plant closing* or *mass layoff*. The law was passed to help ease the transition for workers who lose their jobs in these circumstances. WARN requires employers to give notice not only to employees and unions that will be affected by the job cuts, but also to state government agencies that provide assistance to dislocated workers.

2. Regulated Employers

Only large private employers must comply with WARN, and then only if they engage in

a *plant closing* or *mass layoff* as described by the definitions set forth above.

Employers Covered by WARN

Federal, state and local governments are not covered by WARN and need not comply with its requirements under any circumstances.

Private employers are covered if:
- they have 100 or more employees, not counting *part-time employees*, or
- they have 100 or more employees (including *part-time employees*) who work a combined 4,000 or more hours per week.

Layoffs Covered by WARN

Not every reduction in force by a covered employer triggers WARN's notice requirements. An employer must comply with WARN only if it plans to conduct a:

- *plant closing*
- *mass layoff*, or
- a *plant closing* or *mass layoff* that occurs in stages over any 90-day period. For example, an employer with 150 employees would not have to comply with WARN if it laid off 20 workers in a 30-day period, because this would not constitute a *mass layoff* as defined by WARN. However, if the same employer laid off 20 more workers in each of the two following months, these combined layoffs would total more than 33% of its workforce—and thus constitute a *mass layoff* as defined by WARN. This rule is intended to prevent employers from getting around WARN's requirements by conducting a series of smaller layoffs.

3. Covered Workers

All *affected employees* are entitled to notice under WARN. This includes *part-time* workers.

Consultants or contractors who have a separate employment relationship with, and are paid by, another employer, are not covered by WARN.

WARN does not cover self-employed persons.

4. What's Prohibited: Employers

WARN prohibits employers from carrying out a *plant closing* or *mass layoff* until 60 days after the employer gives written notice of its plans. See "What's Required: Employers," below, for details.

5. What's Required: Employers

If a layoff is covered by WARN, the employer must give written notice of the layoff, 60 days in advance.

Who Is Entitled to Notice
An employer must provide written notice to:
- each affected employee, except those who are union members
- the bargaining representative(s) of all union members who are affected employees
- the state's dislocated worker unit, and
- the local government in the area where the layoff will occur.

Notice Contents
The employer's notice must be based on the best information available at the time notice must be given—if that information proves to be wrong because of subsequent changes in events or inadvertent errors, the employer will not be liable.

The legally required contents of the written notice vary depending on the recipient.

- **Affected employees who are not union members** must be given notice written in language understandable to the employees. The notice must state whether the planned action is expected to be permanent or temporary; whether an entire plant is to be closed; the expected date when the layoff or plant closing will begin and the expected date when the employee receiving the letter will be terminated; whether the employee will have bumping rights (that is, whether the employee can take the job of a less senior employee who isn't targeted for layoff); and the name and telephone number of a company official the employee can contact for more information.

- **Bargaining representatives** must receive notice of the following: the name and address of the employment site where the layoff or *plant closing* will occur; the name and address of a company official to contact for more information; whether the planned action is expected to be permanent or temporary; whether an entire plant is to be closed; the expected date of the first termination and the expected schedule for the remaining terminations; the job titles of positions expected to be affected; and the names of the workers holding those positions.

- **State dislocated worker units and local governments** must receive notice of the following: the name and address of the employment site where the layoff or *plant closing* will occur; the name and address of a company official to contact for more information; the expected date of the first termination and the number of affected employees. In addition, the employer must include the following information in the notice or maintain this information on site and make it available to the dislocated worker unit and local government agency on request: whether the planned action is expected to be permanent or temporary; whether

an entire plant is to be closed; the anticipated schedule for making terminations; whether bumping rights exist; the job titles of positions expected to be affected; the names of the workers holding those positions; the name of each union representing affected employees; and the name and address of the chief elected officer of each union. See Section F, below, for contact information for state dislocated worker units.

6. What's Required: Workers

WARN places no obligations on workers.

7. Exceptions

No Notice Required

WARN does not apply—and therefore, an employer need not give advance notice of a *mass layoff* or *plant closing*—in these circumstances:

- **Temporary facilities or projects.** If an employer closes a facility that was intended to be open only temporarily, or lays off workers who were hired only for a specific project once that project is complete, no notice is required. However, this exception applies only if the laid-off workers understood, when they were hired, that their employment was limited to the duration of the facility or project.

- **Strikes and lockouts.** If a plant closing or *mass layoff* results from a union strike or an employer lockout, no notice is required.

Notice of Less Than 60 Days Allowed

An employer may comply with WARN by giving as much notice as possible under the circumstances—even if the employer can't give 60 days notice—in some cases. If an employer relies on one of these exceptions, it must give as much notice as it can and state (as part of the written notice requirement) its reasons for failing to give the full 60 days notice that would otherwise be required:

- **Natural disasters.** If a natural disaster forces a *mass layoff* or *plant closing*, an employer may give less than 60 days notice.
- **Unforeseeable business circumstances.** If the *plant closing* or *mass layoff* is caused by business circumstances that were not reasonably foreseeable at the time the employer should have given 60 days notice, a shorter notice period is allowed.
- **Faltering company.** If a company is struggling financially at the time it should have given 60 days notice of a *plant closing*, it can give a shorter period of notice. However, the company must show that it was actively seeking business or money that would have allowed it to avoid or postpone the closing, and that it reasonably believed, in good faith, that giving 60 days notice would have precluded it from obtaining the necessary business or money. This exception does not apply to *mass layoffs*.

B. How WARN Is Enforced

1. Individual Complaints

Although the Department of Labor published the regulations that interpret and explain WARN, Congress gave that agency no power to administer or enforce the law. Therefore, there is no administrative agency available to accept or investigate complaints of WARN violations.

The only way affected employees, union representatives or local government units can assert their right to notice under WARN is by filing lawsuits in federal district court.

2. Agency Enforcement

No agency enforces WARN. See "Individual Complaints," above.

C. For Employers: Complying With WARN

1. Reporting Requirements

WARN requires reporting to state dislocated worker units and local governments, as set forth in "What's Required: Employers," above.

2. Recordkeeping Requirements

WARN does not impose any special record-keeping requirements on employers (other than those records that must be kept on-site and available for state dislocated worker units and local governments to inspect—see "What's Required: Employers," above).

However, employers should keep copies of all written notices sent out under WARN—see "Practical Tips," below.

3. Practical Tips

Here are some tips for complying with WARN:

- **Keep complete records.** Although WARN does not require employers to keep any particular records for any length of time, you should keep copies of all written notices you send out pursuant to WARN. This will help you prove that you gave the required notices, should you later have to defend your actions in court.
- **Get a receipt or acknowledgment.** WARN does not require you to deliver your notices in any particular way. However, you can protect yourself from future legal problems by getting some written proof that your notice was received. If you mail your notices, request a signed receipt. If you hand out your notices in person, ask employees to sign a form acknowledging that they received the notice.
- **Watch out for staged layoffs.** If you conduct a series of layoffs, you may have to follow WARN's requirements—even if none of the layoffs, considered alone, would be covered by WARN (see "Regulated Employers," above, for more information).

- **Err on the side of giving notice.** It can be difficult for employers to figure out whether they fall under one of WARN's exceptions, whether a particular employee counts as an *affected employee* entitled to notice or whether a given reduction in force will be permanent or temporary. If you're not sure whether WARN applies, your safest course of action is to give notice as required by the law anyway. This will save you from spending time and money fighting over these details in court—and give your workers a little time to find a new job.

4. Penalties

Employers who violate WARN (by conducting a *plant closing* or *mass layoff* without giving appropriate notice) may be ordered to:

- pay affected workers for all of the pay and benefits lost for the period of violation, up to 60 days (this amount may be reduced by any wages the employee earned during that period and by any payments the employer makes to the employee voluntarily and unconditionally)
- pay a fine of up to $500 for each day of violation, if the employer fails to give notice as required to the state's dislocated worker unit
- pay the attorney fees and court costs of *affected workers* who sue the employer successfully for violating WARN.

D. For Workers: Asserting Rights Under WARN

1. Where to Start

If you believe your employer has violated WARN by failing to give you adequate notice of an impending *plant closing* or *mass layoff*, your first course of action should be to make an internal complaint. Follow your company's complaint policy or, if there is no policy, complain to a human resources representative or a member of management. Even if it's too late for your employer to give you the required notice, you may be able to negotiate pay in lieu of notice (see Section D3, below).

If you are a union member, talk to your shop steward or union representative.

If internal and union complaints don't work, you can file a lawsuit in any federal district court where your employer does business or where the WARN violation occurred.

There is no federal agency that takes complaints of WARN violations.

2. Required Forms

None.

3. Practical Tips

Here are some tips for asserting your rights under WARN:

- **Ask for pay in lieu of notice.** By the time you complain to your employer about a violation of WARN, it's probably too late for your employer to give you the required 60-days' notice. However, your employer may be willing to give pay in lieu of notice—one day's pay for every day of notice you didn't receive—to avoid a lawsuit.

- **Gather information.** Because no government agency investigates WARN complaints, you will have to be your own investigator. It's usually fairly easy to figure out whether your employer and layoff are covered by WARN—that's a simple matter of counting heads. However, if your employer claims that a WARN exception applied to your layoff (for example, that it qualified as a faltering company or that your layoff was not reasonably foreseeable), you will need to find out what your employer knew and when your employer knew it. There are many potential sources of information—company publications, your coworkers, your boss, even the local newspaper or trade publications.

- **Find strength in numbers.** If your employer won't take action on your complaint, talk to your laid-off co-workers and/or to your union representative. If you have to file a lawsuit to enforce your rights, you might want to join a class action lawsuit (one in which all of the laid-off employees sue together) or ask your union to sue on behalf of all affected union members. These group lawsuits allow workers to pool their resources, save time and spread the costs of a lawsuit—and a lawyer—around.

E. Agency Charged With Enforcement & Compliance

No agency has the right to enforce WARN or make sure employers comply with its requirements. However, the Department of Labor issued the regulations interpreting the law, and has some explanatory resources available.

Department of Labor
Employment and Training Administration
Division of Adult Dislocated Workers
Room C5325
200 Constitution Avenue, NW
Washington, DC 20210
Phone: 202-693-3580
http://www.doleta.gov

Agency Resources for Employers and Workers
(These can be obtained either at the Web addresses listed below or at the address and phone number listed above.)

- A list of the names, addresses, telephone numbers and email addresses of the Coordinator of each state's dislocated worker unit
  Dislocated Workers
  http://www.doleta.gov/layoff/e_sdwuc.asp
- A detailed explanation of the rights and obligations created by WARN
  A Guide to Advance Notice of Closings and Layoffs
  http://www.doleta.gov/programs/factsht/warn.asp

F. State Laws Relating to Plant Closings

Final Paycheck Laws

Alabama	Ala. Code § 25-3-5
When law applies	Substantial layoff at or the closing of any plant or industry.
State assistance for employees	Commissioner of Labor to provide seminars to unemployed or underemployed employees on legal rights regarding debts. To lessen the financial burden of closure or layoffs, Commissioner may meet with management and with labor or other organizations, may facilitate communication with creditors and may set up programs to provide financial assistance. No employer or employee group may be required to contribute or participate in such programs.
California	**Cal. Unemp. Ins. Code §§ 15076 to 15077.5**
When law applies	Permanent closing of or substantial layoff at, a plant, facility or enterprise.
State assistance for employees	Private industry councils and the Employment Development Department and its dislocated worker unit shall provide training and assistance for workers who have lost their jobs or received a notice of termination.
Colorado	**Colo. Rev. Stat. § 23-60-306**
When law applies	Plant closings.
State assistance for employees	Workers who have lost their previous jobs because of plant closings are eligible for retraining for new jobs through the State Board for Community Colleges and Occupational Education customized training program.
Connecticut	**Conn. Gen. Stat. Ann. §§ 31-51n, 31-51o**
When law applies	Permanent shutdown or relocation of facility out of state.
Employers affected by requirements	Employers with 100 or more employees at any time during the previous 12-month period.
Severance requirements	Employer must pay for existing group health insurance coverage for employee and dependents for 120 days or until employee is eligible for other group coverage, whichever comes first.
Exceptions	Closure due to bankruptcy.
Hawaii	**Haw. Rev. Stat. §§ 394B-9 to -12; 394B-2 and following**
When law applies	Permanent or partial closing of business; relocation of all or substantial portion of business operations out of state.

Employers affected by requirements	Employers with 50 or more employees at any time during the previous 12-month period.
Severance requirements	Employer must provide 4 weeks dislocated worker allowance as a supplement to unemployment compensation. Amount is the difference between the weekly former wage and the unemployment benefit. Employers who do not follow notice and severance requirements are liable to each employee for 3 months of compensation.
Notification requirements	Employer must provide each employee with written notice 60 days in advance of closing or relocation.
State assistance for employees	Dislocated workers program in Department of Labor and Industrial Relations provides assistance and training for workers who have lost their jobs or received a notice of termination.
Kansas	**Kan. Stat. Ann. §§ 44-616; 44-603**
When law applies	Employers involved in: • manufacture, transportation or preparation of food products or clothing • fuel mining or production • public utilities • transportation must apply to state Secretary of Human Resources for approval before limiting or discontinuing business operations.
Maine	**Me. Rev. Stat. Ann. tit. 26, § 625-B**
When law applies	Business operations are discontinued or relocated at least 100 miles from original location.
Employers affected by requirements	Employers with 100 or more employees at any time during the previous 12-month period.
Severance requirements	Employer must give severance pay of one week for each year of employment to all employees who have worked for at least 3 years, due within one regular pay period after employee's last full day of work.
Notification requirements	Employer must give employees at least 60 days advance notice in writing before relocating a plant. Employer must also notify the director of the Bureau of Labor Standards and municipal officials where the plant is located.
Maryland	**Md. Code Ann., [Lab. & Empl.] §§ 11-301 to -304**
When law applies	Shutdown of workplace or a portion of the operations that results in layoffs of at least 25% of work force or 15 employees, whichever is greater, over any 3-month period.

Employers affected by requirements	Employers with 50 or more employees who have been in business at least one year.
Severance requirements	Employers are encouraged to follow Department of Labor voluntary guidelines for severance pay, continuation of benefits and notification.
Notification requirements	90 days whenever possible.
Exceptions	Bankruptcy, seasonal factors common to industry.
State assistance for employees	Department of Labor will provide onsite unemployment insurance bulk registration (when more than 25 workers are laid off), retraining, job placement and job finding services.
Massachusetts	**Mass. Gen. Laws ch. 149, §§ 179B, 182, 183; ch. 151A, §§ 71A and following**
When law applies	• Closing or reduction of business operations which results or will result in the permanent separation of at least 90% of the employees within 6 months.
	• Sale or transfer of ownership of a company with 50 or more employees.
Employers affected by requirements	• Employers receiving assistance from state business financing or development agencies.
	• Employers with 50 or more employees who sell or transfer control of a business.
Severance requirements	• Employers receiving state agency assistance must make a good faith effort to provide 90 days group health insurance coverage for employees and dependents, at the same payment terms as before plant closing.
	• When a company with 50 or more employees is sold or changes hands, new owner must give severance pay of 2 weeks' compensation for every year of service to employees who have worked at least 3 years. For employees who lose their jobs within 2 years of the sale severance is due within one regular pay period after last day of work; for employees who lose their jobs within one year of sale, due within 4 pay periods after the sale.
Notification requirements	• Employers receiving state agency assistance are expected to provide 90 days notice.
	• Employers with 12 or more employees must notify the Director of Labor and Workforce Development when business changes location.

	• New owner of business with 50 or more employees must provide written notice of rights to each employee and to any collective bargaining representative within 30 days of completion of sale.
State assistance for employees	• Reemployment assistance programs which provide counseling, placement and training are available through the employment and training division of the Department of Workforce Development. • Employees who have worked for a company for at least one year are eligible for up to 13 weeks of reemployment assistance benefits.
Michigan	**Mich. Comp. Laws § 450.732**
When law applies	Permanent shutdown of operations at any establishment where at least 25 persons are employed.
Notification requirements	Department of Labor encourages businesses that are closing or relocating to give notice as soon as possible to the Department, employees, the unions and the community.
State assistance for employees	Department of Labor may study the feasibility of the employees establishing an employee-owned corporation to continue the business.
Minnesota	**Minn. Stat. Ann. § 116L.17**
When law applies	• Plant closing: announced or actual permanent shutdown of a single site. • Substantial layoff: permanent reduction in workforce at a single site not due to plant closing which results in job loss for at least 50 full-time employees during any 30-day period.
Notification requirements	Employers are encouraged to give 60 days notice to the Department of Trade and Economic development.
State assistance for employees	Department of Trade and Economic Development offers customized assistance to employees and businesses through the dislocated worker program.
Missouri	**Mo. Rev. Stat. § 409.516(5)**
When law applies	Business takeovers: any company making a business takeover offer must file a registration statement with the state securities commission disclosing plans for plant closures or major changes in employment policies.

New Hampshire	N.H. Rev. Stat. Ann. § 421-A:4(IV)
When law applies	Business takeovers: any company making a business take-over offer must file a registration statement with the secretary of state and with the target company disclosing plans for plant closures or major changes in employment policies.
New Jersey	**N.J. Stat. Ann. §§ 34:1B-30; 52:27H-95**
When law applies	Potential plant closings.
State assistance for employees	Department of Labor and other agencies mandated to assist workers who want to establish employee ownership plans to save jobs threatened by plant closure. If plant closure would cause significant employment loss to an economically distressed municipality, the Commissioner of Commerce may fund a profitability study of an employee stock ownership plan.
New York	**N.Y. Lab. Law §§ 835 and following; Pub. Auth. Law §§ 1836-a and following; Bus. Corp. Law § 1603(5)**
When law applies	• Plant closing: permanent or temporary shutdown of a single site or one or more facilities or operating units within a single site which results in job loss for at least 25 full-time employees during any 30-day period. (If shutdown causes job losses at other sites, they also count toward the 25.) • Substantial layoff: reduction in workforce at a single site not due to shutdown which results in job loss for at least 33% full-time and 50 part-time employees or 500 full-time employees during any 30-day period. • Business takeovers: any company making a business takeover offer must file a registration statement with the attorney general's New York City office and with the target company disclosing plans for plant closures or major changes in employment policies.
State assistance for employees	• The Department of Labor, in coordination with the Department of Economic Development and the dislocated worker unit, provides rapid response services after a plant closure, including: onsite intervention within 48 hours; basic emergency readjustment services; information about re-training, unemployment insurance and technical assistance. • The Job Development Authority encourages employees of plants that are about to be closed or relocated, to continue to operate them as employee-owned enterprises; state assistance is available.

Ohio	Ohio Rev. Code Ann. §§ 122.13 and following
When law applies	Permanent shutdown of operations at a business with at least 25 employees; relocation of all or substantial portion of operations at least 100 miles from original location.
State assistance for employees	Department of Development has an employee ownership assistance program which provides technical assistance and counseling and will conduct a feasibility study for workers who want to establish employee ownership plans to continue running a business threatened by plant closure.

Oklahoma	Okla. Stat. Ann. tit. 71, § 453(F)(3)
When law applies	Business takeovers: any company making a business takeover offer must file a registration statement with the state securities commission disclosing plans to close or relocate facilities or to make major changes in employment policies.

Oregon	Or. Rev. Stat. §§ 285A.510 to .522; 657.335 to .340
When law applies	• Plant closing: permanent or temporary shutdown of a single site or one or more facilities or operating units within a single site which results in job loss for at least 50 full-time employees during any 30-day period. • Mass layoff: reduction in workforce at a single site not due to shutdown which results in job loss for at least 33% and 50 full-time employees or 500 full-time employees during any 30-day period.
Employers affected by requirements	Employers with 100 or more full-time employees.
Notification requirements	Employers must notify the Department of Community Colleges & Workforce Development of plant closings or mass layoffs.
State assistance for employees	State assistance and professional technical training available to dislocated workers. Workers who are in training are entitled to unemployment compensation and related benefits.

Pennsylvania	43 Pa. Cons. Stat. Ann. §§ 690a.1 and following; 24 Pa. Cons. Stat. Ann. §§ 6201 and following; 70 Pa. Cons. Stat. Ann. § 75(4)
When law applies	Business takeovers: any company making a business takeover offer must file a registration statement 20 days in advance with the state securities commission, the target company and the collective bargaining agent. Must disclose plans for closing down the target company, making major changes in employment policies or changing any collective bargaining agreements.

State assistance for employees	Dislocated workers are eligible for customized job training program through the Department of Labor & Industry and are eligible for assistance to support them while in training.
Rhode Island	**R.I. Gen. Laws § 27-19.1-1**
Severance requirements	Employees and dependents are entitled to at least 18 months continuation of healthcare coverage at own expense. (Length of coverage cannot exceed time of continuous employment.)
South Carolina	**S.C. Code Ann. § 41-1-40**
Employers affected by requirements	Employers who require employees to give notice before quitting work.
Notification requirements	Employers must give same amount of notice they require of employees or at least 2 weeks. Notice must be in writing and posted in every room of the work building. Employers who do not comply are liable to every employee for any damages that result from failure to give notice.
Tennessee	**Tenn. Code Ann. §§ 50-1-601 to -604**
When law applies	Closing, modernization, relocation or new management policy of a workplace or a portion of the operations which permanently or indefinitely lays off 50 or more employees during any 3-month period.
Employers affected by requirements	Employers with 50 to 99 full-time employees within the state.
Notification requirements	Employer must first notify employees who will lose their jobs due to a reduction in operations and then notify the Commissioner of Labor and Workforce Development. Must give circumstances of closing and number of employees laid off. Toll-free telephone line established to encourage employer compliance.
Exceptions	Construction sites; seasonal factors common to industry.
Utah	**Utah Code Ann. § 67-1-12**
When law applies	Defense industry layoffs.
State assistance for employees	Workers in defense or defense-related jobs who are laid off may apply to the Office of Job Training for assistance in retraining or re-education for job skills in demand.
Washington	**Wash. Rev. Code Ann. §§ 50.04.075; 50.12.280; 50.20.042 to .043; 50.70.030 to .050**
When law applies	Employees who have been terminated or received a notice of termination and are unlikely to return to work at their principal occupations or previous industries.

State assistance for employees	The Department of Employment Security offers special training and counseling programs for dislocated workers in aerospace, thermal electric generation and forest products industries in addition to any regular unemployment compensation.
Wisconsin	**Wis. Stat. Ann. § 109.07**
When law applies	• Business closing: permanent or temporary shutdown of an employment site or of one or more facilities or operating units at a site or within one town that affects 25 or more employees. • Mass layoff: reduction in workforce that is not the result of a business closing and that affects at least 25% or 25 employees, whichever is greater, or at least 500 employees. (Does not apply to employees who have worked fewer than 6 of the previous 12 months or who work less than 20 hrs/wk.)
Employers affected by requirements	Employers with 50 or more employees in the state.
Notification requirements	An employer who has decided upon a business closing or mass layoff in this state must give at least 60 days written notice to: • the Dislocated Worker Committee in the Department of Workforce Development • every affected employee • the employees' collective bargaining representative • the highest official of the municipality where the business is located. Employer who does not comply is liable to employees for pay and the value of benefits, from the day that notice was required to the day notice was actually given or business closing or mass layoff occurred, whichever is earlier.
Wyoming	**Wyo. Stat. §§ 27-13-101 to -103**
When law applies	Workers unemployed due to plant closings or substantial plant layoffs.
State assistance for employees	Department of Employment, in conjunction with the department of education, the University of Wyoming and the community college commission, offers occupational transfer and retraining programs and services for displaced workers.

G. Full Text of WARN

U.S. Code
Title 29: Labor
Chapter 23 Worker Adjustment and Retraining Notification

§ 2101. Definitions; exclusions from definition of loss of employment

§ 2102. Notice required before plant closings and mass layoffs

§ 2103. Exemptions

§ 2104. Administration and enforcement of requirements

§ 2105. Procedures in addition to other rights of employees

§ 2106. Procedures encouraged where not required

§ 2107. Authority to prescribe regulations

§ 2108. Effect on other laws

§ 2109. Report on employment and international competitiveness

§ 2101. Definitions; exclusions from definition of loss of employment

(a) Definitions

As used in this chapter—

(1) the term "employer" means any business enterprise that employs—

   (A) 100 or more employees, excluding part-time employees; or

   (B) 100 or more employees who in the aggregate work at least 4,000 hours per week (exclusive of hours of overtime);

(2) the term "plant closing" means the permanent or temporary shutdown of a single site of employment, or one or more facilities or operating units within a single site of employment, if the shutdown results in an employment loss at the single site of employment during any 30-day period for 50 or more employees excluding any part-time employees;

(3) the term "mass layoff" means a reduction in force which—

   (A) is not the result of a plant closing; and

   (B) results in an employment loss at the single site of employment during any 30-day period for—

      (i)

         (I) at least 33 percent of the employees (excluding any part-time employees); and

         (II) at least 50 employees (excluding any part-time employees); or

      (ii) at least 500 employees (excluding any part-time employees);

(4) the term "representative" means an exclusive representative of employees within the meaning of section 159(a) or 158(f) of this title or section 152 of title 45;

(5) the term "affected employees" means employees who may reasonably be expected to experience an employment loss as a consequence of a proposed plant closing or mass layoff by their employer;

(6) subject to subsection (b) of this section, the term "employment loss" means

   (A) an employment termination, other than a discharge for cause, voluntary departure, or retirement,

   (B) a layoff exceeding 6 months, or

   (C) a reduction in hours of work of more than 50 percent during each month of any 6-month period;

(7) the term "unit of local government" means any general purpose political subdivision of a State which has the power to levy taxes and spend funds, as well as general corporate and police powers; and

(8) the term "part-time employee" means an employee who is employed for an average of fewer than 20 hours per week or who has been employed for fewer than 6 of the 12 months preceding the date on which notice is required.

(b) Exclusions from definition of employment loss

(1) In the case of a sale of part or all of an employer's business, the seller shall be responsible for providing notice for any plant closing or mass layoff in accordance with section 2102 of this title, up to and including the effective date of the sale. After the effective date of the sale of part or all of an employer's business, the purchaser shall be responsible for providing notice for any plant closing or mass layoff in accordance with section 2102 of this title. Notwithstanding any other provision of this chapter, any person who is an employee of the seller (other than a part-time employee) as of the effective date of the sale shall be considered an employee of the purchaser immediately after the effective date of the sale.

(2) Notwithstanding subsection (a)(6) of this section, an employee may not be considered to have experienced an employment loss if the closing or layoff is the result of the relocation or consolidation of part or all of the employer's business and, prior to the closing or layoff—

(A) the employer offers to transfer the employee to a different site of employment within a reasonable commuting distance with no more than a 6-month break in employment; or

(B) the employer offers to transfer the employee to any other site of employment regardless of distance with no more than a 6-month break in employment, and the employee accepts within 30 days of the offer or of the closing or layoff, whichever is later

§ 2102. Notice required before plant closings and mass layoffs

(a) Notice to employees, State dislocated worker units, and local governments

An employer shall not order a plant closing or mass layoff until the end of a 60-day period after the employer serves written notice of such an order—

(1) to each representative of the affected employees as of the time of the notice or, if there is no such representative at that time, to each affected employee; and

(2) to the State or entity designated by the State to carry out rapid response activities under section 2864(a)(2)(A) of this title, and the chief elected official of the unit of local government within which such closing or layoff is to occur.

If there is more than one such unit, the unit of local government which the employer shall notify is the unit of local government to which the employer pays the highest taxes for the year preceding the year for which the determination is made.

(b) Reduction of notification period

(1) An employer may order the shutdown of a single site of employment before the conclusion of the 60-day period if as of the time that notice would have been required the employer was actively seeking capital or business which, if obtained, would have enabled the employer to avoid or postpone the shutdown and the employer reasonably and in good faith believed that giving the notice required would have precluded the employer from obtaining the needed capital or business.

(2)

(A) An employer may order a plant closing or mass layoff before the conclusion of the 60-day period if the closing or mass layoff is caused by business circumstances that were not reasonably foreseeable as of the time that notice would have been required.

(B) No notice under this chapter shall be required if the plant closing or mass layoff is due to any form of natural disaster, such as a flood, earthquake, or the drought currently ravaging the farmlands of the United States.

(3) An employer relying on this subsection shall give as much notice as is practicable and at that time shall give a brief statement of the basis for reducing the notification period.

(c) Extension of layoff period

A layoff of more than 6 months which, at its outset, was announced to be a layoff of 6 months or less, shall be treated as an employment loss under this chapter unless—

(1) the extension beyond 6 months is caused by business circumstances (including unforeseeable changes in price or cost) not reasonably foreseeable at the time of the initial layoff; and

(2) notice is given at the time it becomes reasonably foreseeable that the extension beyond 6 months will be required.

(d) Determinations with respect to employment loss

For purposes of this section, in determining whether a plant closing or mass layoff has occurred or will occur, employment losses for 2 or more groups at a single site of employment, each of which is less than the minimum number of employees specified in section 2101(a)(2) or (3) of this title but which in the aggregate exceed that minimum number, and which occur within any 90-day period shall be considered to be a plant closing or mass layoff unless the employer demonstrates that the employment losses are the result of separate and distinct actions and causes and are not an attempt by the employer to evade the requirements of this chapter.

§ 2103. Exemptions

This chapter shall not apply to a plant closing or mass layoff if—

(1) the closing is of a temporary facility or the closing or layoff is the result of the completion of a particular project or undertaking, and the affected employees were hired with the understanding that their employment was limited to the duration of the facility or the project or undertaking; or

(2) the closing or layoff constitutes a strike or constitutes a lockout not intended to evade the requirements of this chapter. Nothing in this chapter shall require an employer to serve written notice pursuant to section 2102(a) of this title when permanently replacing a person who is deemed to be an economic striker under the National

Labor Relations Act (29 U.S.C. 151 et seq.): Provided, That nothing in this chapter shall be deemed to validate or invalidate any judicial or administrative ruling relating to the hiring of permanent replacements for economic strikers under the National Labor Relations Act

§ 2104. Administration and enforcement of requirements

(a) Civil actions against employers

(1) Any employer who orders a plant closing or mass layoff in violation of section 2102 of this title shall be liable to each aggrieved employee who suffers an employment loss as a result of such closing or layoff for—

(A) back pay for each day of violation at a rate of compensation not less than the higher of—

(i) the average regular rate received by such employee during the last 3 years of the employee's employment; or

(ii) the final regular rate received by such employee; and

(B) benefits under an employee benefit plan described in section 1002(3) of this title, including the cost of medical expenses incurred during the employment loss which would have been covered under an employee benefit plan if the employment loss had not occurred.

Such liability shall be calculated for the period of the violation, up to a maximum of 60 days, but in no event for more than one-half the number of days the employee was employed by the employer.

(2) The amount for which an employer is liable under paragraph (1) shall be reduced by—

(A) any wages paid by the employer to the employee for the period of the violation;

(B) any voluntary and unconditional payment by the employer to the employee that is not required by any legal obligation; and

(C) any payment by the employer to a third party or trustee (such as premiums for health benefits or payments to a defined contribution pension plan) on behalf of and attributable to the employee for the period of the violation.

In addition, any liability incurred under paragraph (1) with respect to a defined benefit pension plan may be reduced by crediting the employee with service for all purposes under such a plan for the period of the violation.

(3) Any employer who violates the provisions of section 2102 of this title with respect to a unit of local government shall be subject to a civil penalty of not more than $500 for each day of such violation, except that such penalty shall not apply if the employer pays to each aggrieved employee the amount for which the employer is liable to that employee within 3 weeks from the date the employer orders the shutdown or layoff.

(4) If an employer which has violated this chapter proves to the satisfaction of the court that the act or omission that violated this chapter was in good faith and that the employer had reasonable grounds for believing that the act or omission was not a violation of this chapter the court may, in its discretion, reduce the amount of the liability or penalty provided for in this section.

(5) A person seeking to enforce such liability, including a representative of employees or a unit of local government aggrieved under paragraph (1) or (3), may sue either for such person or for other persons similarly situated, or both, in any district court of the United States for any district in which the violation is alleged to have occurred, or in which the employer transacts business.

(6) In any such suit, the court, in its discretion, may allow the prevailing party a reasonable attorney's fee as part of the costs.

(7) For purposes of this subsection, the term, [1] "aggrieved employee" means an employee who has worked for the employer ordering the plant closing or mass layoff and who, as a result of the failure by the employer to comply with section 2102 of this title, did not receive timely notice either directly or through his or her representative as required by section 2102 of this title.

(b) Exclusivity of remedies

The remedies provided for in this section shall be the exclusive remedies for any violation of this chapter. Under this chapter, a Federal court shall not have authority to enjoin a plant closing or mass layoff.

§ 2105. Procedures in addition to other rights of employees

The rights and remedies provided to employees by this chapter are in addition to, and not in lieu of, any other contractual or statutory rights and remedies of the employees, and are not intended to alter or affect such rights and remedies, except that the period of notification required by this chapter shall run concurrently with any period of notification required by contract or by any other statute

§ 2106. Procedures encouraged where not required

It is the sense of Congress that an employer who is not required to comply with the notice requirements of section 2102 of this title should, to the extent possible, provide notice to its employees about a proposal to close a plant or permanently reduce its workforce.

§ 2107. Authority to prescribe regulations

(a) The Secretary of Labor shall prescribe such regulations as may be necessary to carry out this chapter. Such regulations shall, at a minimum, include interpretative regulations describing the methods by which employers may provide for appropriate service of notice as required by this chapter.

(b) The mailing of notice to an employee's last known address or inclusion of notice in the employee's paycheck will be considered acceptable methods for fulfillment of the employer's obligation to give notice to each affected employee under this chapter.

§ 2108. Effect on other laws

The giving of notice pursuant to this chapter, if done in good faith compliance with this chapter, shall not constitute a violation of the National Labor Relations Act (29 U.S.C. 151 et seq.) or the Railway Labor Act (45 U.S.C. 151 et seq.).

§ 2109. Report on employment and international competitiveness

Two years after August 4, 1988, the Comptroller General shall submit to the Committee on Small Business of both the House and Senate, the Committee on Labor and Human Resources, and the Committee on Education and Labor a report containing a detailed and objective analysis of the effect of this chapter on employers (especially small- and medium-sized businesses), the economy (international competitiveness), and employees (in terms of levels and conditions of employment). The Comptroller General shall assess both costs and benefits, including the effect on productivity, competitiveness, unemployment rates and compensation, and worker retraining and readjustment.

Appendix:

State Resources

Appendix

State Resources

A. State Labor Departments

Alabama
Department of Labor
100 North Union Street
Montgomery, AL 36130-3500
334-242-3460
http://www.alalabor.state.al.us

Alaska
Department of Labor
1111 West Eighth Street
Post Office Box 21149
Juneau, AK 99801-1149
907-465-5980
http://www.labor.state.ak.us

Arizona
Industrial Commission
800 West Washington Street
Phoenix, AZ 85007
602-542-4411
http://www.ica.state.az.us

Arkansas
Department of Labor
10421 West Markham Street
Little Rock, AR 72205
501-682-4500
http://www.state.ar.us/labor

California
Division of Labor Standards Enforcement
Department of Industrial Relations
455 Golden Gate Avenue
8th Floor East
San Francisco, CA 94102
415-557-7878
320 West Fourth Street
Suite 450
Los Angeles, CA 90013
213-620-6330
http://www.dir.ca.gov/DLSE/dlse.html

Colorado
Department of Labor and Employment
1515 Arapahoe Street
Tower 2, Suite 400
Denver, CO 80202
303-318-8000
http://www.coworkforce.com

Connecticut
Department of Labor
200 Folly Brook Boulevard
Wethersfield, CT 06109
860-263-6000
http://www.ctdol.state.ct.us

Delaware
Department of Labor
4425 North Market Street
Wilmington, DE 19802
302-761-8085
http://www.delawareworks.com

District of Columbia
Office of Labor Relations and Collective
Bargaining
441 4th Street, NW
Suite 200S
Washington, DC 20001
202-724-4953
http://dc.gov/agencies

Florida

Department of Labor and Employment
  Security
303 Hartman Building
2012 Capitol Circle, SE
Tallahassee, FL 32399-2152
850-922-7021
http://www2.myflorida.com/les

Georgia

Department of Labor
148 International Boulevard N.E., Suite 600
Atlanta, GA 30303-1751
404-656-3017
http://www.dol.state.ga.us

Hawaii

Department of Labor & Industrial Relations
830 Punchbowl Street
Honolulu, HI 96813
808-586-8865
http://dlir.state.hi.us

Idaho

Department of Labor
317 Main Street
Boise, ID 83735-0600
208-332-3570
http://www.labor.state.id.us

Illinois

Department of Labor
160 North LaSalle St., 13th Floor, Suite C
Chicago, IL 60601
312-793-2800
FAX: 312-793-5257
http://www.state.il.us/agency/idol

Indiana

Department of Labor
402 West Washington
Room W-195
Indianapolis, IN 46204
317-232-2655
http://www.in.gov/labor

Iowa

Iowa Workforce Development
1000 East Grand Avenue
Des Moines, IA 50319-0209
515-281-5387
http://www.state.ia.us/iwd

Kansas

Office of Employment Standards
Department of Human Resources
1430 SW Topeka Blvd., 3rd Floor
Topeka, KS 66612
785-296-4062
http://www.hr.state.ks.us/home-html/
  empstand.htm

Kentucky

Labor Cabinet
U.S. Highway 127 South, Suite 4
Frankfort, KY 40601
502-564-3070
http://www.kylabor.net

Louisiana

Department of Labor
Post Office Box 94094
Baton Rouge, LA 70804
504-342-3202
http://www.ldol.state.la.us

Maine

Department of Labor
45 State House Station
Augusta, ME 04333-0045
207-624-6400
http://www.state.me.us/labor

Maryland

Department of Labor, Licensing and
    Regulation
1100 North Eutaw Street
Baltimore, MD 21201
410-767-2236
http://www.dllr.state.md.us

Massachusetts

Division of Employment and Training
19 Staniford Street
Boston, MA 02114
617-626-5400
http://www.detma.org

Michigan

Consumer and Industry Services
525 W. Ottawa
Post Office Box 30004
Lansing, MI 48909
517-373-1820
http://www.cis.state.mi.us

Minnesota

Department of Labor and Industry
443 Lafayette Road North
St. Paul, MN 55155
651-284-5000
http://www.doli.state.mn.us

Mississippi

Employment Security Commission
1520 West Capitol, Post Office Box 1699
Jackson, MS 39215
601-354-8711
http://www.mesc.state.ms.us

Missouri

Department of Labor and Industrial Relations
3315 West Truman Boulevard, Room 213
Post Office Box 504
Jefferson City, MO 65102-0504
573-751-4091
http://www.dolir.state.mo.us

Montana

Department of Labor and Industry
1327 Lockey Avenue
Helena, MT 59624
406-444-9091
http://dli.state.mt.us

Nebraska

Department of Labor and Safety Standards
301 Centennial Mall South
Lincoln, NE 68509
402-471-2239
http://www.dol.state.ne.us

Nevada

Office of the Labor Commissioner
Department of Business & Industry
555 E. Washington Ave., Ste. 4100
Las Vegas, NV 89101-1050
702-486-2650
http://labor.state.nv.us

New Hampshire
Department of Labor
95 Pleasant Street
Concord, NH 03301
603-271-3176
http://www.labor.state.nh.us

New Jersey
Department of Labor
Post Office Box 110
John Fitch Plaza
Trenton, NJ 08625
609-292-2323
http://www.state.nj.us/labor

New Mexico
Department of Labor
501 Mountain Rd.
Albuquerque, NM 87102
505-841-8983
http://www3.state.nm.us/dol

New York
Department of Labor
State Office Building Campus
Room 500
Albany, NY 12240-0003
518-457-9000
http://www.labor.state.ny.us

North Carolina
Department of Labor
4 West Edenton Street
Raleigh, NC 27601
919-733-7166
http://www.dol.state.nc.us

North Dakota
Department of Labor
600 East Boulevard
Department 406
Bismarck, ND 58505-0340
701-328-2660
http://www.state.nd.us/labor

Ohio
Industrial Commission
30 W. Spring Street
Columbus, OH 43215-2233
614-466-6136
http://www.ic.state.oh.us/index.jsp

Oklahoma
Department of Labor
4001 N. Lincoln Boulevard
Oklahoma City, OK 73105
405-528-1500
http://www.okdol.state.ok.us

Oregon
Bureau of Labor & Industries
800 NE Oregon, #32
Suite 1070
Portland, OR 97232
503-731-4200
http://www.boli.state.or.us

Pennsylvania
Department of Labor & Industry
Room 1700, 7th and Forster Streets
Harrisburg, PA 17120
717-787-5279
http://www.dli.state.pa.us

Rhode Island

Department of Labor

Pastore Government Center

1511 Pontiac Ave.

Cranston, RI 02920

401-462-8000

http://www.dlt.state.ri.us

South Carolina

Department of Labor, Licensing and
Regulation

110 Centerview Drive

Columbia, SC 29210

803-896-4300

http://www.llr.state.sc.us

South Dakota

Department of Labor

700 Governors Drive

Pierre, SD 57501-2291

605-773-3101

http://www.state.sd.us/dol/dol.asp

Tennessee

Department of Labor and Workforce
Development

710 James Robertson Parkway

Nashville, TN 37243

615-741-2257

http://www.state.tn.us/labor-wfd

Texas

Texas Workforce Commission

101 E. 15th Street

Austin, TX 78778

512-463-2222

http://www.twc.state.tx.us

Utah

Labor Commission

160 East 300 South, 3rd Floor

Post Office Box 146600

Salt Lake City, UT 84111

801-530-6800

http://laborcommission.utah.gov

Vermont

Department of Labor and Industry

National Life Building

Drawer 20

Montpelier, VT 05620-3401

802-828-2288

http://www.state.vt.us/labind

Virginia

Department of Labor and Industry

13 South 13th Street

Richmond, VA 23219

804-371-2327

http://www.dli.state.va.us

Washington

Department of Labor and Industries

Post Office Box 44851

Olympia, WA 98504-4851

360-902-4200

http://www.lni.wa.gov

West Virginia

Division of Labor

State Capitol Complex

Bldg. 6 Room B749

Charleston, WV 25305

304-558-7890

http://www.state.wv.us/labor

Wisconsin

Department of Workforce Development
201 E. Washington Avenue GEF-1
Madison, WI 53702
608-266-7552
http://www.dwd.state.wi.us

Wyoming

Labor Standards Office
Department of Employment
Herschler Building, 2nd Floor East
122 West 25th Street
Cheyenne, WY 82002
307-777-7672
http://wydoe.state.wy.us

B. State Fair Employment Practices Agencies

Alabama

None

Alaska

Alaska State Commission for Human Rights
800 A Street, Suite 204
Anchorage, AK 99501-3669
907-274-4692 / 800-478-4692
http://www.gov.state.ak.us/aschr/aschr.htm

Arizona

Civil Rights Division
1275 West Washington Street
Phoenix, AZ 85007
602-542-5263 / 877-491-5742
http://www.attorneygeneral.state.az.us/
civil_rights/index.html

Arkansas

Equal Employment Opportunity Commission
(EEOC)
425 West Capitol
Suite 625
Little Rock, AR 72207
501-324-5060
http://www.eeoc.gov/index.html

California

Department of Fair Employment and Housing
Sacramento District Office
2000 O Street, Suite 120
Sacramento, CA 95814-5212
800-884-1684
http://www.dfeh.ca.gov

Colorado

Civil Rights Division
1560 Broadway, Suite 1050
Denver, CO 80202
303-894-2997 / 800-262-4845
http://www.dora.state.co.us/Civil-Rights

Connecticut

Connecticut Commission on Human Rights
and Opportunities. (CHRO)
21 Grand Street
Hartford, CT 06106
860-541-3400 / 800-477-5737
http://www.state.ct.us/chro

Delaware

Office of Labor Law Enforcement
Division of Industrial Affairs
4225 N. Market Street
Wilmington, DE 19802

302-761-8200

http://www.delawareworks.com/divisions/
   industaffairs/law.enforcement.htm

District of Columbia

Office of Human Rights

441 4th Street, NW, Suite 570 North
Washington, DC 20001
202-727-4559

http://www.ohr.dc.gov/main.shtm

Florida

Commission on Human Relations

325 John Knox Road
Bldg. F, Suite 240
Tallahassee, FL 32303-4149
850-488-7082 / 800-342-8170

http://fchr.state.fl.us

Georgia

Atlanta District Office

U.S. Equal Employment Opportunity
   Commission
100 Alabama Street, Suite 4R30
Atlanta, GA 30303
404-562-6800

http://www.eeoc.gov

Hawaii

Hawai'i Civil Rights Commission

830 Punchbowl Street
Room 411
Honolulu, HI 96813
808-586-8640 (Oahu)
800-468-4644 ext. 68640 (other islands)

http://www.state.hi.us/hcrc

Idaho

Idaho Human Rights Commission

1109 Main Street, Fourth Floor
Boise, ID 83720-0040
208-334-2873 / 888-249-7025

http://www2.state.id.us/ihrc

Illinois

Department of Human Rights

100 West Randolph Street
James R. Thompson Center, # 10-100
Chicago, IL 60601
312-814-6200

http://www.state.il.us/dhr

Indiana

Civil Rights Commission

100 N. Senate Avenue, Room N-103
Indianapolis, IN 46204
317-232-2600 / 800-628-2909

http://www.in.gov/icrc

Iowa

Iowa Civil Rights Commission

211 East Maple Street
Des Moines, IA 50309
515-281-4121 / 800-457-4416

http://www.state.ia.us/government/crc

Kansas

Human Rights Commission

900 SW Jackson
Suite 851 South
Landon State Office Building
Topeka, KS 66612
785-296-3206

http://www.ink.org/public/khrc

Kentucky
Human Rights Commission
332 West Broadway
7th Floor
Louisville, KY 40202
502-595-4024 / 800-292-5566
http://www.state.ky.us/agencies2/kchr

Louisiana
Commission on Human Rights
1001 N. 23rd St., Suite 262
Baton Rouge, LA 70802
225-342-6969
http://www.gov.state.la.us/
    office_detail.asp?id=14

Maine
Human Rights Commission
51 Statehouse Station
Augusta, ME 04333
207-624-6050
http://www.state.me.us/mhrc/index.shtml

Maryland
Commission on Human Relations
William Donald Schaefer Towers
6 Saint Paul Street, Suite 900,
Baltimore, MD 21202
410-767-8600 / 800-637-6247
http://www.mchr.state.md.us

Massachusetts
Commission Against Discrimination
One Ashburton Place, Rm. 601,
Boston, MA 02108
617-727-3990
http://www.state.ma.us/mcad

Michigan
Department of Civil Rights
State of Michigan Plaza Bldg.,
6th Floor.
1200 Sixth Ave.
Detroit, MI 48226
313-256-2663 / 800-482-3604
http://www.mdcr.state.mi.us

Minnesota
Department of Human Rights
Army Corps of Engineers Centre
190 E. 5th Street
Suite 700
St. Paul, MN 55101
651-296-5663 / 800-657-3704
http://www.humanrights.state.mn.us

Mississippi
None

Missouri
Commission on Human Rights
3315 West Truman Boulevard
Jefferson City, MO 65102
573-751-3325
http://www.dolir.state.mo.us/hr

Montana
Human Rights Bureau
Employment Relations Division
Montana Dept. of Labor & Industry
1625 11th Avenue
Helena, MT 59624
406-444-2884
http://erd.dli.state.mt.us/HumanRights/
    HRhome.htm

Nebraska
Equal Opportunity Commission
301 Centennial Mall South
5th Floor
Lincoln, NE 68509
402-471-2024 / 800-642-6112
http://www.nol.org/home/NEOC

Nevada
Equal Rights Commission
2450 Wrondel Way
Suite C
Reno, NV 89509
775-688-1288
http://detr.state.nv.us/nerc

New Hampshire
Commission for Human Rights
2 Chenell Drive
Concord, NH 03301
603-271-2767
http://webster.state.nh.us/hrc

New Jersey
Division of Civil Rights
31 Clinton Street
Newark, NJ 07102
973-648-2700
http://www.state.nj.us/lps/dcr

New Mexico
Human Rights Division
1596 Pacheco St.
Santa Fe, NM 87505
505-827-6838 / 800-566-9471
http://www.dol.state.nm.us/dol_hrd.html

New York
Division of Human Rights
One Fordham Plaza, 4th Floor
Bronx, NY 10458
718-741-8400
http://www.nysdhr.com

North Carolina
Employment Discrimination Bureau
North Carolina Department of Labor
4 W. Edenton St.
Raleigh, NC 27601-1092
919-807-2827
http://www.dol.state.nc.us/edb/edb.htm

North Dakota
Human Rights Division
Department of Labor
600 East Boulevard Avenue, Dept. 406
Bismarck ND 58505
701-328-2660 / 800-582-8032
http://www.state.nd.us/labor/services/human-
rights

Ohio
Civil Rights Commission
1111 East Broad Street, 3rd Floor
Columbus, OH 43205
614-466-2785 / 888-278-7101
http://www.state.oh.us/crc

Oklahoma
Human Rights Commission
Jim Thorpe Building, Room 480
2101 North Lincoln Boulevard
Oklahoma City, OK 73105

405-521-2360
http://www.onenet.net/~ohrc2

Oregon

Civil Rights Division
Bureau of Labor and Industries
800 NE Oregon Street #32, Suite 1070,
Portland, OR 97232
503-731-4200
http://www.boli.state.or.us/civil/index.html

Pennsylvania

Human Relations Commission
711 State Office Building
1400 Spring Garden Street
Philadelphia, PA 19130
215-560-2496
http://www.phrc.state.pa.us

Rhode Island

Commission for Human Rights
10 Abbott Park Place
Providence, RI 02903-3768
401-277-2661
http://www.state.ri.us/manual/data/queries/
    stdept_.idc?id=16

South Carolina

Human Affairs Commission
2611 Forest Drive, Suite 200
Columbia, SC 29204
803-737-7800 / 800-521-0725
http://www.state.sc.us/schac

South Dakota

Division of Human Rights
118 West Capitol Ave.

Pierre, SD 57501
605-773-4493
http://www.state.sd.us/dcr/hr/HR_HOM.htm

Tennessee

Human Rights Commission
531 Henley Street
Room 701
Knoxville, TN 37902
865-594-6500 / 800-251-3589
http://www.state.tn.us/humanrights

Texas

Commission on Human Rights
6330 Highway 290 East, Suite 250
Austin, TX 78711
512-437-3450 / 888-452-4778
http://tchr.state.tx.us

Utah

Anti-Discrimination & Labor Division
Labor Commission
160 East 300 South
3rd Floor
Salt Lake City, UT 84111
801-530-6801 / 800-222-1238
http://laborcommission.utah.gov/
    Utah_Antidiscrimination_Labo/
    utah_antidiscrimination_labo.htm

Vermont

Attorney General's Office
Civil Rights Division
109 State Street
Montpelier, VT 05609
802-828-3657 / 888-745-9195
http://www.state.vt.us/atg/civil%20rights.htm

Virginia

Council on Human Rights

Suite 1202, Washington Building

1100 Bank Street

Richmond, VA 23219

804-225-2292

http://www.chr.state.va.us

Washington

Human Rights Commission

Melbourne Tower, #921

1511 Third Avenue

Seattle, WA 98101

206-464-6500 / 800-605-7324

http://www.wa.gov/hrc

West Virginia

Human Rights Commission

1321 Plaza East, Room 108A

Charleston, WV 25301

304-558-2616 / 888-676-5546

http://www.state.wv.us/wvhrc

Wisconsin

Department of Workforce Development

Equal Rights Division

1 South Pinckney Street

Room 320

Madison, WI 53708

608-266-6860

http://www.dwd.state.wi.us/er

Wyoming

Department of Employment

Labor Standards Office

1510 E. Pershing Blvd.

Suite 2015

Cheyenne, WY 82002

307-777-7261

http://wydoe.state.wy.us/doe.asp?ID=3

Index

G

H

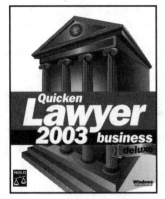

Remember:

Little publishers have big ears.
We really listen to you.

Take 2 Minutes & Give Us Your 2 cents

Your comments make a big difference in the development and revision of Nolo books and software. Please take a few minutes and register your Nolo product—and your comments—with us. Not only will your input make a difference, you'll receive special offers available only to registered owners of Nolo products on our newest books and software. Register now by:

PHONE
1-800-728-3555

FAX
1-800-645-0895

EMAIL
cs@nolo.com

or **MAIL** us
this registration card

fold here

Registration Card

NAME _____ DATE _____

ADDRESS _____

_____

CITY _____ STATE _____ ZIP _____

PHONE _____ EMAIL _____

WHERE DID YOU HEAR ABOUT THIS PRODUCT? _____

WHERE DID YOU PURCHASE THIS PRODUCT? _____

DID YOU CONSULT A LAWYER? (PLEASE CIRCLE ONE)   YES   NO   NOT APPLICABLE

DID YOU FIND THIS BOOK HELPFUL?   (VERY)   5   4   3   2   1   (NOT AT ALL)

COMMENTS _____

_____

_____

WAS IT EASY TO USE?   (VERY EASY)   5   4   3   2   1   (VERY DIFFICULT)

We occasionally make our mailing list available to carefully selected companies whose products may be of interest to you.

❏ If you do not wish to receive mailings from these companies, please check this box.

❏ You can quote me in future Nolo promotional materials.
   Daytime phone number _____.

FELW 1.0

Nolo *in the* NEWS

"Nolo helps lay people perform legal tasks without the aid—or fees—of lawyers."

—USA TODAY

Nolo books are ...*"written in plain language, free of legal mumbo jumbo, and spiced with witty personal observations."*

—ASSOCIATED PRESS

"...Nolo publications...guide people simply through the how, when, where and why of law."

—WASHINGTON POST

"Increasingly, people who are not lawyers are performing tasks usually regarded as legal work... And consumers, using books like Nolo's, do routine legal work themselves."

—NEW YORK TIMES

"...All of [Nolo's] books are easy-to-understand, are updated regularly, provide pull-out forms...and are often quite moving in their sense of compassion for the struggles of the lay reader."

—SAN FRANCISCO CHRONICLE

fold here

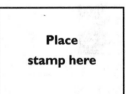

Place
stamp here

Nolo
950 Parker Street
Berkeley, CA 94710-9867

Attn: FELW 1.0